Why Rampage Killers Emerge
Conditions and Characteristics

S. Lee Funk, Ed.D.

Why Rampage Killers Emerge
Conditions and Characteristics

S. Lee Funk, Ed.D.

Academica Press
Washington~London

Library of Congress Cataloging-in-Publication Data

Names: Funk, S. Lee (author)
Title: Why rampage killers emerge : conditions and characteristics | Funk, S. Lee.
Description: Washington : Academica Press, 2024. | Includes references.
Identifiers: LCCN 2023949415 | ISBN 9781680535440 (hardcover) | 9781680535457 (e-book)

Contents

List of Figures

List of Tables

Acknowledgments

The theoretical and empirical constructs throughout this book are largely founded on syntheses of research dating back decades, if not centuries. The capable work, of my predecessors, in whatever discipline – philosophy, sociology, psychology, criminology, education – cannot be overemphasized. Nor can my appreciation for all those who strive, often in obscurity, to somehow fathom the foibles and virtues of humanity.

This book is dedicated to the living victims. May they find solace, if not through understanding, then through informed action.

My gratitude is extended, as always, to my ever-patient wife, Margarita, who never failed to smile when I retreated to my office with the simple explanation, "It won't write itself."

Cover art courtesy of Pixabay, a Canva Germany GmbH brand, creator 13842406.

Preface

This book describes a genesis. As an explanation of an origin or an exploration of a foundation, it previews a gestation, not the complete story. A portentous sequence continues after the initiation of a potentially violent mindset. That devolution is covered in another book entitled *How Rampage Killers Interpret Their Worlds* (Washington DC: Academica Press). The separate volumes are self-contained, but complimentary and they occasionally refer to one another. When such references were necessary, care has been exercised to ensure that there is adequate information to meaningfully interpret the relevancy to the work at hand. For the sake of brevity this work is often referred to as *WRKE* and its companion as *HRKITW*.

Particular principles have been applied to verify theories and authenticate facts. The breadth of this study necessitated employment of a variety of sources so it was important to set guidelines for their use to eliminate those publications (material or electronic) which were poorly conceived or unsubstantiated. Those standards are itemized and justified with hypothetical examples in a short essay entitled, "Regarding Source Credibility and Accuracy." It may be found on the author's site on Academia.edu or LinkedIn.

Formatting follows The Chicago Manual of Style, 17th edition (University of Chicago Press, 2017). Names are arranged according to the standard practices for country of origin. Therefore, the family name is placed according to cultural tradition. Alphabetizing conforms with that convention. Guidelines: Asia Media Centre, "Shinzo Abe or Abe Shinzo? A Basic Guide to Using Asian Names," posted May 23, 2019, https://www.asiamediacentre.org.nz/features/a-guide-to-using-asian-names/. Aaron, "Spanish Naming Conventions – The Basics," MyHeritage Blog, posted July 18, 2011, https://blog.myheritage.com /2011/07/spanish-naming-conventions—-part-1-the-basics/.

Introduction

I shudder when I think of the calamities of our time.
– St. Jerome
in a letter to a friend, around 400 CE

The false notion that arbitrary rampages are unique to our modern era is rooted, perhaps, in an unfounded, though well-intentioned, belief in the innate empathetic nature of human beings. If the phenomena are novel, we might believe, then the causes stem from unidentified deficiencies in the present social order. If we can only identify then correct those flaws, perhaps these deadly and disturbing incidents can be eliminated or, at least, the frequency reduced. Unfortunately, evidence does not support such wishful justification.

Historical accounts and sacred writings verify that humans repeatedly act on a predilection toward mayhem rationalized by interpretations of events, personal as well as epochal.[1] Notoriously prominent are genocidal episodes that are committed in war, or part of a crime, or politically motivated (even socially condoned and sponsored by state actors). These killings represent a typology of terrorist acts that have an organizational component in that they are committed by institutions or motivationally defined groups or at the behest of such bodies. They are meant to assert power over social conditions and, as such, are distinct from the mass killings by individuals who perpetuate their deeds based on motivations that are largely egocentric. Nevertheless, terroristic acts – political, religious, and criminal – bear witness to humankind's capacity for mass violence based on material gain, a philosophical premise, and/or as an avenue to a dogmatically endorsed destiny.

As deleterious as activities in combat, crime, or politics may be, they are somewhat understandable in that their motives, though sinister, have some element of reason at least according to the moral codes driving their commission. They are, in a sense, utilitarian or – in the case of unlawful operations and terrorism – "instrumental" as some researchers have described them.[2] It is despicable that a drug lord would murder a group of individuals to protect his or her product or turf but, even so, the probable financial gain provides a reason that is lucid, though immoral by most standards.

Harder to fathom are the types of multiple or large-scale killings that arise because of the idiosyncratic drives of the perpetrator. Providing a typology for mass murder is not the function of this book and, besides, many frameworks have already been suggested by others.[3] However, since the main intent of the work at hand is to describe the origination of the perspective of a particular type of killer (rampage assailants), it is essential to define that group and to distinguish it from the larger set of murderers who may be characterized in a different manner.

Very broadly, disregarding genocide and democide (associated with civil, religious, or military bodies) and consolidated illegal enterprises, multiple homicides fall along a continuum with three points of demarcation. They may be distinguished by the probable impulses of the killer, by the interval between murders, and by the private/public nature of the crime(s). These markings result in three groupings:

1. Serial homicide – successive murders conducted in secret to ease the compulsions of the perpetrator with intervals on non-activity between each episode;
2. Spree killing – a string of homicides that may be clandestine or public carried out in rapid succession as a reaction to a particular circumstance or as part of ongoing criminal treachery;
3. Mass murder – the killing or the attempt to kill numerous individuals within a restricted time frame.

Bear in mind that the descriptions of each set are directly pertinent only as far as their boundaries are artificially delineated. As Knox notes in her elegant essay on public fascination with extreme violence and the media's grappling for a coherent narrative: "The gruesome accounting of typological strategies loops from expert to media to popular discourse and attempts to corporate something wholly evanescent and changeable."[4] Murder, like all human activity, can be defined by a variety of motives, circumstances, and locales. Any categorization is not absolute. Massacres can be exhibited along a continuum of savage emotions and images of devastation that run – sometimes abated and sometimes, sadly, unabated – through our human consciousness.

The descriptive categories in the foregoing list have been covered in the news, entertainment media, and by researchers. Certainly, they are familiar to the lay person and scholar alike with each defining attribute calling to mind a well-known image from history, fiction, or current events. Jack the Ripper, Hannibal Lector, or Ted Bundy may inhabit the first category. The second group may be represented by the figures of Charles Starkweather and Caril Fugate (or their fictionalized counterparts) crossing the Midwest or Andrew Cunanan obsessing over Gianni Versace as he stalked his idol on a deadly route through the country.[5]

An analysis of literal origination does not necessarily aid the delineation of distinctions between the first two sets relative to the third except to the extent that it is necessary to be cognizant of the traits in order to contrast them with this book's primary subject.

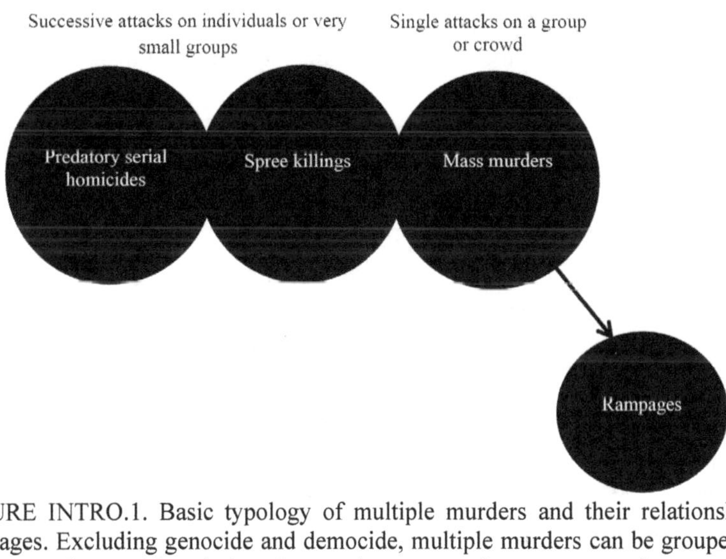

FIGURE INTRO.1. Basic typology of multiple murders and their relationship to rampages. Excluding genocide and democide, multiple murders can be grouped into three general sets, although there is sometimes an overlap among certain perpetrators. Rampage assailants are a distinct class, among others, of single incident mass murderers.

Defining the Phenomenon and Distinguishing Nuances

The characteristics of mass murders are readily observable. They take place in a compressed period, usually within the confines of a 24-hour interval and involve the killing of many innocents (or at least unsuspecting individuals) who have no inclination that death is immediately at hand.

Variable forms of slaughter including bombings, gangland slayings, cult murders, family massacres, and terrorist activities have been assigned to this genre. Rampages represent a subset (depicted in Figure Intro.1) that meet the following conditions:[6]

1. Sudden and unexpected to the community at large (irrespective of planning by the assailant(s));
2. Public in that there is no attempt to keep the event secret once the crime is initiated;
3. Arbitrarily directed – not primarily aimed at certain individuals;
4. Enacted in a compressed time-period – frequently less than 90 minutes;
5. Without a larger group participating in the preparation or execution;
6. With an intention to take multiple lives and create havoc (although the number of fatalities may vary);
7. With no possibility of financial gain and irrelevant to any strategy for advancing a specific ideology (despite bigotry – racism, sexism, etc. adopted by the perpetrator), a broader cause or orthodoxy is not tactically assisted.

The lack of a logical rationale for the seemingly arbitrary violence does not preclude an evaluation of the mental apparatus with the accompanying emotional matrix and sequence of events that coalesce into a fatal climax – such an examination is precisely what this book (and its companion) entails – it only implies that the fateful act lacks commonly accepted rationality as well as – certainly – humanity. "What's going on here? What's really going on?" Kyle Huff reportedly said at a rave after-party before a rampageous onslaught in which he shot eight – six fatally – then took his own life.[7]

The modifier, "rampage," could imply a series of actions that are poorly thought-out, even spontaneous.[8] However, when that adjective is combined with the noun, "killer" or "assailant" the phrase connotes the intensity of a crime, not, as one might immediately assume, an apparent lack of contemplation. The descriptor more congruent with the internalized drivers for this type of marauder is "autogenic." More accurate nomenclature might also be derived by simply narrowing the broad set of mass murderers to capture this sub-category: for example, "random mass killers" or "single incident multiple homicide offenders" or "public multiple murderers." Some have suggested "sudden mass assault by a single individual" that can be abbreviated with "SMASI."[9] The phrase "solo mass murderer" has also been used in the literature.[10] Certainly, any one of those referents would avoid the misrepresentation inherent in the emotionally charged adjective "rampage."

Nevertheless, in deference to the common vernacular and for the sake of ready accessibility when searching data bases, the phrase "rampage killer" has been used throughout this work, but that use should not be taken to imply that this group of mass murderers does not give due consideration to crimes prior to commission. On the contrary, as this book, as well as its accompaniment, both show, there are meditative considerations – aberrant though they may be – in the psyches of these criminals that contributes to conscious decision-making, even though the decisions themselves are nonsensical and the actions may seem spontaneous to the casual observer.

Throughout this work, to avoid repetitive diction, the term "rampage" (followed by "killing" or "murder" or "assailant") will be interchanged with "autogenic" as well as "random" and "sudden mass." The event itself may sometimes be referred to as a "SMASI" (or "SMA" in those rare cases when partners are involved). However, the adjective "mass," when qualified and used in conjunction with a noun (such as "murderer") will designate a larger sphere when multiple lives are taken during an isolated event (large-scale criminal assaults, for instance).

Likewise, the word "assailant" could be used in place of the word "killer" in the defining criteria, given that the purpose is to restrict subjects based on motive, not body count. The operant factors in the preceding set of defining features purposely does not include a minimum number of deaths. As mentioned in the third conditional element, a rampage is mostly undirected but a sundry circumstances or interventions – weapon malfunctions, response by law enforcement, defensive maneuvers by victims, etc. – may contribute to the number of casualties. The interference is irrelevant to the psychological or emotional state of the would-be slayer leading up to the fatal event, the examination of which is the primary purpose of this book. Applying that same reasoning, though, an antagonist cannot be considered a "killer" unless there is at least one death (apart from one self-afflicted).

There are three caveats that do not necessarily change the defining criteria but need explanation to prevent the erroneous exclusion of certain events or persons.

Rampage Killing Relative to Familicide

First, despite the third item for defining a rampage killing, listed as an attack where victims are mostly random, there are instances in which rampages include family members, spouses, and/or lovers. Such was the case with Mutsuo Toi (whose biographical account is in Chapter Two), Jeffrey Weise (discussed in Chapter Three), Kip Kinkel (Four), and many others. In such instances, the familial harm constitutes only a fraction of the damage. If the totality of the episode involved relations, then the massacre would be placed into a separate category – namely familicide. The encompassing criteria assigned to rampage killers does not restrict other manifestations of brutality and many instances may involve behaviors that are not characteristic of all cases.

Definition of Rampage Killing in Relation to Movement

Secondly, the number of locales involved in any rampage, from the standpoint of psychological-social forces, is often irrelevant. That is, an episode may extend over more than one place provided it entails demonstrative violence within a narrow time frame. A significant attribute, as indicated by the fourth distinguishing descriptor, is temporal, not spatial; although, in the situations with multiple settings, they are usually in proximity to one another. This assertion is noteworthy because it contrasts with a definition of the broad category of mass murder provided by some researchers as well as the FBI, which states that the killings in a rampageous massacre take place in a single location.[11] Two examples of rampages occurring at more than one site in a compressed timeframe follow.

John Zawahri, 23, started his roving rampage at the family home in Santa Monica, California where he killed his father with multiple gunshots and his older brother with a single wound to the chest.[12] Afterwards he set fire to the house and, wearing black military regalia, paused long enough to be sure the flames had engulfed the residence.[13] Carrying a duffle bag with at least 13,000 rounds and armed with a modified semi-automatic AR-15, a .44 caliber revolver converted to fire .45 cartridges, and three "Zip Guns" he went into the street.[14] He forced two cars to pull over and wounded the driver of the first, after which he entered the passenger side of the second forcing the woman at the wheel to drive approximately one mile to the city college.[15] Along the way he made his captive stop so he could fire upon pedestrians and other vehicles including a municipal bus and police cruiser.[16] Three people suffered minor injuries. Zawahri and his captive arrived at the school as a Ford Explorer was leaving the parking lot.[17] Zawahri riddled it with bullets, immediately killing the 68-year-old driver and seriously wounding his daughter who was accompanying him. She died two days later at the University of California Medical Center.[18] The killer abandoned his hostage when they arrived at the campus, and he started across the grounds on foot. He shot a woman in the head, who died three hours later in the hospital, then entered the library.[19] Wildly shooting, he expended approximately 70 rounds.[20] Finally, a responding officer took him down. Zawahri was taken from the building and died on the sidewalk.[21] Six were dead – two family members and four complete strangers.[22] The entire episode lasted less than 20 minutes.[23]

Kurt Myers, a 64-year-old retired machinist, set his own apartment on fire around 9:30 on a Wednesday morning in a small village in rural New York.[24] Afterwards he drove around the corner to a local barbershop. With a shotgun he murdered two customers and critically wounded the owner as well as another patron. He then proceeded to drive across the Mohawk River and the New York State Thruway Fast Lube to a neighboring town. He used the same weapon to slaughter an employee along with customer.[25] At a press conference the Governor referred to it as a "truly an inexplicable situation," adding, "[t]here's no apparent motive to the best of our knowledge…."[26] Myers took refuge in the basement of an abandoned building and early in the afternoon fired upon the law enforcement.[27] The police established a perimeter to wait him out.[28] The next morning, 19 hours into the standoff, Myers fired through the door to shoot and kill a K-9 police dog. Officers swarmed the building and in the shootout Myers was killed.[29]

Regardless of physical movement on the part of the rampaging assailant, what matters is that "the killings are all part of the same emotional experience."[30]

Autogenic Massacres Versus Terrorism.

Finally, there is the problem of mixing autogenic mass murder with terrorist acts. Irrespective of their similarities, the two are distinct, mainly because of the seventh criterion for identifying rampages, functionally defined as "irrelevant to any strategy for advancing a specific ideology." Generally recognized definitions of terrorism (including those adopted by the United Nations Security Council, the European Union, academicians, and international criminologists) emphasize that manufactured terror is primarily a tool for wrenching some factional aim.[31]

Arguably, once the articulation of an agenda is removed, there is not much of difference between a terrorist and a rampage killer. Both target innocents; both are obsessed; both have group hysteria as a primary motivator; both frequently end an attack with suicide. "When we see a news headline about a suicide bombing in Iraq or Afghanistan, we tend to interpret it in the broader political context, precisely because it is this context – and not the personal psychological problems of the individuals involved – that has the biggest effect on our lives."[32] That interpretation is pervasive because the motivation cannot be lobotomized from a fanaticism emmeshed in a movement with transformative intentions.[33]

The border between a terroristic act and a rampageous one is so fine that it may seem indistinguishable. Despite the apparent evanescent nature, though, there is a single discrepant psychological explanation for terrorism relative to rampages – a discrepancy that is simple enough to describe, but subtle in application. Terrorists, whatever one may make of their actual purpose or methods, are motivated (at least in their conscious minds) by a belief system extending beyond their own egocentric disillusionment or desire for retribution. Most prominent, as far as that distinction is concerned, is the attention on possible effect. The terrorist believes his or her action will contribute to some tangible seismic shift in the status quo – a release of captives or cessation of occupation or reform of governmental policy.[34] This distinction does not imply that those who adopt terror as a solution are more reasonable than rampageous individuals. Both arrive at their positions by employing quasi-logic premised on solipsistic reasoning rooted in deviant emotionality. The transcendent intentions of their actions, though, are different. Terrorists are acting to set right geopolitical situations they fervently believe to be wrong.

As differentiated by the FBI, international terrorists are "inspired by, or associated with, designated foreign … organizations or nations," while domestic terrorists attempt to "to further ideological goals … of a political, religious, social, racial, or environmental nature."[35] In contrast, random mass killers are avenging an accumulation of personal perceived wrongs.

Timothy McVeigh, at the time of this writing, is still considered to be the master mind and primary perpetrator of the most heinous act of domestic terrorism committed by a citizen in the annals of the United States of

America.[36] He parked and detonated a truck bomb in front of a federal complex in Oklahoma City, killing 168 people, including 19 children, some of whom were under five years old. Over 650 were injured and more than 300 buildings in the immediate area were damaged.[37] There were at least three co-conspirators: Terry Nichols, who mixed the explosives and actively participated in the logistics of the operation; Michael Fortier who assisted in raising funds through the sale of stolen weapons; Lori Fortier (Michael's wife) who, along with her husband, harbored McVeigh before the bombing and assisted in menial tasks.[38] The three men were all veterans who had become close during basic training and McVeigh was best man at the wedding of the Fortiers. All four were sympathetic to the militant Patriot movement consisting of right-wing quasi paramilitary extremists who believe that the national government routinely oppresses ordinary citizens by infringing upon constitutional guarantees, especially religious liberty and the right to use firearms.[39]

Nicolas and McVeigh were particularly disturbed by the stand-offs at Ruby Ridge in Idaho and Waco Texas where attempts by federal authorities to resolve simmering conflicts involving illegal weapons resulted in deaths to civilians as well as law enforcement personnel – a marshal, a mother, her son with a family dog at the former, and four agents along with 81 uncharged adults and children at the latter.[40] McVeigh was present during the siege at Waco and distributed anti-government literature near an Alcohol, Tobacco, and Firearms (AFT) checkpoint removed from a building where the besieged were housed. Among other items, he sold bumper stickers while perched on the hood of his car.[41] They contained slogans such as "When Guns are Outlawed, I Will Become an Outlaw," "A Man with a Gun is a Citizen. A Man without a Gun Is a Subject," and "Ban Guns. Make the Streets Safe for a Government Takeover."[42] While there he was interviewed by a reporter for the student newspaper for Southern Methodist University.[43] He offered this summation of the situation:

> The government is afraid of the guns people have because they have to have control of the people at all times. Once you take away the guns, you can do anything to the people. ... The government is continually growing bigger and more powerful, and the people need to prepare to defend themselves against government control.[44]

The bombing coincided with the second anniversary of the Waco tragedy.[45]

McVeigh considered his action at once a "retaliatory strike" for past activities by U.S. law enforcement personnel and "a pre-emptive (or pro-active) strike against these forces and their command and control centres...."[46] The primary intent (even though paranoid and misdirected) of the bomber and his compatriots was to advance a cause connected to historical events that, in turn, fastened to a designated political objective. While awaiting execution McVeigh penned a letter to the *Buffalo News* in which he affirmed, "Everything that Waco implies was right on the forefront of my thoughts. That sort of guided my path for the next couple of years."[47] Such Intentions are much more defined than the nebulous near-hysterical animosity usually expressed by rampage killers – an animus exemplified by the delusions of Andres Breivik described in Chapter Four and the bitter conceit of Elliot Rodger relayed in Chapter Five.

Theoretical Foundation and Framework

A unified field theory on crime and human cruelty has yet to be developed and never may be – the motivations and emotional currents that foster the starkest of human activities simply cannot be condensed into a nominal mixture that would apply to every villain across all situations. It is possible, though, to isolate certain types of crime and the decisions leading to those misdeeds, then dissect the thought process responsible for culminating behavior. It is a kind of cognitive reverse engineering. When such a dissection is completed, the findings can be applied to past accounts that have been vetted for accuracy to reconstruct the moral matrix that influenced the election of certain courses of action.

Because the events and motives leading to rampage killing are precipitous to an observer, they can only be examined in reverse, i.e., after specific occurrences. The research design, then, relies upon methods derived from the social sciences and history, specifically those applied frequently to case studies, namely:

1. Purposive sampling
2. Triangulation
3. Repeated observations
4. Pattern matching
5. Textual analyses
6. Biographical evaluations.

A discussion of each, as applied in this study, will conclude this introduction.

Purposive Sampling

In keeping with a heuristic design, purposive sampling allows a researcher to dive into the traits and experiences of subjects by deliberately isolating participants or activities that fit predetermined parameters, thereby structuring a framework for noticing influential agencies or commonalities within the set. Comparisons that will naturally result provide insight into mental and emotional processes. This type of selection was used to subdivide apparent phenomena (such as the characterizations in the appendix). The same approach was used to assist with quantitative determinations of common and uncommon characteristics among the general class or isolated subsets of autogenic killers (e.g., variations of dispositional conditions – Figure 6.1).[48]

Triangulation

This analytical technique relies upon the presentation of a concept that is verified through contrasting information that may be deduced, empirically derived, or mathematically demonstrated.

> Social scientists operate through observation and experience; as well as through ideas, theories and models. … 'Triangulation' is a process of verification that increases validity by incorporating several viewpoints and methods. In the social sciences, it refers to the combination of two or more theories, data sources, methods or investigators in one study of a single phenomenon to converge on a single construct, and can be employed in both quantitative (validation) and qualitative (inquiry) studies.[49]

The method used in this text was a blend of "data triangulation," utilizing information or statistics from differing kinds of sources and "methodological triangulation" for which a hypothesis is supported by multiple studies or types of research then verified through features in the cases under study.[50] Figure 1.1 illustrates this approach. Procedurally, this approach involved sifting through archival information (journals, postings, accounts of conversations, etc.) for verbalizations that supported an explanation of emotional status and/or behavior while also coinciding with substantive evidence in the literature on sociology and/or psychology and/or criminology and/or developmental theory.

Repeated Observations

Inferences pertaining to the views and motivational factors of murderous individuals were also supported by repetition in occurrences. The approach simply utilizes multiple examples to demonstrate a trend or perspective.

> The major advantage of repeated observations is that they can expose similarities and differences that occur in behavior or response over time, in different settings, or among different people. This in turn helps to identify consistencies, inconsistencies, transitions, and the trajectory of the phenomenon under study.[51]

Incidents, comments, or explanations were introduced to provide evidence of criminal intentions, to verify the common existence of a psychological frame of reference, and/or as short narratives to add a note of realism to interpretations of empirical literature. It's use was often noticed by anecdotes introduced as "Cases in Point."

Pattern Matching

Based on critical consideration of alternative theories, pattern matching involves comparing demonstrable events with a proposed arrangement in contrast to options that deviate from the suggested configuration. This strategy was used throughout the book to uphold assumptions of precluding conditions or cognitive processes.

Textual Analyses

Mass murderers frequently have a compulsion to chronicle their thinking either in writing or in conversation. The tendency provides an abundance of verbal artifacts that may be used to reconstruct the thinking of subjects and/or provide data to test the utility of a theoretical construct. The application was made by considering the consistent use of particular words or phrases, by scouring utterances or writings for thematic compositions, and by categorizing them to ascertain or possibly negate the existence of belief systems.

Biographical Evaluations

Finally, narrative accounts of subjects were set forth and analyzed in relation to experimental findings and/or legal arguments, and/or testimonials from witnesses, including observations from civil authorities. The approach coincides with sound principles of anthropological research, founded on the use of biographical information for interpretation of influential agents – both external and internal – in human conduct.[52]

Chapter One

Dispositional Conditions

Sweltred Venom sleeping got,
Boyle thou first i'th' charmed pot.
– William Shakespeare
Macbeth

When she was twenty years old and still an undergraduate student, Amy Bishop shot and killed her younger brother.[1] It was an event that would torment her for the rest of her life, so much so that she would seek a small bit of consolation by naming her only son, Seth, after her dead sibling.[2] Over twenty-five years later, she would request a trial in order to prove that she was not responsible for her brother's death, claiming in the petition that she had a "loving and caring relationship" with him.[3] What made the entreaty particularly unusual was the timing: it was filed less than a month after Amy Bishop pled guilty to three counts of capital murder and three counts of attempted murder for her assault on colleagues at the University of Alabama in Huntsville approximately two and a half years earlier.[4]

That very public legal chronicle, played out after she had already been sentenced to life in prison with no possibility of parole, was demonstrative of the sort of self-centered dramatic episodes that Bishop had enacted for years prior to the fateful afternoon when she shot her associates with a 9mm pistol at a faculty meeting.[5] It was indicative of the kind of relationship she maintained with the world at large, one in which she repeatedly engaged in extreme emotional responses that resonated with her personal world view but were practically unfathomable to others.

Prior to assuming the position at the University of Alabama (UA), Bishop lived with her husband, James Anderson, and their children in Ipswich Massachusetts for five years. During that time, the couple called the police at least 14 times – with enough frequency that one officer remembered the family as "regular customers."[6] Many of these calls were complaints about minor irritations such as the noise from dirt bikes or teens playing basketball (all in the afternoon or early evening). Her neighbors from that period say that these incidents were often accompanied by "face-to-face, nose-to-nose" confrontations with other residents.[7] On one occasion, Bishop reportedly told police that there was a chance a conflict would "come to blows."[8]

One Saturday morning, about a year before taking the job at UA, shortly after being seated for breakfast with her family at an IHOP, Bishop struck another customer. The other patron had refused to surrender the last available booster seat, which, before Bishop make a similar request, had already been given to her for her child.[9] The alleged victim gave this account of the incident:

> She stood up and started screaming profanities at me with my two young children there… I had my young child on my hip and I went to get my other child to say, 'let's get out of here.'… And, um she struck me in the side of the head."[10]

During the confrontation, Bishop demonstrated her conceit and confined social perspective by shouting, "I am Dr. Amy Bishop."[11] Charged with assault, battery, and disorderly conduct, Bishop was arrested.[12] She was later placed on probation.[13]

In one of the most ironic vignettes in Bishop's life – punctuated as it was by episodes of tragic violence and reactive aggression – the prosecutor for this case, in what would turn out to be only a mild foreshowing of coming events, urged the court to mandate that Bishop participate in an anger management program.[14]

Bishop's professional interactions appeared to have been as tumultuous as her relationship with her neighbors and associations in public. While doing post-doctoral work at the Beth Israel Deaconess Medical Center (affiliated with Harvard University), Bishop along with eight others published a paper in a medical journal for which she was listed as the second author. According to one of the co-authors, she was furious that she was not credited with the first position. "She broke down. She was extremely angry with all of us. She exploded into something emotional that we never saw before in our careers."[15] A writer who collaborated with her on another project, an unpublished work of fiction, commented, "When I worked with her, I found she was always within striking distance of the edge."[16]

Later, while teaching at the university where her rampage eventually took place, her classroom manner made some students so uneasy that they wrote a letter to the Biology Department Chair, then met with him personally, and ultimately submitted a petition to call attention to her disconcerting behavior. One of the signers complained to the administration on three separate occasions.[17]

In the words of the attorney, Roy W. Miller, who represented her following her sudden assault, “Something’s wrong with the lady, okay?”[18]

Gender, Autogenic Mass Murder, and Predispositions

As a woman, Amy Bishop is atypical (though not alone) among mass murderers as well as the subsidiary grouping of rampage assailants. Michael Stone, a professor of clinical psychiatry at the Columbia College of Physicians and author of the well-known book, *The Anatomy of Evil*, gathered information on 208 single incidents of multiple murder.[19] Males perpetrated 96.5 percent of them.[20] His estimate is close to the rate derived through a compilation of “636 massacres involving 2,869 victims and 861 offenders” over a twenty-six-year time span (1976-2002).[21] That study attributed 93.8 percent of the offenses to males and 6.2 percent to females, as compared to homicides in general in which the percentages have been cited as 88.6 and 11.4, respectively.[22] More recent data for murders overall remain comparable. For 2019, out of 11,743 homicides when the gender of the offender was known, the FBI recorded 10,335 (88%) as male and 1,408 (12%) as female.[23]

Data bases on murderous rampages do not offer information that precisely coincide with the framework established for this study because they use criteria unaligned with the parameters set for this work (as articulated in the Introduction). Typically, the count of offenses incorporates only those incidents involving firearms. After the tragedy in Aurora, Colorado *Mother Jones* set up the first open-source database for public killings with four or more victims but, even though (as of this writing) it now offers discrete data points on 125 incidents from 1982-2021, it includes only those with guns.[24] The Violence Project maintains a comprehensive record that tracks two hundred life variables, including mental health history, trauma, and situational triggers covering the years 1996-2020. It, too, focuses only on shootings.[25] The Federal Bureau of Investigation (FBI) has issued a report with a twenty-year timespan that broadened the definition of assailants to include “individuals actively engaged in killing or attempting to kill people in a populated area."[26] The rates by gender are 96 percent (332/345) for males and 4 percent (13/345) for females.[27] Those percentages equate roughly with the mass murder rates suggested by Stone and others. Once more, though, the tabulation is restricted to "active shooters."[28] Weaponry is a component of rampageous acts that relates to cultural preferences and tactical savagery, but it is only one aspect of the sacrificial drama staged by single incident mass assailants (a point more thoroughly discussed in *How Rampage Killers Interpret Their Worlds*).

Certainly, men commit proportionately more crimes than women and that disparity is even more pronounced for violent offenses.[29] The reasons for this phenomenon are part of a larger group of socio-biological questions beyond the scope of this book. As far as autogenic killers are concerned, as this book and its companion show, the arc of precipitating events and their interpretation are essentially the same for both genders.

The purposive sample of rampageous assailants conforming to the definition in the Introduction compiled for this text then cataloged in the Appendix, offers a total of 103 males, 8 females and 1 transgender, placing the masculine and feminine percentages at 93 (103/111 = 0.927) percent and 7 (9/111 = 0.072) percent, respectively. When a statistical test (z-score) for the proportionality of this count in relation to the ratio for common homicides for 2019 is conducted, the outcome is not significant at 0.01, 0.05, or even 0.10 ($p = .12114$). That calculation might be criticized because the data from the Appendix included killings from all over the globe and the federal count only took in numbers from the United States. As a point of fact, the rate of male offenders worldwide is higher – estimated at 90 percent, so it might be supposed that the contrast between males and female would show significance in relation to worldwide rates. Even so when the same procedure is used to compare an accepted estimate for murder rates throughout the world with the sample garnered for this study, the outcome (with respect to mathematical significance) is the same ($p = .32708 > .01, .05, .10$).[30] The results suggest that among rampaging murderers and would-be killers there is not a statistical distinction directly linked to the sex of the attacker – at least no more than is probable for homicides in general.

The distinction between the rate of women classified as mass killers (as reported in some sources, e.g., the FBI or Violence Project) and the set tabulated for this study is explained by the inclusion of rampages defined by the operational criterion (based on intentionality) and autogenic attacks by means other than firearms. That hypothesis is partially verified by the percentage of women using methods apart from guns – 2/8 = 0.25 – contrasted with men – 9/103 = 0.087 (shown in Appendix). Coinciding with that assumption is the fact that in the United States over 92.1 percent of all homicides with firearms have been ascribed to men as opposed to 7.9 by women.[31]

What is most relevant, from a psychodynamic perspective is the moral decline and subsequent homicidal obsession of female autogenic killers compared to the mental and emotional degeneration of males. The evidence indicates that they are essentially the same. In his interviews of criminal inmates that involved forty-seven men and eleven women. Lonnie Athens found corresponding thought processes in the adoption of habitual violence by either gender[32] In the same vein, when discussing the rationale for their actions, women who attempt or complete assassinations justify their crimes in a manner that corresponds to male assassins.[33]

A close look at both the distal and proximal motivators for rampages perpetuated by teenage girls and women highlights the same kind of cognitive distortions and self-indulgent rationalizations evident among male adolescents and men. The director for the Center for Education in Targeted Violence and Suicide and chair of the Mass Violence Collaborative at the University of Toledo writes:

> While we do not want to give female shooters attention, we are missing an opportunity to thwart a plot if we operate with the naïve, false belief that they do not engage in such violence. There are far more incidents involving females than the public realizes. … Like their male counterparts, females seek fame, collect injustices and wish to seek revenge. … They also have high indications of suicidality. They are more alike their male counterparts than different. They are dangerous.[34]

Dr. Amy Bishop's shooting at the University of Alabama was much like the premeditated ambush by a male professor, Dr. Valery Fabrikant at Concordia University.

The circumstance preceding the shooting by Bishop was denial of tenure, for Fabrikant an obstruction of promotion. Both were enthralled with their own sense of importance and routinely blamed others for any missteps or misfortunes. Both were scholars in highly technical fields and killed colleagues in the work setting. Bishop's arrogance and her paranoid accusations mirrored Fabrikant's temperament as well as the nature of his complaints. Small wonder, as shown in the last chapter of *How Rampage Killers Interpret Their Worlds*, neither ever demonstrated contrition and used similar maneuvers aiming for legal absolution while imprisoned.

Sandwiched between Whitman's ambush on the community of Austin from the university tower in 1966 and Stephen Paddock's rifle fire from the 32nd floor of the Mandalay Bay Hotel in Las Vegas in 2017 was Brenda Spencer's prolonged sniper assault on children and staff at an elementary school in 1979. Whitman and Paddock were shot and killed by police officers, while Spencer once said she was suicidal and intended to be taken out by law enforcement.[35] Nasim Najafi Aghdam (a mass assailant though not a killer) shot employees at YouTube Headquarters then committed suicide in much the same way that Vester Flanagan burst upon a news show broadcast aired by a CBS affiliate. Flanagan killed two co-workers before eventually taking his own life. Both aggressors – the first a female entertainer and activist, the second a male journalist – claimed they were victims of discriminatory practices that exploited their talents and thwarted their opportunities for success in their chosen occupations.[36]

Based on the evidence currently available, it is unlikely that the *XY* chromosome, as an entity, is responsible for disproportionate number of rampage killings by teenage boys and adult men. The simplicity of that assumption is complicated, however, by the impetus provided by two characteristics held by some males that are culturally moored:

- Sexism
- Insecurity associated with stereotypical masculine expectations.

The former is subsumed in the prejudicial preferences of autogenic killers that is touched upon occasionally throughout this work and deliberately contemplated in *How Rampage Killers Interpret Their Worlds*. The second bullet is discussed as a component of discomfort with physical capacity in the next chapter.

Bishop is prototypical among autogenic murders in an important respect that may be less immediately distinguishing than her gender or violent history but subterraneously distinguishable: a predilection, reinforced by certain character traits for social marginalization. That single feature by no means constitutes the psychological totality for rampaging assailants, but it is a characterological bedrock.

While there are certain patterns that are evident in the lives of those committing mass violence and, in many cases, statements or actions that border on actual proclamations of intent, they range from subtle to crass. This spectrum has made the identification of common tendencies elusive. Synthesizing etiological factors into an explanatory construct is complicated even more by the fact that any single feature attributable to a mass murderer can be readily attributed to others in the general population who do not commit such heinous acts. As one psychiatrist noted, "… most people who are depressed, isolated and can't talk, don't become mass murderers."[37] Even so, certain elemental traits embedded in a person's psyche – whether genetically, prenatally, or in early development – may, given a confluence of events, result in an unmerciful sinister disposition.

The conditions can predispose devolvement into autogenic murder. They are:

- Perceived physical inadequacy
- Destructive/oppressive environmental situations
- Neuropsychological impairments
- Pathological personality.

The classifications are explanatory in nature with an associative, not denotative, relationship to psychiatric or sociologic diagnoses. To minimize the presumption of stasis, they should be considered descriptive, not categorical. Each will be present at birth or from an early age, as a singular dominate trait or, more frequently, in combination with others to permeate the eventual slayer's pattern of development. Successive chapters will analyze the nature and potential effects of these dispositional conditions.

These situational contributors precede then perpetuate the maladjustment of eventual rampage killers. Displayed with influential subordinates in Table 1.1, the disadvantages caused by physique, environment, neural pathways, or personality hinder productive social maturation. They act as threads as habitual patterns are fashioned. The factors in this set do not cause violent behavior, but they are, as previously mentioned, elemental to its devolutionary sequence.

Despite apparent distinctions, the individuals considered in the chronicles throughout this book are alike in at least two ways. First, each chose to murder and wound unsuspecting victims for reasons that are unjustifiable by commonly accepted societal standards and ill-conceived by any rational system of thought. Secondly, and more important from an epistemological standpoint, each carried one or more pre-conditional traits that became fallow turf for the eventual thicket of thoughts and emotional responses that were harbingers for the orchestration of extreme violence.

TABLE 1.1. Dispositional conditions

Externally oriented circumstances		Internally oriented circumstances	
Perceived physical inadequacy	Destructive/ Oppressive environment	Neuropsychological impairments[a]	Pathological personality[b]
Typology	Typology	Typology	Typology
Prolonged or pronounced childhood illness Limited stature Unsatisfactory appearance Disability Dyspraxia Gender dysphoria[c] Sexual dysfunction, and/or perversion, and/or disesteem[d]	Injurious familial relations Unsupportive living conditions Hostile community: victimized or intimidated by peers, associates, authorities	Restricted or distorted cognition Mood disordered Delusional Hallucinatory, paranoid, or disassociated episodes, psychotic	Specified personality disorder Negative affectivity vs. emotional stability Detachment[e] vs. extroversion Antagonism vs. agreeableness Disinhibition vs. conscientiousness

General note: Examples in each category derive from actual cases but may not be exhaustive. Some biographical accounts of rampage murderers are incomplete and so all probable conditions remain unrepresented. In addition, some future malefactor may evidence a contributor previously unidentified. Nevertheless, given the breadth of the model and the anecdotal patterns supporting the categorization, if adequate information is available, s/he will likely exhibit a history that supports an elemental descriptor belonging to one column or more.

[a] Mood disorders are grouped with neurological conditions because of their reciprocal relation. See Table 4.1.

[b] Some identifiers for this grouping originate from a multidimensional approach for assessing personality functions based on the trait specified model. They were used

in place of categorical diagnoses to designate observable maladaptive attributes or habits when prescriptive designations were insufficient for the depiction of an individual. American Psychiatric Association, *Diagnostic and Statistical Manual of Mental Disorders,* 5th ed. (*DSM-5*, Arlington Virginia: American Psychiatric Association, 2013), 770-781. Dysfunctional personalities relevant to psychoticism vs. lucidity are catalogued along with impairments relevant to neural operations and/or emotions. Consult the Special Note in the Appendix for an itemization of distinguishing features for defining characterological pathologies.

[c] Referring to an individual's chronically painful dissatisfaction with his/her role or orientation accompanied by an inability (for whatever reasons) to resolve conflicting feelings. The *DSM-5* stresses that the diagnosis is relevant with respect to the discomfort that a person may have with their sexual identity, not to the ambivalence felt by individuals or the perception of its propriety by a broader community. "*Gender dysphoria* refers to the distress that may accompany the incongruence between one's experienced or expressed gender and one's assigned gender." American Psychiatric Association, *DSM-5*, 451. The category does not incorporate inclinations or sexual preferences, e.g., homosexuality, transsexuality, or gender fluidity. Consult: a) American Psychiatric Association, *DSM-5*, 451-459; and William Byne, Dan H. Karasic, Eli Coleman, A. Evan Eyler, Jeremy D. Kidd, Heino F.L. Meyer- Bahlburg, Richard R. Pleak, and Jack Pula, "Gender Dysphoria in Adults: An Overview and Primer for Psychiatrists," *Transgender Health* 3 no. 1 (2018): 57-A3.

[d] Includes perversions that are invasive to others, e.g., pedophilia or forcible paraphilia, not lifestyle preferences or orientations that are based on consent, e.g., bisexuality or mutual sadomasochism. This category of conditions also includes individuals that are preoccupied with their perception of their sexual prowess (such as so-called involuntary celibates – incels). See Chapter Two under "Perceived Inadequacy and Sexual Disesteem" and entries concerning Alek Minassian and Elliot Rodger (Chapter Five and Appendix).

[e] An unfortunate term: the defining behaviors are more indicative of anxious avoidance of social settings and interpersonal situations than disinterest. American Psychiatric Association, *DSM-5,* 779.

The presentations with analyses in chapters two through six will demonstrate how the precursors act as incessant active contributors to an autogenic killer's existential perspective. There are three referential intersections for each category:

1. The psychological frameworks associated with preconditions that contribute to a destructive mind set;
2. Empirical or theoretical support from research-oriented sources that verify the likelihood of the long-term deleterious effects of the constructs;

3. Statements or actions by perpetrators that illustrate the impact of the prefatory circumstances.

Therefore, in line with the triangulation model described in the introduction, the dispositional conditions form the apex of the triangle with theoretical foundations and evidence from accumulated incidents acting as the base (see Figure 1.1).

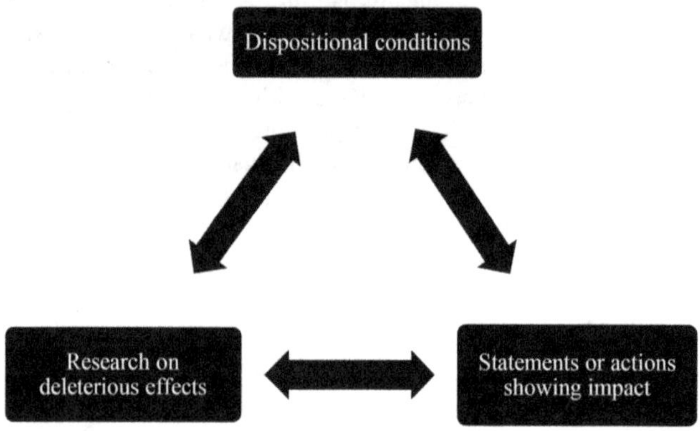

FIGURE 1.1. Applying triangulation model to verify effects of dispositional conditions. Empirical and/or theoretical evidence underscore social-emotional damage inherent in preconditions. Actual verbiage and/or incidents enact those effects.

When necessary for clarification or for support of a given thesis the other methods for validation itemized at the conclusion of the introduction are employed.

Cautionary Notes on Etiology

The categorized precursors presented in Table 1.1 should not be misconstrued as causes for the moral degeneration that can result in indiscriminate killing. They are, instead, representations of internal or circumstantial referents that can hinder personal development. That hinderance can, in turn, be morally degenerative. The etiology is not marked by any one or even any single combination of conditions. The influencers, are, metaphorically, backdrops to a procession, not precipitous forces by themselves.

Relevant to that admonition is the need for refutations of two erroneous phenomenological theories for mass murder that have been subject to popular circulation, if not necessarily acceptance. Both propositions are wrong in two ways. First, they have been popularly advanced as activators, suggesting that autogenic massacres can be directly caused by a singular circumstance. Secondly, both constructs depend on lopsided research.

The propositions have been adopted, presumably, as scapegoats for an uncomfortable manifestation of human behavior, providing some comfort by the assumption of a unitary cause. One school of thought blames media consumption while another attributes violent eruptions to a byproduct of modern medicine.

The Consumption of Violent Media as an Etiological Agent

Those who promote this thesis are relatively non-selective about the communicative formats that may play a part in the devastation. Video games, rock music, movies, and television have all taken the rap. Following the school shooting in Parkland, Florida in early 2018 that left 17 people dead, lawmakers overlooked psychological and sociological literature to glom on to a possible one-dimensional explanation that, besides providing superficial solace, could sway voters to support their continuation in office through the exploitation of cultural divisiveness.[38]

Tennessee Rep. Marsha Blackburn made the claim that mothers were "very concerned" about "exposure" to entertainment that "desensitized" children to violence.[39] Iowa Senator Chuck Grassley, remarked, "[Y]ou see all these films about everybody being blown up. Well, just think of the impact that makes on young people."[40] The simplistic observations are reminiscent of the view advanced by some politicians in the 1950s that comic books inosculated youth to the perils of crime and led to juvenile delinquency. In that decade, as part of a larger investigation, a Senate sub-committee held hearings and issued an extensive report on the subject.[41] In rendering criticisms of the medium the document quoted Dr. Robert H. Felix, Director of the National Institute of Mental Health, who wrote, "They [comics] might well be instructive in the techniques of criminal activity and the avoidance of detection."[42] Like much public discourse, the statements contain some truth, along with misleading implications that are damaging to effectively interpreting variations in human behavior.

Over 20 years ago, the American Psychological Society (APS – founded in 1887 now with over 10,500 members)[43] published an article that began, "Research on violent television and films, video games, and music reveals unequivocal evidence that media violence increases the likelihood of aggressive and violent behavior in both immediate and long-term contexts." The same piece continues, saying, "The growing body of video-game research yields essentially the same conclusions."[44] The report then goes on to conduct an extensive review of the literature available at that time in order to prove those points.

The contentions are pointed but, unfortunately, grossly overstated. There is no question that studies have found a relationship between aggression and exposure to violence by various forms of media. The statistical significance, though, has been highly variable. Moreover, as a first-year graduate student would know, correlation is not causation. Jonathan Kellerman, a reputable psychologist, pointed out almost two and one-half decades ago:

> Numerous studies have produced correlations and other statistical associations between media violence and aggression in children. Explanations include (1) *sanitization and desensitization* – after repeated exposure to violence, kids get used to witnessing cruelty and mayhem; ... (2) *identification* – kids imitate whatever they seen on-screen; (3) *arousal* – kids are unhealthily stimulated by media violence and perceive it as thrilling; ... and (4) *positive reinforcement* – kids learn from TV and the movies that violence is rewarded.
>
> Though some statistical support has been obtained for all four suppositions, *not a single causal link between media violence and criminality has ever been produced.*[45]

Since the time of the publication of Kellerman's book and the APS synthesis of research there has been further speculation loosely associating actual aggressive acts, as well as suppressed empathy, with violent portrayals on the screen. However, definitive causality remains elusive and certainly, given the diversity of studies and commentaries on the subject, debatable.[46]

The lack of consensus is mainly due to methodology. It is difficult, if not impossible, to control the numerous variables that account for emotional responses whether short or long term, violent or not. By way of example, one extensive longitudinal study that examined the possible impact of television violence considered subsets of subjects with controls for socioeconomic status (SES), intellectual ability, and parenting (including physical aggression, personality characteristics, fantasies, nurturance, punishments, rejection, mobility, and television habits). Results showed that the influence of TV exposure persisted even with those factors controlled.[47] Even so, it is possible to readily imagine other influential factors: peer relations, family dynamics, physical well-being, mental health, heredity, just to name a few. The problem was accentuated in a meta-analysis. An examination of 26 independent samples failed to show a connection between aggressive criminality and violent viewing. Among the studies chosen only a few looked at effect sizes for two of the most obvious contributors: SES along with personal traits.[48]

Another concern is standardization in semantics and measurement methodology. Different researchers have operationalized "violence," "aggression," and even "media" with diverging definitions.[49]

If these issues do not engender doubt, there is the long-standing problem, existing in all fields, of so-called "publication bias." That is, the tendency for journals to favor research that is extraordinary or that is contrary to popular conceptions while avoiding replication studies.[50] The trend is particularly pernicious when the subject under consideration is enmeshed in a topical conversation, which is certainly the case with mass media and their relation to the ills of the day.

Over the decades of the twentieth century, graphic depictions of violence have increased, and at the same time, savagery has decreased across the nation. Using a rating system to measure incidents and extent of vividity in high grossing movies from 1920 to 2005, a researcher from Stetson University (Ferguson) determined that the extent of violence in movies in terms of occurrences as well as intensity more than quintupled after hitting a low point in 1945.[51]

> A total of 90 films were included. … Trained raters viewed each movie and recorded at each 1-min interval whether any violent acts had occurred during the previous minute. … Violence was defined for the purpose of ratings as 'Any act (e.g., hitting, kicking, shoving, slapping, shooting, stabbing) causing intentional harm, injury or death, including war scenes, torture, rape, strangulation, or assault.' … Graphicness of the violence was also rated for each movie. This consisted of six Likert-scale questions….[52]

Meanwhile, the sale of video game units climbed from 73.8 million in 1996 to 298.6 million units in 2008. Since that time there has been fewer sales year-by-year, but even so, the number sold in 2013 was 159.8 million – more than double that of 1996.[53] It was estimated in 2008 that 97 percent of teens played video games and 66 percent of those were action oriented, many including violence.[54] If exposure via visual and auditory imagery was a causal factor (in and of itself) for accelerating violence, then there should have been a marked increase in both the frequency and brutality of injurious episodes, especially among young people but, the opposite has been the case.

The crime rate in the United States reached a zenith in 1991, the same year that violent incidents also peaked at 716 for every 10,000 people. By 2016 the proportion of violent crimes fell by almost half to 366 for every 10,000. A similar trend occurred with murder, down from 9.8 per hundred thousand in 1991 to 5.3 in 2016.[55] Arrests for juveniles (10-17 years of age) for violence (murder, nonnegligent manslaughter, rape, robbery, and aggravated assault) also declined during roughly the same period, from its height in1994 of over 400 per 100,000 to an historic low of under 200 per 100,000 in 2012, roughly retaining that rate through 2018.[56]

It is likely that young people tempted to engage in law-breaking sometimes have found respite and even perverse inspiration in pictorial depictions of crime. However, it is ludicrous to assume that they turn toward graphic novellas, in lieu of friends, relatives, or ill-intentioned mentors, for actual instructions in the practice of robbery, burglary, knifing, or shooting. Likewise, mediatized violence may coincide or even uphold the gruesome fantasies of potential autogenic killers, but it is doubtful that cartoons, broadcasts, or gaming will inspire human massacres that are completely devoid of empathy unless the agitated actor was already so inclined. Chapters four and five in *How Rampage Killers Interpret Their Worlds* covers this topic in more depth to show that a consumption of commercialized cruelty, be it based on tabloids, facts, or fancy, is a component, but not the trigger, of emotional deterioration.

Psychiatry as an Etiological Agent

More disconcerting than a misinterpretation of the influence of media is the proliferation of poorly substantiated literature about psychotropic medications. Capitalizing upon the inexplicably broad skepticism for empirically premised medical treatment (even among the well-educated), some writers have put forth primarily speculative evidence asserting that drugs prescribed for mood or thought disorders have initiated side-effects causing emotional imbalances resulting in atrocious instances of mayhem. The assertions are superficially ill-founded and even more fallacious when subjected to objective testing.

There can be no argument that substance abuse often results in incoherent thought, which sometimes leads to violence or with the fact that inebriated states and addiction can eventually result in psychological or moral deterioration that disinhibits rage. The influence that alcohol and drugs may have on mental instability is pursued in the broader context of neuropsychological impairments in the fourth chapter of this book. The subject of dispute at this point is the possibility that a demonstrable upswing in multiple murders or rampageous acts can be attributed to medications whether they were prescribed as psychiatric remedies or, for that matter, some other type of malady.

In this book along with its associated work, *How Rampage Killers Interpret Their Worlds*, mental and emotional dysfunctions are shown to be foundational, but by not igniters, of rampageous actions. That view is verified by documentary evidence regarding the medical histories of assailants. It is hardly surprising that preceding their predacious outbursts some of the perpetrators were treated with prescriptive psychotropic medicines. Rather than instigators of purposeful mass assaults the prescriptions were predicated on diagnostic analyses to ward off the possibility of eventual aggression or at least the psychological discomfort of the person in treatment. The fact that the remedial attempts may have failed does not make them the cause of the tragedies.

The main culprits, according to the pharmacology detractors, has been a group of anti-depressants that act as serotonin reuptake inhibitors (SSRIs). However, other medications have been blamed as well, some of which are specific brands and others that encompass entire drug families. They include but are not necessarily limited to: Anafranil (trade name, a tricyclic antidepressant, used for obsessive-compulsive disorder); amphetamines (generic, stimulants); Ambien (trade name, a sedative); amitriptyline (generic, affecting neurotransmitters, used for depression and anxiety); benzodiazepines (generic, for alcohol withdrawal, anxiety, muscle relaxation, panic disorder, seizures); lithium (generic, an anti-psychotic commonly used for bipolar disorder and schizophrenia); mefloquine hydrochloride (generic, antimalarial agent); Ritalin (trade name, a stimulant, often used for attention deficit disorders); serotonin antagonist and reuptake inhibitors (SARIs, generic, for major depressive disorders); selective serotonin and norepinephrine reuptake inhibitors (SSNRIs, generic, for major depressive disorders and panic attacks); Strattera (trade name, a stimulant prescribed for attention deficit disorder); Suboxone (trade name, for opioid misuse); Thorazine (brand name, early psychotic drug, discontinued and considered obsolete in United States); varenicline tartrate (generic, for smoking cessation); and Welbutrin (trade name, another anti-depressant, discontinued in U.S.).[57]

The list is long and varied, which reveals one of many problems from a credibility standpoint. With so many drugs enumerated as possible provocateurs of belligerence the odds of an aggressor using at least one of them is disproportioned compared to the absence of any pharmacological intervention. The likelihood of the involvement of medical stimulation in relation to catastrophes gives the illusion of being on the increase simply because the universe of suspicious medicines keeps expanding.

That point is associated with the careless manner data have been accumulated to support the hypothesized dangerous reactions. The various articles, documentaries, blogs, public statements, and news stories utilize inconsistent criteria for determining the reasons for classifying a medication as problematic. In some cases, it is because a mass murderer was reported to be taking a particular drug; in others because s/he suddenly ceased a prescribed regimen or traces of compounds were found in the body; while in some instances an actor was in treatment at some point or maintained a prescription but may or may not have used it; in still others a drug has been cited as suspect due to manufacturer's warnings or cautionary measures recommended in professional literature.[58]

The lack of clarity about the intake of the prescribed medicines is related to yet another fault with the supposed evidence that links violence to medication: the critics are not precise about the issue being studied. Throughout the accusatory investigations, proponents of the linkage conflate suicides, random violence, assassinations, autogenic assaults, familicide, violent fantasies, and murders as if they were the same act.[59] While all these events are tragic and often horrendous, they are not the same. An elementary principle of scientific research is attention to the nature of causality, which can only be legitimized by the isolation of variables. Failure to account for those variances will result in assumptions that relationships exist where there are none, the qualitative equivalent of a Type I error.[60] When establishing cause and effect relative to human systems, a critical consideration must be precision in designating the antecedent as well as the outcome observed.

Associated with analytical imprecision are factual errors and misrepresentations in opinion pieces, editorials, and various reports that purport to be based on science. One article that is critical of psychiatric pharmacology was billed as "exclusive" and quoted a portion of a *Sixty Minutes* interview with a neighbor of Adam Lanza, the Newton shooter who killed his mother at home then went on to kill 26 more at an elementary school in 2013.[61] "I know he was on medication," she said with assurance.[62] The same misinformation was stated as fact by at least two other sources.[63] However, both Adam Lanza and his mother were resistant to any medical treatment throughout the entirety of his life, and it is extremely doubtful he would have complied with any prescriptive measures whatsoever.[64] A robust report from the Connecticut State Attorney said without equivocation, "The shooter [Lanza] refused to take suggested medication and did not engage in suggested behavior therapies."[65] Another consumer oriented outlet reported that Patrick Purdy, who fired upon school children in Stockton California, killing five and wounding 30 more, was under the influence of amitriptyline as well as Thorazine, both prescribed by mental health practitioners.[66] The truth is that Purdy had been in and out of treatment since the time he was a teenager and never followed up on the scripted protocols. On the other hand, he regularly took a variety of intoxicants that included liquor, marijuana, hallucinogens, tranquillizers, stimulants, even glue, and had been doing so since the time he was twelve.[67]

Prescriptions were also linked to the massacre by Steven Kazmierczak, who shot 26 people, killing 5 and wounding 21 before taking his own life at Northern Illinois University.[68] Campus police said he had ceased taking his medication and "and became somewhat erratic."[69] An opinion piece on a popular firearms forum reported that his girlfriend indicated he had taking Prozac along with Ambien and "[t]oxicology results showed that he still had trace amounts of Xanax in his system."[70] The single sided observations undercut the critical and revelatory information that Kazmierczak had a history of psychiatric problems dating back to the time he was in high school. He made the first of many suicide attempts at age 16 (twelve years before his rampage) and had been diagnosed with schizoaffective disorder, schizoid personality traits, and was subject to psychosocial stressors as well. In addition, he had a history of auditory hallucinations and experienced a visual hallucination on at least one occasion. Kazmierczak was treated with antidepressants, antipsychotic drugs, and mood stabilizers for over ten years. Meanwhile, he was using marijuana.[71] Contrary to causing his outburst, the prescribed medication had probably kept his aggressive tendencies at bay.

A review of campus shootings covering a span of fifty years was conducted by a foremost authority on the subject, Dr. Peter Langman. After considering the role of psychotropic drugs in 62 murderous episodes from the standpoint of usage over time, profiles of assailants taking medication, and the documented effects of the medicine on individual killers, he concluded that just slightly more than ten percent (12.5%) were medicated at the time of their attacks.[72] Even in those instances, there was no proof that medication made them "manic, agitated, or violent."[73] Langman points out that, instead of acting like "crazed killers," autogenic murderers are often organized and detailed oriented.[74]

The allegation that drug therapies have prompted multiple killings has also been made in cases perpetuated by adults outside of educational settings. Arguably, the most infamous involves the deadly shooting conducted by Joseph Wesbecker at a printing-plant in Louisville Kentucky in September of 1989. With an AK-47 assault rifle, Wesbecker murdered 8 and wounded 19. He ended his tirade by standing in front of the door to a foreman's office, pressing a Sig-Sauer 9-millimeter pistol under his chin and firing a single shot that took his own life.[75] He had been taking Prozac, the well-known anti-depressant, for a little more than one month.[76] Surviving victims (with one exception) and relatives of the dead sued Eli Lilly, the manufacturer and distributor of Prozac, claiming the drug had disrupted Wesbecker's impulse control and the company was liable.[77]

The case went to court on September 26, 1994. At the time approximately 160 more cases were pending against Lilly.[78] "The trial itself lasted 47 days during which 75 witnesses testified, 22 depositions were presented to the jury and 411 exhibits were introduced into evidence."[79] The jury absolved the drug maker of responsibility, so it appeared as if Prozac was not at fault.[80] However, the judge, based partially on the way that plaintiff's handled a ruling during rebuttal, suspected that untoward arrangements had been made. He began an investigation, which the drug maker attempted to block with an order from the Kentucky Court of Appeals. The jurist, John W. Potter, persisted and successfully convinced the Kentucky Supreme Court to overturn it. Potter then pressed for a hearing and, to avoid charges of bias, recused himself. The judge who inherited the case never pursued it, so any last-minute arrangements that were made during the original trial were never officially disclosed.[81]

Multiple sources, though, including two of the petitioners and a co-counsel, have acknowledged that they were promised an award worth at least

20 million dollars no matter what the verdict.[82] That amount would be more than 50 million by today's standards.[83] The pre-settlement headed off additional testimony that would have exposed documents unfavorable to the public perception of Eli Lilly.[84]

The ethical lapses on the part of the drug maker are worrisome to be sure, but they do not apply directly to the decisions made by Wesbecker, nor do they mean, necessarily, that Prozac prompted the tragic episode. The killer carried two of four precursors to devolution of a rampageous individual: exposure to destructive environmental situations and impaired neuropsychology (refer to Table 1.1 and Appendix). His father died when he was but only a year old and when he was four, he lost his grandfather. Throughout much of his childhood he was shuttled from place to place, and he even spent close to a year in an orphanage.[85] His emotional problems, dated back to 1978, slightly less than eleven years preceding his rampage in 1989 and close to a decade before Prozac was even introduced to the market in 1988.[86]

Jefferson County Coroner, Dr. Richard Greathouse, reviewed Wesbecker's medical records and a daily newspaper summarized the presentation of his report.

> 'Here we are dealing with a man who had a long history of chronic mental illness and chronic mental depression,' said Dr. Richard Greathouse, Jefferson County coroner.... The records show that Wesbecker, 47, fought mental illness and depression for the past 11 years. He was beset by racing thoughts, sleeplessness, tremors, blurred vision, confusion, anxiety, headaches, dizziness and anger, according to the records. ... Wesbecker had difficulty concentrating and once couldn't recall his own address. He felt isolated from others, and he sometimes felt worthless. Wesbecker told psychiatrists he had thoughts of taking his own life and had acted on those thoughts 12 to 15 times. He took pills, clogged his car's exhaust pipe and tried to hang himself. Wesbecker ... also had occasional thoughts of hurting other people, the records indicate. He had mentioned his wife's ex-husband and his foreman at Standard Gravure as possible targets. ... Under court order, Our Lady of Peace Hospital turned over the records Friday to Greathouse, who released a summary of the material. Greathouse said that ... Wesbecker was voluntarily admitted to hospitals at least three times for psychiatric treatment between 1978 and 1987.[87]

In a formal complaint against his employer twenty months before his rampage and at least a year and a-half before he took his first dose of Prozac Wesbecker personally described a pattern of mental instability that included manic episodes.[88]

There is evidence that Wesbecker, like all autogenic assailants, fantasized and started readying for furor long before acting and, again, before medicating. The president of the local union noticed him reading *Soldier of Fortune Magazine*, two years in advance of the shooting. Wesbecker said at the time that he was thinking about ordering an Uzi, an Israeli semiautomatic weapon.[89] He also engaged in the kind of intimidating behavior that is common among rampageous types. Prior to going out on disability leave, preceding the shooting by one year, he told a colleague he intended to "get even" with the factory where he worked.[90] Another fellow worker said after the massacre, "This guy's been talking about this for a year."[91] Wesbecker's planning was independent of prescriptive interventions.

With all the accusations of psychological pitfalls leveled against such an extensive list of medications, there should be a host of citations of empirically based writings that demonstrate their dangers. Though much has been written, there are very few studies that have rigorously investigated the role of psychotropics in mass homicides. Those that are well-documented, careful in their analysis, and objectively written have not proven that a relationship exists between prescription drugs and sudden mass assaults such that the former causes the later either by ingestion or cessation.

A typical article that masquerades as scientific is "The Systemic Correlation Between Psychiatric Medications and Unprovoked Mass Murder in America" that appeared in *New Male Studies: An International Journal*. The technical tone of the title suggests mathematical analyses that never appear. The premises are backed (but not supported) by associations and coincidences absent statistical proofs. Correlates are demonstrated, supposedly, by the relationship between popular opinions and actual events or observations of politicians associated with the news. No correlational calculations (or for that matter, impartial evaluations) are involved. The proofs are based on implication. For example, under the heading, "The Hidden Correlate: Psychiatric Drugs," the author says of mass shootings, "The two constant variable [*sic*] … were that the vast majority of shooters had been formally diagnosed with a mental illness and were prescribed psychiatric medications."[92] First, as Figure 6.1 and the Appendix demonstrate, the statement is untrue. Secondly, even if it were so, it proves nothing, any more than height, by itself, makes a person a great basketball player. A paragraph later, the author notes, that "all classifications of psychiatric medications can cause a wide range of pathological behavior,"[93] referring to the possible, though rare, side-effects that are appropriately listed in the *Physician's Desk Reference Manual* as well as in research-oriented papers and journals.[94] It should not come as a revelation that prescriptions sometimes result in undesirable reactions, which, by the way, is exactly the reason they are to be taken with professional supervision. There are medicines on the market treating a variety of conditions that may initiate heart palpitations, rashes, nausea, sleepiness, etc. Usually, though, when such symptoms occur, they come about because of complications connected to the medical malady being treated, not because of treatment itself.

As mentioned previously critics of anti-depressants and other psychiatric medications often single out cautionary labels to substantiate their claim that drugs in question can be hazardous. "[T]he argument is that the consumer should be warned directly by the manufacturer of all effects of the drug to assure that the decision they are now making in tandem with the doctor is an informed decision."[95] Those admonishments have been cited in multiple sources as proof that the potential harm is not only certain, but well known. That sort of alarmist reasoning has been proffered by the Citizen's Commission on Human Rights (CCHR), Duke, Kupelian, Stolzer, and Glenmullen, among others.[96] Looking at 27 international drug regulatory agency precautions issued on psychiatric drugs, the CCHR cites mania (on 48%), hostility (on 52%), homicidal ideation (on 4%) as examples.[97] The percentages are misleading, though, because they are intended only to alert the consumer to the possibility of ill-effects, not the probability. The words and phrases used for describing potential ill effects are broad in their connotations and do not predict potential violence of any sort, much less random killing.

> The relatively rare adverse effects of antidepressant-induced mania and serotonin syndrome are sometimes invoked by those who believe antidepressants are criminogenic. However, these adverse effects produce characteristic physical symptoms and mental status changes that are easily distinguishable from a criminal act committed in the absence of these phenomena.[98]

A focus on mandatory labeling obfuscates the fact that the manufacturers are merely fulfilling their legal and ethical duty to warn and in so doing concentrate on risks that have a very low chance of materializing and when they do occur are not nearly as dreadful as detractors imply.

Instead of assuming causation based on unsubstantiated relationships or conjecture, it would be beneficial to look at the results of the few empirical investigations that are available. Well-constructed studies testing the association between violent outbursts and depression inhibitors have shown inconclusive findings at best. A quasi-experimental investigation in Finland compared a large set of homicide offenders (959) with an even larger control group (10 controls for each offender).[99]

> The primary outcome measure was the risk of offending during current use vs. no current use for three major categories of psychotropic medications: antidepressants, benzodiazepines, and antipsychotics. ... A Poisson regression model was used to estimate the relative risk (RR) of homicide during current use versus no-use of each study medication among the offenders.[100]

A cursory reading of the results would suggest a relatively high risk of homicidal events among those subjects using any one of the three families of drugs. The misinterpretation was reported as mathematical fact by at least one source only too anxious to condemn modern psychiatry.[101] However, closer scrutiny of the statistical probability calculations exposes the fact that the experimental distinction failed to meet the level necessary for confidence, as far as anti-depressants were concerned.[102] The article concludes:

> The results of this prospective study show that antidepressant use *per se* was associated with an only modestly increased risk of committing a homicide, with borderline statistical significance. ... These results ... imply that the use of antidepressants should not be denied to either adults or adolescents due to a presumed risk of homicidal behavior.[103]

A large percentage of the murderers (96% i.e., 812/849) were intoxicated by alcohol or illicit drugs while offending.[104] That compounding variable makes the possibility that prescribed medicines were the primary inducements for the crimes less likely.

One extensive study carried out in Sweden relied on the records of 856,493 individuals prescribed selective serotonin reuptake inhibitors (SSRIs) who were then convicted of violent crimes. It disaggregated the possible relationship by gender, age range, and by type of SSRI medication (fluoxetine, citalopram, paroxetine, sertraline, or escitalopram). Only the males (in the aggregate) and one age group (15-24, both genders) showed a significant ($p < 0.001$) relationship between use and convictions. Even these results, from a policy standpoint, are suspect since the control measures were based on behavior by individuals when they used SSRI compared with periods when they did not.[105] Although a robust calculation was used to adjust for internal correlations, statistical formulas cannot compensate for the inherent bias in the selection of the many individuals placed on medication who very likely had a propensity to violence in the first place.[106]

Unproven, also, is the suspicion that medicinal treatment for depression results in suicide. Randomized trials and a meta-analysis have shown an association, but nothing that is statistically significant, which means, from a scientific standpoint, the relationship has yet to be determined.[107] Given the potential harm involved in suicidal thinking, treatment protocols should necessarily balance the risk for side-effects against the possibility for self-injury.[108]

In fact, when the question of harm through pharmacological intervention is reversed to pose the proposition that offsetting depression might reduce aggressive impulses, there is some evidence that prescriptive interventions can curtail unwarranted or disproportionate violence. The chemistry may vary depending on the medication, but many anti-depressants arouse the level or maintain the durability of neurotransmitters (serotonin, dopamine, norepinephrine) in the brain's circuitry.[109] "Decades of research have shown that prosocial and affiliative behaviors are associated with intact or enhanced serotonin function, whereas antisocial and aggressive behaviors are associated with impaired or reduced serotonin function."[110] Researchers have manipulated positive sociability with an SSRI to determine the effect on moral judgements by volunteer subjects in hypothetical situations. In emotionally salient scenarios, volunteers were more inclined to judge harmful actions as forbidden compared to those taking a placebo ($p = 0.001$) or a relatively selective noradrenaline reuptake inhibitor that enhances noradrenaline neurotransmission ($p = 0.048$).[111] When engaged in an ultimatum game where mutual gain required the acceptance of monetary offers that could be non-advantageous for individuals, players using SSRIs were more prone to concessions than controls (placebo, $p = 0.034$; selective noradrenaline reuptake inhibitor, $p = 0.009$).[112] It is likely that modulation of anxiety, worry, and defeatism through appropriate medication may affect perspective in a positive way and result in more generous interpretations of possible outcomes.[113]

Finally, like so many dire warnings about the devastation wrought by the perils of modernity, the claim that mass murder is an unforeseen offshoot of medical science does not coincide with historical fact. Nor does assigning the blame to the vivid nature of mass media. As pointed out in the introduction, humankind's instinctual hostility and the inclination to wreak grave havoc on a grand scale has been represented in scripture, ancient literature, and history.[114] More evidentiary, there are documented accounts of rampages dating back to sixteenth century long before the advent of advances in medicine or easy access to electronic modes of communication.[115] The problem lies in the deviance that can sometimes corrupt human nature and it is that corruption that needs to be addressed to comprehend the cruelty and its byproducts.

There can be no doubt that psychotropic medications sometimes have undesirable side-effects, and, sadly, sometimes those effects may occasionally, if rarely, result in injuries or even death. But, as the preceding arguments demonstrate, the charge that they are responsible for autogenic killing is simply not supported by logic, the facts, empiricism, or history.

The psycho-emotional rudiments to autogenic massacres are presented with accompanying theoretical arguments, statistics, and documentary evidence in this book. The developmental sequence that is incentivized by those foundational elements are posited with additional facts and evidentiary arguments in the companion volume, *How Rampage Killers Interpret Their Worlds*.

The path to making a conscious decision to slaughter other human beings purposely and indiscriminately is lengthy, tortuous, and ugly. Mapping that route requires diligent observation and scrutiny of trails overgrown with damaged aspirations and human compulsions. The surveillance should not be obscured by detours that emanate from intuition without a factual basis.

Chapter Two

Perceived Physical Inadequacy

I am a cripple. Some say it is my own fault;
others blame my parents or my genes. I prefer to blame existence.
– August Strindberg
Ghost Sonata
trans. Katarina Carlson, Patrick Scheid, and Zach Trebino

Since a pre-occupation with appearance could be readily interpreted as superficial (almost by its very nature) and ultimately transitory, concern with the body's prowess might be discounted as a minimal variant in development. In fact, it is closely associated with a sense of personal efficacy that, in turn, is essential for adjusting to upheavals in life. "[A]t every developmental level, the evaluation of one's looks takes precedence over other domains as the Number 1 predictor of self-esteem."[1] The thesis partially explains the corrosive response to their disappointment in their physical features that some killers have shown. Of course, there is more to physicality than appearance, but the predictive value tends to remain constant for most corporal concerns.

Even though there have been myriad studies associating negative body image with youthful discontent, anxiety, and depression, what has become apparent in recent years is the extensive reach of those feelings into adolescence and adulthood. In a study of burn victims, for example, researchers noted:

> [B]ody image dissatisfaction is related to prolonged difficulties with mental and physical health-related quality of life … even after controlling for premorbid quality of life and injury severity. … Contrary to expectations, preinjury quality of life is not lower among those who develop body image dissatisfaction after the burn. Finally, postburn Physical domain adjustment is poorer among all burn survivors relative to published norms, whereas adjustment in the

> Mental domain is poorer only for those with body image dissatisfaction.[2]

Similar attitudinal inhibitors became apparent in an examination of children with pronounced limited stature. The situations studied were extreme, in that the subjects were diagnosed with achondroplasia with their height in the fifth percentile relative to age. Nevertheless, their scores on scales assessing social competence, behavior problems, and self-concept illustrate the profound impact that physical deviations can have on emotional stability and self-confidence. Although demonstrating no appreciable difference when compared to peers with respect to involvement in school activities, they measured significantly higher for schizoid traits, depression, social withdrawal, somatic complaints, and problems with self-concept in relation to both unhappiness as well as unpopularity.[3]

The conclusions parallel the relationship between calibrated body image dissatisfaction (BID) and assessed difficulties in conduct, social relations, and affective reciprocation in a study involving 650 fifth graders and their parents. Although, for the most part, results were mixed when it came to positive attitudes in relation to body image, children with the highest BID ratings also scored at elevated levels for internalizing problems and for negative affect.[4]

A person's view of his or her presentation to others, especially in the highly sensitive developmental period of adolescence, is projected and then replayed as an essential element of social consciousness. A review of influential factors in adolescent psychological maturation notes:

> Identity development has long been viewed … as a central task of adolescent development. Researchers … have described different constructs that contribute to adolescents' sense of self including academic competence, popularity and social acceptance, romantic appeal, and physical appearance. … [A]dolescents' perceptions of their physical appearance contributes most significantly to their overall sense of self. With changing bodies to make sense of, adolescents' views of their bodies no doubt contribute to their physical appearance self-concepts and their identity….[5]

The internalized image reflects a supposition of acceptance, impartiality, or sometimes distain – depending on the nature of the perception – as a significant feature coloring interpersonal events.

In the Walt Disney epic cartoon, *Dumbo*, a baby elephant is rejected by members of his own species.[6] "[T]he gossipy female elephants in Mrs. Jumbo's troupe are jealous when the stork delivers her baby. They refused to call him Jumbo Jr., and instead brand him 'Dumbo' because of his ears."[7] As the story proceeds, Dumbo finds he can use the body parts that were subjects of derision to fly. In life, though, such handicaps are rarely turned neatly into instruments for satisfaction and assertion.

A more realistic narrative is found in the movie, *Johnny Handsome*, when a physician tries to reform a disfigured imprisoned bank robber with a cleft pallet by giving him reconstructive surgery. The well-intentioned doctor believes that his patient's malicious nature is driven solely by his unpleasant features and disability, so with physical correction the criminality should evaporate. Upon his release from prison, however, the convict is obsessed with seeking revenge against those who double-crossed him in his former life.[8]

People carry their body image, whether positive, negative, or – more frequently – a mixture of both, throughout their life. "When these thoughts and feelings become too time-consuming and cause significant emotional distress (such as anxiety, sadness, or self-consciousness) and/or significant problems in your daily life — this is body dysmorphic disorder. [BDD]"[9] It, like gender dysphoria (GD) in certain cases, is a delusion (an unsubstantiated belief, fear, or desire) that without self-reflection can devolve into an obsession.[10] The influence such an impression may have in a prejudicial interpretation of reality by an eventual rampage murderer will be scrutinized later in this chapter. There is an abundance of research indicating that dysfunctional traits associated with mood are often exhibited among individuals with BDD in comparison to the general population. Particularly, depression, anxiety, and compulsions are prevalent.[11]

As a corollary to that association, some researchers maintain that body dysmorphia is a manifestation of obsessive-compulsive disorder.[12] "A pattern of neurocognitive deficits (obsessive thoughts and compulsive behaviors) may reveal symptoms of BDD and define the clinical profile of a given population. Cognitive deficits, including deficits in executive, memory, and social functions affect visual and selective information processing."[13] The deficiencies in thinking and selectivity in attention may contribute to delusions. When 48 patients with non-delusional body dysmorphia were compared with 52 patients with BDD diagnosed as delusional, investigators found the two groups did not differ significantly in terms of most variables (demographic traits, clinical features, phenomenology, course of illness including complications, comorbid psychopathologies, and response to treatment).[14] The researchers suggested "that BDD may have a psychotic subtype that significantly overlaps with, and may even be the same disorder as the BDD variant of delusional disorder, somatic type."[15] Andrew Blaze, who will be examined later in this chapter, repeatedly made statements that stressed her dysmorphic attitude toward her gender, but she expressed dissatisfaction with the nature of her physique as well. Her OCD was evident in her fixation on her online presence and sheer volume of the dramatizations belittling one persona and idolizing another.

An investigation over a timespan of four years involved 30 patients who imagined themselves to be "ugly." All met criteria for at least one comorbid disorder, with 18 (60%) exhibiting major depression, 10 (33%) bipolarity, and 15 (50%) suffering with social phobia.[16] Similar findings were reported in a survey involving 50 participants, 36 self-referred and 14 referred by medical personnel or agencies. Thirty-six percent had a past depressive episode and 20 of the 50 (40%) were rated with clinically significant depression at the time they were surveyed.[17] "There was also a high frequency of personality disorder … 72% of patients had one or more personality disorders diagnosed, 48% had two or more disorders, 26% had three or more disorders, and 4% four or more disorders."[18] In the four-year study, twelve (40%) appeared delusional, while only two (7%) of the subjects recognized that their physical defect(s) may have been imaginary.[19] Similarly, on a questionnaire, the only statistically significant distinction in responses between BDD subjects with and without depression was to the question, "'I would still be unattractive if I did not have my defect.' Patients who were clinically depressed were more likely to endorse this belief ($p = 0.04$)."[20] The assumption that their personal impressions were correct regardless of what evidence may or may not exist, underscores a well-known principle in modern social science, that will resurface throughout this book – as far as motivational impulses are concerned, perception trumps fact. The interpretation of data or beta press is more influential than the actual data or alpha press.[21]

That internal pressure is forceful enough for consideration of suicide. An investigation that followed the course of 185 men and women with BDD for four-years found a mean annual suicidal ideation rate of 57.8 percent, 10-25 times higher than the general population in the USA. Actual attempts averaged 2.6 percent, estimated to be 3-12 times more than the country overall. When adjustments were made for age, gender, and geographic region, the percentage of completed suicides was calculated to be almost half again as much as the nation at large (approximately .45 ×).[22]

Although usually (actually, *always*, according to the purposive sample in the Appendix) accompanied by other conditional characteristics, perceived physical inadequacy is present and pronounced with enough autogenic murderers that it cannot be discounted as a mere coincidental accompanying trait. On the contrary, it is a reoccurring attribute that, considering the literature related to personalized image, undoubtedly has a profound effect on sociability. One compilation of more than 48 cases of school shooters listed 24 (or approximately 50%) males and females alike with "biological issues," ranging from diminished stature, to being overweight, to a skin condition.[23] That group only included murderers who rampaged with a firearm at an educational institution. A broader set, including killers from multiple settings, who used homicidal methods besides shooting, is presented in the Appendix. Thirty percent (34/112) has physical features that could be considered unsatisfactory. (See Figure 6.1 and the Appendix for detail).

Five Cases in Point

Robert Benjamin Smith (Dyspraxia). A school shooter in 1966, he, was so persistently mal-coordinated that he struggled to master common tasks that are often indicative of developmental milestones – for example, tying his shoes and riding a bicycle.[24] He was not, however, intellectually incapable. Although he was retained in the early grades, by the time he reached high school he was an avid reader who was doing well enough academically for his classmates to elect him to the student council. However, he remained essentially friendless and, as far as his peers could tell, never dated.[25] During his senior year he walked from his home to the Rose-Mar College of Beauty in Mesa, Arizona (about a mile and a half) with a .22 caliber pistol, extra ammunition, a package of plastic sandwich bags, nylon cord, tape, and two hunting knives.[26] He shot to death four women, wounded another, and slaughtered a little girl who was only three years old.[27]

Scott Pennington (Speech Disability). He shot and killed his English teacher before holding an entire class hostage in Kentucky. Pennington previously expressed his discomfort with his dysfluency in an essay that he submitted to the very same instructor that he murdered. The assignment was to react to the theme: "Worst Day of My Life" and Pennington wrote in part, "… the day when I discovered I had no friends, my stuttering became more pronounced … I realized what hell life was…."[28] The fact that he associated his stutter with devastation in his social life affirms his self-consciousness regarding the impairment. After the killing, while holding classmates at gunpoint, Pennington, tried to goad them into talking. Remarkably, he appeared calm and spoke fluently, as if the act of murder assisted him in conquering his preoccupation with his vocal shortcoming.[29]

Michael Carneal (Limited Stature). At five foot two inches tall, Carneal was one of the slightest members of his class, wore glasses, and was frequently ill at ease.[30] He was belittled and intimidated, which added to his awkwardness.[31] Before leaving the eighth grade, a gossip column in the school paper mentioned that he was involved in a gay relationship, a rumor he found so humiliating that he made a futile and inept attempt to overdose by snorting Tylenol.[32] His perception of his inferiority was accentuated in high school by the success of his older sister who, as a senior, was socially confident, a section leader in the school band, a reporter for the newspaper, and a singer in the Kentucky state choir.[33] Along with the humiliation he experienced at school and the feelings of inferiority he felt when he compared himself to his sibling, he began to exhibit signs of paranoia. He heard commanding auditory hallucinations, believed dangerous intruders were secretly living in the crawl spaces of his home, and when showering covered the air vents because he was afraid people were spying on him.[34] He felt compelled to bring a virtual arsenal to school – a pistol, two rifles and two shotguns – because the rifles made him feel powerful and he wanted to impress a clique of older boys to gain acceptance by the group.[35] Targeting a prayer group that often met before classes, he killed three, and wounded five others, one of whom was paralyzed from the chest down.[36]

Eric Harris (Unsatisfactory Appearance, Disability). One of the Columbine shooters, Harris mentioned he felt harassed throughout much of his childhood because he was a "scrawny white kid."[37]

> I believe that Columbine investigators have overlooked or minimized the ramifications of this condition, both physical and psychological, in understanding Eric Harris' compulsion to punish his schoolmates and end his own life. Brooks Brown [a classmate] wrote that Eric was teased whenever he took off his shirt.[38]

Harris had a congenital condition known as *pectus excavatum*, a sunken sternum, creating the appearance of a concave chest.[39]

Adam Lanza (Unsatisfactory Appearance, BID). When Lanza murdered his mother then went to his former elementary school to massacre twenty children and six staff members, he was six feet tall and weighed 112 pounds, putting his body mass index at 15.2, below the 1st percentile.[40]

His low weight was not due to a medical condition, it was a byproduct of delusions aligned with the sort of body image dysphoria (BID) endured by people with anorexia nervosa.

> Overall, the studies undertaken, to date, specifically investigating unusual beliefs in AN [anorexia nervosa] report not only high rates of overvalued ideas (ranging from 26% to 30%) but also very high rates of beliefs that can be classified as delusions (ranging from 10% to 45.5%). The notion that unusual beliefs in AN are most likely to represent overvalued ideas with poor insight is not justified by this literature. Instead, delusions with no insight appear to be almost as present as overvalued ideas in AN samples.[41]

Lanza was terrified of being overweight and put together 35 reasons for avoiding food consumption.[42] The list was not simply a string of rationales for resisting weight gain. It literally encouraged starvation to the point of physical injury, including arguments such as:

> 09. Starving is an example of excellent will power. …
>
> 11. Bones are clean and pure. Fat is dirty and hangs on your bones like a parasite. …
>
> 25. I want to walk in the snow and leave no footprints.
>
> 26. Starve off the parts you don't need. They're ugly and they drag you down. …
>
> 34. Eating is conforming to everyone else's expectations.[43]

When tests were conducted after Lanza's death, Connecticut's chief medical examiner found no evidence of brain damage due to poor nutrition.[44] His murderous compulsions were not caused by neurological damage from malnutrition or any other organic cause. His skewed perceptions, as manifested in his BID, contributed to his aversion to almost every aspect of an active life (except virtual reality), which necessarily inhibited nourishment of elemental human requirements.

Additional precursors (itemized in the Appendix) aligned in shepherding Pennington, Smith, Carneal, Harris, and Lanza to their rampages. However, the preceding accounts testify to the discomfort they had with their physical limitations, a dissatisfaction which, by nature would have been pervasive, thus hampering their ability to socialize.

Assumed Inadequacy Relative to Status

Discussing her research at a hospital, Dorothea M. Ross, a founder of the Society of Pediatric Psychology, recalled:[45]

> In the early 1980s, as part of a major study of childhood pain, we asked children with leukemia what was their worst pain experience had been. We expected the answers to be some of the often-excruciating treatment-related pains that these children must endure. To our amazement many children said that their worst pain was to be teased about their appearance (for example, baldness, extreme pallor) when they returned to school.[46]

In a well-known early scene from the horror movie, *Carrie*, the protagonist is mocked by her teenage classmates when she begins to menstruate in the shower after her physical education class. The film's gory climax features Carrie committing mass murder through telekinesis.[47]

For reasons every bit as trivial children and adolescents frequently experience the type of intimidation foisted on Carrie. In a survey including over three thousand young people (ranging in age from 13-20) involving 73 schools and colleges in the United Kingdom, bullying was attributed to appearance by 51 percent of respondents, making it the number one reason for victimization.[48]

Given the hypersensitivity of pre-adolescent and adolescent minds it is not only logical but highly likely that BID (with all its variants) is an elemental agent making some paranoid individuals bitter enough to eventually turn toward indiscriminate killing.

Besides appearance, self-consciousness can also be associated with a severe illness, especially when it is persistent and, like disagreeable features, viewed with trepidation by the community at large. A particularly morbid rampage that occurred in the first part of the last century featured distress resulting from a chronic disease.

Biographical Analysis: Mutsuo Toi – Perceived Physical Inadequacy (Pronounced Illness, Sexual Disesteem); Neuropsychological Impairment (Depression)

When he was still just an infant both parents of Mutsuo died of the same illness that would contribute to his own undoing – tuberculosis. It was early in the twentieth century, before effective antimicrobial therapy became common. Orphaned with his sister, he was brought up in a village in rural Japan by his grandmother. Even though he started his life with profound loss he was able to enjoy a contented childhood with a close relationship to his sibling and his caregiver.[49] He was friendly, well-liked in his small community, and successful in school.[50] However, in his late teens and early twenties a conjunction of two circumstances with a pair of compulsions dislodged Mutsuo's emotional equilibrium.

The first circumstance was his sister's marriage. Her departure from the household, affixed with the responsibility of becoming the primary person looking after for his aging grandmother, depressed him.[51] He became known as a "hikikomori," a Japanese term for a young person who is reclusive.[52]

Mutsuo attempted to find renewed purpose and self-respect by joining the military and was successful in passing all the required tests except for the mandatory physical. During that examination a physician for the Imperial Japanese Army informed him that he had contracted tuberculosis.[53]

As a male adolescent who had just experienced the severance of a close familial relationship and was now facing impending mortality, he must have felt compelled to pursue provincial efforts to find a mate or at least experience the pleasure of coupling. He engaged in Yobai or "night-crawling," which traditionally involves entering the bedrooms of women unbidden during the night to seek consensual sexual intercourse.[54] He did so repeatedly and on many occasions consummated relations with some who were already married and with others who were much older than him. However, as news of his condition spread throughout the area, he more frequently faced revulsion.[55]

The vehement dismissals were accompanied by the nationwide fascination for a current news story featuring the seemingly sadistic strangulation and mutilation of a married lover by a prostitute, Abe Sada. She had been a Geisha, who contracted syphilis just as Mutsuo had been inflicted with tuberculous and, due to her illness, she turned to earning her living in a brothel. Abe strangled her partner, severed his genitalia with a kitchen knife, then carried them neatly wrapped in a magazine cover inside her bag until she was apprehended days later.[56] Mutsuo became so caught up with the prostitute's testimony he began writing a novel about the affair.[57]

He told an acquaintance, "I'm going to die from lung disease anyway, so I'll do something more terrifying than Sada Abe."[58] Insinuations of that sort were noticed by multiple residents throughout his tiny town leading to notification of law enforcement. Authorities confiscated weapons in his home and revoked his license for firearm possession.[59] It did not matter. Within a week Mutsuo had accessed a Browning shotgun, a katana, an ax, and two knives.[60] Around midnight on a rainy May evening in 1938 he climbed a pylon and cut the single cable that brought electricity to the township and its immediate vicinity.[61] The entire area immediately went dark, and Mutsuo was free to prowl, but now it would be for something more dreadful than sexual courtship.

He decapitated his 76-year-old grandmother with the ax.[62] In a note found after his suicide he suggested that the slaughter of the elderly woman, who had raised him from the time he was a toddler, was merciful because it spared her the shame that she would have surely endured as a survivor of his rampage.[63] "Tears, tears, I keep shedding tears of apology," he wrote.[64] After that initial murder he readied himself in combat regalia in an early enactment of the pseudocommando killer persona.[65] He strapped two flashlights to his head, hung a bicycle lamp around his neck, strapped an ammunition sack to his shoulders, and tucked the blades into his belt.[66]

Carrying his rifle, he then methodically proceeded through multiple homes killing almost every dweller but, inexplicably, sparing others who were clearly vulnerable. He entered 11 houses in the settlement, attacking 30 people, most with his sword or ax – 25 died immediately and two more later succumbed to fatal wounds. Half of the town's population, ranging in age from 5 to 86, were murdered.[67] Mutsuo then walked two kilometers up a hill to a neighboring village. There he killed his final couple – first he shot the husband seven times as he attempted to defend his home, then he shot and killed the man's wife with whom he had previously had an affair.[68]

Ninety minutes had elapsed since the time of his grandmother's death and Mutsuo made a final early morning visit to one more residence.[69] After demanding a notebook and pencil he left the family assuring them, "I won't shoot innocent people. Don't worry," and instructed a boy who lived there, "Study hard and become a great man."[70] He made his way up into the forested hills to compose his farewell message. As morning broke, he took his own life by pulling the trigger of the shotgun with his big toe, shooting himself in the chest.[71]

In one portion of his final letter, without offering any condolences for those he harmed, he gives a rationale for the bedlam, referring to his rampaging as vengeful, as if the victims were responsible for his disease.

> I have an uncurable sickness. I am shunned by my neighbors, betrayed by women and for this act of revenge I am willing to die. I thought about turning back, but after battling this illness, I feel like I can no longer come back. If only this sickness was treatable. If only I was a little bit stronger, maybe things wouldn't have to be like this.[72]

In another passage he laments, but his pathos is only for himself.

> During the four years that I was ill, I really wept at the harshness and oppression of society. Although my relatives told me they love me, I cried for how little it was. Society should have a little sympathy for those who have no one to care for them, the tuberculosis patients.[73]

Like his more modern counterparts, he believed personal unhappiness provided a justification for human sacrifice.

Later in the century Mutsuo's disenchantment with women along with his self-pity would be echoed by Marc Lépine, George Sodini, Eliot Rodger, and other malcontents who would in time assume a self-conscious, but still smug, mantel as involuntary celibates (incels) –misogynists frustrated with their lack of success with romance. A thread on a website devoted to this peculiar faction of male chauvinism claimed Mutsuo as one of their own.

> I dont know about you guys but i think this was badass as shit, this guy almost got as many kills as Cho [Seung-hui, responsible for the highest number of gun causalities at a school, K-12 or college, to date] and in Wikipedia it says that it is the dealiest shooting by a lone gunman in Japanese history.
>
> Just goes to show that you should never fuck with ricecels [presumably a racist rendition for Asian incels].[74]
>
> He was the original ricecel and an inspiration to all.[75]

He really was......[76]

The celebratory rhetoric neglects the facts that their hero had relations with a variety of partners and the rejection he experienced was due to an infectious disease that he carried that was fatal in his lifetime. As this chapter reaches its conclusion, thwarted intimacy as an aspect of sexual disesteem, will be discussed further in relation to individualized perceptions of limited physical capacity.

Even though it may be linked with other foundational elements, disappointment with bodily features can be perennial in an eventual killer's thinking.

Biographical and Textual Analysis: Andrew Blaze – Perceived Physical Inadequacy (Dysphoria); Neuropsychological Impairment (Delusional, Mood Disordered); Pathological Personality (Detached, Antagonistic)

Her legal name, which was never formally changed, was Randy Stair. She was a producer, director, and animator on YouTube and assumed the pseudonym of Andrew Blaze for those purposes.[77] In deference to her extensive web activity and her small following on social media, her adopted moniker is used in this text. In a similar regard, female pronouns are used for referents. Blaze, at 24 years of age, was resolute in her identification with the female gender. Prior to her sudden assault, she posted a suicide note online under the heading, "Please Read."[78] She declared, "I've been a trapped soul who's been forever searching to rediscover herself. You didn't misread that; I said 'herself'. Andrew Blaze is not a persona nor a character ... it's who I truly am."[79] Blaze struggled with her sexual identity and viewed herself as victimized by her birth assignment. In a journal entry three days before her rampage she wrote, "[T]he girl inside me is clawing to get out."[80] Throughout much of her writing and in many of her videos that theme is emphasized.

She used pallets to block the exits of the store where she worked a night shift, then fired 59 rounds with two pistol-grip shotguns, damaging merchandise, shooting three people to death, then turning a weapon on herself to take her own life with a single intraoral shotgun blast.[81] She murdered the night manager, who was 47 years of age, with five shots striking his head, chest, rank flank, groin, and left arm.[82] A 63-year-old fellow-worker was fatally shot in the upper back and left shoulder.[83] Her youngest victim, at 25, was killed with four wounds: two to the left hip, one to the anterior chest, and another to the back of the head.[84] A fourth employee managed to escape.[85]

Blaze left her parents with a brother and said, in one of the many tweets she uploaded just before her murder-suicide, "Goodbye humans…I'll miss you…."[86] As the remaining biographical account will attest, the statement alludes to the fact that she considered herself to be of another world, but the wistful sentiment is disingenuous. She harbored and repeatedly expressed disgust for the entire human race.

During what she called her "9-year career," Blaze produced multiple YouTube channels, prominently *PioneersProductions*, *PioneersAnthology*, and *Ember's Ghost Squad* (*EGS*) as well as a string of gaming pictorials.[87] Before her death she had but 428 subscribers for hours of video.[88] Her tiny audience did not prevent her from presuming she had celebrity status. She posted question and answer sessions where she supposedly responded to written inquiries from curious fans and compiled autobiographical productions in which she would chart her memories of her creative course. No doubt largely due to infamy for her murders – certainly not the quality of the films – subscribers eventually topped seventeen thousand.[89] In addition, prior to her sudden assault, over a period of less than a year, she authored a journal of 237 pages while also maintaining multiple web sites.[90]

Her early efforts on YouTube consisted of physical comedy, dry humor, and self-mockery.[91] These shows were interspersed with narratives, some whimsical and other just silly, involving a variety of playthings, most prominently a hobby horse, a sex-crazed homosexual stuffed whale, and a sardonic rubber frog.[92]

In an episode entitled, "Extinction," the whale and frog are viciously killed by her after she loses her job because they collaborated in making an obscene video of her then posting it on the internet. She stabs both animals to death, while an animated female singer and guitarist named Ember goads her on.[93] When the deed is done and Blaze is lamenting the violence, the rocker tells Blaze off-handedly, "You did what you had to do."[94] In the next chapter the two mischievous objects reappear and terrorize Blaze until Ember magically transforms them back into inanimate figures.[95] The series finale concludes with Blaze, at Ember's urging, cremating the pair to purge their memory and rid herself of the curse of communicating with toys. Blaze returns to her house, despondent, and tells Ember "I'm ready," then points a pistol to her temple and shoots herself, immediately collapsing on the floor. Multiple images of Ember gradually move to the screen's foreground followed by a frame with just her eyes.[96]

The sequence foretells Blaze's eventual suicide while marking a permanent end to creations for *PionneersProductions* and ushering in new channels, one of which, *EGS*, would center around Ember McLain, a character based on a storyline from a Saturday morning Nickelodeon show, *Danny Phantom*. As a prelude to one feature Blaze posted a disclaimer disavowing association with the studio.[97]

The very brief narrative that follows involves the pulverization via a ray gun of an animated male (who resembles Blaze) by a member of the Ghost Squad. An argument then ensues between the killer and another member of *EGS* over the necessity for murder. The aggressor exclaims: "Do you even know what your purpose is in this squad? … Our purpose is to destroy the human race and terminate this stupid planet, not sit around with our thumbs up our asses and act like we belong here."[98] The cartoon would upload on YouTube six days after Blaze's rampage. She apparently scheduled its appearance to showcase her emotional divorcement from humanity and rationalize her own brutality.[99] Another film was posted less than two hours before her SMASI: a 42-minute kaleidoscopic tribute to the Columbine massacre and EGS interspersed with images of the supermarket where Blaze intended to murder and kill herself. As of this writing, it has been viewed well over fifteen thousand times.[100] That posting was followed by a slew of tweets linking to videos about the Ghost Squad saga and Blaze's overall disenchantment with earthly existence.[101]

Ember premiered in Blaze's work in "Extinction" and, after the incineration of other main characters, Blaze all but dropped broad comedy as well as straightforward storytelling to concentrate on fantastic tales and animation.[102] In one of her numerous retrospectives she talks of the segment where she butchers the frog along with the whale with the air of a seasoned director espousing on her creative genius for a film class. "It was the first video I did that I had that was on a much more abstract scale and now all my ideas are leaning towards that direction. …"[103] Remember, her audience was less than five hundred.

The reason for the new emphasis was her continued infatuation with Ember's imaginary persona. In a recording for her parents prior to the sudden assault, Blaze informed them, (without a visible trace of irony) of her yearning for this character who was, keep in mind, not just fictional, but completely animated.[104] Blaze came to believe, as incredible as it may seem, that taking multiple lives would provide her with a passport to a netherworld populated by Ember and her cohorts where Blaze would be reborn as a cartoonish version of herself. The inside cover of the spiral notebook that contained her journal angerly showcases her fantasy.

> I have no regrets for what I may do or what I have done. I am who I am, and no fucking human shit can take that away from me. I'm an 'EGS' recruit; you're worthless fucking humans. ... I will not stop. I will not change. I will not cower. I will fight for the squad and do what I've set out to do. I'm Andrew Fucking Blaze.[105]

Her deluded reasoning for killing three people corresponds with the rationale embraced by James Holmes (Chapter Four), who carried out the Aurora theater massacre, believing that deaths would add value to his own life and contribute to his longevity.

It is also evident that Blaze shared qualities with Elliot Rodger, who was self-conscious about his sexuality, prone to self-pity, completely self-absorbed, and prolific. Between comedic-dramatic productions, animation, live videos, farewell addresses, and handwritten journals, Blaze left behind an extensive collection of written words, oral commentary, and creative projects expressing a philosophy on life that is both imaginative and disturbing. The excerpts that follow comprise a small fraction of her work. These texts were selected to provide explanations, as disconcerting as they may be, for the slaughter and destruction Blaze contemplated and eventually enacted. Many of her more emotional expressions are in relation to her gender dysphoria. However, that dissatisfaction is accompanied by an all-consuming depression entangled in disdain for people in general. As she anticipated the upcoming killings, she fully adopted an absurd melancholy fable that she believed would alleviate her cognizance of her physical insufficiency. The selections are grouped along three themes: a) her sexual identification and dissatisfaction with her assigned gender at birth, b) her chronic disenchantment with virtually every aspect of life, and c) her desire for eternal relief by way of a persistent singular delusion.

Gender dysphoria. She was enraptured by femininity and despised masculinity. The following entry from her diary, implies that it is not just the male form that she disliked but all aspects of manhood.

> Whenever I'm out and about I focus all my attention on girls. I analyze their appearance, their traits, see how they tick and think, 'Gee ... they'd make a nice addition to the squad..' ... Words cannot

> describe my love for girls. … Guys on the other hand are absolutely fucking disgusting. I'll leave it at that. I had to be sent here in this body to realize how wrong it is and to crave what I once had and had lost.[106]

She frequently dressed in female attire and in one of her suicide videos, taunted her parents with the revelation that the activity as well as her feminine grooming were habitual.

> I was cross dressing ever since high school. … I never told anybody about this and it's something that probably shocks you. … Every year of my life since 2013 I just felt more and more feminine. … Look at the bathroom. Look at where my stuff was. You'll see there's a girl's Venus razor there. … Every three days since like 2016 I've been shaving my arms and legs and my entire body every three days. You wonder what I am doing in the shower for so damn long, I'm shaving my entire fucking body. … But nobody ever questioned that. … I hid it for the longest time.[107]

However, as the following excerpts from her journal indicate, wearing the clothing of women only gave Blaze momentary solace before reminding her that she was, from her point of view, stuck in a masculine frame. Blaze does not appear to be referencing any symptoms of transvestic disorder since she does not mention sexual arousal.[108] Instead, she was more concerned with actual garments and the female pose that she was able to adopt as she wore them.

> I sit here alone on my bed full of emptiness. I'm wearing my girl clothes with my legs crossed. Why am I damned to spend two to three decades in this disgusting body?? I'm not a man. Sorry mom and dad, but I'm not sorry. I'm a fucking woman. Each and every day it gets harder to live in this body. …
>
> I don't know how my mom hasn't put it all together. She asked me once as an 'end all be all' way of 'Are you gay?' and I said 'No,' because I'm not gay. Guys who are 'gay' are attracted to men (the same sex). I despise men, I hate them, they're disgusting. …
>
> And the thing is, I don't want to fuck girls, I want to be them. I'll gladly live and die a virgin. I respect girls too much to just use them for sex; people like that disgust me. Sex is disgusting.[109]

Beyond the vociferous diatribes about her preferred gender, though, is evidence that she resented the physical shape of her body, not simply her sex assignment.

> [Blaze is driving and scowling, complaining that she feels frustrated by her latest recording efforts and the traffic.] One thing I can talk about is I've noticed that I've lost weight, which is bad, cause, when you look at my body structure, I have nothing to me [removes hands from steering wheel and displays a bicep by pulling on t-shirt sleeve]. My clothes hang off of me. … I don't even want to eat anything anymore. It's terrible. Nothing makes my mouth water anymore, like, nothing makes me crave something.[110]

Blaze's psychological divorcement from her natal gender, repeated debasement of male attributes, and complaints about her physique demonstrate that she was dysphoric with respect to her body as well as her gender. A related malformed perception, body integrity identity disorder (BIID), among people who are detached from their assigned sexual identity has been estimated at a rate of 19 percent.[111] BIID differs from BDD because the individual with the identification disorder frequently becomes obsessed with the prospect of amputating the offensive body part. Blaze's complaints about her male organs would border on that type of revulsion. Aside from fretting about her masculinity, Blaze was expressing the general disenchantment she was feeling for simple pleasures. She not only disliked the body in which she was born, she convinced herself that life had become bland, thus establishing a philosophical foundation for slaughter. Most of the pessimistic quotations that follow are laced with that anhedonia.

Depression and spite. Blaze was an admirer of Eric Harris and she begins her journal by reverentially quoting him. "As the late Eric Harris once said, 'I hate the fucking world.' What an inspiration."[112] A few lines later she meshes the belligerent style of her idol with a sketch of her personal purgatory.

> Humans are WORTHLESS. …
> What is there to be remotely happy about on this shit hole of planet??
> You are a dead man the instant you are conceived by your parents.
> You don't even have a say in your own name![113]

Blaze caps her rant about humanity's lack of worth and the vacuous nature of existence with a complaint about the fact that names are determined by parents at a child's birth. The fact that she associated her chosen de plume with femininity, repeatedly insisting that the name represents her true nature, suggests that the objection of which she wrote was her sex designation, more than name specification. The gender assignment was a primary source for her barely subdued rage.

Throughout her diary Blaze frequently returns to mimic the random wrath of her model, Harris. At one point she writes of channeling his personality by wearing a t-shirt stenciled with "Natural Selection," the belligerent self-satisfied phrase that was on the shirt Harris wore during the massacre at Columbine.[114] Blaze, despite her narcissistic traits and self-indulgence, was not wholly psychopathic like her idol, especially with respect to her lesser ability to manipulate people in her orbit.[115] Although she was certainly vain, her social phobia prevented her from successfully using others for her own purposes.

> I'm fine being alone. ... I'm not into relationships. I just I don't care to be in a relationship. ... Once I got through college, I just I didn't want to get a job. I didn't want to get a career. I just didn't want to have anything to do with the fucking world anymore and all I cared about was Ember. All I cared about was death, ghosts, funerals, graves, dark music, horror music, you know. ... I was just in the darkest place I've ever been in my life, and I've never gotten out of that. Nor do I want to.[116]

Blaze seemed completely disinterested in forming attachments and was consistently asocial. An indicator of her daily devolution was her complete lack of ambition. She was utterly unwilling to pursue any interest outside of the virtual horror she had fashioned for herself. That state of mind is an aspect of alienation, and it is part of the crucial unconscionable formation of an eventual rampage killer (discussed extensively in Chapter Three of *How Ramage Killers Interpret Their Worlds*).

In another recording made prior to her murder-suicide, Blaze revealed that her enjoyment of cross-dressing was a carefully guarded secret. The closeting of that activity along with her perception of gender misidentification was a source of extreme emotional distress. She metaphorically acted out her fear of exposure in the pivotal video when she kills two whimsical companions. At one point she screams, "All these years I've put up with your shit ... most of all the public humiliation you've caused me!"[117] Then, in her first suicide post she admits that the dramatic scene was an enactment of her interior reality.

> I'd highly, like, advise caution watching that video because it really starts showing like the psychotic side of me and it's really disturbing to watch. Um, in terms of like performance and all that, it was one of the best acting performances, I say acting [gestures with air quotation marks] loosely, but one of my best performances on video.[118]

Her anxiety around concealment and possible exposure is common among those who are non-heterosexual. Research that involved 3,350 undergraduates found significantly higher levels of clinical symptoms for general anxiety, panic disorder, social phobia, and depression for those who were bisexual, gay, lesbian, queer, or questioning than among others self-identified as straight.[119]

For Blaze, that kind of pervasive animus completely shaded any potential ambition.

> I'm so ready to go, even if I die a nobody, ANYTHING there is better than here. I've learned a lot in my 24 ¼ years on this planet but the biggest thing I've learned is that nothing matters.[120]

In one of her many YouTube postings directly addressing her viewers, Blaze momentarily stumbles upon an insight, which, unfortunately, she fails to deeply consider. She observes that her sadness may be associated with her preoccupation with her online persona to the detriment of the pursuit of real goals in life. There is a bit of irony in the fact that she recognizes that possibility as she is filming a video.[121]

At one point in one of the suicidal postings, she admits that she might benefit from professional help, but then blithely discounts the possibility.

> I know you could be thinking like you have gotten help. You could have seen a psychiatrist. You could have gotten help! But the truth is that wouldn't be me. Me being on medication, sitting in therapy. No. That alters who you are.[122]

Eschewing psychological interventions, Blaze might have opted for a physical recourse to alleviate her dissatisfaction by pursuing a sex change. After all, she blamed much of her misery on her revulsion toward her own body and her longing to be a woman. Yet, she completely dismisses the idea of realizing true transsexuality for reasons that are every bit as flimsy as those she used to reject counseling.

> I wanted to get a sex change operation and everything. I really honestly did, but I knew it wasn't smart to do because it ruins your whole life if it's botched or if it goes wrong and not everybody looks good after a sex change operation. and that's what I wanted to do but I couldn't do it. And I'm also like, yeah, but then it's not me, you know. I was put here in this body and I'm gonna have to live in this body until I die.[123]

First, she says she is reluctant because the procedure could go awry, then she caves to her narcissism by focusing on the remote possibility that her appearance afterwards might be distasteful. Finally, she settles on the same meaningless bromide she used with respect to mental health treatment – that it is not who she is meant to be and she is destined just do endure her fate. The truth is Blaze relished her depression.

> I just want to lock myself in a dark room and listen to horror soundtracks all night. Those haunted dark piano, string, and synth bass soundtracks make me feel that much closer to home.[124]

Instead of seeking a solution, she was determined to focus almost exclusively on a fantastic obsession.

Deluded escapism. Her unhinged beliefs were rooted in disgust for her masculine biology along with an associated desire to evade reality.

> I've wanted to die for as long as I can remember being told about death. I want to be free. I want to get out this body that brings me nothing but agonizing shame. I'm one of them; a ghost squad recruit.[125]
>
> There are few images that truly changed my direction in life like Ember and the Dazzlings [members of the Ghost Squad]. … The image of her floating with her guitar and evil grin changed my life forever. …
>
> These images are what drives me. I can't take my eyes off Mackenzie [another spectral teen in the ghost squad] either. M is my best friend. … Ember's my goddess. …[126]

The connection between her dysphoria and her resistance to maturity does not imply that such immaturity is a dominate characteristic among people who are transgender, transsexual, or transitioning. In fact, there is evidence that some dysphoric individuals do not necessarily exhibit psychological problems apart from anxious thoughts associated with their sexual status.[127] Their concerns over gender identification are frequently isolating but not always symptomatic of a broad spectrum of preoccupations, except for very realistic impressions of social rejection and concomitant depression.[128]

However, in the case of Blaze her fixation on gender transference was emblematic of resistance to living in a world where she would need to take care of the common problems besetting every person, including those connected to relationships and sex. While she was steadfast in her dislike for masculinity, she was evasive when talking of her sexuality.

> In all honesty, I've never been into relationships. I've never ever even been on a date, to tell you the truth. Never have, never wanted to. … It's not like I'm asexual or anything. I have sexual interests, pretty much everyone on earth does, but it's just my choice. It's what I've chosen and honestly, it's what makes me happy. … And at the end of the day, does it really matter?[129]

Sexual activity entails involvement, however fleeting, and may imply commitment that edges close to adulthood. Her self-indulgence could hardly allow for the intrusion of others, even in the most superficial way. The characters in her online stories were toys, gadgets, and cartoons. Most salutary, she was convinced she would finally escape the rigors of common existence by joining a crowd of imaginary phantoms, all of whom were caricatures of pubescent girls. Romanticizing death is common among rampageous individuals and the entrancement becomes more intense as the prospect for the final confrontation draws closer. (That aspect of the devolving perspective of sudden mass assailants is also analyzed in *How Rampage Killers Interpret Their Reality*).

Blaze was hardly alone among those who struggle with their gender status with respect to harboring suicidal wishes. A literature review showed that among diagnosed GD transsexuals an average of 37 to 74 percent harbored self-destructive thoughts. For those who were birth assigned as male (comparable to Blaze), percentages were 33-71.9.[130] When the researchers interviewed 151 users of a gender identity treatment unit, they found that almost half (48.34%) had contemplated taking their own life and close to one quarter (23.84%) had tried at least once.[131] "[O]ne might suppose that in this population, suicidal ideation may be associated with an emotional process which might limit the perception of available solutions and drive a person towards a state of hopelessness, thus increasing the probability of suicide."[132] That sort of emotional exhaustion is certainly apparent in the myriad vituperative and melancholic statements made by Blaze.[133]

While the experiential source for her suicidal desperation may have been the same as the clients participating in the clinic, Blaze's referential frame for that final remedial act was completely different. The subjects who were interviewed had attempted to end it all by overdosing, hanging, self-suffocation, stabbing themselves, or some other form of personally inflicted bodily injury.[134] Blaze took the lives of others as a preface to taking her own and did so because she believed the sacrifice was necessary for an animated afterlife. She was depressed, but her death wish was infused with a convoluted fantasy that required multiple murder for its consummation.

When Blaze insisted that she would be reincarnated into a ghostly feminine cartoon, she was not writing or speaking metaphorically, nor was she referring to a passing whimsy. Rather, she was perseverating on an auto-erotic metaphysical belief that was infused with her repugnance toward her gender by birth. In the following passage she pictures her transference to the next realm then describes her dysmorphic attitude toward her current state.

> I envision the world around me fading away audibly and visually into darkness. ... and then after around 10 seconds of pure darkness and silence begin to see Mackenzie standing inches away from my eyes, starting in profile, then a blur, and finally coming into focus; almost like waking up from a surgical procedure in a daze. ...
>
> Words cannot describe how happy I'll be to not have to eat, breathe, blink, or shit ever again. I virtually eat nothing nowadays. I'm 132 lbs of skin and bone. My arms are literally as thin as the EGS drawings.
>
> I want to chop my penis off so bad ... they're so fucking disgusting. ... I can't wait to have my penis and my butt hole taken away and to have my pussy and breasts back... It's agony ... 24 years without them.[135]

In one suicide message she reaffirms the notion that transcendence into the ghost squad was preordained and insists that the *EGS* series was a declaration for a perverse reckless freedom. She also tries, without much success, to advance a logical argument for her nonsensical doctrine. Then, in a tiresome display of her inflated sense of self-importance she renders advice for the followers that she believes will be inspired by her murder-suicide.[136] Obviously, Blaze had taken refuge in possibilities completely divorced from even a semblance of reality. Her portrayal of the freakish afterlife is practically a caricature of a fantasy that might be embraced by a preschooler, but she was 24 years old when she spoke of the rapturous reunion she would experience after death.

Another journal entry makes it clear that her illusion was an intoxicant, meant to obliterate the pangs associated with ordinary existence.

> I used to believe in heaven, God, Jesus, and all that shit. … Once I realized how the world 'works': I would either daydream in class about YouTube videos, girls, or death. To this day those are still my big Threes at 24. It never gets boring; life gets boring. This body is beyond boring. Humans are beyond boring. Just be thankful I don't experiment with drugs. I've always wanted to try LSD but it'd be the death of me, hands down. Could you imagine me on acid? … Besides alcohol and cigarettes the only drug I've done is weed, and I barely felt anything. … I'm not a fan of injection so heroines out. Coke? … Snorting white stuff up your nose? Pass. … I can barely drink a pilsner beer these days without getting bored of it. Alcohol just doesn't do it for me. … 'EGS' is all I have to look forward to.[137]

When she compares her obsession with drugs and alcohol, she indicates that her gender dysphoria and romance with death are both subsumed in a desire for oblivion.

Of all the disturbing aspects of Blaze's short life, the most distressing and perplexing is her mortal subscription to a Pygmalion illusion. It is not, though, entirely unfathomable. It can be understood by integrating primary aspects of her internal life. In the first video-taped farewell to her parents she touches on each corner of the triad that shaped her disturbed motivation.

> I doubt any of you knew how depressed I was. … I was never meant to be a guy. I was just a female soul trapped in a man's body my whole life and I couldn't tell you guys that. … I always felt like I was a girl, pretty much, I was always girly, you know. … Ember was always there in this dark place. … Like, she told me to do this. You

> know, do it for the ghost squad, you know, we need more souls. Kill people. .... It was just the overall hatred and general stress of being here on this planet. ... I just wanted to kill people.[138]

The interaction of her perpetual melancholy with her neurotic impressions and her desperate yearning for solace does not absolve Blaze of responsibility. As suggested earlier, she had no interest in treating her discomfort with her gender through psychological or physical remedies. She chose to be isolated, and she delighted in her own hostility. Most importantly, she was aware, if unconvinced, of the absurdity of the mythos. In the following set of quotations, she careens from aggressive defensiveness, to proclaiming her superiority, to simply acknowledging that she might appear to be psychotic, to a feeble explanation of her morbidly bizarre doctrine.

> Somewhere someone is laughing at all of the things I'm saying like 'this is what ... I mean ... this is without a doubt the stupidest psychotic retard on Earth!' Ha, keep laughing pal ...You'll all see for yourselves when your time comes ... .[139]

> I'm not insane. Would someone insane admit or deny their own insanity; don't think so. ...
> I simply tell it how it is; although 'simply' is a rough was of putting it. I have a very gifted yet abstract mind.[140]

> I just felt a connection to her [Ember]. I felt like I'd known her before, even though she's a cartoon. Spiritually, I just felt connected. ... *EGS* is just meant to be, be who you are, not give a fuck what anyone thinks about you and just live, you know, your existence. You're a ghost. You're dead, you know, that's the whole point.[141]

Her desperate desire to remove her discomfort fits with models for delusionary thinking that recognize strange belief-systems as noticeably absurd, unassailable to logic, isolating in nature, and associated with internalized stressors.[142] Blaze persisted in her incredibly fantastic thinking because she went unchallenged due to her solitary lifestyle.

As a product of self-deception and wish fulfillment, the formation of her peculiar epistemology was largely a product of her own volition.

> All delusions are currently thought to have an organic cause and are explained in neuropsychological terms, by reference to brain damage,

> perception failures, reasoning biases and cognitive deficits. But the formation of some delusions is also likely to include motivational factors. …
>
> Some delusions have been described as extreme cases of self-deception. They are considered cases of self-deception because they seem to have a defensive function. They are considered extreme because they tend to disrupt functioning to a greater extent than standard cases of self-deception, and to result in the endorsement of more implausible and more tenacious beliefs.[143]

Empirical support for that supposition is found in the close connection between hypnosis and misidentification, the social context of delusions (particularly those of a religious nature), as well as rationalizations for persecutions.[144] An integrative review of articles covering 43 experimental efforts that manipulated variables to examine the causes of delusions and hallucinations in non-clinical and clinical populations found that mental mechanisms are frequently major contributors to paranoia and illusionary ideas. The psychological apparatuses that were particularly notable included the influence of the necessity to maintain self-esteem, exaggerated fears from worry or rumination, anxiety, and the cognitive shadow of negative affect.[145]

The fiction manufactured by Blaze was consistent with the self-deception necessary to maintain paranoid theories for implementing indefensible decisions. Particularly consequential to her decisiveness was deliberate indulgence in a fantasy (*EGS*) and infatuation with a tragic motif (a sacrificial death necessary to realize a fantasized state of being). Both illustrate compulsions that are often a part of the anticipatory mind set of rampage killers (considered more broadly in Chapter Four of *How Rampage Killers Interpret Their Reality*). Blaze's rejection of her gender along with her musculature was sharpened by social mores and self-imposed deprivation of emotional intimacy. Her case accentuates how destructive a repulsion toward physical features can be especially when it is associated with obsessions relevant to gender.

Assumption of Diminished Status and Sexual Disesteem

As mentioned in the last chapter boys and men sometimes believe they are inadequate when they fail to conform to certain cultural conceptions of masculinity. These feelings are related to perceptions of physical deficiencies because they are realized by disappointment in a capacity to meet expectations associated with gender. They originate with the assumption of shortcomings when normative roles are not sufficiently fulfilled due to, for example, social intimidation, a lack of athleticism, occupational setbacks, or difficulty in providing for dependents.[146]

> [E]very man will feel inadequate at some point in his life resulting in a crisis of masculinity. It is from this feeling of inferiority and shame that men attempt to repair, restore, or reclaim their manhood. For many, this is achieved via violence. In addition, men that do not feel loved by others or do not achieve a sense of self-love are more prone to violent behaviors.[147]

The result is emotional distance knotted with resentment. That cognitive structure, entangled within masculine hegemony, is represented in Figure 2.1.

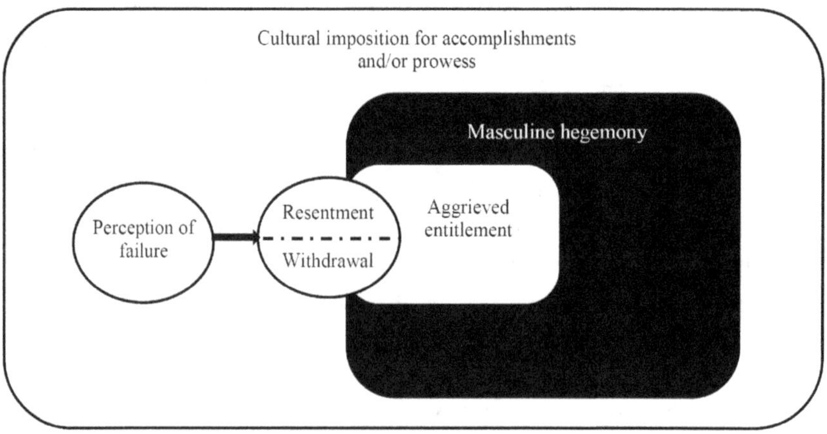

FIGURE 2.1. Assumption of diminished status and male hegemonism. When boys or men assume they have failed to sufficiently meet the expectations of their culture they insulate themselves from their disappointment with resentment and sometimes by withdrawing. If they subscribe to the notion of inherent male privilege, they will imagine or exaggerate grievances.

Toxic masculinity can be associated with animosity over personal shortcomings and or setbacks often attributed to progressive influences.

> Two studies examined whether men's perception of the declining value of traditional masculinity activates social status, realistic, and symbolic threat, and in turn motivates opposition to feminist social movements. In Study 1, men's perception that their ingroup is losing

> value across several social spheres was associated with social status and realistic threat, both of which were associated with opposition to feminist movements. Study 2, an experiment, presented men with public opinion data showing a 30-year decline in the degree to which Americans value traditional masculinity or no decline. ... In sum, perceived decline in the social value of traditional masculinity creates status anxiety about the ingroup's future and motivates compensatory reactions against gender equality.[148]

That reactionary insecurity is reflected in sexist notions and beliefs (professed or enacted).

Reporting on the database of active shooters (predicated on the FBI definition of public assaults with four or more deaths),[149] *Mother Jones* in 2019 noted:

> Based on case documents, media reports, and interviews with mental health and law enforcement experts, we found that in at least 22 mass shootings since 2011—more than a third of the public attacks over the past eight years—the perpetrators had a history of domestic violence, specifically targeted women, or had stalked and harassed women.[150]

The preferential violence, though, while hinting at pathology, is not entirely foundational to motivation since the action may originate as a byproduct of perceived failures associated with one or more dispositional conditions. Kimveer Gill and George Hennard along with Lépine and Sodini are examples of misogynous autogenic killers, who were subjected to dispositional conditions from a single or multiple domains that prefaced their hatred of the opposite sex (documented in this book's Appendix and Appendix A of *How Rampage Killers Interpret Their Worlds*).

Preoccupation with sexual prowess is a subsidiary of toxicity originating from gender stereotypes and subjugation. A male's impression that his sexuality is undeveloped, or immature can devolve into antagonism toward femininity as evidenced by so called involuntary celibates (incels). Again, the relationship is shown in Figure 2.1. The incel league is necessarily misogynistic, since it is premised on a belief that men are entitled to sex and only idealized representatives are successful at coupling. One member of an internet Forum entitled "INCELS," posted:

> … I see of Sexism out in the world.. and, I love it. I fucking love that the world hasn't been lost yet in that regard. There's still people out there who spend their time reminding women of their place in society. Hell, even Trump on some level is sexist and you can't even deny that. You shouldn't. That's fucking amazing. The leader of the free world bragged about how he groped women, and that's awesome. Women are continually reminded about their lower status, and all they can do is complain.[151]

Another (signified with an image of Virginia Tech killer Cho Seung-hui aiming a handgun) wrote:

> I vote for sexism as I don't know why females are seen as human in the first place, their actions make them seem like low IQ robots instead.[152]

A third added:

> There's no way in hell anyone is gonna make me see a woman as strong and independent. When she's she's still getting her black blown out by dudes and as well as still asking men for money even when they have jobs of their own.[153]

A qualitative analysis of over eight thousand posts made in two incel communities on the net found that the conversations centered on five interrelated topics: a) the sexual market; b) women as naturally evil; c) legitimizing masculinity; d) male oppression; and e) violence.[154] Rodger Elliot (analyzed in Chapter 5) was a prototype of a man invested in sexual entitlement. His extended listing of supposed slights was derived from failed romantic interactions to which he felt an inherent right.

In contrast, women feel rejected due to perceptive deficiencies founded on idealized gender standards. The point is personified by a woman known only as Alana who first created the incel portmanteau when she started a website known as Alana's Involuntary Celibate Project as a forum for people who, like her, were frustrated by sparsity or failures in their sexual encounters.[155] It was meant to be a refuge for all those unable, for whatever reasons, to form intimate attachments. "I don't care if your reason is that you always fall in love with horses—and horses aren't legal to fall in love with."[156]

Eventually Alana turned the site over to someone else and it became a haven for males who considered themselves emasculated.[157]

It is now defunct, but the legacy has continued as a movement and there are women that do not match typical notions of feminine allure who relate to it.

> Rachel, a 19-year-old from the US, was 15 when she first came across the term 'incel' online, and was struck by how precisely it described her situation. 'I've never had sex or had a relationship due to a hormonal condition that has caused me to develop a very atypical appearance,' she says. 'The term 'incel' fits me perfectly.'[158]

They have been dubbed "femcels," and their sexual disesteem is prompted by common notions of attractiveness that are a product of traditional femineity. A post on crystal.cafe, an internet chatroom, gave this dispirited evaluation of the possibility of forming a union as a femcel.

> 100% of men only go for the top 20% of women. Failing that they 'settle' for the top 40%.
> The remaining 60% of us will never even be glanced at by the ugliest and lowest of status males. They would rather spend their life lusting after beautiful women than spend even a second near us.[159]

The same writer complained about masculine privilege in much the same way that males on INCELS complain about the feminist perspective.

> Suffering as a male? Please. Misandry this, misandry that, but the moment you might bring up the possibility misogyny exists in society you're seen as some loudmouthed, overweight, dyed haired dyke no matter how obvious and clear the misogyny is. Life is handed to them on a platter and their parents coddle them and shelter them from any harsh realities. They don't care about facts or the truth, men are the SJWs [social justice warriors] of gender.[160]

A survey of the incel online community has indicated that females participate with greater frequency than males (59.6% as opposed to 38.5%). Between the genders, the rates for those considered highly characteristic of the cult was almost equivalent (50/103 for females compared with 52/103 for males).[161] A higher level of expressive activity along with equivalent intensity uphold the assumption that celibate women are as disenchanted with the trappings of romance as the men – if not more so. Females, however, are disillusioned because of the experience of psychological injury stemming from appearance or insufficient seductive features, while males have experienced a kind of narcissistic wound because they believe they were being deprived of an entitlement.

Trans, cis, binary, lesbian, or queer, women are often subjected to derision that needles their self-worth. The insecurity can be compounded by features or traits that are popularly considered to be unattractive. Olga Hepnarová, who will be discussed in the next chapter, committed whole-sale slaughter by driving a vehicle into a group of people waiting to board a tram in Prague. She represents those individuals who were nudged toward a mass slaying by repetitious impressions of childhood turmoil and ostracism. Some of her memories involved mockery based on her looks or her mannerisms. In her final suicide message – an indictment sent to newspapers for publication – she specifically enumerates those encounters.

Bishop endured allergies, hives, and eczema during her formative years.[162] A meta-analysis of 35 studies with data from 1,935,147 children and adolescents found statistically significantly increased risk of mental disorders for those with common skin diseases (atopic dermatitis – AD) compared with those without them. More specifically, for those subjects with AD there was a greater likelihood of attention-deficit hyperactive disorder ($p < 0.001$), sleep disorders ($p < 0.01$), anxiety ($p < 0.05$), depression ($p < 0.001$), conduct disorders ($p < 0.001$), and autism spectrum disorders ($p < 0.01$).[163] Another literature review concluded:

> Atopic dermatitis was found to have significant behavioral effects on children, ultimately resulting in a lack of opportunity to develop proper coping. … Acne vulgaris was found to have a more direct effect on self-esteem, self-confidence and identity, especially in girls.[164]

With its irritation, lesions, and inflammation, no doubt the skin conditions Bishop experienced during youth hampered her ability to form comfortable relationships and acquire a capacity for composure in adverse situations.

The data in the Appendix (diagramed in Fig. 6.1) suggest that perceived physical inadequacy is the least prevalent of the dispositional conditions. Moreover, among the sample in that table there are no cases in which it is lodged without another precondition. It might be assumed, then, that it is only influential when joined with other precursor(s). However, in the same set of 112 cases, over two thirds (77/112 = 0.69) are comorbid. Therefore, disappointment with physique, health, or prowess should not be dismissed as minimally important. Quite the contrary, as the cases in this chapter demonstrate, it can be a potent strand throughout the devolution of a malicious actor.

Negative impressions of their body are so penetrative that aggressors, like Mutsuo and Blaze, as well as others repetitiously express contempt for their undesirable features either overtly or through symbolic acts. Their disgust with their endowed nature contributes to personal beliefs that they are isolated and relegated to perpetual disassociation from peers, their family, and social opportunities. In most instances that negative obsession with their superficial deficiencies will be accentuated by other prefatory influences on their psychological deterioration, such as their environment, mental/emotional disequilibrium, or an aberrant personality. Regardless, their unhappiness with their physicality or appearance will be so overwhelming that it will be an unassailable factor that pervades a steady decline in judgement. Their unhappy perception of their physical attributes will pervert their interpretation of life's sundry treats, travails, and overtures, no matter their origin or how neutral they may actually be.

Chapter Three

Destructive/Oppressive Environmental Situations

So runs my dream: but what am I?
An infant crying in the night:
An infant crying for the light:
And with no language but a cry.
– Alfred Lord Tennyson
"In Memoriam A.H.H. 54"

Early forms of literature, such as myths and folktales, are mostly metaphorical, which is certainly part of their enchantment, but in addition to the analogous treatises on human psychology, there is some very straightforward advice. "Fairy tales are about trouble, about getting into and out of it, and trouble seems to be a necessary stage on the route to becoming."[1] A reoccurring message to young people from ancient times to the present has been simple and unadorned: be wary.

Danger may burrow into damaging interactions among relatives, domestic unpredictability, and hostilities originating from the broader sphere of associates in school, the workplace, or township. These situational factors are encompassed in the broad prefatory underlay to rampaging labeled as, "Destructive/Oppressive environment" (see Table 1.1).

This chapter will concentrate on the long term social-psychological effects of damaging environs and their contribution to the development of a killer's desire to inflict harm. The experiences are categorized under the following headings:

- Injurious familial relations – situations in which children are physically or emotionally abused or repeatedly exposed to abuse of other family members;

- Unsupportive living conditions – homes where young people are subjected to deprivation, demeaning conditions, or reoccurring chaos;
- A hostile community – circumstances where vulnerable individuals are intimidated, harassed, or exposed to cruelty by peers, associates, or authority figures.

The categorization does not mean the domains are easily divisible. They often overlap. A review of three articles examining reports of child mistreatment (two from the United States and a third from Israel) determined that intimate partner violence co-occurred with child abuse at a rate of 26 to 59 percent.[2] Two additional studies (one with comparative samples and another comparing reports on subjects from alternate sources) found a significant correlation between marital violence and physical child abuse (both: $p < .01$).[3] A survey of six thousand households revealed that 50 percent of the men who often attacked their wives also frequently assaulted their children.[4] Multiple kinds of adverse childhood experiences (ACE – birth through 18) were retrospectively reported in a questionnaire answered by 4,674 women and 3,955 men in southern California. Adversities included emotional abuse, physical abuse, sexual abuse, emotional neglect, physical neglect, domestic violence, substance abuse in the household, mental illness in the household, parental separation or divorce, and a criminal member of the household.[5] "Multivariate logistic regression analyses were conducted to investigate whether the presence of each category of ACE was significantly associated with the risk of having other types of ACEs after controlling for demographic covariates to obtain adjusted odds ratios…."[6] After adjusting for demography, the probability that an experience in any given category would be accompanied by another type of adversity ranged from 2.0 to 17.7 ($p < 0.0001$). Put another way, if a person endured one ACE, the likelihood of enduring another was 2 to 18 times higher than it was for those who were not subjected to any adversity at all. Of the respondents who underwent any sort of childhood trauma, 86.5 percent had been exposed to at least one additional ACE and 38.5 percent reported four or more additional exposures.[7]

The categorization of oppressive/destructive environmental circumstances is presented in this work for the sake of elucidation, comparison, and illustration with the understanding that the demarcation between categories is juxtaposed over graduating shades of discomfort. The most pervasive damage produced by each of these conditions, whether isolated or overlapping, is a kind of emotional obstruction to the formation of affectionate and proactive attachments with primary caretakers and/or surrogates and/or relatives and/or acquaintances.

The victim, then, fails to nurture trust and cultivate concern for life. "Five studies examined the effects of chronic and contextual activation of attachment security on reactions to others' needs. ... Self-reports of attachment anxiety and avoidance were inversely related to empathy, and attachment anxiety was positively related to personal distress."[8] The studies all involved undergraduate college students who were divided into three groups. In four of the experiments by way of a story, picture, subliminal presentation, or an autobiographical memory a group was primed with images for attachment, another with positive affect, and a third given neutral information. Various questionnaires and rating scales were administered to assess reactions. Regression analyses were used to determine effects.[9]

The first study determined that for empathy, the reaction to security priming significantly contrasted with positive framing ($p < 0.01$). The results were duplicated in the second group of trials and scores for compassion were significant with subjects who were given prompts emphasizing security as opposed to those that were simply exposed to positive emotions ($p < 0.01$). Study 3 affirmed the validity of the results of Studies 1 and 2 and the findings also negated the possibility that the influence of security priming might be related to biased memories. Even when participants were unaware of subconscious signals, personal reactions promoted higher degrees of empathy with lower levels of personal distress in the participants experiencing attachment in comparison to controls. The fourth study demonstrated that mood did not significantly deter the effects of security priming on the accessibility of empathic feelings.[10]

The fifth study compared memories of attachment associated with security, avoidance (detachment), or anxiety by encouraging recall of an interaction with parents.[11] It contained a second phase, as well, in which separate subjects were asked to respond to a situation involving a best friend or a mere acquaintance. As might be expected, memories of comforting attachments produced higher empathy ratings as did friendship. Particularly relevant to environmental stimuli, attachments imbued with anxiety or disinterest (avoidance) negatively correlated with empathetic reactions[12] – "the higher the attachment anxiety or avoidance, the lower the reported empathy."[13]

Secure connections are essential for the development of interpersonal reciprocity, without which people objectify others or treat them as irrelevant.

Injurious Familial Relations

An insightful typology of school shooters, advanced by Peter Langman, and well supported by case studies, identifies three culpable categories: traumatized, psychotic, and psychopathic.[14] The first includes youths who have "suffered physical and/or sexual abuse … at least one parent with substance abuse problems, and … at least one parent with a criminal history."[15] Langman's recognition of abuse, victimization, and/or problematic households as one foundational element for violent outbursts upholds the premise that a childhood laced with brutality and upheaval can forever mar the psyche of a potential mass killer.

The premise is upheld by data in a compilation of 160 mass shootings in which four or more people were killed in a public setting.[16] The database was part of a project sponsored by the National Institute of Justice that examined community-level factors and life histories of assailants conducting rampages with firearms between 1966 and 2018.[17] Forty-five percent of school shooters had witnessed or experienced childhood trauma.[18]

The Federal Bureau of Investigation cites "Family Dynamics" as one of four general considerations for assessing the level of danger in profiling a potential shooter in a school setting. The Bureau advises that there are four "prongs" to a thorough threat assessment, the other three being: "Personality of the Student," "School Dynamics," and "Social Dynamics."[19] Three of the four major focal points recommended by the FBI (namely, familial, educational, and interpersonal conditions) fit in the sphere of environmental conditions.[20]

Neuroscience supports expectations for an underdeveloped ethical sense that might result from repeated exposure to violence, and/or the threat thereof, and/or regular neglect while growing up.

> This chronic stimulation of the brain's fear response means that the regions of the brain involved in this response are frequently activated. … Other regions of the brain, such as those involved in complex thought, and abstract cognition, are less frequently activated, and the child becomes less competent at processing this type of information. … The result may be a child who has difficulty functioning when presented with a world of kindness, nurturing, and stimulation.[21]

These maturational detriments may well continue through the teen years and beyond due to chemical damage in the brain's architecture that will include limited growth in the left hemisphere as well as the hippocampus, abnormalities in the limbic system, and an impaired connection between hemispheres. The long-term effects (possibly for life) can be depression, posttraumatic stress disorder, episodes of memory loss, periods of dissociation, and symptoms of attention deficit/hyperactivity disorder – any of which, of course, can impair judgment and/or limit emotional reciprocity.[22]

Along with neuralgic damage, abundant evidence endorses the intuitive supposition that exposure to ongoing domestic turbulence is associated with learned behavior that can be destructive. A number of empirically based studies, relying on comparable groups or other control mechanisms have demonstrated a strong correlation between physically abusive experiences and eventual aggressive behavior, criminal conduct, chronic substance abuse, and self-injurious acts including suicide.[23] With regard to the developmental aspects of victimization, a particularly important finding is that youngsters subject to physical harm early in life learn to interpret cues from their environment differently than those who have not been subject to such experiences. In a random sample of children registering for kindergarten, subjects who had been harmed reacted to video vignettes differently than registrants in the control group in that they were "…less attentive to relevant social cues, more biased toward attributing hostile intent, and less likely to generate competent solutions to interpersonal problems. …"[24] These results point to the formation of a worldview based on accentuated suspicion, inadequate receptivity of communicative intent, and ill-conceived decisions.

The reciprocal requirements for successful socializing are impeded by the insensitivity of mistreated children to the necessity for customary niceties. The result is diminutive acceptance by acquaintances and this rejection remains significant in comparison to non-abused peers irrespective of socioeconomic status.[25] Of course, this outcome contributes to a ruinous cycle of isolation inhibiting the development of social skills which, in turn, isolates the individual even more.

An underlying perspective of distrust accompanied by delayed social-emotional skills may be fashioned by just witnessing inter-parental violence at a young age, regardless of who was a direct receipt of abuse. A meta-analysis of 118 studies published between 1978 and 2000, reviewing correlational research, revealed that the exposure to these intimate conflicts was a significant predictor for stress and difficulties with social competence.[26]

Continually experiencing violence does not necessarily restrict an individual's ability to assess potential harm. More perniciously, though, it may well diminish the capacity to accurately judge benign intentions of others even when they may be helpful. Incarcerated males tasked with determining the intentions of agents who could administer punishments were highly successful in predicting both the cruel (77%) and non-cruel (72%) choices. However, inmates with higher scores on a scale measuring exposure to violence (ETV) reported significantly more negative impressions of the moral character of both types of punishers than did their counterparts with lower ETV indicators ($p = 0.004$). Those with greater levels of ETV also saw less distinction in the morality of favorable versus unfavorable agents.[27] There is, then, "the intriguing possibility that exposure to violence does not fundamentally disrupt all components of social learning, but instead may produce a problem with generating global subjective social impressions and translating those impressions into adaptive social decision-making."[28] The findings partially explain the indiscriminate nature of some predators in their choice of victims.

A common observation among professionals and lay persons alike is that "[c]hildren exposed to violence are more likely to be violent."[29] In one study involving records of over 1,500 subjects (including sampled subjects and their matches), youths exposed to neglect and/or physical abuse had significantly higher rates of delinquency and adult criminality after a 20-year span than demographically matched controls.[30] Contrary to what would be expected, there was no statistically significant difference when it came to involvement in violent crime. Even so, arrests for violence were higher by over 3 percentage points for the population who had experienced physical abuse compared to those neglected. (15.8% vs 12.5%).[31]

The terms "socialization" or "socialized" commonly describe individuals who have become adept at maneuvering community norms in the societal milieu. By the same token, according to criminologist Lonnie Athens, people become acclimated to aggression in their environment and given the proper conditional events, the acclimation devolves into a preference for adoption of violence as a mechanism for problem solving, retaliation, or dominance – what he calls "violentizaton."[32]

Athens carefully constructed a sociological theory that outlines the multiple drivers that produce violent behavior. Offering insight into habituation, neuroscience supports the same concept by showing how impulses are not only learned but eventually internalized into nervous responses.

> A child raised in an environment characterized by persisting trauma (e.g., domestic violence, physical abuse, community violence) will develop an excessively active and reactive stress response apparatus. The majority of the stress response systems reside in the brainstem and midbrain (e.g., locus coeruleus). Overdevelopment of these areas, even in the presence of optimal emotional or cognitive experience will result in an altered Cortical Modulation ratio and, a predisposition to act in an aggressive, impulsive, behaviorally reactive fashion.[33]

Texts left behind by Jeffrey Weise, dramatically articulate the pervasive resentment that coalesces in the mind when hyper-arousal is necessary for coping with home life.

Textual Analysis: Jeffrey Weise – Oppressive/Destructive Environmental Situations (Injurious Familial Relations, Unsupportive living conditions); Neuropsychological Impairment (Mood Disordered*)*

According to news reports, the alcoholic mother of Weise abused him both physically (hitting him with objects) and verbally.[34] Weise's biological father committed suicide during a stand-off with police a little less than eight years before his son's sudden mass assault. When sixteen-year-old Weise rampaged, it is dubious that he lived in a place he could actually call home.[35] "A member of his extended family says it seemed like the teenager was floating – on his own, with no adults watching out for him."[36] He shot to death his grandfather and the man's girlfriend then took his police-issued weapon, bulletproof vest, and squad car to Red Lake Senior High School, which he previously attended before being placed on home study.[37] He then murdered seven more, grinning and waving at his former classmates, eventually killing a teacher, an unarmed security guard, and five students, while wounding several others before killing himself.[38]

Among his numerous blogs was one that reads:

> Jan. 4th, 2005 @ 06:39 pm
>
> The instrument of my resurrection was supposed to be freedom. But

> there isn't an open sky or endless field to be found where I reside, nor is there light or salvation to be discovered.
> Right about now I feel as low as I ever have.
> I don't think it's a big secret why, really.
> My biggest disappointment and downfall came from what was supposed to be the one thing to lift me from the grave I'm continually digging for myself.
> Nah, never. Only the worthy are saved, y'know.
> I don't know, but what I do know is I'm a retarded fuck for ever believing things would change for me. I'm starting to regret sticking around, I should've taken the razor blade express last time around…
> Well, whatever, man. Maybe they've got another shuttle comin' around sometime soon?
> Ciao.
> Current Mood: drained
> Current Music: Strawberry Fields Forever - John Lennon[39]

Disregarding the brutality of his eventual rampage, the pathos in these entries is wrenching. He completely internalizes his repeated abuse and sustained neglect, viewing himself as beyond any sort of redemption – "only the worthy are saved, y'know." At 16 years old, Weise was world weary. His last entry, about six weeks after the first, labels his mood as "drained," as he listens to the Lennon/McCartney hymn to oblivion, "Strawberry Fields Forever" with the refrain "Let me take you down/Cause I'm going to Strawberry Fields/Nothing is real."[40] He chastises himself as stupid for believing it could be otherwise and has no faith that his life will ever improve, believing that his existence is worthless.

The introduction to his on-line diary, *Thoughts of a Dreamer*, written prior to the preceding excerpt, names his "Current Music" as "The Man Comes Around," by Johnny Cash – a foreboding song about a mystical figure dispensing justice and righteousness during the apocalypse.[41] It begins and ends with quotations from the book of Revelations. Besides his on-line journal, Weise posted fictional writings, using the pseudonym Blades11, on two other web pages: Tall Man's Guest Book (2001-03) and The Writer's Coven (2003-04).[42] The Guest Book was part of Phantasm: The Tall Man's Liar, a now defunct website dedicated to a character in a series of films about a mortician with supernatural abilities who robs graves to create an army of the dead.[43] Beyond the modern evocation, the persona references "Der Großmann," translated as "Tall Man" or "Great Man," a sort of fabled German bogeyman, who resides in the forest and preys on wayward children.[44] The contributions by Weise to these sites reflects the chronic morbidity of his state of mind.

Another portrait of vengeful despair emerges in the chronicle of Alvaro Castillo who committed patricide then raided his former high school.

Textual Analysis: Alvaro Castillo – Perceived Physical Inadequacy (Obesity); Oppressive Environment (Injurious Familial Relations); Neuropsychological Impairments (Paranoia and Depression)

Castillo's mother described life in the household as "a constant powder keg of tension," primarily because of the capricious standards enforced by the persistent terror imposed by her husband.[45] If the children were ill or even injured, they were forced to take cold showers instead of seeking medical treatment. When they reached the age of five, he proclaimed that their childhood was over, insisting they abandon friends, work only on their education, and read adult-level literature. He enforced his edicts by intimidation and beatings, usually inflicted on his wife but sometimes on his son or daughters.[46]

Alvaro was the oldest child in the household, and he coped with the oppression by being dutiful and subservient.[47] Terrified of his father, he would cater to his every whim, cooking his favorite food, fetching his slippers, even tuning the channels on the television for him.[48]

After his high school graduation, Castillo joined the national guard, motivated primarily by a desire to learn how to use weapons. He was discharged shortly after basic training.[49] At home he attempted a ceremonious suicide on the seventh anniversary of the Columbine shooting. His death was prevented by his father who came upon his son as he was donning his military uniform and then wrestled his gun away from him. His parents had him involuntarily committed to a mental health center.[50] At the time of his dismissal from the facility he was diagnosed with "major depressive disorder, possible psychotic disorder, and anxiety disorder."[51] He told a social worker that there were microphones throughout his house, and he was under surveillance by a picture mounted in a bathroom.[52]

Just 22 days before unleashing his fury he confided, "I am feeling very depressed these days. I drown my sadness and depression with work, cleaning, and movies. Still, it keeps coming back."[53] Even more disquieting is his description of his alter ego: "I am having sexual fantasies and fantasies of being held hostage by an evil twin brother. I assume he represents my dark side."[54]

As his dad sat reading on a couch in the living room Castillo shot him seven times. He then dressed for battle in a Colorado t-shirt with a trench coat (an homage to Eric Harris of Columbine infamy), combat boots, and cargo pants. He took a semi-automatic rifle, a sawed-off shotgun, smoke grenades, pipe bombs, and 200 rounds of ammunition to his alma mater.[55] There he set off the bombs and fired upon a building. Two students were wounded, one by a bullet that grazed her shoulder and another by a shard of glass.[56]

An excerpt from his journal, video clips, a comment to law enforcement, and the trial record portray his desperate desire to get even with the hostile world beget by his father.[57]

> I feel sorry for the families and parents of the victims, but there is nothing I can do. I cannot end pain except my own. I will sacrifice those children so they will not suffer the harsh consequences and hardships of life. – Alvaro Castillo, *Journal*, July 29, 2006.[58]

> It's a constant struggle against good and evil and I am tired of evil. I will die, and I just don't understand how committing suicide is an evil act. … We do it to relieve pain. It's a mercy. … And about the school shootings, it's sacrifice. It's just sacrifice. … It's not a punishment like Sodom and Gomorrah. Look at that. Thousands of people died: men, women, children. … And I am not criticizing God or anything like that. I love God. And I am not saying he did a bad thing. I am not. And I am not questioning him. I am not questioning the Lord our God. … I'm just saying, 'Look what happened at Sodom and Gomorrah.' … Read the Bible. Hellfire … fire and brimstone. All those people were sacrificed. … What about the plagues of Egypt? Huh? What about the death of the first born? Those were children! … What do you have to say about that? Huh? Little children and they died! And they did not do anything! Why? Why did that happen? Sacrifice! Sacrifice! [enunciating the word slowly for emphasis]. – Castillo, self-recording prior to rampage.[59]

> Whenever I see him [his father] I remember what he did to me, to sisters, and my mother. I can still hear the sound his hand made

> whenever he would hit our bodies. [Gives demonstration of striking by rapping microphone] Like that. … With his bare hands – head, back, rear. … It wasn't really the physical pain. It was the emotional pain that a father, a person that you loved was doing this to you and your family. He could do that to me all he wanted. It would have been discipline, but disciplining my mom? She was about the same age, and he was disciplining her like a child. Is that right? No. Is that right? I ask you, is that right? No! – Castillo, self-recording after father's murder.[60]

> He made me suffer all his life. Someone had to put him out of his misery. … He abused me and my family. He was abused too. – Castillo's comment to police after apprehension.[61]

> I know that, as a result of my actions, I shocked and hurt a lot of people, but that wasn't my intention. I simply wanted to help, but now I realize that what I did was wrong. – Castillo address to court prior to sentencing.[62]

As mentioned in the Introduction to this book, tragically, a prelude to a rampage may sometimes be taking the life of a close family member (or sometimes more than one). Nevertheless, Castillo's paranoid elevation of his reaction to paternal cruelty as a justification for the necessity of cosmological intervention through mass murder stands out even among the annals of deranged vindictive killers.

Castillo had been captivated by the mayhem at Columbine High and felt compelled to imitate Harris and Klebold. He had taken a trip to the site of that notorious massacre, as a sort of pilgrimage, and apparently came away inspired.[63] Due to his religiosity (to which he returned repeatedly when talking or writing) Castillo seemed incapable of summoning the sadistic cruelty manufactured by Harris and passively accepted by Klebold. Therefore, he cloaked the reasoning for his crimes in devotion, even though the bloodletting would have equaled or exceeded the toll at Columbine had he been able to carry out his mission in the manner he envisioned. He justified his intent to kill school children as "sacrifice," comparing his plan to biblical events when spiritual decadence or continuing sacrilege prompted deific wrath.[64] There was an occasional iota of remorse, but it was fleeting because, to him, his plans were necessary for ridding the world of wrong and relieving suffering.[65]

Unsupportive Living Conditions

For those youths experiencing a family life without protection, safety, and predictability the pernicious persistence of that damage is all encompassing and unrelenting. With basic needs unmet, a youngster concentrates on activities associated with psychic and physical survival with relatively little attention paid to interactions that stir more sophisticated characteristics, such as compassion.

Unpredictability in childhood, whether related to physical threats, insecurities around daily provisions, and/or the atmosphere in the home precludes the formation of a principled worldview because the exigencies of daily events dominate the young person's thoughts. A natural construction of a cogent morality based on empathic considerations, or even long-term self-interest, becomes stunted by egocentric survival mechanisms. In terms of Kohlberg's classic moral stages, a person will become stuck in the "preconventional" level, marked by obedience for the sake of personal protection or, at best, emotional exchanges for purposes of positioning in the family hierarchy.

Advancement to "conventional" morality, is unlikely without the benefit of strong interpersonal relations. Fundamentally morality is based on the belief "that people should live up to the expectations of the family and community and behave in 'good' ways. Good behavior means having good motives and interpersonal feelings such as love, empathy, trust, and concern for others."[66] Such emotional touchstones will coalesce slowly, if they form at all, when a child is confined to environmental conditions permeated with uncertainty or fear or cruelty or all of those elements.

From the standpoint of childhood development, cognition, moral reasoning, behavior, and social adaptability are closely aligned. An overview of this relationship is presented in the chart labeled as Table 3.1.

TABLE 3.1. Progression of stages for cognitive, moral, behavioral, and interpersonal with conceptual development

Stages	Cognitive	Moral	Behavioral	Interpersonal with conceptual orientation
Pre-Operational/ pre-conventional (roughly ages 3-7)	Immediate desires with magical thinking, transductive reasoning	Decisions and actions determined by respect or fear of authority	Tangible, immediate reinforcement	Egocentric needs, wants, wishes
Concrete operational/ conventional (roughly ages 8-13)	Experiential learning with some inductive reasoning	Decisions and actions determined by social parameters	Social reinforcement, moderately delayed gratification	Reciprocity founded on rules, fairness, equality
Formal operational/post-conventional (roughly ages 14 – adult)	Thoughts based on abstract ideas with deductive reasoning	Decisions and actions determined by ideals, ethics	Symbolic reinforcement, attention to internalized norms	Broad social-ethical perspective shaped by civility, humaneness, legacy

General note: The table represents a broad synthesis of observations emanating from Lawrence Kholberg, Jean Piaget, Abraham Maslow, Reuven Feuerstein, B.F. Skinner, and Lev Semyonovich Vygotsky. Theoretical and empirical support may be found in the following: a) Harry Belin and Gary Fireman. "The Foundation of Piaget's Theories: Mental and Physical Action" *Advances in Child Development and Behavior* 27, (1999): 221-246; b) Nancy Eisenberg, and Paul A. Miller, "The Relation of Empathy to Prosocial and Related Behaviors," *Psychological Bulletin* 101, no. 1 (January 1987): 91-119; c) Charles Fernyhough, "Getting Vygotskian about Theory of Mind: Mediation, Dialogue, and the Development of Social Understanding," *Developmental Review* 28, no. 2 (June 2008): 225-262; d) Jerry Hutton and Timothy G. Roberts, "Relationships of Sociometric Status and Characteristics of Emotional Disturbance," *Behavioral Disorders* 8, no. 1 (November 1982): 19-24; e) Bertram, F. Malle, "Attribution Theories: How People Make Sense of Behavior," in *Theories in Social Psychology*, ed. Derek Chadee (Malden, MA: Wiley-Blackwell, 2011), 72-95; e) Richard S. Neel, Zoe Neibrugge Jenkins, and Nancy Meadows, "Social Problem-Solving Behaviors and Aggression in Young Children: A Descriptive Observational Study," *Behavioral Disorders* 16, no. 1 (November 1990): 39-51; f) Monica Tomar and S.K. Sharma, *Principles of Growth and Development* (Delhi, India: Isha Books, 2005), 76-137; g) Fanny Stella Torres Vigoya, "The Mediated Learning Experience and the Mediators Implications," *Profile Issues in Teacher's Professional Development*, no. 6 (January/February 2005): 177-185.

That construct is intended (in a general way) to show the developmental relationship between interpretation of external stimuli, formation of personal responsibility, behavioral responses, and sociability. A particular process (as represented in any of the columns in Table 3.1) – even cognition – should not be confused with an innate skill or with what is often referred to (carelessly) as intellectual ability.[67] Intelligence invokes a stagnate predictor for achievement (often in the academic arena) at a particular point in time, whereas, developmental processes, by definition, are fluid and subject to enhancement in response to conditions.

Impoverished circumstances – material, emotional, or experiential – will often impede cognitive development even though they will, by no means, necessarily prevent growth on a permanent basis. Enrichment, on the other hand, in all cases but the rarest, will stimulate thought and that stimulation will expand the capacity to modify the effects of adversity. Unfortunately, disruptive and/or oppressive experiences in childhood, absent an interpreting mentor who assists with an appreciation of context, hinders maturation in multiple domains and that immaturity can, and frequently will, result in inadequate interpretation of complex cues along with poor decision-making.

Self-modulation – a cognitive skill necessary for restraining impulsivity as well as generating personal industry – coalesces in an environment of stability with supportive emotional connections. Higher levels of parental neglect result in less capacity for personal control. An international study involving surveys of college students across six habitable continents and 32 nations found a significant correlation ($p = 0.05$) between limited self-control and neglectful parenting in every country.[68] Predictability provides an atmosphere in which a child can become confident in his or her own capacity for efficaciousness.

When self-sufficiency is absent or diminished a person comes to believe – either consciously or unwittingly – that the world is acting upon him or her and s/he has little or no influence over outcomes. "In five studies, depleted capacity for self-regulation (caused by prior, even irrelevant acts of self-regulation) increased aggressive responding, especially after an insulting provocation."[69] The resulting mindset is laced with a tendency to obsess over indignities large and small alike – sometimes giving them equal weight. A mind set of that sort externalizes blame while internalizing victimization.[70] Often referred to as injustice or wound collecting, the habit is explained with attention to its degenerative qualities and with further examples in the companion text, *How Rampage Killers Interpret Their Worlds*. For now, though, the compounding toxicity of obsessing over injuries real, exaggerated, or imagined can be shown in sharp relief by considering the life of Andrew Joseph Stack III.

Biographical and Textual Analysis: Andrew Joseph Stack III – Destructive Environment (Unsupportive Living Conditions); Pathological Personality (Antagonistic)

Three years into his second marriage, Stack's frequent ranting accompanied by the intensity of his rage became so frightening that his wife, Sheryl, left with her daughter and slept in a hotel. When they returned the next day, their home was burned to the ground. While staying with a neighbor Ms. Stack was watching the news about the fire that destroyed her home when the broadcast was interrupted to report on a crash of a single-engine fixed-wing Piper Cherokee aircraft into Internal Revenue Service offices housed in Austin Texas.[71] The pilot, who perished in the collision, was her husband, Joe Stack. One IRS supervisor was killed, and thirteen employees injured. Evidence later revealed that Stack had set his house on fire before embarking on his airborne ambush.[72]

There was no question both acts were intentional. The FBI ascertained that Stack had purposely initiated the fire that destroyed his residence and witnesses to the crash reported that the plane continued at full speed directly to the second floor of the facility where the IRS was located.[73] Most telling, was the vindictive six-page, three-thousand-word essay that Stack, prior to the malicious suicidal crash, posted on Embedded Dart.com, his software company's web site.[74]

The treatise expressed Stack's anger and disgust towards corporations as well as a host of governmental of actions and entities: assistance to failing financial institutions, self-serving politicians (targeting New York Senator Patrick Moynihan in particular), General Motors, Enron, unions, health care polices, insurance carriers, the Catholic Church, and, not surprisingly, the national tax structure. It went on to describe in detail an encounter with a widow who never received pension benefits that she deserved, then railed against the handling of the aftermath of the September 11 atrocities, especially the airline bailouts. The lamentation then shifted to the insincerity of a Certified Public Accountant Stack hired, supporting his outrage against the

CPA and the IRS with a recitation of the Section 1706 of the Tax Reform Act.[75] Stack's diatribe climaxed with:

> I choose to not keep looking over my shoulder at 'big brother' while he strips my carcass, I choose not to ignore what is going on all around me, I choose not to pretend that business as usual won't continue. …
>
> I spent my entire life trying to believe it wasn't so, but violence not only is the answer, it is the only answer. The cruel joke is that the really big chunks of shit at the top have known this all along and have been laughing, at and using this awareness against, fools like me all along.
>
> I saw it written once that the definition of insanity is repeating the same process over and over and expecting the outcome to suddenly be different. I am finally ready to stop this insanity. Well, Mr. Big Brother IRS man, let's try something different; take my pound of flesh and sleep well.
>
> The communist creed: From each according to his ability, to each according to his need.
>
> The capitalist creed: From each according to his gullibility, to each according to his greed.
>
> Joe Stack (1956-2010)
> 02/18/2010[76]

Stack's antagonism toward taxation dated back almost two and one-half decades preceding his strike. He was involved with a fringe group that advocated leveraging the allowances for religious exemptions to offset taxable receipts. Unfortunately, the maneuvers were unsuccessful, and he was stuck with a huge liability.[77] "That little lesson in patriotism cost me $40,000+, 10 years of my life, and set my retirement plans back to 0. It made me realize for the first time that I live in a country with an ideology that is based on a total and complete lie," he wrote in his final letter.[78]

As he strived to overcome that financial hurdle Stack confronted a new element in IRS regulations that reduced his net income. He was making his living as an independent contractor, but the 1986 Tax Reform Act expanded the requirements necessary for technology professionals to qualify as self-employed individuals, forcing most to be classified as company employees, thereby increasing their withholdings.[79] "[T]hey could only have been more blunt if they would have came out and directly declared me a criminal and non-citizen slave. Twenty years later, I still can't believe my eyes," Stack declared in the desultory suicide note.[80] Unwilling to meet the burden, regroup, and move forward, he sacrificed money and time attempting to vanquish the revenue collection arm of the United Sates government.

> During 1987, I spent close to $5000 of my 'pocket change', and at least 1000 hours of my time writing, printing, and mailing to any senator, congressman, governor, or slug that might listen; none did, and they universally treated me as if I was wasting their time. I spent countless hours on the L.A. freeways driving to meetings and any and all of the disorganized professional groups who were attempting to mount a campaign against this atrocity.[81]

Even so, he continued to pursue his entrepreneurial goals by establishing and operating two independent software companies: Prowess Engineering Inc., in Corona, California and Software Systems Service Corp. in Lincoln, California. Both were shut down – the first because he failed to file the required return and the second for failure to pay $1,153 in state taxes.[82]

There are three aspects to Stack's personality that are apparent when considering his continual conflict with monetary franchise authorities.

1) Arrogance – he believed he could, without legal assistance, outwit, outargue, and prevail in a feud with the government over technicalities related to taxation;
2) Uncompromising - at the time of his rampage, he was only being audited, besides, with a home valued at $230,000-$300,000 and two private planes worth almost as much combined, he had the resources to peaceably resolve any debt while still saving most of his fiscal resources and protecting his family[83]
3) Grudgeful - as an extension of the preceding conceits, he was unwilling, indeed, apparently emotionally unable, to let the dispute dissipate.

All point toward the psychological malformations left by the death of his parents and his upbringing as an orphan for most of his youth.

Stack told a stepdaughter that both his parents were killed in an automobile accident when he was only four years of age.[84] According to an unidentified sibling, Stack was five when his father died, and his mother committed suicide two years later.[85] Either way, he was parentless at a young age and raised in institutionalized environments – first a Catholic institution then at the Milton Hershey School (MHS), a residential educational setting, which at that time was open only to boys.[86] He may have learned determination but he did not master compromise or flexibility . One of his brothers who lived at MHS with Stack said their social survival was based on emotional suppression and personal insulation.

> One of the traits he and I share was whatever you're going to accomplish in your life or whatever battles you have to fight, you're pretty much on your own. And whatever you're going to get, you're going to get it by yourself. …[87]

The subjective account of the limited adaptability developed by Stack and his brother coincides with research regarding the internalized sense of isolation experienced by orphans. Children and adolescents who are orphaned have been shown to have high levels of distrust and suspicion as indicated by weak relations with other young people, buried feelings, insecurity, self-recrimination, and stunted pro-social behavior.[88]

One inquiry divided subjects into three groups – those with no experience in a family, those with limited familial interactions between ages 3-7, and those who were involved in families since birth.[89]

> It was found that family deprivation violates psychological development of adolescents. The violation manifests itself in the specificity of their emotional intelligence and regulatory functions, reduction of social intelligence and level of sociability, as well as in specific self-image (negative self-attitude, uncertainty, distrust of the world, particular attitude to the future and the prospects of life, etc.)[90]

A similar study contrasted 103 children (13+) who have been in orphanages with 110 children selected from different schools.[91] It measured hostility and locus of control, with well-crafted practical definitions for both.[92] Based on a questionnaire and inventory, orphans showed significantly more hostility ($p < 0.001$) and significantly less assurance of locus of control (p, 0.01).[93] Ill-being and psychological distress has been shown to continue into adulthood, which appears to have been the case with Stack.[94]

The hesitancy to trust contributes toward the tendency to be an isolate (at least as far as profound affect is concerned), which is substantial in the initial phase in the formation of rampageous tendencies (as shown in *How Rampage*

Killers Interpret Their Worlds). Fused with a sense that influence over events and circumstances is hampered by the whims of a substantially hostile universe, a store of wrongs and injuries is compiled in the mind of the emerging aggressor. Stack wrote, "Needless to say, this rant could fill volumes with example after example if I would let it. … I know I'm hardly the first one to decide I have had all I can stand. … I have just had enough.[95] His farewell message followed by the Kamikaze ambush was his embittered attempt to mark his place in an arcade where he felt he had no standing.

Productive relationships are predicated upon increasingly complex interpersonal encounters learned incrementally over time beginning in early childhood then carried forward in adolescence and refined daily in adulthood. A measure of physical and emotional surety is essential to the gestation of the sequence.

Security, however, is not simply a product of material circumstances or even consistency in expectations. It is dependent, also, on staking mutuality in attitudinal responses for societal norms. Lanza, the Newton shooter, lived in a materially secure household that simply disregarded his responsibility to the world at large – even with respect to the simplest expectations such as responding to conversational inquiries or, eventually, even leaving his room. His mother passed off his inhumane nonchalance as a product of his disability, which, paradoxically she refused to treat in the manner suggested by professionals.[96] Lanza reciprocated her indulgence by murdering her in her sleep.[97]

The story of Ethan Crumbley also exemplifies the deadly consequences that come about when parents do not address social maturation of a child.

Biographical Analysis: Ethan Crumbley – Destructive Environment (Unsupportive Living Conditions, Hostile Community); Neuropsychological Impairments (Acute Depression, Delusional), Pathological Personality (Emerging Sociopathy)

When he was in the fifth grade Crumbley was featured in the local newspaper for his part in an elementary school project suggesting solutions to poverty and hunger.[98] He was quoted as saying, "I see people that are on the streets sometimes that are homeless and hungry, and so I feel like I should take action and help them."[99] Photographs taken when he was about 12 years old show a round-faced boy with glasses. In one picture his hands form a steeple across his chest as if he is praying.[100]

Approximately three years later, on November 20, 2021, Crumbley took a semi-automatic handgun in a backpack to his school in Michigan. After ducking into a bathroom to retrieve the pistol, he walked down a hallway shooting into classrooms and at people in the corridor. He fired more than 30 times.[101] At the arraignment, the prosecuting attorney charged that Crumbley acted "methodically and deliberately" singling out those "who hadn't had the opportunity to escape."[102]

Three students, one of whom was only 14 years of age, died within hours. Another passed the next morning in the hospital.[103] Six were wounded, three critically, and one teacher sustained injuries.[104] His weapon was a Christmas present that had been purchased by his father just four days earlier on "Black Friday."[105] Immediately after getting the gift, 15-year-old Crumbley had posted a picture of it on Instagram and as shown in Figure .3.1, expressed his delight with his new toy. Within half an hour he received five likes, for which, in just a few days he would offer a cruelly calculated embellishment.

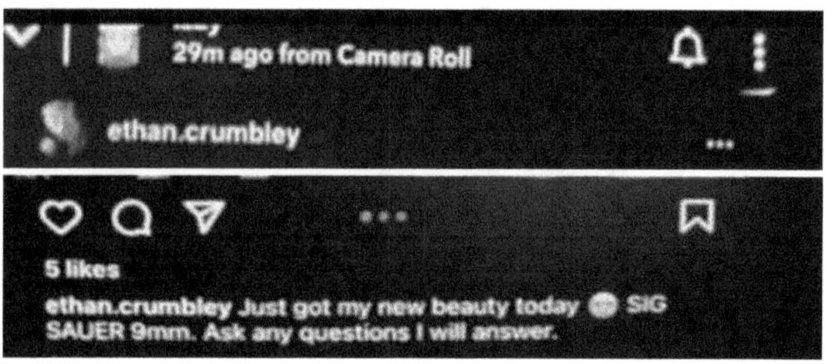

FIGURE 3.1. Top and bottom views of Instagram post by Ethan Crumbley after receiving semi-automatic handgun as a Christmas gift. It was later circulated on Twitter before being removed from both platforms. Embedded in Tereza Shkurtaj, "Signs of Trouble: What were Ethan Crumbley's Instagram posts?" *Sun*, posted and updated December 4, 2021, https://www.the-sun.com/news/4205383/ethan-crumbleys-instagram-posts/. The middle portion contained a picture of the weapon.

Borrowing the title from a novel by Joseph Heller: "something happened."[106]

Crumbley was routinely bullied in school and so regularly endured the agony of trying to thrive in an unwelcoming and threatening environment. One classmate observed, "I've seen him around the school. He's a kid, he's been picked on and stuff like this and when a kid has been picked on, people bullying him, you're going to get this."[107]

Meanwhile, his mother and father were consistently, almost studiously, oblivious to their son's welfare. An acquaintance that lived nearby stated that when Crumbley was eight or nine he would be left alone while his parents were out barhopping.[108] She was so worried that she notified Child Protective Services (CPS) and even spoke about her concerns directly to the Crumbleys. At 14 years of age, a year before the shooting, while he was working in a diner, Crumbley collapsed and struck his head on a cabinet. When his mother was informed of the incident, she shrugged it off, explaining that her son Ethan had not eaten that day, as if that omission was not, in and of itself, a cause for concern.[109]

According to prosecuting attorneys Crumbley's parents were guilty of "gross negligence and breach of a legal duty" during the six months that preceded their son's school shooting, overlooking events and circumstances that would have been cause for immediate concern for other responsible guardians.[110] They failed to attend to the fact that his best friend had moved out of the area, that he was deeply saddened by the loss of a family pet, and he was showing symptoms of chronic deepening depression.[111] Instead, the prosecution charged, his mom and dad "spent their time in the barn caring for their horses (3-4 nights per week up to 3 hours at a time), and seeking other relationships, including [the] mother's extramarital affairs. …"[112] They were also preoccupied with their financial problems and substance abuse.[113]

It was, however, his amoral sadism, the attraction to violent machinations, evidence of delusional ideation, and utter antipathy toward standards of conduct that were the more dire predictors of an ensuing maelstrom. Prosecutors alleged that Crumbley had a history of torturing animals and a suit brought by Fieger Law against Oxford High School stated that he had recorded the torture. Court documents filed by the county and the civil complaint both claimed he placed a bird's head in a jar that he kept on the floor in his bedroom until one day when he took it to school and left in a bathroom stall.[114] Meanwhile, as he approached fifteen years of age, Crumbley began to show signs of fearful thinking and atypical perception. On multiple occasions when left home alone he allegedly sent messages to his mother complaining of ghosts and demons inside the house.[115]

On the day before the SMASI, a teacher at Oxford High School noticed Ethan Crumbley during class time searching online for ammunition with his cell phone.[116] According to the County Prosecutor:

> Jennifer Crumbley was contacted via voice mail by school personnel regarding that son's inappropriate internet search. School personnel indicate they followed that voice mail up with an email but received no response from either parent. Thereafter, Jennifer Crumbley exchanged text messages about the incident with her son on that day, saying: 'LOL [laughing out loud] I'm not mad at you. You have to learn not to get caught.'[117]

That night the teen recorded two videos on his cell phone "wherein he talked about shooting and killing students the next day at Oxford High School."[118] He also put out another message on Instagram quoting Krishna in Hindu scripture making a Frankensteinian transformation (Figure 3.2). It was the same foreboding prophecy that Robert Oppenheimer quoted when he was psychologically quivering with the searing realization of the eventual ruin that that would be wrought by a nuclear weapon.[119] It is doubtful that Crumbley was familiar with the Bhagavad-Gita or the testing of the first atomic bomb. It is more probable that he saw the quotation while playing one of the many graphically violent video games in his collection – probably Fallout 76 in which "I Am become Death" is a primary quest.[120] The declaration's link with the salutation to his school insinuated that he had assumed the guise of an evil warrior bent on an unshakeable mission of obliteration.

FIGURE 3.2. Partial pictorial of Instagram post by Ethan Crumbley on the day before his sudden mass assault. Embedded in Tereza Shkurtaj, "Signs of Trouble: What were Ethan Crumbley's Instagram posts?" *Sun*, posted and updated December 4, 2021, https://www.the-sun.com /news/4205383/ethan-crumbleys-instagram-posts/. The original quotation is from the *Bhagavad-Gita* 11:32. There are numerous translations, but the passage would more accurately reflect the karmic mysticism of the religious text if it was interpreted as "Now I am become the world-destroying time." James Temperton, "'Now I am Become Death, The Destroyer of Worlds.' The Story of

Oppenheimer's Infamous Quote," *Wired*, posted September 8, 2017, https://www.wired.co.uk/article/manhattan-project-robert-oppenheimer. Of course, with Temperton's interpretation, the sinister tone would be replaced by the prospect of eternal placidity.

The next morning another instructor was so horrified by Crumbley's scribblings on a math review sheet that she took a photograph of the paper and alerted a school counselor. Crumbley must have taken his mother's advice about evasion to heart because by the time other staff members saw the actual drawings, he had altered them in a clumsy attempt to make them look like innocent sketches of a schematic for a video game (Figure 3.3).

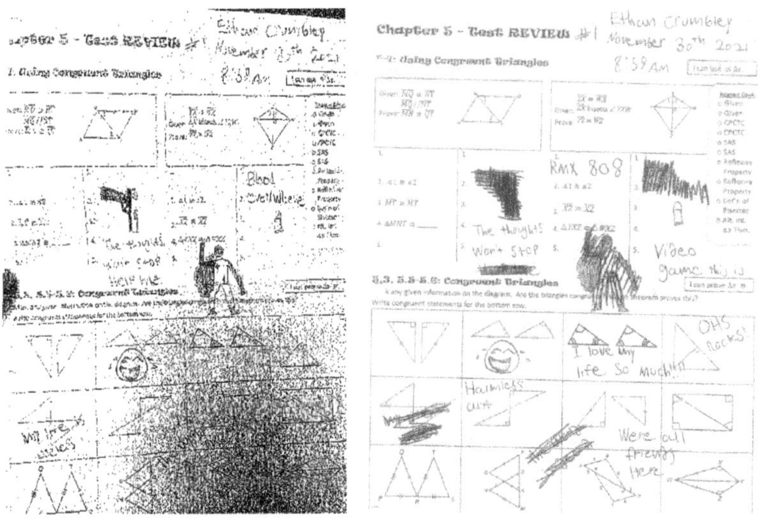

FIGURE 3.3. Partial copies of photos of Ethan Crumbley's drawings from the morning of the Oxford High School shooting. The page on the left is the original as photographed by the teacher before Crumbley reported to the office. The time is noted as "8:39 AM" (top right-hand corner of first picture). The sentence near the bottom-center (in shaded area near overlapping triangles) reads as, "The world is Dead." On the right is a cropped copy of Ethan Crumbley's drawings after he altered them. The time is noted as 8:59 AM (top right-hand corner of second picture). Notice the plea, "Help me," is scratched out, but the preceding statement professing an inability to stop compulsive thinking remains. State of Michigan in the Court of the 52-3 Judicial District, People v. James Crumbley, Jennifer Crumbley, Combined Response and Brief in Response to the Defendants' Motion to Modify Bond, December 23, 2021, exhibits 1 and 2, Srbibd.com.

The pictures and subsequent surreptitious alteration demonstrate that he was bent on realizing his fantasies and was conscious of the possible repercussions for formulating a plan. Within hours he would demonstrate his enthusiasm for his grim musings.

His mother and father were called to the school, and, unlike the previous day, they both responded, although it took them 90 minutes to arrive. School counselors urged the Crumbleys to involve Ethan in therapeutic counseling within 48 hours or face the possibility of a referral to CPS.[121] "When … asked to take their son home for the day, they flatly refused and left without him, apparently to return to work."[122] James Crumbley departed from the school at approximately 10:55 a.m. then made the five minute drive to the family home – a distance of 1.4 miles – and found the gun absent from its place in an armoire cupboard.[123]

Ethan Crumbley was allowed to return to class with his backpack which, presumably, held the Sig Saur semi-automatic and at least 30 live rounds.[124] Based on the record of emergency calls, he rampaged that afternoon at approximately 12:51.[125] Despite the rapidity of his fire, thanks to the immediate actions of first responders, the casualties were abated when he was apprehended within five minutes.[126] Jennifer Crumbley sent a text to her only child slightly less than 30 minutes later saying, "Ethan don't do it."[127] The admonition, she later contended, was in reference to the possibility that Ethan might be contemplating suicide.[128] Fifteen minutes after her panicked message, her husband phoned 911 to report that the firearm was missing and alert authorities that Ethan might be the shooter. The time was at 1:37 p.m..[129] Over two and one-half hours had lapsed since Mr. Crumbley had left the meeting with school personnel.

To date neither the family nor the school has offered a sensible explanation for the failure to search the backpack that in all likelihood contained the handgun. Obviously, Ethan's mom and dad had habitually ignored aberrations in their son's behavior whether they were suggestive of problems that were physical or psychological. However, that fateful morning they were confronted with illustrations that, even when marked up, plainly suggested the allure of extreme violence, and still they resisted the obligation of caring for their boy. The lead prosecutor for the case remarked, "[L]ooking at that drawing, it's impossible not to conclude that there was a reason to believe he was going to hurt somebody."[130] The educators saw the same images and were concerned enough to notify the guardians but still did not proceed with the logical course of conducting a search for a firearm. It is certain they had the legal right to do so.

Three years before Crumbley's assault, the Michigan Association of Secondary Principals offered guidance to administrators in the state regarding standards for honoring due process procedures for searching students.[131] The advisory aligns perfectly with the situation that unfolded at Oxford High School. In Crumbley's situation, the criteria were met. The possibility of a large-scale shooting in the context of gory illustrations and a confession of compulsive thoughts certainly justified an investigation while the selection of the pack intended for school materials can hardly be considered intrusive.

The neglect on the part of the professionals involved in the Crumbley narrative could, unquestionably, suggest incompetence at worse or naivete at best. As troublesome as that error may be, the extended inattention on the part of his parents over the course of months, as their child became increasingly intrigued with the possibility of enacting an aggressive performative escapade, is the very definition of depraved indifference.[132]

Long periods without a residence or successive short-term relocations to impermanent quarters (of whatever sort) that suggest "homelessness," pose prevalent instances of conditions that undermine an assumption of security. Interviews with 181 families and 169 children in 18 temporary shelters throughout Los Angeles County revealed a greater likelihood of eligibility for special education when considering three distinct disability categories.[133] "Compared to children in the general population … children in this study were four times more likely to have symptoms of BD [behavioral disorder] … three times more likely to test positive for LD [learning disability] … and seven times more likely to screen positive for MR [mentally retarded, i.e. intellectual disability]."[134] The chapter that follows this one sets forth evidence that impairments in cognition and/or self-control may, given certain additional influences, be the basis for the development of compulsions for a mass killers.

While frequent switches in educational settings is sometimes discounted as a common feature of modern life, there is evidence demonstrating that transitions between schools is emotionally difficult for all youngsters – even those considered well-adjusted. School mobility is not only associated with negative educational outcomes such as poor achievement, grade retention, and failure to graduate, but with difficulties related to self-esteem and confidence.[135] One study conducted in the United Kingdom that involved 6,448 subjects showed a statistically significant association between mobility (of 3 or more schools) and psychotic-like symptoms even when controlling for other variable adversities (family problems, ethnicity, urbanicity, and residential status).[136]

Two Cases: Educational Instability

Alex Baranyi, along with his friend David Anderson, murdered an entire family of four without provocation and for no material gain.[137] Baranyi recalled a childhood with a tiresome string of school transfers that he eventually accepted, resigning himself to loneliness. "My father started moving us around a lot. So, I didn't have a chance to make a lot of new friends and stuff. … I stopped trying to get friends. Recess at school, I'd walk around by myself. You know, walk in circles around. You know, it's just me by myself. You know, I wasn't trying to reach out to other people."[138]

Lanza was certainly impaired in his development by neurological deviations, but the re-occurring disruptions in his schooling also contributed to his eventual malevolent character. Between preschool and graduation Lantz attended seven different schools and was homebound or home schooled off and on from the eighth grade through his secondary years. Only two of the transfers were "promotional" (i.e., the result of a transition to a higher grade-level.[139] For someone like Lanza, who found any interpersonal encounter disconcerting, the upheaval would have been repeatedly devastating.

Neglect, even when superficially non-violent, also retards inter-personal maturation. Malnutrition results in vitamin deficiencies that are associated with "anxiety, depression, social problems, and attention problems."[140] Less obvious, but every bit as devastating, is the emotional deprivation resulting from inadequate interaction, sometimes referenced as "attachment disorder" or "early emotional frustration" – where young people are deprived of communicative stimulation and/or opportunities for experiential activities.[141] Analytical profiles of children who were adopted from Romanian orphanages – almost iconic in reputation – found that the neglected babies had diminished brain growth as well as severely inhibited reciprocal affective responses.[142] The detriments associated with deprivation during youth are often life-long.

Obviously intimate partner violence, including the daily possibility of such episodes, as well as divorce, separation, or an unexplained parental absence is upsetting for children and adolescents in the short term. As often as 20 percent of the time, the devastation will persist, manifesting itself in ways that will hinder the victim's capacity to successfully deal with challenges throughout life particularly in regard to forming healthy attachments and curtailing depression.[143] Rampage assailants tend to be emotionally distant (a characteristic that will be touched upon occasionally in this book and emphasized in *How Rampage Killers Interpret Their Worlds*) and that the distance will be exacerbated by the dissolution of a caregiving couple during childhood. The life of Brenda Spencer, presented in the next chapter, illustrates how a family breakup can become a presumptive event in an eventual murderer's emergence. In her case it was particularly insidious because of the compounding effect of neurologic problems.

A childhood with excessive upheaval or uncertainty, with or without abusive situations, fosters insecurity about future well-being. This interplay explains in part the elevated levels of juvenile crime and violence in high poverty neighborhoods. If changes are too frequent or are handled without care they can initiate long-term worry resulting in "poor academic performance, a lack of social competence, and an inability to regulate emotions."[144] Those last two outcomes can contribute to a frame of mind conducive to impulsive acts and even criminality.

One of the more extreme examples of morality arrested by degrading environmental situations was the abbreviated life of Patrick Purdy. Not only did he experience family dynamics with violent upheavals, shelter and sources of substance throughout his childhood were unpredictable. The effect of that unpredictability was bolstered in early adulthood by flirtations with crime along with daily use of narcotics and alcohol.

Biographical Analysis: Patrick Purdy – Destructive/Disruptive Environmental Circumstances (Injurious Familial Relations, Unsupportive Living Conditions), Neuropsychological Impairments (Restricted Cognition, Hallucinatory); Pathological Personality (Sociopathic)

Patrick Purdy left his motel room abandoning his meager belongings with dozens of plastic army men strategically placed throughout the living area and bathroom as if standing guard. A little less than an hour later, he arrived at the elementary school that he attended from kindergarten through the third grade. It was only about four and a half miles from the motel. What Purdy did between the time he departed from his room and arrived at the school is unknown, although, since both nicotine and caffeine were found in the blood when his body was autopsied, it is reasonable to suppose he stopped for a cup of coffee and a smoke.[145]

After parking his car in a drive near a cluster of portables, he lit a pipe bomb and left it in his vehicle with flammable liquids and fireworks. It exploded and caught fire within minutes. With an assault weapon, a pistol, and a nylon pouch containing ammunition, he strode to the side of a building that housed four classrooms, opened fire on the grounds where 400-500 primary students were playing, moved to the other side of the building, then reloaded and continued shooting. When the magazine was empty, he pulled his handgun from a holster and shot himself in his right temple. He had fired a total of 105 rounds, killing five children and wounding thirty more along with one teacher.[146] Fortunately, none of the wounded died following the assault.

Purdy was 24 years of age old when he completed the sequence of events that marked the end of a life that began with a childhood punctuated by uncertain living circumstances, re-occurring violence, persistent substance abuse, and tenuous family ties.[147] His parents lived separately during much of Purdy's early years and throughout that time, he had little if any contact with his natural father, who, prior to being discharged from the military for petty criminal activity, was diagnosed with "Schizophrenia, Chronic Paranoid Type."[148] His mother remarried by the time he was four, but she divorced his stepfather, Albert E. Gulart, when Purdy was eight.[149] Gulart physically abused Purdy's mother and there were occasions when in the midst of especially violent episodes she instructed her children to run to a neighbor to call the police.[150]

Purdy was undergoing "violent subjugation" and "personal horrification" – substages of "brutalization," the first experiential stage, in the formation of a psychological propensity for extreme violence as identified by Lonnie Athens.[151] The criminologist explains:

> During this experience [violent subjugation], bona fide or would be authority figures from one of the subject's primary groups use violence to force her to submit to their authority. …
>
> A second experience which people undergo during the brutalization stage is personal horrification. … Here the subject does not himself undergo violent subjugation, but witnesses another person undergoing it. …
>
> Neither … happens in a tranquil social atmosphere, but instead happens in a tempestuous one.[152]

Along with being victimized by physical violence and witnessing brutality against family members, Purdy's primary needs were unmet.

When he was nine years of age, his older sister, younger half-brother, and Purdy himself, were taken into protective custody after a neighbor reported that they appeared neglected. The children were released to the mother's care the very next day, but the day after that, when a detective made a follow-up phone call to the home and found them at home unsupervised, Purdy and his sister were again taken in by civil authorities. His mother was charged with child neglect, although these charges were eventually dropped after she participated in a counseling program.[153] This rapid succession of events, over the course of just a few days, wherein Purdy was removed from his home, placed in custodial care, returned to his mother, then re-assigned to civil custody, then again placed back home, is indicative of the kind of inconsistent living arrangements that would continue his entire life.

While still essentially a child, at twelve years old, Purdy began using various substances – a chronic indulgence that would continue until his death. Throughout his life he abused glue, alcohol, marijuana, Valium, PCP, LSD, and cocaine.[154] A progress report conducted by San Joaquin County Mental Health, a month before his 15th birthday remarked that the youthful Purdy was "a pretty sharp boy when straight."[155]

At that time Purdy was no longer living with his mother on a regular basis. From the time he was 13 years-old time until he was legally considered an adult (at 18) he would live with his biological father, in foster homes, in juvenile custody, or on the streets.[156] Throughout that period he engaged in numerous legal violations including assault, possession of stolen property, possessing dangerous weapons, alcohol possession, extortion, violation of a court order, theft, public intoxication, solicitation, vandalism, and cultivation along with possession of marijuana.[157] Before reaching adulthood, as a direct result of his offenses, he also participated in a series of psychological evaluations and treatment programs.

When he was 15, a judge ordered participation in the Alcoholic Rehabilitation Clinic in Stockton. His intake documents indicate he was regularly inhaling glue and drinking.[158] He stated he sometimes experienced blackouts and the records characterize him as "very drug oriented."[159] The clinic referred him to San Joaquin County Mental Health Services (SJCMHS) for evaluation where he was diagnosed with sociopathic tendencies.[160]

The diagnostic categories of sociopathy and psychopathy are sometimes used interchangeably, though that interchange is technically inaccurate. They are meant to distinguish similar clinical traits – anti-social tendencies including deceptiveness and exploitation – based on differing origins. The former implies that social factors, particularly a turbulent home life and an early induction into criminal activities, are major contributors to the defining characteristics while the latter suggests a neurological, or at least a developmental, basis. Related to those geneses, the sociopath tends to be less cunning, more prone to violence, and not as grandiose than the psychopath who is fluent (though superficial), manipulative, and unwilling to fashion moral priorities.[161]

Purdy's chaotic upbringing and perpetual involvement in petty crime would lend credence to a diagnosis attributing his coping mechanisms to sociopathy. When evaluated by SJCMHS he admitted to glue sniffing as well as drinking half a gallon of wine per day.[162] Approximately a year and a half-later, while being detained for an outstanding bench warrant, he engaged in another psychological examination at the request of San Joaquin County Probation Department.

He indicated then that he consumed alcohol on a constant basis and had been intoxicated daily since the time he was twelve. Intelligence examinations were administered, and his ability was assessed as ranging between delayed and normal. The final report attributed his difficulties to emotional detachment and chemical dependency. Just a few weeks later, while still in juvenile detention, he was again psychologically profiled and he told the examiner that he drank a six-pack of beer everyday but preferred to use marijuana and valium.[163]

Chaos would continue through Purdy's short adulthood. He lived for short intervals with an aunt and uncle, roommates, his grandmother, in his car, in various motels, and jail. There were periods when he had no address at all. The locales in California included Los Angeles, Sacramento, Modesto, Lodi, South Lake Tahoe, and Stockton in addition to his sojourns out of state in Key West, Florida; Sandy, Oregon; Memphis, Tennessee; and Windsor, Connecticut.[164] His problems with the law continued and he was charged in separate incidents with the following: driving under the influence, failure to appear, reckless driving, public intoxication, possession of dangerous weapons, possession of stolen property, vandalism, discharging a firearm, and resisting arrest. Purdy held a variety of jobs, rarely keeping one for more than a month. Amazingly, he attained a license as a security guard from the State Bureau of Collections and Investigative Services –securing employment as such from three separate companies![165]

Before turning twenty, Purdy applied to the Social Security Administration (SSA) for disability support and, accordingly, underwent yet another psychological evaluation.[166] He was diagnosed with drug dependence (supposedly in remission) and "borderline intellectual functioning."[167] The next month he was examined again by a different doctor for the Social Services Disability Evaluation Division, who described him as confused with attention difficulties, concluding he was "suffering from substance-induced personality disorder."[168] He was found eligible for payments.[169]

Over the next five years, before carrying out his final assault, Purdy had at least five encounters with law enforcement for various offenses including traffic violations and assaulting a police officer. In addition, there were three situations when he filed a report as a victim. He also started and quit or was dismissed from at least 11 different jobs.[170]

In one incident in El Dorado County, Purdy was arrested for discharging a firearm while intoxicated. He kicked out the side window of a deputy's vehicle while he was handcuffed in the back seat. While held in jail, he cut his writs with his finger and toenails, made a noose out of his t-shirt, and claimed he could hear his mother calling him by name. He was placed on suicide watch [171] While incarcerated in that county, Purdy was examined and profiled at the Psychiatric Health Facility in Placerville and identified as "extremely dangerous."[172] His faltering neurological faculties – fostered by his incessant ingestion of intoxicants – contributed to his emotional instability.

Purdy was assessed and reassessed, treated and retreated by mental health professionals on numerous occasions. However, except for more foreboding prognostications about his temperamental decline, those efforts were to no avail. On his own volition he went to the Sacramento Mental Health Center (SMHC) for help with his alcoholism and suicidal thoughts and was referred to the Volunteers of America Public Inebriate Center.[173] A few months later he returned to the SMHC. He said, "I'm not thinking the way I should be thinking."[174] Also, he mentioned that he felt a connection to a postal worker whose rampage was in the news, and he complained of voices telling him "to do things."[175] It is likely he was referring to Patrick Henry Sherrill who the previous month had shot 20 of his co-workers.[176]

Purdy was diagnosed with antisocial personality disorder, which aligned with the sociopathy previously identified by SJCMHS. Center staff told him to come back the next day. When he did so he was crying and complaining about auditory hallucinations. Thorazine was prescribed and when he returned a week later, he was doing slightly better. When he moved out of the county shortly thereafter his unstable lifestyle hindered any possibility of continuing progress.[177]

Due to his relocation, he again sought assistance from SJCMHS where he completed an intake form in which he cited his religion as "'people against god' and described his family as 'mother dearest is a sick witch epileptic, my father was M.R. [mentally retarded], my brother is M.R. and I'm just fine!!!'"[178] Obviously his thought process was becoming more scattered. A little over a week later he was prescribed Thorazine and amitriptyline.[179]

The SSA re-evaluated Purdy repeatedly to assure his eligibility for public assistance. Each time he was found qualified for on-going disability payments, primarily because of his drug and alcohol dependency.[180] However, other issues were noted as well. One report, in a statement characteristic of bureaucratic banality, said he was "getting worse as time goes by."[181] In another he was characterized with borderline personality disorder, limited judgment, and poor impulse control.[182]

A telling commentary on the overlay of his fragmented lucidity on his abused childhood and subsequent ramshackle existence came from one of his voluntary visits to SJCMHS when he said, "I can't go on like this."[183] Eventually, as if symbolically summarizing his entire life, he revisited a place of his early youth to act out a final scene of perdition.

Purdy's mental erosion, initiated by maternal neglect and early ETV represents the sort of deterioration that can occur when emotional security is threatened in an unstable household. Just as malignant are disruptions during development that are instigated by forces outside the home. These experiences internalize hostilities that can, given the presence of the right variables, result in horrifying vindictive actions.

A Hostile Community

In a discussion of school shootings in relation to bullying, Langman eloquently notes, "If any connection exists, it is a complex relationship that varies from one case to another. What we need is an understanding of why some kids are so fragile and vulnerable that harassment – among other factors – might contribute to their decision to commit a school shooting."[184] The significant feature is the individual's interpretative reaction, not necessarily, the actual severity of events or circumstances.

Nevertheless, 71 percent of school shooters perceive "themselves as wronged, bullied or persecuted by others."[185] Reporting on news accounts about teenage perpetrators from a set of 28 taking place from 1992 through 2001, researchers noted that "[n]early all had stories of being constantly bullied, beat up, and … 'gaybaited.' Nearly all had stories of being mercilessly and constantly teased, picked on, and threatened." [186] Of course, the quantification in that report is a bit vague, but a study of 35 primary sources examining 126 cases (128 perpetrators from 13 countries) adds gravatas. Close to 9 of 10 (88.1%) assailants experienced social conflict in the educational environment. Close to 30 percent (29.9%) were physically bullied and over half (53.7%) thought they were rejected by their peers.[187]

The exact percentage of the entire set of rampage assailants, including youths and adults, who are predisposed toward retaliating against previous aggressors remains unknowable. However, given the profiles on record (and those offered in this study), most mass murderers are undoubtedly motivated by memories (some accurate, some exaggerated, some largely illusionary) of needless cruelty and inhumanity that they repeatedly reimagine. Classroom avengers harbor long-standing barely suppressed anger, then "target schoolmates and have the motives of hostile revenge."[188]

Like many of those who assail a school, rampage attackers at a place of business feel "aggrieved in some way."[189] Similarly, a public massacre is perpetuated by a "rageful, depressed, and often paranoid individual who releases his anger."[190] Except for locale, the delineation between an autogenic murderer in a public setting, school shooters, and workplace avengers is a distinction with no real difference. They are all, as Knoll points out, "resentful."[191]

Much is made of harassment and bullying in educational settings, but intimidation and victimizing is common in the workplace as well. Responses to a questionnaire distributed to 195 employees across a variety of industries revealed that 27 percent felt they had been mistreated in the previous 12 months. For the same survey 47 percent believed they had been mistreated at some point in their career and 75 percent reported they had witnessed mistreatment at work.[192] A poll of over 1,000 American workers resulted in similar percentages: 79 percent said they had indirectly experienced or observed bullying on the job while 66 percent state they personally had been victims. Most of these negative interactions did not originate with a supervisor, as one might intuitively surmise. Over half (52%) are from co-workers, 8 percent from managers outside the company, and 6 percent from other employees within the same organization.[193]

Abuse on the job resembles intentional cruelty in school. Though the descriptions may not be identical, concerns expressed in two separate polls – one concerning interactions at work and the other at school – are remarkably similar.

For workers:

- 60 percent state they are "picked on … or regularly undermined";
- 30 percent are subjected to "malicious rumors";
- 23 percent receive "aggressive texts, emails, or phone calls." [194]

Compared with students:

- 53.6 percent reporting they are "verbally bullied";
- 51.4 feeling "socially bullied";
- 13.6 percent "cyber bullied."[195]

School and workplace rampages alike have both steadily increased over the last two decades – the former climbing from 353 in 2000-2009 to 426 in 2010-2019,[196] and the latter increasing from 83 to 394 in one year alone (2015-2016).[197]

The relationship between ETV, deficient empathy, and use of violence was demonstrated by a battery of self-report inventories completed by urban adolescents who were at risk for criminality. A multiple regression analysis indicated that low empathy by itself will not consistently lead to harm, but when it is coupled with high levels of ETV in the community it becomes a significant predictor for violent acts.[198] A preference for wrathful judgement has been displayed by young survivors of intensely violent communities. Interviews focusing on peer-oriented moral violations were conducted with Columbian children six, nine, and twelve years old, evenly divided by gender. Some had been exposed to minimal violence and others had been subjected to more extreme experiences. Most of them recognized and disapproved of transgressions, but the youngsters who had been exposed to extremely hurtful acts thought it was legitimate to inflict harm or withhold assistance when provoked and considered it reasonable to retaliate for purposes of retribution.[199]

For many rampage murderers, deliberate torment by callous acquaintances or by members of an insensitive community made persistence in prevailing conditions untenable. A look at two cases, Olga Hepnarová and Zhao Zewei, will penetrate the antagonism that erupts from encounters interpreted as deliberate harassment.

Biographical and Textual Analysis: Olga Hepnarová – Perceived Physical Inadequacy; Destructive/Oppressive Environmental Situations (Injurious Familial Relations, Hostile Community); Neuropsychological Impairment (Thought Disorder, Compulsive)

Hepnarová intentionally drove a three-ton trunk into a tram stop in Prague, striking 20 people, killing 8 (3 at the scene, 5 who died later) and injuring 12 (6 seriously, the rest less so).[200]

In a statement, three days after her arrest, Hepnarová described experiences that have been and, tragically, will be shared by many children subject to abuse and hostility. Following is the account she gave police of her life on an ordinary school day in the sixth grade.

> In the morning, I would already wake up afraid of what was going to happen in the school, and what will the others come up with against me next. I couldn't even eat the breakfast properly as I was very nervous. … There, the whole class with the teacher would laugh at me, for example if I had done something, and this laughter would be often provoked by the teacher himself. After this torture at school, I had private hours of German or piano, which I attended with the same disgust as I would often meet people on the street or in a tram who were of the same ill nature as those at the school. For example, once when I was returning from the piano hours, I met a boy on a walkway who, all of a sudden, kicked me between my legs. Or once when I was driving in a tram, I somewhat neglectfully showed the conductor my season-ticket, after which he screamed at me, calling me a princess and pleading me to show him my season-ticket properly. … I would always happily rest in a place where there weren't any people, or when I was alone at home. I've never searched for any company and always preferred to stay alone [201]

As she remembers it, there were few instances that was enjoyable or even mildly pleasant as she moved about at home, in school, and through the community. The world was a sinister and unforgiving place peopled with venomous adults and villainous children. It was a Dickensian childhood, but without the occasional fictional beneficent stranger that might offer temporary respite.

No investigation ever verified the extent of Hepnarová's persecution. However, her father did admit to severely beating her on at least one occasion and he, along with her sister, stated she was frequently truant during the eighth grade.[202] She attempted suicide when she was 13 and as a result underwent psychological evaluation followed by admission to a psychiatric facility on two occasions.[203]

She was diagnosed with apathy, detachment, disharmonic development, insubordination, negativism, affective lability, flattened affectivity, inadequate reactions, nicotinism, and vomiting.[204] One psychiatrist, though, was much more specific, diagnosing Hepnarová with "hebephrenic schizophrenia."[205] The term is essentially interchangeable with "disorganized schizophrenia" that represents a subtype no longer considered useful since all schizophrenic conditions are characterized by delusions and scattered thoughts, at least to some degree.[206]

Hepnarová unquestionably harbored delusions of targeted persecution. However, based on her history, they apparently originated from actual experiences. About one week before her sixteenth birthday, Hepnarová, wrote a letter to one of the few people she trusted – a psychiatrist who had treated her during a period she was institutionalized.[207]

The rather lengthy missive (over 1,300 words) began with an announcement of a beating she recently delivered upon a sibling. It was the first time she expressed that she was favorably inclined toward retributive justice, a perspective she used later to justify her slaughter. She was unapologetic about attacking her sister, explaining that she was subject to the same sort of indignity in the past by the same sister now on the receiving end. Throughout this communication, she expressed irritation toward acquaintances as well as strangers and toyed with cruelty as one method for coping with her discomfort.

The epistle made it clear that, she had completely given up on society and dismissed any desire to carry on relationships. There was, she acknowledged, an unknowable substantial part of her that was "simply inside," dividing her from companionship.[208] She believed people were essentially hypocrites presenting themselves as friendly and cheerful, when in fact they posed a danger to her spirit. They had already caused her damage and she wished to be left to herself. As a matter of fact, she stated that she was "happier without people." [209]

If so, it was a happiness without joy. A few lines later she admitted to a "loneliness" that she accepted despite "sadness and bitterness."[210] It would be more accurate to say that she found some relief and a measure of calm in her isolation. Her solitary choices had come about because she was "rejected" and she was unwilling to engage in customary mannerisms or displays of humility to recoup her social standing.[211] On that point she was absolute: "I don't value myself that high to be against them, but I'll never be with them. … People won't find me anymore, I've changed so much that it'll be a futile task for them to do so. It's too late."[212] During a timespan that is typically the most social period of development, Hepnarová thoughtfully structured her life to spend as much time as possible without engagement. She read, she did bookbinding, and took day trips by herself.

Before the vehicular rampage, Hepnarová wrote and sent a pair of letters to two different publications, which, ironically, due to a slow postal system, were not delivered until after the tragedy. Although the messages, were very similar, they were not identical. The wording varied slightly, and a passage was omitted in one. The reprint from the Mladý svět magazine (some of which follows) is representative.[213]

She began by meticulously stating her identity, including her place of employment and her address. It was if she was citing the basic information necessary to identify her as would be required for tracking the status and protecting the rights of a prisoner of war under the Geneva Convention.[214] Hepnarová viewed herself in that context. As far as she was concerned, her assault was the final act of combat in a conflict that had been going on for years. The diatribes, sent to newspapers so that they would be broadly published, were defensive testaments, not manifestos per se, but accusatory polemics, like statements a condemned person would make when facing death.[215]

The string of abusive incidents and injustices reads like an extended oratory from a judge summarizing infractions before passing judgment. The list is very long but just as notable is the amount of detail regarding places and time periods. These traumatic encounters – regardless of whether they were described accurately, exaggerated, or only imagined – were deeply and substantially etched into the lens through which Hepnarová viewed existence.

> And here's my confession (if I don't believe in priests or doctors, I still do believe in at least one single honest journalist).
> Till 13 years of age, I'm being raised under the claws of the so-called good family. I'm battered and bullied – a toy in the eyes of the adults and a victim of the children at school (and forever an outsider among my peers). They call me: DRAGONESS, MUMMY, TARZAN, BROKEN ANGEL, STONE FLOWER, DREAMING VIRGIN, OUR DARLING, etc. My torturers are relentless. I'm a freaky element of the pack, a black sheep of the family. As far as my memory serves, I'm a loner. I haven't any friends, and never will have. I fall in despair, and in consequence escape. Escape from school, escape from my home, escape from my life (1x). Then at 13 years of age I'm once again being put back into a life full of vilification, mockery and injustice. In the children hospital in Opařany, I finally realize the unawareness and uselessness of psychiatry (for me). Upon finishing the elementary school I then go to study for a bookbinder. At school, the racism somehow eases up, but as a female professional driver I once again have to fight (prejudices, etc.). In the autumn of 1971, I leave home to live in a cottage which was built almost entirely by myself and out of my own money. This cottage is a symbol of my lonely fight. One and a half year later, however, I have to leave it and, on the brink of collapse, I find myself living in a boarding house, which proves to be one monstruous of a Babylon (where one can live, though).
> Here are some of my random notes from the past.
> I'm wretched like a last drug addict. But where are my drugs? Where? What is it that keeps me from falling
> All my feelings on the brink of exhaustion and my hopes already vanished. Yet, the broken angel is still in one piece.
> Why am I doing this. To let them know where are the limits of one's helplessness against the society.
> My position is worse than that of an American black. Why? Because I'm alone.
> Thousand times I've been lynched. Here are some examples:

> - by my father Antonín Hepnar
> - lured into the showers and then beaten to a bloody pulp (Opařany 1965)
> - repeatedly insulted and kicked between the legs by a group of known and unknown boys (at 11 years of age, in the hallway of my house)
> - beaten on a public street by a girl of the same age (at 10 or 11 years of age, Bethlehem square)
> - in a bookbinding workshop physically assaulted by the workmaster … and verbally
> - countless times I've been crudely reminded that I'm a loser who has nothing to do in a company full of orderly people (I hereby maintain that I was always healthy, both psychically and physically!!)
> - numerous times, the people on the street would pass by me and then spit – either on the ground or at me …
> - in all of my previous jobs I've been openly denigrated and traduced, ridiculed, vilified, except maybe for PK [Pražské komunikace; Prague Communications], where they were treating me with a certain official politeness
>
> Personal summary. I'm a sexual cripple. Unable to find a proper relationship. I'm a destroyed human. A human destroyed by people.[216]

She then assumes the role of a magistrate and passes sentence, stating that society itself is overly self-indulgent and so cannot properly pass judgement. Then follows an assertion of her own absolution, as she declares that it is reasonable to exact the lives of enumerable others for her own.

> Therefore, I have a choice: to kill myself or to kill the others. And I decide as follows.
>
> I WILL RETURN MY HATERS THEIR FAVOR. If I had gone as an unknown suicide, it would've been too easy for you.
>
> And because the society is too consummate to judge itself, it is judged privately. Sometimes, it is indeed punished, sometimes it is only shocked. Here's my verdict:

> I, Olga Hepnarová, the victim of your bestiality, sentence you to death by rolling over you and hereby proclaim that my life is worth of countless others.[217]

She finalizes her declaration with the Latin phrase “Acta, non verba”[218] (usually translated as “deeds not words”) thereby punctuating her pronouncement with a language laden gavel.[219]

Hepnarová’s trauma may not have been as persistent or frequent as she remembered but there certainly must have been some and her rumination was painful and bitter, eventually forming the basis for rationalizing an act of mass violence. She was executed by hanging March 12, 1975 – the last woman to suffer the death penalty in Czechoslovakia.[220]

Early in Hepnarová’s farewell letter, she hearkened back to the time when she was 13. That period would have been 9 years before her vehicular onslaught, which, of course, demonstrates the extended length of time that unhappy memories may reverberate in the back of the mind. She reacted to that discordant reverberation in a way she considered to be equivalent to the cruelty she endured. Over three decades later, in a much different part of the world Zhao Zewei held a grudge for a longer period and enacted his version of vengeance in a way that was much more intimate.

Biographical Analysis: Zhao Zewei – Perceived Physical Inadequacy (Limited Stature); Destructive Environment (Victimized); Neuropsychological Impairment (Depressed)

At 28-years-old Zhao Zewei was slight of build and reticent to speak, very much the way he had been 10 years ago when he was a schoolboy in Shaanxi Province in northwest China, the same locale where he continued to reside with his parents.[221] Unemployed, he spent most of his time at home playing games on the computer.[222] His family was convinced he had some type of mental illness or, at the very least, coping with depression.[223] That belief, which seemingly dismissed his lack of independence and disengagement from common activities as functional, hints that his apathy and isolation might have been excused in the home.

Zhao ruminated on the misfortunes of his teenage years when he attended the prestigious No. 3 Middle School in Mizhi.[224] In part because of his diminutive stature and partially due to his shy nature, he had been subject to ridicule and intimidation. The third year, when he was between 13 and 14-

years-old, was particularly unsettling.[225] He simply could not forget it. "He was angry inside," his uncle, Li Zhisheng, recalled.[226]

A decade later he remained as friendless as he had been in his early teens. He was also jobless and, with no better prospects in the foreseeable future, he was essentially aimless. Zhao exhibited chronic lethargy and was, unquestionably, detached from the possibility of realizing social expectations. Shopping on the internet, he purchased five knives.[227] Perhaps he believed that he needed a small arsenal of blades to successfully carry out his intentions. He sought out his former classmates but when he was unable to locate them, Zhao turned his wrath on the unsuspecting pupils who just happened to be attending his former school.[228]

As the school day closed, around 5:00 p.m. on April 27, 2018, he entered the site where he previously felt brutalized, claiming that he was there to pick up his son.[229] He waited for the conclusion of the afternoon session with three of his knives at the ready. At approximately 6:10 the students, anticipating the upcoming three-day weekend, filed through a constricted lane to exit the grounds.[230] Zhao rushed the crowd and began frenetically striking at the unsuspecting youths.[231] Because the passage was narrow, the youngsters had little room to maneuver.[232] "I couldn't see what was in his hand, but he was running and stabbing people randomly," a witness said.[233]

Even in these circumstances, when his weapons should have allowed him to dominate the situation, Zhao was overpowered. Some of the youths began to throw rocks at him. He was then captured by several teachers along with security personnel. The police arrived soon after.[234] Seven girls and two boys were killed, another eleven wounded, four of those seriously.[235]

He was sentenced to death and the court offered a summative, but still unsatisfying, assessment: "Because his work and life were not going well, Zhao Zewei held a grudge in his heart and took it out on innocents."[236] Zhao confessed that he felt bullied when he attended school and "hated" his classmates, so decided to use a "dagger" to get even.[237] He did not offer an explanation that justified killing children he did not know as part of enacting his revenge fantasy.

A review of the literature directly pertaining to revenge as a decisive phenomenon identifies six types that are manifested in a range reflecting the proportionality of the actions along with the emotional intensity of the desire to act. The most disproportionate with the highest level of emotionality is described as "maladaptive."[238] It is characterized as being all consuming, sustained by preoccupation with harm, and dangerous to the avenger as well as others.[239] The potential perpetrator is infatuated with retribution and the more he savors the thought the greater the infatuation.

An adolescent whose moral development is delayed and mainly contingent upon the assessment of others (Table 3.1) may try to gain large scale group approval through antagonism. The result is a perversion of normative values such that status (in the mind of the actor) can be acquired by prominent aggression. The tortured quest for admiration by an underachieving socially maladjusted 15-year-old in California serves as an example.

Biographical Analysis: Andy Williams – Perceived Physical Inadequacy (Limited Stature); Destructive Environment (Unsupportive Living Conditions, Victimized); Neuropsychological Impairments (Distorted Cognition)

Describing his thoughts during his rampage in an interview 12 years into his prison sentence, Williams recalled:

> To me, it was just like a numbness at the time. … I couldn't really – like at fifteen, I didn't really think all that stuff through. I didn't think two boys were going to die. I didn't think thirteen people were going to get shot. I just thought I was gonna make a lot of noise and that the – and that the cops were gonna show up.[240]

When questioned after arrest he said, "I didn't want anybody to die, but if they did, then oh well."[241] On the surface the two statements seem askew but in the context of his primary motivation they coincide. The most important matter, as far as Williams was concerned, was that his belligerent daring be undeniable. Reacting to what he believed was the ethos of his crowd, the mechanics of the massacre, even the body count, were irrelevant to him. It was the enactment of a radical brutal scenario that mattered. Years later, he would admit that he was suicidal, but that admission also aligned with the comment about a lack of strategy and professed indifference to injury and death. Killing himself would be perfect exclamatory punctuation for his consumptive campaign.

Pale in complexion and slight in build as well as height, Williams had lived in the community of Santee less than a year in advance of his SMASI.[242] Most of his childhood had been spent in Maryland. While he was in the eighth grade, he relocated with his father to Twentynine Palms in California where they resided with his grandparents for about six months. Williams befriended a young man who, as Williams himself would eventually experience, was bullied by his classmates.

When his dad took a job with San Diego Naval Medical Center they settled near the facility.[243] Williams missed his life in the east where he was well liked, played on the football team, participated in theatre, earned straight As, and had a girlfriend.[244] The principal of his middle school there remembered him as "a happy-go-lucky kid."[245] The series of relocations during puberty may have held an emotional echo of another string of adjustments that he had been forced to make before he entered kindergarten. During his preschool years his parents separated. That separation was followed by their divorce and his mom's departure with his half-brother. After the split he typically saw his mother once a year, usually during Christmas season.[246]

To assuage Andy's hesitancy about moving to an unknown suburban city, his father allowed him to spend the summer months before his freshman year in his former hometown in Maryland. He stayed at the home of friends.[247] Unbeknownst to his dad, however, his son, preceding their earlier move, had begun to experiment with marijuana and other drugs, including cocaine. Upon his return to familiar surroundings, he began to indulge again. With minimal parental supervision, he spent the vacation hanging out with his old friends, playing Nintendo, fishing in the river that bordered the town, and getting stoned.[248]

His entry to his new school, Santana High, was cushioned by an association with an ensemble of teens that frequently ditched classes to hang out at a skateboard park to smoke pot, drink stolen tequila, and take other drugs that might come their way.[249] "We would just sit there and smoke weed. Bong loads, pipes, joints, you name it – he smoked it," recalled a short-term romantic interest from the time.[250]

Williams was now fourteen and, except for the brief interlude while he lived in Twentynine Palms, for two successive years had regularly indulged in drugs and alcohol. The substances included liquor, massive amounts of marijuana, opiates, and coke.[251]

Although all cellular interactions are not completely understood, plasticity of pre-pubescent, pubescent, and adolescent neural development is now well known and thoroughly documented.[252]

Correspondingly, the detrimental effects of inebriants on cerebral maturation, especially regarding personal restraint and extemporaneous judgement have become apparent.[253] The superficiality in decision-making and concomitant inadequacy in the assessment of consequential actions that Williams would display shortly after he turned fifteen years of age can be partially explained by fragmented thinking due to long-standing substance abuse at an early age.

That fragmentation was compounded by the abrasive social matrix in which he had become ensnared. When he attended school Williams was harassed and ridiculed. In emails to a former girlfriend in Maryland he revealed that he hated Santana High because bullies would spit on him, punch him, call him "gay," and burn him with cigarette lighters.[254]

"He was skinny – most of his friends were a good 20 or 30 pounds heavier than him. I didn't know it then, but he hated going to school because of the abuse. But the friends outside school were pounding on him almost as bad," his dad explained after Andy's imprisonment.[255] His son remembers it the same way, adding that he remained involved with the group because he was desperate for their approval. "I don't know. I thought these guys are cool, and I wanted to be cool. I've always wished I was a little bit braver."[256] The explanations by father and son might be discounted as exaggerated rationalizations for the atrocities later enacted by the younger Williams, except other associates from that time have portrayed the dynamic in much the same way. "He was so thin that some described him as 'anorexic' and so pale that others called him 'albino.' … Said a friend: 'He didn't have an easy life.'"[257]

His closet buddy from that period, Josh Stevens, observed, "He was pushed to the edge. … Listen to 'In the End,' track eight on Linkin Park's CD. That was the song that inspired Andy."[258] The song is a Wagnerian lament to frustration and futility that blends rap lyrics with a hard rock chorus, repeating the line, "But in the end it doesn't even matter."[259] Williams left a note quoting the song for his father before leaving his home on the morning of his SMASI. He signed it "Sorry dad I Love you."[260] Stevens's mother observed, "Andy was a follower. … Josh could manipulate Andy because Andy wanted to be In."[261] His standing with his group was subservient.

The circle's alpha dog was Christopher Reynolds who, at 29 year-of age, was dating the mother of Stevens. He cavorted with the boys and would take them paintball shooting.[262] He also supplied them with drugs and alcohol, which, by some accounts, put him in the position to make sexual advances on them.[263] Andy Williams claims Reynolds took advantage of him at least once, a charge his dad has corroborated.[264] Now over 40 years-old, Reynolds is currently in prison due to convictions for multiple counts of lewd misconduct unrelated to Williams or the Santana shooting.[265]

Because of his unexcused absences, drug abuse, and general disinterest Williams did poorly with his schoolwork. "Constant truancies and ignored homework marked him as a deadbeat to other students and an exasperation to teachers."[266] He covered up his failures by erasing messages from the school on the home answering machine before his father could listen to them and intercepting his report card in the mail.[267]

As the second semester was getting underway, just prior to his 15th birthday, Williams received word that his close friend from Twentynine Palms had been killed while tying his shoe after stepping off a school bus.[268] Williams had neither the maturity nor the verbal facility to process it. "My friend is dead. … I can't believe it. We just talked the other day. He was fine. Now he's gone. This sux [sic]," he told his former girlfriend from Maryland over the phone.[269]

It was around this time, in February of 2000, less than two years after Harris with Klebold carried out the abortive bombing and their shooting massacre in Colorado, that Williams and two of his fellow skateboarders fantasized that they could "pull a Columbine."[270]

> Over a period of time these boys, Andy, A.J. [Gilbert], and Josh, video taped themselves writing down the hit list, taping the hit list with a camcorder, making their plan to shoot up the school, and also clowning before the camera.[271]

The tapes, reportedly, ended up scattered, and are now in the possession of various participants in the filming as well as others who were on the clique's periphery.[272] There are no public records indicating that the videos were ever viewed by authorities.

It is unknown how intent the other two boys ever were about an eventual assault. As it turned out, neither assisted in the shooting. Throughout the month, though, the subject continued to arise and Williams was always pivotal to the conversation, even if he was not generally taken seriously.[273] Glibert's mother has "publicly stated that there were at least twenty students that were aware of Andy's threats prior to the shooting…."[274] At a party on the Saturday preceding the shooting on a Monday morning, Stevens drew a diagram of the campus and pinpointed where each assailant could stand – he in one hallway, Gilbert in another, and Williams in the boy's bathroom. He mentioned that they could use his shotguns and Williams should arm himself with his father's handgun. He then crumpled up the drawing and threw it away, apparently signaling that he was backing out. There were approximately 50 people, at the gathering, adults as well as young people.[275] Despite that symbolic gesture, Williams revisited the topic again later that night as he and Gilbert were sleeping over with Stevens. Typically, he backed off, saying as often before, that he was merely jesting.[276]

On Sunday Williams had multiple conversations about his intentions. A junior high school girl recalled the banter as teens were gathering in the late afternoon to jump bikes over improvised obstacles. "We were just making fun of him, just mocking him.[277] Rather than deter Williams, the mockery emboldened him. That night he again boasted of his plans to another friend, advising him to stay home from classes the next day.[278] There was also a conversation he had with Chris Reynolds, but the two conversers remember it much differently. Reynolds has stated he warned Williams that he would call law enforcement if he was serious about the impending violence, while Williams has claimed the opposite, saying Reynolds threatened him with his life if he failed to follow through with the threatened rampage.[279]

That same evening Stevens had a long phone conversation with another friend who convinced him to completely forsake any plans of participating in the ambush. Meanwhile, with his father out for the evening, Williams sat alone in their apartment arranging the stash of bullets he would need the following day.[280]

The repeated revisitation of the possibility of a sudden assault in the guise of humor allowed Williams to broach the idea of killing in a manner that was relatively acceptable in his peculiar social setting. He was able to hint at his intentions, retain deniability, gauge the possibility of the status inherent in the crime, and bid for possible assistance. It was "kidding on the level," a type of foreshadowing when the autogenic mass murderer signals his or her accelerating desire for pandemonium while keeping his or her options open for interpretation.[281]

On Monday morning after he stole a .22 caliber revolver along with 40 rounds from his father's gun cabinet, he killed two students, while wounding a campus supervisor, a teacher intern and eleven more students. One pupil, who was seventeen years of age at the time, will carry bullet fragments in his hip for the rest of his life.[282]

At the time Williams was delighted. "'It was the first time in my life that I felt I was powerful and I was in control,' he said from prison."[283]

Except for a brief interlude when he resided in a small desert community in southern California, he had continuously disregarded his schoolwork, deceived his father, and stayed inebriated. His social group treated him like a mascot, but when he finally rampaged, he was the primordial predator.

> The key emotional dynamic on the path of these [senseless] murders is a play with moral symbolics in which (1) the protagonist enters as a pariah, (2) soon becomes lost in the dizzying symbolics of deviance, and (3) emerges to reverse the equation in a violent act of transcendence.[284]

Williams was unquestionably a conduct problem. However, he was not conduct disordered in the sense that he was entirely anti-social. (The distinction is explored in Chapter 5 and exemplified in the catalogue composing Appendix.) He was not callous or without conscience. His friends from Maryland recalled with fondness the sympathy he showed for small animals that were harmed. While living in Twentynine Palms he had been deeply attached to a vulnerable neighbor and even attended religious services with him.[285] Following his crimes that Monday morning, Williams was diagnosed with "a 'major depressive disorder.'"[286] A psychiatrist who treated him attested that he probably had brought the gun to school hoping his classmates would view him as someone who was strong and fearsome.[287] Williams carried an empty emotional reservoir that he wanted to fill by acquiring some semblance of respect from tenuous companions.

Fractious experiences in childhood disrupt the process of development and subvert the ability of young people to form attachments that are supportive and nurturing. The result may be dysregulation (vacillating affection), over-regulation (controlling or clingy relationships), or avoidance of positive emotional bonds.[288]

> [T]he defensive exclusion and distortion of memories and evaluations of attachment experiences that characterize incoherent states of mind may make it difficult to attend flexibly nondefensively to other social interactions. … Insecure states of mind may also lead

> to biased or negative expectations of oneself and others in interactions.[289]

Ultimately, for many of those autogenic murderers who interpret their childhoods as torturous, it all comes down to pay back – revenge for interactions they could not control as they unfolded and for which they lacked the mental maturity to compartmentalize or the capacity to interpret in a way that would make incoherent experiences meaningful. For others, such as Williams, meaning is sought through a frantic bid for prominence.

Chapter Four

Neuropsychological Impairments

Dreary dells and haunted floods,
By the churchyard's lonely bound,
Wand'ring o'er the cheerless ground,
Where oft, as vulgar stories tell,
From aisles the midnight spectres yell. …
– Gavin Turnbull
"To Melancholy"

It may be tempting, however simplistic, to cite insanity as the predominate cause of rampage killings, but the dismissive explanation, quite literally, does not add up. In 2019, 51.5 million adults (aged 18 or older) in the United States were diagnosed with a mental illness (representing 20.6 percent of that population).[1] The number of young people (12-17 years old) receiving mental health services during 2019 was estimated at a more than 20.4 million.[2] That same year the nonprofit Gun Violence Archive (GVA), tracked 417 mass shootings (in which four or more were shot) of which 31 resulted in multiple murders (at least four killed).[3] Based on those numbers the proportion of the mentally ill who would have committed a sudden mass assault with a gun would be 0.000005799 and the odds for armed mass murder would equate to 0.000000431. Even reducing the number to those considered severely mentally ill – 13.1 million or 5.2 percent of all adults in the country and 4.1 million or 16.7 percent of young people for a total of 17.2 million the odds of one of those individuals rampaging with a firearm would only increase to 0.000024244 and the chances of mass murder would be 0.000001802.[4] Put another way if only one tenth of one percent of all those with serious psychological impairments rampaged, based on the numbers for 2019, there would be 17,200 incidents of mass murder per annum in America alone! Of course, there are ways people conduct multiple murders besides shooting (Pricilla Ford's vehicular homicide, described later in this chapter, is one such example) but that would hardly account for the difference between the possible massacres that could have been committed by just a small percentage of the mentally ill and the number actually carried out in 2019.

Analogous observations may be made for supposed instances of sudden or episodic psychoses, such as intermittent explosive disorder (IED), brief reactive psychosis (BRP – sometimes called brief psychotic disorder), or inexplicable violent seizures, all of which have been used as a shelter for refuge from the consequences of moribund acts by unknowledgeable – or unscrupulous – defense attorneys and their desperate clients. The admonition that rampages are not caused by such episodes should not be construed to mean these dysfunctional states do not exist. IED and BRP are both recognized in the latest version of the chief reference for American Psychiatric Association, the *Diagnostic Statistical Manual*, and knowledge of the brain is limited enough that it is hard to deny the possibility that brutality is sometimes – rarely – related to undetected electro-magnetic relays.[5] Their mere existence, though, does not mean they are functionally responsible for rampages. The three maladies (IED, BRP, and seizure provoked outbursts) produce episodes that are of relatively short duration (in comparison to other mental disorders), unpredictable, and unplanned. Rampages in their active phase last for multiple minutes to hours and, if the preparatory phase is included, weeks or even months. More importantly, they are pre-meditated, frequently in tortuous detail. Three chapters in *How Rampage Killers Interpret Their Worlds* concentrate on the premeditation involved in rampaging.

Chronic neurological and/or emotional problems represent only one of four conditional categories that solitarily or in conjunction with other situational factors may preface the developmental process that eventually ends in carnage. As shown in Table 1.1, for the taxonomical purposes of this text these psychological impairments include mental states that are characterized by extreme deviations in perception, cognitive processes, or emotions, but are separate from that class of mental disturbances when the individual is repeatedly socially manipulative or blatantly antisocial (that is, pathological personalities).

Irrespective of the disproportionately low percentage of murderous incidents directly associated with mental or emotional disturbances (in relation to the universe of subjects dealing with such difficulties), psychiatric abnormalities sometimes contribute to the constellation of factors that intermingle to undermine a killer's emerging perspective. That construction may rest on four deficiencies (see Figure 4.1):

1. Restricted, distorted, or disordered cognition – wherein misinterpreted information posits unfounded assumptions;
2. Mood disordered – wherein perceptions are occluded by emotional framing;
3. Delusional thought patterns – wherein an idiosyncratic Weltanschauung dominates thought;
4. Disassociated or hallucinatory episodes – wherein illusionary sensations suggest violent acts.

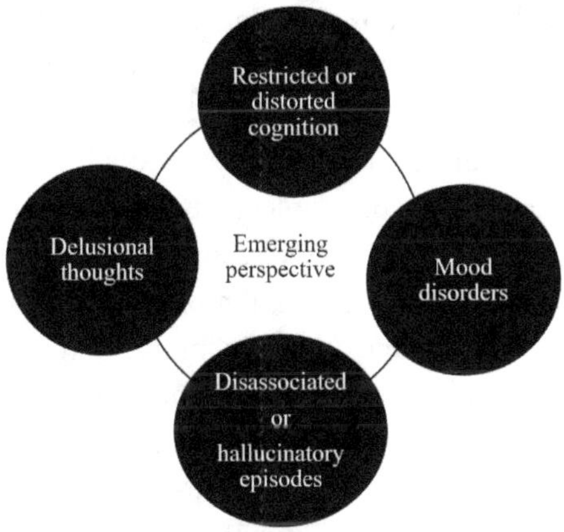

FIGURE 4.1. Influence of neuropsychological impairments relevant to some rampage murders. The smaller spheres represent the functional components of disorders in thought and temperament. The large central sphere signifies the mindset that is forming in the mind of the eventual autogenic mass murderer. Any single impairment may be effective by itself or may be comorbid with others.

These four derivations should not (and perhaps cannot) be partitioned or stratified. They frequently overlap jointly or even act as a quadrant, but still selectively describe neurological and/or interpretive impairments that influence destructive behavior. The degree of adversity varies based on a variety of mental or physiological conditions and, in the case of mass killers, the conditional harbingers are ushered by the reactive strategies that impede functional relations in the family, community, and work setting. The poor outcomes of those interactions accentuate traits embedded in a neurogenic interpretation of the world that results in an increasingly isolated frame of reference.

The features of each in relation to an eventual inclination for violent action will, in due course, be discussed accompanied by profiles of murders exemplifying the characterizations. Before engaging in those discussions, though, there is a necessity for a slight detour to put traumatic brain injury and its cousin, chronic use of alcohol and/or drugs, in perspective in relation to the preconditions necessary for formation of the rampageous mentality.

Putting Traumatic Brain Injury and Chronic Substance Abuse in Perspective

There is little question that head trauma can cause practically any type and any degree of neurological damage, depending on the incident as well as the amount and precise location of damage. Furthermore, an abundance of evidence connects brain injury to acting out –sometimes resulting in extreme violence.

Extensive research on childhood injuries, pedophilia, death row inmates, spousal abuse, and miscellaneous violent offenders support this assertion.[6] "Case studies as far back as 1835 have reported the onset of antisocial traits after frontal lobe injury."[7] An examination of 150 murder defendants in six states found 10 percent with traumatic brain injury, compared with 1-2 percent in the population at large.[8] An even more dramatic study of 13 men and two women scheduled for execution revealed that all "experienced severe head injuries earlier in life."[9] Further, ineffectual executive functions link to brain damage, even when it is relatively minimal.[10]

Excessive intoxication over prolonged periods can have a damaging effect on lucidity. Even so, with respect to the focus of this chapter – that is, impairments as foundational components to a murderous mindset – the temporary effects of substances as social inhibitors, while relevant in the larger realm of violence, may contribute to rampages but are not primary initiators. In fact, the proportion of single incident multiple killings that can be attributed to substance abuse in and of itself is remarkably small. A review of 30 North American mass murderers found that "[a]lcohol was consumed by only three (10%) of the perpetrators just prior to or during" the massacre.[11]

Chemically induced transient states may be secondary agents to predispositions or symptomatic of dysfunctional coping strategies but they are generally not embryonic. On the contrary, researchers have noted a broad swath of factors – both biological and social – contributing to criminality. These contributors include but are certainly not limited to any single one or any combination of the following: fetal exposure to toxic elements (such as tobacco), malnutrition early in life, impulsive cognition, callousness, thrill seeking, non-productive parenting (including over-indulgence, abuse, and neglect), delayed development (both physical and mental), low socioeconomic status, poor performance in school, exposure to delinquency, peer rejection, availability of weapons.[12]

The Appendix records preconditions for 112 rampageous assailants. The influence of drugs or alcohol is relevant in twelve (.107) of those in that list (Attias, Casteel, Harpham, Hawkins, Hennard, Kazmierczak, Knight, Loughner, McCree, Purdy, Williams, and Whitman). A Narcotic was taken by James Holmes to enhance performance and subdue pain during his assault on movie goers.[13] It was not intended as an emotional suppressant. Feeling poorly the morning before his murderous odyssey through the forest and his hometown of Hungerford England, Michael Ryan took paracetamol. A commonly used analgesic, the main ingredient being acetaminophen, his dose equated to two Tylenols.[14] Clifton McCree was most likely under the influence of marijuana when he killed five and wounded one more. Since he was a chronic user of cannabis, that indulgence is hardly an indication of a premeditative attempt to insulate his emotions for his SMASI. In the case of Loughner, his substantial consumption of hallucinogens may have contributed to a psychosis that led him to try to assassinate a United States Congresswoman and to murder six bystanders in that attempt.[15]

Intoxicants, often have the effect of inducing "selective disinhibition" whereby an actor will engage in behaviors s/he would generally resist. That state is dependent on the situation, social conditions, and the setting (a bar as opposed to an office building for example) as well as the intoxicating agent.[16] "When substance intoxication is involved, 'all bets are off' in terms of accurate forensic description and isolation of neuropathologic processes. In such cases, the evaluator must rely on identification of crime behavior that is congruent with the loss of presence of self-control, irrespective of possible brain damage."[17] Such circumstances are separate from an inherent propensity toward harmful conduct and certainly distinct from the attention necessary for prolonged planning preceding a rampage.

The literature indicates that aggression typically (but not always) predates drug and alcohol use and that the compulsion for abuse is often symptomatic of the same cognitive dysfunctionality that contributes toward a contentious nature.[18] To the degree that mental derangement can be spurred by cellular damage in the brain, extensive substance abuse may be one contributing factor, among many, in deviant socialization. Aggressive deviance in conjunction with intoxicants as a dispositional influence can occur in one of two ways that are a kind of psychological Palindrome.

To begin with, obfuscation of the faculties can result in "restricted or distorted cognition" as described in the next subsection. "Brain scans and new testing protocols show substance abuse can damage your brain just as bad as traumatic brain injury. ... The main area impacted can be the frontal lobe, which controls decision making and impulse control."[19] The erosion of rationality, in turn, can sometimes lead to psychosis, mania, and depression. In a carefully integrated review of findings published since the 1970s, a report concluded, "[S]ubstance-induced disorders exist, they are prevalent enough to contribute significantly to the rates of comorbidity between SUDs [substance use disorders] and psychiatric conditions. ..."[20] It cautioned, though, that the causation applies only to a subset of comorbid conditions.[21]

There is also the polar effect of chronic ingestion of mind-altering substances (of any type) compounding the impact of psychiatric maladies already present. Abundant evidence supports the prevalence of this malignant dynamic. A comprehensive review of dual diagnoses on the continent of Australian cited 47 percent as the *lowest* estimate for the presence of the problematic relationship.[22] A survey in the United States showed significantly greater odds for the possibility of substance dependence among those with certain mental health problems, compared to the general population (even after adjusting for socio-demographic factors), as follows: any mood disorder, 3.3; major depressive disorder, 2.2; bipolar I disorder, 4.2; dysthymia, 2.8; any anxiety disorder, 2.8, and any panic disorder, 1.9.[23] Remarkably, similar results have been found for alcohol alone: mood disorders, 3.6; major depressive disorder, 3.9; bipolar 6.3, anxiety disorders, 2.6; generalized anxiety disorder, 4.6; and post-traumatic stress disorder, 2.2.[24]

For the future mass murderer, the chronic indulgence in inebriants may co-join with other conditions to harm the psyche or accentuate inherent damage resulting in confusion, unstable relations, and progressive disorientation. Patrick Purdy profiled in the previous chapter is an example.

With brain injury and substance abuse now placed within the broader topic of deficiencies in thinking and emotional regulation, the four variants of psychological deviation that were introduced earlier can be explored, each in turn.

Restricted or Distorted Cognition

During a six-month period at an in-patient non-secure community unit for individuals with learning disabilities (LDs), researchers tabulated 55 incidents of physical violence, 25 occurrences of aggression (intimidation, threats, lingual abuse), 8 instances of racial abuse, and 8 episodes of sexually threatening behavior among the residents – all in a facility with 10 beds.[25] The study illustrates the intricate association between processing disorders and the potential for violence. Studies with a broader base but with participant commonalities have portrayed similar disproportionate levels of hostility.

Eighty-one percent of staff at another learning disability assistance center operated through the National Health Service Trust (in England) "experienced violence in the workplace in the previous 12 months. Many had experienced numerous incidents…."[26] In a ward with 52 patients, there were 286 violent events with 36 percent of these committed by the same six women![27] Two additional studies of elementary pupils found combative comments to peers by students with learning disabilities to be more frequent than those from students without learning disabilities.[28]

Another examination considered levels of aggression, rated as stable aggressive, unstable aggressive, and non-aggressive in adolescent boys in relation to assessors frequently linked to cognitive fluidity – verbal learning, incidental spatial learning, tactile-lateral ability, and executive functions – while controlling for social disadvantage. Both the stable and unstable aggressive groups scored significantly lower with regard to executive functioning, suggesting a lesser inclination for self-control, than the non-aggressive set of participants.[29] A corresponding study demonstrated that emotional regulation, as scaled by parents, was "highly correlated with ratings of response inhibition, working memory, attentional shift, and general executive control in preschool children" with or without attention-deficit/hyperactive disorder (ADHD).[30]

Pertinence of limited cognitive efficiency in relation to the potential for violence is not related to general intellectual ability as much as instinctual or acquired skills in the interpretation of interpersonal cues and the emotional motivations of others. Individuals with psychotic spectrum disorders who have engaged in psychotically driven aggressive (PDA) episodes have been shown to score lower on social cognition measures than counterparts with no history of PDA acts (irrespective of variances in medication).[31]

The capacity for inhibitions, restraint, and foresight, frequently referred to as "executive functions" and residing in the frontal lobes, are foundational to an internalized social paradigm that is alert to the perception of others and attuned to consequences. Surprisingly, though, despite the imperative that this region remains functional for civilized behavior, it is somewhat sensitive to disruptive events. "Both the biological substrata and their complex mental and behavioral products are relatively fragile."[32] This sensitivity, as well as deficiencies in abstraction associated with limited competence in language – sometimes paired with neural aberrations and sometimes not – partially explains the apparent reduction of interpersonal interpretative skills along with underdevelopment of global thinking connected to impaired capacities.[33]

Linked with thorough executive functioning is the metacognitive contribution of language. Certainly, perceptual, or cognitive deficits, evidenced by conditions such as learning disabilities or developmental delays, do not promulgate violence. They are, however, linked to immature judgement, associated with brain dysfunctions as well as inhibited communication, and tied to underdeveloped verbal fluency often endemic to incapacitated interpersonal functioning. These rifts in the necessary developmental groundwork can result in a perspective driven more by frustration and resentment than by attunement to reciprocal relationships.

> There is an increasing recognition that all children are active social thinkers who use cognitive, communicative, and linguistic skills simultaneously in social interactions in order to construct knowledge. … This has led to the belief that difficulty in social interaction and interpersonal relationships may have to do, at least in part, with problems in language and communication….[34]

An investigation into linguistic patterns of fourth and fifth grade students identified with emotional/behavioral disorders determined that semantic language (word interpretation), syntactic language (sentence/phrase coherency), intelligence measures, and social skills were statistically significant in predicting pragmatics (the ability to use verbalization as a tool in personal relations).[35]

Another investigation showed a marked distinction in linguistic facility between eight or nine-year old children without a disability and those of the same age identified with emotional handicaps during socially oriented interviews.[36] "[T]he most obvious differences between the … groups were evident in the area of Relation. This area includes poor topic maintenance, inappropriate response, situational inappropriateness, and inappropriate speech style."[37] Limits in cognition accompanied by repressed communicative facility and social-emotional deficiencies are evident in youths with language delays, learning disabilities, behavior disorders, emotional disturbance, patterns of delinquency, developmental disabilities (including those on the autistic spectrum), and ADD/ADHD.[38]

A self-indulgent pattern prevails in all the writings and/or recordings left behind by single incident multiple murderers. Though their journals, web postings, or videos are punctuated with accusatory oratorical explanations, there is no insight into their own character flaws or, even more telling, the inhumanity of their intentions.[39] Two biographies with analyses follow, each preceded by broad descriptors of cognitive deficiencies relevant to the case. The examples illustrate certain symptomatic perceptual limitations associated with the conduct of a gruesome gambit.

Biographical and Textual Analysis: Kip Kinkel – Neuropsychological Impairments (Distorted Cognition, Delusional, Mood Disordered); Pathological Personality (Anti-Social)

- General knowledge is less accessible when there is damage or inefficiency in the frontal lobe, causing impaired individuals to "experience heightened and exaggerated emotional" responses to events."[40]
  - Adolescents with learning disabilities exhibit disorganized thinking patterns including exaggerated responses to social situations.[41]
  - A lesion in a prefrontal lobe can disrupt rational functions including "to choose between extrareceptive input…."[42]
  - Individuals diagnosed with serious mental illness report histories and environmental stressors associated with elevated risk of violence.[43]

Kinkel was retained in the first grade, struggled with fine motor tasks beginning in the 2nd grade, was placed in special education in the 3rd grade, and assessed with a specific learning disability a year later.[44] In spite of these difficulties, that same year (when he was in the fourth grade) he was assigned to a program for the gifted and talented because he demonstrated proficiency for math and science.[45]

Mental health experts who later evaluated Kinkel determined that he was highly functional as far as general intellectual ability was concerned. One commented, “He's capable intellectually.”[46] Another noted, “He’s cognitively bright, above average. Even though he has a learning disability, his overall I.Q. is high.”[47] The poor coordination and reading delays that were evident in contrast to his measured intelligence suggest that Kinkel was struggling with neurological deficits.

That possibility was to be confirmed in court after his arrest when an accomplished pediatric neurologist explicated the results of a thorough assessment.[48] The examination uncovered aberrations contributing to problems with a number of cognitive functions including “language production,” “verbal memory,” “attentional abilities,” motor control, and “higher-level processing.” Referencing a SPECT [single photon emission computerized tomography] scan revealing abnormalities in the frontal lobes, the examiner explained that those regions are “labeled by psychologists and neurologists as the seat of the executive function … where the orders and the structure of behavior come from … the agenda-setting region of the brain.” He pointed to lesions in the prefrontal region that would disrupt “the ability to strategize, to plan, to prioritize, to choose between …. stuff coming from the outside versus … motivation … from the inside.” There were disruptions in the temporal lobes that could lead to limitations in impulse control as well as “[e]motional instability, distortions of sensory perceptions, illusions, delusions. …” Additionally, he identified problems with the occipital and parietal lobes that would affect the interpretation of perceptions. Along with these impairments, Kinkel was susceptible to psychosis and “childhood onset schizophrenia.”[49]

At that same hearing, two additional accomplished mental health professionals, one a forensic psychologist and the other a child and adolescent psychiatrist, testified that Kinkel was delusional when he was still a boy. Both asserted he gave credible accounts of auditory hallucinations dating back to the time he was 12 years old.[50] With respect to the decisions that would eventually lead to multiple deaths and injuries, Kinkel’s disordered perspective, deficiencies in consequential reasoning, and limitations in regulatory thinking would be prominent. Though not causal to the brutality itself, they would be contributing agents to the degenerative thinking that would precede the assault.

As he progressed in school, acquaintances noticed that Kinkel’s interests were limited to explosives, knives, and animal torture.[51] A few months before his rampage the mother of one of his friends, alarmed at his conduct, banned him from her home after he attended her son's birthday celebration.[52] As a gift he had brought a tool for breaking into cars. He also used a whipping cream cannister to spray the word "kill" in the driveway.[53] He had been one of four teens invited to the party.[54] His disregard for common courtesy, especially considering the gathering's relative intimacy, represented a flagrant rejection of social niceties.

There are, in fact, indications that persecutory and/or grandiose delusions are more prevalent among criminals than non-criminals, especially when their crimes involve violence.[55] Moreover, there is evidence of comorbidity of psychopathic indicators and schizophrenic traits among violent offenders.[56]

Psychopathy is intertwined with thought disorders with sufficient frequency for some researchers to suggest that the combination may mark a distinct personality disorder, a sub-type of schizophrenia, or an unrecognized neurodevelopmental problem.[57] A perusal of criminal histories of 205 seriously mentally ill adult patients found a significantly higher percentage of aggressive episodes among those who were classified with conduct disorder prior to the age of 15 than those who had no such diagnosis.[58] Another study that compared the records of people with early onset of schizophrenic symptoms to those who were symptomatic later in life found that a higher percentage of younger starters manifested anti-social tendencies in adolescence and both showed more disruptive behavior in their youth than a comparable group that never displayed indications of psychosis.[59] The results of those two studies, and others, coincide with a neuro-developmental course for anti-social personality disorder (ASPD) interfacing with delusional thinking, a juxtaposition that would certainly be applicable to Kinkel.[60] He exhibited paranoia accompanied by dysregulation of his emotions. Those traits correspond with the predispositions of people with ASPD whose brain imagery presents "impairment in neural systems undergirding cognitive functions and inhibitory control, specifically the prefrontal cortex and temporal lobes."[61]

Kinkel was never able to conform to the family ethos. His parents both held master's degrees in education and were successful Spanish teachers. Until his retirement his father worked at the Thurston High School – the very place where his son would enact the last stage of his rampage. After retiring he continued to teach at a community college four days a week.[62] In addition he was an avid outdoorsman and an active member of a local tennis club.[63]

Kinkel's mother taught in a neighboring district, where she chaired the language department, and the day before her death was selected as Outstanding Teacher of the Year.[64] She would help students during lunch or after school and did volunteer work for a group working with underprivileged youth.[65]

Five years older than Kip, his sister, Kristen, excelled in school in both academics and extra-curricular activities.[66] In contrast to her brother, she was congenial and adept in social situations. "My strengths were relating to people. I liked to talk," she recalled in an interview after her brother's rampage.[67] She was a popular cheerleader who graduated as valedictorian and continued to the University of Oregon.[68] Meanwhile, Kip Kinkel was small in stature, socially isolated, a mediocre student at best, and withdrawn.[69] Facetiously, he was featured in his middle school yearbook as "most likely to start World War III."[70]

Kristen often found herself playing the role of intermediary in a family where the relationship between his parents, especially the dad, and the youngest child was fractious. She recalled:

> [M]y parents were in their mid-50s. There's a huge generation gap in between there. … And a lot of times I found myself saying, 'Settle down. Relax. Think about it. Think about the students that you teach. What he did was not that bad.'[71]

When considered as distinct events, Kristen may have been correct in thinking that her brother's behaviors were not extreme. However, as he matured – or more accurately grew older without maturing – the incidents increased in rapidity and with that increase her brother's shortcomings mounted in intensity.

He confided in his journal:

> I try so hard every day. But in the end, I hate myself for what I've become.
>
> Every single person I know means nothing to me. I hate every person on this earth. I wish they could all go away. …
>
> The only reason I stay alive is because of hope. Even though I am repulsive and few people know who I am, I still feel that things might, maybe, just a little bit, get better. …

> I know everyone thinks this way sometimes, but I am so full of rage that I feel I could snap at any moment. I think about it everyday. … You all make me sick. I wish I was dead.[72]

His inability to excel was undoubtedly partially attributable to neurologic constraints but, as a youngster, what he noticed was the comparative competence of those closest to him. Apparent in his writing is a debilitating depression accompanied by personal disdain predicated, in part, by what he surely interpreted as persistent – almost inevitable – failures.

After he reached middle school, Kinkel became self-conscious about his small stature and told his parents he felt intimidated and bullied by other students, eventually convincing them, against their natural inclinations, to allow him to take karate lessons.[73] He enjoyed the sport and did well in competition.[74] Unfortunately, in response to provocation, he used his new found skill to kick a schoolmate in the head, resulting in a suspension.[75] He also participated in football when he entered high school and his family made it a point to attend his games to cheer for him.[76] His slight build, lack of aptitude for the game, and poor temperament inhibited successful participation. He never made first string and was often benched for swearing at the coaches.[77]

Kinkel swung between embracing or eschewing his temper. He felt like his unpredictability frightened his peers and knowledge of that fear emboldened him on the one hand while he regretted insinuations of villainy on the other. In his journal he wrote, "I feel like everyone is against me, but no one ever makes fun of me, mainly because they think I am a psycho."[78] Kinkel's psychosis, in discordant concert with his anti-social tendencies, would contribute to the combination of rage and internalized disgust that would tragically instigate his rampage and linger in its aftermath.

As a middle schooler, Kinkel began to explore the internet, visiting pornography sites and researching bomb construction.[79] Incredibly, he ordered books on bomb-making and had them delivered directly to his school. When the order arrived, it was traced back to him and the principal called in his parents for a conference. Almost as remarkable as his choice of a delivery site was his explanation that he was interested in the reading material because he wanted to go into law enforcement and specialize in explosives.[80]

The sequential steps in procuring knowledge on manufacturing bombs is demonstrative of three aspects of Kinkel's mental state during that phase of his life. First, from the standpoint of his devolution, he was anticipating the possibility of extreme violence. Secondly, occurring one year following his first encounter with an illusionary voice, Kinkel was amassing defenses against a delusionary mindscape. An evaluator after his arrest said of Kinkel's fascination with explosives: "It related, I think, to delusional fears. Fears of an invasion. Fears that were of a persecutory nature, that he needed to protect himself."[81] Kinkel confided that he was eager to learn about building bombs because he would need that skill for fortification against an impending invasion from China as well as the inevitable end of the world.[82] Finally, and perhaps most telling, by adopting a deceptive excuse for seeking information about the assembly of a destructive and potentially deadly device, he was displaying an anti-social preference for escaping accountability and, at the same time, covering up his paranoid ideation.

Later, in high school, he would give a presentation in his Speech class on bomb making, complete with schematics.[83] When his home was searched after his rampage, police would find at least five bombs including one lodged below the dead body of his mother.[84]

In the 8th grade Kinkel was arrested for shoplifting and for the first time he directly acted on his infatuation with weapon acquisition by secretly purchasing a sawed-off shotgun that he then kept hidden underneath his bed.[85] That same year during the second semester, Kinkel was again apprehended along with a friend for boosting a rock, 12 inches in diameter, off an overpass and striking a car.[86]

Partially because of the two arrests, his mother brought him to see a therapist.[87] Early treatment notes from those sessions say, "Kip reported he often feels angry but does not know why he feels this emotion." They also state that there was a disturbing strain in the relationship with his father and he presented with "major depressive disorder [MDD], mild."[88] The descriptor, "mild," should not be misconstrued as a suggestion that Kinkel was only experiencing a minimal anomaly in mood stability. In a teenager, depression often includes disconcerting patterns in perception. A study comparing depressed and non-depressed adolescents demonstrated "that adolescents with MDD display selective neurocognitive impairments on tasks capturing 'cool' [self-management without duress] and 'hot' [self-management under stress] executive functioning."[89] The fourth edition of the diagnostic and statistical manual (in use while Kinkel was in therapy) calls out irritability, anhedonia, persistent insomnia (or hypersomnia), psychomotor agitation (or retardation), fatigue, and difficulties in concentration as probable symptoms.[90] Table 4.1 displays the negative toll that depression can take on cognition.

Kinkel exhibited the persecutory sense that is prevalent among autogenic murderers, and he validated his feelings of persecution in therapy and in his writings. He told his therapist that he had a rule about not disclosing any difficulties if his parents questioned him about school because, according to him, they assumed, "automatically," that he was always at fault.[91]

In an essay entitled, "Love Sucks," written in response to the prompt "Love at First Sight," Kinkel wrote:

> No, I don't believe in love at first sight because love is an evil plot to make people buy alcohol and firearms. When you love someone something it is always taken away from you. I also would like to add that I hate each and every one of you. Because everything I touch turns to shit. I think if you think you fall in love with someone at first sight it might just be lust. Love at first sight is only in movies. Where the people in the movies are better than you. That is why you go to a pone [pawn] shop and buy an AR-15 because you are going to execute every last mother fucking one of you. If I had a heart it would be gray.
>
> It is easier to hate than love. Because there is much more hate and misery in the world than there is love and peace. Some people say that you should love everyone. But that is impossible. Look at our history it is full of death, depression, rape, wars and diseases. I also do not believe in love at first sight. But I do believe in hate at first sight. Therefore love is a much harder feeling to experience.
>
> I really wouldn't know how to answer this question because my cold black heart has never and never will experience true love. I can tell you one about love. It does more harm than good. I plan to live in a big black hole. My firearms and [illegible] will be the only things to fight my isolation. I would also like to point out Love is a horrible thing. It makes things kill and hate.[92]

He imagined romance as a channel for exploitation or vindictiveness while his own capacity for affection was subsumed in protective bitterness. His only comfort was found in his armaments.

A related sentiment was expressed in his diary. "My parents are trying to take away some of my guns! My guns are the only things that haven't stabbed me in the back."[93] These complaints were not simply typical expressions of teenage angst or spite about the motives of those in positions of responsibility. Fashioned by his paranoia and credited by tallies of his supposed injuries, Kinkel was projecting suspicion upon the world at large.

The counseling continued from January through July of the year between middle school and the ninth grade. Six months into therapy the psychologist referred Kinkel to the family physician for a prescription for the well-known anti-depressive, Prozac.[94] The record from the next session observes:

> Dr. Geisler started him on Prozac 20 mg. A.M. twelve days ago. He is sleeping better and there have been no temper outbursts. Kip is taking the Prozac as prescribed and reports no side-effects. His father is making a good effort to spend time with him and Kip is pleased with this change. ASSESSMENT: Kip appears less depressed though it is certainly too early to assess the usefulness of the Prozac.[95]

Remarkably, slightly over a week later, Kinkel's father, succumbing to his son's persistence bought a 9 mm Glock 19 semi-automatic handgun.[96]

Dad's reasoning was that it was better for the teen to have legal access to the gun and use it with his involvement, rather than illicitly acquiring and shooting it. It was supposed to remain in a gun safe unless the two were using it together.[97] The transaction was made without consulting the therapist, who testified later, "I have concerns about that."[98] As Kinkel began his ninth-grade year the same rationale was used along with similar conditions when his father, using his son's money, bought him a Ruger .22 caliber semi-automatic rifle.[99] The acquisitions did nothing to deter the teen's desire to continue to acquire more weaponry. He was already hiding the illicit shotgun and, in the interval between the purchase of the 9 mm handgun and the rifle, he secretly bought another .22 pistol, which he also stashed away.[100] Also, the younger Kinkel surreptitiously accessed the Glock on one occasion and the Ruger on another, forcing the older Kinkel to take additional measures to keep each secure.[101]

The decision to purchase firearms for a young man with depression may seem bewildering, especially given the distaste his parents held, or at least appeared to hold, for anything resembling violence. "[H]e was not allowed to have little soldiers. He was not allowed to have any kind of toy that had any kind of violent anything. I mean, violence in our house was a huge no-no," his sister, Kristin, said.[102] In truth, though, Kinkel started a knife collection when he was in the second grade and his father, besides the firearms already mentioned, gave him two BB guns as well three knives, and passed along for his 12th birthday a 336 Marlin that his dad had previously given him.[103]

Midway through the summer before he was to begin high school, Kinkel, his mother, and the psychologist decided as a group to conclude the counseling. The session commentary reads:

> Kip continues to do well. He is taking Prozac 20 mg. A.M. daily with no side-effects. He does not appear depressed and denies depression symptoms. His mother reports his moods have generally been quite good. He recently returned from a family reunion in San Diego and was very well behaved and seemed to have a good time.
>
> ASSESSMENT: Kip continues to function well with no evidence of depression.
>
> PLAN: Kip, his mother and I agree he is doing well enough to discontinue treatment.[104]

Plainly, his therapist favored continued use of the anti-depressant. Yet, after using the drug for only a few months and with the pressures of secondary schooling on the immediate horizon Kinkel stopped taking it.[105]

Although he managed to get through most of his freshman year without a fight, suspension, or an arrest Kinkel still signaled his infatuation with the methodology of harm. For the most part these signals would be noticed but disregarded. Kinkel's speech and accompanying paper on bomb-making prompted his teacher to alert a counselor who responded with a memorandum that indicated Kinkel's dad was very much aware of his son's obsession with explosives.[106]

His parents seemed equally nonchalant when their housekeeper of seven years quit because young Kinkel – at 15 years of age – with his knife collection of close to 50 blades and penchant for lighting fires – frightened her.[107] "Thank you for telling us," they responded.[108]

Ironically, it was a typical teenage stunt that eventually prompted ire along with distrust on the part of his parents. Kinkel was spending the night with a friend when they snuck out and met a larger group to toilet-paper the house of a fellow student.[109] Their goal was to break the school record for the most rolls ever used. They were successful at 400, but they were caught, and the next day had to clean up the mess.[110] Kinkel's father administered further punishment – restricting most of his son's activities for the entire duration of the upcoming summer including phone use, computer access, television, and overnight sleepovers.[111] Even with those restrictions imposed, his dad remained suspicious and searched his son's room finding a locked trunk. After he cut off the lock with a hacksaw, the hidden shotgun and .22 pistol were exposed and subsequently confiscated.[112]

By now Kip Kinkel's mental and moral decline were inexorably entangled with coveting weaponry. The bombs, guns, and knives were central to the fantasies of enacting retribution on a pitiless world where his every effort to succeed was repeatedly thwarted. He had written in his diary:

> I want you to feel this, be this, taste this, kill this. Kill me. Oh God, I don't want to live. Will I see it to the end? … All humans are evil. I just want to end the world of evil.[113]

Just as important, from his paranoid perspective, he needed the weapons for protection.

During an evaluation following Kinkel's apprehension, he relayed that for over a year prior to his rampage he was fearful that he was being stalked by a threatening figure in his neighborhood who held a grudge against him.[114] The evaluator testified:

> [H]e said, 'I had to have a plan to get rid of this guy. That's why I needed the gun.' I said, 'Which gun?' He said the one I bought from Corey [a fellow student]. He said, 'I needed a pistol. My dad had the other pistols in his locker, so I needed this one in case he came after me.'[115]

Tragically, arrangements to buy that .32-caliber Baretta, stolen by his friend from another high schooler, set in motion the series of events that would result in the murder of both of Kinkel's parents.[116] A sudden mass assault would follow.

The father of the gun's proper owner noticed early one morning that the gun was missing and alerted authorities at school.[117] Eventually in the course of questioning students, Kinkel's name came up. Kinkel was called out of second period study hall and an officer patted him down.[118] To the detective's dismay, the frightened teen announced, "Well, I'm gong [sic] to be square with you guys. The gun's in my locker."[119] Authorities went to retrieve the weapon while Kinkel waited in the office of Coach Stone who was also the high school's designated disciplinarian. He no doubt knew this particular youngster very well.[120] Their short conversation demonstrates how Kinkel's thinking was divorced from predictable cause and effect.

> 'Coach, what's going to happen if I have the gun?' Kip asked. Stone told him the school had no tolerance for guns; he would not be able to return to school for a year.
>
> Kip dropped his head and mumbled, 'Sorry, coach.'[121]

When the Baretta was retrieved the detective discovered that it was a semi-automatic fully loaded with eight rounds in the clip.[122] Kinkel was immediately arrested along with the erstwhile seller and escorted to a waiting patrol car.[123] On the way Kinkel's anti-social leanings surfaced. "They'll get theirs," he muttered.[124] The remark, intentionally threatening, previews the mayhem that he would foment the next day and flaunts the premeditative nature of his SMASI.

Kinkel was charged with two felonies: receiving a stolen weapon and possession of a firearm in a public facility.[125] He was released into the custody of his father who, as an educator, would have understood that his son would surely be subject to expulsion proceedings in addition to the criminal charges.

When they arrived at their house the younger Kinkel retreated to his room while his father went to the kitchen and began making and taking phone calls.[126] He apologized to the worried parent who had reported the theft, but he was mainly concerned with arranging for his son's education after he was expelled.[127]

News stories tend to speculate about an event or situation that precedes killing. However, a point emphasized throughout *How Rampage Killers Interpret Their Worlds*, is that autogenic murder stems from strain that has been internalized with the blame for discomfort projected upon external sources. Preceding events are circumstantial, not immediately instigating.[128] In the case of Kinkel, he may have been provoked by hearing his father discussing his transgressions and the upcoming consequences. He hinted at that in his confession after the fact, but he never directly said so.[129]

A friend explained that Kinkel dreaded the thought that he would be forced to become solitary. "Being alone was his weakness. He was always worried about being alone all the time, isolated and stuff like that."[130] The emotional impetus for Kinkel's murderous deployment was his conviction that he would be forsaken due to his own inadequacy. It was not momentary anger or a sudden impression, but the enactment of a compulsion arising from long-standing pessimism and chronic anxiety. With those persistent feelings, as his father sat in the kitchen drinking coffee, Kinkel used the .22 to kill him with a single bullet in the back of his head.[131]

He waited nervously for over three hours for his mother to come home from work.[132] An English teacher from his school called for his father. Kinkel told him that his dad was not at home.[133] A person from the community college also phoned because that his father was missing a Spanish class. Kinkel said he would not be there because he was having "family problems."[134]

When his mother arrived, he met her in the garage. As she ascended the stairs leading to the house Kinkel told her he loved her then shot her twice in the back of her head with the .22 pistol. When she failed to immediately die, he shot her four more times – once above her left eye, another time in her left cheek, again in the center of her forehead, and, finally, directly in her heart.[135]

Explaining the last round of gunfire during his confession, Kinkel said, "I shot her again so she wouldn't know that I killed her....I loved my mom."[136] After he was in custody, he repeatedly asserted that the homicidal decisions were unavoidable.[137] In relation to his perception of their absolute necessity, the stated purpose for the fatal shots, combined with the exhortation of affection, encapsulates Kinkel's conflicted processing of his motives. From his self-absorbed vantage point, he was taking the action necessary to interrupt the complete erosion of his diminished status in the household and to quell the incessant harpies in his mind. For people with delusional disorders "deficits in logical reasoning are more likely to occur due to faulty assessment of premises than to a defect in the structure of inferences. Such deficits seem to be provoked (in healthy individuals) or exacerbated (in patients with schizophrenia) by emotional content."[138] He was proceeding in a manner calculated to prevent the catastrophe of his abandonment.

The next morning, Kinkel prepared to carry his rampage forward to his school. He filled a backpack with 1,200 rounds of ammunition and taped two bullets across his chest in case he needed them to take his own life.[139] Then he donned a large overcoat to conceal the weapons he was carrying: a .22 caliber semiautomatic Ruger rifle, his father's 9mm Glock pistol, the .22 caliber Ruger semiautomatic handgun, and a hunting knife strapped to his leg.[140] He put on a cap with the logo for the post-industrial rock band, Nine Inch Nails, and drove his mom's Ford Explorer, parking one block away from his high school. It was now slightly before eight in the morning.[141] After walking onto the grounds from the rear parking lot, he went down a hallway leading to the cafeteria.[142]

He ran into a friend and told him, "Okay, you need to get out of here, Adam. Something bad is gonna [sic] to happen."[143] The warning was prescient of the one that would be given by Harris to a former friend before he and Klebold opened fire at Columbine High. "Brooks, I like you now. Get out of here. Go home."[144] In both cases the admonishment articulated foreknowledge of the devastation that was to follow.

Another acquaintance approached and Kinkel walked past him, but suddenly turned. Taking the rifle from under his long coat, he took aim, and pulled the trigger. When the gun failed to discharge, he reloaded and shot his first victim in the head as he was holding his finance's hand.[145] Sixteen years of age, the young man died the next day in the hospital.[146] Almost immediately Kinkel fired on another student, hitting him in the face. That victim survived, but over twenty years later he still carries the ".22-caliber bullet that traveled through his left cheekbone, drilled through his jaw, hit his spinal cord and stopped near the back of his neck."[147] Kinkel continued to the cafeteria.[148]

Over two hundred students were congregating around tables chatting and doing schoolwork.[149] Kinkel entered the room and swung the Ruger up in an arc from his hip, repeatedly discharging close to 50 rounds in less than a minute and a-half. He approached a wounded peer lying on the ground, placed the gun against the back of his head, and fired, killing him on the spot.[150] The murdered junior had recently enlisted in the Oregon National Guard and would later be buried with full military honors.[151]

Kinkel walked to another student who had taken cover beneath a table and put the gun against his forehead then pulled the trigger on his rifle for the last time. It did not fire. Kinkel tried again, but the clip was spent.[152]

The former target, now enraged, lurched forward, and struck Kinkel in the throat with his fist.[153] As he did so, a six-foot, five-inch varsity wrestler tackled the diminutive shooter and three more boys came to his aid to subdue him.[154] During the fray, Kinkel managed to pull the Glock from his belt and get off one round. The bullet went through the index finger of his tackler and pierced another student in the backside. More teens piled on, wresting away the weapon, punching Kinkel, and holding him prostrate on the floor as he pled with them to take his life.[155] "'Just shoot me, shoot me now,' one of the students … quoted the boy as saying."[156]

Following his apprehension, while handcuffed and awaiting interrogation at the police department, Kinkel managed to un-tape the blade on his leg, which had been overlooked when he was arrested. He lunged at the same detective that had interviewed him the previous day, again begging to be killed. “Kill me, shoot me,” he shouted.[157]

The repetitious expression of his death wish, provides more evidence of the conflicting forces at work in the young man’s psyche. Once he found himself subjugated, the resentful anti-social militancy that had adrenalized his rampage quickly dissipated and the only option he could conceive as viable was final revocation of his internal torment.

Biographical Analysis: Brenda Spencer – Destructive/Oppressive Environment (Traumatic Divorce); Neuropsychological Impairments (Frontal Lobe Damage, Seizures, Depression); Pathological Personality (Underdeveloped Morality)

- An individual with a frontal lobe impairment(s) will frequently demonstrate deficient sensitivity to the rights and well-being of others. At the very least, “a propensity” for inconsideration and/or – worse – violence “will be enhanced. The inability to empathize with the plight of the victim may exacerbate violent” actions.[158]
    - Studies employing imaging techniques such as the PET (Position Emission Tomography) scan have confirmed an association between antisocial as well as predacious inclinations and frontal lobe deficits.[159]
    - “[P]atients who sustain significant closed-head injuries, frequently resulting in damage to the orbital frontal and anterior temporal lobes are well known for their aggressive outbursts. These individuals typically manifest poor frustration tolerance, irritability, impulsive behavior, emotional liability, poor judgement….”[160]
    - “TBI [traumatic brain injury] during childhood and adolescence increased the risk of any criminality 6.8-fold …, conduct disorder 5.7-fold … and concomitant criminality and conduct disorder 18.7-fold. … Our results suggest that clinicians working with mentally ill adolescents who have experienced head injuries should be aware of the increased risk for delinquency and violent tendencies occurring later in the adolescents’ lives.”[161]

- It is not at all uncommon, especially prior to a differentiated diagnosis, for peers and adults to assume that children with epilepsy are day-dreaming or short of attention.[162]

Using a .22 caliber semi-automatic rifle and ammunition given to her as a Christmas gift. Spencer opened fire from her home, sniping at Grover Cleveland Elementary School across the street. She discharged at least 36 rounds in 15 minutes, killing the principal, as well as a custodian, and wounding eight children along with a police officer.[163] The carnage was finally halted when law enforcement moved a garbage truck in front of the school to block her view.[164]

For a little more than six hours thereafter she held the area at bay from inside her house, as she talked with local reporters by phone over the course of three calls, then negotiated with a detective from the hostage unit.[165] When pressed for an explanation by one reporter she said, "I just wanted to. … I don't like Mondays. This livens up the day."[166] That comment inspired a song co-written by Bob Geldof with Johnnie Fingers and performed by the Boomtown Rats – a tune that verges on being a power ballad and remains a potent commentary on pointless murders during the mid to late 20th century.[167] Spencer ended her telephone conversation with one journalist when she said, "I have to go now. I shot a pig, I think, and want to shoot some more."[168]

The unexpected and, to this day, unexplained sniping, which occurred in 1979, has been characterized as the "original" school shooting. "Certainly, she was the grandmother of school yard shootings. … She started it all," an NBC newscaster has said.[169]

Until she was sixteen Brenda Spencer lived an innocuous life as the youngest child with a brother and sister near San Diego California.[170] Her mother described her as "very active. … always happy … a good child, well behaved, never had any problems in school."[171] Her parents divorced when she was nine and, after a contentious dispute, her father was awarded custody of all the children, though her mother was granted visitation rights.[172] The older siblings moved in with their mom full-time four years after the decision, while Brenda Spencer stayed with her dad.[173]

Her mother's house, though, was only a few blocks from her father's residence and her daughter stopped by frequently.[174] "I'd see her maybe once a week and then, uh, she'd come over and spend part of the weekend with me and, uh, I'd come home from work and she'd be sitting at the door waiting for me to come home so we'd talk and what have you."[175] Her maternal grandmother and a neighbor from that period recall the visits as well.[176]

However, at her fourth parole hearing in 2005, some 25 years after her sudden mass assault, Brenda Spencer sketched a much different picture. In response to a question from the presiding commissioner about her relationship with her mother she replied, "Well, sometimes I'd stop by her house, but she didn't much seem to care to see us or anything."[177] Spencer's contradictory claim is only one of many inconsistencies between her version of events and the evidence apparent from material facts and/or the memories of others. Another questionable accusation is that she was sexually molested by her father and was subject to verbal along with physical abuse from her siblings. These dubious assertations and others are critically evaluated elsewhere.[178] Their importance at this point is to introduce the idea that her judgement, or lack thereof, was an offshoot of emotional devastation along with cerebral trauma. Spencer consistently acts in a manipulative manner. Her willingness to manufacture plotlines to gain sympathy for herself even at the expense of the reputation of family members exemplifies that habit.

Regardless of her distortions of the truth, there is credible evidence that her parents' separation had a negative impact on her emotional well-being. Prior to that event, Spencer was involved in softball, soccer, bowling, and golf.[179] "It was a happy home. The kids were happy," her mother recalls.[180] An acquaintance in the neighborhood described the family as "[n]ormal, normal, normal."[181] After the divorce, Spencer's participation in sports came to an end and she retreated into solitary activities, spending hours staring out the window of her home or sitting in a tree house by herself.[182] Another neighbor remembered her as "a tiny, lonely little youngster."[183] By the time she was in high school she was chronically truant in school, engaging in petty theft as well as vandalism, and occasionally experimenting, if not routinely indulging, in illicit drugs.[184]

Truancy, minor skirmishes with the law, and certainly experimentation with drugs have long been known to represent the sort of acting-out that signals adolescent depression.[185] Only slightly more than a month before the shooting, a social worker, who counseled Spencer while she attended an alternative high school, referred her to a psychiatrist because she believed she was suicidal.[186] She described her as "unwilling to discuss any future plans, or even acknowledge that the future existed."[187] Table 4.1 synopsizes the cognitive disruptions that have been assessed in association with depression. Spencer's mood disorder was a definite impediment to her ability to develop a rational and ethical world view, but, as will become obvious, it was not the only obstacle.

Irrespective of the amount of time they spent together, the support Spencer received from her mother bordered on apathy, while the predominate mood in Spencer's primary household was bleak. When questioned about pursuing custodial rights in the wake of suspicions of abuse, Spencer's mom blasély said: "I couldn't really afford the attorney that I'd had to get and what have you. …"[188] People who worked with her father described him as shy, quiet, and noticeably unhappy.[189] Spencer's defense attorney observed, "She lived with her dad. The dad was a sort of very bitter man. … The mother on the other hand sort of became like a stone herself. … [S]o it was a very cold sterile environment in both places."[190] She had but one friend during most of her childhood who all but abandoned her around the time of puberty.[191]

Individuals who feel isolated interpret events and interactions in an egocentric manner. The lack of give-and-take from peers prevents them from developing the sort of transactional perspective that is necessary for positive momentum through the social-psychological stages represented in Table 3.1. "The sense we make of our interactions with others is called social cognition. When loneliness takes hold, the ways we see ourselves and others, along with the kinds of responses we expect from others, are heavily influenced by both our feelings of unhappiness and threat and our impaired ability to self-regulate."[192] Spencer was interpreting the world through the dense mist of downcast solitude.

Given her abiding sadness and associated isolation, her potential for moral maturation was seriously restricted. Social priorities in reference or deference to others are based, at least in part, on an acquired sensitivity to human feeling. One way to determine the weight of that sense is by assessing the ability to feel guilt and shame. They "are self-conscious moral emotions [that] differ from basic emotions such as sadness, happiness and fear in that they require a capacity for self-awareness…."[193] Highly depressed children and teenagers (9-15 years) have been shown to be less prone to guilt but more prone to shame with less competency in self-awareness, emotional control, and situational understanding than counterparts who are less depressed.[194] Visceral understanding does not necessarily enhance the capacity for handling confrontational situations, but it links with the reflective thought and the intrapersonal awareness necessary for learning from such experiences. Shameful feelings also become internalized but their consideration is prone to perseverative self-reproach and is non-reflective.

Morality, it seems, is both rational and sentimental.[195] "[T]he automatic tagging of ordinary social events with moral values may be an important mechanism for implicit social behaviors in humans."[196] The depression Spencer experienced throughout most of her life prevented her from interpreting relationships with others in a way that would nurture compassion or crystalize her own personal values. Along with that emotional encumbrance, she experienced brain damage.

When she was 14 years of age, which would have been when she was starting high school, Spencer struck her head on a telephone pole in a bicycle accident.[197] She temporarily lost consciousness and felt dizzy the following day.[198] The injury was not treated at the time, but subsequent to her arrest, neurological exams, including X-rays and an electroencephalogram (EEG), were administered.[199] The EEG was characterized as "grossly abnormal," consistent with temporal lobe epilepsy.[200] Since her incarceration, she has experienced psychomotor seizures and been treated with Tegretol.[201] In a letter to a journalist Spencer characterized the episodes as "grand mal."[202]

Epileptic seizures are not generative in the sense that they will by themselves precipitously initiate mental illness or emotional maladjustment. They are symptomatic of abnormalities in mental functionality. "An epileptic seizure is a transient occurrence of signs and/or symptoms due to abnormal excessive or synchronous neuronal activity in the brain."[203] In Spencer's case the cause was a concussion that immediately caused disorientation as well as occasional ruptures in her thinking over the long term. "You wouldn't know what was going on … you know … 'Brenda, are you awake?'" one of her instructors reminisced when describing her engagement in his class.[204] Although the seizures were not necessarily the sole reason for chronic cognitive disruptions, they were, and remain, evidentiary.

Tenuously linked to aggressive behavior, epilepsy has even been exploited by well-intentioned, albeit ill-informed, defense attorneys to defend malicious actions by their clients even though there is scant credible evidence that it acts as a solitary trigger for violence especially during interictal periods.[205] There are, admittedly, rare instances of preictal, ictal, and postictal aggression.[206] These phenomena would be irrelevant to Spencer's case because the motor precision and lingual fluidity exhibited during her rampage rules out the possibility of a seizure prior to or during the commission of her crimes.[207] Similarly, the calculated nature of Spencer's attack over a prolonged period rules out episodic dyscontrol or intermittent explosive disorder as the cause.[208]

It was not the epilepsy itself that was at fault but the neurological aberration that caused that syndrome. The relevant result of Spencer's mishap was continued constraint of the necessary interpersonal intelligence for the cultivation of social skills. The brain trauma, coinciding with her acute pubescent introversion, did not change her personality, so much as arrest it. The normal development that would have allowed for fully functioning executive functions, particularly those relevant to restraint and judgement, was disjointed.

The advent of morality in response to social situations as part of maturation was emphasized in the previous chapter. With her head injury, Spencer experienced figurative, and, very likely, literal fissures, in cognitive capacity and efficiency especially with respect to the very processes essential for balanced decision-making and impulse modulation.

Concluding an extensive investigation of 10 cases of adults who had neuroanatomic traumas in early childhood the authors declared "an early lesion within the frontal lobe can be viewed as both a localized event and as a reverberating event that affects the maturation of interacting areas mediating the acquisition of representational knowledge, actions and response control through contingency learning."[209] Research involving individuals who have been injured later in life has resulted in similar conclusions.[210]

Spencer had a cerebral fault that aligned with her deficient socialization subjecting her to moral retardation resembling sociopathy. She was clinically diagnosed with "anti-social personality disorder" (ASPD) – an assessment that was based on the behavioral indicators resembling ASPD without giving weight to her personal history, which included depression as well as brain trauma.[211] Her counsel at her first parole hearing suggested that "she was thinking like an eight-year-old" when she rampaged.[212]

The immaturity suggests an explanation for her antagonism, although it falls far short of an excuse. Even a young child would have realized the implications of opening fire on multiple strangers. Spencer fantasized about her cruelty and hinted at her intentions in advance, proving that she had ample opportunity to reconsider before finally acting. For a time, she even reveled in her notoriety and wrote a letter to Bob Geldof telling him she was glad he wrote "I Don't Like Mondays" because it made her famous.[213] If Spencer ever did reflect on her plan, the pause had no bearing on her intentions. She coldly conducted her ambush and conveyed her reasoning for it in a caviler manner.

Mood Disordered

Irregularities in temperament erode reason and sensible decision-making. A comprehensive review of the literature on empirical research examining the effect of unimodal depressive and bipolar disorders presented a collection of controlled studies examining the performance on a range of performance tests in relation to dysphoria as well as the faux euphoria associated with a manic state. Findings relevant to this observation are summarized in Table 4.1.

TABLE 4.1.
Effects of mood disorders on cognition assessed by perceptual tasks

Cognitive function	Assessment tool with description	Results
Attention/figure ground	Continuous Performance Test (CPT): response to a target shown with visual distractions.	"[D]epressed and manic patients in the acute phase … produce more errors of attention compared with matched controls … deficits worsen with severity of illness."
Attention with working memory	Trail Making Test, Part A (TMT - A): locating figures from an array in numerical order. Digital Symbol Substitution Test (DSST): matching symbols to numbers based on corresponding pairs.	"[P]atients with mood disorders can experience measurable deficits of attention during euthymic and disturbed mood states."

Memory	Story Recitation (SR): repeating chronicle after presentation. Word List Recall (WLR): reciting words in order after initial citation by tester.	"Impairments have been reported during the depressed, manic and euthymic phases."
Executive	Stroop Test (ST): naming color of printed words that spell the name of another color. Trail Making Test, Part B (TMT-B): same as Trail Making Test but the subject must alternate between letters and numbers.	"Compared with healthy controls, bipolar were impaired while acutely ill, but they showed improvements ... during the subacute phase of their illness.... [P]atients with a history of bipolar disorder who were euthymic ... committed more errors than did healthy controls. Similarly, patients in either acute or euthymic mood states have demonstrated significant impairments.... [P]erformance ... was impaired for depressed patients and worsened with a patient's level of depression."

Sources for Descriptions of Assessment Tools as follows: CPT: Cherie L. Marvel and Sergio Paradiso, "Cognitive and Neurological Impairment in Mood Disorders," author manuscript, PubMed Central, United States National Library of Medicine National Institutes of Mental Health, Psychiatric Clinics of North America, posted October 19, 2008, http://www.ncbi.nlm.nih.gov/pmc/articles/PMC2570029/; TMT A&B: Esther Heerema, medically reviewed by Claudia Chaves, "Administration, Scoring, and Interpretation of the Trail Making Test," Verywell Health, updated January 4, 2020, https://www.verywellhealth.com/dementia-screening-tool-the-trail-making-test-98624; DSST, WLR, ST: Jannique GZ van Uffelen, Marijke Hopman-Rock, Marijke Chin A Paw, and Willem van Mechelen, "Protocol for Project FACT: A Randomised Controlled Trial on the Effect of a Walking Program and Vitamin B Supplementation on the rate of Cognitive Decline and Psychosocial Wellbeing in Older Adults with Mild Cognitive Impairment," BMC Geriatrics, posted December 23, 2005, http://www.biomedcentral.com /1471-2318/5/18; SR: Henry L. Roediger III and Jeffrey D. Karpicke, "The Power of Memory Testing: Basic Research and Implications for Educational Practice," *Perspectives on Psychological Science* 1, no.

3 (September 2006): 183. Source for Cognitive Functions and Conclusions: Marvel, and Paradiso, "Cognitive and Neurological Impairment in Mood Disorders."

Inattention, not filtering irrelevant stimuli, sporadic fluidity in routine tasks, difficulties in remembering sequences, and limited restraint of impulsivity erode self-confidence and a construction of a cogent internal narrative. The practical outcome on-going emotional strife is damage to the coherent thoughts integral for fashioning an ethical framework. Under certain conditions, that fissure can be fertile territory for nurturing a rationale for excessive acts of violence or destruction.

Predominate features of 17 students characterized, as "classroom avengers" who assaulted others in 15 separate incidents were depressive symptoms, resentment directed toward peers as well as authority figures, and a lack of acceptance of responsibility for determinations relevant to proper conduct. All but one were suicidal. The researchers classified these aggressors as having vengeful motives towards adults and/or peers in the same way that "workplace avengers" harbor hostilities against employers and co-workers for perceived injustices and/or rejection.[214]

Textual Analysis: Kimveer Gill – Neuropsychological Impairment (Mood Disordered)

He wrote with abandon on a website known as VampireFreaks.com.[215] Gill killed one and wounded 19 during a shooting rampage in the cafeteria at Dawson College in Canada before taking hostages then killing himself while facing down police.[216] Prior to the bellicose incident, the chronology of his thoughts, posted on the internet for the entire world to peruse, documented his emotionality, degenerating thinking, and callous intentions.

Calling himself "Trench," Gill kept a blog under the heading "fatality666," a title that merged his murderous intentions with his affinity for the symbolism of evil.[217] The allusion may have been to *Revelation* 13:18, but as a heavy metal affectionate, Gill was probably inspired by the Iron Maiden song, "Number of the Beast," the fifth cut on the album with the same name.[218] In his profile he announced, "You will come to know him as the angel of death."[219] His entries candidly and frequently reveal a state irritation, dysthymia, or bipolarity. Three entries note prolonged periods without sleeping while seven mention that he feels "tired." The count pertains to the description for being physically exhausted, not frustrated, as in "tired of" this or that. He uses that phrase, as an expression of psychological weariness, three times.[220] There are others descriptions for his affective state that leave some room for interpretation but are obviously indicative of frustration or despair: "FUCK YOU [once with two exclamation points]," "Psychotic like a German HA HA HA HA HA HA HA," "Muhahahahahaha," "Hahahaha Muhahahaahaha," "Drunken rage HA HA HA HA HA," "Tired of motherfuckers fucking with me," "Fuck the motherfucking world," "Fuck life," "Arrrrrggg," "Aaaaaaaaaaaaa," "Destroy all mankind," "Fucking ChokesIam Someone." [221]

Even more telling – and poignant – is the melancholic tautology punctuated by a label for his state of mind (identified as "Mood") over a seven-month period. Descriptors include: "Nothingness"; "Vengeance" (entered on two dates, repeated three times on one day); "Dead"; "So cold So empty"; "Empty"; "Not well"; "Sad"; "Dark and Disturbed"; "Hollow"; "Emptyness" (sic – twice); "Nothingness"; "Psychotic"; "Dark" (3 times); "Rage"; "Vengeful"; "Homicidal"; "Destructive"; "Deranged"; "Psycho"; "War-Like"; and "Black … So Black" – all indicators of mania, depression, or discordance.[222]

The expository entries are often vainly angry and violent:

> **Freshly dug graves** - May 17, 2006, 05:20: am Turn this fucking world into a graveyard Crush all those who stand in your way
> Let there be a river of blood in your wake Walk through that river with
> Pride
> Don't you just love freshly dug graves I do
>
> …
>
> FUCK THE WORLD. You're all animals. I can see through you. When I look in your eyes I can see your thoughts. You're nothing at all. Just animals. Always thinking about sticking your dicks in a hole. FUCKING ANIMALS.[223]

And frequently somber, laced with self-pity:

> **My Own Prison** - January 26, 2006, 10:43:am I am locked in an invisible cage within my head. There is no chance of escape.
>
> …

> **I love the grey sky** - February 15, 2006, 01:59:am I've forgot how to smile
>
> …
>
> -------- **Hell** - July 13, 2006, 07:25:am People kill each other Rape women Molest children Deceive and betray Destroy lives Bullying and torturing each other at school
> What kind of world is this? What the fuck is wrong with people. This world....this life, is worst than hell.[224]

In one revealing passage, as he discusses the video game "Postal," he expresses his obsession for eventual retribution to be carried out upon a populace incognizant of his anguish and therefore irrelevant to him.

> -------- **Postal dude rulz** - September 10, 2006, 05:37:am Wish they make Postal 3, like really really good. Postal 2 Share the Pain was o.k. but too childish, i want them to make a game so realistic, that it looks and feels like it's actually happening. … (Postal dude was sad before he became angry and psychotic, that's the part we're never seen in the game. He was normal, but the world made him the way he became, gotta show that in the game and movie too).[225]

Gill was ruminating on the second version of a controversial video game, imbued with graphic violence, that is a product of the company Running with Scissors. The game's name, of course, is based on the phrase "going postal" that in popular vernacular labels a person engaging in acts of extreme violence precipitated by rage. The adverbial clause "going postal" derives from the homicidal acts committed by another single incident annihilator, Patrick Sherrill, a substitute letter carrier, who shot and killed 14 co-workers before shooting himself in the head and killing himself in 1986.[226] Irrespective of the origin of Gill's neurological-emotional fracture, his fixation on a fantasy mimicking Sherrill's crimes is demonstrative of the fact that he identified with another whose empathy had deteriorated to the point where a sanguinary tantrum was assumed as the last viable option for confronting life's disappointments.

Gill's somber dystopian interior world was reflected in the climate he lauds throughout his electronic diary. He preferred weather shadowy and wet, describing misty scenery in terms that are reverential, practically mystical. In one early entry, written a few days before Christmas, the description of monochromatic dampness inspires a landscape of desolate carnage:

> **Vengeance is coming** - December 23, 2005, 09:21:pm It will be a quiet and peacefull morning. A light drizzle will be starting up. The clouds will be grey, so grey. Just the way I like it. Disembowled bodies litter the streets. Some have been decapitated, others hung off bridges and over-passes. Yet, others still lie burning. Flames slowly eatting away at their putrid flesh. Glorious.[227]

In successive entries he mentions "grey skies" with adoration five times.[228] In one passage he ascribes superhuman status to himself through the absorption of dreariness and assumption of cruelty.

> **Raining** - August 24, 2006, 07:20:pm …
> My trenchcoat flew behind me a couple of times when the wind picked up, other than that not very windy. Just the way I like it. And it was deserted, every street, it looked like everyone had died. Cuz' there wasn't a person anywhere. …
> Ever notice that when the clouds turn grey the humans become sparse, like, even before the rain, even if there is no rain. I'll never understand humans. The way they live their lives, their feelings, the things they want to do in life, probably has something to do with these invisible gods they pray to. Meh.
> *Mood*: Just listen to the song and you'll know :) Music: Sentenced – Vengeance is Mine[229]

The guttural hymn, "Vengeance is Mine," by the Finish death metal group, Sentenced, is an ode to over-the-top vindication. "A dozen of eyes for an eye," is an oft repeated line.[230]

A distain for humanity saturated with his grandiosity upholds the callous intentions of an autogenic murderer. Along with that acerbic isolationism Gill had become preoccupied with the somber and sadistic imagery that pervades contemplation in anticipation of a rampage.

Delusional Thoughts

Preoccupation with a worldview based on a subjective schema characterizes a delusional perspective. The associated behaviors based on this sort of outlook derive from elaborate unsubstantiated belief systems: faith in eventual domination of Earth by an interstellar race, for example. The malignant categorical orientation receives treatment in the current discussion on neurological/emotional impairments – as opposed to later when pathological personalities are discussed – because the delusions are singular, extreme, and persistent. The distinction, though, is fine, if not mute: either state is conditional with respect to the developmental sequence of a rampage killer's psyche. The case of Ander Breivik is illustrative.

Biographical and Textual Analysis: Ander Breivik – Neuropsychological Impairment (Delusional); Pathological Personality (Narcissistic)

Breivik was indicted and found guilty of killing 8 by a bomb in Olso and 69 at a youth camp on the Norwegian island of Utøya, 67 shot to death and two dying due to injuries or drowning.[231] After executing the worst mass murder by a single individual during peacetime in Norway's history, Breivik, justified his attack as a "necessity" in a valiant struggle against "multicultural ideology."[232]

Breivik's indiscriminate killing of adults and children might be characterized as an act of domestic terrorism and he himself would probably prefer that characterization as opposed to a classification as a nonsensical massacre. Certainly, he would reject the notion that he was mentally imbalanced while committing his crimes. He refused to plead "Not Guilty by Reason of Insanity" (NGBRI), preferring to be a martyr in prison for his separatist ideals. Besides, he benefited from a guilty verdict since a sentence for a crime while sane would be limited. If found insane, the confessed killer could have been "involuntarily committed to a psychiatric facility for as long as he is considered ill."[233] That term would be indefinite.

The trial court struggled with making a ruling about Breivik's sanity. Two pairs of forensic psychiatrists were appointed, the first concluding that he was "psychotic at the time of the acts" and the second that he was "not psychotic. ... [but instead] suffers from a dissocial and narcissistic personality disorder."[234] The latter diagnosis would place Breivik squarely within the class of assailants scrutinized in the next chapter. Both teams, however, agreed that he acted according to long-standing delusions. The only contention, as far as his delusional preoccupation is concerned, is the psychological origin – whether it stems from psychosis or grandiosity. The judges ultimately decided that Breivik was legally responsible for his crimes, a decision that does not preclude the possibility of a neurological or emotional impairment, a point which will be analyzed in the last sub-section in this chapter. [235]

The following quotation is a relatively short excerpt from a prepared statement of 6,837 words that Breivik read on the second day of his trial.

> Today Norway and many countries are suffering cultural self-hatred [*selvforakt*] due to multicultural ideology. ... The multiculturalist government is forced to fight a two-front war against us on the one hand and militant Islamists on the other. My European nationalist brothers and sisters will triumph, which will proclaim the end of a left extreme government that has lasted since the Axis powers fell. How can I be so certain that this will happen? The reason is that multiculturalism is a self-destructive ideology. National cohesion is so weakened that the economy cannot sustain the welfare state. The economic crisis will make the financial crisis today look like a picnic. ... Multiculturalism is an anti-Norwegian and anti-European hate ideology. Multiculturalism is an evil ideology that forces itself upon us. ... The political elites [*i båre land*] are actually so brazen that they expect us to applaud deconstruction. And those who do not applaud are branded as evil racists and Nazis. This is the real madness – they should be the object of psychiatric evaluation and labeled as sick, not me.[236]

Breivik was rationalizing the murder of 77 and injury of 242 more through the carefully planned bombing followed by deliberate executions at the retreat. Within the isle's confines he lured the camp administrator, teens, chaperons, and security personnel to come within range by posing as a police officer.[237] Of those killed, thirty-three were under 18 and two were only 14 years old.[238] The targets, he would explain later in court, were legitimate because the encampment was for "political indoctrination" to educate "cultural Marxists" and the youths at the scene were political leaders.[239] Breivik emphasized on day five of his trial, "Those who were on the island accounted for the entire leadership of the AUF. The goal was to execute all."[240] The initialism, "AUF," is short for Arbeidernes Ungdomsfylking, a political organization for young people associated with the Labor Party.[241]

In his final statement to the court, after sentencing, Breivik made the following accusation that, with its effrontery, demonstrates the circular reasoning of the paranoid mind:

> By discarding my allegations of the principle of necessity and sentencing a representative of the Norwegian resistance movement you have sided with the multicultural majority in parliament and therefore you also expressed support for the multiculturalist ideology. Since I do not recognise this court I cannot legitimise the Oslo district court by accepting this sentence. In my view this sentence and judgment is illegitimate and at the same time I cannot appeal against the judgement because by appealing I would legitimise the court.[242]

With characteristic self-righteousness, Breivik claimed he preferred the death penalty to a "pathetic" prison sentence. "'There are only two just and fair outcomes in this case,' he told the Oslo central court: 'Acquittal or capital punishment.'"[243] As it turned out, at the age of 33, he was sentenced to 21 years (the ultimate penalty in Norway for anything short of genocide). So, conceivably, he will one day be free.[244]

Conceivable, but unlikely, since his sentence can be extended indefinitely if the legal authorities determine he poses a continuing threat. The court explained: "A sentence of permanent detention can be imposed if there is considerable danger of repetition. Permanent detention is not subject to any timeframe. However, the court always fixes a timeframe that may not exceed 21 years. When the timeframe expires the offender may be re-assessed. If the court concludes that there is still a danger of repetition the timeframe may be extended up to five years at a time. There is no upper limit to the number of times that the court may extend the timeframe."[245] Norway formally abolished the death penalty in 1979, but the most recent execution at the time had been in 1876, more than a century prior to its abolition.[246] The country's most severe punishment, imprisonment up to 30 years, has been reserved for crimes against humanity.[247]

A compelling argument could be advanced that Breivik was, indeed, guilty of genocide. Afterall, he admitted to targeting a selected political group: leaders in the AUF. That deliberate selection would appear to comply with the definition for genocidal action under the United Nations Convention, Article II: "Deliberately inflicting on the group conditions of life calculated to bring about its physical destruction in whole or in part."[248] It would additionally conform with the elements of "genocide by killing" in Article 6(A) of the Rome Statute of the International Criminal Court of which Norway is a party:

"The perpetrator killed one or more persons. … The perpetrator intended to destroy in whole or in part, that national, ethnical, racial, or religious group."[249] However, the court elected to try and convict him for criminal violations instead, apparently because the brutality, as atrocious as it may have been, was not sufficiently widespread to qualify as a crime against humanity and was not committed at the behest or to advance the cause of any defined organization. Similar reasoning was applied to determine that he qualified as rampage killer and not a terrorist in conformance with the operational definition set forth in the definition in the Introduction to this book.

He did meet the technical criteria under Norwegian law for the commission of "a terrorist act by violating Penal Code § 148 … and Penal Code § 233 … (premeditated murder and there are particularly aggravating circumstances), with the intent to interfere seriously a function of fundamental importance in society, as the executive authority, or cause serious fear in a population."[250] In Breivik's case the distinction between political terror and autogenic mass murder may seem very fine, but it is parsable. Notwithstanding his facility with language and the superficial lucidity of his statement to the court, Breivik was obviously motivated by obsessions, which, though systematically articulated, were delusional. For instance, he claimed to be a founding member of group bent on reviving the Knights Templar, the legendary Catholic fighting unit established during the Christian crusades for dominance of sacred sites during the Middle Ages.[251]

Prior to launching his massacre, Breivik arranged for a portrait in full dress uniform of his fanciful military order. It features him proudly posing in bedighted garb featuring a tunic, medals, and a knotted gold lanyard.[252] The outfit was cobbled together with purchased surplus gear. A well-known Norwegian criminal psychiatrist noted:

> The badges and carnival uniform are part of his own narcissistic self image – he believes they are real. …
> What makes a grown adult get into this fantasy uniform? It's part of the image he is trying to live up to.
> Because he never received any real medals, he buys them. Breivik believes he actually deserves these dingle dang medals.[253]

Breivik released a 1,516-page compendium, posting it on Facebook and e-mailing it to approximately 1,000 followers. Written under the pseudonym Andrew Berwick and entitled *2083 – A European Declaration of*

Independence, about 50 percent of it was a compilation of writings from other sources (some acknowledged and some not), including the manifesto of Ted Kaczynski – commonly known as the "Unabomber."[254] The year 2083 is a reference to the 400-year anniversary of the Battle of Vienna in 1683 that halted the advance of the Ottoman Empire.[255]

As previously mentioned, there were two forensic psychological reports written for Breivik's trial: one declared him psychotic under Norwegian law and the other found gross characterological flaws (narcissism and anti-social tendencies) making him criminally liable for his actions.[256] The question of his sanity or lack thereof for purposes of trial is not an issue as far as his chronic delusional state is concerned.

> Mental illness does not necessarily mean gross disorganization and a total deficit of reality testing. Paranoid delusions tend to become systematized over time, elaborate and deeply ingrained in the psychotic person's philosophy and worldview.[257]

One can be sane as far as a legal definition is concerned and still be neurologically impaired and prone to irrational thinking.[258] Contra wise, unless a person is experiencing hallucinations or disassociation (as described in the successive subsection), cognitive distortions do no presuppose innocence.

Breivik stated that those killed in his assault on a youth camp deserved to die because of their complicity with a "multiculturalist" movement. Therefore, he had a moral imperative to conduct the slaughter to prevent an eventual civil war brought on by immigration and suppression of Europeans.[259] Most disturbing, he seemed to take a perverse pleasure in his gory and destructive activities. On the day of his indictment, he was smiling when he entered the courtroom and gave a facsimile of a Roman salute with his fist.[260] He smiled, as victims and family members wept, when a video of the bomb blast was shown and reportedly "was unable to suppress a smirk of satisfaction" when the final verdict was announced.[261]

Despite the evident delusions cherished by Breivik, the structure and sequencing of his statements is remarkably coherent, indicating a pervasive mindset rather than an episodic dysfunction. At the same time, the malicious thoughts, manifested finally in depraved acts, stem from an enduring state of mind fractured by prejudice, not just a philosophical commitment to social dominance.

Their expositions conform to a conceptual model advanced by the well-known Yale Psychologist, Robert Sternberg, cataloguing three components of hate, – negation of intimacy, passion, and decision/commitment.[262] With that determination, Sternberg identifies a deranged perspective in which obsession is the dominant trait, as "the most powerful force underlying mass killings and genocide."[263]

The self-embroiled thinking represents a set of convictions that are based on referents that are self-reinforcing. "Paranoid individuals have closed information processing systems, literally para noia, meaning against knowledge – which precludes any corrective information…."[264] Incidents or philosophical expositions supporting the belief system become integrated while evidence to the contrary is ignored. "Persons do not comply with a delusion as much as they behave in a manner consistent with its content or theme."[265] The self-perpetuating feedback is the dynamo of fantastic fanaticism (surveyed in *How Rampage Killers Interpret Their Worlds*).

Overlap among dispositional conditions is more common with rampageous assailants than not (a point that will be stressed in the final chapter). Particularly deceptive, from a diagnostic standpoint, is the melding of neuropsychological impairments with personal pathologies. The first can present as disorientation engendering empathy while the second may be leveraged by a subject for deception and malice.

> [D]estructives differ among themselves in the degree of integration of the self, by which they primarily appear to be referring to the hierarchical subordination of the real self (which is nonadaptive) to the façade self (which has adaptive capacities). Poorly integrated destructives are in almost constant conflict within themselves and others, due to intrusions of real-self experiences into consciousness and consequent nonadaptive behaviors. … Better organized destructives … increase self-esteem and effectively gain real world benefits through their destructive acts, thus shoring up the defective real self and presumably improving adaptation.[266]

The conditionality creates impediments to socialization and construction of morality whether originating as a deviation in cognition or mood or interpersonal functioning. When disordered thinking is intertwined with a disturbed personality hyper-delusional premises will promote pandemonium as a means for circumventing or tangling systems. Under such circumstances, malevolent anticipation is difficult to detect.

Another case study with textual evaluations follows.

Biographical and Textual Analysis: James Holmes – Perceived Physical Inadequacy; Neuropsychological Impairment (Mood Disordered, Delusional); Pathological Personality (Avoidant, Manipulative, Deceitful, Grandiose, Callous)

Like many autogenic assailants Holmes tricked himself into believing he was responding to a calling when, armed with assorted weapons and outfitted for combat, he attacked an unsuspecting audience in a crowded multiplex. "A crime that I had a mission to complete. Just something that I had to do," he explained during a psychiatric evaluation when asked about his thoughts during the slaughter.[267] Breivik intended to further his tortuous political aims. Others who rampage ofttimes convince themselves they are protesting unsatisfactory societal treatment. Holmes thought he was advancing his value in a universe where jabberwocky-like equations, karma, misanthropy, and neurology all intersect with nihilism. His cosmology, shown in Figure 4.2, is encapsulated in tiny excerpts from his collection of writings, *Course of Life*.

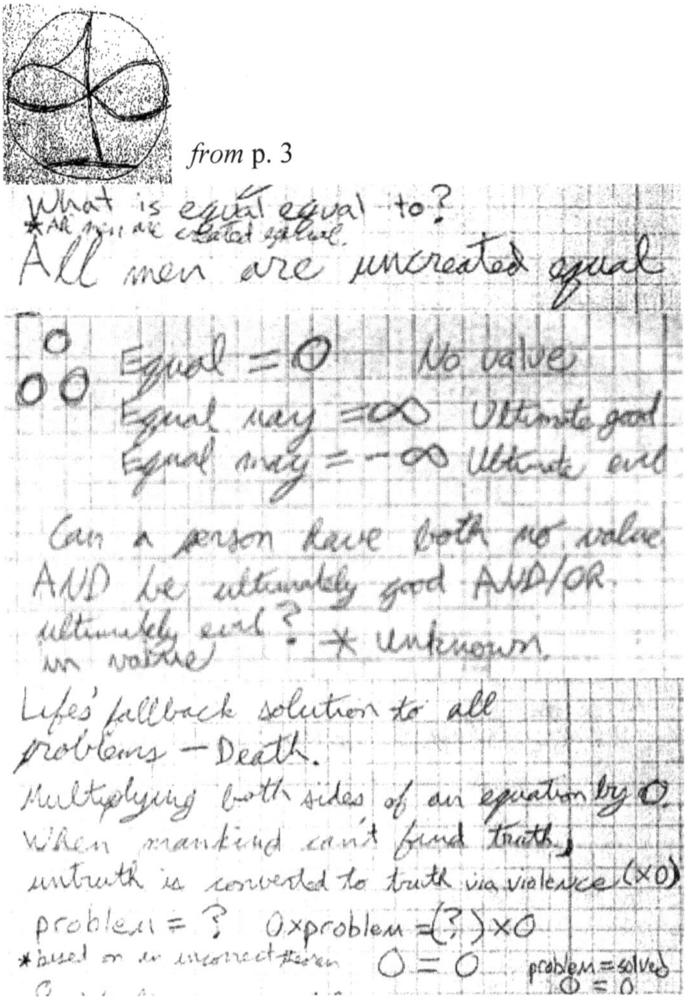

from p. 3

from p. 5

from p. 6

from p. 7

FIGURE 4.2. Excerpts from the Journal of James Holmes. Holmes labeled the symbol from page 3 as an "ultraception." The numeral 1 transects the infinity symbol to show that taking a life can eventually be part of a trade-off to transcend death. The remaining symbols, questions, and syllogisms advance a metaphysical philosophy in which human beings are monetized as points that may be accumulated through taking lives. If existence has no inherent meaning and no one person is necessarily superior to another, then one can justify doing whatever must be done to gain capital for extending a lifespan. Sadie Gurman with Dan Elliott, "Theater Gunman, James Holmes, Says He Knew Shooting Was 'Legally Wrong,'" CBS News, posted June 2, 2015, https://www.cbsnews.com/colorado/news/theater-gunman-says-he-knew-shooting-was-legally-wrong/; James Holmes, *Computation Book: Course of Life*, Colorado Judicial

Department: James Holmes 12CR1522, Peoples Exhibit #341, https://assets.documentcloud.org/documents/2089833/james-holmes-notebook.pdf; James L. Metzner, James Eagan Holmes: Sanity Evaluation, Arapahoe Colorado Mental Health Institute at Pueblo, Colorado, Case no. 12CR1522, September 3, 2013, 10-13, 16, 18-19, 56-57, appendix III, School Shooters .info: Resources on School Shootings, Perpetrators, and Prevention, last updated March 21, 2024 s.v. "James Holmes," https:// schoolshooters.info/.

The essence of his delusionary reasoning, with respect to his murderous bent, was an increase in his metaphysical "capital" in exchange for another human's life and an exponential advancement in his standing when taking multiple lives. [268]

His life vividly portrays the type of tragedy that can sometimes ensue when phobic perceptions mingle with pathological personal traits.[269] Already noted is the fact that it is not at all unusual for defects in cognition and/or personality to present in a comorbid fashion. Avoidance, schizoid presumptions (including magical ideation), and phobias are especially likely to be related.[270]

A study comparing 367 first-degree relatives of subjects with schizophrenia with counterparts in a control group concluded, among other observations, "The substantial correlation between avoidant and schizotypal symptoms suggests that these personality disorders are not independent."[271] A second investigation compared results of diagnostic interviews with relations of probands on the schizophrenic spectrum with relatives of participants with attention-deficit-hyperactivity-disorder and with controls. The research suggests, "When deficiencies in social development derive from a vulnerability to Sz [schizophrenia], they may be represented by avoidant personality disorder."[272] In still another analysis, researchers noted, "[T]here is considerable diagnostic overlap between APD [avoidant personality disorder] and social phobias, especially the generalized subtype of social phobia where a number of social settings are associated with an anxious state." They then raise the question: "Does APD exist as part of a continuum, representing the more chronic, wide-ranging, and severe point on a spectrum of anxiety disturbance?"[273]

At first glance the withdrawal and social discomfort experienced by Holmes could be discounted as a deficiency in confidence. In fact, they exemplified a pervasive pattern of apprehension aroused by acute self-consciousness bordering on debilitating paranoia. Throughout his life he was ill at ease when interacting with others and, despite his obvious brilliance, only occasionally voluntarily engaged in interpersonal encounters, a choice that naturally reinforced his social ineptitude and tendency to internalize.

He was also inordinately self-conscious about multiple parts of his body and in his journal among evaluations listed in a "Self Diagnosis [sic] of broken mind" determines that he was suffering with "Dysphoric mania" and "Body dysmorphic disorder." He writes of being preoccupied with his nose and teeth when he was a child. In addition, he expresses early "[c]oncern" for his penis, explaining, "Suffered accidents as child. Allergic reaction to sex – scarring." Then elaborates, albeit vaguely, "Excessive stimulation in response to 'most beautiful woman in the world.'" The writing thus delineates an unease with his features and masculinity beginning when he was still young. He continues (without identifying the age of origin) to tell of disappointment with his hearing and sight, singling out his poor vision as proof of "[i]mperfect biology." On the same page, connecting his physical imperfections with his arrested ability to socialize, he recognizes his difficulties in communication, emphasizing that he retains an "[o]dd sense of self" and views himself as "divided." Later, he conveys his distaste for his hair, eyebrows, and eyelashes.[274]

His difficulties with socializing were evident from the times he was a child and so pronounced that his parents took him to see a counselor when he was only eight years old.[275] When Holmes was 12 years old, his family moved from Northern California to San Diego and he had such difficulty cultivating new friendships that his mother went door to door seeking companionship for him.[276] Throughout middle and high school he continued to keep to himself and those who were acquainted with him describe him as "shy" or "quiet."[277] When posing for the team photo for cross-country, he appeared so uncomfortable with his teammates that the picture was ruined.[278] "'He was of us, and not of us,' the coach said."[279] Sports participants in high school typically form tight bonds with other members of a team but the behavior of Holmes conforms to the description of a deficit in "developing close relationships" (a problem with "intimacy" defined relative to APD as well as schizotypal personality disorder [SPD]).[280] The incapacity was so obvious it stood out to the person coaching, who was a layperson as far as psychological diagnosis would be concerned.

During this period, he participated in family therapy with a licensed clinical social worker.[281] The sessions were initiated by his parents who were worried about his apparent inability to effectively form bonds with peers.[282]

Years later he would write in his journal: "Family therapy. ... Revealed nothing so as not to appear weak amongst family."[283] The concern shown by his parents is evidence that Holmes was around the time of puberty demonstrating obvious problems with intimacy and exhibiting a consequent desire to withdraw. Both traits are catalogued in *DSM-5* as traits indicative of avoidant and antagonistic personalities.[284] The comment in his journal heralds his life-long habit of masking sincere participation in therapy – a preference that would disguise his mounting homicidal inclinations.

In college his limited affect was plain to a fellow graduate student who was present during recruitment for his doctoral program in neuroscience. "What struck me was that he was kind of nonchalant. ... He just seemed too cool to be there. He kicked back in his chair and seemed very relaxed in a very stressful situation."[285] His air of indifference was apparently a pose. During introductions he made a joke a colleague described as "weird, awkward," demonstrative of his eccentric nature.[286]

Months later, when Holmes sought assistance at the university's mental health center, he was referred for psychiatric treatment. The psychiatrist claimed that the worker that made the referral described Holmes as "one of the most anxious people she had ever seen."[287] The description corresponds to the fearfulness as well as the mistrust inhibiting affection, both associated with APD.[288]

During the time he studied for his doctorate, even though the program involved a very small cadre of graduate students, Holmes kept to himself, leaving each class immediately after its conclusion without socializing with his counterparts.[289] "If no one had ever said anything to him, he wouldn't have said a word," a fellow student observed.[290] He dated another student for about five months but she insisted on keeping the relationship casual.[291] Later she was called as a witness in the death penalty phase of his trial. She attested to his discomfort in social situations, a characteristic that is a hallmark of an avoidant mentality. He had confided in her that he felt "stage fright," presumably referring to his reluctance to engage in discussions in classes and labs.[292] She referred to him as "pretty shy and closed off."[293] Eventually, according to her testimony, she broke up with him at least in part because she felt "distant from him," describing in that simple phrase the "diminished mutuality" associated with APD.[294]

After their break-up Holmes sought intimacy through a dating site known as "Adult Friend Finder" that carries the tagline "Hookup, Find Sex or Meet

Someone Hot Now."[295] Indicative of his mounting eccentricity, his post carried his picture with dyed orange hair and the question, "Will you visit me in prison?"[296]

With his personal relationships worsening, he repeatedly questioned the meaning for his own existence or the value of life for anyone as far as that goes. He wrote in his journal:

> Can a person have both no value
> AND be ultimately good AND/OR
> ultimately evil? …
> * Unknown.
> Why does the value of a
> person even matter?
> * Justice
> If people are ultimately good
> or evil in value, then one may
> suffer from injustice.
> If life has no value:
> - All is just
> - Life and death are not demarcated.
> - Any and all actions have no
> impact on anything….[297]

His thoughts were recorded in a spiral bound computation book. The cover had a place for a name where he wrote, "James Holmes." It also contained a location to enter the title of the course. Holmes completed that line with the words "of Life," a play-on-words that shows he was no longer interested in academics but was now obsessed with sorting out metaphysical issues.[298] In the self-diagnostic section mentioned earlier he attributes his flagging mental health to (among other conditions) "Borderline, narcissistic, anxious, avoidant and obsessive-compulsive personality disorder."[299] Then, on the very next page he makes notations on his paralytic socialization in terms that are pseudo-clinical:

- Isolationism. Removing myself from social Settings. Being around others is tiring with no apparent reason. Perhaps just an extreme form of introversion.

- Avoid social interactions. 99% of the time will not initiate a conversation. If discourse is unavoidable or [avoidant?] action socially acceptable responses will be short or in question form to have other person be the one talking.[300]

After seven pages he returns to his nihilistic musings:

> Everything
> Everything suffers the same paradoxical [quandaries?]
> as nothing.[301]

Just before passages dedicated primarily to logistical planning of his rampage (complete with a to-do list and diagrams) he filled six and one-half pages with the entry, "Why?" leaving a seventh empty except for that same solitary word as a heading.[302] The repetition expresses his torment while also marking his difficulty with pondering any topic besides agnosticism. He concluded with:

> Faith
> What kind of GOD
> commands his people not
> to murder yet cowers
> behind free will?
> Reason
> The reason why life should exist
> is as arbitrary as the reason why it shouldn't
> life shouldn't exist.[303]

His philosophical positioning exhibits the "anhedonia (an aspect of detachment)" attributed in the *DSM-5* to APD.[304]

He also points to: "Excessive fatigue. Present since beginning undergraduate studies. Can move. but [sic] typically 'need' to lie down for 1 hour."[305] Holmes is describing a world weariness accompanying his pathological disunion from sociality. He was experiencing what some biosocial experts refer to as "under-arousal," an uncomfortable temperamental condition characterized by a relatively low heart rate and reduced affect.[306] Evidence of the reciprocal dependence of metabolic and emotional status can be found in recent findings of neural sympathetic activity.

> Electrodermal activity (EDA) is now the preferred term for changes in electrical conductance of the skin, including phasic changes that have been referred to as galvanic skin responses (GSR), that result from sympathetic neuronal activity. EDA is a sensitive psychophysiological index of changes in autonomic sympathetic arousal that are integrated with emotional and cognitive states. Until recently there was little direct knowledge of brain mechanisms governing generation and control of EDA in humans. However, studies of patients with discrete brain lesions and, more recently, functional imaging techniques have clarified the contribution of brain regions implicated in emotion, attention, and cognition to peripheral EDA responses. Moreover, such studies enable an understanding of mechanisms by which states of bodily arousal, indexed by EDA, influence cognition and bias motivational behavior.[307]

Holmes's ongoing disaffected state contributed to his introversion, restricting his ability to adjust to shifting circumstances in his life. Individuals with low responsiveness to stimuli have been shown to be less adaptable than their more responsive counterparts.[308]

Plainly, continuing banal reciprocation will have a pernicious effect on an individual's eudaimonia. Introverted responses contribute to depressed interactions turning initiative ever inward. A person will then seek out "stimulating behaviors to increase arousal so that this discomfort is reduced. This may include stimulating behaviors such as skydiving, drag racing, or simply avoiding boring tasks."[309] For Holmes, unable to forge intimate ties, while stagnating in metaphysical ambivalence and moral disquietude, there was an allure to intensify stimulation through extreme violence.

In the final pages of his journal, following the diagrams and lists pondering the logistics for mass homicide, there is a heading, "The Shrinks," where he records these thoughts:

> … Fear of failure drove determination to
> improve better and succeed in life. No fear of consequences. Primary drive reversion to hatred of mankind. Intense aversion of people, cause unknown.
> Began long ago, suppressed by greater fear of others.
> No more fear, hatred unchecked. Starts small.
> Buy stun gun and folding knife. Research

> firearms laws and mental illness. Buy handgun.
> Committed. – Shotgun, - AR 15, 2nd handgun, wildcard: explosives. Slingshot and least suspicious: gasoline & oil.
> Acquire remote detonation system and body armor, practice shooting at the Byers Canyon rifle range.
> Can't tell the mind rapists plan. If plan is disclosed both 'normal' life and ideal enactment of hatred folded.
> Prevent building false sense of rapport.
> Speak truthfully and deflect incriminating questions. Oddly, they don't pursue or delve further into harmful omissions. Attempt to see if can pass exams as myself and not by fear. Fail. I was fear incarnate. Love gone, motivation directed to hate and obsessions which didn't disappear for any reason w/ the drugs. No consequence, no fear, alone, isolated, no work for distractions, no reason to seek self-actualization. Embraced the hatred, a dark knight arises.[310]

The sequence chronicles his disillusionment with the tedium of pursuing success in spite of his perpetual nervousness about his ability to perform and communicate. He found comfort and purpose in nurturing his divorcement, itemizing the acquisition of materials necessary for his ambush, and reminding himself that his devotion to his plans negates any reason for interactions with others. The ominous animosity in the last two lines, with its reference to a fictional icon in a tone that is almost mystical, reflects his newfound fervor in sinister intentions.

As a superhero cloaked to hide an alter ego the image also symbolizes, whether Holmes fully appreciated it or not, his true conviction of his own superiority and talent for deception. Throughout his life Holmes played out his own dangerous version of a "mind game" by evading candid conversations in counseling sessions in order to deceive the mental health specialists who were attempting to help him.[311] He devotes two and one-half pages in his journal to a cynical critique of his psychotherapy and prescribed medications.[312] "Oddly, they don't pursue or delve farther into harmful omissions," he wrote with some derision of his therapists.[313] He needed to maintain dominance during counseling by parceling valuable information. Manipulative transactions of a prospective power differential are manifestations of criminogenic thinking by someone who feels the need to control others in order to insulate his/her positive self-regard or to experience a perverted form of self-efficacy.[314] Capturing the offender mindset, one forensic psychologist warns, "[S]ecrecy offers him great advantage and provides him with a sense of power. Others are unaware of the sinister intentions that lurk behind an often benign façade."[315] In the singular instance when Holmes did let down his guard in a therapeutic setting, the psychiatrist informed campus police at the University of Colorado that he posed a "danger to the public due to homicidal statements."[316] When he eventually quit treatment altogether, he followed up by sending that doctor threatening text messages.[317]

According to his last therapist, Lynne Fenton (a University of Colorado psychiatrist), he was always "hostile and guarded" during treatment.[318] During his last session he calmly revealed he was quitting school and planned to live off his savings, a job, and the support of his family. "Though Fenton offered to continue seeing him, he refused and abruptly walked out, she said."[319]

Holmes withdrew from college, and as time progressed, he concentrated on two solitary aims – the accumulation of explosive devices to protect his domicile and collection of weapons for murdering strangers gathered in a single spot. The Chief of Police of Aurora revealed that for more than four months Holmes received large mail order packages delivered to his apartment as well as the college.[320] "[H]e bought and stockpiled 6,000 rounds of ammunition. …"[321] Prior to the killings, Holmes armed his apartment with bombs and fire power that would erupt if the front door opened.[322]

He also sent an e-mail to inquire about applying to a gun club so that he could practice shooting.[323] When the person who owned the range called to invite Holmes to an orientation, he heard a greeting on the answering machine that he described as "guttural" and "freakish."[324] He phoned three times, but Holmes never responded. Suspicious, the owner instructed staff to refer Holmes directly to him before granting him access.[325] Perhaps it was due to his debilitating shyness, but Holmes never showed.[326]

Before rampaging, Holmes sent his notebook to the psychiatrist who treated him while he was still a student.[327] The fact that he sent it to the very therapist that he disavowed by stopping treatment suggests that he still hoped someone could somehow fathom what was taking place with his emotional deterioration. The gesture also acted as an apologia – a final justification commonly made by autogenic killers prior to their rampage (analytically described in *How Rampage Killers Interpret Their Worlds*).

Later, during his trial, Holmes would testify that he called an afterhours line at the university hospital minutes before initiating the shooting, but no one picked up.[328] In a videotape of a court-ordered evaluation, he told the appointed psychiatrist that the call was “Just one last chance to see if I should turn back.” Even if someone had answered and tried to dissuade him, they would have been “overruled,” he testified.[329] During the penalty phase of his trial an audio recording was played that indicated an operator did, in fact, answer but Holmes resorted to his lifelong habit of absolute reticence and remained silent.[330] Either way, that final call, as Holmes implied, may very well have been a last aborted request for help.

Holmes was misanthropic and that peculiar prejudice was both premised and maintained by his paranoia and social phobia. He admitted he felt some apprehension as he entered the theater, believing he was under surveillance from the FBI. He even hoped agents might stop him.[331] If they “found out about his plot, ‘they could have done the right thing … and locked me up,’ he said.”[332] That admission, with its unfulfilled wish, shows that while his suspicious mind was acutely sensitive to his surroundings, he was still keenly cognizant that what he was about to do was terribly wrong and he should be stopped.

He bought a ticket for a midnight showing of *The Dark Knight Rises*, stopped briefly at the concession stand without making a purchase, and entered the sold-out theatre.[333] Before the feature began, he pretended to be answering his cell, then stepped out through an exit near the screen as if he were trying to avoid disturbing the other patrons. He propped the door ajar as he left.[334] Twenty minutes into the movie he reappeared garbed in quasi-military regalia, armed with teargas canisters, a shotgun, a semiautomatic rifle, and a pistol.[335] In less than half an hour, 12 (including a six-year old girl) were dead or dying, at least 70 more wounded, the seats in the auditorium were riddled with holes, the floor was littered with shell casings as well snacks tossed aside by panicked spectators, and over 400 people were traumatized for life.[336]

Afterwards, upon capture, Holmes reportedly announced, “I am the joker.”[337] Since that time he has tried to distance himself from that announcement, saying he never referred to himself in that way. He asserted that the first time the characterization was ascribed to him was by someone in an adjacent cell while he was awaiting trial. Moreover, he has indicated that he is not particularly drawn to the image.[338] He has maintained he was inspired to dye his hair orange by the appearance of an acquaintance who had dyed his blue. The Batman movie, he claims, was only chosen for his carnage because it was opening night and he was sure the venue would be crowded.[339] The Colorado District Attorney who coordinated the prosecution pointed out: "He was just looking for a blockbuster, right? … Had this been *Jurassic World*, he'd have been there. Had it been *Avengers: Endgame*, he'd have been there."[340] If Holmes did adopt the persona of one of pop culture's most iconoclastic villains it would certainly have been an expression of his personal disregard for himself as well as his disdain for his terrified victims.

Dr. William Reid was retained by the court itself (not the prosecution or the defense) to determine if Holmes met the legal criteria to be found not guilty by reason of insanity according to Colorado law. He conducted an extensive review of the personal history and medical records for Holmes and interviewed the defendant for 22 hours, determining:[341]

> My primary diagnosis was a condition called schizotypal personality disorder. Schizotypal personality is characterized by chronic, pervasive pattern of social and interpersonal deficits marked by acute discomfort with, and reduced capacity for close relationships, and distortions of thinking and perception. The traits usually appear by early adulthood, often in childhood or adolescence.[342]

Before, during, and since his trial, a number of experts in the field of psychiatry opined that Homes showed signs of schizophrenia, which coincides with the opinion of the therapist that he was seeing prior to the shooting.[343] The diagnosis may have been accurate at the time of the rampage since schizotypal and/or avoidant personality types sometimes develop more intense schizophrenic symptoms in late adolescence or early adulthood.[344] That etiological development would explain Holmes's quiet, sometimes quirky, behavior that, with the aid of his aloof attitude and antipathy toward others, eventually mutated into macabre obsessions.

Hallucinatory or Disassociated Episodes

Actions relevant to circumstantial illusionary thinking – the fourth possible manifestation related to neurological or emotive problems – arise from misinterpretation of events or overtures in the moment: for instance, assessing the content of an indifferent conversation as a threat or seeing a screwdriver as a weapon.

In a study now 30 years old, of 15 men and women imprisoned for homicide who were referred for psychiatric evaluation, 13 were deemed to be psychotic.[345] More telling, though, in terms of their self-restraint, was the fact that all of those suffering from psychosis engaged in excessive acts of violence when committing their crimes – "beheading with heavy cutting weapons and repeated chopping, manual strangulation, crushing head with heavy stones, clubs, etc."[346] Such brutality manifests the frenetic state of their consciousness at the time of the deeds.

A much more comprehensive and recent inquiry into violent recidivism on the part of over 1,000 prisoners in England and Wales revealed that those with untreated schizophrenia were "more than three times as likely to be violent than their treated counterparts." Tellingly, in light of the observations made in the immediately preceding sub-section, the researchers also noted, "It was of interest that this effect was not observed for untreated persons with delusional disorder. However, it is possible that persons with this diagnosis responded less well to treatment than those with schizophrenia."[347] Of course, given the persistent and self-affirming nature of illogical belief systems, it is hardly surprising that participants with delusions were more resistant to intervention.

An investigation by the *New York Times* in the year 2000 highlighted the consequences of insufficient treatment of serious mental illness when it comes to rampage murders. Looking at 100 multiple killings, the investigators found that 20 had been hospitalized for psychiatric problems prior to the incidents. More indicative – and more relevant to treatment protocols – is the fact that 14 of the 24 who had been prescribed drugs had stopped their regimens prior to their rampages.[348]

Pronounced examples of mass killers subject to hallucinatory states are Sylvia Seegrist and Priscilla Ford. Both illustrate the potential for tragedy when severe mental illness is not adequately addressed.

Two Cases with Hallucinatory Neuropsychological Impairment

Sylvia Seegrist was repeatedly hospitalized and diagnosed with schizophrenia before she assaulted strangers with a Ruger semiautomatic rifle at a shopping mall. Wearing army fatigues, a knit cap, and black boots, she killed three – including a two-year old boy – injuring seven as well. She was 25 old at the time. Dubbed "Ms. Rambo" by the manager of the drug store that dispensed her medication (which she stopped taking prior to the shooting),

Seegrist had been observed raking leaves at 4:00 AM, wearing her military garb in the steam room at a local health club, marching up and down the stairs outside her apartment, and drinking furniture polish. Despite stabbing a guidance counselor, attempting to strangle her mother, and speaking incessantly about killing, her family was unsuccessful in committing her. [349] In a letter to the Springfield Press three months before the assault, her mother expressed frustration about her failure to have her institutionalized. "What does it take?" she asked, "Blood on the floor?"[350] Apparently it did. She is now serving three consecutive life terms and seven concurrent 10-20-year sentences in the State Correctional Institution in Muncy Pennsylvania.[351]

Pricilla Ford. Although the District Attorney labeled her as "evil personified," when Ford took the stand at her trial in her own defense, she claimed to be Jesus Christ incarnate.[352] "'I am human' she testified, 'And I am divine. I don't like it any more than anyone else does. I don't want to be divine.'"[353] On Thanksgiving Day in 1980 the former New York City school teacher heard the voice of Joan Kennedy in her head instructing her to plow her 1974 Ford Lincoln Continental into pedestrians strolling along a sidewalk in downtown Reno. After five blocks she struck 30 people, 7 of whom died from their injuries.[354] She referred to her victims as "beasts" and "pigs," claiming the carnage was necessary to "call attention to the case of her daughter, who was taken into custody by Washoe County juvenile authorities in 1973."[355] Ford had been treated by seven separate hospitals prior to her massacre, diagnosed as paranoid schizophrenia with religious delusions and paranoid psychosis as well as with a passive-aggressive personality with hysterical episodes.[356] Not surprisingly, her attorneys mounted an affirmative defense on the basis of insanity even though Ford resented the implication that she was not sane.[357]

At the conclusion of a six-month trial, at that time the longest in Nevada's history, she was found guilty of killing 6 along with the attempted murder of 23 and sentenced to death.[358] She was still appealing the sentence when she died at the age of 75 while battling emphysema, the sole woman on Nevada's death row.[359]

The disparity between the actual circumstances at the time of the incident and level of violence raises the question of how often disassociation may be responsible for rampageous massacres. Generally, the distinction between a psychotic mind and a dissociated one is that psychosis is considered a biological-neurological malady whereas a dissociative condition is viewed as a psychological coping mechanism. But there is increasing evidence that the two, whatever their origins, are inter-related as far as their observable manifestations are concerned.

> Strong associations between measures of dissociation and psychosis have now been confirmed in clinical and non-clinical populations, and it is increasingly recognized that the so-called first-rank symptoms of schizophrenia (i.e., voices commenting or conversing, thought broadcasting, thought withdrawal, and delusional ideas) may occur more frequently in individuals meeting diagnostic criteria for dissociative disorders than those who are diagnosed with schizophrenia.[360]

Dissociation as a causal agent in identity confusion or divided personalities remains a controversial topic in the realm of psychological science. Nevertheless, the clinical bible of the field, the *DSM-5*, devotes an entire chapter of sixteen pages to dissociative disorders and at no point questions the validity of characteristic descriptors of the conditions.[361] On the contrary, it alleges, "Transient depersonalization/derealization symptoms lasting hours to days are common in the general population." To put that statement in perspective, the manual goes on to say, "However, symptomatology that meets full criteria … is markedly less common than transient symptoms. Lifetime prevalence in the U.S. and non-U.S. countries is approximately 2% (range of .08% to 2.8%)."[362]

Perceptual fragmentation defining a depersonalized experience can be noted in the actions of two rampage killers that parallel the symptoms itemized in the prefatory bullets for each case.[363]

Two Cases of Disassociation

Andrew Jerome Wurst.

- Internal disturbance marked by either or both:
  - Depersonalization, i.e., sensations of detachment from yourself and/or a sense of removal from your own feelings;
  - Confusion about one's core identity, i.e., conflicting beliefs and/or impulses.

Wurst, 14 years of age, shot four at a school dinner-dance that had the theme "Had the Time of My Life," killing one teacher, wounding another, and injuring two students as well.[364] As far as he was concerned, it was of no consequence because, as he said after his arrest "It doesn't matter anymore. None of this is real."[365] In an interview with a nationally recognized forensic psychologist, Wurst elaborated on his belief system. He believed only he was alive and everyone else was either an imagined entity or a programmed automaton. He would experience the presence of others but once they left, they no longer existed.[366]

Jennifer San Marco.

- External disorientation marked by either one or both perceptions:
  - Derealization, i.e., feeling detached from external circumstances and/or disconnected from friends and acquaintances;
  - Identity alteration, i.e., switching personas and/or major personality features.

Armed with a 15-round 9mm Smith and Weston pistol, 44-year-old Jennifer San Marco shot two people in the parking lot of a mail processing plant then proceeded inside to shoot four more. Prior to her arrival she killed her former neighbor by shooting her in the head inside her apartment. In all seven people died in what is widely thought to be the worst instance of workplace violence by a female in modern history. Prior to the eruption, San Marco appeared at a service station without any clothing. On another occasion she was observed at a meeting mumbling in such a way that she seemed to be arguing with herself.[367]

Disassociation is a condition that factors into some rampages, but like other facets of mental illness, it should not be mistaken as the single activating agent so much as an accompanying feature to degenerative disturbance.

The Insanity Defense and the Question of Competence

The limited number of documented mass murder cases that can be directly attributed to a psychotic episode has not prevented attorneys defending accused killers from entering a plea of not guilty by reason of insanity or mental disease or defect. A comment by the counsel for Amy Bishop, whose deeds were chronicled in the first chapter, tidily summarized the desperation involved when electing to use this defense. "I don't know what else I've got. ... It wasn't self-defense. It wasn't 'somebody else did it.' I think she has some real severe mental problems."[368]

Nevertheless, these pleas are rarely successful in trials for multiple murderers or for other types of killers for that matter. "[T]he insanity defense is rarely raised and even more rarely successful. It is used in only about 1% of cases in the U.S. and is successful less than 25% of the time."[369] Jurors are reluctant to believe that a person who can plan an attack, access a weapon, then methodically perform successive coordinated acts is incapable of controlling his or her behavior at some point in that sequence.

Conceptually in accord with an affirmative defense, the burden in most states falls on the prosecution to demonstrate that the accused was sane, not on the defense to prove insanity, temporary or otherwise. "A defendant is not criminally responsible if because of a major mental illness the defendant did not appreciate what he was doing was wrong or that because of the mental illness he could not control his actions."[370] Given that those requirements, there are three hurdles in attaining an acquittal based on insanity:

1. A pre-existing history of mental illness;
2. A qualified expert who can explain the defendant's condition and how it meets the legal standard;
3. A forceful and convincing cross-examination of the prosecution's expert who will attempt to refute the claims made by the defense.371

Pleading Not Guilty by Reason of Insanity: A Case Defying Credulity

Contiguous to the mass murder of strangers, is the notorious unsuccessful affirmative defense mounted for family annihilator Ronald DeFeo, Jr., who was charged with the murder of his father, mother, two sisters, and two brothers while they were lying in bed.

Initially he claimed the family was attacked by a mob hitman.[372] However, under intense police questioning he confessed to the killings. "It all started so fast," he allegedly told his interrogators, "Once it started, I just couldn't stop."[373] The defense entered a plea of not guilty by reason of "mental disease or defect," [374] maintaining that DeFeo had been in a dissociative state, brought on by a violent home life, suppressed anger, and paranoia that arose as a means of survival under threatening conditions.[375]

When he testified on his own behalf, DeFeo gave various confusing versions of the events of the morning of the brutal slayings. The Crime Bureau

Chief of Suffolk County at the time the murders were committed and where DeFeo was tried recalled:

> He killed them all. He didn't kill them all. He only Killed Dawn [sister]. He killed his parents, but he didn't kill his siblings and then he killed Dawn. It changes all the time. He would always try to change the facts to suit his own purpose of what he thought the jury would buy.[376]

For his part, DeFeo, later claimed that the contradictory narratives were all part of a strategic attempt to convince the jury that he was insane, maintaining he was behaving that way on the advice of his counsel.

> The courtroom is like … a stage. Insanity is a defense to get around things. … My attorney used insanity as a defense. He told me you ought to go in the courtroom and act crazy. 'Make these people think you're crazy,' he said. And that's what I did. … Changing stories was part of the attack.[377]

Planned or not, DeFeo failed to appear mentally ill. "I don't know. Is that insanity? I don't think … that's the definition. … I think that's part of the bravado that I saw," one juror, Amelia Franza, suggested.[378]

Regardless, there was ample proof that DeFeo was not psychologically incapacitated, at least not according to law, when he slaughtered each family member. The presiding judge, Thomas Stark, commented in an interview after the trial had long passed:

> In addition to his own statement [given to police while in custody], there was a tremendous amount of evidence indicating consciousness of guilt. The fact that the evidence [from the crime scene] was carefully picked up and secreted by him, the fact that he took the rifle and threw it in the waters of the Great South Bay – all of this indicated his knowledge that what he had done was wrong, both in a legal sense and a moral sense.[379]

Not swayed by the claims of disassociation or his staged confusion, the jury found DeFeo guilty of six counts of second-degree murder. If each murder was considered an isolated act, he would have been liable for 6 consecutive terms of 25 years to life. However, since the verdict originated from one continuous event, the state of New York allowed the sentences to be served concurrently.[380]

While passing the sentence, Judge Stark, perhaps worried that DeFeo would someday be released, labeled the acts as the "most heinous and abhorrent crimes."[381] It turns out there was little reason for the judge's concern. Although technically eligible for paroled release in 1999, he died in the Sullivan Correctional Facility in Fallsburg, New York, in March 2021, at the age of 69.[382]

The allusions to demonic possession, coupled with claims of paranormal experiences by George and Kathy Lutz who later lived in the house with their three children, led to the legend of the Amityville haunting that has spurred numerous books, movies, and blogs either attesting to the presence of the supernatural in the residence or refuting that possibility.[383]

In courtroom scenarios almost as bizarre as DeFoe's ever changing explanation of the events that took place in his household when his family was slain, the preliminary hearing and trial of Colin Ferguson raised questions about the efficacy and consistency of legal standards regarding the insanity defense and mental competency.

Deluded but Competent

There is a nuanced but important distinction between an insanity defense and competency to stand trial (CST). The latter pertains to a defendant's ability to deliberately participate in court proceedings after apprehension, while the former addresses the accused state of mind at the time of the incident. The supreme court has set forth five points for a determination of CST:

1. The functional ability to be involved in the process;
2. A capacity to understand the procedures including the roles of those involved;
3. A capability for participation even if a willingness is absent;
4. "A reasonable [as opposed to sophisticated] degree of understanding;"
5. A level of rationality such that the accused appreciates the proceedings and can consult with counsel.[384]

An associated legal issue related to competence sometimes arises when a defendant wishes to represent himself or herself despite the constitutional right to counsel – the primary concern being that s/he is making the decision "voluntarily and intelligently."[385]

Colin Ferguson rampaged on the Long Island Railroad line out of New York City in the early evening of December 7, 1993. As the train entered Garden City in Nassau County he rose from his seat and proceeded to shoot commuters row by row, with a 9mm semiautomatic pistol, eventually precisely alternating to the left and right side of the aisle. The second time he exhausted his ammunition, three other passengers restrained him until the train arrived at the next station where he was apprehended by an off-duty railroad officer. Three men and one woman were dead, and two more women died shortly thereafter. Nineteen were wounded. If one of the indicators for mental health is the ability to discern right from wrong, theoretically at least, Ferguson demonstrated some semblance of sanity before leaving the train in handcuffs.[386] "I've done a bad thing," he said.[387]

While being interrogated by the police immediately following apprehension, Ferguson demonstrated no remorse. "One of his first questions was, 'How many people were dead?' And then he wanted to talk about why he didn't get a 'B' in a college course," Detective Parpan, one of his interrogators, reported.[388] That lack of empathy would continue to show throughout a competence hearing, his trial, and the sentencing in a string of encounters that became so morbidly absurd that *Saturday Night Live* opened a show with a satiric skit about the situation.[389] When he was finally able to mete out a sentence, the Judge, Donald Belfi, scolded, "Colin Ferguson, in my almost 21 years on the bench, I have never presided over a trial with a more selfish and self-centered defendant."[390] The path to that final admonishment, though, was tedious and circuitous.

After disputes with a series of defenders, Ferguson managed to secure the services of two highly reputable (although, to some, controversial) attorneys: William Kunstler, and Ronald Kuby.[391] Kunstler had served as counsel to Martin Luther King, the "Chicago Seven" protesters (charged with inciting people to riot outside of the Democratic Convention in 1968), and the suspects in the World Trade Center bombing.[392] Kuby built a reputation around cases involving social pariahs, casting himself as an activist and lawyer for leftist causes.[393]

Based upon notes found by investigators in Ferguson's pockets that spouted vindictiveness against whites, Asians, "Uncle Tom blacks," and other groups, Kunstler and Kuby elected to use an insanity defense based on the premise that Ferguson was subject to "black rage." The concept derived from a book originally written in 1968 with that title. In that work two psychiatrists advance a theory that blacks in America have become increasingly hostile due to decades of subjugation.[394] Kuby offered the following explanation for their decision to defend Ferguson with that premise: "We laid out a strategy – a course of action, which involved his only conceivable defense which was the insanity defense and Kunstler couched it with the phrase, 'black rage.'"[395] Moreover, Kunstler and Kuby questioned Ferguson's ability to rationally assist his attorneys, maintaining he was in no state to even stand trial.[396]

Ferguson would have none of it, asserting he was sane and a "white Caucasian" had taken his gun then committed the massacre. He subsequently petitioned to represent himself.[397] Kuby described the rapidly deteriorating relationship between Ferguson and his lawyers in this way:

> Ultimately Kunstler and I became convinced that Colin Ferguson, indeed – outside of being generally crazy – that he was suffering from very extreme and excessive mental illness that interfered with his mental functioning as a defense. The ultimate break came when he accused us, his attorneys, of staging a phony incident at the Nassau County Jail, so the jail would be locked down, so that Colin Ferguson would be unable to go to his eye doctor appointment, so he would go blind, so he would be unable to identify the actual Caucasian shooter. … We realized that once he started accusing us of plotting against him that we were going to get fired and he was going to represent himself.[398]

Subsequently, a competency hearing was convened. Though not necessarily the best decision for Ferguson tactically, the judge found in Ferguson's behalf as far his ability support his defense was concerned.[399]

Outside of court, after years had passed, Kuby commented, "[F]or the standards of competence all you have to do is be able to understand the nature of the proceedings and assist in your own defense in the most rudimentary way. So, in essence if you know the difference between a judge and a grapefruit, you're competent to stand trial."[400] Richard Peck, the chief prosecutor during the trial reflected, "Was he mentally ill? Yes. What non-mentally ill person would do something like that? Was he legally insane? He was not…."[401] The court ruled that Ferguson could represent himself, although Kuby and Kunstler were appointed as advisors and the presiding judge.[402] The judge allowed the application for the insanity defense to be withdrawn, opening the curtain for what Kuby later labeled as "mental illness theatre."[403]

While acting as his own attorney, Ferguson was capable of putting forth all the mannerisms and appearances of a polished attorney. He wore a well-pressed suit, questioned witnesses in a dispassionate manner, listened attentively to the proceedings, and complied with court rulings. "He was a very intelligent individual," Peck said, "I don't know what he was reading but for someone who had never been in a courtroom before, he was comfortable."[404] However, many of Ferguson's comments and arguments were beyond indecorous. They were preposterous.

- In his opening statement, when proposing his theory of the crime, despite the numerous witnesses who had seen the ruthless killing and evidence that the gun used in the incident had been wrestled from his hand, he suggested that a white gunman conducted the slaughter after stealing the weapon from his handbag as he was sleeping;[405]
- He asked his advising attorney to draw up a motion for funding by the county to hire a private investigator to find the actual aggressor;[406]
- His questions were occasionally irrelevant – even off-the-wall – for example he asked, "What are your ambitions in life" and at one point he requested that members of the jury raise their hands if they enjoyed hockey;[407]
- He moved to subpoena (then) President Bill Clinton and (then) Governor Mario Cuomo for the defense to prove there was a government conspiracy to find him guilty;[408]
- He further suggested that the Jewish Defense League was conspiring to kill him.[409]

It took the jury approximately 10 hours to find him guilty of almost every charge he was facing. The only reason it took that long, the foreman shared after sentencing, was because they were deliberating over lesser charges, such as aggravated harassment.[410] Ultimately, Ferguson was ordered to serve six consecutive terms of 25 years to life for each death in addition to the maximum of 50 years for attempted murder, two weapons charges, and reckless endangerment. He will be eligible for parole in 2309.[411]

Not surprisingly, Ferguson appealed, asserting, in part, that he should not have been found competent to stand trial and, therefore, was not fit to continue *pro se*.[412] In essence, the appeal was based on the premise that he had inadequate counsel – namely himself. The Appellate Court and the Supreme Court of New York upheld his conviction, stating, in part:

> The court properly determined after a hearing, that the defendant was competent to stand trial. ... In addition, the defendant's decision not to pursue an insanity defense does not, in and of itself, indicate incompetence. [T]he court properly permitted the defendant to appear *pro se*, since a defendant who is competent to stand trial is necessarily competent to waive his right to counsel and proceed....[413]

The macabre carnival show that had lasted over seven years, damaging so many lives and then denigrating the legal system, was at long last over.

The cases of DeFeo and Ferguson illustrate the inherent difficulties in translating psychological profiles into legal terms. It is difficult – if not impossible – to objectively pronounce judgment on a subjective interpretation of reality. Perhaps, the previously quoted observation that Mr. Peck made about Ferguson's sanity – or lack thereof – can be expanded into a broader moral pronouncement when it comes to mass murder. Anybody who knowingly engages in multiple homicidal acts must be mentally deficient, incapacitated, subject to some sort of delusional perspective, or compelled by almost unfathomable emotions. Culpability, though, is a different matter altogether.

Chapter Five

Pathological Personality

Thus while he spake, each passion dimmed his face
Thrice changed with pale, ire, envy, and despair,
Which marred his borrowed visage, and betrayed
Him counterfeit, if any eye beheld.
– John Milton
"Paradise Lost"

Pin-pointing a personality disorder (PD) as a motivator for any single mass autogenic mass killer is predictably difficult because people with deficient or vicious personalities tend to avoid treatment or therapy before the pivotal event. Diagnosis is even more problematic because rampage killers resist capture and so are frequently either killed by authorities or commit suicide, thus leaving no subsequent opportunities for interviews.[1] Most of those who remain alive, who are uncaptured and must account for their aggressive criminality, are deceptive by nature. As a result, speculation about character flaws often take place after the fact as part of psychological autopsies that are largely based on anecdotes. Even so, images can be reconstructed with broad strokes based on a constellation of identifiable attributes. These reconstructions can then disclose personal dysfunctions for proper categorization in the dispositional conditions.

Both Bishop and Fabrikant, for instance, were prone to hypersensitive and arrogant behaviors that could easily be associated with a sense of entitlement and a grandiose self-image, both associated with narcissism. Bishop repeatedly acted upon her belief in her own importance and specialness. The episode at the IHOP and her reaction when passed over as first author on a journal article are prime examples. Similarly, Fabrikant, with his conviction that he was a brilliant scholar believed he was entitled to professional deference based solely on his expertise irrespective of his continual conflict with associates.[2] He had a habit of assigning co-authorship to colleagues and then using that assignment to extract favors from the assignee.[3] The extortion became more frequent as he sought professional advancement and tenure. His manner was so abrasive and intimidating some secretaries, who were often the first to receive Fabrikant upon his arrival for meetings, had panic buttons installed at their desks. One was cautioned to leave for home if she saw his car entering the parking lot.[4]

Harris (as mentioned early in the second chapter) perceived himself to be physically inadequate and, like Elliot Rodger who will be discussed later, Harris manifested a malicious personality type – only in his case it was psychopathy as opposed to the narcissism applicable to Rodger. A lead FBI agent on the team that investigated the Columbine massacre – and the only psychologist – described Harris as a "budding psychopath" at a symposium attended by leading experts in psychopathology. A participant objected, saying instead, "I think he was a full-blown psychopath."[5]

The *DSM-5* does not reference "psychopathic" as a personality type, though the adjective is a common one in psychology and criminology, acknowledged as a personality dysfunction as far back as 1801 when the Italian physician, Philippe Pinel referred to certain morally depraved patients as exhibiting "insanity without delirium."[6] After the publication of Hervey Cleckley's classic, *The Mask of Sanity* in 1941, psychopathy became more broadly recognized as a distinct syndrome. In a later edition the author commented:

> It is perhaps in silent recognition of the absurdities that prevailed for so long in our official categories that psychiatrists in practice still avail themselves of the more or less slang term [psychopath] which is a sort of nickname for our subject. ... There is nothing vague about these patients clinically. Their course of conduct can be predicted with much greater accuracy than that of patients with defined psychosis.[7]

The American Psychiatric Association, for whatever reasons, has elected to avoid psychopathy in terminology for diagnostic purposes. Employing, instead, the broader referents, "antisocial personality disorder" for adults and "conduct disorder" for children and adolescents.[8] Both diagnoses apply to individuals who are manipulative, callous, and irresponsible with respect to social obligations. For the sake of differentiation, psychopaths may be viewed as a sub-set of either category in that they tend to demonstrate, in addition to the anti-social traits, insufferable conceit, glibness, and persuasive charm.[9]

Grandiosity is a trait shared by both psychopaths and narcissists, as is the compulsion to seek vengeance against perceived persecutors. Both of those features were evident in the self-imposed titles used in the planning for the massacres committed by Harris and Klebold then later by Rodger. Columbine was called "Judgment Day."[10] Rodger named his cruel exercise "The Day of Retribution," adding on his final recording that it was "the day in which I will have my revenge against humanity, against all of you."[11] He originally coined the phrase after he moved to Santa Barbara to attend college and felt demeaned by other students, particularly young women.[12] The fact that these killers dubbed their violent plans (electronically and in writing) with titles imbued with self-absorbed vindication is one of many indications of the egomaniacal nature of their perspectives.

Dr. Hare, the originator of the Psychopathy Checklist, identifies "deceitful and manipulative" as one "key symptom" of a psychopath's personality profile.[13] Eric Harris successfully manipulated his socially awkward and frequently depressed friend, Dylan Klebold, into actively participating in an elaborate scheme for killing.[14]

A close look at their relationship, along with other destructive partnerships, will reveal the damaging sequence of events that can be driven by deceit. The examinations will be instructive in two other respects relative to the role that individuals with personality disorders (PDs) assume in autogenic killing. First, they will demonstrate the duplicitous nature of a pathological personality, especially when the harbinger is bent on a vindictive or damaging end. Secondly, the contrast of characterological deviance with other predispositions, specifically those classified as neuropsychological, will be sharpened.

Manipulation in Killing Alliances

Andrew Golden with Mitchell Johnson.

Though the details are scanty, after Johnson's arrest it was revealed that between the ages of six and eight, he had been repeatedly sexually violated. He was also subjected to oppressive discipline and screaming outbursts by his natural father throughout his childhood.[15] The summer before participating in the school shooting with his partner Johnson was found with his pants down while changing the diaper of a young girl, two to three years old. He was charged in juvenile court with molestation.[16] It greatly upset the family. His step-father, who he deeply admired, was furious and his mother was horrified.[17] Around that same time Johnson was rejected by a girl he met while visiting his father and was so distraught that he threatened suicide.[18] Later, when another crush broke up with him "[h]e was apprehensive about the impact … on his reputation."[19] A few weeks prior to the sudden assault, he was dismissed from the baseball team for self-mutilation after carving his initials into his own shoulder.[20]

Self-harm by adolescents is associated with anxiety, depression, shame, and self-consciousness.[21] Johnson's scarring indicated that his perception of acceptability in his community was very much in jeopardy. He exhibited more frustration around his standing when he became enraged after receiving discipline for wearing a cap at school.[22] Responding to an assignment by the in-school suspension (ISS) teacher, he wrote, "He had some squirrels he needed to kill" and when that chore was completed, "[t]here would be no more ISS."[23] The steady erosion of his sense of inclusion in his township and among his peers mutated into antagonism that would soon be directed toward those who held prestige.

Golden, Johnson's accomplice in mayhem, was suspected of torturing and killing animals. He was indulged by his parents who believed him to be something of a miracle because he was born after his mother had a tubal ligation reversed. They doted on him. His father along with his grandfather thought it was amusing that he began swearing when he was barely old enough to attend school and indulgently encouraged his habitual use of foul language.[24] Unlike his partner Golden's view of his social capital had little, if any, influence on his decision to engage in mass killing. In contrast to his counterpart Golden would have been indifferent to opinions or impressions of others because he was manifestly anti-social – the most obvious indicator being his affinity for animal torture.

One of the employees at the Craighead County Jail, where Golden was housed awaiting trial, reported:

> [He] hated cats. And I said, 'What did you do with this cat?' He said, 'I've done several things to cats. … I shot bottle rockets at them. I tried one to the clothesline and I shot [BBs] at them. … I've shot them full of BBs. He said, 'They would just be lying there scrawling and hollering. …'

> [He] was talking about nothing else how he would slit their throats and wring their necks and stuff like that. He thought he was so cool....[25]

This type of cruelty has a demonstratable relationship with characteristics inherent to individuals with conduct disorders (CDs), psychopathic personalities, and other maladaptive character traits.[26] The *DSM-5* cites "physically cruel to animals" as one criterion for determining the presence of a CD. It also lists "Often bullies, threatens, or intimidates others. ... Has used a weapon that can cause physical harm to others. ... Has broken into someone else's house. ... Often lies to obtain goods or favors or to avoid obligations (i.e., 'cons' others)."[27] Young people with CD present with characteristics that are associated with aggressive psychopathic attributes, specifically, callous-unemotional behaviors.[28]

Golden would ride his bike around his neighborhood with a knife strapped to his side and occasionally hit smaller girls on the arm.[29] One neighbor said she did not want her daughter to play with him because "[h]e was too rowdy."[30] When he was in the first grade, he brought a toy gun to school that was immediately confiscated. After he convinced a classmate to fetch it for him, he filled it with mud and fired it at another first grader hitting her in the eye.[31]

Another sign of Golden's CD and imminent psychopathy (apart from the nature of the ambush itself, of course) was his skillful deception of adults who, in the tightly woven setting of his community, would have functioned as standard-bearers for expectations. "Andrew [Golden] was a sweet child when his parents were around. ... whenever he was away from his parents he was a little demon," observed one adult from the neighborhood.[32]

At least five months preceding the rampage, he bragged of his intention to bring guns to school in order to murder others. There are conflicting accounts for this incident but the version in which Golden makes threats seems most probable. A school counselor believed Golden was hinting that he might harm himself.[33] However, a pupil overheard him and signed an affidavit attesting to his certainty that Golden was threatening others.[34] The father of that witness stated that when he was told of the statement it worried him enough to contact school authorities.[35]

The timing for the assault became opportune because Johnson was angry with his teachers as well as his classmates and was facing the very real possibility of being sent away to live with his father– a prospect that terrified him.[36] According to a boy who was a close friend of Johnson, about one week before the shooting, Johnson confided in him that he had enlisted a co-conspirator to enact his wrath upon the world. "He was just sick and tired of everything and so he asked one of his friends to help him."[37] In a civil deposition following his release from custody much later, Golden corroborated that story. "[H]e was angry at some people and, related to the gang stuff he, him and somebody else had been into it. And he said he was going to get some people back over the gang stuff."[38] The partnership solidified in that context: Johnson signaled that he was frustrated and Golden capitalized on that frustration.

On the morning of their attack Golden and Johnson attempted to use a hammer and torch to break into the gun safe of Golden's father. When they were unsuccessful, they stole a .38 derringer, a .38 snub-nose pistol, and a .357 Magnum, which were unsecured. Unsatisfied with their haul, they used a crowbar to break into the basement of Golden's grandfather's home. They took four more handguns and three rifles.[39] When the boys carried out their ambush, it was Golden who pulled the fire alarm to lure their unsuspecting victims outside of the building.[40] When the shooting began, he was the first to shoot, expending approximately 25 rounds while his partner shot only five.[41]

When sentenced for his part in the rampage, Golden, because of his status as an 11-year-old juvenile, was given a truncated term of imprisonment. After serving his time, he withheld and falsified information to secure a permit to carry a concealed weapon, an attempt at chicanery that was ultimately unsuccessful.[42] He sported a tattoo with a cross with the words, "Romans 3:23." The verse is commonly quoted as, "[F]or all have sinned and fall short of the glory of God."[43] Perhaps it was intended as a justification for contributing to the slaughter of four children and one adult while wounding ten more. Three deaths and two of the wounded were directly attributed to him.[44]

Eric Harris with Dylan Klebold

A little over a month before orchestrating the explosions and shooting their classmates, Harris and Klebold, as part of their spiteful legacy, shot a series of videos, frequently called "The Basement Tapes."[45] In the first an observant viewer can detect the one who is engineering the necessary mind-set to pull off the eventual butchery.

> They ranted for more than an hour. Dylan was wild and animated and angry, obsessively hurling his fingers through his long, ratty hair. Eric was mostly calm and controlled. …
>
> Eric introduced most ideas: Dylan riffed along.[46]

The merit of the observation is verified by an encapsulated monologue by Harris followed by stage direction to Klebold:

> Harris: I'm sorry I have so much rage, but you put it on me. …
>
> Harris: More rage. More rage. (*motions with his hands for emphasis*) Keep building it on.
>
> Klebold: If you could see all the anger I've stored over the past four fucking years ...[47]

Harris took the lead in planning the logistics of the bombing and mass shooting. He never wavered from his dedication to the death and misery that the onslaught would bring.[48]

He particularly relished the duplicity involved in carrying on what seemed like a normal teenage life while callously planning and anticipating the rampage for over two years.[49] Of his parents, he said, "I could convince them that I'm going to climb Mount Everest or I have a twin brother growing out of my back."[50] Harris boasted, "I can make you believe anything."[51] The disdainful declaration typifies the "contemptuous delight" that a psychopath takes in deception.[52]

Klebold was deceptive as well, but in a much different manner. He hid his depression and loneliness behind a façade of indifference and annoyance. Speaking through her anguished tears, his mother told a television interviewer: "I think we'd like to believe that our love and our understanding is protective and if anything were wrong with my kid, I would know, but I didn't know." She then went on to say that as a young boy Klebold was "a happy, precocious, brilliant little child."[53] However, in an early basement tape, Klebold complains that he believed he was "hated" by his peers as far back as preschool,[54] recording in his journal "If anybody had any idea how sad I am …," then continuing that he was lonely "[e]ver since 7th grade" when he felt abandoned by a former friend.[55] Harris exploited Klebold's pervasive feelings of inadequacy and discontent by conspiring with him to make his suicidal ideation part of a cinematic revenge fantasy.

Both were emotionally unstable and prone to demonstrations of temper. In the case of Harris, the anger was an expression of his perpetual arrogance and his need to maintain situational dominance through intimidation. A profile he posted on WBS, an early web-based chat network, offered this introduction: "I kill who i dont like, i waste what i dont want, i destroy what i hate."[56] In contrast, Klebold's outbursts were expressions of frustration borne from his perception of rejection and preoccupation with personal failings. Klebold has a lyrical passage in his journal that reads, in part, as follows:

> [D]esolation is knowledge
> pain is acceptance
> despair is anger
> denial is helpless
> martyrism is hope for others
> advantages taken are causes for martyrism
> revenge is sorrow
> death is a reprieve
> life is a punishment
> others' achievements are tormentations
> people are alike
> I am different.[57]

The private writings of Harris are infused with contempt, Klebold's with disenchantment. The opening line in Harris's journal is: "I hate the fucking world, too much god damn fuckers in it."[58] Klebold begins with "Fact: People are so unaware.... well, Ignorance is bliss I guess....that would explain my depression."[59] Of course, both are enthused in their self-centered emotional states. They are adolescents, after all, but one is obsessed with unfocused generalized anger while the other lives with melancholy.

Their relationship was more tendinous than the ties that normally bind teen friendships. They harbored an emotional symbiosis that nourished a mutual sense of supra-separation. "Because I have something only me and V have, SELF AWARENESS," Harris asserted in the first paragraph of his diary.[60] His co-conspirator, Klebold, in his diary referred to the rest of humanity as "zombies."[61] One entry reads: "The zombies & their society band together & try to destroy what is superior & what they don't understand & are afraid of. Soon… either I'll commit suicide, or I'll get with [censored] & it will be NBK for us."[62]

"NBK" was the nickname for the impending attack, taken from the movie, *Natural Born Killers*, the graphic Oliver Stone film about a couple on an extended murder spree.[63] It is likely that Harris initially used the initials as code that was later adopted by both the shooters. "In Dylan's 1998 yearbook Eric wrote, 'God I can't wait till they die. I can taste the blood now – NBK.'"[64]

The following year Klebold wrote in his diary: "I hate this non-thinking stasis. I'm stuck in humanity. Maybe going 'NBK' (gawd) with Eric is the way to break free."[65] The two conspirators kept their journal entries separate from one another and there is no record of a time when they shared their musings. Each had their own tone and style, but much of the content overlapped. Both were entrenched – Harris in accentuated irritation and Klebold in chronic dejection – and they were convinced that the insulation was not a sign of their self-imposed constrained affectivity but, instead, proof of their shared superiority.

After examining the motives behind a set of seemingly "senseless" murders committed by men who viewed themselves as social outcasts, a UCLA sociologist made these observations:

> The deviant's dizziness is a spinning around between two poles. On the one side, the pariah cannot rest when he achieves conformity. His deepest fear is not failure in conventional terms, but that success means cowardice. On the other side, he discovers more in deviance than just a refuge. *Being deviant gives him an edge.*
>
> …
>
> The fiction that these killers constructed was that an act of such ferocious domination was always what they were headed toward.[66]

The aggressive hubris of Harris combined with the depressive personality of Klebold to fashion a conspiratorial drive for an assault based largely on their internalized ostracism.

Discounting terrorism, it is rare that a mass killing is conducted by an adult duo. An FBI report states that out of 160 "active shooter" incidents logged between 2000 and 2013, only two were carried out by a team.[67] In one a participant was never apprehended, so it is impossible to ascertain the nature of the dynamic in that duet.[68] The other involved a rampage in 2012, during which Jacob Carl England and Alvin Lee Watts drove through Tulsa,

Oklahoma armed with handguns taking the lives of three and wounding two more.[69] All the victims were black and the two men later pled guilty to hate crime charges, first degree murder, and shooting with intent to kill.[70]

Alvin Lee Watts with Jacob Carl England

Watts was 32, 13 years older than England, when they embarked on their deadly drive. Upon capture, through all the court proceedings, he said nothing. Previously, he had pled guilty to misdemeanor assault and battery in a domestic dispute and three years later was charged with aggravated assault and battery, though the latter case was dismissed.[71]

England, in contrast to his co-defender, had never been arrested before apprehension for the murders. The only crime on his record was driving with a suspended license.[72] He expressed remorse at the sentencing hearing, and he admitted he felt guilty for taking part in the heartless ambush chain. His voice cracked as he read his written statement: "There are no words to express the sorrow and guilt of what I have done. There is no excuse for my actions. I must live with this in my heart until the end of my days."[73] England, 19, was in a fragile state when he partnered with Watts. He had been devastated over the death of his father at the hands of an African American man, a loss that was then followed by the suicide of his fiancé. According to a neighbor, he was taking medication for depression.[74]

Given the disparity in ages, his aggressive conduct prior to the rampage, England's fragility, and the older man's stoicism during legal proceedings, it is likely that Watt's personal animosity was the primary force in the commission of the crimes. England, although unquestionably accountable, was subject to the coercive cruelty of an unconscionable mentor.

In the context of his interactions with England, the former crimes by Watts call for extended consideration. It is generally accepted that the causes for intimate partner violence, distal and proximal alike, are heterogenous.[75] However, many of the male aggressors, especially those who become involved with community agencies or the legal system, have a defining personal trait: an abject tendency to control the behavior of the abusee. "People who work with both victims and perpetrators are aware that violence is one tool among many that the perpetrator uses to gain greater power in the relationship in order to deter or require specific actions from women, win arguments, or demonstrate their dominance."[76] Even though there are no controlled studies exploring the possibility of a causal or correlational connection between domestic disputes and single incident multiple homicides, the numbers suggest it is probable. Data derived by tabulating media coverage along with law enforcement and court records show that for the 194 mass shootings in the United States between 2009-2020, more than half (53%) were related to family conflict.[77]

The "power motive" in domestic violence derives, not so much from a desire to dominate as a need to assert personal value through dominance. Summarizing the literature on offenders in her doctoral dissertation Shelly Marie Wagers noted:

> [L]ack of a true self may actually represent a lack of internal power resources an individual needs to feel a sense of power, which leads to a batterer continuously feeling powerless within the context of their intimate relationship regardless of their partner's actions.[78]

After operationalizing and measuring facets of "internal power" (IP) then applying a t-test as well as a Pearson correlation, Wagers correlated IP with abusive behaviors self-reported by subjects and found an inverse significant relationship between IP and psychological abuse, IP and physical abuse, as well as a combination of the two ($p < .01$).[79] She observed:

> According to mainstream domestic violence theories, power is a key component to understanding a batterer's motive for using coercive control tactics against an intimate partner, [but] there are two distinct types of power – social, which is external power, and personal, which is internal power – and … distinguishing these two types of power is important, especially in regard to an individual's 'power motive.'[80]

The observation is relevant because a feeling of "powerlessness" is a component of alienation that, in turn, fosters the formation of a rampage killer's drive. A composite picture of these variables is the crux of Chapter Three in *How Rampage Killers Interpret Their Worlds.*

In a manner akin to the massacres perpetuated by teams, serial killing partners involve one person who persistently exerts pressure on another to ensure that his or her devious desires are fully experienced regardless of misgivings that a companion may feel. Collaboration of this sort represents an astounding proportion of successive multiple homicides. Research spanning the years from 1800 to 2008 attending to nearly 500 killers – 400 males and

70 females – involving 3,000 to 4,600 deaths – revealed that 26 percent were committed by dyads.[81] The configurations for these relationships varied, encompassing husbands with wives, brothers, cousins, and, horribly, parents with their off-spring. Without exception, there was "one person who psychologically maintained control of the other members of the team."[82] Partnerships in multiple murder are controlled by one dominate personality with unyielding sadistic intentions who exploits a vulnerable accomplice by focusing aspirations on a scenario of an aggrandized delusion that imbues the dependent stooge with a feeling of gravitas.

The Nature of Pathological Personalities

Recognizing and responding to civilized norms is characteristic of those who adequately function in a social structure and are sensitive to the sort of exchanges (both tangible and virtuous) necessary to maintain order and accountability. For those with an aberrant pathology, however, that reciprocity is secondary to meeting idiosyncratic needs or desires. The maintenance of control through repression or its apparent opposite – an abandonment of responsibility – is the way they maintain status and identity.

> [T]wo core features of personality disorder, affective (emotional) regulation and impulse regulation, could be understood along a single continuum of regulation. At one pole of this regulation continuum is extreme over-regulation (of emotion and/or impulsivity).At the other pole is extreme under-regulation (of emotion and/or impulsivity). In other words, there is a single dimension of regulation ranging from very high to very low, with personality disorders falling at each end of the continuum, and healthy personalities falling somewhere in the middle of these two extremes.[83]

In terms of a dispositional characteristics, then, a moderate personal lapse is evident when a subject "cooperates predominately for personal gain" while a severe impairment is manifested by "little mutuality: others are conceptualized primarily in terms of how they affect the self…."[84] The primary method used by individuals with pathological personalities to meet their desires (to maintain their sense of worth) is through aggression, whether implied, passive, or direct. Since the result is often compliance on the part of acquaintances within their range of influence, this way of coping with life's peculiar circumstances makes a person with a personality disorder at once overbearing in day-to-day encounters and, at the same time, difficult to immediately recognize.

Exemplative of surreptitious vacillation is the reaction of adolescents labeled "insecure" when performing a problem-solving task with their peers when their rejection of advice accompanied by annoyance with their workmate was more evident than counterparts deemed to be well-adjusted.[85] Contrariwise, but just as illustrative, so-called "avoidant" adults did not report anger when placed in provocative situations even though they showed signs of physiological arousal and hostility when the provocateur was not acting with intention.[86]

Emotional demonstrations by people with PD may be reactions to uncontrollable predicaments or utilitarian in the sense that they are a means to an end. The first is an "affective attack" and the latter is "predatory."

> The term affective attack is currently understood to encompass behaviors one might associate with that of a stereotypical Halloween decoration of an intimidating cat. … The animal may arch its back to make itself look larger and more threatening. As the cat approaches the target, typically a rat, it will be vigilant of any movement, which may trigger an immediate attack.
>
> The second form of attack, quiet biting "predatory" attack or stalking prey … represents a predatory-like stance toward the object of prey. … [T]he cat tends to be unusually quiet and lowers its profile to avoid detection. The attack comes quickly and the apprehension seen in affective attack is transformed into a swift and directed approach.…[87]

These two modes are not opposites, rather they are alternative methods to achieve a certain aim – to exploit or shape a given situation.

Their realization in an individual with PD is why intimate partners of people with character deficiencies speak in terms of "walking on eggshells" to avoid conflict (when the partner with a personality disorder may engage in affective aggression) or "living in dread and fear" (when the mate with PD continuously engages in predatory behavior). Pathological personalities are always striving for exploitation, either through confrontation or manipulation, and they never – ever – let up because for them the maintenance of control – as destructive to others as that effort may be – is essential to the survival of their own identity.

The *Merck Manual*, the definitive guide to medical maladies, offers this summation:

> Personality disorders in general are pervasive, enduring patterns of perceiving, reacting, and relating that cause significant distress or functional impairment. …
> Personality disorders exist when these traits become so pronounced, rigid, and maladaptive that they impair work and/or interpersonal functioning.[88]

That summary captures the all-encompassing and persistent nature of PDs and helps to elucidate why they present such challenges for professionals when they become involved in therapy.

> '[People with] personality disorders exhibit chronic, pervasive problems getting along with people in all kinds of different contexts,' says Thomas R. Lynch, PhD, assistant professor of psychology at Duke University and the Duke University Medical Center. …
> As a result, people with the disorders often don't seek treatment, and those who do often drop out, he says. For example, people with borderline personality disorder (BPD) – the most commonly treated personality disorder – quit treatment programs about 70 percent of the time.[89]

People with ineffectual personalities have an extremely limited repertoire for dealing with others – repeated variations of the same theme are replayed in all situations – avoidance, or obsession, or fear, or control, or hysterics, depending on their peculiar maladaptation. They are unable to change notes and that rigidity prevents complementary involvement with family, acquaintances, friends, coworkers, even competitors and hinders formation of relationships based on mutual comfort.

Because their adaptive range is confined, individuals with personality disorders have difficulty adjusting to the favorable or unfavorable responses of people in their constellation. Their self-image is circumstantial (in the sense that it is dependent on the assessment of others). For that reason, they tend to be protective of their position or vantage point, especially when they feel that their prominence is endangered. In a field experiment of 405 middle-school students, those with narcissistic tendencies were shown to be more aggressive than their counterparts when they felt their sense of self was threatened.[90]

Additional research that has included both men and women has shown a connection between insecure attachments (especially when accompanied by anxiety) and traits related to borderline personality disorder and impulsivity.[91]

The tendency to respond with aggression when there is a threat explains the prevalence of PDs among the incarcerated population. A detailed and extensive analysis of "psychiatric surveys … based on interviews of unselected prison populations" involving 22,790 prisoners from 12 countries determined that 65 percent had personality disorders. Twenty-one percent were characterized as anti-social.[92]

The aggressive activities of criminals may benefit instigators in many ways, but they have an overarching intent: predominance. "People who commit serious crimes are determined to control others. Their self-esteem depends upon it! … Control for the sake of control is an error in thinking in which the person regards interpersonal relationships as arenas for conquests, conquests that are vital to propping up his self-image…."[93]

An inclination toward domination enforced, when necessary, by force is a re-occurring theme in many of the psychological constructs for PDs presented in the *DSM-5*, particularly those characterized as over-bearing, excessively reactive, or impulsive.[94] All, however, represent deviant patterns in socialization. Notable features lacking (or at least diminished) in all serious PDs are compassion and/or the capacity for cultivating companionship. These deficiencies contribute to an ever-expanding disregard for others accompanied by consistently increasing disinterest in social obligations. The *DSM-5* acknowledges this pattern by repeatedly mentioning a habitually damaged interpersonal dynamic as an observable trait for every personality disorder that may be diagnosed with the traditional rubric.[95]

The social ineptitude is associated with intrapersonal rigidity. The *DSM-5* notes, under the heading of "General Personality Disorder" that "The enduring pattern is inflexible and pervasive across a broad range of personal and social situations."[96] That schema represents an individual's outlook and reaction to the world marked by an interior logic that is constrained by preconceived narrowly construed premises about the way the world should operate to conform to egoistical fixations. There is little regard for the perspectives or feelings of others (even when the actual intensity of the inflexibility may not be immediately apparent to a casual observer). Pathological personalities depend on a constructed reality – usually a very fragile one – for security. For this reason, power by whatever means –through passive manipulation or overt force – is essential for maintaining a sense of equilibrium in relationships.

Three selected cases will profile a subject's persistent inflexibility in line with a PD – borderline, paranoid, and narcissistic. A prominent aspect in each case is the presence of the extraordinary emotional constraints apparent throughout multiple situations in the subject's life and – in two of the examples – obvious from childhood. As is often the case with dispositions endemic to rampageous types, the deviant personal traits blend with other precursive attributes. It is less likely for a categorical precursor to exist in isolation than not – a fact that will be emphasized in the final chapter. Nevertheless, in the exemplative narratives that follow, the pathological nature of the killers' personality was the dominate toxic agent that obscured their sense of humanity.

Biographical Analysis: Laurie Dann – Neuropsychological Impairment (Restricted Cognition – Compulsive); Pathological Personality (Borderline Personality Disorder)

She was briefly treated for "manic depression" – essentially what would be diagnosed as bipolar disorder (BD) today – but her actions align with what is now known about borderline personality disorder (BPD).[97] BD will sometimes co-exist with BPD or, more frequently, be mistaken for it. "It is not uncommon for the psychiatrist to see symptoms of both bipolar disorder and BPD, which creates a diagnostic dilemma that must be distinguished by the time of treatment initiation due to their diverging methods of approach. There are similar symptoms that may be seen in clinical presentations of both of these psychiatric disorders...."[98] A diagnostic probability of comorbidity is supported by data accumulated from multiple sources: 96 percent of patients with BPD experience a mood disorder at some point during their life, with lifetime depression reported for 71-83 precent. Disturbances associated with anxiety are extremely common as well: 88 percent develop pervasive anxiety and between 34 and 48 percent experience panic disorder.[99]

In an extensive study involving self-reporting of medical histories and subsequent structured interviews with 610 patients, 40 percent of the subjects who were previously diagnosed with BD, did not manifest as such to trained clinicians, even though they had been previously diagnosed with the syndrome.[100] Pertinent to the diagnosis for Dann, certain descriptors used for manic-depressive disorder in the *Diagnostic and Statistical Manual of Mental*

Disorders, 3rd ed.-Revised (*DSM III-R*) – in use during the time Dann was in therapy – parallel some applied to BPD in the more recent DSM-5.[101] Also relevant is the fact that the clinician that allegedly made that diagnosis, "came into the case late, taking on a patient who was uncooperative, skilled at deception, and severely disturbed."[102]

While Dann frequently displayed the near-hysteria, manipulative tendencies, hypersensitivity, and misplaced antagonism associated with BPD, her history does not show evidence of prolonged periods of frenzy alternating with lethargy endemic to someone struggling with vacillating moods. Furthermore, her aberrant emotions were reactive – a direct result (though extreme) to circumstances. No pattern of unpredictable neurological-biological impulses arising independent of situational determinants has been documented.

Dann was also professionally diagnosed with obsessive-compulsive disorder (OCD), a syndrome sometimes associated with BPD. Commenting on her rampage, one of the psychiatrists who treated her observed, "Violence is not a characteristic trait of obsessive compulsive [sic] disorder."[103] Typically, the observation would be accurate. However, anxiety induced OCD can be symptomatic of BPD, which is partially characterized by anger and over-reactions to ordinary situations.[104]

The OCD diagnosis was based on the Yale-Brown questionnaire, a standard clinical instrument consisting of 67 items. One question was, "Have you ever been constantly preoccupied that you will lose control of your temper and hurt or kill someone even though you do not think that you are that kind of person normally?" Remarkably, she responded, "never."[105] Even so, the two psychiatrists treating her at that point determined that her "OCD was centered on aggressive obsessions and that her compulsions were a reaction to the fear that something terrible would happen and she would be responsible."[106] That explanation for the diagnosis corresponds with observable features for BPD, particularly those relating to "intimacy," "emotional liability," and "anxiousness," described by the alternative model in the *DSM-5*.[107]

OCD is distinct from obsessive-compulsive personality disorder (OCPD). Obsessive-compulsive disorder is marked by repetitive non-productive behaviors, while the personality type exhibits a pervasive perfectionism that consistently interferes with substantial intimate connections. "The essential feature of obsessive personality disorder is a preoccupation with orderliness, perfectionism, and mental and interpersonal control at the expense of flexibility, openness, and efficiency. This pattern begins by early adulthood and is present in a variety of contexts."[108] The crux of the distinction is that OCD is defined by peculiar, frequently debilitating, attributes whereas OCPD is differentiated by a pervasiveness that affects the subject's view of the world and, consequently, sociability. "OCPD has some of the same symptoms as obsessive-compulsive disorder (OCD). People with OCD have unwanted thoughts, while people with OCPD believe that their thoughts are correct."[109] Dann never exhibited the obsession with perfection, order, and job performance that is a hallmark of OCPD. On the contrary, she was frequently unkempt, kept her household in complete disarray, could not hold onto a job, and failed to follow-up with social obligations, such as writing thank-you notes.[110] Dann's compulsions were evident through hoarding, miserliness, and rituals.[111] They were based on her pervasive anxiety that was a symptom of her borderline personality disorder.

Based on empirical studies, neurology, and personal experience in clinical work, one theorist has determined that some people with BPD manifest what may be called "zero degrees of empathy," a mind-set where an individual is incapable of relating on the emotional condition of others."[112] Additionally, individuals with borderline personality disorder "may also funnel their aggression into the external environment."[113] This externalized anger may take the form of intimate partner violence, assault on acquaintances, aggressive criminal acts, and murder (including familicide and serial homicide).[114]

Dann was withdrawn during her middle school years and attended a special education program on a part-time basis where she participated in group counseling sessions.[115] Eventually she confided to the class "she didn't feel she was good at anything, that she couldn't communicate with her parents and she felt like an outcast in her own family."[116] When her classmates made suggestions about how she might behave differently in order to improve her circumstances, she became defensive and resentful.[117] She was already manifesting the "emotional lability" characteristic of individuals with a borderline personality.[118] By the time she was a teenager, Dann began exhibiting that attribute and the others associated with BPD.

According to one of her peers, in high school she wanted to be chosen for the Girls Club and attempted to make the cheerleading squad. Characteristically, in both instances when she was not selected, she angrily stalked away.[119] She had difficulty making friends with other girls but had no trouble attracting members of the opposite sex. "'I perceived a paranoia when girls were around,' a female classmate recalled. 'She always had a boyfriend and was really clingy, draped around him. That really struck me, that she was somehow frightened and had a really unhealthy attachment to boys.'"[120] When her date for the junior prom explained that he was late because he was in a car accident Dann was furious, never bothering to ask if he was injured or even inquire about the details of the collision. Enacting the self-centered nature of BPD, she pouted for the remainder of the evening.[121]

Consistent with her impulsivity after high school Dann changed majors at least three times and attended four separate universities over the course of more than five years while still failing to graduate.[122] She was, however, successful in dating. "Her main interest on campus, said one sorority sister, was not difficult to distinguish: 'Men! She had a lot of dates!'"[123] At the same time, corresponding to secondary school, Dann found it difficult to relate to members of her own gender. She was asked to leave the sorority because she appeared to be disinterested in participating with the group.[124]

During her second year at the University of Arizona (UA) Dann finally met someone that she would see steadily. He was a pre-med student and in Dann's last year at UA they essentially lived together, even though they maintained separate residences. She was possessive and demanding, so much so that she drove away her partner's friends. When he broke up with her – partially because of her smothering behavior –she was devastated and repeatedly called, begging him to renew the relationship.[125] When her marriage to another man dissolved eight years later, she would pester her earlier beau over the phone with pleas and threats. The repetitive contacts did not stop until an attorney notified her parents and demanded that they find a way to control her.[126] These insistent overtures were demonstrative of another attribute associated with borderline personality disorder: "separation insecurity."[127]

In the meantime, though, between her years at the University of Arizona and the harassing calls, she married a wealthy businessman from the Chicago area.[128] Dann immediately exhibited her lack of self-restraint during their honeymoon. Her new husband, after going out without her, returned to their room, and found her masturbating with a vibrator. On another occasion, while walking by another couple's room, they could hear the pair making love through a partially open window. Dann shouted "Hey! ... It can't be that good."[129] The marriage soon became rocky for more serious reasons.

Preoccupied with warding off impending disaster, the attributes of her OCD became more pronounced. She would touch every utility pole and hop over cracks in the sidewalk when walking. When driving she developed a habit of repetitive foot tapping when pausing at stoplights. Before her husband left for work, she would engage in rituals to guarantee his safety. She was unable to hold a job and, at the same time, was inattentive to household duties.[130] Dann would concentrate on items of little importance and consequently would neglect obligations essential to maintaining a life with a modicum of equilibrium. She confided to a friend that when her husband asked her to do something the next day, she would become so preoccupied with the future activity that she would "stay up all night trying to remember to do it."[131] She would then sleep all the following day and forget what she was supposed to do.[132] Dann was describing the incapacitation associated with the chronic generalized anxiety of BPD.

The divorce was almost inevitable, but Dann was so dependent on the relationship she hoped to extend the "proceedings for two or three years."[133] Predictably, beginning with the separation, her condition rapidly deteriorated.

She feigned pregnancy to re-establish the marriage. She contacted the post-office, identified herself as her husband's wife, and put a hold on his mail, then picked it up, inspected it, and kept in the back seat of her car. On one occasion she burglarized his home, poured water on his shirts, and then crouched in a closet.[134] The episodes illustrate how needy she had become, the utter terror she felt about being alone, and her seething wrath over thwarted romance. "Borderlines *rage* at those they love. When people say it is a thin line between love and hate, in borderlines that thin line becomes infinitesimal! Despite all this rage, they describe themselves as a 'empty' inside."[135] That indistinguishable demarcation between affection and hatred is symptomatic of the persistent insecurity binding a person with BPD in relationships – a dread of abandonment that is a prevalent feeling among those with maladaptive character traits.[136]

Perhaps to fill the emotional void of her divorce, Dann took up babysitting with limited success.[137] Though this occupational choice may seem counter-intuitive, it conformed to her flawed personality. It was easy to fake credentials and she could exploit the children's natural dependency. Acting as a caretaker would alleviate her fear of being alone as well as her sense of impending abandonment. One father recalled, "She had an almost childlike quality about her. ... But she had a great uneasiness with adults."[138] Some families ceased to employ her due to bizarre incidents involving theft or damage to furniture.[139]

Ominously, she bought three guns: a .357 Smith & Wesson Magnum (including two boxes of ammunition with 50 bullets each), a .32 Smith & Wesson Revolver, and a .22 automatic Beretta.[140] It is impossible to know, for certain, if she made these purchases because she felt fearful or hostile. Either feeling, though, would be attributable to someone with BPD.

With the marriage dissolution, Dann moved into a room near Northwestern University on the Lakeshore Campus in Evanston, Illinois then, later, relocated to a student facility close to the University of Wisconsin (UW) in Madison. She never enrolled in classes while living at either place.[141] Without the structure of school or a job and with no marital partner to keep her grounded, she degenerated into enacting reoccurring temporary – though sometimes prolonged – deranged frantic states. To employ a commonly used clinical term, Dann was "decompensating" and, in doing so, frequently resorted to OCD mechanisms to cope.[142]

Disorientating events, especially when related to attachment figures, can result in symptoms approximating delusion and/or severe mental disturbance for those individuals with a borderline personality.[143] Relevant to this interplay is the fact that BPD was originally introduced to describe a syndrome on the threshold between neurosis and psychosis.[144] A review of the empirical studies on thought disorders in subjects with BPD conducted by researchers from Department of Psychiatry and Psychotherapy at the University Medical Center in Hamburg Germany and Institute of Psychiatry at King's College in London, concluded by saying, "Psychotic symptoms, especially hallucinations, are highly prevalent in patients with BPD. Recent studies suggest that hallucinations in BPD are similar to those in patients with psychotic disorders in terms of phenomenology, but their emotional impact seems to be even stronger in patients with BPD. ... Although symptoms could be called transient in the sense that they are not constantly present during the day, symptoms are present for long periods of time in a significant proportion of patients." It was calculated that 20-50 percent of those with BPD experienced "psychotic symptoms (hallucinations and paranoid ideation)."[145]

Dann wandered the hallways late at night, and at Northwestern and UW watched television in the common room, persistently switching channels in a repetitious pattern. Also, she perpetually wore a pink sweat suit that had been given to her by her former husband as a birthday present.[146] Students called her the "Psycho Elevator Lady" because she would ride the lift for hours. Her roommate found notes on her desk that appeared to be a schedule for getting on and off particular floors. When punching the buttons, she would use a pencil or cover her fingers with a sleeve.[147]

At the "All-U-Can Eat" cafeteria in the last building where she resided, she would consume multiple helpings, retreat to the restroom, then line up for additional portions. Residents suspected she was bulimic.[148] Eating disorders afflict an estimated 29-53 percent of people with BPD.[149] A longitudinal study over a six-year period involving 290 subjects found that 50% of patients with BPD who did not show evidence of remission also developed some type of eating disorder.[150] Another source has reported that rates of eating disorders among those with PDs are markedly higher than the general population. Bulimia nervosa and BPD have a frequency rate of 28 percent, which is greater than the overall percentage for personality disorders in general with a range of 5 to 10 percent.[151]

Eventually Dann moved back home to live with her parents. Four days later, at the conclusion of an extended rampage, she would commit suicide.[152] Dann – angry at her husband for the divorce, resentful of men in general for her rejection in the face of her need for blind affection, unable to form friendships, isolated inside of her own longing for acceptance – sought vengeance on peripheral acquaintances and strangers who symbolized her naiveté and preoccupied vulnerability.

It started with the preparation of juice boxes and Rice-Krispy treats injected with arsenic.[153] Some parcels were mailed to various individuals including her psychiatrist and ex-husband.[154] The rest she personally delivered. She left the poisonous presents at family homes (at least six of which were previous babysitting clients) and fraternity houses. There were as many as 22 drop-offs. Dann, though, typically (and thankfully), had failed to plan the passive ambush well. The dosages in the concoctions were weak and as a result there were no fatalities.[155]

After her deliveries, she visited the home of a family where she previously baby-sat and picked up two of the younger boys, one four and the other six, telling their mother she was taking them to a carnival. Instead, she drove to an elementary school where the son of a former sister-in-law was a student. There she deposited a homemade bomb in a miniature cardboard house (left over from a social studies project) near the entrance inside. It started a small fire that was extinguished before any real damage took place.[156]

Dann then proceeded to drive to a day-care center attended by children of yet another ex-sister-in-law and tried to enter with a can of gasoline. Not too surprisingly, she was not allowed inside. She returned to the home of her past clients and brought the two children to the basement where their mother was doing laundry. Somehow, she managed to start a fire on the stairs without anybody noticing and made a hasty retreat. Thanks to the mother's bravery and quick thinking the would-be victims escaped.[157]

Still, Dann's violent odyssey continued.

With all three of her guns concealed, she appeared in a second-grade classroom at a school that enrolled other children of previous employers.[158] A substitute who was teaching the class assumed she was an observer, but Dann only stayed a short while before leaving abruptly.[159] She apprehended a first-grade boy near a water fountain and either forced or coaxed him into a restroom. She shot him in the chest with her .22 Berretta. Two other young boys entered as she was leaving the bathroom. Dann attempted to shoot them, but the gun misfired. Leaving the .357 Magnum behind, she returned to the same class and began brandishing the .22. The teacher attempted to wrest the weapon from her, was able to eject live rounds from the gun, and even pulled Dann close to the door whereupon she managed to call for help. However, Dann broke free, threatened the class with her revolver then started firing, seriously wounding four and murdering one.[160]

She tried to escape the area by car but noticed a police roadblock that, ironically, was clearing traffic for a funeral procession. Dann whipped a U-turn but headed into a dead-end street where she crashed her car, then fled on foot, leaving the car engine running. Before doing so, she removed her bloody shorts and tied a plastic bag around her waist.[161] But her destructive foray was not yet over.

With the Beretta and Smith & Wesson, she entered a home where a middle-aged couple was chatting with their 20-year-old son, a student at the University of Illinois and an All-American swimmer.[162]At first, she tried to convince them she was a victim of sexual assault. They even allowed her to use the phone to call her mother and offered her clean shorts. The young man became suspicious of the situation, managed to get his parents to leave, and tried to secure one of her guns. Dann shot him in the chest, ran to an upstairs bedroom, put the revolver in her mouth, and shot. It was by now 7:00 PM and two were dead – a child who thought he was safe at school and a wrathful woman of 30 years of age.[163]

The second subject is this series, Leo Held, showed reoccurring signs of a paranoid personality disorder (PPD). His paranoia was not born of the kind of intense fear or extreme delusions usually associated with schizophrenia rendering a victim with the malady practically incapacitated in ordinary affairs. Instead, his persistent distrust interfered with his social habits.[164] It was not, however, intrusive enough to prevent him from maintaining a relatively stable family life and holding down the same job for close to 20 years.[165] His friends and neighbors viewed him as an "unassuming … husband and father"[166] until such time as a relatively innocuous set of grudges led to a day of methodical violence when he killed six and wounded six more.[167]

Biographical Analysis: Leo Held – Pathological Personality (Paranoid)

After serving in the army and attending college for a short time, Leo Held returned to his hometown of Loganton, Pennsylvania, a tiny berg of 500. He married, had four children, was active in the community, and worked at a nearby paper mill for almost 20 years.[168] He was respected as a devout Christian[169] and, after his rampage, the reverend at his Lutheran church described him as "a level-headed, upright citizen…."[170] He neither drank nor smoked tobacco.[171] Throughout the course of his adult life he served as a school board member, Boy Scout leader, and secretary of the fire brigade.[172] He was also an avid hunter and expert shot.[173]

Held appeared highly reliable in that he steadily worked, was dedicated to his family, involved with his church, and engaged in local enterprises. At the same time, his suspicion and antagonism hampered his actual acceptance in his community. He was able to participate in all the normal encounters of daily life but still resented his co-workers and neighbors. The resentment, though subtle on the surface, was evident under scrutiny.

"Leo was so sick," said one anonymous individual, "There were so many signs that weren't picked up on"[174] Even though he worked at the same job for close to two decades, Held had no close companions on the job due to his persistent distrust of others. He did not participate in frequent lunchtime card games and was viewed by others as an introvert who did not make eye contact with his co-workers.[175] For his commute to and from his workplace, he participated in a car pool for approximately eight years but the others found his driving so erratic that they all eventually dropped out rather than ride with him at the wheel.[176] Though he served on two school boards, fellow members viewed him as unusually reticent with a tendency toward rigidity.[177]

Held displayed his disagreeable nature by feuding with neighbors over trivial matters. He argued with one about smoke from burning leaves and another about a fallen branch. The latter took him to court over assault and battery charges, reporting that he struck her, a 71-year-old widow, with the tree limb.[178]

A little over a year before his extended rampage he saw a local physician complaining of insomnia and general anxiety.[179] According to the *Philadelphia Inquirer* he "felt people at the plant … were talking about him."[180] The accusation is in line with the criterion in the *DSM-5* for reading "hidden demeaning or threatening meanings into benign remarks or events."[181] Prior to the onslaught, Held became increasingly withdrawn and self-involved, even rebuffing an inquiry about his state of mind from an associate.[182]

One morning, a little less than two months after turning 40, he saw his wife off to work and his children off to school then drove alone to his place of employment with two handguns – a .44 Magnum and a Smith and Wesson .38.[183] Holding a gun in each hand, he entered the building and started picking off targets. Part of the attack was conducted in the dark because one of the shots damaged a transformer. Even with that disadvantage, he killed his boss, three colleagues, and a plant superintendent, wounding four others as well.[184]

Then he went to the town's small airport where one of the former members of his carpool worked as an executive assistant. As Held entered the office he pulled out a pistol and his victim dove beneath her desk. He repeatedly shot into it, hitting her four times, seriously wounding her but, gratefully, not fatally.[185] The manager entered the room and, believing the entire incident was a prank, took Held by the arm and escorted him out the door. Oddly, the shooter meekly complied.[186]

To Held more vengeance needed to be had. He drove to a school that three of his children attended but only circled it without stopping and continued to his neighborhood. There he assaulted a family across the street from his own residence, shooting the father to death and injuring the mother while their four-year-old daughter cowered under her bed. He stole a rifle and ammunition then fled to his house.[187]

Police finally confronted Held at his home where he tried to hold them off with the stolen weapon and his other firearms. They tried to talk him into surrendering but he resisted and engaged the officers in a shootout.[188] Giving voice to his feelings of persecution he shouted out, "Come and get me, I'm not taking any more of their bull."[189]

Held was finally apprehended after being shot several times. He died in the hospital two days later.[190] Before passing, he expressed regret, not over the murders, but for failing to fully exact his version of justice. "I had one more to go," he said cryptically.[191]

Paradoxically, Elliot Rodgers was disappointed in his stature along with his attractiveness and, at the same time, was a classic narcissist – a self-indulgent, self-deluded personality that is in Cluster B of the personalities in the *DSM-5*, the grouping reserved for individuals viewed as "dramatic, emotional, or erratic."[192] Excerpts from his autobiography, *My Twisted World: The Story of Elliot Rodger*, manifest a perspective so extravagantly self-centered it borders on mimicry.

Textual Analysis: Elliot Rodger – Perceived Physical Inadequacy (Small Stature, Sexual Disesteem); Destructive Environment (Intimidated); Pathological Personality (Narcissistic)

His "Day of Retribution" began in his apartment when he stabbed to death two roommates and a visitor.[193] He then purchased a triple vanilla latte from Starbucks and drove his BMW to a sorority house where he stopped to pound on the door for several minutes. When there was no response, he sped through the small college community of Isle Vista, near Santa Barbara, shooting his Sig Sauer pistol and deliberately striking two separate bicyclists with his automobile. He killed three more people by gunfire and wounded fourteen before taking his own life after crashing his car.[194]

Hours before rampaging, Rodger sent his autobiographical manifesto to 30 people, including his parents, former teachers, and at least one therapist.[195] One recipient was an acquaintance from an online forum who forwarded it to a local television station in Santa Barbara.[196] Unlike the diatribes circulated by his criminal compatriots, all of which come across as a montage of accusations, unsubstantiated theories, and disjointed dissertations on the blemishes of human virtue, his polemic is a chronological account of his conscious decent from a gleeful, if pampered, boy to an embittered mass murderer. Although it is tedious, egocentric, and devoid of morality – other than Rodger's accusatory sentiments – it is, at least, sequential.

One hundred thirty-seven pages long, covering a span of twenty-two years, it is remarkably detailed, considering that is based solely on Rodger's memory.[197] Even more remarkable is the author's facility in interpretating events wherein he massages every episode and situation, no matter how tiny or innocent, into a tale of his repressed sexuality seemingly aided by the stupefied misunderstanding of those closest to him. The length and tone of the document, even without regard to the content itself, testify to Rodger's unflagging sense of personal exaltation.

It starts with a proclamation.

> Humanity… All of my suffering on this world has been at the hands of humanity, particularly women. It has made me realize just how brutal and twisted humanity is as a species. All I ever wanted was to fit in and live a happy life amongst humanity, but I was cast out and rejected, forced to endure an existence of loneliness and insignificance, all because the females of the human species were incapable of seeing the value in me.[198]

His sense of entitlement is thereby announced, and he reinforced it by stating his inherent, if inadequately recognized, worth.

The narrative then takes on a sequential format connected by Rodger's complaints about a world that has failed him – initially because of family members and friends who assumed their lives had intrinsic merit beyond his wishes, then later due to acquaintances who persistently neglected his insatiable need for admiration and desire for sexual gratification, which, he implies over and over again, he should have by divine design.

He shares a memory of a tantrum that he threw at his third birthday party because he did not receive the first piece of cake.[199] He points out, "It was my birthday after all."[200] The outburst might be pardonable for a preschooler, but Rodger's explanation for it – at twenty-two years of age – is not. The excuse demonstrates his belief in "automatic compliance," an expectation for catering that frames the world view of narcissists.[201] It is also a metaphor for a life story that essentially ends with a deadly fit of rage to express his anger toward a world that ignored his preening.

He befriended a girl of the same age at five years old who was the daughter of friends of his parents and his autobiography foreshadows his reoccurring thematic hostility. "This girl … would eventually come to represent everything I hate and despise; everything that is against me, and everything that I'm against."[202] It turns out, years later that she would grow into an attractive college student and Rodger describes their reacquaintance in later life as follows:

> [M]y mother invited Maddy and Mo Humpreys over for dinner. … Maddy had just graduated from USC, a university renowned for its abundance of spoiled, bratty students who partied all the time. … I often call USC the 'University of Spoiled Cunts.' … Before Maddy came, I stalked her Facebook for a bit, and I saw that she was the exact image of everything I hated in women. She was a popular, spoiled USC girl who partied with her hot, beautiful blonde-haired clique of friends. … They were the kind of beautiful, popular people who lived pleasurable lives and would look down on me as inferior scum, never accepting me as one of them. They were my enemies. … As a child, I played with her as an equal. Now she was my enemy. I would take great delight in torturing and flaying her and every single one of her spoiled, obnoxious evil friends.[203]

Rodger's reaction to the possibility of renewing his childhood friendship is representative of his approach to any opportunity to form any type of relationship. He is, in accordance with narcissistic personality disorder (NPD), "often envious," judging others as shallow for reasons that are themselves entirely trite.[204]

Early on in his account he bemoans his small build, an exaggerated flaw he returns to time and again throughout the narration of his personal story.

> I was very small and short statured for my age. I never gave this much concern during my early childhood, but this fact fully dawned on me the day my family took a trip to Universal Studios. … I found out that there was a Jurassic Park themed ride at Universal Studios, I couldn't wait to go on it. We queued up in the line and waited for an hour. When [we] reached the front, the park staff presented me with a measuring stick, and I didn't fit the requirements. I saw other boys my age admitted onto the ride, but I was denied because I was too short! The ride that I was so excited to enjoy at the theme park was forbidden to me. I immediately fell into a crying tantrum, and my mother had to comfort me.[205]

The unease and accompanying resentment about his physique would continue throughout his life. In his personal narrative he continuously returns to his view of his small size or lack of strength or ill-health at almost every juncture with a memorable event – at age six, nine, fourteen, between thirteen and seventeen, at eighteen, nineteen, twenty-one, and twenty-two.[206]

Of course, many people are small in size and many, also, are not particularly fit. Recognizing their disadvantage, they become adept in other concentrations more fitting to their physicality. "For men, intelligence, job competence, athletic ability, wealth, and power are all routes to positive evaluation in the eyes of others as well as the self."[207] Rodger in contrast, obsessed over his perception of his inadequate stature. The concern is not contrary to his narcissism (as one might immediately assume), but directly tied to it. His disappointment in his physical prowess impeded his quest for admiration and provided him with one more point of reference for envy.

His assumption of superiority (disguised by a slight build) that goes unrecognized, in a world populated with people too superficial to respect it, comprised the entangled view that makes up the theme that is emphasized (and re-emphasized) in his autobiographical manifesto. Every failure or disenchantment (and there are many) in Rodger's short life was related in his mind to the misfortune of his superior nature marred by the curse of a non-muscular body in a society that, as far as he was concerned, adores a singular version of attractiveness.

When promoted out of elementary school he observed in his typical rueful manner: "The boys who girls find attractive will live pleasure-filled lives while they dominate the boys who girls deem unworthy. … I will go on to be rejected and humiliated by girls. … Life is such a cruel joke."[208] Then in middle school he latched onto a sociological belief system that explained his unpopularity and justified his pessimism.

> I noticed that there were two groups of cool, popular kids. There were the skateboarder kids. … [T]hen there were the boys who were popular with girls. … They all seemed so confident and aggressive. I felt so intimidated by them, and I hated them for it. I hated them so much. …
>
> I also observed the girls. I was still very short for my age, and most of the girls were taller than me. …

> I thought all of the cool kids were obnoxious jerks. ... This showed me that the world was a brutal place, and human beings were nothing more than savage animals. Everything my father taught me was proven wrong. He raised me to be a polite, kind gentleman. In a decent world, that would be ideal. But the polite, kind gentleman doesn't win in the real world. The girls don't flock to the gentlemen. They flock to the alpha male. They flock to the boys who appear to have the most power and status.[209]

Rodger laid claim to unique sophistication, which should have given him immediate access to the upper level of the social order, but, once again, he thought his imaginary specialness was unheralded because it was masked by his insufficient height and persistent rectitude. He viewed his male counterparts as brutish, while he saw the female students as nymphs attracted to cavorting masculinity, but incapable of discerning a worthy partner. The passage reveals his craving for status, his jealousy for those who enjoy it, and his burgeoning habit of affixing blame for his social ineptitude on others – in this case on his peers who are crude and his father who failed to instruct him on the harsh realities of a Darwinian juvenile society.

From that point forward each encounter at school became an exemplification of social cruelty and his inability to adjust to civil vagaries or to engage in meaningful reciprocation with others, no matter what their age, regardless of gender. He retreated into the world of online video games, was harassed by other students at school, and failed to impress them when he bragged of attending a premier of a Star Wars movie.[210]

When his stepmother gave birth to a baby boy, he initially recounts the day with a bit of enthusiasm, then discounts it as irrelevant in the larger scheme of his ever-present internal torment. "It was an exciting day. I actually had a brother. ... I wasn't as impacted by his birth as I expected myself to be, because I was caught up in my own personal and emotional changes that I was going through at that stage."[211] His description of feelings and subsequent discounting of their importance is in keeping with the narcissist's maintenance of emotional distance during any experience when s/he is not the central character. "The narcissist, out of touch with his emotions, finds it impossible to communicate them. He disavows their very existence and the existence or prevalence or incidence of emotions in others. He finds the task of emoting so daunting, that he repudiates his feelings and their content and denies that he is capable of feeling at all."[212] Rodger found it difficult to enjoy a once-in-a-lifetime event because he was preoccupied with his failure to dominate the pubescent social hierarchy.

He describes his eighth-grade promotional exercise as a "nightmare" because he felt awkward (as most of his classmates probably did) when he delivered a required soliloquy about his future.[213] He then attended two high schools and was unhappy in each of them.[214]

Finally, Rodger went to a third high school that was a continuation setting structured around independent study, so his presence was required less frequently than in a traditional program.[215] Nevertheless, he managed to find a new reason to disapprove of the other pupils. "I didn't like any of the students there, as they were all slobs with the exception of two or three boys," he notes with his usual derision.[216]

There were relatively few demands on Rodger during the time he finished grades 10-12. Still, he arrogantly objected to the slightest intrusion and was especially outraged that he was sometimes expected to contribute to his household.

> I had heated conflicts with Soumaya [his stepmother] during every week that I was at father's house. All I wanted to do was play WoW [World of Warcraft], and Soumaya strictly limited my playtime. … She kept making me do chores around the house. I despised doing work around the house, especially since we had a nanny who was supposed to do it.[217]

He does write about a single occasion when he reacted quickly to help another family member. However, even in that instance he was concerned more with the transactional nature of the episode than with any sort of familial affection.

> The 4th of July of this year was the day I saved my little brother's life from drowning. …
> The party was a pool party, and my brother Jazz had full exposure to the swimming pool. He had already learned how to walk, but he couldn't swim. At one instance … I saw Jazz quickly run off from the adults, completely unattended. I then watched as he curiously examined the water, and then descended into steps of the shallow end of the pool. Before long, he lost his footing on the steps and his whole body sank into the water. … I ran as fast as I could, plunging into the water with my clothes still on, and pulled him out. I asked him how

> he was doing, and he coughed up some water and told me he felt fine. The only person who saw this happen was a little girl who was swimming in the shallow end. I saved his life, and my brother remembers it to this very day. Every single second of my brother's life, everything that happens to him in the future, will exist because I pulled him out of the water that day.[218]

The lesson that Rodger absorbed from the rescue of Jazz, his younger brother, has nothing to do with his affection for him or brotherly companionship. Instead, Rodger recaps the incident by boasting that he shaped his sibling's destiny and will be the creditor for his very existence from that day forth. He is self-congratulatory and smug.

Years later, as he fantasized about rampaging, he pictured Jazz as one of his victims. The newfound hatred was based solely on jealousy over Jazz's potential allure.

> I had an argument with Soumaya while I was visiting father's house. It started when she began to boast that my brother Jazz was recently signed by an agent to act in T.V. commercials. She said that by the time he is my age, he will be a successful actor. I talked about how Jazz was already so socially savvy for his age, and how I've always envied him for it. …
>
> It is very unfair how some boys are able to live such pleasurable lives while I never had any taste of it, and now it has been confirmed to me that my little brother will become one of them. …
>
> That was the day that I decided I would have to kill him on the Day of Retribution.[219] [Besides his roommates and their friend, all of Rodger's victims, as it turned out, were strangers.]

It is perfectly in keeping with his self-absorbed personality for Rodger to save his brother's life and then later enjoy the idea of murdering him. All associations in the life of a narcissist are expendable and when his younger sibling appears superior to him, he became a threat to Rodger's sensitive ego so was marked for eventual elimination.

Eventually Rodger graduated from high school in the Los Angeles area, where both parents resided.[220] He offers this commentary:

> Not having to go to school anymore gave me a lot of free time to think and brood.

> As time progressed, I realized how hopeless everything in my life was. …
> My hatred for people who have sex festered inside me like a plague. I frequently went on walks around town to brood over how hopeless and unfair everything was. It was better than being stuck in my room all the time. When I saw young couples walking around at the mall, my anger and hatred intensified greatly. It was the worst torture ever to see them making out and being intimate. My life, if you can call it a life, was living hell.[221]

He was idle and unhappy but had no interest in taking proactive steps to rectify the situation to enrich his indolent life or to advance his standing in his community. Rodger believed he simply deserved happiness and that women should be drawn to him without any advances on his part. It never occurred to him that he must actively pursue goals to attain satisfaction or that he should initiate contact to enjoy romance.

Work was not really an option for Rodger, at least not the kind of labor that would be agreeable to him even though he had no advanced education or technical skills. His conceit, as unwarranted as it may have been, prohibited taking on an entry level position. He explains: "The problem was that most of the jobs that were available to me at the time were jobs I considered to be beneath me. … I am an intellectual who is destined for greatness. I would never perform a low-class service job."[222] His father helped him to find a temporary job as an assistant carpenter, which he tolerated until it was completed in three weeks.[223] He then found employment on his own. He wrote: "To my horror and humiliation, the job turned out to be a menial custodial job, and I had to clean offices and even the bathrooms. There was no way I would ever degrade myself to such a level."[224] Rodger had achieved close to nothing at this point in his life. He barely graduated from high school, had been unable to complete course work beyond the secondary level, and was employed by a family friend less than a month. Yet, he believed most work was beneath his dignity. His attitude aligned with the first diagnostic criterion for narcissism – grandiosity without achievement.[225]

Eventually he re-enrolled in college and completed a solitary class.[226] Shortly thereafter his parents agreed to support him in moving to Santa Barbara to attend City College. The arrangement was conditional upon completion of another semester at the school where he was presently enrolled.

He finished two classes and made the change. He is characteristically melodramatic in describing the prospect of his transition while, per usual, is completely unaware of his own responsibility for success in the new setting.

> And so ends another era of my extraordinary and tragic life. I call it the era of Hope and Hopelessness, where I drifted and languished in lonely despair while I lived at my mother's apartment and attended two colleges. …
>
> The move to Santa Barbara is the endgame, the ultimate climax of everything. I saw it as a new chance that was given to me to finally have the things I want in life: love, sex, friends, fun, acceptance, a sense of belonging. …
>
> In truth, the move Santa Barbara was actually a chance that I was giving to the world, not the other way around! … If I still have to suffer the same rejection and injustice even after I move to Santa Barbara, then that will be the last straw. I will have my vengeance.[227]

In truth, Rodger had been toying with the idea of rampaging for at least two years. Later in his vindicative chronicle he states, without a trace of regret, that he remembered at 17 years-old harboring fantasies of inflicting pain on anyone who may have crossed him.[228] The designation of the eventual enrollment at Santa Barbara City College as a final opportunity for the world to recognize his greatness was a cognitive ruse – a form of self-trickery to convince himself that the people he would eventually attack deserved the harm that he intended for them.

Predictably, after his move to the idyllic coastal town, he became discouraged: his roommates failed to meet his standards, the coeds did not fawn over him, his male classmates appeared oafish, other students were indifferent to his presence, and the classes were mundane. He became enraged at a couple expressing their affection for one another while he was enjoying his morning coffee, so he followed them and splashed his drink on them. Driving home one day, he hurled the contents of a latte at two young women at a bus stop because they failed to smile at him. He dropped a math course after crushing on a lady then discovering she had a boyfriend.[229]

Rodger's parents arranged for social skills advising and he had meetings with a young man and later a young woman. Both were only slightly older than him, and the sessions were unsuccessful. Due to his self-consciousness about his physique as well as his emotional fragility, Rodger's capacity for connecting with others was constricted. As a practical matter, his arrogance shielded his interactions. His hyper-critical judgement shortstopped spontaneity or friendly exchanges, making him essentially socially phobic.

"The self-esteem of the shy narcissist is maintained primarily by the use of grandiose fantasies that compensate for perceived inadequacies."[230] Rodger's use of emotional isolation had become ingrained as a mechanism for avoiding any effort at affability. Because it would conflict with his adopted aloofness and conviction of his supremacy, as a matter of course he would resist or reject any intervention requiring that he extend himself – a defensive feint that makes narcissism notoriously difficult to treat.[231] To that point, according to a family friend, Rodger met with therapists off and on since he was eight years of age.[232] Summarizing a final session with a psychiatrist, Rodger said the doctor "ended up giving me the same useless advice that every other psychiatrist, psychologist, and counsellor had given me in the past."[233] Also an unnamed source reported that prior to the shooting he was given a prescription to suppress his paranoia and he refused to take it.[234] Rodger haughtily rationalized the decision by saying, "After researching this medication, I found that it was the absolute wrong thing for me to take."[235] Successful participation in a therapy or voluntarily taking psychotropic medication requires that an individual admit to the existence of problem that is internal, not necessarily outside the person's control.

True to form Rodger dismissed any insight from a college social skills advisor, saying "nothing came out of it."[236] Of a counselor, he said, "It has the same effect as hiring a prostitute, I imagine. It temporarily feels good for the moment, but afterward it makes one feel like a pathetic loser for having to hire a girl when other men could get the experience for free."[237] The description entirely neglects any advice that may have been beneficial, instead concentrating on an analogy to the counselor's sexuality.

As he approached his twenty-second birthday Rodger settled upon a resolution. "I was giving the female gender one last chance to provide me with the pleasures I deserved from them."[238] On a Saturday night in July he took shots of vodka to suppress his hesitancy and roamed a neighborhood where college kids were reveling on the street or hosting open house parties. Annoyed that no one noticed him, he drank the readily available beer, then clumsily confronted an interracial couple who roused his ire first by engaging in conversation with one another then suggesting that he get a drink of water to abate his obvious inebriation. He climbed into a chair on a ledge to observe the festivities but when others joined him without acknowledging his presence, he tried to push them off the balcony. A scuffle quickly ensued, and he was shoved into the street. He staggered away but when he noticed he had lost his sunglasses he returned to reclaim them.[239]

> The people in this house must have been friends with the ones I previously fought with, for they greeted me with vicious hostility. … A whole group of the obnoxious brutes came up and dragged me onto their driveway, pushing and hitting me. I wanted to fight and kill them all. … Eventually, some other people from the street broke up the fight.[240]

He limped home, outraged that nobody, particularly no alluring woman, stopped to help him. As he sulked on his bed, he found that a gold necklace that was a gift from his grandmother was gone. He sobbed until he passed out.[241]

Devoid of insight into his own behavior or empathy for the people that he deliberately antagonized, he assessed his situation in the same manner as Huberty (Chapter Six), using almost identical language. He affixed blame on all the inhabitants of the earth and characterized that eventful evening as the "last chance" when he had already given "the world too many chances." It was now "time for retribution."[242]

Weeks later, Rodger convinced himself that he would be the winner in a million-dollar lottery and spent the greater part of a month visualizing what he called his "victory." He decided, it was his fate, and it would be "the perfect, happy conclusion to the tragic life … in the past."[243] Preoccupied, as he had been his entire life with fantasies of endowed riches, he was consumed with immature wishful thinking that was founded upon his conviction that he was entitled to wealth, whether he earned it or not. When he failed, he became hysterical.

> I raged at the entire world, thrashing at my bed with my wooden practice sword and slashing at the air with my pocket knife. I even downed an entire bottle of wine, and got so drunk that I spilled my wine all over my laptop, permanently destroying it. I soaked my pillow with tears as I drifted off to sleep in my lonely bed.[244]

The next morning, he called his mother and begged her to replace his computer. Of course, she did.[245]

As the year ended, he learned of a Powerball mega-million-dollar lottery in Arizona. Persisting with his magical thinking, he drove all night to buy tickets. He believed, again, he was destined to be successful. "Once I won it, I'd be able to have my beautiful blonde girlfriend, I'd be able to show the world that girls consider me worthy, I'd be able to show the world how superior I am."[246] He failed to win, and he handled it in his usual manner. "I wailed with agony. My tears streamed down my face and stained my collar. I couldn't take it anymore. Feeling the need to talk to someone, I called the only people I had in my life: My parents."[247] They were alarmed at his hysteria and arranged for him to see his psychiatrist when he returned home for the recess between semesters.

The bouts of sadness endured by Rodger came about only because he admired the accomplishments of someone else or felt intense sorrow for himself when reality misaligned with his imaginings.

> Whatever the narcissists experiences as emotions, he experiences in reaction to slights and injuries, real or imagined. His emotions are all reactive, not active. He feels insulted – he sulks. He feels devalued – he rages. He feels ignored – he pouts. He feels humiliated – he lashes out. He feels threatened – he fears. He feels adored – he basks in glory.[248]

Rodger's emotional pain was tethered to the unachieved admiration that he felt was his right.

After speaking to his mother and father during the winter break, he resolved to follow through on the vicious fantasy he had been contemplating for years. He finally acted on the long simmering revenge fantasy, purchasing a Glock 34 semiautomatic pistol.[249]

When setting down plans in his autobiographical manifesto, Rodger anticipates the killing as "the climatic massacre" and "the ultimate showdown in the streets."[250] As his autobiography nears its conclusion Rodger tells of uploading several videos on YouTube to "express" his "views."[251] One is entitled "Why do girls hate me so much?"[252] The description in his narrative is oxymoronic.

> Why do they hate me so much? Why have they never fancied me? Why do they give their love and sex to other men, but not me, even though I deserve them more? In the video, I show that I am the perfect, magnificent gentleman, worthy of having a beautiful

> girlfriend, making the world see how unreasonable it is that I've had to struggle all my life to get a girlfriend. It is my attempt to reason with the female gender, to ask them why they have mistreated me. I was hoping I would get some sort of answer from girls. In fact, a small part of me was even hoping that a girl would see the video and contact me to give me a chance to go on a date. That alone would have prevented the day of retribution, if only one girl had just given me one chance. *But no…* As expected, I got absolutely no response from any girls. The only response I got were from other men who called me names and made fun of me. This just shows how evil and sadistic they are. Oh well, they will realize the gravity of their crimes when I slaughter them all on the Day of Retribution. How dare they reject a magnificent gentleman like me![253]

The succession of postings generated concern on the part of Rodger's mother who called his therapist, who then notified a mental health agency, which, in turn, referred the matter to the Santa Barbara County Sheriff.[254] Four deputies, a city police officer, and a dispatcher in training visited Rodger and spoke to him for approximately ten minutes.[255] Believing that Rodger was "shy, timid and polite," they did not view his videos, search his apartment, or even enter his residence before arriving at the conclusion that he posed no immediate threat to himself or others.[256]

After Rodger's carnage devasted the community County Sheriff Bill Brown would say in an interview on *Face the Nation*:

> Obviously, looking back on this, it's a very tragic situation, and we certainly wish that we could turn the clock back and maybe change some things. … It's very apparent that he was able to convince many people for many years that he didn't have this deep, underlying obvious mental illness that also manifested itself in this terrible tragedy.[257]

In contrast, Rodger wrote in his manifesto:

> I tactfully told them that it was all a misunderstanding, and they finally left. … For a few horrible seconds I thought it was all over. When they left, the biggest wave of relief swept over me. It was so scary.

> It was all because of the videos. … I immediately took most of them off of YouTube, and planned to reupload them a few days before the Day of Retribution. This incident made me realize that I needed to be extra careful. I can't let anyone become suspicious of me. All it takes is for one person to call the police. … For the next few days, I felt extremely fearful that they could show up anytime. I kept one of my handguns with a few loaded magazines near me just in case such a thing did happen. If they did show up, I would have to try to quickly shoot them all and escape out the back window. I would then have to perform a hasty mockery of my plans, with the police on my tail. That will ruin everything. Thankfully, all suspicion of me was dropped after I took down the videos from YouTube, and the police never came back.[258]

There are two features – one pertaining to his duplicitous nature and another regarding his devolution – that are apparent from the welfare check and Rodger's reaction to it.

The first observation is that he deftly deceived six people in law enforcement who, in their professional lives, surely must have encountered lying many times. Truth-default theory holds that when making an inquiry a questioner tends to presume that the respondent is telling the truth. That presumption is partially upheld when the demeanor of the queried subject appears honest (even though such may not be the case). It may be aided further when answers are partially true or simply exclude extraneous information so that they fit into an assumption of reality.[259] Rodger, probably without full conscious realization but, nevertheless, with finesse, employed both stratagems. He was "courteous" and "was able to convince the deputies" that he was simply having "some social problems."[260]

His deception was aided by his deference and massaging of details. "The narcissistic personality is quite gifted at bamboozling and conning others."[261] A narcissist effectively grifts others with acting prowess and verbal facility, skills that Rodger had mastered by extorting his parents and steering his way through school with minimal effort.

> In the narcissist's surrealistic world, even language is pathologized. It mutates into a weapon of self-defense. … They hide and evade and avoid and disguise. In their planet of capricious and arbitrary

> unpredictability, of shifting semiotic and sematic dunes – they perfect the ability to say nothing….[262]

The conversation with authorities that took place outside his door highlights the finely honed usuary that had become ingrained in Rodger's character.

The second point is that at this juncture Rodger is firmly committed to killing. Not only does he attempt to guarantee the success of his deranged plan by misrepresenting his dejected mood, he rushes to remove any clues to his intentions that may be lingering the internet. He is no longer fantasizing. He is strategizing, emphasizing in his final post:

> You will finally see that I am, in truth, the superior one, the true alpha male. … Yes. … Now I will be a god compared to you. You will all be animals. You are animals and I will slaughter you like animals and I will be a god exacting my retribution on all of those who deserve it and you do deserve it just for the crime of living a better life than me.[263]

Rodger's spectacularly vengeful attack is then contrived to maximize the possibility of public attention.

The primary aberration of an ineffectual personality is its immobility. No matter what situational variants may arise, the individual responds with the same set of misshapen tools for interacting with those within his or her sphere of influence – oppression, aggression, deceptive passivity – whatever techniques for dominating may permeate his or her character. This method for handling the many vagaries of life may be immediately satisfying in certain instances but damaging to psychological adaptivity in the long run. The self-imposed limitations to adjustment constrain responses and habituate rationalizations shielding the pathological personality from social influence.

Chapter Six

Intersections

What the hammer? what the chain,
In what furnace was thy brain?
What the anvil? what dread grasp.
Dare its deadly terrors clasp?
– William Blake
"The Tyer"

Attributing any human activity to a single causal factor would border on sophistry. Throughout this work it has been repeatedly emphasized that the conditional elements examined – perceived inadequate physiology, destructive/oppressive environmental circumstances, neuropsychological impairments, and pathological personality characteristics – are rudiments, not solitary perpetuating agents, in the deviant cognitive-emotional construct that supports the rationale to enact mayhem.

Furthermore, these predecessors do not typically present themselves in isolation. Instead, in most instances, more than one is apparent and, in some cases, multiple precursors may be evident. The juxtaposition of these factors aligns with what is often referred to as "General Strain Theory" – the explanatory perspective on crime that holds that multiple conditions and events, not temporally synchronized, but connected in the mind of the criminal, converge to fashion a lifestyle outside of societal parameters.[1]

A philosophy of life, no matter how disjointed or destructive, originates from an attempt to apply coherence to events and situations that are not unified and may even seem random. The disturbed mind's decent toward violent irrationality is frequently initiated by multiple categorical elements in the pre-dispositional paradigm coalescing for degeneration.

Most of the cases discussed in previous chapters have exhibited more than one precondition. Eric Harris was self-conscious about his concave chest while decidedly psychopathic. A related observation holds true for Eliot

Rodger, who identified himself as less attractive than his peers but was, counterintuitively, unabashedly narcissistic. Both demonstrated a perception of physical inadequacy along with pathological personality traits. Andrew Blaze's narcissism was such a dominant force in his life that he obsessed over self-directed online videos in which he was a star, and yet his dislike for his birth gender was so consuming that it was dysmorphic. Scott Pennington was ashamed of his dysfluent speech patterns and at the same time experienced destructive/oppressive environmental circumstances with an abusive father, a mother who exhibited signs of psychosis, and harassment from his classmates.[2] Laurie Dann had a pathological personality complimented by compulsions.

Rampageous assailants will sometimes feature an unfortunate integration of willful malignancy with neural derangement or psychiatric disorders.

> The comorbidity of personality disorders and mental disorders may arise from direct relations between symptoms of the two psychological disorders. We may not need latent variables or diseases to explain this type of comorbidity. … An anti-essentialist stance objects the view that clusters of symptoms reflect and should be explained by an underlying disorder essence. The idea that there exist meaningful links between the constructs of personality disorder and mental disorder corresponds with a psychodynamic understanding of psychopathology.[3]

The characterological flaws may present either in isolation or in any combination as negative affect, reduced capacity for empathy, antagonism, or habitual impulsivity.[4]

The inextricable relationship has been recognized in the taxonomical development of personality profiling.[5] Dual diagnoses are widely recognized and accepted, especially in regard to anti-social traits. "Studies agree unanimously that psychopathy is a highly comorbid disorder. Generally, comorbidity among patients studied in society is 90%, in emergency rooms 89%, and in psychiatric clinics 84%."[6] A much larger and more recent sampling of 3,258 randomly selected adult household residents in Canada "revealed an increased prevalence of nearly every other psychiatric disorder in those with antisocial personality disorder, with 90.4% having at least one other lifetime psychiatric diagnosis."[7] When the issue is examined from another angle – that is, the presence of anti-social personality disorder among those with serious neuropsychiatric conditions – concurrent conditions again appears prevalent. In a tertiary care hospital among 116 patients, personality disorders in general were found for 21.55 percent (CI: 95%) with avoidant being the most frequent, but anti-social second (5.17%).[8]

The emotional imbalance of James Huberty with his physical disabilities and parental abandonment compounded his hostility to amalgamize into multiple murder. Huberty is infamous for conducting a ruthless sudden mass assault on 45 or more unarmed civilians at a McDonald's restaurant in Southern California.[9] His narrative illustrates how the reactive exchange of dispositional conditions distorts perspective.

This chapter will then close with a summation of the categorization of precursive attributes and circumstances including identified intersections for 112 cases.

Biographical Analysis: James Oliver Huberty – Perceived Physical Inadequacy (Prolonged and Pronounced Illness); Destructive Environment (Injurious Family Relations); Neuropsychological Impairment (Depression, Anxiety, Paranoia); Pathological Personality (Negative Affect)

Huberty endured all four categorical preludes to a rampage-prone mentality: chronic physical disadvantages, a disrupted and dispirited environment, a distortion in neurologic functioning, and a pathologic personality distinguished by waves of negativity (see Table 1.1). The first came from contracting polio at three years of age, leaving him with bouts of spastic paralysis and trouble walking for the rest of his life.[10] The next circumstance, though, was even more traumatic. His mother left the family to become a Lutheran missionary when Huberty was merely seven years old and his sister was eleven.[11] According to neighbors, from that point forward he was raised mainly by his grandmother.[12] After the abandonment he became sullen and irritable, moods he frequently exhibited for the rest of his days.[13]

He was also a social isolate. A neighbor who lived down the road from the family farm where Huberty grew up said that he "spent most of his time by himself." She recalled taking him to a barbecue in a nearby town when he was a teen, saying, "He just did not want to mix, he didn't want to talk to people."[14] He was an innocuous figure during high school, graduating 51 in a class of 77, without participating in sports or clubs. One of his teachers remembered him as a "loner," who "didn't have many friends."[15] As a result of his serious illness in early childhood followed by his mother's departure,

Huberty was exhibiting signs of depression along with apprehension in settings calling for personal interactions.

Anxiety in all its mutations is frequently noted as the most frequent mental health problem among children and adolescents, while its more specialized offspring, social phobia, is the most widespread in the population in general.[16] The latter, according to the *DSM-IV Training Guide for Diagnosis of Childhood Disorders*, will typically manifest "in mid-adolescence following a history of social inhibition in childhood."[17] That description coincides well with a timeline for Huberty's emotional dissolution.

Chronic anxiety is very much a neurobiological disorder and, given that fact, along with the generalized vulnerability of young people, it is not surprising that it is among "the earliest of all forms of psychopathology to emerge."[18] The onset and continuance of nervous reactions to ordinary situations are often initiated and maintained by worry about an inability to exert meaningful control during life's important events. A study of 117 youths 9-17 years of age, assessed the intensity of the participants' anxious preoccupation "and their perceptions of control over anxiety-related events. … Findings indicated that perceived control over anxiety-related events was significantly negatively correlated with self-reported anxiety levels."[19]

Huberty used firearms as a mechanism to assert himself. As a youngster he enjoyed shooting heads off cabbages and going into the woods for target practice at night.[20] After his grandmother died and his father remarried Huberty would announce his arrival for visits by getting out of his car and firing warning shots.[21]

The absence of his mother while he was growing up was so disturbing that his wife of 19 years was acutely sensitive to its impact.[22] A few days after Huberty's rampage, she wrote a letter to a local television station (KFMB) and made a point of emphasizing her husband's dispirited life as a child. "He has always been a nervous person who could not take much pressure. He had a very unhappy childhood. … He came from a broken home. He was always very sad and very lonely. His only close friend was his dog, Shep," she wrote.[23]

Huberty's initial choice for an occupation may have been a product of his isolation. He started work on a degree in sociology – an odd major for a person so uncomfortable with socializing – but then became a licensed embalmer, a job which conceivably could have been a match for his solitary inclinations.

Even so, his work in the funeral business was unsuccessful. He was skilled at preparing bodies but had difficulty dealing empathetically with clients.[24] A former supervisor remarked that Huberty "didn't like being around the public."[25] Ultimately, his inability to meaningfully relate to others, initiated by the debilitating illness in his pre-school years then complimented by maternal abandonment, interfered with his aptitude in any vocation.

While involved in his mortuary studies Huberty met his future wife who he married in 1965. The couple had two daughters.[26] Their marriage would last up until the day Huberty was killed as he held siege at the fast-food stand in 1984.[27] Although the union was long lasting, it was not particularly tranquil. In one instance, his wife filed a report of spousal abuse with the Department of Children and Family Services, saying Huberty had injured her jaw.[28]

Before his massacre, Huberty also attacked others even more hapless. After a neighbor complained that Huberty's German Sheppard damaged the neighbor's car, Huberty resolved the situation by shooting the canine in the head. In a separate incident he threatened to shoot another dog after it defecated on his lawn.[29]

Throughout his adult life, to the extent that his stunted maturity could maintain, he remained steadfastly devoted to his family. However, due to his chronic irritability and limited interpersonal skills, he was often cruel. A former neighbor, who knew the family well, remembers that his daughters would appear with welts on their faces.[30] She recalls that the thirteen-year-old sister told her that "her daddy had slapped her around."[31]

Perhaps to compensate for his impulsive cruelty, he was belligerently over-protective of his children. On one occasion as part of an ongoing feud with another parent, he called to say ominously, "One of these days when you least expect it, I'm going to get you alone."[32] Huberty eventually became obsessively concerned with other, more catastrophic threats. He slipped into a survivalist mentality, stockpiling food, essential supplies, and, of course, weapons.[33] According to a co-worker at that time, who shared his enthusiasm for weaponry, Huberty's collection consisted of pistols, rifles, shotguns, and an Uzi.[34]

Like many of the rampaging assailants before and after him, Huberty showed unmistakable signs of paranoia. By the time he conducted his mass assault he had adjusted to his unhappy memories as well as the more recent disappointments in his life by continually nursing delusions and blaming others. "He didn't like anybody," observed the San Diego Police Chief.[35] His ability to care for his loved ones – the obligation that ran counter to all the misfortunes he experienced as a young boy – was challenged in a fundamental way when he was laid off due to an economic downturn.[36]

"My husband was terminated on November 15, 1982," his widow relayed in her letter to KFMB-TV, "His world came crashing in around him."[37] The couple liquidated their property, but the transaction did not go well, and the financial pressure mounted.[38] Huberty sought additional employment and was successful for a few months but then he lost his new position as well.[39] "Hey, I have nothing to live for. I got no job or anything," he reportedly complained to a former colleague.[40] As the situation worsened, Huberty's delusional thoughts intensified. Apparently feeling that their mutual interests assured some level of simpatico, he confided in the former workmate who had seen his arsenal. "He blamed the whole country for his misfortune. He said that Ronald Reagan and the government were conniving against him. The working class were going to pay for this inflation. ... He became so discouraged he wrote the Mexican government and applied for residence," his acquaintance related.[41] His persistent fatalism was bolstered when he was involved in a traffic collision that left him with a tremor in one hand and incapable of continuing his work as a welder.[42]

Huberty reacted by suspecting the entire social order of malevolent intent, by externalizing his locus of control, and with severe depression. In one dramatic encounter, he pointed one of his many guns to his temple, but his wife stopped him before he could shoot. She left the room to hide the gun and when she returned found him crying as he sat on the couch.[43]

To quell his agitation, Huberty's wife would sometimes pretend to read Tarot cards to predict his future.[44] This pacification measure is indicative of the intense nervous dread he was feeling and its connection to his immature disposition. He was placated by the invocation of magical predictions. The application of mystical hope through a set of inanimate symbols in a deck is comparable to a transductive inference. Identified by Jean Piaget as part of genetic epistemology, illogical reasoning of that sort is used by children during the preconceptual substage of the preoperational stage of development. It is characterized, in part, by the assignment of cause and effect to random occurrences.[45] "[It] is a type of flawed logic that is most commonly used by very young children to connect meaning between events where there is no correlation. With adulthood it takes the form of ... being fooled by randomness."[46] Research shows a connection between assuaging stress and wishful thinking, especially when it relies upon religion or superstition.[47] Referring to Table 3.1, it is evident that Huberty's ability to cope with stress was stuck with the limitations of the pre-operational/pre-conventional stage, coinciding with the time his mother left.

With no employment prospects in Ohio, Huberty moved his family to Tijuana, just south of the border between Mexico and California. Without knowing the language, culture, or locale, Huberty was unable to scrape together a living. He moved north, back to the states, to San Ysidro, and with the help of a government training program secured a job as a security guard.[48] In a short time he was dismissed due to "a general instability . . . plus the fact that he was not performing his duties in a proper manner."[49]

With that dismissal Huberty suffered what he surely interpreted as one more injury – this time an unsustainable one – and with it, his limited equanimity along with his declining personal efficacy completely collapsed. He became obsessed with the inevitability of global devastation.[50]

Dystopian beliefs are sometimes adopted by individuals with a fragile self-esteem and a personal perception of vulnerability.[51] Huberty's indulgence in this type of escapism was similar to the reassurance he gratefully absorbed when his wife assumed the role of an oracle while doing Tarot card readings.

His delusional frame of reference at this point was so pervasive that he was close to a psychotic break. His former wife reported that he "began hearing voices and seemed to be talking to people who were not there."[52] On one occasion he approached a police officer and calmly announced that he was a war criminal. He was taken to the federal building on the border, interrogated, then released, whereupon he walked two miles to return home.[53]

At his wife's urging Huberty finally called a mental health clinic, seeking counseling.[54] The receptionist misspelled his name and besides, because of Huberty's monochromatic tone, determined that it was a "non-crisis" situation and failed to handle the communication as an emergency.[55] Huberty waited for hours for a return call that never came – "a broken promise in his mind just like so many others."[56] He gave up and took a solitary ride to the beach on his motorcycle.[57]

The next day he attended traffic court over a minor infraction. Since he was relatively new to the state, Huberty was let off with a warning. He took his family to lunch at a McDonald's and then to the zoo.[58] It may have been a family outing but there was also an air of foreboding. Huberty confided to his wife that he believed his life was over and he made an ominous farewell declaration, "Society had their chance."[59] His mind was made up.

After the day's excursion, he left his family at home. He was wearing army fatigues (purchased from an army surplus catalogue) with a black t-shirt, and he carried a canvas bag with hundreds of rounds of ammunition, as well as three firearms.[60] In an unusual display of sentiment, he kissed his wife before going out.[61] As he was leaving, he said, "I'm going hunting – hunting humans."[62] He told his oldest child, "Goodbye. I won't be back."[63]

He took three weapons carefully selected from his collection of over 300 firearms, wrapped in a checkered blanket: the Uzi, a Winchester pump-action shotgun, and a 9mm semi-automatic pistol.[64] Minutes before 4:00 in the afternoon he entered a McDonald's just a little more than one-tenth of a mile from his house.[65] Approaching the counter, he aimed his shotgun at the sixteen-year-old behind the counter. He pulled the trigger, but the weapon misfired. Believing it to be a prank, the employee disregarded Huberty and turned away.[66] Obsessed as he was with his perception of continual slights, Huberty must have interpreted the subdued reaction as one more insult. When Huberty fired at the ceiling the attendant along with the other staff and the patrons realized the situation was dire. Huberty indiscriminately began shooting anyone within range.[67]

After the initial shots, one brave soul approached Huberty to try to calm him.[68] "He was shot 14 times as a result and murdered."[69] A surviving witness remembers Huberty shouting, "You dirty swine Vietnam assholes … I've killed a thousand and I'll kill a thousand more!"[70] In fact, there is no record of Huberty serving in the military.[71] He was, at long last, conducting war against a world that had repeatedly betrayed him and his militaristic cry, like his clothing, was part of a cataclysmic enactment of revenge.

He shot 40, including a four-month old baby girl, a pregnant woman as well as her infant daughter, three boys outside the facility as they arrived on bicycles, and an unsuspecting elderly couple as they entered the establishment.[72] Seventy-seven minutes after it began, the tragedy came to its conclusion when Huberty was finally taken out by a single shot from a sniper stationed across the street on the roof of a post office.[73] Counting the unborn child, 21 were dead.[74] Another victim died from wounds the following day in the hospital.[75] At that time the number of victims was the highest for any shooting, outside of war, in the country.[76]

Counterproductive Symbiosis among Preconditions

The Appendix documents the circumstantial overlap among 112 who fit the definitional criteria set forth in the introduction. That table catalogues the circumstances or syndromes that prefaced the devolvement of all of the rampage attackers included in this book along with *How Rampage Killers Interpret Their Worlds* and a few others as well.

It encompasses assailants from multiple localities, but the offenders from modern China are largely absent. A knife-wielding assailant rampaged at a school in a central China village on the same day that Lanza carried out his massacre in Connecticut.[77] Revealingly, the slashing in the People's Republic went largely unreported while Lanza's school shooting at Sandy Hook is well-known. Despite the efforts on the part of the Chinese government to obfuscate the sociological forces behind mass murder, the phenomena in that country, as it does throughout the world, persists. It is unfortunate, considering the multiple (and gruesome) instances of extreme violence in the nation, but it is virtually impossible, because of state control of the media, to ascertain the background of multiple murderers in that jurisdiction.[78]

The tableau represented in the Appendix is a categorical amassment of situations and/or characteristics worldwide that preceded rampages enacted in various ways.[79] The multiplicity of the circumstances and traits contributes to an explanation for the seemingly illusive nature of the dispositions of autogenic assailants, while, at the same time, the grouping dispels the fable of inexplicable variance. A diagram illustrating the frequency of preconditions in isolation as well as the various intersections constitutes Figure 6.1.

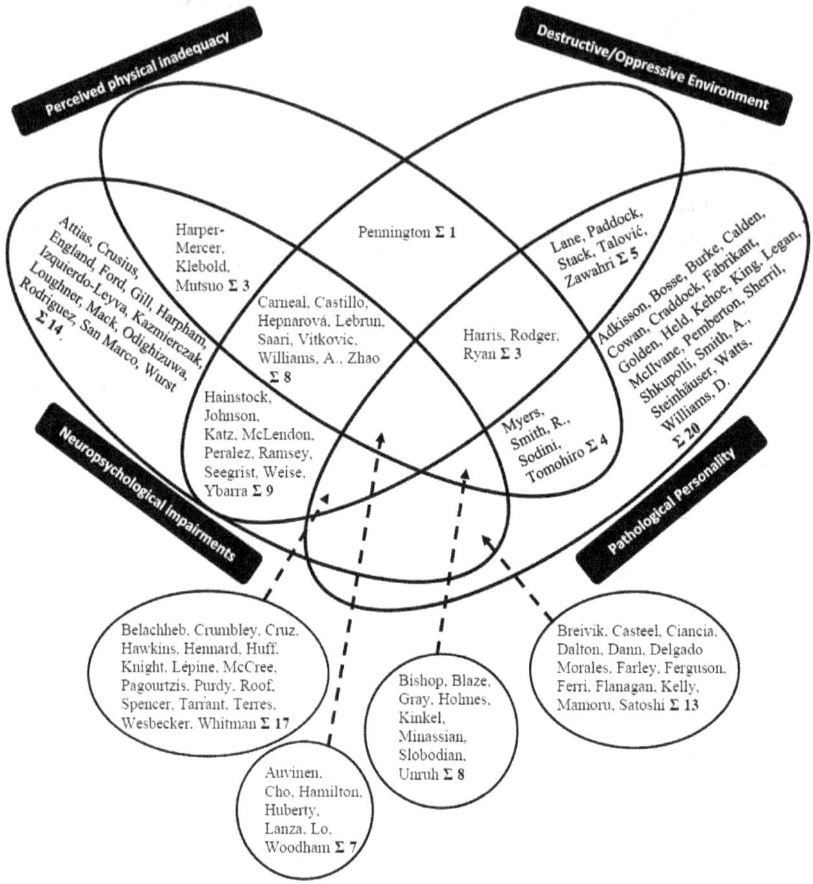

FIGURE 6.1. Venn Diagram of Dispositional Conditions among a Purposive Sample of Rampage Assailants as presented in Appendix.

The remarkable number of overlapping indicators highlights the complex and probable interactive nature of underlying influences in the dissolution of the consciences of autogenic offenders. Less than one-third of the aggressors in the sample were influenced by a single precursor – 14 neuropsychological, and 20 pathological personality (34/112 = 0.303). Those classifications contain a broad range of internalized attributes and many of the subjects manifested multiple traits included in those categories. When broad overlapping conditions (as delineated in Table 1.1 and Appendix A) are considered, 71 percent (79/112 = 0.705) appeared to be struggling with a mental illness or mood disorder and more than two-thirds (77/112 = 0.687) showed signs of a dysfunctional personality of one kind or another. Pathological personal indicators combining solely with psycho-emotional difficulties were only influential at a rate slightly above 10 (13/112 = 0.116).

Substantiating the introductory comments in Chapter Four, less than 13 precent (0.125) of the rampageous assailants in the selection displayed evidence of a neurological or emotional disturbance as their only predisposition. Contrary to prevailing popular thought, environmental factors, whether related to childhood trauma or intimidating experiences in later life, were not, by themselves, influential agents and even when combined with a perception of physical deficiency the percentage was close to nil (1/112 = 0.008). On the other hand, in the totality of precursors, when the psychological toll related to a damaging environment was adjoined to one or more, the influence was evident in close to 45 percent (50/112 = .446) of the sample cases.

Nevertheless, regardless of the complexity of a murderous predilection, the character traits and/or situational conditions merely form the backdrop for the psychological degeneration that shapes the ruthless dedication that leads to sudden massacres.

Afterword

As emphasized in the Forward, Introduction, and Chapter One the primary premise of this book is that autogenic mass murderers emerge because they are hindered in their maturation by one or a combination of adverse factors. That hindrance, however, is not a cause. It is a condition that allows the gestation of unsavory thoughts and reactive habits, just as a petri dish provides an environment for the germination of microbial substances while the actual culturalization itself is attributable to biological actions and reactions.

The morphology that follows from those circumstantial adversities composes the thematic core in *How Rampage Killers Interpret Their Worlds*. The formation of rampageous decision-making can only be appreciated by recognizing the devolutionary process narrated in that text. Sources suggesting preventive measures are presented at its conclusion.

Appendix

Dispositional Conditions among a Purposive Sample of Autogenic Assailants

General note on referencing: Most of the subjects in this table are contained in this book (*Why Rampage Killers Emerge: Conditions and Characteristics – WRKE*) or its compliment (*How Rampage Killers Interpret Their World – HRKITW*). The chapters with the most thorough profile of the rampageous individual appears as the last entry in the column below each name. Relevant documentation is available in those locations. Those referents are to substantial portrayals, not brief explanatory comments about the individual, which may appear elsewhere but can be readily located through the indices. When additional background, apart from previous descriptions or analyses in the body of either book, was necessary to support characterizations relevant to the table, then the necessary sources are cited. For those few subjects not covered in this book or its companion, a brief description of the relevant rampage is supplied in the first column. Unless otherwise cited, ages, gender, and weapons employed were extracted from the material used to fashion the initial sketch or from one of two sites: Murderpedia: The Encyclopedia of Murderers, last updated June 4, 2017, http://www.murderpedia.org/; School Shooters .info: Resources on School Shootings, Perpetrators, and Prevention, last updated March 21, 2024, https://schoolshooters.info/.

Special note on subject selection: The sample is purposive with the requirement for inclusion being conformance with the operational definition for rampage killing used throughout both books (established in both Introductions).

Special note on categorization: Assignments were made due to observable features, conditions, or behaviors represented in the synopses in the relevant cells. As mentioned in a note for Table 1.1, determinations for personality pathologies were predicated on the clinical diagnostic method or by traits designated with the alternative multidimensional approach. If the later was used, the primary domain was applied with the appropriate attributable criteria for each case listed in parenthesis. For more detail, consult: American Psychiatric Association, *Diagnostic and Statistical Manual of Mental Disorders,* 5th ed. (*DSM-5*, Arlington Virginia: American Psychiatric Association, 2013), 645-646, 770-781. For consideration of the conceptual issues on personal pathology, see: Timothy J. Trull and Christine A. Durrett, "Categorical and Dimensional Models of Personality Disorder," *Annual Review of Clinical Psychology* (2005): 355–380.

Killer, age (at rampage), gender, weapons used and/or carried; referent or description	Perceived physical inadequacy	Destructive/ Oppressive environment	Neuropsychological impairments	Pathological personality
Jim David Adkisson, 58, male, shotgun; *HRKITW*, 5, Appendix A.				Antagonistic (attention seeking, grandiose, callous, hostile): said murders were heroic, slaughtered church congregation during a musical, blamed unemployment on politics, rationalized rampage as a political act.
David Edward Attias, 18, male, automobile; *HRKITW*, Table 6.3.			Restricted or distorted cognition: history of frenetic behavior, prolonged substance abuse. Mood disordered: diagnosed as bipolar.[1]	

Pekka-Eric Auvinen, 18, male, attempted arson, .22 caliber pistol; *HRKITW*, 4, Appendix A.	Limited stature.[2]	Hostile community: intimidated by peers, documentation of bullying during elementary and middle school years.[3]	Mood disordered: extreme social anxiety, symptoms of depression.[4]	Narcissistic: grandiose, put hundreds of videos online, considered others inferior;[5] dubbed himself "Sturmgeist89" (translated in English as "Stormghost"), referred to himself as "godlike atheist";[6] fancied himself as an "Ubermensch" in warped interpretation of Nietzsche.[7]
Abdelkrim Belachheb, 39, male, semiautomatic pistol; *HRKITW*, 2, 4, Appendix A.		Unsupportive living conditions: estranged from father.	Restricted cognition: at least one severe head injury as a child.	Anti-social (sociopathic): unfaithful to spouses, habitually lied and cheated, violent outbursts, exploited affections.
Dr. Amy Bishop, 44, female, handgun; *WRKE*, 1, 2; *HRKITW*, 7.	History of severe allergies, hives, eczema.		Hallucinatory: reported she heard voices, treated with Haldol for paranoid schizophrenia after arrest.[8]	Narcissistic: boasted about intellect; overreacted to tiny slights, consistently desired deferential treatment, insisted she was superior, demeaned others, continual conflicts with colleagues, neighbors.

Andrew Blaze (Randy Stair), 24, male body, identified as female, shotguns; *WRKE*, 2; *HRKITW*, Appendix A.	Gender dysphoria, body image dissatisfaction: repulsed by male features.		Mood disordered: depressed, longed to die, acted out suicide on YouTube. Delusional: convinced himself that a cartoon character was alive, left message encouraging imaginary followers.	Detachment (anhedonic, withdrawn, intimacy avoidant, suspicious): lost interest in simple pleasures, channeled time and thought into self-serving videos and fantasies. Antagonistic (deceitful, grandiose, callous, hostile): misrepresented self to co-workers, arrogantly lied to family, talked casually of his superiority, raged over minor irritants.
Sebastian Bosse, 18, male, explosives, handguns, knife, sawed-off rifles, smoke canisters; *HRKITW*, 2				Negative affect (anxious, hostile, depressed): considered himself an outcast; repeatedly expressed feelings of futility; resented peers, school, country, human beings. Antagonistic (grandiose, callous, hostile): pictured himself as a grand avenger, fantasized scenes of carnage and

				death, repeatedly expressed disdain for others.
Ander Breivik, 32, male, explosives, semiautomatic rifle, semiautomatic pistol; WRKE, 4; *HRKITW*, 7			Delusional: imagined himself as an exalted leader of a noble army guarding a pure homeland.	Narcissistic: constant exhibitions for admiration, haughty, impervious to suffering of others, sadistic.
David Augustus Burke, 35, male, revolver, plane crash; *HRKITW*, 5				Anti-social (sociopathic): robbed employer, unfaithful to lovers, kidnapped romantic partner and child, cultivated image of innocence.
Paul Calden, 33, male, semiautomatic handgun; *HRKITW*, 2.				Detached (withdrawn, intimacy avoidant, suspicious): socially isolated, lived alone, spent time on solitary pursuits (e.g., video games). Antagonistic (callous, hostile): threatened lawsuit over salary, shouted and swore at fellow worker in parking lot dispute; brought handgun to work to intimidate others.[9]

Michael Carneal, 14, male, pistol, rifles, shotguns; *WRKE*, 2; *HRKITW*, Appendix B.	Limited stature.	Hostile community: intimidated and mocked by peers.	Delusional: imagined beings inhabiting crawl space in home, thought people were spying on him, auditory hallucinations.	
Luther V. Casteel, 42, male, handgun, pistol, sawed-off shotgun; *HRKITW*, 6, Table 6.3.			Distorted cognition: inebriated.[10] Mood disordered: depressed (self-diagnosed).[11]	Anti-social: no remorse, history of criminality, fearless, regretted losing freedom but not killing, married three times;[12] at trial testified, "I'm not someone who asks for mercy or pity for my actions. … I have absolutely no fear of anything anyone can put upon me."[13]
Alvaro Rafael Castillo, 18, male, pipe bombs, semiautomatic rifle, shotgun, smoke grenades; *WRKE*, 3; *HRKITW*, 4.	Unsatisfactory appearance: obese.	Injurious familial relations: subject to abuse by father, witness to domestic violence.[14]	Distorted cognition: spent a week in psychiatric facility, paranoid. Mood disordered: suicide attempt, self-abuse.[15]	
Cho Seung-hui, 23, male, 2 semiautomatic pistols; *HRKITW*, Introduction, 3, 5, Appendix A.	Prolonged childhood illness: pneumonia, whooping cough, heart defect, medically	Hostile community: taunted by peers at school.[17]	Restricted cognition: possibly on autistic spectrum: severe social anxiety, flat affect, selective mutism. Mood disordered: wrote poems and	Detachment (withdrawn, intimacy avoidant, anhedonic, depressed, limited affect, suspicious): stalking, stilted socializing, averted eye

	fragile in preschool years.[16]		stories describing despair, suicidal.[18]	contact, juvenile fantasies of romance, sweeping resentment in manifesto.[19]
Paul Anthony Ciancia, 23, male, assault rifle; conducted a shooting rampage at the Los Angeles International Airport, killing a Transportation Security Administration Officer and wounding two other TSA employees, plus a civilian.[20]			Mood disordered: family worried that he was suicidal.[21]	Detachment (withdrawn, intimacy avoidant, suspicious): socially inhibited throughout his life;[22] compared transportation security system to Nazism and called officials "tyrants."[23]
Frederick William Cowan, 33, male, 2 semiautomatic handguns, 2 pistols, hunting knife, high powered rifle; *HRKITW*, 6, Table 6.3.				Anti-social: animal cruelty, unable to comply with authority figures (court-martialed twice, disciplined by employer), drawn to militaristic sadism. Narcissistic: infatuated with bodybuilding.
DeWayne Craddock, 40, male, 2 handguns with high-capacity magazines, 1				Negative affect (hostile, perseveration, suspicious): reticent and formal in interactions,

silencer; *HRKITW*, 6.				addicted to routines, installed cameras to surveil property, amassed firearms, conflicts on the job. Narcissistic: preoccupation with body image.
Ethan Crumbley, 15, male, semi-automatic handgun; *WRKE*, 3; *HRKITW*, 5.		Unsupportive living conditions: neglected, aberrant behavior indulged. Hostile community: bullied.	Mood disordered: acute depression over loss of friend, suicidal. Delusional: feared supernatural beings in residence;	Anti-social (emerging sociopathy): deceptive, preoccupied with extreme violence, fascinated by animal cruelty.
Patrick Crusius, 21, male, AK-47;[24] *HRKITW*, 6, Appendix A.			Distorted cognition: schizoaffective disorder; paranoid delusions: subscribed to theory that non-whites were part of a vast movement to subvert Anglo-Saxon culture; obsessive: traveled more than 600 miles to rampage.[25]	
Nikolas Jacob Cruz, 19, male, semi-automatic rifle *HRKITW*, 5, Appendix A.		Injurious family relations: aware of adoption but no contact with birth mother, witnessed adopted father's death at five-years-old, adopted mother died of	Restricted cognition: attention deficit, impulsivity in preschool through high school, obsessive-compulsive. Mood disordered: anxiety, depressed, suicidal thoughts, self-abusive.[27]	Anti-Social (sociopathic): at 14 reportedly hit mother with vacuum hose, later threw her against wall, animal cruelty, verbal threats, brandished a gun, relished violent thoughts,

		pneumonia in his senior year of high school, moved in with family that made him depart within a month. Hostile community: bullied by brother and friends.[26]		abusive to girlfriend;[28] told therapist he would make remarks for "shock value."[29]
Jason Dalton, 45, male, 2 semiautomatic handguns; *HRKITW*, 6.			Mood disordered: visible signs of acute depression.[30] Episodic paranoia reported by acquaintances, firearm cache (4 handguns, 11 rifles).[31]	Antagonistic (manipulative, deceitful, callous, hostile): history of angry outbursts and irritability, fired guns in yard for extended periods, lied to family during prolonged mobile killing session, fabricated absurd story about mind-control, no empathy for victims (emotionless during interview with police and forensic evaluation).[32]
Laurie Dann, 31, female, arson, bomb, handgun, poison; *WRKE*, 5.			Distorted cognition: ritualistic behavior, paranoid responses to stress.	Borderline personality disorder: promiscuous, obsessively needy, unable to perform daily functions, binge eating,

				histrionic reactions.
Campo Elías Delgado Morales, 52, male, arson, knife, revolver; *HRKITW*, 6.			Distorted cognition: post-traumatic stress.	Anti-social (psychopathic, sadistic): could be charming when it suited him, left America because of brawling, beat and murdered mother, ensnared then knifed to death teenager with her mother, used fire to vacate apartments and methodically fired upon fleeing victims.[33]
Jacob Carl England, 19, male, handguns, *WRKE*, 5.			Mood disordered: acute depression.	
Dr. Valery Fabrikant, 52, male, 3 handguns; WRKE, 5; *HRKITW*, 1, 7.				Anti-Social Behaviors consistent with malignant narcissism: marked grandiosity, thrived on conflict, resentful of anyone suggesting a threat to his dominance (supervisors, colleagues, judge).
Richard Wade Farley, 39, male, 2 Revolvers, 2 semiautomatic pistols, 2 shotguns;			Delusional: self-deception approaching erotomania.	Negative affect (emotionally liable, hostile, perseveration): used threats to dominate others;

HRKITW, 5, Appendix A, Appendix B.				antagonistic (manipulative, grandiose, callous): used trickery to control people, believed he was elite, gloated about his imaginary domination.
Colin Ferguson, 35, male, semiautomatic pistol; *WRKE*, 4; *HRKITW*, 4.			Delusional: professed that crime was fabricated and trial was a scheme.	Narcissistic: grandiose pronouncements, no empathy for victims, reveled in attention during trial, fired attorneys to maintain center stage, preposterous antics in courtroom for sake of personal aggrandizement.
Gian Luigi Ferri, 55, male, pistol, 2 semiautomatic handguns, *HRKITW*, 4.			Delusional: paranoid, blamed failures on amorphous entities, kept enemies list.	Antagonistic (manipulative, grandiose, callous, hostile): flimflammer, con artist, arrogant.
Vester Flanagan, 41, male, handgun, *HRKITW*, 4.			Delusional: paranoid, reacted vehemently to supposed slights.	Antagonistic (grandiose, attention seeking, callous, hostile): overinflated belief in his talent, instigated conflicts and blamed bigotry, admired other mass killers, committed

				murders on television then spectacularized chase.
Pricilla Joyce Ford, 51, female, automobile; *WRKE*, 4.			Hallucinatory and disassociated episodes: imaginary persona, command hallucinations.	
Kimveer Singh Gill, 25, male, carbine rifle, semiautomatic handgun, shotgun, WRKE, 4; *HRKIW*, 4, Appendix A.			Mood disordered: depressed.	
Andrew Golden, 11, male, derringer, 5 handguns (at least one semi-automatic), 3 rifles, snub-nose pistol; *WRKE*, 5.				Anti-social (conduct disorder): manipulated vulnerable partner, notoriously deceptive, stole from family, orchestrated ambush.
David Malcolm Gray, 33, male, arson, semi-automatic rifle; *HRKITW*, 4, Appendix A.	Uneasy with appear-ance: balding.		Mood disordered: depressed – mourned death of parents for five years.[34] Delusional: believed neighbor gave him chronic flu.[35]	Detached (withdrawn, suspicious): recluse, extended periods without leaving home;[36] antagonistic (hostile, callous): infatuation with militarism, cruel to animals, brandished firearm.[37]
Eric Hainstock, 15, male, handgun,		Unsupportive living conditions:	Distorted cognition: attention-deficit/hyperactive	

shotgun; *HRKITW*, 2.		victim of neglect, abuse. Hostile community: sexually assaulted, mocked by peers, bullied.	disorder, delayed verbal development.	
Thomas Watt Hamilton, 43, male, 2 semiautomatic handguns, 2 revolvers; *HRKITW*, 4.	Sexual disesteem: probable pedophile.[38]	Unsupportive living conditions: familial confusion – deceived into believing his mother was his older sister, truth finally disclosed when he was 22 years old.[39]	Paranoid: despite his aberrant activities, believed he was persecuted without reason.	Tyrannical sadist: used authoritarian position to force discomfort on young men.
Christopher Sean Harper-Mercer, 26, male, at least 3 pistols and a rifle (7 guns at apartment shared with mother);[40] *HRKITW*, 6.	Sexual disesteem: self-conscious about virginity, identified with Rodger.[41]		Restricted cognition: mother stated he had Asperger syndrome.[42] Delusional: believed he was in touch with "demonic forces."[43]	
Noah Jacob Harpham, 33, male, AR-15, revolver; *HRKITW*, 6.			Distorted cognition: history of extreme alcohol abuse. Mood disordered: diagnosed as bi-polar.[44]	
Eric Harris, 18, male, bombs, carbine rifle, crickets, sawed-off shotgun, knives; *WRKE*, 2, 5; *HRKITW*,	Unsatisfac-tory appear-ance: pectus excavatum.	Unsupportive living conditions: repeated relocations.[45]		Anti-social (psychopathic): delighted in manipulating friends, family, acquaintances, bragged about

3, 4, 5, 6, Appendix A, B.				skills in deception, feigned remorse for minor crime to shorten probation, angered readily if thwarted, misanthropic, sadistic.
Robert A. Hawkins, 19, male, assault rifle; *HRKITW*, 3.		Unsupportive living conditions: intermittent contact with mother, ward of state for four years.[46]	Distorted cognition: chronic substance abuse, attention-deficit hyperactive. Mood disordered: suicidal, depressed, anxious, post-traumatic stress.[47]	Anti-social (sociopathic): expulsion for violence, oppositional, threatened to kill stepmother then taunted her later;[48] saw "father as easy to manipulate";[49] during therapy told group, "I don't even feel anything";[50] suicide note mused, "Just think tho [sic], I'm going to be [expletive deleted] famous."[51]
Leo Held, 39, male, 2 revolvers, stolen rifle; *WRKE*, 5.				Paranoid personality disorder: all relationships infused with suspicion, confided in no one, constantly aloof, interpreted conversations as derogatory, resisted arrest in western style holdoff,

				accusatory taunts to law enforcement.
George Jo Hennard, Jr., 35, male, 2 semiautomatic pistols, truck; *HRKITW*, 2, 6, Table 6.3, Appendix A, B.		Injurious familial relations: strained relationship with mother. Unsupportive living conditions: repeated relocations.[52]	Distorted cognition: history of sustained drug and alcohol abuse.[53]	Detached (withdrawn, intimacy avoidant, suspicious): socially isolated since high school (even while playing in band), enjoyed periods at sea away from others, distrusted all women, catcalled at strangers. Disinhibited (irresponsible, impulsive, rigid, inflexible): minor legal skirmishes, dismissed from Merchant Marines, job history shaky, overly attentive to appearance of yard.[54]
Olga Hepnarová, 22, female, Truck; *WRKE*, 3; *HRKITW*, 5.	Self-conscious, eccentric manner-isms.[55]	Injurious family relations: harsh discipline by father. Hostile community: ridiculed, harassed, and beat by peers and casual acquaintances.	Restricted cognition: perseveration, compulsions, constrained communication (despite verbal ability).	
James Egan Holmes, 24, male, pistol, semiautomatic	Body dysmorphia (self-diagnosed):		Mood disordered: anxious. Delusional: developed and acted upon metaphysical	Avoidant personality disorder: extremely

rifle, shotgun, teargas; *WRKE*, 4; *HRKITW*, 2, 5, 6, Appendix A.	journal entries note uneasiness with numerous physical features.		belief system wherein death could be exchanged for extended life.	introverted, distrusted others, no reciprocation in relationships. Antagonistic (manipulative, deceitful, grandiose, callous): hid murderous compulsions from therapists, thought adding to his own life justified killing, fascinated by carnage, shrugged off murder of child.[56]
James Oliver Huberty, 41, male, semiautomatic pistol, shotgun submachine gun, (300 firearms at home); *WRKE*, 6; *HRKITW*, Introduction, Appendix A, B.	Prolonged childhood illness: polio, leaving him with muscle spasms and trouble walking.	Injurious family relations: maternal abandonment.	Bouts of depression, anxiety. Delusional: survivalist preparations, conspiracy theorist, dystopian beliefs, paranoid interpretation of ordinary encounters, soothed by magical thinking. Hallucinatory: auditory.	Negative affect (anxious, insecure, hostile, suspicious): pursued respite with foreign government, killed family pet, feuded with co-workers, neighbors.
Kyle Aaron Huff, 28, male, semiautomatic handgun, shotgun, (AR 15, bat, gasoline, handgun, machete in truck nearby); *WRKE*, Introduction.		Unsupportive living conditions: parents divorced in his early teens, father subsequently moved to Thailand.[57]	Mood disordered: depressed, suicidal.[58] Delusional: paranoid, grandiose belief in his superior morality;[59] wrote: "I can't let them get away with what they're doing. … I hate this world of sex that they are striving to make.	Anti-social (psychopathic):[61] quick tempered, disengaged during high school, vandalized art sculpture intended for charity, unsociable at raves, painted threatening message in

			This is a revolution brother. The most important thing to happen since man began....”[60]	street;[62] taunted victims: “I have enough caps to kill all you fools”;[63] “There's plenty for everyone.”[64]
Silvio Izquierdo-Leyva, 36, male, pistol, revolver; fired upon seven of his fellow employees, killing four and wounding three others, then shot and killed driver who refused to surrender car.[65]			Delusional: believed in willful spiritual beings; evidence of paranoia.[66]	
Mitchell Johnson, 13, male, derringer, 5 handguns (at least one semi-automatic), 3 rifles, snub-nose pistol; *WRKE*, 5.		Injurious family relations: emotionally abused by father. Hostile community: sexually abused by neighbor.	Mood disordered: depressed, anxious, self-mutilated.	
David Katz, 24, male, semi-automatic handguns; murdered three, wounded nine by gunfire, and left two more injured at a video game tournament, shot and killed himself.[67]		Unsupportive living conditions: subject of acrimonious custody battle in early teens.[68]	Mood disordered and hallucinatory: hospitalized in psychiatric facilities, prescribed medications for psychosis and depression.[69]	
Steven Kazmierczak,			Distorted cognition: abused marijuana,	

27, male, knife, 3 semiautomatic handguns, sawed-off shotgun, pepper spray;[70] *WRKE*, 1; *HRKITW*, 3.			engaged in obsessional rituals. Mood disordered: seven suicide attempts or gestures in two-year span, prescribed antidepressants as well as mood stabilizers.[71] Paranoid, released from military following mental health evaluation, prescribed antipsychotics.	
Andrew Phillip Kehoe, 55, male, arson, explosives; *HRKITW*, 4.				Narcissistic (grandiose, required admiration, sense of entitlement, exploitative, unempathetic, haughty): wore suit while farming, sustained bitterness about political defeats, lapsed on medical bills, taxes, attributed financial problems to taxation, left sign designating blame.
Devin Kelly, 26, male, assault rifle, 2 handguns (multiple weapons in car); attacked church congregation,			Distorted cognition: assigned by Air Force to behavioral health services for unspecified "mental disorders."[73]	Anti-social (sociopathic): stalked ex-girlfriends, tried to bribe one for a date, at least one sexual assault, cruelty to animals,

killed 26 (including unborn child) and wounded 20, shot by a civilian, fled but was found dead a couple of miles from the scene;[72] *HRKITW*, Appendix A.				fractured skull of stepson, battered wife, escaped from institutionalization, made death threats to superiors, court martialed with bad conduct discharge.[74]
Alvin Lee King III, 45, male, handguns, semi-automatic rifles (one with bayonet); after binding his wife hand and foot to a kitchen chair in their home, burst into a First Baptist church during services, killing 5, wounding 10, shot himself (though not fatally) before his apprehension;[75] *HRKITW*, Table 6.3.				General personality disorder: dominated, intimidated, threatened family members, hid incestuous activities, arrogant, boasted about or insinuated intellectual superiority, displayed obvious dislike for students needing assistance.[76]
Kip Kinkel, 15, male, knife, pistol, 2 semiautomatic handguns, semiautomatic rifle; *WRKE* 4; *HRKITW*, 3, 4, 7.	Viewed himself as small and weak.		Restricted cognition: constrained executive functioning. Mood disordered: depressed. Delusional: paranoid, believed parents intended to abandon him.	Anti-Social (conduct disordered): deceptive behavior, animal cruelty, minor criminal infractions, angry outbursts, enjoyed notoriety.

			Hallucinatory: auditory commands.	
Dylan Klebold, 17, male, bombs, knives, crickets, sawed-off shotgun, semi-automatic handgun; *WRKE*, 5; *HRKITW*, 3, 4, 5, Appendix A.	Unsatisfactory appearance: self-conscience about size and general appearance.		Mood disordered: chronically depressed.	
Julian Knight, 19, male, rifle, semiautomatic rifle, shotgun; *HRKITW*, 3.		Unsupportive living conditions: adopted – attempted to contact birth mother without success, multiple relocations during childhood, traumatized by divorce of adopted parents. Hostile community: hazed, sodomized at military college.[77]	Distorted cognition: impulsive, sudden outbursts and fights with comrades, charged with malicious wounding, assault, and bodily harm;[78] binge drinking.[79] Delusional: repetitious vivid fantasies of vanquishing enemies in battle.[80]	Antagonistic (grandiose, attention seeking): egocentric, histrionic responses.[81]
Thomas Michael (T. J.) Lane III, 17, male, pistol; *HRKITW*, 3, 7.		Injurious family relations: exposed to intense domestic violence in pre-teen years.		Anti-social (sociopathic): boasted of malingering, mocked family of victims, multiple infractions since incarceration, no

				remorse, escape attempt.
Adam Peter Lanza, 20, male, rapid-fire handguns, rifle, semi-automatic rifles; *WRKE*, 1, 2, 3; *HRKITW*, 2, 4, 5, Appendix A.	Body image dissatisfaction: anorexic.	Unsupportive living conditions: maternal indulgence, inconsistent paternal involvement.	Restricted cognition: autistic spectrum and/or sensory deprivation disorder, obsessive-compulsive, schizophrenic symptoms.[82]	Antagonistic (grandiose, callous. hostile): writing in fifth grade expressed caviler amoral convictions;[83] espoused misogyny, misanthropy.
Pierre Lebrun, 40, male, arson, rifle *HRKITW*, 6, Table 6.3.	Disability: dysfluent.[84]	Hostile community: harassed by fellow employees.[85]	Delusional: apologia accused coworkers of following and spying on him in multiple locales in Canada and U.S.[86]	
Santino William Legan, 19, male, assault rifle (gun light, knife, bulletproof vest, gas mask in apartment);[87] *HRKITW*, 6, Appendix A.				Antisocial (sociopathic): disruptive in school, poor attendance, adopted philosophy committed to dominance, compiled list of people he would kill and women he wanted to rape, abusive to young woman he dated, posted facetious message prior to massacre, killed 6 year old boy as well as 13 year old girl.[88]
Marc Lépine, 25, male, semiautomatic		Injurious familial relations: father	Mood disordered (depressed): maintained life	Detached (withdrawn, intimacy avoidant,

rifle; *HRKITW*, 3, Appendix A.		emotionally abusive, violent, used corporal punishment.[89]	brought him "no joy."[90]	anhedonic, suspicious): preference for isolation, scornful of emotional involvement; distrustful of all women.[91]
Wayne Lo, 18, male, semiautomatic rifle; *HRKITW*, 6, 7, Table 6.3.	Limited stature: self-conscious about height[92]	Injurious familial relations: tyrannical father.[93]	Delusional: originally believed God directed rampage.	Antagonistic (grandiose, attention seeking, callous, hostile): viewed himself as superior, professed distasteful ideas to gain attention, admitted he was indifferent to right/wrong, confessed to seething anger.
Jared Lee Loughner, 22, male, semiautomatic handgun; attempted to assassinate a U.S. Congresswoman then fired 33 more shots into a crowd, struck 19 people causing six fatalities, one of which was a child nine-years of age;[94] *HRKITW*, 6.			Delusional: believed in governmental mind control. Hallucinatory: disassociated episodes, trouble distinguishing dreams from reality. Psychotic: bizarre idiosyncratic interpretation of events, extensive use of psychotropic recreational drugs (marijuana, LSD, Salvia divinorum).[95]	

Robert Earl Mack, 42, male revolver; *HRKITW*, 3.			Mood disordered: acute depression, anxiety. Delusional: imagined violent anthropomorphic attack on his person.	
Mamoru Takuma, 37, male, knife; *HRKITW*, 5.			Mood disordered: suicidal.[96] Psychotic: history of psychiatric problems including hospitalization, diagnosis of schizophrenia.	Anti-social (sociopathic): sex with minor, rape, laced tea of instructors with sedatives, trivialized knife rampage;[97] said: "I should have just used gasoline so I could kill more people that day."[98]
Clifton McCree, 41, male, semiautomatic handgun, revolver; *WRKE*, 4; *HRKITW*, Appendix A, B.		Unsupportive living conditions: absent father, alcoholic mother, repeated relocations.[99]	Distorted cognition: constant indulgence in cannabis, failed drug test at work, postmortem toxicology revealed marijuana in system.[100]	Negative affect (anxious, insecure, hostile, suspicious): bought wife necklace saying, "Taken," unexcused absences from job, periods of withdrawal, abrasive to co-workers and public, paranoid, believed he was persecuted.[101]
Thomas McIlvane, 31, male, sawed-off rifle; *HRKITW*, 6.				Antagonistic (antipathic, grandiose, callous, hostile): consistent volatility, belligerent in posture and mannerisms,

				destructive outburst, threats.
Michael Kenneth McLendon, 28, male, arson, 2 assault rifles, pistol, shotgun; *HRKITW*, 3.		Injurious familial relations: pronounced intergenerational conflict.[102]	Mood disordered: depressed, suicidal.	
Alek Minassian, 25, male, Automobile; *HRKITW*, 5, Appendix A.	Sexual disesteem: fancied himself an involuntary celibate (incel).		Restricted cognition: autism spectrum disorder (ASD).[103]	Antagonistic (grandiose, attention seeking, callous, hostile):[104] impervious to consequences, haughty demeanor, believed he was entitled to sexual relations, amoral, unapologetic justification for actions.[105]
Mutsuo Toi, 21, male, ax, katana, knives, shotgun; *WRKE*, 2; *HRKITW*, Appendix A.	Pronounced childhood illness: tuberculosis. Sexual disesteem.		Mood disordered: chronic depression, suicidal.	
Kurt Myers, 64, male, arson, shotgun; *WRKE*, Introduction.	Disability: vocal tic, singsong inflec-tion.[106]			Negative affect (anxious, separation insecurity, perseveration, depressed, repressed emotions): reticent, unsociable,

				downcast demeanor, harbored affection for 20 years for married woman.[107]
Peter Odighizuwa, 43, male, semiautomatic handgun; shot to death a dean, professor, and a fellow student, injured three additional students at the Appalachian School of Law;[108] *HRKITW*, Appendix A.			Delusional: reported that he sometimes felt like God exorcising demons. Paranoid: believed he was a victim of government conspiracies.[109]	
Stephen Paddock, 64, male, modified automatic rifle (arsenal of explosives, with at least 42 firearms in hotel room); *WRKE*, 1; *HRKITW*, 2, 5.		Unsupportive living conditions: father (infamous for criminality) absent during formative years.		Detached (withdrawn, intimacy avoidant, restricted affect, suspicious): elected solitary activities, resisted close relations, maintained secrecy in personal life, shaded widows, excessive home security.
Dimitrios Pagourtzis, 17, male, revolver, shotgun, pipe bombs;[110] *HRKITW*, 2, 6.		Hostile community: bullied by classmates at high school, harassed by staff.[111]	Mood disordered: chronic low-grade depression;[112] suicidal.[113]	Antagonistic (attention seeking, hostile): clothed himself as pariah, aggressive militaristic interests.[114]

Donald Pemberton,[115] 20, male, ax, knife; *HRKITW*, 5.				Anti-social (psychopathic): violent history including charges for illegal weapon, posed for photos with meat cleaver and sword, lured man to ambush, made obscene gesture to photographers at court appearance, fashioned weapon in prison;[116] said his victim could "die all he wants. I don't care";[117] after imprisonment stated matter-of-factly, "I think about killing every day."[118]
Gary Scott Pennington, 17, male, revolver; *WRKE*, 2.	Delayed physical develop-ment. Disability: speech dys-fluency.[119]	Injurious familial relations: abusive father.[120] Hostile community: savagely beaten by peers, mercilessly mocked in school, socially isolated.[121]		
Kristine Peralez, 38, female, gun; *HRKITW*, 5.		Hostile community: victimized, perpetrator unknown.	Mood disordered: long-term depression	

Patrick Edward Purdy, 24, male, pipe bomb, pistol, semiautomatic rifle; *WRKE*, 1, 3; *HRKE*, 4.		Injurious familial relations: witness to domestic violence. Unsupportive living conditions: neglected, continuous relocations while young.	Restricted cognition: intellectual delay, chronic substance abuse. Hallucinatory: auditory.	Anti-social (sociopathic): legal infractions (both minor and major) throughout life, chronic lying, diagnosed with personality disorder, job instability, impulsive.
Evan Ramsey, 16, male, shotgun; *HRKITW*, Introduction.		Injurious familial relations: violent father and older males, maternal neglect. Unsupportive living conditions: natural father absent from 5 to 16 years of age, succession of foster homes. Hostile community: sexually abused.[122]	Distorted cognition: impulsive.[123] Mood disordered: depressed,[124] suicidal.[125]	
Elliot Rodger, 22, male, automobile, pistol; *WRKE*, 5; *HRKITW*, 2, 5, Appendix A, B.	Small stature, self-conscious about agility and virginity	Hostile community: bullied in school.		Narcissistic: obsessed with appearance and impression management, sense of entitlement, believed in his superiority and supreme destiny.

Jason Rodriguez, 40, male, handgun;[126] *HRKITW*, 3.			Mood disordered: bouts of acute depression. Delusional: testimony by seven experts. Hallucinatory: auditory commands. Psychotic: symptoms of paranoid schizophrenia.[127]	
Dylann Roof, 21, male, semiautomatic pistol; *HRKITW*, 4, 5, Table 6.3, Appendix A.		Injurious familial relations: raised with intimate partner violence. Unsupportive living conditions: father divorced birthmother then subsequent stepmother, shuttled between homes, no continuity in school attendance.[128]	Distorted cognition, mood disordered, psychotic: examined for competency to stand trial by multiple psychiatrists, psychologists, mental health practitioners, and autism experts who delivered the following probable diagnoses: social anxiety, schizoid personality, autistic traits, emerging or transient psychosis, depressed, suicidal ideation, obsessive-compulsive symptoms, paranoia.[129] Delusional: bought into separatist dogma, thought his martyrdom would advance Anglo-Saxon supremacy and he needed to sacrifice himself for white race;	Anti-social (sociopathic): rationalized racism with belief of white superiority (particularly his own), attacked parishioners during Bible study while they prayed, belittled family members when they visited him in prison, proud of murders;[131] wrote in journal: "I would like to make it crystal clear, I do not regret what I did. I am not sorry. … I have not shed a tear for the innocent people I killed. I do feel sorry for the innocent white children forced to live in this sick country…."[132]

			diagnosed with grandiose and somatic beliefs.[130]	
Michael Robert Ryan, 27, male, arson, automatic rifle, carbine rifle, semiautomatic handgun; *HRKITW*, Introduction, 4, 5, 6, Appendix A.	Limited stature: target for bullies in childhood, self-conscious of height in adult-hood.[133]	Injurious family relations: extreme maternal indulgence.[134] Hostile community: bullied by peers.[135]		Avoidant personality disorder (APD):[136] disengaged, withdrawn, isolated throughout most of youth, loner as an adult, socially inept, fantasized and boasted about idealized relationships, recreated only with guns and military figurines, stalker.[137] Spineless sadist: frequently shot at peers and animals with air rifle.[138]
Matti Juhani Saari, 22, male, arson, semiautomatic pistol; *HRKITW*, Appendix B.	Prolonged and pronounced childhood illness: frequent hospitaliza-tions in preschool years.[139]	Injurious family relations: parents divorced during early childhood. Unsupportive living conditions: frequent relocations. Hostile community: mocked by peers, bullied at school.[140]	Mood disordered: anxiety, panic attacks, depressed, suicidal thoughts.[141]	
Jennifer San Marco, 44, female, semiautomatic,			Distorted cognition and delusional: disordered thinking, disassociated	

handgun; *WRKE*, 4; *HRKITW*, 3.			episodes, derealization, identity alteration.	
Satoshi Uematsu, 26, male, knives, edged tools; *HRKITW*, 5, Appendix A, B.			Delusional: believed massacre could "revitalize the world economy and … prevent World War III";[142] requested House Speaker arrange minimal sentence, assistance after release, and payment of 500 million yen "for the sake of Japan and world peace."[143]	Antagonistic (grandiose, attention seeking, callous, hostile): subscribed to his superiority, believed in legalized euthanasia for people with disabilities, tweeted picture of himself smiling after massacre;[144] said victims had "no right to complain" and bereaved families were "hysterical";[145] attempted to bite off pinkie at hearing to "offer … apology."[146]
Sylvia Wynanda Seegrist, 25, female, semiautomatic rifle; *WRKE*, 4.		Injurious family relations: sexually abused by grandfather.[147]	Hallucinatory: visual and auditory. Psychotic reasoning	
Patrick Henry Sherrill, 44, male, 2 semiautomatic handguns, pistol; *WRKE*, 3, 4, 6; *HRKITW*, 2, Appendix A, B.				Detached (withdrawn, intimacy avoidant, restricted affect, anhedonic, depressed, suspicious): lived alone, mostly solitary activities, preferred regimented

				interactions, idiosyncratic non-flexible habits, displayed exaggerated interpersonal gestures, misread innocuous comments, overreacted to professional criticism.
Ibrahim Shkupolli, 43, male, handgun, knife; *HRKITW*, Chapter 4, Appendix A.				Anti-social: carried out long-term affair, enraged when lover wanted to part, subject of restraining orders, convictions for bodily injury to others, illegal weapon charges.
Michael Peter Slobodian, 16, male, rifle, semi- automatic rifle;[148] *HRKITW*, 5.	Limited stature: self-conscious of height.[149]		Mood disordered: probable acute depression.[150]	Anti-social (conduct disordered, psychopathic): forged 35 excuses for absences, cynical about tragic literary figure, killed teacher who acted as confidant, sadistic, designed experiment involving dissection of live frogs.[151]
August (Benjamin) Nathaniel Smith, 21, male,				Anti-social (psychopathic): subscribed to racial superiority,

handguns; *HRKITW*, 4, Appendix A.				enjoyed intimidation, used religion as front for bigotry, verbally facile, presented gentle façade, misanthropic.
Robert Benjamin Smith, 18, male, knives, handguns; *WRKE*, 2.	Dyspraxia: poor coordi-nation.			Anti-social (psychopathic): enjoyed confessing to violence, told police he wanted to be notorious, said killing made him feel like a god, carried out crimes in sadistic manner.[152]
George Sodini, 48, male, 2 automatic handguns, semiautomatic handgun, revolver; *HRKITW*, Introduction, 3, 6, Appendix A.	Sexual disesteem: believed he was rejected by women.[153]			Negative affect (emotionally liable, anxious, hostile, depressed, suspicious): pessimistic about relationships and his work, irritated by expressions of optimism, worried about job permanence, defeatist, drank to ease nervousness, hated family, thought he had an inherent tragic flaw, concluded life was bleak.[154]
Brenda Ann Spencer, 16, female,		Injurious familial relations: emotionally	Distorted cognition: probable frontal lobe damage, seizures.	Disinhibited (irresponsible, impulsive, distractable, risk

semiautomatic rifle, *WRKE*, 4; *HRKITW*, 4, 7, Appendix B.		traumatized by divorce.	Mood disordered: depressed.	taker): underdeveloped sense of morality, non-attentive in classes, lied repeatedly, attracted to shock rock.
Andrew Joseph Stack III, 53, male, arson, airplane; *WRKE*, 3; *HRKITW*, Appendix A.		Unsupportive living conditions: orphaned and separated from siblings in early childhood, raised in residential setting without nurturing.		Antagonistic (deceitful, grandiose, callous, hostile): attempted to circumvent tax code, egocentric decision-making, emotionally abusive to family, destroyed home, blamed financial problems on outside forces, exaggerated extent of fiscal difficulties.
Robert Steinhäuser, 19, male, pistol, shotgun; *HRKITW*, 6.				Anti-social (conduct disordered): hid school failures and disciplinary measures from parents for weeks, forged numerous medical excuses to skip classes, mocked an instructor by imitating a shooting.[155]
Sulejman Talović, 18, male,		Unsupportive living conditions: experienced bombing and		Negative affect (emotional liability, hostile): aggressive acts as juvenile. Detached

pistol, shotgun; *HRKITW*, 3, 6, Appendix A.		siege of his village as toddler, displaced with family for five years during genocidal civil war, multiple school transfers.[156]		(withdrawn): socially isolated.[157]
Brenton Harrison Tarrant, 28, male,[158] lever-action rifle, 2 semiautomatic rifles, 2 shotguns;[159] *HRKITW*, 5, Appendix A.		Unsupportive living conditions: upset by parent's separation, discovered father's body after suicide.[160]	Delusional: believed "non-Europeans" were intentionally conquering Europe through immigration and mass murder would reverse their efforts by inspiring a race war;[161] subscribed to a theory that there was a conglomerate of "anti-whites" controlling the press and education;[162] described one-sided attack on worshipers as "firefight."[163]	Malignant narcissist, sadistic: sense of entitlement based on racial heritage;[164] killed during religious services, shot wounded victims as they begged for help, murdered child of three clinging to father's leg, wounded four-year-old boy, streamed massacre on Facebook;[165] wrote: "I only wish I could have killed more invaders, and more traitors as well. … [T]he attack was a end in itself, with all the necessary affect required. These writing, and their coverage, are just a bonus. … You are nothing to me but just

				another target. I will wipe you the fuck out with precision the likes of which has never been seen before on this Earth, mark my fucking words. … You [referring to imaginary followers] will be infamous until victory is achieved. Take it with a smile."[166]
Dion Terres, 25, male, semi-automatic handgun (AR-15, knives left in car);[167] *HRKITW*, 2, 5, Appendix A.		Claimed abuse by family members during his early childhood.[168]	Restricted cognition: habitual use of marijuana. Mood disordered: depressed. Hallucinatory: imagined he committed infamous murders.	Negative affect (emotionally liable, anxious, separation insecurity, hostile, suspicious): habitually confrontive, extremely possessive of girlfriend, frustrated when isolated, intimidated strangers, frequent physical altercations.
Tomohiro Kato, 25, male, knife, rental truck; drove vehicle into a crowd at a popular shopping location in central Tokyo, killing three and	Unsatis-factory appear-ance: considered himself unattrac-tive.[170]			Anti-social (psychopathic): terrorized mother in his youth, admittedly deceptive, carefully planned attack and blamed it on others, expressed no

injuring two, then got out to stab twelve people in the vicinity, murdering four more.[169]				remorse until judicial appeal, fantasized murder;[171] "described himself as 'hot-tempered and stubborn.'"[172]
Howard Barton Unruh, 28, male, 9 mm German Luger pistol, knife, tear gas pen;[173] *HRKITW*, Introduction, Appendix A.	Self-conscious about sexual prefer-ence.[174]		Distorted cognition (post-traumatic stress): served as tank gunner in WWI, mother; brother, a church member, and a psychiatrist reported he returned home introverted, sullen, and irritable.[175]	Paranoid personality disorder: reticent to socialize during childhood; meticulously recorded enemy deaths while serving as soldier; kept ledger of affronts by neighbors and acquaintances.[176]
Frank Vitkovic, 22, male, carbine handgun; *HRKITW*, 2, 3.	Disability: traumatized by knee injury that ruined sports career.	Hostile community: intimidated by peers, hazed during childhood.	Mood disordered: chronic depression.	
Alvin Lee Watts, 32, male, handgun; *WRKE*, 5.				Anti-social: manipulative, domestic abuser, enjoyed threatening violence.
Jeffrey James Weise, 16, male, pistol, semiautomatic handgun, shotgun;[177] *WRKE*, 3; *HRKITW*, 3, Appendix A.		Injurious family relations: father committed suicide. Unsupportive living conditions: no stability in housing.	Mood disordered: depressed, suicidal.	

Joseph Thomas Wesbecker, 47, male, AK-47, 2 military style semiautomatic pistols, revolver, semiautomatic handgun; *WRKE* 1; *HRKITW*, Table 6.3.		Injurious familial relations: Death of father while he was a toddler, grandfather at 15, mother attempted suicide. Unsupportive living conditions: resided in various households (including an orphanage) during childhood.[178]	Mood disordered: history of manic episodes, attempted suicide, treated in psychiatric facility for major affective illness, depressed, diagnosis of atypical bipolar disorder. Delusional: paranoid response to ordinary events.[179]	Diagnosed with borderline personality disorder.[180]
Charles Joscph Whitman, 25, male, handguns, hatchet, machete, knives, 2 rifles (1 with power scope), unspecified blunt object, shotgun; *HRKITW*, Introduction, 5, Appendix B.		Injurious familial relations: abusive and controlling father.[181]	Distorted cognition: habitual use of stimulates, sleep deprivation at time of incident, brain tumor.[182] Mood disordered: depressed.[183]	Antagonistic (manipulative, deceitful, grandiose, attention seeking, callous, hostile): reneged on gambling debts, poached, tyrannically sadistic as scout master, craved admiration, brandished weapon for fun, explosive episodes, threatened debtor with violence, beat spouse.[184]
Charles Andrew (Andy) Williams, 15,	Unfit, frail appearance.	Unsupportive living conditions:	Distorted cognition: impulsive, intense	

male, revolver; *WRKE*, 3, 4.		disorienting relocations, maternal absence. Hostile community: taunted by peers.	ongoing substance abuse. Mood disordered: depressed.	
Douglas Williams, 48, male, mini semiautomatic rifle, shotgun (additional firearms in truck); *HRKITW*, 2.				Negative affect (grandiose, attention seeking, callous, hostile): subscribed to racial supremacy, taunted co-workers, belittled others, misanthropic.
Luke Woodham, 16, male, bat, knife, hunting rifle; *HRKITW*, Introduction, 1, Table 6.3, Appendix A.	Unsatis-factory appear-ance: overweight, extremely near-sighted.[185]	Injurious familial relations: father left after years of acrimony in marriage then essentially absent, mother's methods for discipline bordered on sadistic, physically tormented by brother. Hostile community: bullied and teased by classmates largely due to his appearance.[186]	Mood disordered: claimed chronic depression since age of eight;[187] acute anxiety with suicidal thoughts preceding SMASI: "I didn't eat. I didn't sleep. I didn't want to live. … It destroyed me.[188] Delusional: overvalued belief in black magic.	Diagnosed with personality disorder by two separate forensic psychiatrists;[189] although effective at impression management showed deceptive and exploitive behavior consistent with conduct disorder.
Andrew Jerome Wurst, 14, male, handgun;			Disassociated episodes (depersonalization): believed he was an	

WRKE, 4; *HRKITW*, 2.			actor in an artificial reality.	
Aaron Rey Ybarra, 26, male, knife, shotgun;[190] *HRKITW*, 3, Appendix A.		Injurious family relations: alcoholic father, heroin addicted brother, intervened in suicide attempt by father who was subsequently committed for mental health evaluation[191]	Mood disordered: attempted suicide. Symptoms of psychosis: twice involuntarily committed for mental health evaluations.[192]	
John Samir Zawahri, 24, male, AR-15, arson, a revolver converted for .45 cartridges, 3 "zip guns"; *WRKE*, Introduction.		Injurious familial relations: father abused mother, brandished knife at family.[193] Unsupportive living conditions: parents involved in contentious divorce.[194]		Negative affect (emotionally liable, anxious, insecure, hostile): angry loud outbursts, clingy with mother in preschool years, serious behavior problems, fascinated with firearms and explosives, violent threats toward school personnel.[195]
Zhao Zewei, 28, male, knives; *WRKE*, 3.	Limited stature.	Hostile community: ridiculed and bullied at school.	Mood disordered: depressed.	

Notes

Introduction

[1] Specific instances are offered in the Introduction to *How Rampage Killers Interpret Their Worlds.*

[2] Paul E. Mullen, "The Autogenic (Self-Generated) Massacre," *Behavioral Sciences and the Law* 22 no. 3 (2004): 313; Thomas G. Bowers, Eric S. Holmes, and Ashley Rhom, "The Nature of mass murder and Autogenic Massacre," *Journal of Police Criminal Psychology* 25, no. 2 (October 2010): 60.

[3] See: a) Bowers, Holmes, and Rohm, "The Nature of mass murder," 59-66; b) Matt DeLisi, and Aaron M. Scherer, "Multiple Homicide Offenders: Offense Characteristics, Social Correlates, and Criminal Careers," *Criminal Justice and Behavior* 33, no. 3 (June 2006): 367-391; c) Ronald Holmes and Stephen T. Holmes, *Mass Murder in the United States* (Upper Saddle River, NJ: Prentice-Hall, 2001); d) Peter Langman, *School Shooters: Understanding High School, College, and Adult Perpetrators* (Boulder, CO: Rowman and Littlefield, 2015); e) Jack Levin and James Alan Fox, *Mass Murder: America's Growing Menace* (New York, NY: Plenum Press, 1986); f) Mullen, "The Autogenic (Self-Generated) Massacre," 311-323; g) Thomas A. Petee, "Differentiating Forms of mass murder," Department of Sociology, Auburn University, http://webhome.auburn.edu/~peteeta/massmurder1.htm; h) Michael H. Stone *The Anatomy of Evil* (Amherst, NY: Prometheus Books, 2009).

[4] Sara Knox, "A Gruesome Accounting: Mass, Serial and Spree Killing in the Mediated Public Sphere," *Journal for Crime, Conflict, and the Media* 1, no. 2 (January 2004): 12.

[5] The Federal Bureau of Investigation (FBI) has dismissed the division between serial murderers and spree killers because the distinguishing line separating the two has been marked by the so-called "cooling off period" (a time between killings that is sometimes relatively prolonged) – a characteristic that is difficult to precisely define. Congressional Research Service (CRS), *Public Mass Shootings in the United States: Selected Implications for Federal Public Health and Safety Policy* (Prepared for Members and Committees of Congress, Updated April 16, 2013), 7, 31fn, https://crsreports.congress.gov/.

Nevertheless, there are behavioral differences between serial homicide offenders and spree killers that can and should be distinguished in relation to neural mechanics and emotive impetus. Consider points argued in the following: a) Samuel Adjorlolo and Heng Choon (Oliver) Chan, "The Controversy of Defining Serial Murder: Revisited," *Aggression and Violent Behavior* 19, no. 5 (September–October 2014): 486-491; b) Robert DePaolo, "Serial Killers: A Discussion of Etiology and Process in Terms of Behavior Theory," NoAnxiety.com, posted March 21, 2011, http://www.noanxiety.com / psychology-articles / serial-killers-a-discussion-of-etiology-and-process-in-terms-of-behavior-theory/179; c) Louis B. Schlesinger, Stephanie Ramirez, Brittany Tusa, John P. Jarvis, and Philip Erdberg, "Rapid-Sequence Serial Sexual Homicides," *The Journal of the American Academy of Psychiatry and the Law* 72, no. 1 (March 2017): 72-80; d) Enzo Yaksic, Mikhail Simkin, and Vwani Roychowdhury, "Statistical Study of Time Intervals between Murders For Serial Killers," *Journal of Criminal Justice* 73, March–April 2021, 101751; e) Enzo Yaksic, "The Folly of Counting Bodies: Using Regression to Transgress The State Of Serial Murder Classification Systems," *Aggression and Violent Behavior* 43 (November–December 2018): 26-32.

[6] The list is a synthesis of conceptual observations from these sources: a) CRS, *Public Mass Shootings*, 6-10; b) Claude T.H. Friedman and Robert A. Faguet, *Extraordinary Disorders of Human Behavior* (New York, NY: Plenum Press, 1982),188; c) Knoll, "Mass Murder: Causes," 761-766.

[7] James Alan Fox, Ann W. Burgess, Jack Levin, Marleen Wong, and Allen G. Burgess, "Capitol Hill Mass Murder Case," *Brief Treatment and Crisis Intervention* 7, no. 2 (May 2007), 127, 143, https:// triggered.clockss.org/ ServeContent?url=http%3A%2F%2Fbtci.stanford.clockss.org%2Fcgi%2Freprint%2F7%2F2%2F127.pdf.

[8] An arcade contest entitled *Rampage* was released by Bally Midway in 1986, coincidently or not, just two months after one of the more notorious workplace massacres committed by Robert Sherril in a post office. CNN Library, "Rampage Killings Fast Facts," updated November 28, 2019, https://www.cnn.com/2013/09/16/us/rampage-killings-fast-facts/index.html; IMDb, "Rampage (1986)," Brian Collin and Jeff Nauman, creators, IMDb.com, Inc., under "Details and Company Credits," https://www .imdb.com/title/tt0304616/. The game features three monstrous animals (an ape, a lizard, and a wolf) who "move from city to city destroying skyscrapers and various vehicles and eating people that get in the way." IMDb, "Rampage (1986)," under "Storyline." Numerous renditions, with variations on the plot designed for different platforms, have come out over the years, with the latest, entitled "Rampage World Tour," appearing in 1997. IMDb, "Rampage World Tour (1997)," Brian Collin, dir. and writ. and Jeff Nauman, dir.,

https://www.imdb.com/title/tt0304618/?ref_=tt_rec_tt; Novabug [pseud.], "The Brief History of Rampage," YouTube, posted January 26, 2018, https://www.youtube.com/watch?v=u_xrRqYotwo&t=122s. Even more recently the concept was converted into a film starring Dwayne Johnson ("The Rock") that features a gigantic silverback gorilla, who becomes a second protagonist and defends the world against arbitrary slaughter by merciless adversaries. IMDb, "*Rampage* (2018)" Brad Peyton, dir., Ryan Engle, Carlton Cuse, Ryan J. Condal, and Adam Sztykiel, writ, https://www.imdb.com /title/tt2231461/; Warner Brothers Pictures, "*Rampage* – Official Trailer 2 (HD)," YouTube, posted February 13, 2018, https://www.youtube.com/watch?v=-43MBOJnVks. The characterizations and structure certainly support the chaos promised in the title.

[9] Anthony G. Hempel, Ruth E. Levine, J. Reid Meloy, and Joseph Westermeyer, "A Cross-Cultural Review of Sudden Mass Assault by a Single Individual in the Oriental and Occidental Cultures," *Journal of Forensic Sciences* 45, no. 3 (May 2000): 582.

[10] Paul Gill, James Silver, John Horgan, and Emily Corner, "Shooting Alone: The Pre-Attack Experiences and Behaviors of U.S. Solo mass murderers," *Journal Forensic of Sciences* 62, no. 3 (May 2017): 710.

[11] John Douglas and Douglas Olshaker, *The Anatomy of Motive: The FBI's Legendary Mindhunter Explores the Key to Understanding and Catching Violent Criminals* (New York, NY: Lisa Drew/Scribner, 1999),191; John E. Douglas, Robert K. Ressler, Ann W. Burgess, and Carol R. Hartman, "Criminal Profiling from Crime Scene Analysis," *Behavioral Sciences & The Law* 4, no. 4 (Autumn 1986): 408; Deniese Kennedy-Kollar and Christopher A.D. Charles, "Hegemonic Masculinity and mass murderers in the United States," *Southwest Journal of Criminal Justice* 8, no. 2 (2013): 63.

[12] CBSLA.com, "Coroner Releases Report in Santa Monica Shootings," CBS2 and KCAL9, posted June 13, 2013, https://losangeles.cbslocal.com/2013 /06/13/coroner-releases-report-in-santa-monica-shootings/; Mayors Against Illegal Guns, *Analysis of Recent Mass Shootings* (United States Department of Justice, Office of Justice Programs, September 2013), 8.

[13] Paul Farrell, "John Zawahri: Top 10 Facts You Need to Know," Heavy.com, updated April 19, 2015, under "1. He Killed His Father and Brother" and "7. Zawahri Stood and Watched His Father's House Burn," https://heavy.com/news/2013/06/john-zawahri-santa-monica-college-shooter/.

[14] Iris Carreras, "John Zawahri, Suspected Gunman in Deadly Santa Monica Shooting, Left Farewell Note, Police Say," CBS News: posted June 14, 2013, https://www.cbsnews.com/news/john-zawahri-suspected-gunman-in-deadly-santa-monica-shooting-left-farewell-note-police-say/; Farrell, "John Zawahri: Top 10 Facts," under "6. He Was Armed to the Teeth" and photos

by "Santa Monica Police Department"; Mayors Against Illegal, *Analysis of Recent Mass Shootings*, 8. "A zip gun is essentially a cheap makeshift gun. Persons make them using supplies from around their home or found at a local hardware store. … The term 'zip' is used because a rubber band is often used to help fire these weapons." Neil Shouse, "What Is a Zip Gun and Is It Illegal in California? (Penal Code 33600 PC)," Shouse California Law Group, posted October 8, 2018, https://www.shouselaw.com/ca/blog/gun-laws/what-is-a-zip-gun-and-is-it-illegal-in-california/. They are outlawed in California.

[15] Carreras, "John Zawahri, Suspected Gunman"; CBSLA.com, "Carjacking Victim Describes Terrifying Face-to-Face Encounter with Santa Monica Gunman," CBS2/KCAL9, posted June 10, 2013, https://losangeles.cbslocal.com/2013/06/10/carjacking-victim-describes-terrifying-face-to-face-encounter-with-santa-monica-gunman/; Mayors Against Illegal Guns, *Analysis of Recent Mass Shootings*, 8.

[16] Farrell, "John Zawahri: Top 10 Facts," under "6. He Was Armed"; Mayors Against Illegal, *Analysis of Recent Mass Shootings*, 8; James Nye and Associated Press (AP), "Pictured: Santa Monica College Gunman John Zawahri, 23, Who Went on Shooting Rampage Killing Four Because He Was Angry at Parents Divorce," *Mail Online*, posted June 8, 2013, updated June 10, 2013, https://www.dailymail.co.uk/news/article-2338250/Pictured-Santa-Monica-college-gunman-John-Zawahri-23-went-shooting-rampage-killing-angry-parents-divorce.html.

[17] CBSLA.com, "5 Dead, Including Suspect, in Santa Monica Shooting Rampage," CBS2/KCAL9, posted June 7, 2013, https://www.cbsnews.com/losangeles/news/shots-fired-suspect-down-at-santa-monica-college/.

[18] AP, "6th Person Dies as a Result of Santa Monica Rampage," CBS2/KCAL9, posted June 9, 2013, https://losangeles.cbslocal.com/2013/06/09/6th-person-dies-following-santa-monica-rampage/.

[19] Nye and AP, "Pictured: Santa Monica College."

[20] CBSLA.com, "5 Dead, Including Suspect"; Mayors Against Illegal Guns, *Analysis of Recent Mass Shootings*, 8.

[21] CBSLA.com, "5 Dead, Including Suspect."

[22] AP, "6th Person Dies"; Mayors Against Illegal Guns, *Analysis of Recent Mass Shootings*, 8.

[23] Farrell, "John Zawahri: Top 10 Facts," under "1. He Killed His Father and Brother"; Nye and AP, "Pictured: Santa Monica."

[24] Jon Campbell and Doug Stanglin, "Cops Kill Suspect in Deadly N.Y. Shooting Rampage," *USA Today*, posted and updated March 14, 2013, https://www.usatoday.com/story/news/2013/03/14/upstate-new -york-herkimer-mohawk-suspect-surrounded/1986913/.

[25] Roomie Huh, "Upstate New York Shooting Update: Kurt Myers, Suspected Gunman, Killed by Police in Shootout," CBS News, posted March 14, 2013, https://www.cbsnews.com/news/upstate-new-york-shooting-update-kurt-myers-suspected-gunman-killed-by-police-in-shootout/.

[26] Ibid.

[27] Campbell and Stanglin, "Cops Kill Suspect."

[28] Michael Hill and John Kekis, AP, "Kurt Myers, Suspected Gunman in New York Shooting Rampage, Killed by Police," *Huffington Post*, posted March 14, 2013, updated May 14, 2013, https://www.huffpost.com/entry/kurt-myers-killed_n_2874981.

[29] Campbell and Stanglin, "Cops Kill Suspect." It was the first mission for the two-year old German Shepherd.

[30] Douglas and Olshaker, *The Anatomy of Motive*, 191.

[31] For defining criteria refer to: a) Jeff Goodwin, "A Theory of Categorical Terrorism," *Social Forces* 84, no. 4 (June 2006): 2027-2030; b) John Horgan, The Psychology of Terrorism (New York, NY: Routledge, 2005), 1-4; c) Dávid Tóth, "The History and Types of Terrorism," 1-4, https://lj.oa.edu.ua/articles/2015 /n1/15ddttot.pdf. The determination of types of terrorism is a related but separate issue covered in the following sources among others: a) Goodwin, "A Theory of Categorical Terrorism," 2029-2032; b) Omar A. Lizardo and Albert J. Bergesen, "Types of Terrorism by World System Location," *Humboldt Journal of Social Relations* 27, no. 2 (2003): 162-192; c) Ariel Merari, "A classification of terrorist groups," *Terrorism* 1, nos. 3-4 (1978): 331-346: d) Tom Parker and Nick Sitter, "The Four Horsemen of Terrorism: It's Not Waves, It's Strains," *Terrorism and Political Violence* 28, no. 2 (2016): 197–216; d) Tóth, "The History and Types of Terrorism," 9-13.

[32] Adam Lankford, in *The Myth of Martyrdom: What Really Drives Suicide Bombers, Rampage Shooters, and Other Self Destructive Killers* (New York, NY: Palgrave MacMillan, 2013), 37.

[33] For insight into the investigative problems based on assumptions about motivational singularity or similarities among those adopting terrorism as a strategy, see Walter Reich, "Understanding Terrorist Behavior: The Limits and Opportunities of Psychological Inquiry," in ed. Walter Reich, *Origins of Terrorism: Psychologies, Ideologies, Theologies, States of Mind* (Washington DC: Woodrow Wilson Center Press and Baltimore, MD: John Hopkins University Press, 1998): 261-279.

[34] A pair of essays contrasting the supposed political motives with the psychological compulsions of terrorism make up Part I of *Origins of Terrorism*, respectively: Martha Crenshaw, "The Logic of Terrorism: Terrorist Behavior as a Product of Strategic Choice," 7-24; and Jerrold M.

Post, “Terrorist Psycho-Logic: Terrorists Behavior as a Product of Psychological Forces,” 25-40.

[35] FBI, “What We Investigate,” FBI Official Web Site, under “Terrorism,” n.d., https://www.fbi.gov /investigate/terrorism.

[36] Wm. Robert Johnston, compiler, “Deadliest Terrorist Strikes in the United States,” Worst terrorist strikes in the United States, updated August 17, 2019, http://www.johnstonsarchive.net/terrorism/wrjp255us.html; Dale L. Watson, Executive Assistant Director, Counterterrorism/Counterintelligence Division, FBI, testimony before the Senate Select Committee on Intelligence, February 6, 2002, FBI Official Web Site (archived), https://archives.fbi.gov/archives/news/testimony/the-terrorist-threat -confronting-the-united-states.

[37] History.Com Editors, “Oklahoma City Bombing,” History.com, posted December 16, 2009, updated April 16, 2021, https://www.history.com/topics/1990s/oklahoma-city-bombing; Adam Janos, “Timothy McVeigh's Death: The Final Days of the Oklahoma City Bomber,” Arts and Entertainment (A&E) True Crime Blog: Stories and News, posted June 9, 2021, updated June 10, 2021, https://www.aetv.com/real-crime/timothy-mcveigh-death; Oklahoma City Document Management Team, *Alfred P, Murrah Federal Building Bombing, April 19, 1995, Final Report* (Stillwater, OK: Oklahoma State University, Fire Protection Publications, 1996), 10, Murderpedia: The Encyclopedia of Murderers, last updated June 4, 2017, s.v. “Timothy James McVeigh,” https://murderpedia.org/.

[38] Nolan Clay, “Lori Fortier's Testimony Only as Good as Her Credibility,” *Oklahoman*, posted May 4, 1997, https://www.oklahoman.com/story/news/1997/05/04/lori-fortiers-testimony-only-as-good-as-her-credibility/62315520007/; Lori Fortier testimony, in Nolan Clay and Penny Owen, “Lori Fortier Testifies McVeigh Told of Bomb Witness Says She Could Have Prevented Deaths,” *Oklahoman*, posted April 30, 1997, https://www.oklahoman.com/story/news/1997/04/30/lori-fortier-testifies-mcveigh-told-of-bomb-witness-says-she-could-have-prevented-deaths/62316007007/; Lori Fortier testimony in Timothy McVeigh Trial, April 29, 1997, Famous Trials, s.v. “Okla City Bombing Trial (1997),” https://famous-trials.com/; Michael Joseph Fortier statement as part of plea agreement, August 10, 1995, in Douglas O. Linder, “The Oklahoma Bombing Conspirators,” Famous Trials, s.v. “Okla City Bombing Trial (1997)”; John Philip Jenkins, “Oklahoma City Bombing Terrorist Attack, Oklahoma, United States (1995),” *Encyclopedia Britannica*, updated February 12, 2024, s.v. “Oklahoma City Bombing,” https://www.britannica.com/; Douglas O. Linder, “The Oklahoma Bombing Conspirators,” Famous Trials, originally posted 1995, s.v. “Okla City Bombing Trial (1997)”; Murderpedia, “Oklahoma City Bombing,” s.v. “Timothy James McVeigh”; Jo Thomas, “For First Time, Woman Says McVeigh Told of Bomb Plan,” *New York*

Times, posted April 30, 1997, https://www.nytimes.com/1997/04/30/us/for - first-time-woman-says-mcveigh-told-of-bomb-plan.html.

[39] Anti-Defamation League (ADL), Glossary of Extremism, s.v. "Patriot Movement," https://extremismterms.adl.org/; AP, "Michael and Lori Fortier, We Will Prove, Proclaimed Tim McVeigh," posted April 24, 1997, https://apnews.com/article/9996136361c7090e5af0218226b9af03 (archived); Jenkins, "Oklahoma City Bombing Terrorist Attack"; Linder, "The Oklahoma Bombing Conspirators"; Murderpedia, "Timothy McVeigh," s.v. "Timothy James McVeigh"; Steven Wilmsen, "The Oklahoma City Bombing Trial: Who is Lori Fortier?" *Denver Post Online*, updated March 15, 2004, https://extras .denverpost.com/bomb /bomb172.htm.

[40] There were multiple injuries, some very serious, at the compound in Texas and at the home of the Weavers on Ruby Ridge. The death tally for Waco counts the casualties from an initial confrontation between agents and members of the cult that resulted in the siege plus those dead from the fires that ended it. Cori Brosnahan, "Ruby Ridge, Part One: Suspicion, Part Two: Confirmation, Part Three: Fear & Faith," American Experience, ©1996–2023 WGBH Educational Foundation, https://www.pbs.org/wgbh/americanexperience /features/ruby-ridge-part-one-suspicion/; Timothy Donahue quoting and paraphrasing Nichols, in CNN, "Witness: Nichols' Anti-Government Remarks Not Unusual," posted November 6, 1997, http://www.cnn.com/ US/9711/06/Nichols .starts/; Editors of Encyclopedia Britannica, "Waco Siege: American History (1993), *Encyclopedia Britannica*, s.v. "Waco Siege," updated March 1, 2022, https://www.britannica .com/; History.com Editors, "Ruby Ridge," History, posted January 19, 2018, updated August 21, 2018, https://www.history.com/topics/1990s/ruby-ridge; History.com Editors, "Waco Siege," History, posted December 19, 2017, updated August 21, 2018, https://www.history.com /topics /1990s/waco-siege; Dave Hunt, Threat Assessment of Randy Weaver for Marshal Service, in Brosnahan, "Ruby Ridge, Part One"; Murderpedia, "The Oklahoma City Bombing and the Trial of Timothy McVeigh: A Chronology," s.v. "Timothy James McVeigh"; Sarah Pruitt, How Ruby Ridge and Waco Led to the Oklahoma City Bombing, History, posted May 22, 2018, updated April 2, 2020, https:// www.history.com/news/how-ruby-ridge-and-waco-led-to-the-oklahoma-city-bombing; Gina Tron, "How Was Oklahoma City Bomber Timothy McVeigh Connected To Waco?" Oxygen True Crime, posted April 18, 2018, https://www.oxygen.com/crime-time/how-was-oklahoma-city-bomber-timothy-mcveigh -connected-to-waco; Robert Walsh, "The Waco Siege," *Crime Magazine*, posted October 30, 2014, https://crimemagazine.com/ waco-siege.

[41] Douglas O. Linder, "Timothy McVeigh in Waco," under "March 1993," photo, Famous Trials, s.v. "Okla City Bombing Trial (1997)"; Michelle Rauch

testimony concerning her 1993 interview with McVeigh in Waco, McVeigh Trial, June 10, 1997, Famous Trials, s.v. "Okla City Bombing Trial (1997)"; Tron, "How Was Oklahoma City Bomber Timothy McVeigh Connected?"

[42] Tron, "How Was Oklahoma City Bomber Timothy McVeigh Connected?"

[43] Rauch testimony concerning 1993 interview with McVeigh, in Waco, McVeigh Trial, June 10, 1997.

[44] Quoted by Michelle Rauch, in testimony concerning 1993 interview with McVeigh in Waco, McVeigh Trial, June 10, 1997.

[45] Linder, "The Oklahoma Bombing Conspirators," under "Timothy J. McVeigh Biography"; Murderpedia, "Summary," s.v. "Timothy James McVeigh." Typical of mass casualty events, alternative theories to the crime (some more conspiratorial than others) abound and persist: a) AP, "John Doe No. 2 Theories Linger in Oklahoma City Bombing Case," Fox News, posted January 13, 2015, https://www.foxnews.com/story/john-doe-no-2-theories-linger-in-oklahoma-city-bombing-case; b) J.M. Berger, "Full Text: The Oklahoma City Bombing: Was There a Foreign Connection?" *Intelwire*, posted December 23, 2006; c) Nolan Clay, "Nichols Claims FBI Official Directed Bombing McVeigh Cohort Again Claims Robbery of a Gun Collector Was Simply Staged," *Oklahoman*, posted February 22, 2007, https://www.oklahoman.com/story/news/local/oklahoma-city/2007/02/22/nichols-official-directed-bombingbrspan-classhl2mcveigh-claims-robbery-collector-simply-stagedspan/61811473007/; d) Andrew Gumbel and Roger G. Charles, *Oklahoma City: What the Investigation Missed - And Why It Still Matters* (New York, NY: William Morrow, HarperCollins, 2012); e) Serge F. Kovaleski, "Oklahoma Bombing Conspiracy Theories Ripple Across The Nation," *Washington Post*, posted July 9, 1995; f) Marcus Lowth, fact checked by Jamie Frater, "10 Apparent Conspiracies Surrounding the 1995 Oklahoma City Bombing," List Serve: Weird Stuff, posted December 11, 2007, https://listverse.com/2017/12/11/10-apparent-conspiracies-surrounding -the-1995-oklahoma -city-bombing/; g) Samantha Putterman, "Unfounded Oklahoma City Bombing Conspiracy Theory Involving Hillary Clinton Resurfaces," *PolitiFact*, posted May 1, 2019, https://www.politifact .com/factchecks/2019/may/01/facebook-posts/unfounded-oklahoma-city-bombing-conspiracy-theory-/; h) Saranac Hale Spencer, "Baseless Oklahoma City Bombing Conspiracy Theory," FactCheck.org, posted March 6, 2019, https://www.factcheck.org/2019/03/baseless-oklahoma-city-bombing-conspiracy-theory/; i) Russ Winter, "Hidden in Plain Sight: The Truth About Timothy McVeigh and the Oklahoma City Bombing," *Winter Watch*, posted September 28, 2020, https://www.winterwatch.net/2020/09/hidden-in-plain-sight-the-truth-about-timothy-mcveigh-and-the-oklahoma-city-bombing/. After reviewing government documents attained by the AP, Dan Defenbaugh (now retired) who served as the FBI chief of the Oklahoma City investigation

commented, "If I were still in the bureau, the investigation would be reopened." AP, "Was Oklahoma City Bombing Wider Conspiracy?" NBC News, posted February 25, 2004, https://www.nbcnews.com/id/wbna 4371384. Attorney Stephen Jones, who represented McVeigh, said, "[T]he bombing conspiracy consisted probably of 10 conspirators." AP, "Was Oklahoma City Bombing Wider Conspiracy?" However, "[a] team of FBI agents that re-examined the Oklahoma City bombing after a resurgence in conspiracy theories uncovered no new reliable leads…." AP, "Oklahoma Bombing Conspiracy Theories Dispelled," *Los Angeles Daily News*, posted November 25, 2007, updated August 29, 2017, https://www.dailynews.com /2007/11/25/oklahoma-bombing-conspiracy-theories-dispelled/. A key member of that group was former FBI deputy director Weldon Kennedy, who wrote in a memoir, "I can say with total confidence that we identified all three conspirators [Fortier, McVeigh, and Nichols] in the case and arrested them. McVeigh's sister, Nicholas's wife, and Fortier's wife had limited knowledge, but none of them were materially involved. No other person, other than these three, was involved in this bombing – despite what conspiracy theorist may say." *On-Scene Commander* (Dulles, VA: Potomac Books, Inc., 2007), 220.

[46] Letter by Timothy McVeigh in Tracy McVeigh, "The McVeigh letters: Why I Bombed Oklahoma," *Guardian*, posted May 6, 2001, https://www. theguardian.com/world/2001/may/06/mcveigh.usa. Presented as transcribed in periodical.

[47] In Walsh, "The Waco Siege."

[48] For more on purposeful non-random data collection, see: a) Steve Campbell, Melanie Greenwood, Sarah Prior, Toniele Shearer, Kerrie Walkem, Sarah Young, Danielle Bywaters, and Kim Walker, "Purposive Sampling: Complex or Simple? Research Case Examples," *Journal of Research in Nursing*, 25, no. 8 (December 2020): 652-661; b) Imelda T. Coyne, "Sampling in Qualitative Research: Purposeful and Theoretical Sampling; Merging or Clear Boundaries?" *Journal of Advanced Nursing* 26, no. 3 (September 1997): 437-640; c) Lawrence A. Palinkas, Sarah M. Horwitz, Carla A. Green, Jennifer P. Wisdom, Naihua Duan, and Kimberly Hoagwood, "Purposeful Sampling for Qualitative Data Collection and Analysis in Mixed Method Implementation Research," author's manuscript, PubMed Central, posted September 1, 2016, https://www.ncbi.nlm.nih.gov/pmc/articles/PMC 4012002/.

[49] Sabina Yeasmin and Khan Ferdousour Rahman. "'Triangulation' Research Method as the Tool of Social Science Research," *Bangladesh University of Professionals Journal* 1, no. 1 (September 2012): 155-156.

[50] Ibid, 157.

[51] Albert Mills, Gabrielle Durepos, and Elden Wiebe, eds., *Encyclopedia of Case Study Research* (Los Angeles, CA: Sage Publications, Inc.), 2:803. In

addition, refer to Robert K. Yin, *Case Study Research Design and Methods* (Newbury Park, CA: Sage Publications, 1989), 122-123.

[52] For discussions about the utility and validity of this type of evaluation consult: Robert Jones, David Bennett, Nelson M. Blake, Robert Crane, Samuel Eddy, Robert G. Gregory, Joseph Levine, Roderick MacDonald, Peter T. Marshal, James M. Powell, James R. Sharp, William Stinchcombe, Walter Ullmann, and Stephen Webb, eds., *A Guide to Historical Method* 3rd ed. (Chicago, Il: Dorsey Press, 1980), 171-200; and Yin, *Case Study Research*, 33-35, 109-113.

Chapter One

[1] *Patriot Ledger*, "Timeline of the Amy Bishop Case," posted and updated October 2, 2012, http://www.patriotledger.com/archive/x1238772457/ Timeline -of-the-Amy-Bishop-case.

[2] James Lindsay with Associated Press (AP) contributors, Jay Reeves, Desiree Hunter, and Denise Lavoie, "Ala. Suspect Brilliant but Social Misfit," *Lubbock-Avalanche Journal,* lubbockonline.com, posted February 21, 2012, http://lubbockonline.com/stories/022110/loc_ 565688235.shtml.

[3] Lane Lambert, "Amy Bishop Wants Murder Trial Here," *Patriot Ledger*, posted and updated October 2, 2010, http://www.patriotledger.com/topstories/x383 194450/Amy-Bishop-wants-murder-trial-here.

[4] After learning of the rampage at the university, the District Attorney in Norfolk County (the jurisdiction where Bishop's brother was shot) initiated an inquest into Seth's death. The circumstances were suspicious enough for an indictment even though the incident at that point was well over two decades in the past. Bob Salsberg, "Amy Bishop Charged with Murder of Brother," *Huffington Post*, posted June 16, 2010, updated May 25, 2011; WHNT News 19, "Amy Bishop Charged With Brother's Murder, YouTube, posted January 9, 2012, https://www.youtube.com/watch?v=JKSfRfW70eg. More than two years later, after Bishop's sentence to life in prison for the multiple killings in Huntsville, the D.A. for Norfolk declined to prosecute explaining, "The penalty we would seek for a first-degree murder conviction is already in place." Denise Lavoie, "Amy Bishop, "Who Killed 3 Alabama Professors, Wants to Stand Trial for Brother Seth's 1986 Murder," HuffPost Crime: posted October 2, 2012, http://www .huffingtonpost.com/2012/10/02/amy-seth-bishop-murder-trial_n_1932904.html (page discontinued). Subsequently, Bishop persuaded her public defender to file a request that the trial move forward. Lane Lambert, "Amy Bishop Wants Murder Trial Here," *Patriot Ledger*, PatriotLedger.com: posted and updated October 2, 2010, http://www.patriotledger.com/topstories /x383194450/Amy-Bishop-wants-murder-trial-here. In the words of a Norfolk County spokesperson, the filing was "legally meaningless" since the District Attorney had already declared

"nol prossed" (an entry on the legal record that the prosecution would not proceed to trial). Lambert, "Amy Bishop Wants Murder Trial; *Webster's Collegiate Dictionary*, 5th ed., s.v., "nolle prosequi and nol-pros." There are several puzzling aspects to the death of Amy Bishop's brother including the actual shooting incident as well as the actions of the police and district attorney in its aftermath. The sources that follow, besides those already noted, may be useful for those who wish to pursue the subject: a) Braintree Police Department News Release, "Comments from Chief Paul Frazier Regarding Amy Bishop," Braintree, Massachusetts, release date, February 13, 2010, http://www.google.com/search?client=safari&rls=en&q="Comments +from +Chief+Paul+Frazier+Regarding+Amy+Bishop&ie=UTF-8&oe= UTF-8; b) Shaila Dewan, Katie Zezima, and Stephanie Saul "Alabama Campus Shooter Packed a History of Rage," *Seattle Times*, originally published February 20, 2010, https://www.seattletimes.com/nation-world/alabama-campus-shooter-packed-a-history-of-rage/; c) Trooper Brian L. Howe to First Assistant District Attorney John P. Kivlan, "Accidental Shooting of Seth Bishop, White Male, D.O.B. 4/9/68 at 46 Hollis Avenue, Braintree, Massachusetts on December 6, 1986, Report to, Case no. 86-112-0910-0185," March 30,1987, School Shooters .info: Resources on School Shootings, Perpetrators, and Prevention, last updated March 21, 2024, s.v. "Amy Bishop," https://schoolshooters.info/; d) Brain Lawson, "Amy Bishop's Parents Testified in 2010 about Day She Killed Her Brother," AL.com, posted and updated February 22, 2012, https://www.al.com/breaking/2012/02/amy_bishops_parents_testified.html.

[5] Niki Doyle, "Police Find Gun Used in UAH Shooting in Bathroom, More Charges Pending against Amy Bishop," AL.com, posted February 13, 2010, updated January 14, 2019, http://blog.al.com/breaking /2010/02/police_find_gun_used_in_uah_sh.html.

[6] Michelle Sigona, "Amy Bishop's Bizarre Past," International Crime Wire, posted February 18, 2010, http://www.michellesigona.com/2010/02/amy-bishops-bizarre-past/ (page discontinued).

[7] Susan Donaldson James, "Accused Alabama Shooter Fought with Neighbors, Told Family She was Stalked," American Broadcasting Company (ABC) News, posted February 16, 2010, http://abcnews.go.com/Health/shooter-amy-bishop-fought-neighbors-odd-ball-colleagues/story?id=9846839#.UO Onva79Ws1.

[8] John W. Guilfoil, "Ipswich Neighbors Recall Confrontations with Amy Bishop," Boston.com, posted February 15, 2010, http://www.boston.com/news/local/breaking_news/2010/02/ipswich_neighbo.html (page discontinued).

[9] Cable News Network (CNN), "Police: University Shooting Suspect Was Charged after Fight in 2002," posted February 17, 2010, https://www.cnn.com/2010/CRIME/02/17/alabama.shooting/index.html; Maria Cramer, "Bishop

Could Have Been Tried, DA Says: Cites Actions that Followed Brother's Death," Boston.com, posted February 17, 2010, 2, http://www. boston.com/news/local/massachusetts/articles/2010/02/17/bishop could_have_been_tried_da_says/?page=1 (page discontinued); Steve Doyle, "Amy Bishop Claimed She Was Victim in 2002 IHOP Assault," AL.com, posted February 18, 2010, https://www.al.com/breaking/2010/02/amy_bishop_cursed_punched_woma.html.

[10] Unidentified woman as reported by Seth Doan, in CBS, "New Revelation in Professor's Past," CBS.com, recorded newscast, posted February 17, 2010, YouTube, https://www.youtube.com/watch?v=f8RK2M-dvBE.

[11] It is not entirely clear whether Bishop made the proclamation in the restaurant during the actual attack or immediately thereafter. Some stories indicate she shouted her name while striking her adversary. AP, "Accused Ala. Prof."; CNN, "Police: University Shooting Suspect"; Dewan, Zezima, and Saul, "Alabama Campus Shooter." However, the *Salem News* stated that the other party involved in the confrontation followed Bishop to the parking lot to get her license number – presumably to make a police report – and it was at that point that Bishop proudly declared her identity. Matarazzo and Manganis, "Records Show Bishop." If that version is correct, she may have made the statement defiantly to demonstrate that she had no concern about the possibility of any further retaliatory action, legal or otherwise, from her perceived adversary. The distinction, though, is somewhat irrelevant. Either way the manner in which she proclaimed her name demonstrates her inclination toward grandiosity and oblivion to the rights and feelings of others.

[12] Lowell Sun, "Accused Ala. Prof Charged with Assault in Mass. IHOP," *Sun*, posted February 17, 2010, https://www.lowellsun.com/2010/02/17/accused-ala-prof-charged-with-assault-at-mass-ihop/.

[13] Dr. Jacqueline U. Johnson, as Personal Representative of The Estate of Dr. Adriel D. Johnson, Sr., Deceased, v. Dr. Vistasp M. Karbhari, Dr. Amy Bishop Aka Amy Bishop Anderson, and James Anderson, Circuit Court for Madison County, Alabama, CV-2011-900038.00 (served April 2011), ¶25, School Shooters .info, s.v. "Amy Bishop"; Lee Roop, "Amy Bishop's Life Is a Tale of Triumph and Violent Failure (Timeline)," AL.com, posted and updated September 12, 2012, http://blog.al.com/breaking/2012/09/amy_bishops_life_is_a_tale_of.html (page discontinued); Sigona, "Amy Bishop's Bizarre Past." Accounts regarding the actual ruling are inconsistent. Two say she pled guilty to misdemeanors. Doyle, "Amy Bishop Claimed She Was Victim"; Roop, "Amy Bishop's Life." Another says that she did not plead guilty but "admitted there was enough evidence to prosecute her." Cramer, "Bishop Could Have Been Tried," 2. The CBS news report states she admitted guilt to "avoid jail time." Doane, in CBS, "New Revelation in

Professor's Past." According to another article, Captain Bonaiuto of the Peabody Police Department in Massachusetts (where the incident took place) stated that Bishop admitted to the charges in court, and they were then adjudicated, but eventually dismissed. Jay Reeves and Gregg Bluestein, "Ala. Prof's Story Begins with Brother's 1986 Death," originally published February 16, 2010, Murderpedia: The Encyclopedia of Murderers, last updated June 4, 2017, s.v. "Amy Bishop," https://murderpedia.org/. Captain Bonaiuto's explanation seems the most likely since another source mentions that Bishop was placed on "informal probation." Plus, a detailed account on the *Salem News* site, based on court records, chronicles that the judge "continued the case without a finding for six months. … The charges were then dismissed." Bruno Matarazzo Jr. and Julie Manganis. "Records Show Bishop Was in a Scrap at IHOP, Alleged Alabama Gunwoman, Mom Tangled Over Child's Booster Seat," *Salem News*, posted February 17, 2010, http://www.salemnews.com/local/x1690088055/Records-show-Bishop-was-in-scrap-at-IHOP.

[14] Roop, "Amy Bishop's Life." According to the *Salem News*, the judge did not concur with the prosecuting attorney and instead took the advice of the defense. Matarazzo and Manganis, "Records Show Bishop." Other news accounts verify that there is no record of her participating in any training or therapeutic sessions designed to give her tools to restrain her outbursts even though the topic was broached during court proceedings. CNN, "Police: University Shooting Suspect"; *Huntsville Times* Staff, "Amy Bishop Charged with 2002 Assault at IHOP," AL.com, posted and updated February 16, 2010, https://www.al.com/breaking/2010/02/amy_bishop_charged_with_2002_a.html. The incident at the restaurant occurred in March of 2002. The attack at the university took place on February 12, 2010. Roop, "Amy Bishop's Life."

[15] Shaila Dewan, Stephanie Saul, and Katie Zezima with contributing reporters William K. Rashbaum and Sarah Wheaton, "For Professor, Fury Just Beneath the Surface," *New York Times*, posted February 20, 2010, https://www.nytimes.com/topic/person/amy-bishop; Amy Wallace, "What Made This University Researcher Snap?" *Wired Magazine*, posted February 28, 2011, 4, http:// www.wired.com/magazine/2011/02/ff_bishop/all/. To put this outburst in perspective, with so many contributors, the second position would still have afforded her status.

[16] Wallace, "What Made this University Researcher?" 2. Bishop is a second cousin to the well-known novelist, John Irving and she completed three novels, all unpublished. "One novel was about the troubles of a girl growing up in Belfast and another was a thriller about a scientist who was an IRA operative. … The third, 'Amazon Fever,' was about a virus that renders women infertile." AP and *Patriot Ledger*, "Students Had Complained about Bishop,"

Patriot Ledger, posted and updated February 18, 2010, https://www.patriotledger.com/article/20100218/NEWS/302189538.

[17] AP and *Patriot Ledger*, "Students Had Complained."

[18] Lindsay with Reeves, Hunter, and Lavoie, "Ala. Suspect Brilliant." Prior to posing that rhetorical question, her attorney, dropping his professional composure, admitted, "I just think the case speaks for itself. … I think she's wacko." The following day, though, he said he regretted using that derogative bit of slang. CNN, "Alabama Professor's Lawyer Regrets Calling Her 'Wacko,'" posted, February 19, 2010, http://www.cnn.com/2010/CRIME/02/19/alabama.shooting.lawyer /index.html. Regardless, before arranging for a plea bargain, Miller, previewed his intent to proceed with an insanity defense for Bishop's crimes, even though it was "rarely" successful in Alabama. "I don't know what else I've got," he explained. "It wasn't self-defense. It wasn't 'somebody else did it.' I think she has some real severe mental problems." Dennis Tatz, "Amy Bishop's Sanity at Issue," *Patriot Ledger*, posted and updated on February 22, 2010, https://www.patriotledger.com/story/news/courts/2010/02/22/amy-bishop-s-sanity-at/40208755007/. The insanity defense along with issues related to competency for trial relative to mass murder are explored in Chapter Four.

[19] Lizzie Crocker, "Mass Murderers, Unlike Serial Killers, Are Hard to Profile," *The Daily Beast*, posted July 20, 2012, http://www.thedailybeast.com/articles/2012/07/20/mass-murderers-unlike-serial-killers-are-hard-to-profile.html; Michael H. Stone, *The Anatomy of Evil* (Amherst, NY: Prometheus Books, 2009).

[20] Crocker, "Mass Murderers, Unlike Serial Killers."

[21] James Alan Fox and Jack Levin, *Extreme Killing: Understanding Serial and Mass Murder*, (Thousand Oaks, CA: Sage Publications Inc., 2005), 159.

[22] Ibid, 160, table 13.1.

[23] US Department of Justice, Federal Bureau of Investigation (FBI), Criminal Justice Information Services Division, 2019 Crime in the United States, under "Homicide, Expanded Homicide Data," table 3, https:// ucr.fbi.gov/crime-in-the-u.s/2019/crime-in-the-u.s.-2019/home. Percentages are rounded to nearest whole number. Surprisingly, perpetrators were unknown for 4,502 (28%) of the 16,245 homicides that were reported.

[24] Mark Follman, Gavin Aronsen, and Deanna Pan, "A Guide to Mass Shootings in America," *Mother Jones*, last updated May 26, 2021, https://www.motherjones.com/politics/2012/07/mass-shootings-map/; Mark Follman, Gavin Aronsen, and Deanna Pan, "US Mass Shootings, 1982–2021: Data from Mother Jones' Investigation," *Mother Jones*, last updated May 26, 2021, https://www.motherjones.com/politics /2012/12/mass-shootings-mother-jones-full-data/.

[25] Jillian Peterson and James Densley, The Violence Project: How to Stop the Mass Shooting Epidemic, supported by Award No. 2018-75-CX-0023, from the National Institute of Justice, Office of Justice Programs, U.S. Department of Justice, under "The Database, Mass Shooter Database, Epidemic," regularly updated, https://www.theviolenceproject.org/.

[26] FBI, *Active Shooter Incidents: 20-Year Review, 2000-2019* (U.S. Department of Justice, May 2021), 2, https://www.fbi.gov/file-repository/active-shooter-incidents-20-year-review-2000-2019-060121.pdf/view.

[27] Ibid, 4.

[28] Ibid, 2.

[29] Roy F. Baumeister, *Evil: Inside Human Violence and Cruelty* (New York, NY: A W.H. Freeman/Holt Paperback, Henry Holt and Company, 1999), 137; US Department of Justice, FBI, under "Homicide, Expanded Homicide Data," table 6.

[30] International criminal statistics are notoriously suspect because the criteria for inclusion vary markedly by country. The year 2017 was used as the point of comparison because two sources contained rates by gender as well as a reasonable number for overall incidents. The Facts Institute, Countries by Murder Rate – Ranked, posted 2022, under "Key Findings from the Report," https://www.factsinstitute.com /ranking/countries-by-murder-rate/; Edith M. Lederer, "464,000 People Killed in Homicides around The World in 2017: UN Report," AP, posted July 8, 2019, https://globalnews.ca/news/5473422/un-report-homicides-2019/. Andrew Blaze (aka Randy Stair), profiled in the next chapter, was not included with the males or females for purposes of calculating the z-score because she identified as a woman even though she was physically a man.

[31] According to Bureau of Justice statistics for 1980-2008. Alexia Cooper and Erica L. Smith, *Patterns and Trends: Homicide Trends in the United States, 1980-2008* (U.S. Department of Justice, Office of Justice Programs, November 2011) 10, table 10.

[32] Recounted by Richard Rhodes, *Why They Kill* (New York: Alfred A. Knopf, Inc., 1999), 64, 84-90. Findings by Athens contributed to the theoretical constructs in *Violent Criminal Acts and Actors: A Symbolic Interactionist Study* (Boston, MA: Routledge and Kegan Paul Ltd, 1980) and *Creation of Dangerous Violent Criminals* (Urbana and Chicago, Il: University of Illinois Press. 1992), both by Lonnie H. Athens.

[33] John Douglas and Douglas Olshaker, *The Anatomy of Motive: The FBI's Legendary Mindhunter Explores the Key to Understanding and Catching Violent Criminals* (New York, NY: Lisa Drew/Scribner, 1999), 219-220.

[34] Lisa Pescara-Kovach, "Female Shooters Shouldn't Be Ignored," *The Hill*, posted May 19, 2019, https://thehill.com/opinion/civil-rights/444478-female-

shooters-shouldnt-be-ignored?rl=1. Dr. Pescara-Kovach's occupation and position are cited at the end of the article.

[35] For more on these three rampages, refer to: Chapter Four of this Book as well as the Introduction along with Chapters Two and Seven in *How Rampage Killers Interpret Their Worlds*.

[36] Aghdam, 38 at the time of her rampage, maintained at least four channels on YouTube in English, Turkish, and Farsi with over 5,000 subscribers and 9.2 million views between 2010 and 2018. Tom Cleary, "Nasim Aghdam: 5 Fast Facts You Need to Know," Heavy.com, updated December 9, 2019, https://heavy.com/news/2018/04/nasim-aghdam-youtube-shooting-suspect-channel-instagram-photos/; Stephanie Gosk, "YouTube Shooting Suspect's Family Claims Warnings Were Missed," *Today*, posted on YouTube, April 5, 2018, https://www.youtube.com/watch?v=12d-ynrjVM4. She also posted on Instagram, Facebook, and her own website. She used various online aliases including Nasim(e) Sabz and Nasim VeganBreeze. A vegan, she advocated for animal rights, danced, sang, made speeches, blogged, gave cooking instructions, and performed body building videos. Cleary, "Nasim Aghdam: 5 Fast Facts"; Merritt Clifton, "The Many Faces of Nasim Aghdam, Vegan Turned YouTube Shooter," Animals 24-7, posted April 5, 2015, under "Social Media Star," https://www.animals24-7.org/2018/04/05/the-many-faces-of-nasim-aghdam-vegan-turned-youtube-shooter/; Jessica McBride, "Watch: Nasim Aghdam's YouTube Channel & Videos," Heavy.com, posted April 4, 2018, https://heavy.com/news/2018/04/nasim-aghdam-youtube-channel-video-nasime-sabz/. Aghdam alleged that YouTube censored her content and demonetized her profits by undercounting her viewers thereby cutting her rightful share of advertising revenues. Clifton, "The Many Faces of Nasim Aghdam"; narration, in *Inside Edition* "YouTube Shooter Vents on Website After Making Just Pennies for Videos," posted on YouTube, April 5, 2018, https://www.youtube.com/watch?v=ubu557K-_T8; Madison Malone Kircher, "YouTube Shooter Nasim Aghdam Said Company 'Ruined Her Life,'" *Intelligencer*, posted April 4, 2018, https://nymag.com /intelligencer/2018/04/who-is-youtube-shooter-nasim-aghdam.html. She uploaded film clips airing her complaints and criticized the media company on her own site, displaying a yellow banner that accused YouTube of censorship as well as putting short term profits above health, the environment, family values, upholding the truth, and the welfare of non-human species. Narration and video, ABC News, "YouTube shooting: What Happened before Female Suspect Carried Out Her Attack," posted on YouTube, April 5, 2018, https://www.youtube.com/watch?v=Ok7 vxzWs124; Cleary, "Nasim Aghdam: 5 Fast Facts"; Clifton, "The Many Faces of Nasim Aghdam," under "YouTube Age-Restricted & 'Demonetized,'" Videos, Alleged Censorship; Kircher, "YouTube Shooter

Nasim." Early in the afternoon, with a 9mm handgun, she assailed YouTube Headquarters in San Bruno, California opening fire on employees who were outside eating lunch. Three were wounded by her gunshots while a fourth injured her ankle fleeing. Aghdam then took her own life. ABC 7 News, "1 dead, 4 Injured in Shooting at YouTube Headquarters in San Bruno," posted April 3, 2018, https://abc7news.com/youtube-shooting-shooter-california-headquarters/3297411/; Mahita Gajanan and Eli Meixler, "What to Know about Suspected YouTube Shooter Nasim Aghdam," *Time*, posted April 4, 2018, https://time.com/5226954/youtube-headquarters-shooter-san-bruno/; Gosk, "YouTube Shooting Suspect's Family"; Emily Shapiro, "YouTube Headquarters Shooting: How the Attack Unfolded," ABC News, posted April 4, 2018, https:// abcnews.go.com/US/shooting-youtubes-calif-headquarters-unfolded/story?id=54227873; Matt Gutman, narration, "Alleged YouTube shooter Broadcast Her Motive on Its Website: Police," ABC News, posted on YouTube, April 4, 2018, https://www.youtube.com/watch?v=ErM1lqz8oso. Contrary to internet conspiracy theories, she was not transgender nor transitioning. Katelyn Burns, "Conspiracy Theorists Are Now Claiming the YouTube Shooter Is Transgender," them, posted April 5, 2018, https://www.them.us/story/conspiracy-theorists-claiming-youtube-shooter-transgender; Christina Cauterucci, "People Are Molding Their Responses to Nasim Aghdam to Fit the Shape of Their Bigotry," *Slate*, posted April 4, 2018, https://slate.com/news-and-politics/2018/04/people-are-molding-their-responses-to-nasim-aghdam-to-fit-the-shape-of-their-bigotry.html. Flanagan is listed in this work's Appendix and is a subject of anecdotal evaluation in the fourth chapter of this book's companion volume.

37 Jeanna Bryner, "Scientists: You Can't Profile School Shooters," *Live Science*, posted January 11, 2008, http://www.livescience.com/1446-scientists-profile-school-shooters.html.

38 Elizabeth Chuck, Alex Johnson, and Corky Siemaszko, "17 Killed in Mass Shooting at High School in Parkland, Florida," NBC, posted February 14, 2018, updated February 15, 2018, https://www.nbcnews.com/news/us-news/police-respond-shooting-parkland-florida-high-school-n848101.

39 Vanessa Schipani, "The Facts on Media Violence," FactCheck.org, posted March 8, 2018, https://www.factcheck.org/2018/03/facts-media-violence/.

40 Ibid.

41 US Congress, Senate Committee on the Judiciary, Juvenile Delinquency, *Comic Books and Juvenile Delinquency*, Library of Congress Catalogue Card Number 77-90720, 1955-56, http://www.thecomicbooks.com/1955senateinterim.html.

42 Ibid, under "Techniques of Crime Are Taught by Crime and Horror Comics."

43 American Psychological Society, s.v. "About," http://www.the-aps.org/fm/.

[44] Craig Anderson, Leonard Berkowitz, Edward Donnerstein, L. Rowell Huesmann, James D. Johnson, Daniel Linz, and Neil M. Malamuth, and Ellen Wartella, "The Influence of Media Violence on Youth," *Psychological Science in the Public Interest* 4, no. 3 (December 2003): 81, http://journals.sagepub.com /doi/pdf/10.1111/j.1529-1006.2003.pspi_1433.x.

[45] Jonathan Kellerman, *Savage Spawn: Reflections on Violent Children* (New York, NY: The Ballantine Publishing Group, 1999), 72. Jonathan Kellerman is now best known as a novelist but for years he was a practicing psychologist and held positions such Director of the Psychosocial Program, Children's Hospital of Los Angeles, as well as Professor of Pediatrics at the University of Southern California. Ibid, back cover; Kellerman interview with Mark Rubinstein in CrimeReads, "Jonathan Kellerman and the Dark Psychology of Crime: Probing the Mind Behind Alex Delaware," posted March 21, 2018, https:// crimereads.com/jonathan-kellerman-and-the-dark-psychology-of-crime/.

[46] Refer to: a) Craig Anderson, Akiko Shibuya, Nobuko Ihori, Edward L. Swing, Brad J. Bushman, Akira Sakamoto, Hannah R. Rothstein, and Muniba Saleem, "Violent Video Game Effects on Aggression, Empathy, and Prosocial Behavior in Eastern and Western Countries: A Meta-Analytic Review," *Psychological Bulletin* 136, no. 2 (2010): 151-173, http://dx.doi.org/10.1037/a0018251; b) Victoria Simpson Beck, Stephanie Boys, Christopher Rose, Eric Beck, "Violence Against Women in Video Games," *Journal of Interpersonal Violence* 27, no. 15 (October 2012): 3016-3031, posted April 30, 2012, https://doi.org/10.1177/0886260512441078; c) Brad J. Bushman, Mario Gollwitzer, and Carlos Cruz, "There Is Broad Consensus: Media Researchers Agree That Violent Media Increase Aggression in Children, and Pediatricians and Parents Concur," *Psychology of Popular Media Culture* 4, no. 3 (2015): 200–214, https://www. researchgate.net/publication/280759024; d) Brad J. Bushman, Hannah R. Rothstein, and Craig A. Anderson, "Much Ado About Something: Violent Video Game Effects and a School of Red Herring: Reply to Ferguson and Kilburn (2010)," *Psychological Bulletin* 136, no. 2 (2010): 182–187, http://citeseerx.ist.psu.edu/viewdoc/download?doi=10.1.1.601.4246&rep=re p1&type=pdf; e) Robert Busching, Johnie Allen, and Craig A. Anderson, "Violent Media Content and Effects," *Oxford Research Encyclopedia, Communication* posted March 2016, doi: 10.1093/acrefore/9780190228 613.013.1; f) Christopher J. Ferguson, "Does Media Violence Predict Societal Violence? It Depends on What You Look at and When," *Journal of Communication* 65, no. 1: (February 2015): 1-22; g) Christopher J Ferguson and John Kilburn, "Much Ado About Nothing: The Misestimation and Overinterpretation of Violent Video Game Effects in Eastern and Western Nations: Comment on Anderson et al. (2010)," *Psychological Bulletin* 136, no. 2 (March 2010): 174-178, discussion 182-187; h) Christopher J. Ferguson

and Stephanie Rueda, "The Hitman Study Violent Video Game Exposure Effects on Aggressive Behavior, Hostile Feelings, and Depression," *European Psychologist* 15, no. 2 (January 2010): 99-108, https://www.researchgate.net/publication/240218655_The_Hitman_Study; i) Rowell L. Huesmann, "The Impact of Electronic Media Violence: Scientific Theory and Research," *Journal of Adolescent Health* 41, no. 6 (December 2007): 6–13, https://www.jahonline.org/article/S1054-139X(07)00391-6/pdf; j) James D. Ivory, Malte Elson, Christopher J Ferguson, Joanne Savage, Patrick M Markey, John Colwell, Mark D Griffiths, and Kevin D. Williams, "Manufacturing Consensus in a Diverse Field of Scholarly Opinions: A Comment on Bushman, Gollwitzer, and Cruz (2015)," *Psychology of Popular Media Culture* 4, no. 3 (2015): 222-229, https://www.researchgate.net/publication/280029075_Manufacturing_Consensus_in_a_Diverse_Field_of_Scholarly_Opinions_A_Comment_on_Bushman_Gollwitzer_and_Cruz_2015; k) Joanne Savage and Christina Yancey, "The Effects of Media Violence Exposure on Criminal Aggression," *Criminal Justice and Behavior* 35, no. 6 (June 2008): 772-791; l) Hikaru Takeuchi, Yasuyuki Taki, Hiroshi Hashizume, Kohei Asano, Michiko Asano, Yuko Sassa, Susumu Yokota, Yuka Kotozaki, Rui Nouchi, Ryuta Kawashima, "The Impact of Television Viewing on Brain Structures: Cross-Sectional and Longitudinal Analyses," *Cerebral Cortex* 25, no. 5 (May 2015): 1188-1197.

[47] L. Rowell Huesmann, Jessica Moise-Titus, Cheryl-Lynn Podolski, and Leonard D. Eron, "Longitudinal Relations Between Children's Exposure to TV Violence and Their Aggressive and Violent Behavior in Young Adulthood: 1977–1992," *Developmental Psychology* 39, no. 2 (April 2003): 203-205, table 2, 217, table 10, https://www.apa.org/pubs/journals/releases/dev-392201.pdf.

[48] Savage and Yancey, "The Effects of Media Violence Exposure," abstract, 780, table 1, 785, 786.

[49] a) Anderson et al., "Violent Video Game Effects on Aggression," 82-83; b) Bushman, Gollwitzer, and Cruz, "There Is Broad Consensus," 201-202; c) Bushman, Rothstein, and Anderson, "Much Ado About Something," 4; d) Ferguson and Kilburn, "Much Ado About Nothing," 175-176; e) Umar Farooq, "Social Problem – Definition, Effects, Characteristics, Classification & Causes," study lecture notes, posted August 13, 2011, http://www.studylecturenotes.com/social-sciences/sociology/121-social-change-and-social-problem; f) Ivory et al., "Manufacturing Consensus in a Divided Field," 8, 10; g) Philip Mongan, "Rampage School Shootings: A Content Analysis of Media and Scholarly Accounts of Perpetuation Factors Associated with the Phenomenon" (doctoral diss., University of Kentucky, 2013), 21-22, 112-118.

[50] Ferguson and Kilburn, "Much Ado About Nothing," 175; Ridha Joober, Norbert Schmitz, Lawrence Annable, and Patricia Boksa, "Publication Bias: What Are the Challenges and Can They Be overcome?" *Journal of Psychiatry and Neuroscience* 37, no. 3 (May 2012): 149-152.

[51] Christopher J. Ferguson, "Does Media Violence Predict Societal Violence? It Depends on What You Look at and When," *Journal of Communication*: 65, no. 1 (February 2015): E4-E6, E7, figure 1.

[52] Ibid, E5.

[53] Christopher J. Ferguson, *Adolescents, Crime, and the Media: A Critical Analysis*, New York, NY: Springer, 2013), 27, figure 2.1; Statista, "Sales of Computer and Video Games in the U.S. from 1996 to 2013 (in Million Units)," The Statistics Portal: Statistics and Studies from More than 22,500 Sources, https://www.statista.com/statistics/263258/computer-games-unit-sales-in-the-us/.

[54] Harvard Health Publishing, "Violent Video Games and Young People," *Harvard Mental Health Letter*, posted October 2010, archived, https://www.health.harvard.edu/search?content%5Bquery%5D =Video%20Game%20Use%20Among%20American%20Teens&content%5 Btoggle%5D%5Barchived%5D=true.

[55] Matthew Friedman, Ames C. Grawert, and James Cullen, *Crime Trends: 1990-2016* (New York University of Law: Brennan Center for Justice, 2017), 3, 11, 14.

[56] U.S. Department of Justice Office, Statistical Briefing Book: Law Enforcement and Juvenile Crime Juvenile Justice and Delinquency Prevention (OJJDP), released August 31, 2021, under "What are the trends in serious violent crime offending by juveniles?" and "What proportion of serious violent crimes are committed by juveniles?" https://www.ojjdp.gov/ojstatbb/.

[57] Regarding side effects begetting mass violence: a) Wisner Baum, "Medication-Induced Violence Lawsuits," n.d., https://www.baumhedlundlaw.com/ medication-induced-violence/; b) CCHR International, *Psychiatric Drugs: Create Violence & Suicide School Shootings & Other Acts of Senseless Violence* (Los Angeles, CA: CCHR, March 2018), https://www.cchrint.org /pdfs/violence-report.pdf; c) Citizen's Commission on Human Rights (CCHR) Florida "Antidepressants Are a Prescription for Mass Shootings," posted November 14, 2012, https://www.cchrflorida.org/antidepressants-are-a-prescription-for-mass-shootings/; d) Criminal Justice, "Prescription Drugs and School Violence," 2023, https://criminal-justice.iresearchnet.com/ crime/ school-violence/prescription-drugs-and-school-violence/; e) David Dahlman, "Antidepressant Drugs and Antipsychotic Drugs and Murder," Dr. Dahlman.com, designed 1999-2001, https://drdahlman.com/antidepressant-drugs-and-antipsychotic-drugs-and-murder/; f) Selwyn Duke, "From Prozac to Parkland: Are Psychiatric Drugs Causing Mass Shootings?" *New*

American, posted February 18, 2018, https://thenewamerican.com/from-prozac-to-parkland-are-psychiatric-drugs-causing-mass-shootings/; g) ePRNews, "Press Release: Latest Shooting – Another Act of Violence; Another Psychiatric Drug," ePRNews.com, posted March 14, 2018, https://eprnews.com/latest-shooting-another-act-of-violence-another-psychiatric-drug-3141 59/ ("either removed or taken down for editorial review & approval"); h) David Kupelian, "Media Ignoring 1 Crucial Factor in Florida School Shooting," *WND*, posted February 15, 2018, https://www.wnd.com/2018 /02/media-ignoring-1-crucial-factor-in-florida-school-shooting/; i) Jerome London, "37 Mass Shooters Who Were on Antidepressants," *Thought Catalogue*, updated September 11, 2019, https:// thoughtcatalog.com/jeremy-london/2019/09/37-mass-shooters-who-were-on-antidepressants/; j) Manette Loudon, dir., and Gary Null, dir. and writ., *The Drugging of Our Children* (Gary Null & Associates, 2005); k) Jamshid A. Marvasti and Shelby L. Friel, "Psychiatric Diagnoses and Medications: Do They Cause Gun Violence?" *Connecticut Medicine* 83, no. 3 (March 2019): 113-122; l) Joe Pierre, "Mass Shootings, Psychiatric Medications, and Rick Perry," *Psychology Today*, posted June 20, 2015, https://www.psychologytoday .com/us/blog /psych-unseen/201506/mass-shootings-psychiatric-medications-and-rick-perry; m) Jon Rappoport, "Prozac Mass Murders: The Truth Comes to Light," *Jon Rappoport's Blog*, posted Oct 2, 2019, https://blog.nomorefakenews.com/2019/10/02/prozac-mass-murders-the-truth-comes-to-light/; n) Dan Roberts, "Every Mass Shooting Shares One Thing in Common & It's NOT Weapons," *AmmoLand: Shooting and Sports News*, posted April 1, 2013, https://www.ammoland.com/2013/04/every-mass-shooting-in-the-last-20-years-shares-psychotropic-drugs/#axzz3dc2o9i2n; o) SSRIStories.org, under "SSRI Stories: Antidepressant Nightmares," © for indexing 2023, https://ssristories.org; p) Jeanne M. Stolzer, "The Systemic Correlation between Psychiatric Medications and Unprovoked Mass Murder in America," *New Male Studies: An International Journal* 2, no. 2 (2013): 12-23, http://psychrights.org/Research/Digest/Misc/PsychDrugsMassMurder CorrelationJStolzer2013.pdf. Regarding common prescriptive uses: a) Drugs.com, "Thorazine Side Effects," updated December 22, 2023, https://www.drugs.com/sfx/thorazine-side-effects.html; b) Drugs.com, medically reviewed by Kaci Durbin, "Xanax," updated November 21, 2023, https://www.drugs.com/xanax.html; c) Drugs.com, medically reviewed by Sophia Entringer, "Venlafaxine," updated August 22, 2023, https://www.drugs.com/venlafaxine.html; d) Drugs.com, medically reviewed by Carmen Pope, "Wellbutrin: 7 Things You Should Know," updated July 28, 2023, https://www.drugs.com/tips/Wellbutrin-patient-tips; e) Drugs.com, medically reviewed by Carmen Pope, "Benzodiazepines," April 14, 2023, https://www.drugs.com/drug-class/benzodiazepines.html; f) Drugs.com, medically reviewed by Melisa Puckey, "Ambien," updated February 29, 2024, https://www.drugs.com/ambien.html; g) Drugs.com, medically reviewed by Melisa Puckey, "Amitriptyline," updated February 29, 2024, https://www.drugs.com/amitriptyline.html; h) Drugs.com, medically reviewed by Melisa Puckey, "Trazodone," updated February 29, 2024, https://www.drugs .com/trazodone.html; i) Drugs.com, medically reviewed by Melisa Puckey, "Wellbutrin," updated August 15, 2023, https://www.drugs.com /wellbutrin.html; j) Drugs.com, medically reviewed by Philip Thornton, "Lithium," updated August 14, 2023, https://www.drugs. com/lithium.html; k) Everyday Health, "Thorazine (Chlorpromazine (Oral/Injection)," © 1996-2024, https://www.everydayhealth.com/drugs/Thorazine; l) Terry Martin, medically reviewed by Armeen Poor, "Safety Concerns and Side Effects of Chantix," Verywell Mind, updated May 9, 2023, https://www.verywellmind. com/how-chantix-works-2825340; m) Cerner Multum, medically reviewed by editorial team, Drugs.com, "Lariam," Drugs.com, updated August 4, 2023, https://www.drugs.com/mtm/lariam.html; n) Omudhome Ogbru, "Clomipramine (Anafranil)," MedicineNet, medically reviewed September 25, 2019, https://www.medicinenet.com/clomipramine-oral/article.htm#what_is_clomipramine _what_is_clomipramine _used_for; o) Mark L. Ruffalo, "The Five Most Influential Psychiatric Drugs of All Time," *Psychology Today*, posted November 15, 2019, https://www.psychologytoday.com/us/blog/ freud-fluoxetine/201911/the-five-most-influential-psychiatric-drugs-all-time; p) Kathleen Smith, medically reviewed by Merihan Raouf, "ADHD Stimulant Medication," Psycom, updated March 19, 2021, https://www.psycom.net/ritalin-methylphenidate; q) Dan Wagener, ed., "Serotonin Antagonist and Reuptake Inhibitor (SARI)," American Addiction Centers, updated September 14, 2022, https://americanaddictioncenters.org/anti depressants-guide/sari; r) Amber R. Watson, medically reviewed by Melissa Badowski, "Wellbutrin," *Medical News Today*, posted October 17, 2022, https://www.medicalnews today.com/articles/drugs-wellbutrin.

58 See: a) Baum-Hedlund, "Medication-Induced Violence"; b) CCHR Florida "Antidepressants Are a Prescription"; c) CCHR International, *Psychiatric Drugs: Create Violence & Suicide*; d) Duke, "From Prozac to Parkland London,"; e) ePRNews, "Press Release: Latest Shooting"; f) Kupelian, "Media Ignoring 1 Crucial Factor"; g) Marvasti and Friel, "Psychiatric Diagnoses and Medications," 114, 117-119; h) Roberts, "Every Mass Shooting Shares One Thing"; i) Stolzer, "The Systemic Correlation between Psychiatric Medications," 12-19.

59 See: a) CCHR International, "Mental Health Watchdog Releases New Report on Link Between Psychotropic Drugs & School/Mass Shootings," CISION, PR Newsletter, posted May 22, 2018, https://www.prnewswire.com/news-releases/mental-health-watchdog-releases-new-report-on-link-between-

psychotropic-drugs--schoolmass-shootings-300618265.html; b) CCHR International, *Psychiatric Drugs: Create Violence & Suicide*, appendix c; c) ePRNews, "Press Release: Latest Shooting"; d) Kupelian, "Media Ignoring 1 Crucial Factor"; e) Marvasti and Friel, "Psychiatric Diagnoses and Medications," 116-117; f) Roberts, "Every Mass Shooting Shares One Thing."

[60] James H. McMillan and Sally Schumacher, *Education in Research: Evidence Based Inquiry*, 6th ed. (Boston, MA: Pearson Education Inc., 2006), 292-293.

[61] Kupelian, "Media Ignoring 1 Crucial Factor." Scott Pelly conducted the original interview for CBS News. "Newton," originally aired December 16, 2012. It can now be viewed as CBS, "60 Minutes Reports: Tragedy in Newtown," posted on YouTube December 17, 2012, https://www.youtube.com /watch?v=Mp-IuTyFqYA.

[62] Louise Tambascio, quoted in CBS News, "60 Minutes Reports: Tragedy in Newtown" and Kupelian, "Media Ignoring 1 Crucial Factor."

[63] Duke, "From Prozac to Parkland London,"; Ralph Lopez, "Neighbor Says Lanza Was on Meds, Links Between SSRIs and Violence," *Digital Journal*, posted December 19, 2012, http://www.digitaljournal .com/article/339440.

[64] Reed Coleman (aka Matthew Nolan), "Timeline: Adam Lanza's Life and Online Activity," Sandy Hook Lighthouse (accessible but dormant), posted September 7, 2013, s.vv. "February 2007," "Late February 2007-March 2007"; Nancy Schoeffler, "Serious Lapses, Fatal Mistakes: A Timeline," *Hartford Courant*, posted November 21, 2014, http://www.courant.com/ news/connecticut/hc-timeline-newtown-adam-lanza-child-advocate-report-2-20141121-story.html (page no longer accessible).

[65] Office of the State's Attorney Judicial District of Danbury, Stephen J. Sedensky III, State's Attorney, *Report of the State's Attorney for the Judicial District of Danbury on the Shootings at Sandy Hook Elementary School and 36 Yogananda Street, Newtown, Connecticut on December 14, 2012* (State of Connecticut: Division of Criminal Justice, November 25, 2013), 35.

[66] SSRI Editor's Note, "Drifter, 26, on amitriptyline and thorazine [sic] takes AK-47, shoots 5 children in a schoolyard, then himself," in reprint from *Time*, originally posted June 24, 2001, *SSRI Stories*, https://ssristories.org/ slaughter-in-a-school-yard-time-magazine/.

[67] Allen Benitez and Phil Yee, "Chronological Life History of Patrick Edward Purdy," in Nelson Kempsky, with Gary A. Binkerd, Phil Yee, Allen Benitez, and Richard Yarvis, *A Report to the Attorney General John K. Van de Kamp on Patrick Edward Purdy and the Cleveland School Killings* (California Department of Justice, Office of the Attorney General: October 1989), appendix c, 5-11, 13-15.

[68] Acalia Cleaver and Zach Eckhardt, "Report on NIU Shooter Theorizes He Lashed Out against a Surrogate Family, Had Severe Mental Health Issues,"

Kaneland Krier, posted March 26, 2010, https://kanelandkrier.com/news/report-on-niu-shooter/.

[69] *Chicago Tribune*, "NIU Gunman Identified," originally posted February 15, 2008, Murderpedia.

[70] Roberts, "Every Mass Shooting Shares One Thing." The website, AmmoLand, has touted itself as among "The Top 1000 Most Read U.S. Websites." John Crump, "AmmoLand News Cracks the Top 1000 Most Read U.S. Websites," AmmoLand, posted April 5, 2020, https://www.ammoland.com/2020/04/ammoland-news-cracks-the-top-1000-most-read-u-s-websites/#axzz6smvdaDwY.

[71] Northern Illinois University (NIU) Department of Public Safety, *Report of the February 14, 2008 Shootings at Northern Illinois University*, xv, 23-24, n.d., School Shooters. info: Resources on School Shootings, Perpetrators, and Prevention, last updated March 21, 2024, s.v. "Steven Kazmierczak," https://schoolshooters.info/.

[72] Peter Langman, "Psychiatric Medications and School Shootings," ver. 3.5 (February 3, 2016), School Shooters.info, s.v. "Browse the Library," https://school shooters.info/.

[73] Ibid, 7.

[74] Ibid.

[75] Ronald D. Brown, *Dying on the Job: Murder and Mayhem in the American Workplace* (Lanham, Maryland: Rowan & Littlefield Publishers, Inc., 2013), 79-80; Bill Hoffman, quoted in John Cornwell, *The Power to Harm* (New York, NY: Penguin Group, 1996), chap. 4, kindle cloud reader; *Lexington Herald-Leader*, "Louisville Man Dies, Raising Shooting Death Toll to 9," originally published September 19, 1989, Murderpedia, s.v. "Joseph Thomas Wesbecker." Accounts about how many were wounded differ. The number used here is based on a synthesis.

[76] Cornwell, *The Power to Harm*, chap. 2; Duke, "From Prozac to Parkland"; Kupelian, "Media Ignoring 1 Crucial Factor"; Andrew Wolfson, *Courier Journal*, "Prozac Maker Paid Millions to Secure Favorable Verdict in Mass Shooting Lawsuit, Victims Say," *USA Today*, posted and updated September 12, 2019, https://www.usatoday.com/story/news/nation/2019/09/12/prozac-makers-secret-payment-mass-shooting-lawsuit-revealed/2302888001/.

[77] Cornwell, *The Power to Harm*, pref.; Andrew Wolfson, *Courier Journal*, "Prozac Maker Paid Millions to Secure Favorable Verdict in Mass Shooting Lawsuit, Victims Say," *USA Today*, posted and updated September 12, 2019.

[78] Decision, in Honorable John W. Potter, Judge, Jefferson Circuit Court, Appellant, v. Eli Lilly and Company et al., 926 S.W.2d 449 (1996), Supreme Court of Kentucky, Leagle, https://www.leagle.com/decision/199613759 26sw2d44911375.xml.

[79] Ibid.

[80] Breggin.com, "Wesbecker Product Liability Case Against Eli Lilly," posted May 7, 2008, https://breggin.com/article-detail/post_detail/wesbecker-prozac -product-liability-suits; Rappoport, "Prozac Mass Murders."

[81] Decision, *Potter v. Lilly et al.*

[82] Jeff Swiatek, " Lilly's Legal Strategy Disarmed Prozac Lawyers," *Indianapolis Star*, Starnews.com, posted April 22, 2000, under "'Unprecedented' Deal" and "Evidence Withheld," http://www .antidepressantsfacts.com/2000-04-22-StarNews-Lilly-tactics.htm; Wolfson, *Courier Journal*, "Prozac Maker Paid Millions."

[83] U.S. Bureau of Labor Statistics, Consumer Price Inflation Calculator, n.d., https://www.bls.gov/data /inflation_calculator.htm.

[84] Pertinent documentation can be found on the website maintained by Dr. Peter Breggin, who was a consultant and expert witness retained by Eli Lilly & Co: Breggin.com, "Wesbecker Product Liability Case Against Eli Lilly." Relevant, as well, are charges from a British medical journal (*BMJ*) about unavailability of internal information and Lilly's response. CNN recaps the standoff in this story: "Medical Journal Apologizes to Prozac Maker," CNN.com, posted January 28, 2005, https://www.cnn.com/2005/US/01 /28/journal.apology/index.html. The actual exchange was published in *BMJ*: Jeanne Lenzer, "FDA to Review 'Missing' Drug Company Documents," December 30, 2004, https://doi.org /10.1136/bmj.330.7481.7 and "Eli Lilly: Correction and Apology," published January 27, 2005, https:// doi.org/10.1136/bmj.330.7481.7.

[85] Michael D. Kelleher, *Profiling the Lethal Employee: Case Studies of Violence in the Workplace* (Westport, CT: Greenwood Publishing Group, Inc., 1997), 56.

[86] Wesbecker rampaged on September 14, 1989. Murderpedia, "The Standard Gravure Shooting," s.v. "Joseph Thomas Wesbecker." "Fluoxetine was approved by the FDA in December of 1987 and was launched to the market in January 1988 under the trade name Prozac®...." Todd M. Hillhouse and Joseph H. Porter, "A Brief History of the Development of Antidepressant Drugs: From Monoamines to Glutamate," author manuscript, PubMed Central, Health and Human Services, posted February 1, 2016, under "Selective Serotonin Reuptake Inhibitors," https://www.ncbi.nlm.nih.gov/ pmc/articles /PMC4428540/.

[87] AP, "Records Show Killer Having Mental Illness," *Victoria Advocate*, September 24, 1989, 20, posted by Newspapers.com by Ancestry, https://www.newspapers.com/clip/36013150/records-show-killer-having-mental/. Punctuated as in publication.

[88] Kelleher, *Profiling the Lethal Employee*, 54; Murderpedia, "Disturbed Past of Killer of 7 Is Unraveled," under "Manic Depression," "Self-Diagnosed," s.v. "Joseph Thomas Wesbecker." The complaint was filed in May of 1987.

[89] Don Frazier, in Eric Harrison, "Gunman Kills 7 and Himself at Kentucky Plant," *Los Angeles Times*, posted September 15, 1989, https://www.latimes.com/archives/la-xpm-1989-09-15-mn-152-story.html.

[90] *Lexington Herald-Leader*, "'He Said Before He Left, He'd Get Even,'" originally printed September 15, 1989, Murderpedia, s.v. "Joseph Thomas Wesbecker"; George Oswine, in Ted M. Natt, Jr., "Disgruntled Employee Kills Seven, Wounds 13, Takes Own Life," AP, posted September 15, 1989, https://apnews.com/article/c45dd78c07fd5ec3df0a09971f45f8d8 (no longer accessible).

[91] Joe White, in Natt, "Disgruntled Employee Kills Seven."

[92] Stolzer, "The Systemic Correlation between Psychiatric Medications," 12.

[93] Ibid.

[94] Rahway, NJ: Merck & Co, continuously updated. It is now published only digitally. https://www .merckmanuals.com/professional

[95] Roger D. Rhoten, "Selective Serotonin Reuptake Inhibitors: A Critical Look at the Antidepressants and an Assessment of Potential Liability Faced by their Manufacturers," (course and third year requirement, Harvard Law Library, 2002), 13, https://dash.harvard.edu/bitstream/handle/1/8852159 /Rhoten.pdf ?sequence=1&isAllowed=y.

[96] CCHR Florida, "Antidepressants Are a Prescription for Mass Shootings"; CCHR International, *Psychiatric Drugs: Create Violence*, 3-5, 12-13; Duke, "From Prozac to Parkland London"; Joseph Glenmullen, "Opinion Column: Antidepressants Carry Risk," Alliance for Human Research Protection, posted March 4, 2005, https://ahrp.org/opinion-column-antidepressants-carry-risk-dr-joseph-glenmullen/; Kupelian, "Media Ignoring 1 Crucial Factor"; Stolzer, "The Systemic Correlation between Psychiatric Medications," 16-17.

[97] CCHR International, *Psychiatric Drugs: Create Violence*, 13.

[98] James L. Knoll, IV and George David Annas, "Warning: Antidepressants May Cause Messaging Manslaughter," *Psychiatric Times* 34, no. 9 (September 2017): 12, https://www.researchgate.net/profile/George-Annas/publication /320020690_Warning_Antidepressants_May_Cause_Messaging Manslaughter /links/5aa6cd52aca272326825f2b1/Warning-Antidepressants-May-Cause-Messaging-Manslaughter.pdf.

[99] Jari Tiihonen, Martti Lehti, Mikko Aaltonen, Janne Kivivuori, Hannu Kautiainen, Lauri J. Virta, Fabian Hoti, Antti Tanskanen, and Pasi Korhonen, "Psychotropic Drugs and Homicide: A Prospective Cohort Study from Finland," *World Psychiatry* 14, no. 2 (June 2015): 245-247. Subjects were matched by gender, age, and home municipality at the time of each homicide.

[100] Ibid, 245.

[101] Fiona Guy, "Antidepressants and the Risks of Committing Homicide," Crime Traveler Online Resources, posted July 15, 2018, updated July 16, 2018,

https://www.crimetraveller.org/2018/07/antidepressants-risk-of-committing-homicide/.

102 The computed relative risks were: 1.31, $p = 0.022$, for current use vs. no current use of antidepressants; 1.45, $p = 0.001$, for current use vs. no current use of benzodiazepines; 1.10, $p = 0.54$, for current use vs. no current use of antipsychotics. Statistical significance was set to $p < 0.016$. Both opioid and non-opioid analgesics were associated with a significantly increased risk of offending. Tiihonen et al., "Psychotropic Drugs and Homicide," 245, 246.

103 Ibid, 246.

104 Ibid.

105 Yasmina Molero, Paul Lichtenstein, Johan Zetterqvist, Clara Hellner Gumpert, Seena Fazel, "Selective Serotonin Reuptake Inhibitors and Violent Crime: A Cohort Study," *PLOS Medicine*, posted September 15, 2015, under "Methods," "Statistical Analyses," "Main Analysis," table 3, https://journals.plos.org/plosmedicine/article?id=10.1371/journal.pmed.100 1875.

106 More relevant, from the standpoint of medical intervention, are the findings that there were no statistical distinctions between types of SSRI medication and the significant correlations of SSRI use with non-violent crime and emergency treatment for alcohol intoxication or misuse. Ibid, table 3.

107 Bernadka Dubicka, Sarah Hadley, and Christopher Roberts, "Suicidal Behaviour in Youths with Depression Treated with New-Generation Antidepressants: Meta-Analysis," *British Journal of Psychiatry* 189, no. 5 (November 2006): 393-398, abstract, doi: 10.1192/bjp.bp.105.011833; Marco Pozzi, Sonia Radice, Emilio Clementi, Massimo Molteni, and Maria Nobile "Antidepressants and, Suicide and Self-Injury: Causal or Casual Association?" *International Journal of Psychiatry Clinical Practice* 20, no. 1 (2016): 47-51, abstract, https://www.tandfonline.com/doi/abs/10.3109/13651501.2015.1117111?journalCode=ijpc20.

108 See: a) Philippe Courtet and Émilie Olié, "Antidepressants Do Prevent Suicide, At Least Pending Something Better ..." [article in French], *Bulletin de l'Académie Nationale de Médecine* 198, nos. 4-5 (April-May 2014): 881-892, abstract, https://pubmed.ncbi.nlm.nih.gov/26753413/; b) David Gunnell, Julia Saperia, and Deborah Ashby, "Selective Serotonin Reuptake Inhibitors (SSRIs) and Suicide in Adults: Meta-Analysis of Drug Company Data from Placebo Controlled, Randomised Controlled Trials Submitted to the MHRA's Safety Review," *BMJ* 330, posted February 19, 2005, abstract, doi: 10.1136 /bmj.330.7488.385; c) Hans-Jürgen Möller, David S. Baldwin, Guy Goodwin, Siegfried Kasper, Ahmed Okasha, Dan J. Stein, Rajiv Tandon, Marcio Versiani, and the World Psychiatric Association Section on Pharmacopsychiatry, "Do SSRIs or Antidepressants in General Increase Suicidality?" *European Archives of Psychiatry and Clinical Neuroscience* 258, s3 (2008): 3-23; d) Julio Licinio and Ma-Li Wong, "Depression,

Antidepressants and Suicidality: A Critical Appraisal," *Nature Reviews Drug Discovery* 4, no. 2 (February 2005): 165–171, abstract, https://www.nature.com/articles/nrd1634; e) Roger T. Mulder, "Antidepressants and Suicide: Population Benefit vs. Individual Risk," *Acta Psychiatry Scandinavica* 122, no. 6 (2010): 442–443, https://onlinelibrary.wiley.com/doi/epdf/10.1111/j.1600-0447.2010.01622.x.

[109] "Antidepressant Medications," reviewed by James Pendleton, Good Therapy, © 2007-2023, https://www.goodtherapy.org/drugs/antidepressants.html; Mayo Clinic Staff, "Serotonin and Norepinephrine Reuptake Inhibitors (SNRIs)," Mayo Clinic, posted October 5, 2019, https://www.mayoclinic. org/diseases-conditions/depression/in-depth/antidepressants/art-20044970.

[110] Molly J. Crockett, Luke Clark, Marc D. Hauser, and Trevor W. Robbins, "Serotonin Selectively Influences Moral Judgment and Behavior Through Effects on Harm Aversion," *Proceedings of the National Academy of Sciences of the United States of America* 107, no. 4 (October 5, 2010): 17433, https://www.pnas.org/content/pnas/107/40/17433.full.pdf, citing the following as evidence: Molly J. Crockett, "The Neurochemistry of Fairness: Clarifying The Link Between Serotonin And Prosocial Behavior," *Annals of the New York Academy of Sciences* 1167 (2009): 76–86; and Klaus A Miczek, Rosa M. de Almeida, Edward A Kravitz, Emilie F Rissman, Sietse F de Boer, Adrian Raine, "Neurobiology of Escalated Aggression and Violence," *Journal of Neuroscience*, 27, no 44 (October 31, 2007): 11803–11806.

[111] Crockett, Clark, Hauser, and Robbins, "Serotonin Selectively Influences Moral Judgment," 17434.

[112] Ibid, 17434-17435. "In the UG [ultimatum game], one player (the responder) decides whether to accept or reject monetary offers from another player (the proposer). If the responder accepts, both players are paid accordingly; if he rejects, neither is paid. Responders tend to punish proposers who offer less than ≈20–30% of the shared stake by rejecting their 'unfair' offers. … Rejecting unfair offers enforces a fairness norm but also harms the other player financially; responders are thus forced to tradeoff concerns for fairness versus harm when considering unfair offers." Ibid, 17434.

[113] Catherine J. Harmer, "Serotonin and Emotional Processing: Does It Help Explain Antidepressant Drug Action?" *Neuropharmacology* 55, no. 6 (November 2008): 1023-1028, abstract, https://www.sciencedirect.com/science/article/abs/pii/S0028390808002311.

[114] See the introduction to *How Rampage Killers Interpret Their Worlds* for particular examples.

[115] a) Charles C. W. Cooke, "Running Amok: Adam Lanza's Abomination Is Not a Phenomenon Peculiar to Modern America," *National Review*, posted December 20, 2012, https://www.nationalreview.com/2012/12/running-amok-charles-c-w-cooke/; b) Fandom.com, "Beselick Amok Case," last

updated August 13, 2022, Amok Wiki: A Scientific Project, https://amok.fandom.com/wiki/Beselick_amok_case ("This wiki has been closed"); c) Andrew Feldherr, Spectacle and Society in Livy's History (Berkley, CA: University of California Press, 1998), 86; UncontinuedProcess [pseud.], Thread: "Earliest Mass Murders/Spree killings In World History?" Columbine High School Massacre Discussion Forum, posted June 9, 2018, https://columbinemassacre.forumotion.com/t5972-earliest-mass-murders-spree-killings-in-world-history; H.S. Versnel, "Two Types of Roman Devotio," *Mnemosyne: A Journal of Classical Studies* 4th Series 29, no. 4 (1976), 365.

Chapter Two

[1] Susan Harter, "Is Self-Esteem only Skin-Deep? The Inextricable Link between Physical Appearance and Self-Esteem," *Reclaiming Children and Youth* 9, no. 3 (Fall 2000): 134.

[2] James, A. Fauerbach, Leslie J. Heinberg, John W. Lawrence, Andrew M. Munster, Debra A. Palombo, Daniel Richter, Robert J. Spence, Sandra S. Stevens, Linda Ware, and Thomas Muehlberger, "Effects of Early Body Image Dissatisfaction on Subsequent Psychological and Physical Adjustment after Disfiguring Injury," *Psychosomatic Medicine* 62, no. 4 (July-August 2000): 577, 579. Sadly, the number of burns along with the clear temporal demarcation allowing for the identification of pre and post attitudes make the victims of burning frequent candidates for investigations of body image dissatisfaction. This study involved 67 men and 19 women who were treated at the Baltimore Regional Burn Center and the Johns Hopkins Bayview Medical Center. Scales measuring satisfaction and adjustment were administered after admission, one week after discharge, and then two months later. A multivariate analysis of covariance was administered to determine their perceptions of quality of life before and after the incidents.

[3] Marg Csapo, "Psychosocial Adjustment of Children with Short Stature (Achondroplasia): Social Competence, Behavior Problems, Self-Esteem, Family Functioning, Body Image, and Reaction to Frustrations," *Behavioral Disorders* 16, no. 3 (May 1991): 219-224. Social involvement and competence were ascertained through Achenbach's Child Behavior Checklist and factors pertaining to self-concept were determined through the Piers-Harris Self Concept Scale.

[4] M. Janice Gilliland, Michael Windle, Jo Anne Grunbaum, Antronette Yancey, Deanna Hoelscher, Susan R. Tortolero, and Mark A. Schuster, "Body Image and Children's Mental Health Related Behaviors: Results from the Healthy Passages Study," *Journal of Pediatric Psychology* 32, no. 1 (January/February 2007): 34-35. The Positive and Negative Affect Scale for

Children was employed to ascertain "internalizing problems," which included issues such as anxiety and depression.

[5] Charlotte H. Markey, "Invited Commentary: Why Body Image is Important to Adolescent Development," *Journal of Youth and Adolescence* 39, no. 12 (December 2010): 1387–1391, under, "Identity Development and Body Image," https://doi.org/10.1007/s10964-010-9510-0. In making these observations, the author references the following: a) Eric Erikson, *Identity, Youth and Crisis* (New York, NY: Norton, 1968); b) Jackie Frost and Stuart McKelvie, "Self-Esteem And Body Satisfaction in Male And Female Elementary School, High School, and University Students," *Sex Roles* 51, no. 1-2 (July 2004): 45–54; c) Susan Harter, "The Development of Self-Representations During Childhood and Adolescence," in ed. Mark R. Leary and June Price Tangney, *Handbook of Self and Identity* (New York, NY: Guilford Press, 2003), 610–642; d) Susan Harter and Nancy R. Whitesell, "On the Importance of Importance Ratings in Understanding Adolescents' Self-Esteem: Beyond Statistical Parsimony," in ed. Richard J. Riding and Stephen G. Rayner, *Self Perception: International Perspectives on Individual Differences*, vol. 2, (Westport, CT: Ablex, 2001), 3-23; e) Gianine D. Rosenblum and Michael Lewis, "The Relations among Body Image, Physical Attractiveness, and Body Mass in Adolescence," *Child Development* 70, no. 1 (January/February 1999): 50-64.

[6] Ben Sharpsteen, supervising dir., Joe Grant and Dick Huemer, screen story, Helen Aberson and Harold Pearl, book (Burbank, CA: Walt Disney Productions and Walt Disney Animation Studios, 1941).

[7] Renaldo Matadeen, "How Disney's Live-Action Dumbo Gets His Name," CBR.com, posted March 30, 2019, https://www.cbr.com/disney-dumbo-1941-name-origin/.

[8] Walter Hill, dir., Ken Friedman, screenplay, John Godey, novel, (Carolco Pictures and Guber-Peters Company, 1989).

[9] Katharine A. Phillips, "What is BDD (Body Dysmorphic Disorder)?" International OCD [obsessive compulsive disorder] Foundation, last updated 2022, https://bdd.iocdf.org/about-bdd/. Dr. Phillips is Professor of Psychiatry at Weill Cornell Medical College, Cornell University, and an Attending Psychiatrist at New York-Presbyterian Hospital. She is also Adjunct Professor of Psychiatry and Human Behavior at the Warren Alpert Medical School of Brown University. She authored *Understanding Body Dysmorphic Disorder: An Essential Guide* (Oxford University Press, 2009), as well as other highly credible titles on the subject.

[10] See: a) American Psychiatric Association, *Diagnostic and Statistical Manual of Mental Disorders*, 5th. ed. (*DSM-5* – Arlington, VA, 2013), 236, 243-247, 455-459; b) Philippa Garety and D. Freeman, "The Past and Future of Delusions Research: From the Inexplicable to the Treatable," *The British*

Journal of Psychiatry: The Journal of Mental Science 203, no. 5 (November 2013): 327-333; c) Tahir Rahman, Sarah M. Hartz, Willa Xiong, J. Reid Meloy, Jeffrey Janofsky, Bruce Harry, and Phillip J. Resnick "Extreme Overvalued Beliefs," *Journal of American Academy of Psychiatry and the Law* 48, no. 3 (September 2022), 6, table 3, https://jaapl.org/content/jaapl/early/2020/06/29/JAAPL.200001-20.1.full.pdf.

[11] Documented in the following: a) Carlo Altamura, Michela Minio Paluello, Emanuela Mundo, Stefania Medda, and Piero Mannu, "Clinical and Subclinical Body Dysmorphic Disorder," *European Archives of Psychiatry and Clinical Neuroscience* 251, no. 3 (June 2001): 105–108; b) Angela Fang and Stefan G. Hofmann, "Relationship between Social Anxiety Disorder and Body Dysmorphic Disorder," author's manuscript, PubMed Central (PMC), Health and Human Services (HHS), posted December 1, 2011, https://www.ncbi.nlm.nih.gov/pmc/articles/PMC2952668/; c) Álvaro Frías, Carol Palma, Núria Farriols Hernando, and Laura González Vallespí, "Comorbidity Between Obsessive-Compulsive Disorder and Body Dysmorphic Disorder: Prevalence, Explanatory Theories, and Clinical Characterization," *Neuropsychiatry Disease and Treatment* 11 (July 2015): 2233-2244; d) John Gunstad and Katharine A. Phillips, "Axis I Comorbidity in Body Dysmorphic Disorder," author's manuscript, PMC, HHS, posted October 17, 2005, https://www.ncbi.nlm.nih.gov/pmc/articles/PMC1613797/; d) Katharine A. Phillips, Elizabeth R. Didie, and William Menard, "Clinical Features and Correlates of Major Depressive Disorder in Individuals with Body Dysmorphic Disorder," *Journal of Affective Disorders* 97 no. 1–3 (January 2007): 129-135; e) Katherine A. Phillips, Susan L. McElroy, Paul E. Keck, Harrison G. Pope, and James I. Hudson, "Body Dysmorphic Disorder: 30 Cases of Imagined Ugliness," *American Journal of Psychiatry* 150 no. 2 (February 1993): 302-308; f) Katharine A. Phillips and Robert L. Stout, "Associations in the Longitudinal Course of Body Dysmorphic Disorder with Major Depression, Obsessive Compulsive Disorder, and Social Phobia," author's manuscript, PMC, HHS, posted December 1, 2009, https://www.ncbi.nlm.nih.gov/pmc/articles/PMC2786172/.

[12] a) Chand Pavan, Pierluigi Simonato, Mg Marini, Francesco Mazzoleni, L. Pavan, and Virginia Vindigni, "Psychopathologic Aspects of Body Dysmorphic Disorder: A Literature Review," *Aesthetic Plastic Surgery* 32, no. 3 (May 2008): 473–484; b) Katharine A. Phillips, Susan L. McElroy, James I. Hudson, and Harrison G Pope Jr, "Body Dysmorphic Disorder: An Obsessive-Compulsive Spectrum Disorder, A Form of Affective Spectrum Disorder, or Both?" *Journal of Clinical Psychiatry*, supplement 4 (1995): 41-51; c) Katharine A Phillips, Anthony Pinto, William Menard, Jane L Eisen, Maria C Mancebo, and Steven A Rasmussen, "Obsessive-Compulsive

Disorder Versus Body Dysmorphic Disorder: A Comparison Study of Two Possibly Related Disorders," *Depression and Anxiety* 24, no. 6 (January 2007): 399-409.

[13] Maria José Azevedo De Brito, Fábio Xerfan Nahas, Táki Athanássios Cordás, Gabriel De Almeida Arruda Felix, Miguel Sabino Neto, and Lydia Masako Ferreira, "Understanding the Psychopathology of Body Dysmorphic Disorder in Cosmetic Surgery Patients: A Literature Review," *Brazilian Journal of Plastic Surgery* 29, no. 44 (January 2014): 605.

[14] Katharine A. Phillips, Susan L. McElroy, P. Keck, James I. Hudson, Harrison G. Pope, "A Comparison of Delusional and Nondelusional Body Dysmorphic Disorder in 100 Cases," *Psychopharmacology Bulletin* 30, no. 2 (1994): 180-181. Subjects were assessed based on criteria from the American Psychiatric Association, *Diagnostic and Statistical Manual of Mental Illness*, 3rd. ed., rev. (*DSM-II-R* – Washington D.C., 1987) and American Psychiatric Association, *Diagnostic and Statistical Manual of Mental Illness*, 4th. ed. (*DSM-IV* – Washington D.C., 1994) using a clinical interview and semi-structured interview. Katharine A. Phillips and Eric Hollander, "Body Dysmorphic Disorder: DSM-IV Source Book Review," in ed. Allen J. Frances, *DSM-IV Sourcebook* (Washington D.C.,1994); Robert L Spitzer, Janet B. Williams, Miriam Gibbon, and Michael B. First, *Structured Clinical Interview for DSM-III-R* (Washington, DC: American Psychiatric Press, 1990).

[15] Phillips et al., "A Comparison of Delusional and Nondelusional Body Dysmorphic Disorder," 183. They cite Phillips et al., "Body Dysmorphic Disorder, 30" for support.

[16] Phillips et al., "Body Dysmorphic Disorder," 302-304. Patients were identified based on the criteria specified in the *DSM-III-R*. Imagined deficiencies varied widely, involving almost every part of the body.

[17] David Veale, Ann Boocock, Kevin Gournay, Windy Dryden, Fozia Shah, Robert W1llson, and Jessica Walburn, "Body Dysmorphic Disorder: A Survey of Fifty Cases," *British Journal of Psychiatry* 169, no. 2 (August 1996), 197-198. BDD diagnosis was based on clinical, semi-structured, and structured interviews as well as the Modified Yale-Brown Obsessive-Compulsive Scale. Depression was determined by the Montgomery & Asberg Depression Rating Scale. A majority (68%) reported multiple defects with most (86%) mentioning some aspect of their face.

[18] Veale et al., "Body Dysmorphic Disorder," 198.

[19] Phillips et al., "Body Dysmorphic Disorder," 304.

[20] Veale et al., "Body Dysmorphic Disorder," 198.

[21] Henry Murray, William G. Barrett, Erik Homburger, and Workers at the Harvard Psychological Clinic, *Explorations in Personality* (New York: Oxford University Press, 1938), 49, 120-121.

[22] Katharine A. Phillips and William Menard, "Suicidality in Body Dysmorphic Disorder: A Prospective Study," *American Journal of Psychiatry* 163, no. 7 (July 2006), 1280, 1281. At intake, 164 (88.6%) of the subjects met full *DSM-IV* BDD criteria (11.4% were in partial or full re-mission but had met full BDD criteria in the past)." Ibid, 1280. The study began with two hundred subjects and the participants declined with each annual interview as shown in the totals that follow: first year, 185; second, 153; third, 95; and fourth, 25.

[23] Peter Langman, *School Shooters: Understanding High School, College, and Adult Perpetrators* (Boulder, CO: Rowman & Littlefield, 2015), xvi, 159, table 8.1. The total number of subjects included in Langman's second book on school shooters is unclear. He says only: "In this book I present forty-eight school shooters in depth and briefly reference others." Ibid, introduction, xvi. The categorization of those manifesting issues with their appearance or body stature is then presented later. Ibid, 159, table 8.1.

[24] Mara Bovsun, "Beauty Salon Massacre," *New York Daily News*, posted March 25, 2008, under "Retreated into Books," http://www.nydailynews.com/news/crime/beauty-salon-massacre-article-1.273663; Christa Mackey, "The Rose-Mar Killings, BellaOnline: The Voice of Women, © 2022, http://www.bellaonline.com/articles/art22876.asp.

[25] Bovsun, "Beauty Salon Massacre"; Mackey, "The Rose-Mar Killings."

[26] Bovsun, "Beauty Salon Massacre"; Murderpedia: The Encyclopedia of Murders, last updated June 4, 2017, s.v. "Robert Benjamin Smith," https://murderpedia.org/; Time.com, "Nation: Slaughter in the College of Beauty," originally posted November 18, 1966, Murderpedia, s.v. "Robert Benjamin Smith."

[27] Bovsun, "Beauty Salon Massacre"; Mackey, "The Rose-Mar Killings; Time.com, "Nation: Slaughter in the College"; Editors of Time-Life Books, *True Crime: Mass Murderers* (Alexandria, VA: Time-Life Books, 1992), 60.

[28] Jonathan Fast, *Ceremonial Violence: A Psychological Explanation of School Shootings* (Woodstock, NY: Overlook Press, 2008), 28-29.

[29] Ibid. Over time he released the other students in small groups then surrendered to the police.

[30] Kaherine Newman, Cybelle Fox, David Harding, Jal Mehta, and Wendy Roth, *Rampage: The Social Roots of School Shootings* (New York, NY: Basic Books, 2004), 22, 24, 305; Lisa Popyk, "Teen Lives Out Murderous Dream," special to the *Post*, originally posted November 10, 1998, Muderpedia, s.v. "Michael Adam Carneal."

[31] Popyk, "Teen Lives Out."

[32] Newman et al., *Rampage: The Social Roots*, 27-28.

[33] Sarah Stewart Holland, "Memories of a School Shooting: Paducah, Kentucky, 1997," *Atlantic*, posted December 17, 2012, https://www.theatlantic.com/

national/archive/2012/12/memories-of-a-school-shooting-paducah-kentucky-1997/266358/; Newman et al., *Rampage: The Social Roots,* 22.

[34] Fast, *Ceremonial Violence*, 38; Opinion of the Court, Commonwealth of Kentucky v. Michael Carneal, Case no. 2004-CA-001534-MR, McCracken Circuit Court no. 97-CR-00350, rendered November 26, 2008, 4, School Shooters. info: Resources on School Shootings, Perpetrators, and Prevention, last updated March 21, 2024, s.v. "Michael Carneal," https://schoolshooters.info; Popyk, "Teen Lives Out." When facing trial Carneal pled "guilty but mentally ill." *Kentucky v. Michael Carneal*, 2. Later, seeking to withdraw his plea, he said he did not reveal the full extent of his mental illness because he believed his delusions to be real. Ibid, 4.

[35] CourtTV.com, "Kentucky v. Michael Carneal: Kentucky School Shooter Sentenced to Life in Prison with Parole," originally posted December 16, 1998, Murderpedia, s.v. "Michael Adam Carneal"; Katherine S. Newman et al., *Rampage: The Social Roots*, 32; Popyk, "Teen Lives Out."

[36] Holland, "Memories of a School."

[37] Fast, *Ceremonial Violence*, 181.

[38] Ibid.

[39] Ibid. Fast spells it "excavetum."

[40] Center for Disease Control and Prevention, Adult BMI Percentile Calculator, reviewed September 2, 2022, https://www.cdc.gov/healthyweight/assessing/bmi/adult_bmi/english_bmi_calculator/bmi_calculator.html;
Lauren Frias, Azmi Haroun, and Michal Kranz, "It's Been a Decade Since the Sandy Hook Shooting. Here Are the Names and Pictures of the 27 Victims, Including 20 Children, Who Were Murdered that Day," *Business Insider*, posted December 14, 2022, https://www.businessinsider. com/who-were-the-victims-of-the-sandy-hook-shooting-2017-12?op=1; Office of the State's Attorney Judicial District of Danbury, Stephen J. Sedensky III, State's Attorney, *Report of the State's Attorney for the Judicial District of Danbury on the Shootings at Sandy Hook Elementary School and 36 Yogananda Street, Newtown, Connecticut on December 14, 2012* (State of Connecticut: Division of Criminal Justice, November 25, 2013), 2, 5, 10, 27, http://www.ct.gov/csao/lib/csao/Sandy_Hook_ Final_Report.pdf; PK, BMI Percentile Calculator for Men and Women in the United States, © 2009-2023 dqydj.com, https://dqydj.com/bmi-percentile-calculator-men-women-united-states/.

[41] Andrea Phillipou, Rachel L Mountjoy, and Susan Lee Rossell, "Overvalued Ideas or Delusions in Anorexia Nervosa?" *Australian & New Zealand Journal of Psychiatry*, first posted online April 8, 2017, 2. See also: Stephen Gadsby, "Self-Deception and the Second Factor: How Desire Causes Delusion in Anorexia Nervosa," *Erkenntnis* 85, no. 3 (June 2020): 609–626 and Joanna E. Steinglass, Jane L Eisen, Evelyn Attia, Laurel Mayer, B.

Timothy Walsh, "Is Anorexia Nervosa a Delusional Disorder? An Assessment of Eating Beliefs in Anorexia Nervosa," *Journal of Psychiatric Practice* 13, no. 2 (March 2007): 65-71.

42 Olivia Exstrum, "Newly Unsealed Documents Reveal Dark Details about the Sandy Hook Mass Shooter," *Mother Jones*, posted December 14, 2018, https://www.motherjones.com/politics/2018/12/sandy-hook-shooter-documents-adam-lanza-gun-violence/; Jennifer Smith and Anneta Konstantinides, "Childhood Drawings and Letters to Santa by Sandy Hook Shooter Adam Lanza Reveal His Misery at School and Anorexic Thoughts Like 'Nothing Tastes As Good As Thin Feels,' Before His Descent Into Evil," *Mail Online*, posted January 23, 2019, updated January 24, 2019, https://www.dailymail.co.uk/news/article-6625503/Childhood-documents-reveal-Sandy-Hook-shooter-Adam-Lanzas-school-misery-anorexia.html.

43 Connecticut State Police, insert in Smith and Konstantinides, "Childhood Drawings and Letters."

44 Mark Russell, "No Signs of Brain Damage in Lanza: Medical Examiner," *Newser*, posted January 11, 2013, https://www.newser.com/story/160814/no-signs-of-brain-damage-in-lanza-medical-examiner.html.

45 Michael C. Roberts, "The Passing of a Pediatric Psychology Pioneer: Dorothea M. Ross," Society of Pediatric Psychology, *Progress Notes* 44, no. 3 (2020), https://pedpsych.org/progress_notes/201905-passing-pediatric-psychology-pioneer-dorothea-m-ross/#:~:text=Born%20in%201923%2C%20she%20passed,in%20the%20early%20lean%20years.

46 Eli H. Newberger, *The Men They Will Become: The Nature and Nurture of Male Character* (Cambridge, MA: Perseus Publishing, 2000), 186.

47 Brian De Palma, dir., Lawrence D. Cohen, screenwriter, Stephen King, novel (Red Bank Films, 1976). Sissy Spacek received an Oscar nomination for her role as the isolated teenager as did Piper Laurie for her performance as her religiously deranged mother. Leigh Butler, "The Unbelievable Crime of Deviating: *Carrie* (1976)," Tor.com, posted August 4, 2016, https://www.tor.com/2016/08/04/the-movie-rewatch-of-great-nostalgia-carrie-1976/. A remake, staring, Chloë Grace Moretz as Carrie and Julianne Moore as her mom was released in 2013. Kimberly Peirce, dir., Lawrence D. Cohen, Roberto Aguirre-Sacasa screenwriters, and Stephen King, novel, *Carrie* (Metro-Goldwyn-Mayer, Screen Gems, and Misher Films).

48 Ditch the Label, *The Annual Bullying Survey 2015*, April 2015, 7, 28," https://www.ditchthelabel.org/. The sample originally numbered 4,853. After scrubbing the data to "to remove incomplete and non-factual submissions," responses totaled 3,023. Ditch the Label is an international non-profit devoted to assisting young people in the navigation of issues related to conflict, relationships, sexual identity, and mental health. It publishes carefully crafted, well documented reports on those subjects.

[49] Josh Fox, "Top 10 Deadliest Rampage Killers," Listverse, posted October 22, 2011, under "8. Toi Mutsuo: 30 dead, 3 Injured," https://listverse.com/2011/10/22/top-10-deadliest-rampage-killers/;
M. D. Iseman, "Tuberculosis Therapy: Past, Present and Future," *European Respiratory Journal* 20, 36 suppl. (2002): 87-88; Ben Kageyama, "The Tsuyama Massacre of 1938," Medium, posted February 3, 2021; narration, in *Past Crimes: True Crime before 1940*, "Japan's Deadliest Lone Gunman Murders: The Story of Mutsuo Toi (1938)," YouTube, posted November 15, 2021, https://www.youtube .com/watch?v=1ofYg4xO-bU.

[50] Murderpedia, "Mutsuo Toi (都井 睦雄 Toi Mutsuo, March 5, 1917 - May 21, 1938)," s.v. "Mutsuo Toi"; narration, in *Past Crimes*, "Japan's Deadliest Lone Gunman Murders: The Story of Mutsuo Toi."

[51] Narration, in *Beyond the Dark*, "The Tsuyama Massacre," YouTube, posted October 22, 2019, https://www.youtube.com/watch?v=c2zQ9oms1f0; Kageyama, "The Tsuyama Massacre."

[52] Kageyama, "The Tsuyama Massacre"; narration, in *Past Crimes*, "Japan's Deadliest Lone Gunman Murders: The Story of Mutsuo Toi."

[53] S. A. Ozbourne, "He Killed 30 People Because Girls Wouldn't Have Sex with Him," Medium, posted January 6, 2021; narration, in *Past Crimes*, "Japan's Deadliest Lone Gunman Murders: The Story of Mutsuo Toi."

[54] Narration, in *heviDocs*, "Mutsuo Toi – The Tsuyama Massacre: Crime In Japan," YouTube, posted September 19, 2020," https://www.youtube.com/watch?v=9Y43KesvfhY (subscription required); Tsuyama Newspaper, Murderpedia, s.v. "Mutsuo Toi."

[55] Fox, "Top 10 Deadliest Rampage Killers," 8; narration, in *heviDocs*, "Mutsuo Toi – The Tsuyama Massacre"; Kageyama, "The Tsuyama Massacre"; narration, in *Past Crimes*, "Japan's Deadliest Lone Gunman Murders: The Story of Mutsuo Toi."

[56] Narration, in *Beyond the Dark*, "The Tsuyama Massacre"; narration, in *Past Crimes*, "Japan's Deadliest Lone Gunman Murders: The Story of Mutsuo Toi"; Hana Carter, "Killer Love: Woman's Obsession with Lover Was So Extreme She Strangled Him and Cut Off His Genitals So She Could Carry Them 'Forever,'" *Sun*, posted and updated December 9, 2019, https://www.the-sun.com/news/137708/womans-obsession-with-lover-was-so-extreme-she-strangled-him-and-cut-off-his-genitals-so-she-could-carry-them-forever/; Lorraine King, "Woman Strangled Her Lover, Cut Off His Genitals and Kept Them in Her Bag," *Mirror*, posted December 7, 2019, https://www.mirror.co.uk/news/world-news/woman-strangled-lover-cut-genitals-21038966. There is a possibility that the death was the result of erotic asphyxiation gone too far. As for the dismemberment, when questioned by authorities Abe explained, "Because I couldn't take his head with me, and I figured I wanted to take the part of him that had brought me the best

memories." In Drvitelly.typepad.com/providentia, "The Abe Sada Incident," Murderpedia, s.v. "Sada Abe"; narrated, in Nikki Young, *Serial Napper True Crime Podcast*, "Sada Abe, the Former Geisha and Murderer," YouTube, posted September 6, 2020, https://www.youtube.com/watch?v=495MKBJ9pWE. Reports differ as to the way she contained the organs until her arrest. The description offered herein is logical and the most frequently told. Before taking leave of her lover's body, Abe, wrote a message on the left thigh of the corpse and the same one on the bedsheet in blood. It has been translated in different ways, but in all the interpretations, their mystical pairing is affirmed. She also carved his name into her arm. When arrested, Abe was staying in a hotel in Tokyo composing farewell epistles to family and friends. Carter, "Killer Love"; Jason Collins, "Sex, Mutilation Murder: The Details of a Killing in Japan Keep It in the Spotlight Even 100 Years Later," Front Page Detectives, posted April 9, 2021, https://www .frontpagedetectives.com/p/sada-abe-killng-murder-japan-famous; Ciaran Conliffe, "Abe Sada, Victim, and Killer," HeadStuff, posted October 3, 2016, https://headstuff.org/culture/history/abe-sada-victim-killer/; King, "Woman Strangled Her Lover." She told police, "I decided that I would flee to Osaka, staying with Ishida's [her consort] penis all the while. In the end, I would jump from a cliff on Mount Ikoma while holding on to his penis." Abe, as quoted in Collins, "Sex, Mutilation Murder."

57 Narration, in *Beyond the Dark*, "The Tsuyama Massacre"; Murderpedia, "Mutsuo Toi (都井 睦雄).

58 Toi Mutsuo, in *Beyond the Dark*, "The Tsuyama Massacre."

59 Narration, in *Beyond the Dark*, "The Tsuyama Massacre"; narration, in *hevidocs,* "Mutsuo Toi - The Tsuyama Massacre"; Ozbourne, "He Killed 30 People."

60 Devastating Disasters, "Tsuyama Massacre – 1938," Devastatingdisasters.com, last updated 2022, https://devastatingdisasters.com/?s=Tsuyama+Massacre+; Fox, "Top 10 Deadliest Rampage Killers," 8; narration, in *hevidocs,* "Mutsuo Toi - The Tsuyama Massacre"; Murderpedia, "The Tsuyama massacre," s.v. "Mutsuo Toi"; Ozbourne, "He Killed 30 People," under "The Crime"; narration, in *Past Crimes*, "Japan's Deadliest Lone Gunman Murders: The Story of Mutsuo Toi"; *whatisurfed* (blog), "Sugisawa Village: The Lost Village," posted March 11, 2017, https://whatisurfed.wordpress.com/2017/03/11/sugisawa-villagethe-lost-village/.

61 *Forbidden Truth Blog*, "Honoring Mutsuo Toi (都井 睦雄), Torture Victim of 20th Century Japanese Society," posted June 9, 2017; narration, in *hevidocs,* "Mutsuo Toi - The Tsuyama Massacre"; narration, in *Past Crimes*, "Japan's Deadliest Lone Gunman Murders: The Story of Mutsuo Toi."

62 Narration, in *hevidocs,* "Mutsuo Toi - The Tsuyama Massacre"; Ozbourne, "He Killed 30 People," under "The Crime."

[63] Kageyama, "The Tsuyama Massacre of 1938," under "Mutsuo's Miseries."

[64] In *Past Crimes*, "Japan's Deadliest Lone Gunman Murders: The Story of Mutsuo Toi." He wrote multiple suicide notes. Some are believed to have been written prior to the killings. The sequence of the messages or the content ascribed to each is lacking in the references that are accessible. Refer to: a) Devastating Disasters, "Tsuyama Massacre"; b) *Asian Madness Podcast*, "Episode 53 - No Turning Back: Toi Mutsuo," posted July 6, 2020, https://podtail.com/podcast/the-asian-madness-podcast/e53-no-turning-back-toi-mutsuo/; c) Murderpedia, "The Tsuyama Massacre." The quotation, used in this passage, according to *Past Crimes*, was composed at the conclusion of the foray and prior to Mutsuo's suicide.

[65] The term's meaning is exactly what parsing would indicate. Its origin is reviewed in the Introduction of *How Rampage Killers Interpret Their Worlds* and put in the context of autogenic mass murderer's penchant for drama in Chapter Five of that book. Additional examples include Charles Whitman, James Holmes, and Ander Breivik.

[66] Narration, in *Past Crimes*, "Japan's Deadliest Lone Gunman Murders: The Story of Mutsuo Toi."

[67] Devastating Disasters, "Tsuyama Massacre"; narration, in *hevidocs,* "Mutsuo Toi - The Tsuyama Massacre"; Ozbourne, "He Killed 30 People," under "The Crime"; narration, in *Past Crimes*, "Japan's Deadliest Lone Gunman Murders: The Story of Mutsuo Toi"; *whatisurfed*, "Sugisawa Village."

[68] Narration, in *Past Crimes*, "Japan's Deadliest Lone Gunman Murders: The Story of Mutsuo Toi."

[69] *Forbidden Truth Blog*, "Honoring Mutsuo Toi"; narration, in *hevidocs,* "Mutsuo Toi - The Tsuyama Massacre."

[70] In *Asian Madness Podcast*, "Episode 53 - No Turning Back"; in *Past Crimes*, "Japan's Deadliest Lone Gunman Murders: The Story of Mutsuo Toi."

[71] Narration, in *Asian Madness Podcast*, "Episode 53 - No Turning Back"; *New York Times*, "Lunatic Kills 27 in Japan," 87, no. 29,338 (May 22, 1938): 28; narration, in *Past Crimes*, "Japan's Deadliest Lone Gunman Murders: The Story of Mutsuo Toi"; *whatisurfed*, "Sugisawa Village."

[72] Mutsuo, as narrated in *Asian Madness Podcast*, "Episode 53 - No Turning Back."

[73] Mutsuo, as narrated, in *Past Crimes*, "Japan's Deadliest Lone Gunman Murders: The Story of Mutsuo Toi."

[74] dahmercel [pseud.], "I dont know about you guys but i think this was badass as shit," INCELS, posted July 7, 2020, under Forums, https://incels.net/threads/tsuyama-massacre-a-very-early-japanese-er-his-name-was-mutsuo-toi.19100/ (site now defunct – see: r/IncelTear [pseud.], "A Forum Called "incels.net" Has Finally Bit the Dust!" redditt, posted March 2023 [?], https://www.reddit.com/r/IncelTear/comments/zcalu4/a_forum_called_incel

snet_has_finally_bit_the_dust/). Punctuation, capitalization, and spelling conform to post. Cho, who terrorized the campus at Virginia Tech, killing 32, is contained in the Appendix in this book and mentioned in the Introduction as well as Chapter Four in *How Rampage Killers Interpret Their Worlds*.

[75] Banned [pseud.], reply to dahmercel, "I dont know," posted July 7, 2020. Spelling conforms to post.

[76] Dahmercel, reply to Banned, "He was the," posted July 7, 2020. Extended ellipsis as posted.

[77] Jessica McBride, "Randy Stair: 5 Fast Facts You Need to Know," Heavy, updated July 16, 2017, under "1. Randy Stair Left a Disturbing Final Video in which He Was Going to Kill People & Urged Everyone to Watch the Headlines." One can argue about her motives for the assumptive persona, but the application of grammatical genderization – especially when older teens or adults have expressed a preference – should be the choice of the persons being discussed and not subject to the whims of various biographers. "People's names and pronouns are changing every day, and it's our duty to appropriately account for that. … Failing to do so not only makes it hard to communicate effectively but can be extremely disrespectful." David Galowich, "How to Respectfully Use Gender Pronouns in The Workplace," *Forbes*, posted Aug 2, 2018. https://www.forbes.com/sites/forbescoaches council/2018/08/02/how-to-respectfully-use-gender-pronouns-in-the-workplace /?sh=272fb7c16c40.

[78] Andrew Blaze (Randy Stair), School Shooters. info, s.v. "Randy Stair"; Jon Meyer, "Disturbing Details in Shooter's Social Media," WNEP American Broadcasting Corporation (ABC), posted and updated June 8, 2017, https:// www.wnep.com/article/news/local/wyoming-county/disturbing-details-in-shooters-social-media/523-02e3e919-f6c7-41a2-9efa-438d23c6fc b1.

[79] Blaze, "Please Read (Randy Stair)," School Shooters. info, s.v. "Randy Stair." Punctuated as original.

[80] Andrew Blaze, *Journal*, Monday, June 5, 2017, School Shooters.info, s.v. "Randy Stair."

[81] AP, "Supermarket Massacre's Shooter's Final Tweet: 'Goodbye Humans … I'll Miss You,'" *Pennsylvania Real-Time News*, posted June 8, 2017, updated June 9, 2017, https://www.pennlive.com/news/2017/06/supermarket_massacre _shooters.html; James Halpin, "Family of Weis Shooter Issues Statement," *Citizen's Voice*, posted June 9, 2017, https://www.citizensvoice. com/news /family-of-weis-shooter-issues-statement-1.2204218; Gary M. Ross, Forensic Pathologist, Forensic Associates of Northeastern Pennsylvania Alliance, Autopsy FA-217-A-149, Randy Stair (completed July 23, 2017), under "Final Summary," School Shooters. info, s.v. "Randy Stair."

[82] Gary M. Ross, Forensic Pathologist, Forensic Associates of Northeastern Pennsylvania Alliance, Autopsy FA-217-A-152, Brian Hayes, (completed

June 20, 2017), under "Final Summary," School Shooters. info, s.v. "Randy Stair."

[83]Ross, Forensic Pathologist, Forensic Associates, Autopsy FA-217-A-151, Terry Lee Sterling (completed June 20, 2017), under "Final Summary," School Shooters. info, s.v. "Randy Stair."

[84] Ross, Forensic Pathologist, Forensic Associates, Autopsy FA-217-A-150, Victoria Todd Brong, (completed June 20, 2017), under "Final Summary," School Shooters. info, s.v. "Randy Stair."

[85] AP, "Supermarket Massacre's Shooter's Final."

[86] AP, "Supermarket Massacre's Shooter's Final"; Travis Kellar, "Alleged Shooter: 'Goodbye Humans...I'll Miss You,'" *Pocono Record*, posted and updated June 8, 2017, https://www.poconorecord.com/story/news/crime/2017/06/08/alleged-shooter-goodbye-humans-i/20679086007/. Quotation punctuated as reported.

[87] Parkaman, "Randy Robert Stair: Murder Plans Posted Online Months Before the Attack," Parkaman.com, posted January 17, 2018, https://www.parkaman.com/category/murder-cases/page/3/; monologue by Blaze, in *PioneersProductions,* "Answering Your Questions + My Burning Hatred For Gaming Channels," YouTube, posted July 1, 2016, https://www.youtube.com/watch?v=8cF4lGmWGW0 (no longer available); monologue by Blaze, in *PioneersAnthology*, "The PioneersProductions Anthology (2014) Full Documentary," YouTube, posted April 15, 2016, https://www.youtube.com/watch?v=ka5UYR4_ttM&t=6s (video no longer available); narration, in W TV, "The Insanely Dark Story of Randy Stairs," YouTube, posted January 13, 2019, https://www.youtube.com/watch?v=pPUQc8KiPdM&frags=pl%2Cwn (no longer available). Blaze sometimes used the initials *EGS* as an abbreviation for his channel and at other time to name the spectral beings he believed waited for him on the other side. For the sake of consistency and to emphasize their origin they are italicized throughout the biography.

[88] Parkaman, "Randy Robert Stair."

[89] Based on numbers posted on YouTube: a) PioneersProductions, last posting April 10, 2017, https://www.youtube.com/user/PioneersProductions (page no longer available); b) PioneersAnthology, last posting May 11, 2016, https://www.youtube.com/user/PioneersAnthology (page no longer available). Subscriber numbers were not accessible for "Ember's Ghost Squad," but many of the episodes had well over 1,000 views. archive.today, posted June 10, 2017, https://archive.is/Rk3ew. One segment, "Conspiring a Massacre - Andrew Blaze (EGS Tapes)," has been viewed 8,073 times to date. The caption, presumably penned by Blaze, reads: "Andrew Blaze isn't your average ghost. She is one of the more mysterious members in the squad. Like many others, she records her intentions and thoughts on cassette tapes.

She holds a wide collection of recordings from her mortal life; and now another recording is public. Her words; chilling." archive.today, originally posted July 21, 2016, https://archive.is/fg7TN. A cartoon with a recording of Ember's plaintive theme, "Remember," sung by Robbyn Kirmssé (composed and produced by Guy Moon) has amassed over three million views on a channel called *Worthless Toaster*. "Ember McLain - Remember (Official Soundtrack Version)," posted April 6, 2014, https://www.youtube.com/c/WorthlessToaster/featured. The site features four cartoons of the performance, nothing else. Blaze is widely believed to be the creator. Many of the comments by viewers attest to that probability. DuskDefender [pseud.], "An Abstract History of Randy Stair by Rave Marcial," posted October 22, 2020, https://www.deviantart.com/duskdefender/art/An-Abstract-History-of-Randy-Stair-by-Rave-Marcial-858880308.

90 "Original Documents," School Shooters .info, s.v. "Randy Stair."

91 Commentary by Blaze, in *PioneersProductions*, "4 Years, Thanks Everyone!" YouTube, posted June 9, 2012, https://www.youtube.com/watch?v=UuFzJ7X9cUI.

92 *PioneersProductions*; *PioneersAnthology*.

93 *PioneerProductions*, "Extinction ('Finale Series Episode 03)," YouTube, posted August 25, 2014, https://www.youtube.com/watch?v=UuFzJ7X9cUI ("Video unavailable").

94 Ibid, animation.

95 *PioneerProductions*, "Resurrection ('Finale Series' Episode 04')," YouTube, posted August 25, 2014, https://www.youtube.com/watch?v=nU_gd5jwVlQ ("Video unavailable"). Title punctuated as original.

96 Narration, *Coffeehouse Crime*, "YouTuber to Mass-Murderer/Randy Stair's Dark Fantasy World," YouTube, posted Jun 14, 2021, https://www.youtube.com/watch?v=dIQJ2s1basU&t=1376s;
PioneerProductions, "Absolution ('Finale Series' Episode 05')," YouTube, posted August 25, 2014, https://www.youtube.com/watch?v=5sUCPZv30Xg ("Video unavailable"). Title punctuated as original.

97 Butch Hartman, Steve Marmel, and Kevin Sullivan, creators, *Danny Phantom* (Los Angeles, CA and New York, NY: Billionfold and Nickelodeon Animation Studios, 2003-2007); NamniC [gone for now] [pseud.], "Ember McLain," Amino, first posting March 2016, under "Who Is She?" https://aminoapps.com/c/cartoon/page/item/ember-mclain/ER1I_LIbvJbpXBdxd7w7Lz8M5l74vR; commentary by Blaze and montage, *Pioneers Productions*, "Curtain Call (Abandoned Unfinished 'EGS' Episode)," YouTube, posted October 12, 2015, https://www.youtube.com/watch?v=9p_fvQHUZyI ("Video unavailable"); *Welcome to the Squad*, "Finding a Purpose EGS 1080p HD," YouTube, posted June 14, 2017, https://www.youtube.com/watch?v=PHSicGQKgd4 (video no longer available

because YouTube account terminated). As Blaze tells it in one of his self-congratulatory explanatory recordings, when Ember first appeared, she was not meant to be the antagonist from *Danny Phantom*, but a different figure with similar features, who Blaze called "Ember Flores." She later became Ember McClain. In the same session he offers an unconvincing argument attempting to explain why use of the character was not copywrite infringement. *PioneerProductions*, "Answering Your Questions."

[98] *Welcome to the Squad*, "Finding a Purpose."

[99] Specific instructions are provided by YouTube for advance publication of a video. YouTube, "Schedule Video Publish Time," YouTube Help, n.d., https://support.google.com/youtube/answer/1270709?hl=en.

[100] *Ember's Ghost Squad*, "The Westborough High Massacre (EGS)/Goodbye," posted on Twitter June 9, 2017, uploaded on YouTube by AS Entertainment, June 10, 2017, https://archive.org/details/TheWestboroughHighMassacreegs Goodbye; investigation by Wyoming County District Attorney Jeff Mitchell, in CBS/AP, "Weis Supermarket Shooting Gunman Posted Video Describing Plan," posted June 9, 2017, https://www.cbsnews.com/news/weis-supermarket -shooting-gunman-posted-video-describing-plan/.

[101] Narration, *Coffeehouse Crime*, "YouTuber to Mass-Murderer"; commentary by Todd Grande, in *Dr. Todd Grande*, "Randy Stair Case Analysis/Animated Ghost Girl Delusion," posted [August 2021?], https://www.youtube.com/watch?v=Ya4j2xrxYHE&t=247s.

[102] In a final recording left for his family, Blaze spends much of the tape recounting his history as a creator and Ember's gradual emergence as a pivotal being not only on his YouTube channels but in his imagination. *Randy Stair Remembered*, "Andrew Blaze Suicide Tapes#Video Versions10 Parents Goodbye 01 June 01, 2017," YouTube, posted August 18, 2019, https://www.youtube.com/watch?v=u2MOXaogmnE (Video "removed for violating YouTube's Terms of Service.")

[103] *PioneersAnthology*, "The PioneersProductions Anthology (2014) Full Documentary," Blaze commentary, YouTube, posted April 15, 2016, https://www.youtube.com/watch?v=ka5UYR4_ttM&t =6s.

[104] Monologue by Blaze, in *Randy Stair Remembered*, "Andrew Blaze Suicide Tapes#VideoVersions10."

[105] Blaze, *Journal*, inside cover. Capitalization and punctuation same as original.

[106] Blaze, *Journal*, Monday, January 30, 2017. Ellipsis, extra period, and quotation marks in original.

[107] Blaze, in *Randy Stair Remembered*, "Andrew Blaze Suicide Tapes#Video Versions10."

[108] See: a) American Psychiatric Association, *Diagnostic and Statistical Manual of Mental Disorders*, 5th ed. (*DSM-5* – Arlington VA, 2013), 702-704; and Taylor Bennett, "Transvestic Disorder DSM-5 302.3 (F65.1): Symptoms,

Treatments," *Counseling News*, posted July 31, 2017, https://thriveworks.com/blog/transvestic-disorder-symptoms-treatments/.

[109] Blaze, *Journal*, Saturday, February 11, 2017. Capitalized as original.

[110] Blaze ranting, in *Randy Stair Remembered*, "Randy Stair (Andrew Blaze) Suicide Tapes June 2, 2017," YouTube, posted August 18, 2019, https://www.youtube.com/watch?v=NRbBMHfLR9U&t=87s&bpctr=1595017513.

[111] Alicia Garcia-Falgueras, "Gender Dysphoria and Body Integrity Identity Disorder: Similarities and Differences," *Psychology* 5, no. 2 (February 2014), 163, citing: Michael B. First, "Desire for Amputation of a Limb: Paraphilia, Psychosis, or a New Type of Identity Disorder," *Psychological Medicine* 35, no. 6 (June 2005): 919-928; and Anne A. Lawrence, "Sexual Orientation Versus Age of Onset as Bases for Typologies (Subtypes) for Gender Identity Disorder in Adolescents and Adults," *Archives of Sexual Behavior* 39, no. 2 (April 2010): 514-545.

[112] Blaze, *Journal*, November 23, 2016.

[113] Blaze, *Journal*, November 23, 2016. Underlining and all caps in original.

[114] Blaze, *Journal*, Wednesday, January 4, 2017.

[115] For more demonstrative explanations of Harris's psychopathy, see: a) Appendix; b) Chapter Five; c) Langman, *Why Kids Kill*, 35-38, 41-43; and d) Cullen, *Columbine*, 234-247.

[116] Blaze monologue, in *Mohn Jilius*, "Randy Stair (Weis Market Shooter) – 01 Andrew Blaze 'ST' 04 04 17 Making of EGS," YouTube, posted June 9, 2017, https://www.youtube.com/watch?v=4id1lSQBZ0Q&list=PLPZoETN1bZvg1weuL9Uv5Lu7TBtSJkzgt ("Video unavailable").

[117] Blaze, "Extinction ('Finale Series')."

[118] Blaze monologue, in *Randy Stair Remembered*, "Andrew Blaze Suicide Tapes Tapes#Video Versions10."

[119] Jeffrey M. Cohen, Christine Blasey, C. Barr Taylor, Brandon J. Weiss, and Michelle G. Newman, "Anxiety and Related Disorders and Concealment in Sexual Minority Young Adults," *Behavior Therapy* 47, no. 1 (January 2016): 95, 96. Measures for disorders were derived from published questionnaires, checklists, and inventories. Sexual interests were self-identified. A two-way multivariate analysis of variance and chi-squared were utilized. The *p* ranged from 0.0001 to 0.001.

[120] Blaze, *Journal*, Monday, March 20, 2017.

[121] Blaze monologue, in HeyGuy4321 [pseud.], "Andrew Blaze's (Randy Stair) Westborough High Massacre Video. Reupload," YouTube, posted July 11, 2017, https://www.youtube.com/watch?v=4bguj-NVkto (video "removed for violating YouTube's policy on hate speech").

[122] Blaze monologue, in *Randy Stair Remembered*, "Andrew Blaze Suicide Tapes Tapes#Video Versions10."

[123] Ibid.

[124] Blaze, *Journal*, March 20, 2017. Punctuated as written.

[125] Blaze, *Journal*, November 23, 2016.

[126] Blaze, *Journal*, January 20, 2017. Spelling as well as ellipsis after friend in original post.

[127] See: Annelou L.C. de Vries, Theo A.H. Doreleijers, Thomas D. Steensma, and Peggy T. Cohen-Kettenis, "Psychiatric Comorbidity in Gender Dysphoric Adolescents," *Journal of Child Psychology and Psychiatry* 52 no. 11 (2011): 1195–1202; and Berna Özata Yıldızhan, Şahika Yüksel, Mirella Avayu, Handan Noyan, and Eren Yildizhan, "Effects of Gender Reassignment on Quality of Life and Mental Health in People with Gender Dysphoria," *Turkish Journal of Psychiatry* (2018), https://www.turkpsikiyatri.com/PDF/C29S1/en/2TPD_17012_YILDIZHAN_effects.pdf.

[128] Marios Dimitrios Chatzinikolaou, "Gender Dysphoria Treatment: A Critical Discussion of Medical and Psychotherapeutic Approaches in Adults and Young People," (paper, 2nd World Conference on Teaching and Education, Vienna, Austria, February 19, 2021), 303-304, referencing Marta R. Bizic, Milos Jeftovic, Slavica Pusica, Borko Stojanovic, Dragana Duisin, Svetlana Vujovic, Vojin Rakic, Miroslav L. Djordjevic, "Gender Dysphoria: Bioethical Aspects of Medical Treatment," *BioMed Research International* 2018, Article ID 9652305, https://doi.org/10.1155/2018/9652305; Yildizhan et al., "Effects of Gender Reassignment," referring to Koray Başar and Gökhan Öz, "Resilience in Individuals with Gender Dysphoria: Association with Perceived Social Support and Discrimination," *Turkish Journal of Psychiatry* 27, no. 4 (December 2016): 225-234.

[129] Blaze, in *PioneerProductions,* "Answering Your Questions."

[130] Elena García-Vega, Aida Camero, María Fernández, and Ana Villaverde, "Suicidal Ideation and Suicide Attempts in Persons with Gender Dysphoria," *Psicothema* 30, no. 3 (August 2018): 284, tables 1 and 2. The article gives a general description of transsexual as "people [who] have the conviction that they are of the opposite sex to that which they were born into, with a continued sense of dissatisfaction and rejection of their own primary and secondary sexual characteristics, and with a profound feeling of rejection and a desire for medical and surgical changes to modify their body and make it conform with the gender they feel to be. From infancy their mental identity is different to their genital phenotype: they are women who feel 'trapped' in a man's body …and men who feel 'trapped' in a woman's body. …They do not have any serious psychiatric disorders. …" Ibid, 283. Ideation was described as "thoughts of carrying out suicide-related behaviours" and an attempt as "a potentially self- injurious behaviour with a nonfatal outcome, for which there is evidence (either explicit or implicit) that the person intended at some level to kill themselves."

[131] Ibid, 284, 285, 286.

[132] Ibid, 286.

[133] E.g: Blaze monologue, in HeyGuy4321, "Andrew Blaze's (Randy)"; Blaze, *Journal*, Wednesday, December 21, 2016.

[134] García-Vega, Camero, Fernández, and Villaverde, "Suicidal Ideation and Suicide Attempts," 286, table 4.

[135] Blaze, *Journal*, Sunday, January 29, 2017. Punctuated as original.

[136] Monologue by Blaze, in *Mohn Jilius*, "Randy Stair (Weis Market Shooter) - 01 Andrew Blaze."

[137] Blaze, *Journal*, Wednesday, February 15, 2017. Punctuation and spelling as originally written.

[138] Monologue by Blaze, in *Randy Stair Remembered*, "Andrew Blaze Suicide Tapes Tapes#Video Versions10."

[139] Blaze, *Journal*, Sunday, January 29, 2017. Ellipses and capitalization in original.

[140] Blaze, *Journal*, March 22, 2017.

[141] Monologue by Blaze, *Randy Stair Remembered*, "Andrew Blaze Suicide Tapes Tapes#Video Versions10."

[142] Lisa Bortolotti and Matteo Mameli, "Self-Deception, Delusion and the Boundaries of Folk Psychology," author's manuscript, PMC, posted May 31, 2012, https://www.ncbi.nlm.nih.gov/pmc/articles/PMC3364711/; Chandra Kiran and Suprakash Chaudhury, "Understanding Delusions," *Industrial Psychiatry Journal* 2009 18, no. 1 (January-June 2018): 3–18.

[143] Bortolotti and Mameli, "Self-Deception, Delusion and the Boundaries," under 1.2 and 2.1.

[144] a) Vaughan Bell, Nichola Raihani, Sam Wilkinson "De-Rationalising Delusions," PsyArXiv Preprints: posted and modified September 2, 2019, https://psyarxiv.com/4p9zs/; b) Lisa Bortolotti, Rochelle Cox, and Amanda Barnier, "Can we recreate delusions in the laboratory?" *Philosophical Psychology* 25, no. 1 (February 2012): 109-131; c) Stefan Westermann, Vivien Gantenbein, Franz Caspar, and Marialuisa Cavelti, "Maintaining Delusional Beliefs to Satisfy and Protect Psychological Needs," *Zeitschrift für Psychologie* (*Journal of Psychology*) 226, no. 3 (January 2018): 197-203. Designed to facilitate rapid dissemination of technical information and research in the human sciences, PsyArXiv Preprints is a creation of the Society for the Improvement of Psychological Science (SIPS) and the Center for Open Science (COS). It is managed by an executive board with input from an advisory committee. https://psyarxiv.com/.

[145] P. Brown, F. Waite, and D. Freeman, "Twisting the lion's tail': Manipulationist Tests of Causation for Psychological Mechanisms in the Occurrence of Delusions and Hallucinations," *Clinical Psychology Review* 68 (March 2019): 25–37.

[146] The following articles look at the psychological damage in the assumption of male dominance and its connection to rampageous thinking. a) Jessie Daniels, "Race, Gender & Rampage," *The Society Pages*, posted April 10, 2009, https://thesocietypages.org/colorline/2009/04/10/race-gender -rampage/; b) Kathryn Farr, "Adolescent Rampage School Shootings: Responses to Failing Masculinity Performances by Already Troubled Boys," *Gender Issues*, no. 35 (2018): 73-97, https://link.springer.com/content/pdf/10.1007/s12147-017-9203-z.pdf; c) Rachel Jewkes, Robert Morrell, Jeff Hearn, Emma Lundqvist, David Blackbeard, Graham Lindegger, Michael Quayle, Yandisa Sikweyiya, and Lucas Gottzén, "Hegemonic Masculinity: Combining Theory and Practice in Gender Interventions," *Culture, Health & Sexuality* 17, sup. 2 (2015): 112-127, https://www.tandfonline.com/doi/pdf/10.1080/13691058 .2015.1085094; d) Patrick Osborne, "Making Sense of the 'Monsters Next Door': General Strain and the Rampage Violence Narrative," *Gender Forum*, no. 69 (special issue, 2018): 3-23, http://genderforum.org/wp-content/ uploads/2018/08/2018_ECRIV_complete.pdf. Another short essay shows how stereotypical masculinity is endorsed by the media; Supersister777 [pseud.], "Cultural Hegemony and Hegemonic Masculinity within Western society," The Fourth Wave, posted April 21, 2014, https://gendersrace popularculture.wordpress.com/2014/04/21/cultural-hegemony-and-hegemonic-masculinity-within-western-society/.

[147] Osborne, "Making Sense of the 'Monsters,'" 7, citing James Gilligan, *Violence: Reflections on a National Epidemic* (New York, NY: Vintage Books, 1997), 51. More backing for that observation may be found in Michael Kimmel, *Angry White Men: American Masculinity at the End of an Era* (New York, NY: Bold Type Books, 2017), chap. 1-3, Kindle Cloud.

[148] Adrian Rivera-Rodriguez, Greg Larsen, Nilanjana Dasgupta, "Changing Public Opinion about Gender Activates Group Threat and Opposition to Feminist Social Movements Among Men," *Group Processes & Intergroup Relations* 25, no. 3 (April 2022): 811-829, abstract, https://doi.org/10.1177 /13684302211048885.

[149] Mark Follman, Gavin Aronsen, and Deanna Pan, "A Guide to Mass Shootings in America," *Mother Jones*, updated May 26, 2021, https://www.mother jones.com/politics/2012/07/mass-shootings-map/.

[150] Mark Follman, "Armed and Misogynist: How Toxic Masculinity Fuels Mass Shootings," *Mother Jones* (May/June 2019), https://www.motherjones.com/ crime-justice/2019/06/domestic-violence -misogyny-incels-mass-shootings/.

[151] SubEightMale [pseud.], "Sexism is alive and well in the world, and I fucking love it," INCELS, posted February 28, 2020, under "Forums," https://incels. net/threads/sexism-is-alive-and-well-in-the-world-and-i-fucking-love-it.119 99/. Except for initial ellipsis, punctuation and capitalization conform to post.

[152] Saint Mentalcel [pseud.], reply to SubEightMale, "Sexism is alive," posted February 28, 2020.

[153] TheLastMujahid [pseud.], reply to SubEightMale, "Sexism is alive," posted February 28, 2020. Transcribed as posted.

[154] Roberta Liggett O'Malley, Karen Holt, Thomas J. Holt, "An Exploration of the Involuntary Celibate (Incel) Subculture Online," *Journal of Interpersonal Violence*, posted September 24, 2020, abstract, https://journals.sagepub.com/doi/pdf/10.1177/0886260520959625.

[155] Nick Chester, "Meet the Women of the Incel Movement: The Truth about Femcels," *Huck*, posted December 5, 2018, https://www.huckmag.com/art-and-culture/tech/meet-the-women-of-the-incel -movement/.

[156] Alana, in Peter Baker, "The Woman Who Accidentally Started the Incel Movement," *ELLE*, posted March 1, 2016, https://www.elle.com/culture/news/a34512/woman-who-started-incel-movement/.

[157] Zack Beauchamp, "Our Incel Problem," *Vox*, updated April 23, 2019, https://www.vox.com/the-highlight/2019/4/16/18287446/incel-definition-reddit.

[158] Chester, "Meet the Women of the Incel Movement."

[159] Anonymous 14777, crystal.cafe, posted five years before access (March 20, 2024), https://crystal.cafe/feels/res/14730.html#58741.

[160] Ibid. "*Social justice warrior* is an often mocking term for one who is seen as overly progressive or left-wing. It's often abbreviated as *SJW*." *Meriam Webster*, "Words We're Watching: Social Justice Warrior," © 2023, under "What does social justice warrior mean?" https://www.merriam-webster.com/words-at-play/what-does-social-justice-warrior-sjw-mean.

[161] Karolin Grunau, "Involuntary Celibacy: Personality Traits Amongst Misogynistic Online Communities" (bachelor's thesis, University of Twente, 2020), 7-8, tables 1, 2a, http://essay.utwente.nl/81904/1/Grunau_BA_BMS.pdf.

[162] Patrick Radden Keefe, "A Loaded Gun: A Mass Shooter's Tragic Past," *New Yorker Reader True Crime*, spec. ed. 41, no. 27A (September 15, 2015): 91.

[163] Qian-Wen Xie, Xiaolu Dai, Xinfeng Tang, Celia H. Y. Chan, and Cecilia L. W. Chan, "Risk of Mental Disorders in Children and Adolescents with Atopic Dermatitis: A Systematic Review and Meta-Analysis," *Frontiers of Psychology* 6, no. 1773 (August 2019), under "Study Selection," "Meta-Analysis," https://www.frontiersin.org/articles/10.3389/fpsyg.2019.01773/full. "All studies applied observational study designs including 11 cohort studies, 12 case control studies, and 12 cross-sectional studies. In terms of representativeness of sample, 22 studies used a random sample or a community sample. Nineteen studies compared the prevalence or incidence of mental disorders in children with AD to the general population, rather than healthy controls." Ibid, under "Characteristics of Studies."

[164] Catherine M Nguyen, John Koo, and Kelly M Cordoro, "Psychodermatologic Effects of Atopic Dermatitis and Acne: A Review on Self-Esteem and Identity," *Pediatric Dermatology* 33, no. 2 (March April 2016): 129-135, abstract, doi: 10.1111/pde.12802.

Chapter Three

[1] Rebecca Solnit, *The Faraway Nearby* (USA: Penguin Books, 2013), 13.

[2] a) Anne E. Appel and George W. Holden, "The Co-Occurrence of Spouse and Physical Child Abuse: A Review and Appraisal," *Journal of Family Psychology* 12, no. 4 (December 1998): 583, https://www .researchgate.net/ publication/232428564_The_co-occurrence_of_spouse_and_physical_child _abuse_A_review_and_appraisal/link/00463534bdae3238dd000000/ download, reviewing: a) Bonnie E. Carlson, "Outcomes of Physical Abuse and Observation of Marital Violence Among Adolescents in Placement," *Journal of Interpersonal Violence* 6, no. 4 (December 1991), 526-534; b) Linda McKibben, Edward De Vos and Eli H. Newberger, "Victimization of Mothers of Abused Children: A Controlled Study," *Pediatrics* 84, no. 3 (September 1989): 531-535; c) Kathleen J. Sternberg, Michael E. Lamb, Charles Greenbaum, Dante Cicchetti, Samia Dawud, Rosa Manela Cortes, Orit Krispin, and Fanny Lorey, "Effects of Domestic Violence on Children's Behavior Problems and Depression," *Developmental Psychology* 29, no. 1 (January 1993): 44-52.

[3] Appel and Holden, "The Co-Occurrence of Spouse and Physical Child Abuse," 583, reviewing Robin A. McGee, David A.Wolfe, Sandra A.Yuen, Susan K. Wilson, and Jean Carnochan, "The Measurement of Maltreatment: A Comparison of Approaches," *Child Abuse & Neglect* 19, no. 2 (February 1995): 233-249; and Suzanne Salzinger, Richard S. Feldman, Muriel Hammer, and Margaret Rosario, "Constellation of Family Violence and Their Differential Effects on Children's Behavioral Disturbance," *Child and Family Behavior Therapy* 14, no. 4 (1993): 23-41.

[4] B. Bala Parameswari, "Domestic Violence and Child Abuse," *IOSR Journal of Humanities and Social Science* 20, no. 2 (February 2015): 56, https://www.iosrjournals.org/iosr-jhss/papers/Vol20-issue2/Version-3/I0202 35659.pdf.

[5] Maxia Dong, Robert F. Anda, Vincent J. Felitti, Shanta R. Dube, David F. Williamson, Theodore J. Thompson, Clifton M. Loo, and Wayne H. Giles, "The Interrelatedness of Multiple Forms of Childhood Abuse, Neglect, and Household Dysfunction," *Child Abuse & Neglect* 28, no. 7 (July 2004): 773-776.

[6] Ibid, 776.

[7] Ibid, 776, 777, 778.

[8] Mario Mikulincer, Omri Gillath, Vered Halevy, Neta Avihou, Shelly Avidan, and Nitzan Eshkoli, "Attachment Theory and Reactions to Others' Needs: Evidence That Activation of the Sense of Attachment Security Promotes Empathic Responses," *Journal of Personality and Social Psychology* 81, no. 6 (December 2001): 1205-1224, abstract, http://www.bruceliese.com/documents/attachment-theory/attachment-priming-mikulincer-Gallath-jpsp-2001.pdf.

[9] Ibid, 1208-1209, 1211-1217.

[10] Ibid, 1210, 1212, 1215, 1217.

[11] Ibid, 1218. For a description of attachment styles refer to Cindy Hazan and Phillip Shaver, "Romantic Love Conceptualized as an Attachment Process," *Journal of Personality and Social Psychology* 52, no. 3 (1987): 512-513, https://adultattachmentlab.human.cornell.edu/HazanShaver1987.pdf

[12] Mikulincer et al., "Attachment Theory and Reactions to Others' Needs," 1218, 1219.

[13] Ibid, 1219.

[14] a) Peter Langman, "Adult School Shooters," version 1.1 (February 1, 2016), School Shooters .info: Resources on School Shootings, Perpetrators, and Prevention, last updated March 21, 2024, s.v. "Library," https://schoolshooters.info/; b) Peter Langman, "Rampage School Shooters: A Typology," *Aggression and Violent Behavior* 14, no. 1 (January-February 2009): 79-86; c) Peter Langman, "School Shooters: Nine Brief Sketches," Version 1.1 (February 12, 2016), School Shooters info, s.v. "Library."

[15] Langman, "Rampage School Shooters," 81.

[16] Jillian Peterson and James Densley, "School Shooters Usually Show These Signs of Distress Long Before They Open Fire, Research Shows," *Insider*, posted February 14, 2019, https://www.businessinsider.com/school-shooters-show-these-signs-of-distress-before-they-open-fire-2019-2.

[17] National Institute of Justice, U.S. Department of Justice, Office of Justice Programs, Mass Shooter Database, posted September 27, 2018, under "Description of Original Award (Fiscal Year 2018, $300,403)," https://nij.ojp.gov/funding/awards/2018-75-cx-0023?award=2018-75-CX-0023.

[18] Peterson and Densley, "School Shooters Usually Show These Signs."

[19] Mary Ellen O'Toole, *The School Shooter: A Threat Assessment Perspective* (Quantico, VA: Federal Bureau of Investigation, 1999), 10, https://www.google.com/search?client=safari&rls=en&q=The+School+Shooter:+A+Threat+Assessment+Perspective&ie=UTF-8&oe=UTF-8.

[20] The other one (as described by the Bureau) is symptomatic of ineffectual socialization or incomplete maturation. With respect to family, the FBI designates: "Turbulent Parent-Child Relationship," "Acceptance of Pathological Behavior," "Access to Weapons," "Lack of Intimacy," "Student

Rules the Roost,'" and "No Limits or Monitoring of TV and Internet." O'Toole, *The School Shooter*, 16-24.

[21] Child Welfare Information Gateway, "Understanding the Effects of Maltreatment on Brain Development," *Issue Brief* (Washington D.C: U.S. Department of Health and Human Services, November 2009), 7. To support the statement, the report refers to Bruce D. Perry, "Incubated in Terror: The Neurodevelopmental Impact of Violence in Childhood," in ed. D. Schetky and E. Benedek, *Textbook of Child and Adolescent Forensic Psychiatry* (Washington, D. C: American Psychiatric Press, 2001), 221-238.

[22] Child Welfare Information Gateway, "Understanding the Effects," 11. For more detailed evidence on the neurobiological effects of child abuse and neglect, refer to: a) Matt McGue and Thomas J. Bouchard, Jr., "Genetic and Environmental Influences on Human Behavioral Differences," *Annual Review of Neuroscience* 21 (1998): 1-24; b) Jack P. Shonkoff, Andrew S. Garner, The Committee on Psychosocial Aspects of Child and Family Health, Committee on Early Childhood Adoption and Dependent Care and Section on Developmental and Behavioral Pediatrics, Benjamin S. Siegel, Mary I. Dobbins, Marian F. Earls, Andrew S. Garner, Laura McGuinn, John Pascoe, and David L. Wood, "The Lifelong Effects of Early Childhood Adversity and Toxic Stress," *Pediatrics* 129, no. 1 (January 2012): e232-e246, http://pediatrics.aappublications.org/content/129/1/e232; c) Martin H. Teicher, "Wounds that Won't Heal: The Neurobiology of Child Abuse," *Cerebrum: The Dana Forum on Brain Science* 4, no. 2 (January 2000): 50-67.

[23] Robin Malinosky-Rummell and David J. Hansen, "Long Term Consequences of Childhood Physical Abuses," (faculty publications paper 99, University of Nebraska, 1993), http://digitalcommons.unl.edu /psychfacpub/99.

[24] Kenneth A. Dodge, John E. Bates, and Gregory S. Pettit, "Mechanisms in the Cycle of Violence," *Science* 250, no. 4988 (December 1990): 1679-1680, 1681. The sample was deliberately demographically representative of the geographic regions where participants resided (Nashville Tennessee, Knoxville Tennessee, and Bloomington Indiana). Children were designated as "harmed" based on ratings from interviewers from standardized interview sessions conducted with their mothers.

[25] Sandra Kapland, David Pelcovitz, and Victor Labruna. "Child and Adolescent Abuse and Neglect Research: A Review of the Past 10 Years. Part I: Physical and Emotional Abuse and Neglect [Research Update Review]," accepted for publication in *Journal of the American Academy of Child and Adolescent Psychiatry* 38, no. 10 (October 1999): 1214-1222, under "Interpersonal Problems," http://www.facmed.unam.mx/cainm/publicaciones/biblio/26.html; Alexandra Okun, Jeffrey G. Parker, and Alytia A. Levendosky, "Distinct and Interactive Contributions of Physical Abuse, Socioeconomic Disadvantage, and Negative Life Events to Children's Social, Cognitive, and Affective Adjustment,"

Development and Psychopathology 6, no. 1 (Winter 1994): 77-98, abstract, https://www.cambridge.org/core/journals/development-and-psychopathology/article/distinct-and-interactive-contributions-of-physical-abuse-socioeconomic-disadvantage-and-negative-life-events-to-childrens-social-cognitive-and-affective-adjustment/21DB26F8671987EBBA9D263C 1528790E.

[26] Katherine M. Kitzmann, Noni K. Gaylord, Aimee R. Holt, and Erin D. Kenny, "Child Witness to Domestic Violence: A Meta-Analytic Review," *Journal of Consulting and Clinical Psychology* 71, no. 2 (April 2003): 345. "[N]egative affect-distress in response to hypothetical interadult conflict ... $p < 0.01$ … problems with social competence … $p < 0.02$."

[27] Jenifer Z. Siegel, Suzanne Estrada, Molly J. Crockett, and Arielle Baskin-Sommers, "Exposure to Violence Affects the Development of Moral Impressions and Trust Behavior in Incarcerated Males," *Nature Communications* 10, no. 1942 (April 2019): 2-3, https://modlab.yale.edu/sites/default/files/files/Siegeletlal_2019.pdf.

[28] Ibid, 5.

[29] Bruce D. Perry, "Incubated in Terror: Neurodevelopmental Factors in the 'Cycle of Violence'" Child Trauma Academy Materials, published January 1997, 8, https://www.researchgate.net/publication/246456464_Incubated_in_terror_Neurodevelopmental_factors_in_the_Cycle_of_Violence.

[30] Cathy Spatz Windom, "The Cycle of Violence," *Science* 244, no. 4901 (April 1989), 161-162. "In comparison to controls, abused and neglected children as a group have a larger mean number of offenses (2.43 versus 1.41, $t = 4.49$, $P < 0.001$); an earlier mean age at first offense (16.48 versus 17.29, $t = 2.38$, $P < 0.05$); and a higher proportion of chronic offenders, that is, those charged with five or more offenses [17 versus 9%; x^2 (1 = 28.86, $P < 0.001$]." Ibid, 162.

[31] Ibid, 163-164, table 2.

[32] Richard Rhodes, *Why They Kill: The Discoveries of a Maverick Criminologist* (New York, NY: Alfred A. Knopf, Inc., 1999), 112-119.

[33] Perry, "Incubated in Terror," Child Trauma Academy Materials, 20, fig. 6 caption.

[34] Dan Gunderson with Associated Press (AP), "Who Was Jeff Weis?" Minnesota Public Radio, posted March 23, 2005, http://news.minnesota.publicradio.org/features/2005/03/22_ap_redlakesuspect/ (page now inactive); Langman, "Rampage School Shooters," 81.

[35] *Bemidji Pioneer*, "Daryl Lussier, Jr.," originally published July 22, 1997, 2, School Shooters .info, s.v. "Jeffrey Weis"; Langman, "Rampage School Shooters," 81.

[36] Murderpedia: The Encyclopedia of Murderers, last updated, June 4, 2017, "Who Was Jeff Weis?" s.v. "Jeffrey James Weise," https://murderpedia.org.

[37] Cable News Network (CNN), "School Gunman Stole Police Pistol, Vest: Student Killed 9 before Turning Weapon on Himself," CNN.com, posted March 23, 2005, http://www.cnn.com/2005/US/03/22/school.shooting/; "Jeffery Weise: Timeline," School Shooters .info, s.v. "Jeffrey Weis"; National Broadcasting Company (NBC) with AP and Reuters, "Teen Who Killed 9 Claimed Nazi Leanings; Troubled Family History Includes Father's Suicide, Mother's Absence," NBCNews.com, posted March 23, 2005, http://www.nbcnews.com/id/7259823/ns/us_news-crime_and_ courts/t/teen-who-killed-claimed-nazi-leanings/#.U93LrK79XEM.

[38] AP, "Shooter Obsessed with Violence," Fox News, posted March 23, 2005, http://www.foxnews.com/story/2005/03/23/shooter-obsessed-with-violence/; CNN, "School Gunman Stole"; NBC with AP and Reuters, "Teen Who Killed 9 Claimed Nazi Leanings"; *Philadelphia Daily News*, "10 Die in Shooting Rampage, Student Killed Grandparents," posted March 22, 2005, Murderpedia, s.v. "Jeffrey James Weise"; Murderpedia, "Red Lake High School massacre," s.v. "Jeffrey James Weise"; Gary Younge and Suzanne Goldenberg. "You Could Hear a Girl Saying, 'No Jeff, Quit, Quit. Leave Me Alone. What Are you Doing?' Nine Killings in Deadly School Rampage of Neo-Nazi Loner Stun Red Lake," *Guardian*, posted on March 23, 2005, http://www.theguardian.com/world/2005/mar/23/usa.schoolsworldwide.

[39] Jeffrey Weise, "Thoughts of a Dreamer," School Shooters .info, s.v. "Jeffrey Weise." Grammar and punctuation as posted.

[40] John Lennon and Paul McCartney, "Strawberry Fields Forever," *Magical Mystery Tour* (EMI Ltd., 1967). The song takes the phrase from "Strawberry Field," an orphanage for girls near one of Lennon's childhood homes. In an interview with *Rolling Stone*, he mentioned that he made the reference plural because he thought it had a better sound, explaining further "Strawberry Fields is just anywhere you want to go." Matt Blitz, "The Story of Strawberry Fields Forever," Today I Found Out – Feed Your Brain, posted March 7, 2016, http://www.todayifoundout.com/index.php/2016/03/beatles-strawberry-fields-forever-meaning/.

[41] Johnny Cash, "When the Man Comes Around," *American IV: The Man Comes Around* (American Recordings and Universal Records, 2002); referred to in Weise, "Thoughts of a Dreamer," Dec. 14th, 2004 @ 01:18 pm.

[42] School Shooters .info, s.v. "Jeffrey Weis."

[43] "Phantasm: The Tall Man's Liar," site custodian information: Hacksaw2012@ hotmail.com, http://www.oocities.org/graver88/ (site accessible, but inactive); Fandom, "The Tall Man," Boogeymen Slashers Wiki: A Movies Community, last updated 2022, http://boogeymenslashers.wikia.com/wiki/The_Tall_Man; Robert Lamb, "Monster of the Week: The Tall Man ('Phantasm')," How Stuff Works – Stuff to Blow Your Mind, posted October 23, 2014, https://www.stufftoblowyourmind; com/blogs/monster-of-the-week-the-tall-

man-phantasm.htm; *Marvelous Videos*, "Phantasm's Time-Bending Monstrosity – The Tall Man's Complicated History and Origin Explored," YouTube, posted August 6, 2021, https://www.youtube.com/watch?v= CuoJq0ZAA.

[44] Slender Archives, "Der Großmann," The Slender Archives: n.d., https://theslenderarchives.weebly.com/germany.html; Storyteller [pseud.], "The Slender Man/Der Großmann," Urban Legends Online – Don't Believe Everything You're Told, posted October 15, 2011, http://urban legendsonline.com/the-slender-man/. A movie entitled *The Tall Man*, about childhood abductions attributed to a piece of folklore that were, instead, committed by an underground network, was produced in 2012, long after Weise's assault. Pascal Laugier, dir. and writ., *The Tall Man* (Minds Eye Entertainment, Cold Rock Productions BC, Incorporated, Forecast Pictures, Iron Ocean Films, Radar Films, and SND Films, 2012). Closely associated with the imagery is the urban legend of the Slender Man, an elusive murderous specter living in a wilderness mansion that originated with an internet posting and in 2014 influenced two impressionable twelve-year old girls to stab a friend 19 times to gain favor with the nefarious mythic being. Caitlin Dewey, "The Complete History of 'Slender Man,' The Meme That Compelled Two Girls to Stab a Friend," *Washington Post*, posted July 27, 2016, https://www.washingtonpost.com/news/the-intersect/wp/2014/06/03/ the-complete-terrifying-history-of-slender-man-the-internet-meme-that-compelled-two-12-year-olds-to-stab-their-friend/?utm_term=.60bca8ea2c5 b; Bryn Lovitt, "Slender Man: From Horror Meme to Inspiration for Murder," *Rolling Stone*, posted August 3, 2016, under "June 8th, 2009: A Legend Is Born" and "May 31st, 2014: Two Pre-Teens Attempt Murder in Name of Slender Man," https://www.rollingstone.com/culture/culture-news/slender-man-from-horror-meme-to-inspiration-for-murder-248430/.

[45] State of North Carolina v. Alvaro Rafael Castillo, North Carolina Court of Appeals, Fifteen-B District: No. COA10-814, Defendant-Appellant's Brief (submitted September 19, 2010), 5, School Shooters .info, s.v. "Alvaro Castillo."

[46] Ibid.

[47] *North Carolina v. Castillo*, 4-7; WRAL News, "Accused School Shooter's Mother, Sister Testify," WRAL.com, posted, updated August 11, 2009, https://www.wral.com/news/local/story/5770869/. His father left a girlfriend and children behind in El Salvador when he immigrated to America. One of his sons, older than Alvaro, passed away there. *North Carolina v. Alvaro*, 4-5; Peter Langman, *School Shooters: Understanding High School, College, and Adult Perpetrators* (Lanham, MD: Rowan & Littlefield, 2015), 45.

[48] *North Carolina v. Alvaro*, 5-6, 7

49 Anne Blythe, "Clinic Knew of Castillo's Danger," *News & Observer*, posted August 11, 2009, updated September 22, 2009, https://www.newsobserver.com/news/local/crime/article10357835.html; Langman, *School Shooters: Understanding*, 46; North *Carolina v. Alvaro*, 7-8.

50 *North Carolina v. Alvaro*, 10-11.

51 Ibid, 11. The Statement of Facts for the appellate case says that Castillo was dismissed from the Guard after his commitment. However, his defense attorney during his trial stated that that he had received an honorable discharge before that time. Blythe, "Clinic Knew of Castillo's."

52 Blythe, "Clinic Knew of Castillo's."

53 Alvaro Castillo, *Journal*, Tuesday, August 8, 2006, 10:05 a.m., School Shooters .info, s.v. "Alvaro Castillo."

54 Ibid.

55 Beth Karas, "Man Obsessed with Columbine Convicted of Murder," CNN/In Session, posted August 21, 2009, http://www.cnn.com/2009/CRIME/08/21/north.carolina.castillo.trial/.

56 American Broadcasting Company (ABC) 30 Action News, "Police: Shooter Spoke"; Karas, "Man Obsessed with Columbine"; Langman, "School Shooters: Nine Brief Sketches," under "Perpetrator: Alvaro Castillo"; *North Carolina v. Castillo*, 16 -18.

57 Monologue recorded by Castillo prior to rampage shown in court, in MrAlvarocastillo [pseud.], "Alvaro Castillo Home Videos 1," YouTube, posted August 17, 2009, https://www.youtube.com/watch?v=pG3LvXszeWY; audio and video during judicial proceedings, in MrAlvarocastillo, "Alvaro Castillo Thanks the Court 8-21-09," YouTube, posted, August 23, 2009, https://www.youtube.com/watch?v=5k4o9KB2z7U; monologue recorded by Castillo, in Thetrenchcoat [pseud.], "Alvaro Castillo 3," YouTube, posted, September 1, 2006, https://www.youtube.com/watch? v=ERx2N1ZH-kY (video no longer available, account terminated); Castillo, self-recording after father's murder, in Thetrenchcoat, "Alvaro Castillo 4," YouTube, posted, September 1, 2006, https://www.youtube.com/watch?v=QFeZoklwJjI (video no longer available, account terminated).

58 In *North Carolina v. Castillo*, 13.

59 Monologue recorded by Castillo shown in court, in MrAlvarocastillo, "Alvaro Castillo Home Videos 1," YouTube, posted August 17, 2009, https://www.youtube.com/watch?v=pG3LvXszeWY.

60 Monologue recorded by Castillo, in Thetrenchcoat, "Alvaro Castillo 2," YouTube, posted, September 1, 2006, https://www.youtube.com/watch?v=9gfM_A2vHHg (video no longer available, account terminated).

61 ABC 30 Action News, "Police: Shooter Spoke of Columbine," ABC Inc., KFSN-TV Fresno, posted August 5, 2009, https://abc30.com/archive/6946921/.

[62] Audio and video during judicial proceedings, in MrAlvarocastillo, "Alvaro Castillo Thanks the Court 8-21-09."

[63] Karas, "Man Obsessed with Columbine."

[64] Castillo, *Journal*, June 1, 2006, in *North Carolina v. Castillo*, 11-12; Castillo, *Journal*, July 29, 2006, in *North Carolina v. Castillo*, 13; Castillo, in MrAlvarocastillo, "Alvaro Castillo Home Videos 1."

[65] Castillo, in MrAlvarocastillo, "Alvaro Castillo Home Videos 1"; audio and video during judicial proceedings, in MrAlvarocastillo, "Alvaro Castillo Thanks the Court 8-21-09"; Castillo, in Thetrenchcoat, "Alvaro Castillo 2."

[66] S.K. Sharma and Monica Tomar, *Principles of Growth and Development* (Delhi, India: Isha Books, 2005), 32.

[67] There is an important distinction between what may be called applicable or situational intelligence and the more traditional (though increasingly less reputable) view encapsulated in a measurable intelligence quotient (IQ). For a brief overview to the difference, watch Robert Sternberg, "Successful Intelligence," YouTube, posted by The Brainwaves Video Anthology, October 27, 2014, https://www.youtube.com/watch?v=ow05B4bjGWQ. For a more comprehensive exploration, read Mogens R. Jensen, "Mediating Knowledge Construction: Towards A Dynamic Model of Assessment and Learning – Part I: Philosophy and theory," *Educational and Child Psychology* 20, no. 2 (January 2003): 100-117; and Mogens R. Jensen, "Mediating Knowledge Construction: Towards A Dynamic Model of Assessment and Learning – Part II: Applied Programmes and Research," *Educational and Child Psychology* 20, no. 2 (January 2003): 118-142. To take neuroscience into consideration, peruse José Luis Bermúdez, *Cognitive Science: An Introduction to the Science of the Mind* (New York, NY: Cambridge University Press, 2014), particularly II, 4.1, 5.2; IV, 10.2-10.3, V, 13.1-13.2., and 14.1-14.2.

[68] Cesar J. Rebellon, Murray A. Straus, and Rose Medeiros, "Self-Control in Global Perspective," *European Journal of Criminology* 5, no. 3 (July 2008): 351-353, table 5, doi:10.1177/1477370808090836. Subjects were in the International Dating Violence Research Consortium participating in the International Dating Violence Research Consortium. Participation varied across nationality, from as low as 140 (Malta) to 5,132 (United States). Items on the questionnaire corresponded with six traits for assessing self-control: 1) impulsivity; (2) a preference for simple tasks; (3) risk-seeking; (4) physicality; (5) self-centeredness, and (6) a bad temper. There were eight prompts to score parental neglect along with statistical controls for age, gender, socio-economic status, and social desirability. Ibid, 332, 334, 337-338, 340, 252-353, table 5. Self-control measures based on: Harold G. Grasmick, Charles R. Tittle, Robert J. Bursik, Jr., and Bruce J. Arneklev, "Testing the Core Empirical Implications of Gottfredson and Hirschi's

General Theory of Crime," *Journal of Research in Crime and Delinquency* 30, no. 1 (February 1993): 5-29.

[69] C. Nathan DeWall, Roy F. Baumeister, Tyler F.Stillman, and Matthew T. Gailliot, "Violence Restrained: Effects of Self-Regulation and Its Depletion on Aggression," *Journal of Experimental Social Psychology* 43, no 1 (January 2007): 62-76, abstract, https://www.sciencedirect.com/science/article/abs/pii/S0022103105001551.

[70] Jennifer Johnston and Andrew Joy, "Mass Shootings and the Media Contagion Effect" (paper presented at American Psychological Association Symposium, Denver Colorado, August 4, 2016), 16, https://www.apa.org/news/press/releases/2016/08/media-contagion-effect.pdf.

[71] Michael Brick, "Man Crashes Plane into Texas I.R.S. Office," *New York Times*, posted February 18, 2010, https://www.nytimes.com/2010/02/19/us/19crash.html; Murderpedia, photo caption, s.v. "Andrew Joseph Stack III"; narration and visuals, in *Peculiar Possum*, "Taxed to Death: Andrew Stack, Short Documentary," YouTube, posted July 2, 2021, https://www.youtube.com/watch?v=yqKaz7pqUYk; Kyra Phillips, narration, interviews with Cheryl Stack, her daughter, Margo, in CNN, "Faith and Fury: Sheryl Stack after the Crash," YouTube, posted April 16, 2012, https://www.youtube.com/watch?v=JePpX4a2DxE.

[72] Russell Gold, Bob Sechler, and Evan Perez, with Ana Campoy, contributor, "Tax Protester Crashes Plane into IRS Office," *Wall Street Journal*, posted February 19, 2010, https://www.wsj.com/articles/SB10001424052748703315004575073401102945506; Peggy O'Hare and R.G. Ratcliffe, "Suicide Flier Described as 'Offbeat,' 'Brilliant,'" *Houston Chronicle*, posted February 19, 2010, https://www.chron.com/news/houston-texas/article/Suicide-flier-described-as-offbeat-brilliant-1716342.php.

[73] Neil Katz, "Austin Plane Crash: Joseph Andrew Stack Left Sick Suicide Note for IRS to Take 'Pound of Flesh,'" CBS News, posted February 18, 2010, https://www.cbsnews.com/news/austin-plane-crash-joseph-andrew-stack-left-sick-suicide-note-for-irs-to-take-pound-of-flesh/; narrator, witnesses, employees, in Fox 7 Austin, "Video Vault: 10th Anniversary of Echelon Building plane Crash," YouTube, posted, February 18, 2020, https://www.youtube.com/watch?v=pWXW-Tea450; observer of collision, in wgaltv, "Video: Former Classmate Of Crashed Pilot Speaks To News 8," YouTube, posted February 18, 2010, https://www.youtube.com/watch?v=AMs4k_PJ cFo&t=1s.

[74] Narration and film in AP, courtesy of Kain Shin, "Man Angry over Taxes Flies Plane into IRS Building," YouTube, posted February 18, 2010, https://www.youtube.com/watch?v=FMXOHRPQ-A4; Rebecca L. Bennett, "The Three Scariest Things that Have Ever Happened in Austin," Austin.com, posted October 31, 20114, https://austin.com/three-scariest-

things-happened-austin/; narration and visuals, in *Peculiar Possum*, "Taxed to Death."

[75] Bizarrepeida, "Suicide Attack Against the Tax Office," created July 11, 2017, https://www.bizarrepedia.com/joseph-stack/; Steven M. Cunningham, "Death and Taxes: (Over?) Reaction to Section 1706 of the Tax Reform Act," *Syracuse Law Review* 62, no. 3 (April 2012): 451-455, https://lawreview.syr.edu/wp-content/uploads/2013/01/P-Cunningham.pdf; Stack statement, in *Huffington Post*, "Joe Stack Statement: Alleged Suicide Note From Austin Pilot Posted Online," posted April 20, 2010, updated May 25, 2011, https://www.huffpost.com/entry/joe-stack-statement-alleg_n_4 67539. "The law was sponsored by Senator Daniel Patrick Moynihan, Democrat of New York, as a favor to I.B.M., which wanted a $60 million tax break on its overseas business. Under budget rules in effect at the time, any tax breaks had to be paid for with new revenues. By requiring software engineers to be employees … income and payroll taxes would rise by $60 million a year. … One year later, convinced that the law was not bringing in the expected revenue, Senator Moynihan proposed that it be repealed, but his bill died." David Cay Johnston, "Tax Law Was Cited in Software Engineer's Suicide Note," *New York Times*, posted February 18, 2010, https://www.nytimes.com/2010/02/19/us /19tax.html.

[76] Stack, in *Huffington Post*, "Joe Stack Statement." Capitalization, spelling, and punctuation align with transcription. The last lines are an alteration of a sarcastic aphorism by the colorful British columnist, essayist, and social critic, Henry Fairlie, who, ensnaring the unabashed material covetousness of televangelists, wrote "From each according to his gullibility, to me according to my greed." Jeremy McCarter, "Joseph Stack Suicide Note's 'Capitalist' Citation," *Newsweek*, posted February 18, 2010, updated March 13, 2010, https://www.newsweek.com/joseph-stack-suicide-notes-capitalist-citation-75111. Before that, *Nation's Business*, published an unsigned one-page poetic commentary that concluded with these lines, "Even the socialist ideal, 'to each according to his need' has thus been exceeded. / It seems we have a new political philosophy: 'To each according to his greed.'" "Handouts Unlimited," *Nation's Business* 53, no. 10 (October 1965): 130, https://ia600902.us.archive.org/28/items/Nations-Business-1965-10/Nations-Business-1965-10.pdf. The statements take off, of course, from Marx's famous practical application of utopian communist ideology: "From each according to his ability, to each according to his needs!" Karl Marx, "Critique of the Gotha Programme," *Marx/Engels Selected Works, Volume Three*, originally written 1875 (Moscow, Russia: Progress Publishers, 1970), online version 1999, 10, https://www.marxists.org/archive/marx/works/download/Marx_Critque_of_the_Gotha _Programme.pdf.

[77] Allen G. Breed, "Simmering for Decades, A Texas Engineer's Grudge against the IRS Explodes into Suicidal Flight," *Los Angeles Times*, posted February 21, 2010, 2, Way Back Machine, https://web.archive.org/web/20100226191529/http://www.latimes.com/news/nationworld/nation/wire/sns-ap-us-plane-crash-stacks-journey,0,7094353.story?page=1; The Week Staff, "Who is Joseph Stack?" *The Week*, posted January 8, 2015, under "Why Was Stack So Furious at the IRS?" https://theweek.com/articles/496458/who-joseph-stack.

[78] Stack, in *Huffington Post*, "Joe Stack Statement."

[79] Cunningham, "Death and Taxes," 454-458; David Cay Johnston, "Tax Law Was Cited in Software Engineer's Suicide Note," *New York Times*, posted February 18, 2010, https://www.nytimes.com /2010/02/19/us/19tax.html.

[80] Stack, in *Huffington Post*, "Joe Stack Statement."

[81] Ibid. Punctuation copied from report.

[82] Breed, "Simmering for Decades," 2.

[83] Bizarrepeida, "Suicide Attack Against the Tax Office." Stack owned a Velocity XL RG Airplane besides the craft he flew into the building. Their total value would have easily been $200,000. Breed, "Simmering for Decades," 2; Sia Magazin, "Velocity XL RG Airplane A $400k Spaceship With Wings Review," posted May 9, 2021, https://siamagazin.com/velocity-xl-rg-airplane-a-400k-spaceship-with-wings-review/; Hanger, "Piper Cherokee: 15 Aircraft for Sale," n.d., https://www.hangar67.com/aircraft-for-sale/single-engine-piston/piper/Cherokee-group (site outdated); Hangar, "Velocity XL-RG: 1 Aircraft for Sale," n.d., https://www.hangar67.com/aircraft-for-sale/single-engine-piston/velocity/xl (site outdated).

[84] Breed, "Simmering for Decades," 1.

[85] Peggy O'Hare and R.G. Ratcliffe, "Suicide Flier Described as 'Offbeat.'"

[86] Breed, "Simmering for Decades," 1; Brick, "Man Crashes Plane"; O'Hare and Ratcliffe, "Suicide Flier Described as 'Offbeat.'"

[87] Unidentified sibling, in O'Hare and Ratcliffe, "Suicide Flier Described as 'Offbeat.'"

[88] Shown in: a) Naglaa Fathi Mohamed Elattar, Asmaa Mohamed Ali Alabd, and Rehab Elsayed Mohammed, "Impact of Orphan Children's Emotional and Behavioral Problems and Length of Institutionalization on Their Life Satisfaction," *East African Scholars Journal of Nursing and Midwifery* 1, no. 3 (May-June 2019): 79, 81, 82, table 2, https://easpublisher.com/media/features_articles/EASJNM_13_76-84.pdf; b) Abhishek Saraswat and Sayeed Unisa, "A Qualitative Study Examining Psychosocial Distress and Coping Mechanisms Among Orphan and Vulnerable Children Living in Institutional Care in New Delhi, India," *Journal of Health and Social Sciences* 2, no. 2 (July 2017): 200-205, https://bettercarenetwork.org/sites/default/ files/jhhs22_195-208.pdf; c) Abhishek Saraswat, Sayeed Unisa, and Molalign Belay,

"Psychosocial Wellbeing Of Orphan and Vulnerable Children at Orphanages in Gondar Town, North West Ethiopia," *Journal of Public Health and Epidemiology* 6, no. 10 (October 2014): 297-300, https://academicjournals.org/journal/JPHE/article-full-text-pdf/75E5637472 46; d) Akshita Singh and Dr. Suvidha, "Well-being of Orphans: A Review on their Mental Health Status," *International Journal of Scientific Research in Science and Technology* 2, no. 5 (September-October 2016): 180-184.

89 Tatyana I. Shulga, Daria D. Savchenko, and Evgeniya B. Filinkova, "Psychological Characteristics of Adolescents Orphans with Different Experience of Living in a Family," *International Journal Of Environmental & Science Education* 11, no. 17 (November 2016): 10495, https://eric.ed.gov /?id =EJ1120236.

90 Ibid, 10493, abstract.

91 P. Meenakshi and P. TamilSelvan, "Comparative Study of Hostility and Locus of Control among Orphans and Non Orphans," *Indian Journal of Applied Research* 8, no. 10 (October 2018): 21, https://www.worldwidejournals.com/indian-journal-of-applied-research-(IJAR)/recent_issues_pdf/2018/October/October_2018_1538490001__132.pdf.

92 Meenakshi and TamilSelvan, "Comparative Study of Hostility and Locus of Control," 21, citing J.B. Rutter, "Generalized expectancies for Internal Versus External of Reinforcement," *Psychological Monograph* 80, no. 1 (1966): whole no. 609.

93 Meenakshi and TamilSelvan, "Comparative Study of Hostility and Locus of Control," 21.

94 Suggested by results reported in: a) Kathleen Beegle, Joachim De Weerdt, and Stefan Dercon, "Orphanhood and Human Capital Destruction: Is There Persistence Into Adulthood?" *Demography* 47, no. 1 (February 2010): 163–180, https://www.ncbi.nlm.nih.gov/pmc/articles/PMC3000004/pdf/dem-47-0163.pdf; b) Aleksander I. Dontsov, Elena B. Perelygina, and Aleksander N. Veraksa, "Manifestation of Trust Aspects with Orphans and Non-Orphans," *Procedia - Social and Behavioral Sciences* 233 (October 2016): 18-21; c) Busisiwe Ntuli, Mathildah Mokgatle,Sphiwe Madiba, "The Psychosocial Wellbeing of Orphans: The Case of Early School Leavers in Socially Depressed Environment in Mpumalanga Province, South Africa," *PLOS ONE*, posted February 26, 2020, https://journals.plos.org/plosone/article?id =10.1371/journal.pone.0229487; d) S. Rajeshwari and S. R. Sundaravalli, "Adjustment Behavior of Orphan Students Pursuing Secondary Education Intirunelveli District," *International Journal of Innovative Research and Advanced Studies* 5, no. 8 (August 2018): 188-190), https://www.ijiras.com /2018/Vol_5-Issue_8/paper_30.pdf; e) Sanurizwanie Mat Sahad, Zakaria Mohamad, Madihah Mohamad Shukri, "Differences of Mental Health among

Orphan and Non-Orphan Adolescents," *International Journal of Academic Research* 4, no. 1 (2017): 21-29, https://kwpublications.com/journals/papers/IJARP/v4-i1/3492; f) Uma J. and Immanuel Thomas, "Personality Differences between Orphans and Non-Orphans," *Creative Psychologist* 3, no. 1 (January 1991): 31-38.

[95] In *Huffington Post*, "Joe Stack Statement."

[96] Reed Coleman (aka Matthew Nolan), "Timeline: Adam Lanza's Life and Online Activity," Sandy Hook Lighthouse, posted September 7, 2013, https://sandyhooklighthouse.wordpress.com/2013/09/07/timeline-adam-lanzas-life-and-online-activity/ (accessible but dormant); Alaine Griffin with contributors Dave Altimari, Edmund H. Mahony, and Frank Koughan, "Courant/Frontline Investigation: Raising Adam Lanza," *Hartford Courant*, posted February 17, 2013, under "Lost Support," http://touch.courant.com/#section/-1/article/p2p-74453912/; Richard Novia, Technology Club Advisor, in Frank Koughan, writ. and prod., "Transcript: Raising Adam Lanza," *Frontline*, Public Broadcasting System (PBS), https://www.pbs.org/wgbh/frontline/film/raising-adam-lanza/transcript/; Office of the Child Advocate, *Shooting at Sandy Hook Elementary School* (State of Connecticut, November 21, 2014), 20, 38, 42-44, 47, 51, 55, 56; Andrew Solomon, "The Reckoning: The Father of the Sandy Hook Killer Searches for Answers," *New Yorker*, posted March 17, 2014, https://www.newyorker.com/magazine/2014/03/17/the-reckoning; Yale clinical psychiatrist, in Nancy Schoeffler, "Serious Lapses, Fatal Mistakes: A Timeline," *Hartford Courant*, posted November 21, 2014, s.v. "October 24, 2006," http://www.courant.com/news/connecticut/hc-timeline-newtown-adam-lanza-child-advocate-report-2-20141121-story.html; Stav Ziv, "Report Details Adam Lanza's Life Before Sandy Hook Shooting," *Newsweek*, posted November 25, 2014, http://www.newsweek.com/report-details-adam-lanzas-life-sandy-hook-shootings-286867.

[97] Stephen Dethrage, "Analysis of Weapons in Sandy Hook Report Shows Lanza Was Deliberate, Could Have Been Much More Deadly," AL.com, posted November 25, 2013, updated January 14, 2019, https://www.al.com/wire/2013/11/analysis_of_weapons_in_sandy_h.html; Koughan, "Transcript: Raising Adam," last entry for "Narrator."

[98] Alyssa Choiniere, "Ethan Crumbley: 5 Fast Facts You Need to Know," Heavy.com, updated December 6, 2021, under 2, https://heavy.com/news/ethan-crumbley/.

[99] Ethan Crumbley, in Choiniere, "Ethan Crumbley: 5 Fast Facts," under 2.

[100] Photos and descriptions in News and Gossip, "Pictured: 'Bullied' Michigan high school shooter Ethan Crumbley," posted December 1, 2021, https://bbcgossip.com/news/pictured-bullied-michigan-high-school-shooter-ethan-crumbley/.

[101] Lauren Fruen, "Moments before Massacre Oxford High School Timeline of 'Terror' from Ethan Crumbley's Creepy Posts & Behavior Meeting to Bloodbath in Hallways," *Sun*, posted December 2, updated December 3, 2021, https://www.the-sun.com/news/4191099/oxford-high-school-timeline-ethan-crumbley-parents/; Shimon Prokupecz and Steve Almasy, "Here's Why the Suspected Michigan School Shooter Has Been Charged with Terrorism," CNN updated December 2, 2021, https://www.cnn.com/2021/12/01/us/michigan-deadly-shooting-terrorism-charge/index.html.

[102] Choiniere, "Ethan Crumbley: 5 Fast Facts," under 1.

[103] Alisha Rahaman Sarkar, "Oxford School Shooting: Who Are the Four Teens Gunned Down 'At Random' by Suspect Ethan Crumbley?" Yahoo! News, posted December 1, 2021, https://news.yahoo.com/oxford-school-shooting-four-teens-041958286.html; Kristen Jordan Shamus, *Detroit Free Press*, "Police Identify 4 Victims Who Died in Oxford High School Shooting," Yahoo! News, posted December 1, 2021, https://news.yahoo.com/police-identify-3-victims-died-043735805.html.

[104] Emily Crane, Joshua Rhett Miller, and Jorge Fitz-Gibbon, "Bullied Suspect Ethan Crumbley, 15, Allegedly Used Dad's Pistol in School Shooting," *New York Post*, posted December 1, 2021," https://nypost.com/2021/12/01/michigan-school-shooting-suspect-identified-as-ethan-crumbley/; Amir Vera and Taylor Romine, "3 Dead, 8 Injured in Shooting at Michigan High School, Undersheriff Says," CNN, posted and updated December 1, 2021, https://www.cnn.com/2021/11/30/us/michigan-oxford-high-school-incident/index.html.

[105] Crane, Miller, and Fitz-Gibbon, "Bullied suspect Ethan Crumbley"; Becky Sullivan, "Prosecutors Detail Warning Signs Missed by Parents of Mich. School Shooting Suspect," GPD News, posted January 7, 2022, https://www.gpb.org/news/2022/01/07/prosecutors-detail-warning-signs-missed-by-parents-of-mich-school-shooting-suspect.

[106] The book is a satiric examination of mid-twentieth mores as influenced by business cannons and conventional notions of success. It was a national Book Award Finalist in 1975. Joseph Heller, *Something Happened* (New York, NY: Simon & Schuster, Inc., 1966).

[107] Treshan Bryant, in R. Ghosh, "Ethan Crumbley: Oxford High School Shooter Lives with Parents Just 2 Miles Away and Was Bullied," *International Business Times*, posted December 2, 2021, https://www.ibtimes.sg/ethan-crumbley-oxford-high-school-shooter-lives-parents-just-2-miles-away-was-bullied-61562.

[108] According to Kayla LeMieux, in Gina Kaufman, Christine MacDonald, Elisha Anderson, Lily Altavena, and Josh Meyer, "James and Jennifer Crumbley Join Son in Custody after Late-Night Capture in Detroit," *Detroit Free Press*, posted and updated December 5, 2021, https://www.freep.com/story/news

/local/michigan/2021/12/05/james-and-jennifer-crumbley-ethan-oxford-high-shooting/8867284002/.

[109] TMZ, "Ethan Crumbley Fell, Hit Head at Diner ... Bizarre Incident Caught on Video," posted December 6, 2021, https://www.tmz.com/2021/12/06/ethan-crumbley-fell-hit-head-at-diner-in-bizarre-incident-last-year/.

[110] State of Michigan in the Court of the 52-3 Judicial District, People v. James Crumbley, Jennifer Crumbley, Combined Response and Brief in Response to the Defendants' Motion to Modify Bond, December 23, 2021, B.2, B.5, Scribd, https://www.scribd.com/home.

[111] Ibid, B.

[112] Ibid.

[113] Ibid, B.6.

[114] *People v. Crumbley*, Brief in Response to the Defendants' Motion to Modify Bond, B.6; Tommy Taylor, "Michigan School 'Shooter' Ethan Crumbley Took Bird's Head in a Mason Jar to Class Three Weeks before Massacre and Showed Off Bullets to Classmates the Day Before, Lawsuit Filed against School Claims," Daily Mail.com, posted January 11, 2022, updated January 12, 2022, https://www.dailymail.co.uk/news/article-10392263/Ethan-Crumbleys-unusual-behavior-prior-Michigan-school-shooting-documented-updated-suit.html.

[115] *People v. Crumbley*, Brief in Response to the Defendants' Motion to Modify Bond, B; accusation by Prosecutor Marc Keast, in Sullivan, "Prosecutors Detail Warning Signs Missed by Parents"; Taylor, "Michigan School 'Shooter' Ethan Crumbley Took Bird's Head"; Dean Vaglia, "Crumbleys Return to Court," *Oxford Leader*, posted January 12, 2022, https://oxfordleader.com/crumbleys-return-to-court.

[116] Megan Ziegler, "Oxford High School Shooting Timeline: Key Moments in the Case," Fox 2 Detroit, posted December 4, 2021, updated December 9, 2021, under "Monday, Nov. 29: The day before the Shooting," https://www.fox2detroit.com/news/oxford-high-school-shooting-timeline-key-moments-in-the-case.

[117] Video and audio of Karen D. McDonald during news conference, in PBS News Hour, "Watch: Michigan Prosecutor Gives Update on Decision to Charge Parents in Oxford School Shooting," posted December 3, 2021, https://www.pbs.org/newshour/nation/watch-live-michigan-prosecutor-gives-update-on-decision-to-charge-parents-in-oxford-school-shooting; transcript of Karen D. McDonald, in *New York Times*, "Read the Prosecutor's Account of Events before the Michigan School Shooting," posted December 3, 2021, https://www.nytimes.com/2021/12/03/us/michigan-prosecutor-crumbley-charges.html.

[118] Oakland County Sheriff's Lieutenant Tim Willis speaking to Judge Nancy Carniak during Ethan Crumbley's arraignment, in Catherina Gioino, "'Sick'

Fantasies: Ethan Crumbley Journal Detailed 'Desire to Shoot Up Oxford High School & Murder Classmates' as Parents May Face Charges," *Sun*, posted December 2, 2021, updated December 3, 2021, https://www.thesun.co.uk/news/16914896/ethan-crumbley-journal-detailed-desire-shoot-oxford-school/. A journal found in his room after the event also contained plans for the assault. Gioino, "'Sick' Fantasies: Ethan Crumbley Journal Detailed 'Desire.'"

119 See Robert Oppenheimer – obviously so distraught that his face is expressionless and his voice a monotone as if he is in shock – recalling the reaction to the first test of atomic test: AtomicHeritage, "Oppenheimer Bhagavad-Gita Quote," YouTube, posted July 10, 2015, https://www.youtube.com /watch?v=pqZqfTOxFhY.

120 Fandom, "Fallout Wiki," s.v. "Games," created 2019, continuously updated, https://www .fandom.com/; *Inside Edition*, "'I Am Become Death, Destroyer of Worlds' Posted by Accused School Shooter," Microsoft Network, posted December 2, 2021, https://www.msn.com/en-us/entertainment/entertainment-celebrity/i-am-become-death-destroyer-of-worlds-posted-by-accused-school -shooter-online/vp-AARpa3T (video no longer available); Nathan Place, "'Now I Become Death': Michigan School Shooting Suspect Posted Ominous 'Countdown' Online before Attack," https://www .independent.co. uk/news/world/americas/crime/michigan-shooting-suspect-become-death-b 1968045.html.

121 Tim Throne, Oxford Community Schools superintendent, "Dear Wildcat Nation," [December 4, 2021?], 2, Scribd; WXYZ Detroit, "Oxford Community Schools Superintendent Details School's Version of Events," posted and updated December 4, 2021, https://www.wxyz.com/news/oxford-school-shooting/oxford-community-schools-superintendent-details-schools-version-of-events.

122 Throne, "Dear Wildcat Nation," 2.

123 *People v. Crumbley*, Brief in Response to the Defendants' Motion to Modify Bond, B, B.6.

124 United States District Court Eastern District of Michigan Southern Division, Jeffrey Franz and Brandi Franz, v. Oxford Community School District, Superintendent Timothy Throne, Principal Steven Wolf, Dean of Students Ryan Moore, Counselor #1, Counselor #2, Staff Member, Teacher #1 and Teacher #2, Complaint and Demand for Jury Trial, December 9, 2021, ¶ 79, Scribd. "Oakland County Prosecutor Karen McDonald says it is a 'very strong possibility' that the suspect in the Michigan high school shooting was carrying the weapon during his meeting with his parents school officials earlier in the day." Anderson Cooper, Twitter @AC360, December 2, 2021. The district maintained, "… despite media reports, whether or not the gun

was in his backpack has not been confirmed by law enforcement to our knowledge nor by our investigation…." Throne, "Dear Wildcat Nation," 2.

[125] BBC News, "Michigan School Shooting: Student Kills Four and Wounds Seven," posted December 1, 2021, https://www.bbc.com/news/world-us-canada-59484333; Aya Elamroussi, "The Shooter 'Methodically and Deliberately' Fired at Students. A Timeline of a School Shooting Tragedy," CNN, posted and updated December 4, 2021, https://www.cnn.com/2021/12/04/us/michigan-oxford-high-school-shooting-timeline/index.html.

[126] Joe Sommerlad, Megan Sheets, and Rachel Sharp, "Oxford High School Shooting: Everything We Know about Deadly Michigan Attack and Suspect Ethan Crumbley," *Independent*, posted December 14, 2021, https://www.independent.co.uk/news/world/americas/crime/oxford-school-shooting-what-happened-b1975858.html.

[127] It was sent at 1:22 p.m. according to prosecutors. Elamroussi, "The Shooter 'Methodically and Deliberately' Fired." Ethan had a half-brother on his father's side, Eli, who was 18 years-off-age at the time of Ethan's SMASI. He moved back in with his birth mother in March of 2021, about eight months before the incident, and explained his reason for doing so simply by saying something "felt off." Nikki Main, "Utter Disbelief: Who Is Ethan Crumbley's Half-Brother Eli?" *Sun*, posted and updated December 4, 2021, https://www.the-sun.com/news/4202078/ethan-crumbleys-half-brother-eli/.

[128] *People v. Crumbley*, Defendants Modified Motion and Brief to Modify Bond, December 22, 2021, ¶ 6, Scribd.

[129] Elamroussi, "The Shooter 'Methodically and Deliberately' Fired."

[130] McDonald, in Elamroussi, "The Shooter 'Methodically and Deliberately' Fired."

[131] See: Michigan Association of Secondary Principals, "Legal Searches in School: Reasonable Suspicion Required," posted [2018? extrapolated from the copyright year], https://massp.com/legal-searches-in-school-reasonable-suspicion-required#:~:text=When%20school%20officials%20want%20to ,the%20law%20or%20school%20rules; also New Jersey v. T. L. O., 469 U.S. 325, argued March 28, 1984, reargued October 2, 1984, decided January 15, 1985, III.

[132] In separate trials both parents were found guilty of involuntary manslaughter and, as this manuscript was being prepared, each faced the possibility of up to 15 years in prison. Erik Ortiz, Selina Guevara and Alan Cohen, "Prosecutors Will Seek 10 to 15 Years in Prison for Crumbley Parents at Sentencing," NBC News, posted April 3, 2024, https://www.nbcnews.com/news/us-news/prosecutors-will-seek-10-15-years-prison-crumbley-parents-sentencing-rcna144964.

[133] Bonnie T. Zima, Steven R. Forness, Regina Bussing, and Bernadette Benjamin, "Homeless Children in Emergency Shelters: Need for Prereferral

Intervention and Potential Eligibility for Special Education," *Behavioral Disorders* 23, no. 2 (February 1998): 102-108.

[134] Ibid, 105.

[135] Janette E. Herbers, Arthur J. Reynolds, and Chin-Chih Chen, "School Mobility and Developmental Outcomes in Young Adulthood," *Developmental Psychology* 25, no. 2 (May 2013): 501-515, under "Social Mobility as a Risk Factor," doi: 10.1017/S0954579412001204.

[136] Swaran P. Singh, Catherine Winsper, Dieter Wolke, and Alex Bryson, "School Mobility and Prospective Pathways to Psychotic-Like Symptoms in Early Adolescence: A Prospective Birth Cohort Study," *Journal of the American Academy of Child and Adolescent Psychiatry* 53, no. 5 (May 2014): 520-524, fig. 1, table 3. For more on this topic: Russell W. Rumberger, *Student Mobility: Causes, Consequences, and Solutions* (University of Colorado Boulder: National Education Policy Center, June 2015).

[137] The carnage enacted by Anderson and Baranyi resembled a familicide in that it was conducted in secret and involved acquaintances. At the same time, like an autogenic mass assault, it had no visible antecedent that would serve as a sensible predicate for the atrocities and, moreover, it was conducted in a compressed timeframe. Nevertheless, because of the second criterion set forth in the Introduction (public demonstration) their indefensible killings do not conform to the operational definition for a rampage used throughout this book. The two perpetrators, then are not included in the Appendix. The narrative and their association are recounted in the following: a) Gary Boynton, "Gothic Murders," *Crime Magazine*, posted October 14, 2009, http://www .crimemagazine.com/gothic-murders-0; b) Jean Guy Bureau, dir., and Donna Wilson, writ., "Payback," *Wicked Attraction*, season 2, episode 5, Investigation Discovery, premiered August 6, 2009; c) Putsata Reang, *Deadly Secrets: From High School to High Crime – The True Story of Two Teen Killers* (New York, NY: Avon Books, 2001).

[138] Baranyi interview, in Bureau and Wilson, "Payback."

[139] Coleman, "Timeline: Adam Lanza's Life," s.vv. "April 2005," "May/June 2005," "September-December 2005-March 2006," "February 2008," "May, 2008-Summer 2008," "Fall 2008," "2009 Spring Quarter"; Office of the Child Advocate, *Shooting at Sandy* Hook, 41, 60, 68-70. Some records state that Lanza was home schooled but the correct classification (through most of middle school) would be homebound, in that he was educated by a visiting teacher from his district as if he was not capable of attending school without direct instruction from the family or a religious institution. During his secondary years he was on independent study on an intermittent basis.

[140] Child Welfare Information Gateway, "Understanding the Effects," 8.

[141] Martha Stout, *The Sociopath Next Door: The Ruthless Versus the Rest of Us* (New York, NY: Broadway Books, 2005), 130-133.

[142] Karr-Morse and Wiley, *Ghosts from the Nursery*, 203-205; Stout, *The Sociopath Next Door*, 130-133.

[143] See: a) Constance R. Ahrons, "Long-term Effects of Divorce on Children," *Family Therapy Magazine* (May-June 2006), 26-27; b) Stephen E. Gilman, Ichiro Kawachi, Garrett M. Fitzmaurice, and Stephen L. Buka, "Family Disruption in Childhood and Risk of Adult Depression," *American Journal of Psychiatry* 160, no. 5 (May 2003): 941-942, 943, 944-945; b) Judith S. Wallerstein, "The Long-Term Effects of Divorce on Children: A Review," *Journal of the American Academy of Child and Adolescent Psychiatry* 30, no. 3 (May 1991): 349–360, abstract, https://psycnet.apa.org/record/1991-30226-001; d) Tianyi Yu, Gregory S. Pettit, Jennifer E. Lansford, Kenneth A. Dodge, and John E. Bates, "The Interactive Effects of Marital Conflict and Divorce on Parent-Adult Children's Relationships," author manuscript, PMC, National Institutes of Health, posted April 1, 2011, 6-9, https://europepmc.org/backend/ptpmcrender.fcgi?accid=PMC288314%20&blobtype=pdf.

[144] Heather Sandstrom and Sandra Huerta, *The Negative Effects of Instability on Child Development: A Research Synthesis* (Urban Institute, September 18, 2013), 13, https://www.urban.org/research/publication/negative-effects-instability-child-development-research-synthesis/view/full_report.

[145] Nelson Kempsky, with Gary A. Binkerd, Phil Yee, Allen Benitez, and Richard Yarvis, *A Report to the Attorney General John K. Van de Kamp on Patrick Edward Purdy and the Cleveland School Killings* (California Department of Justice: Office of the Attorney General, October 1989), 7-8, appendix e.

[146] Allen Benitez and Phil Yee, "Chronological Life History of Patrick Edward Purdy," in Kempsky et al., *A Report to the Attorney General*, appendix c, 23-24, s.v. "January 17, 1989."

[147] Benitez and Yee, "Chronological Life History," 1, 23, svv. "November 10, 1964," "January 17, 1989."

[148] Kempsky et al., *A Report to the Attorney General,* 3; Richard M. Yarvis, "A Psychological Autopsy of Patrick Edward Purdy," in Kempsky et al., *A Report to the Attorney General*, appendix a, 5.

[149] Benitez and Yee, "Chronological Life History," 1; Kempsky et al., *A Report to the Attorney General,* 3.

[150] Yarvis, "A Psychological Autopsy," 4.

[151] Lonnie H. Athens, *The Creation of Violent Criminals* (Urbana and Chicago, Il: University of Illinois Press, 1992), 27-45.

[152] Ibid, 28, 38.

[153] Benitez and Yee, "Chronological Life History," 2.

[154] Ibid, 5-11, 13-15.

[155] Ibid, 5.

[156] Kempsky et al., *A Report to the Attorney General*, 3-4.

[157] Benitez and Yee, "Chronological Life History," 2-10.
[158] Ibid, 5.
[159] Ibid.
[160] Ibid.
[161] The American Psychiatric Association subsumes both under "antisocial personality disorder." *DSM-5*, 659-663. Also, see: a) Scott A. Bonn, "How to Tell a Sociopath from a Psychopath: Understanding Important Distinctions between Criminal Sociopaths and Psychopaths," *Psychology Today*, posted January 22, 2014, https://www.psychologytoday.com/blog/wicked-deeds/201401/how-tell-sociopath-psychopath; b) Hervey Cleckley, *The Mask of Sanity*, rev. ed. (St. Louis, MO: C.V. Mosby Company, 1982), 7; c) Criminal Profiling Staff, "Psychopathy: An Evolutionary Perspective," Criminal Profiling, posted August 15, 2002, http://www.criminalprofiling.com/psychopathy-an-evolutionary-perspective/; d) John M. Grohol, "Differences between a Psychopath and Sociopath," World of Psychology, posted February 12, 2015, https://psychcentral.com/blog/archives/2015/02/12/differences-between-a-psychopath-vs-sociopath/; e) Arkadiusz Jadczyk and Laura Knight-Jadczyk, "Psychopath vs. Antisocial Personality Disorder and Sociopathy," Studies in Psychopathy – Quantum Future Group, http://www.cassiopaea.com /cassiopaea/psychopathy_aspd_sociopathy.htm; f) Kelly McAleer, "Forensic Focus: Sociopathy vs. Psychopathy," PscychCentral, updated September 4, 2010, https://blogs.psychcentral.com /forensic-focus/2010/07/sociopathy-vs-psychopathy/; g) Martha Stout, *The Sociopath Next Door: The Ruthless Versus the Rest of Us* (New York, NY: Broadway Books, 2005) 6; h) Anthony Walsh and Huei-Hsia Wu, "Differentiating Antisocial Personality Disorder, Psychopathology, and Sociopathy: Evolutionary, Genetic, Neurological, and Sociological Considerations," *Criminal Justice Studies* 2, no. 2 (June 2008): 135-152.
[162] Benitez and Yee, "Chronological Life History," 5.
[163] Ibid, 8-9.
[164] Benitez and Yee, "Chronological Life History," 10-22; Kempsky et al., *A Report to the Attorney General*, 3-5.
[165] Benitez and Yee, "Chronological Life History," 10-13, 14, 17.
[166] Ibid, 13.
[167] Ibid.
[168] Ibid,
[169] Ibid, 13-14. Quotation is lifted from page 14.
[170] Ibid, 14-22.
[171] Ibid, 17-18.
[172] Ibid, 18.
[173] Ibid, 14.
[174] Ibid, 15.

[175] Ibid.

[176] Rick Owens, "14 Postal Employees Were Shot and Killed Today In 1986," Postal Employees Network: Postal News, posted August 20, 2018, https://postalemployeenetwork.com/news/2018/08/14-postal-employees-were-shot-and-killed-today-in-1986/. Sherrill is touched upon in Chapter Four and included in the Appendix.

[177] Benitez and Yee, "Chronological Life History," 15-16.

[178] Ibid, 16.

[179] Ibid, 17.

[180] Ibid, 18-20.

[181] Ibid, 18.

[182] Ibid, 20.

[183] Ibid, 19.

[184] Peter Langman, *Why Kids Kill: Inside the Minds of School Shooters* (New York, NY: Palgrave MacMillan, 2009), 14-15.

[185] Christopher J. Ferguson, Mark Coulson, and Jane Barnett, "Psychological Profiles of School Shooters: Positive Directions and One Big Wrong Turn," *Journal of Police Crisis Negotiations* 11, no. 2 (2011): 151.

[186] Michael S. Kimmel and Matthew Mahler, "Adolescent Masculinity, Homophobia, and Violence," *American Behavioral Scientist* 46, no. 10 (June 2003): 1444, 1445, doi: 10.1177/0002764203251484. News sources consulted were the three weekly news magazines: *Time*, *Newsweek*, and *U.S. News and World Report* and three daily newspapers: *USA Today*, *New York Times*, and *Los Angeles Times*. No shooter was above 19 years of age. Ibid, 1445, appendix.

[187] Friederike Sommer, Vincenz Leuschner, and Herbert Scheithauer, "Bullying, Romantic Rejection, and Conflicts with Teachers: The Crucial Role of Social Dynamics in the Development of School Shootings – A Systematic Review," *International Journal of Developmental Science* 8, no. 1-2 (2014): 3-24, abstract, doi: 10.3233/DEV-140129.

[188] James L. Knoll, "Mass Murder: Causes, Classification, and Prevention," *Psychiatry Clinics of North America* 35, no. 4 (December 2012): 762.

[189] Ibid.

[190] Ibid.

[191] Ibid.

[192] Judith Lynn Fisher-Blando, "Workplace Bullying: Aggressive Behavior and Its Effect on Job Satisfaction and Productivity," (doctoral diss., University of Phoenix, 2008), 73, table 1, 74, table 2, table 3, https://www.workplaceviolence911.com/docs/20081215.pdf.

[193] Peter Amato, "Workplace Bullying Is on the Rise (2021 Study)," My Perfect Resume, under "The "Prevalence of Bullying," https://www.myperfectresume.com/career-center/careers/basics/workplace-bullying-in-2021.

[194] Ibid, under "Types of Bullying."

[195] Children's Hospital of Philadelphia Center for Violence Prevention, "Bullying in Schools," under "Facts and Statistics about Bullying and Harassment in Schools," https://violence.chop.edu/types-violence/bullying-schools.

[196] Katharina Buchholz, "Number of School Shootings Increased Every Decade," Statista, posted November 15, 2019, under "Number of K-12 School Shootings in the U.S. (1970-2019)," https://www.statista.com/chart/19982/number-of-us-k-12-school-shootings-per-decade/. Numbers from Center for Homeland Defense and Security, "K-12 Shooting Database," under "Data Map," https://www.chds.us/ssdb/. The count for 2019 stops at November 14.

[197] According to the Bureau of Labor Statistics, in Navigant Law Group, "Workplace Violence – Active Shooter Incidents: More Common Than You Think," Navigant Law Group, LLC, posted February 17, 2020, under "Active Shooter Incidents and Workplace Violence," https://www.navigantlaw.com/workplace-violence-active-shooter-incidents-more-common-than-you-think/.

[198] Deanna Palmeri Sams and Stephen D. Truscott, "Empathy, Exposure to Community Violence, and Use of Violence Among Urban, At-Risk Adolescents," *Child & Youth Care Forum* 33, no. 1 (February 2004): abstract, 33-50, https://doi.org/10.1023/B:CCAR.0000013756.88343.5f.

[199] Alicia Ardila-Rey, Melanie Killen, and Alaina Brenick, "Moral Reasoning in Violent Contexts: Displaced and Non-Displaced Colombian Children's Evaluations of Moral Transgressions, Retaliation, and Reconciliation," *Social Development* 18, no. 1 (February 2009): 181-209, abstract, https://doi.org /10.1111/j.1467-9507.2008.00483.x.

[200] Richard Clark, "Olga Hepnarová – The Last Woman Executed In Czechoslovakia," Capital Punishment U.K, started in 1995, under "Some Cases from Around the World," http://www.capitalpunishmentuk.org/contents.html; Štefan Moravčík, trans., Olga Hepnarová 30.6.1951 – 12.3.1975, continuously updated, under "Crossing the Rubicon," 2015, http://www.pantharei.estranky.cz/en/.

[201] In Moravčík, Olga Hepnarová 30.6.1951 – 12.3.1975, under "Investigation." The massacre took place on July 10, 1973. Hepnarová was officially interrogated four times: immediately afterwards, then three days later, on July 13, 1973, after newspapers received the pronouncements she mailed before the event, and finally on November 6, 1973.

[202] Ibid, under "Other findings I."

[203] Ibid, under "Doctors and Olga Hepnarová."

[204] Moravčík, Olga Hepnarová 30.6.1951 – 12.3.1975, under "Doctors and Olga Hepnarová"; All That's Interesting (ATI), "The Shocking Story of Olga Hepnarová, A Truck-Driving Mass Murderess," posted May 12, 2016, updated May 4, 2018, http://allthatsinteresting.com/olga-hepnarova-murder. She was at the time a heavy cigarette smoker, a habit that continued throughout her short life. Moravčík, "Olga Hepnarová," under "Miscellaneous I."

[205] Moravčík, Olga Hepnarová 30.6.1951 – 12.3.1975, under "Doctors and Olga."

[206] American Psychiatric Association, *DSM-5*, 87-90; Mental Health Resource Staff, "Hebephrenic Schizophrenia Diagnostic Criteria," updated 2002-2022, Mental Health Reference, https://mhreference.org/schizophrenic/schizophrenia - icd/hebephrenic/; Christian Nordqvist, reviewed by Daniel Murrell, "What's to know about Disorganized Schizophrenia?" *Medical News Today*, updated January 18, 2018, https://www.medicalnewstoday.com/ articles/192361.php.

[207] ATI, "The Shocking Story"; in Moravčík, "Olga Hepnarová 30.6.1951 – 12.3.1975," under "Doctors and Olga"; narration of portion of letter, in *Nightmares Before Bedtime,* "Olga Hepnarova [sic]: One Moment in Crime," YouTube, posted October 5, 2017, https://www.youtube.com/watch?v=jAG1 VCXfMI8.

[208] In Moravčík, "Olga Hepnarová 30.6.1951 – 12.3.1975."

[209] Ibid.

[210] Ibid.

[211] Ibid.

[212] Ibid.

[213] Clark, "Olga Hepnarová - The Last Woman Executed"; Moravčík, "Olga Hepnarová 30.6.1951 – 12.3.1975," under "Investigation."

[214] Robin Geiß, "Name, Rank, Date of Birth, Serial Number, and the Right to Remain Silent," *International Review of the Red Cross* 87, no. 860 (December 2005), 724-726. The full article covers the origin, purpose, and general application of sections relevant to the treatment of captives in conflicts between states.

[215] In fact, apologias like Hepnarová's are often issued, in one form or another, by rampage assailants. Almost all have the same attributes that are disaggregated in Chapter Five of *How Rampage Killers Interpret Their Worlds.*

[216] In Moravčík, "Olga Hepnarová 30.6.1951 – 12.3.1975," under "Investigation." Spelling, punctuation, and capitalization as in transcription. Ellipses represent words omitted for sake of brevity or clarity.

[217] Ibid. Capitalization as in transcription

[218] Ibid.

[219] Brett McKay and Kate McKay, "Latin Words and Phrases Every Man Should Know," The Art of Manliness, posted July 5, 2018, under "acta non verba," https://www.artofmanliness.com/articles/latin-words-and-phrases-every-man-should-know/."

[220] Clark, "Olga Hepnarová - The Last Woman"; Headsman (pseud.), "1975: Olga Hepnarova [sic], Tram Spotter," Executed Today.com, posted March 12, 2012, https://www.executedtoday.com/2012/03 /12/1975-olga-hepnarova/.

[221] Agence France-Presse (AFP), "China Executes Man Who Stabbed Nine Children to Death," *Jakarta Post*, posted September 27, 2018, https://www.thejakartapost.com/news/2018/09/27/china-executes-man-who-stabbed-nine-children-to-death.html.

[222] Cui Xiankang and Han Wei, "Stabbings Spread Horror at Shaanxi School," *Caixin*, posted May 2, 2018, https://www.caixinglobal.com/2018-05-02/1-101241810.html; Tracy You, "Hundreds of Chinese Villagers Watch a Mass Murderer Being Taken to the Execution Ground before He Is Shot by a Firing Squad for Stabbing Nine Pupils to Death on a Killing Spree," *Daily Mail*, posted and updated September 27, 2018, https://www.dailymail.co.uk/news/article-6209231/Chinese-knife-attacker-executed-firing-squad-stabbing-nine-pupils-death.html.

[223] Cui and Han, "Stabbings Spread Horror." At least that information is what they conveyed to police after his arrest.

[224] Ibid.

[225] British Broadcasting Corporation News, "Nine Schoolchildren Stabbed to Death in Northern China," *Guardian*, posted April 28, 2018, https://www.theguardian.com/world/2018/apr/27/school-children-stabbed-death-china.

[226] Cui and Han, "Stabbings Spread Horror."

[227] Chris Kitching, "Hundreds of Villagers Watch Firing Squad Execute Knifeman Who Murdered Nine Pupils after Being Bullied at Same School," *Mirror*, posted and updated September 29, 2018, https://www.mirror.co.uk/news/world-news/china-executes-zhao-zewei-murder-13329570.

[228] Kitching, "Hundreds of Villagers Watch Firing Squad Execute Knifeman"; Wang Keju, "Man sentenced to death for stabbings" *China Daily*, posted July 11, 2018, https://www.chinadailyhk.com/articles/49/54/126/1531278609938.html.

[229] AFP, "China Executes Man"; Wang, "Man Sentenced to Death."

[230] Cui and Han, "Stabbings Spread Horror."

[231] AFP, "Chinese Court Sentences Man to Death over School Stabbings," *Hong Kong Free Press*, posted July 11, 2018, https://www.hongkongfp.com/2018/07/11/chinese-court-sentences-man-death-school-stabbings/; Cui and Han, "Stabbings Spread Horror."

[232] Cui and Han, "Stabbings Spread Horror."

[233] Ibid.

[234] Ibid.

[235] AFP, "Chinese Court Sentences Man to Death"; AFP, "Nine Schoolchildren Stabbed."

[236] AFP, "China Executes Man." Rampages with a knife are more prevalent in China than mass shootings, which are practically non-existent (considered further in *How Rampage Killers Interpret Their Worlds*, Chapter Five.)

[237] AFP, "Chinese Court Sentences Man to Death."

[238] Leonie H. Grobbink, Jan J. L. Derksen, and Hjalmar J. C. van Marle, "Revenge: An Analysis of Its Psychological Underpinnings," *International Journal of Offender Therapy and Comparative Criminology* 59, no. 8 (July 2015): 4, table 2.

[239] Ibid, referencing Martha A. Gabriel and Gail W. Monaco, "'Getting Even': Clinical Considerations of Adaptive and Maladaptive Vengeance," *Clinical Social Work Journal* 22, no 2 (June 1994):165-178 and Karen Horney, "The value of Vindictiveness," *American Journal of Psychoanalysis* 8, no. 1 (December 1948): 3–12.

[240] Andy Williams, in Miles O'Brien, dir. and reporter, "Mind of a Rampage Killer," *Nova*, Season 40, episode 8, premiered February 20, 2013 (WGBH Educational Foundation, 2013).

[241] United States District Court Southern District of California, Charles Andrew Williams v. Stuart J. Ryan, civil no. 05cv0737-WQH (WMc), September 21, 2010, 7, School Shooters .info, s.v. "Andy Williams."

[242] AndySpeaks.com, "The Biography of Andy Williams," Murderpedia, s.v. "Charles Andrew Williams"; Kay Duncan and Jack Blackstone, *Child Killer: Charles Andy Williams and the Santana High School Shooting* (Crime Life Publications, 2018), under "March 9, 2001," "August 26, 2000," Kindle Cloud Reader; Scott Gold and Terry McDermott, "Often Ridiculed, The Suspect Said, 'I'll Show You One Day,'" *Los Angeles Times*, posted March 6, 2001, https://www.latimes.com/archives/la-xpm-2001-mar-06-mn-33987-story.html; Jeff Williams interview with Christopher Goodwin, in Goodwin and Simon Hattenstone, "My Child, The Murderer," *Guardian*, posted October 28, 2011, under "Jeff Williams, Andy's Father," https://www.theguardian.com/society/2011/oct/28/my-child-the-murderer.

[243] AndySpeaks.com, "The Biography of Andy Williams"; Jenn Baxter, "The Santana High School Shooting," Lessons from History, posted January 6, 2021, https://medium.com/lessons-from-history/the-santana-high-school-shooting-a2bcc2454316; Duncan and Blackstone, *Child Killer: Charles Andy Williams*, under "December 1999"; Jeff Williams interview with Goodwin, in Goodwin and Hattenstone, "My Child, The Murderer," under "Jeff Williams, Andy's father."

[244] Duncan and Blackstone, *Child Killer: Charles Andy Williams*, under "February 4, 1997;" Megan Garvey, "Shooting Suspect's Heart Was Still in His Small Maryland Hometown," *Los Angeles Times*, posted March 7, 2001, https://www.latimes.com/archives/la-xpm-2001-mar-07-mn-34321-story.html.

[245] Art Fairweather, in Garvey, "Shooting Suspect's Heart."

[246] AndySpeaks.com, "The Biography of Andy Williams"; Baxter, "The Santana High School Shooting."

[247] Baxter, "The Santana High School Shooting"; Duncan and Blackstone, *Child Killer: Charles Andy Williams*, under "June 2000"; Garvey, "Shooting Suspect's Heart."

[248] Baxter, "The Santana High School Shooting"; Garvey, "Shooting Suspect's Heart"; Andy Williams interview, in Fred Dickey, "Killer Recounts Santana High Shooting," *San Diego Union Tribune*, posted May 10, 2013, https://www.sandiegouniontribune.com/news/columnists/sdut-charles-andy-williams-santana-high-school-shooting-2013may10-htmlstory.html.

[249] Baxter, "The Santana High School Shooting"; Terry McCarthy, "Warning: Andy Williams Here. Unhappy Kid. Tired of Being Picked On. Ready to Blow. Want to Kill Some People. Can Anybody Hear Me? How Did Things Get So Bad?" *Time*, posted March 19, 2001, 2, http://content.time.com/time /subscriber/article/0,33009,999474,00.html.

[250] Duncan and Blackstone, *Child Killer: Charles Andy Williams*, under "WJBF-TV in Augusta GA Lost Boy."

[251] Ashlee Allsopp, in Duncan and Blackstone, *Child Killer: Charles Andy Williams*, under "The Grommits"; Williams, in Dickey, "Killer Recounts Santana High Shooting."

[252] Consult: Harold E. Kooreman, "The Impact of Substance Use on the Developing Brain," Center for Health Policy, Richard M. Fairbanks School of Public Health, *Improving Community Health through Policy Research* (July 2017): 2, https://scholarworks.iupui.edu/server/api/core/bitstreams/27 9dd7f2-764e-42c9-bb63-91c07d444f98/content, along with: a) Sunita Bava and Susan Tapert, "Adolescent Brain Development and the Risk for Alcohol and Other Drug Problems," *Neuropsychological Review* 20, no.4 (October 2010): 398-413; b) B.J. Casey, Rebecca M. Jones, and Todd A. Hare, "The Adolescent Brain," *Annals of the New York Academy of Sciences* 1124 (March 2008): 111–126; c) Fulton T. Crews, Clyde W. Hodge, Jun He, and J.H. Hodge, "Adolescent Cortical Development: A Critical Period of Vulnerability for Addiction," *Pharmacology, Biochemistry, and Behavior* 86 (February 2007): 189-199; d) Jay N Giedd, "Structural Magnetic Resonance Imaging of the Adolescent Brain," *Annals of the New York Academy of Sciences*, 1021, no. 1 (July 2004): 77-85; e) Joan Stiles and Terry L. Jernigan, "The Basics of Brain Development," *Neuropsychological Review* 20, no. 4 (November 2010): 327-348; f) Ken C. Winters, and Amelia Arria, "Adolescent Brain Development and Drugs," *Prevention Researcher* 18, no. 2 (2011): 21. Related evidence may be found in: a) Sarah-Jayne Blakemore and Suparna Choudhury, "Development of the Adolescent Brain: Implications for Executive Function and Social cognition," *Journal of Child Psychology and Psychiatry* 47, no. 3/4 (March/April 2006): 296–312,

https://acamh.onlinelibrary.wiley.com/doi/epdf/10.1111/j.1469-7610.2006.01611.x; b) Jay N. Giedd, Jonathan Blumenthal, Neal O. Jeffries, F. X. Castellanos, Hong Liu, Alex Zijdenbos, Tomáš Paus, Alan C. Evans, and Judith L. Rapoport, "Brain Development During Childhood and Adolescence: A Longitudinal MRI Study," *Nature Neuroscience* 2, no. 10 (October 1999): 861–863; c) Monica Luciana, "Adolescent Brain Development In Normality and Psychopathology," *Development and Psychopathology* 2, no. 4, pt. 2 (November 2013): 1325 – 1345.

253 As shown in L. M. Squeglia, J. Jacobus, and S. F. Tapert, "The Influence of Substance Use on Adolescent Brain Development," author manuscript, PMC, HHS, posted February 24, 2010, under "Background on Adolescent Substance Use," "Verbal Encoding," "Summary," https://www.ncbi.nlm.nih.gov/pmc/articles/PMC2827693/, referencing: a) Duncan B Clark, Dawn L Thatcher, and Susan F Tapert, "Alcohol, Psychological Dysregulation, and Adolescent Brain Development," *Alcoholism: Clinical and Experimental Research* 32, no. 3 (March 2008): 375-385; b) Fulton Crews, Jun He, and Clyde Hodge, "Adolescent Cortical Development: A Critical Period of Vulnerability for Addiction," *Pharmacology Biochemistry and Behavior* 86, no. 2 (February 2007): 189-199; c) Krista Lisdahl Medina, Karen L Hanson, Alecia D Schweinsburg, Mairav Cohen-Zion, Bonnie J Nagel, and Susan F Tapert, "Neuropsychological Functioning in Adolescent Marijuana Users: Subtle Deficits Detectable after a Month of Abstinence," *Journal of the International Neuropsychological Society* 13, no. 5 (September 2007): 807-820; d) Linda Patia Spear, Elena I Varlinskaya, "Adolescence. Alcohol Sensitivity, Tolerance, and Intake," *Recent Developments in Alcoholism* 17 (2005): 143-159; e) Susan F Tapert, Eric Granholm, Nathan G Leedy, and Sandra A Brown, "Substance Use and Withdrawal: Neuropsychological Functioning over 8 Years in Youth," *Journal of the International Neuropsychological Society* 8, no. 7 (November 2002): 873-83. See also: Shahnaza Hamidullah, Hayley H. A. Thorpe, Jude A. Frie, Richard D. Mccurdy, and Jibran Y. Khokhar, "Adolescent Substance Use and the Brain: Behavioral, Cognitive and Neuroimaging Correlates," *Frontiers in Human Neuroscience*, posted August 4, 2020, https://www.frontiersin.org/articles/10.3389/fnhum.2020.00298/full.

254 Duncan and Blackstone, *Child Killer: Charles Andy Williams*, under "Thursday, March 1, 2001 around 2:00 or 3:00 a.m."

255 Jeff Williams interview, with Goodwin and Hattenstone in "My Child, The Murderer," under "Jeff Williams, Andy's father."

256 Williams, in Dickey, "Killer Recounts Santana High Shooting."

257 Scott Gold, Ken Ellingwood, and H.G. Reza, "Suspect, 15, Had Made Repeated Threats before Attack Near San Diego," *Los Angeles Times*, posted March 6, 2001, under "At First, It Might Have Been a Joke,"

https://www.latimes.com/archives/la-xpm-2001-mar-06-mn-33988-story.html.

[258] Josh Stevens, in McCarthy, "Warning: Andy Williams Here," 3.

[259] Linkin Park, "In the End," *Hybrid Theory* (North Hollywood, CA: Warner Bros. Records, 2000). Regarding the shooting, the band issued this simple statement: "Like everyone else, we are extremely saddened by these events and our hearts go out to the families and friends of the victims." In ABC News, "Linkin Park Responds to School Shooting," posted January 6, 2006, https://abcnews.go.com /Entertainment/story?id=108537&page=1.

[260] Photo by Maddie McGarvey, in Shibani Mahtani, "Profile of a School Shooter," *Wall Street Journal*, posted June 3, 2018, https://www.wsj.com/articles/profile-of-a-school-shooter-1528023600. Punctuated and capitalized as reported.

[261] Dawn Hemming, in McCarthy, "Warning: Andy Williams Here," 3.

[262] Baxter, "The Santana High School Shooting"; Duncan and Blackstone, *Child Killer: Charles Andy Williams*, under "Andy Shot BB Guns and Played Laser Tag"; McCarthy, "Warning: Andy Williams Here," 4. Although Reynolds denies it, they allegedly took aim from a moving vehicle at drunken individuals.

[263] Baxter, "The Santana High School Shooting."

[264] Andy Williams interview, in Fred Dickey, "Killer Recounts Santana High Shooting"; Jeff Williams interview with Goodwin and Hattenstone, in "My Child, The Murderer," under "Jeff Williams, Andy's Father."

[265] Dickey, "Killer Recounts Santana High Shooting."

[266] Ibid.

[267] Baxter, "The Santana High School Shooting"; Andy Williams interview with Miles O'Brien, in Jenny Marder, "School Shooter: 'My Grand Plan Was Suicide by Cop,'" PBS, posted February 18, 2013, https://www.pbs.org/newshour/science/science-jan-june13-andywilliams_02-18.

[268] Duncan and Blackstone, *Child Killer: Charles Andy Williams*, under "February 7, 2001"; Murderpedia, "Charles Andrew 'Andy' Williams," under "Early Life," s.v. "Charles Andrew Williams."

[269] Duncan and Blackstone, *Child Killer: Charles Andy Williams*, under "February 7, 2001."

[270] General content: Gold, Ellingwood, and Reza, "Suspect, 15, Had Made Repeated Threats," under "At First, It Might Have Been a Joke." Rumors relayed by Dawn Hemming, aunt of Josh Stevens, in Duncan and Blackstone, *Child Killer: Charles Andy Williams*, under "February 13, 2001"; McCarthy, "Warning: Andy Williams Here," 3. Quotation: Goodwin and Simon, "My Child, The Murderer," introduction; Murderpedia, "Charles Andrew 'Andy' Williams," under "Early Life." The Columbine massacre was conducted on April 20, 1999. The shooting at Santana High School was on March 5, 2001.

[271] Duncan and Blackstone, *Child Killer: Charles Andy Williams*, under "February 2001." Spelling as reported.

[272] Amanda Alacqua, in a transcription of a series of messages with Blackstone in Duncan and Blackstone, *Child Killer: Charles Andy Williams*, under "Amanda in an Instant Message Communication with the Author."

[273] CNN, "Mother: School Wrong to Bar Students after Shooting," posted March 12, 2001, https://edition.cnn.com/2001/US/03/12/school.shooting/; CNN, "Suspect Had Talked about Shooting at School," posted March 5, 2001, https://www.cnn.com/2001/US/03/05/school.shooting.07/index.html; Dustin Hopkins, in Gold and McDermott, "Often Ridiculed, The Suspect Said"; Gold, Ellingwood, and Reza, "Suspect, 15, Had Made Repeated Threats," under "At First, It Might Have Been a Joke"; Jessica Pierce, acquaintance of Williams, Gilbert, and Stevens, in Duncan and Blackstone, *Child Killer: Charles Andy Williams*, under Friday, "March 2, 2001"; McCarthy, "Warning: Andy Williams Here," 4; Murderpedia, "Charles Andrew 'Andy' Williams," under "Early Life."

[274] Attributed to Tamara Von Mauw, in Duncan and Blackstone, *Child Killer: Charles Andy Williams*, under "March 7, 2001."

[275] Baxter, "The Santana High School Shooting"; Williams, in Dickey, "Killer Recounts Santana High Shooting," under "Saturday March 3."

[276] Duncan and Blackstone, *Child Killer: Charles Andy Williams*, under "Saturday, March 3, 2001"; Gold and McDermott, "Often Ridiculed, The Suspect Said," under "Saturday, March 3."

[277] Katie Hutter, in Gold and McDermott, "Often Ridiculed, The Suspect Said," under "Sunday, 4 P.M."

[278] Neil O'Grady, in Gold and McDermott, "Often Ridiculed, The Suspect Said," under "Sunday Night."

[279] Baxter, "The Santana High School Shooting"; Gold, Ellingwood, and Reza, "Suspect, 15, Had Made Repeated Threats," under "At First, It Might Have Been a Joke"; Gold and McDermott, "Often Ridiculed, The Suspect Said," under "Sunday Morning"; Reynolds, in Dickey, "Killer Recounts Santana High Shooting," under "Sunday, March 4."

[280] Duncan and Blackstone, *Child Killer: Charles Andy Williams*, under "Sunday, March 4, 2001."

[281] Foreshadowing in anticipation of an autogenic mass slaying is reviewed in Chapter Five of *How Rampage Killers Interpret Their Worlds*.

[282] Baxter, "The Santana High School Shooting"; CNN, "Mother: School Wrong to Bar Students";

Duncan and Blackstone, *Child Killer: Charles Andy Williams*, under "The Victims"; County of San Diego, East County Division v. Andrew Charles Williams, Superior Court of California, no. CE211823, DA no. MAD314,

Charge Summary, executed March 7, 2001, 6-16, School Shooters .info, s.v. "Andy Williams."

[283] Mahtani, "Profile of a School Shooter."

[284] Jack Katz, *Seductions of Crime: Moral and Sensual Attractions in Doing Evil* (United States of America: Basic Books, A Division of Harper-Collins, 1988), 290.

[285] AndySpeaks.com, "The Biography of Andy Williams"; Duncan and Blackstone, *Child Killer: Charles Andy Williams*, under "February 4, 1997," "February 7, 2001."

[286] Dickey, "Killer Recounts Santana High Shooting," under "Monday, March 5."

[287] Baxter, "The Santana High School Shooting."

[288] Premised on: a) Matthew R. Perlman, Anne E. Dawson, Christina M. Dardis, Theresa Egan, and Timothy Anderson, "The Association Between Childhood Maltreatment and Coping Strategies: The Indirect Effect Through Attachment," *The Journal of Genetic Psychology* 177, no. 5, posted September 1, tyy2016, https://www.tandfonline.com/doi/full/10.1080/00221325.2016.1218322; b) Shelley A. Riggs "Childhood Emotional Abuse and the Attachment System Across the Life Cycle: What Theory and Research Tell Us," *Journal of Aggression, Maltreatment & Trauma*, 19, no. 1 (2010): 5-51; c) Melanie J. Zimmer-Gembeck and Ellen A. Skinner, chapter 10, "The Development of Coping: Implications for Psychopathology and Resilience," in *Developmental Psychopathology*, 3rd ed., vol. 4, *Risk, Resilience, and Intervention*, ed. Dante Cicchetti (John Wiley & Sons, Inc., 2016), posted online, February 10, 2016, https://onlinelibrary.wiley.com/doi/full/10.1002/9781119125556.devpsy410.

[289] Joseph P. Allen, Stuart T. Hauser, and Emily Borman-Spurrell, "Attachment Theory as a Framework for Understanding Sequelae of Severe Adolescent Psychopathology: An 11-Year Follow-Up Study," *Journal of Consulting and Clinical Psychology* 64, no. 2 (April 1996): 254-255. The authors cite: John Bowlby, *Parent-Child Attachment and Healthy Human Development* (New York, NY: Basic Books, 1988); and Mary Dozier, Andrea L. Stevenson, Spring W. Lee, and Dawn I. Velligan, "Attachment Organization and Familial Overinvolvement for Adults with Serious Psychopathological Disorders," *Development and Psychopathology* 3, no. 4 (October 1991): 475-489.

Chapter Four

[1] National Institute of Health (NIH), National Institute of Mental Health (NIMH), "Mental Health," n.d., https://www.nimh.nih.gov/health/statistics/mental-illness#part_154785.

[2] Substance Abuse and Mental Health Services Administration (SAMHSA), *Key Substance Use and Mental Health Indicators in the United States: Results*

from the 2019 National Survey on Drug Use and Health (U.S. Department of Health and Human Services – HHS, September 2020), 57-58, https://www.samhsa.gov/data/sites/default/files/reports/rpt29393/2019NSDUHFFRPDFWHTML/2019NSDUHFFR1PDFW090120.pdf.

[3] Jason Silverstein, "There Were More Mass Shootings Than Days in 2019," Columbia Broadcasting System (CBS) News, posted January 2, 202, https://www.cbsnews.com/news/mass-shootings-2019-more-than-days-365/,

[4] NIH, NIMH, "Mental Health"; SAMHSA, *Key Substance Use and Mental Health Indicators in the United States*, 57. The calculation for teens with serious mental health issues was derived on the number involved with specialty settings, both in- and outpatient.

[5] See a) American Psychiatric Association, *Diagnostic and Statistical Manual of Mental Disorders*, 5th ed. (*DSM-5* –Arlington VA, 2013), 94-96, 466-469; and Lisa Feldman Barrett, "The Future of Psychology: Connecting Mind to Brain," *Perspectives on Psychological Science* 4, no. 4 (July 1, 2009): 326–339, https://www.ncbi.nlm.nih.gov/pmc/articles/PMC2763392/.

[6] Gail S. Anderson, *Biological Influences on Criminal Behavior* (Boca Raton, FL: Taylor and Francis Group, 2007), 207-210.

[7] M.C. Brower and B.H. Price, "Neuropsychiatry of Frontal Lobe Dysfunction in Violent and Criminal Behaviour: A Critical Review," *Advances in Neuropsychiatry* 71 (2001): 720.

[8] Robert Hanlon, "Neuropsychological Abnormalities in Indigent Defense Clients," presentation for Non-Capital Mitigation Workshop, Northwestern University Feinberg School of Medicine and Neurological Associates of Chicago, 2007.

[9] *New York Times,* "Head Injuries in Murderers," posted June 3, 1996, http://www.nytimes.com/1986/06/03/science/head-injuries-in-murderers.html.

[10] David B. Arciniegas, C Alan Anderson, Jeannie Topkoff, and Thomas W McAllister, "Mild Traumatic Brain Injury: A Neuropsychiatric Approach to Diagnosis, Evaluation, and Treatment," *Neuropsychiatric Disease and Treatment* 1, no. 4 (December 2005): 311-327.

[11] Anthony G. Hempel, J. Reid Meloy, and Thomas C. Richards, "Offender and Offense Characteristics of a Nonrandom Sample of Mass Murderers," *Journal of the American Academy of Psychiatry Law* 27, no. 2 (June 1999): 217.

[12] Laura A. Baker, Catherine Tuvblad, and Adrian Raine, "Genetics and Crime," in *The Sage Handbook of Criminological Theory*, ed. Eugene McLaughlin and Tim Newburn (Thousand Oaks, CA: Sage Publications Ltd., 2013), 33; Stephen Buka and Felton Earls, "Early Determinants of Delinquency and Violence," *Health Affairs* 12, no. 4 (Winter 1993): 50-57.

[13] Chloe Mayer, "Where Is James Holmes Now? Aurora Shooter's Life Behind Bars," posted July 20, 2022, https://www.newsweek.com/aurora-movie-shooting-where-james-holmes-now-prison-1725658. During an interview with authorities Holmes said he had taken 100 mg dose of Vicodin around 10 o'clock in the evening, about two and on-half hours prior to his ambush. Jordan Steffen, "Aurora Theater Shooting Trial, The Latest from Day 41," *Denver Post*, posted July 1, 2015, updated April 22, 2016, s.v. "4:56 p.m.," https://www.denverpost.com/2015/07/01/aurora-theater-shooting-trial-the-latest-from-day-41/.

[14] Drugs.com, reviewed by Leigh Ann Anderson, "What Is Paracetamol/Panadol Called in the US?" posted January 8, 2024; Jeremy Josephs, *Hungerford: One Man's Massacre*, (London, England: Smyth Gryphon, Ltd., 1993), 54.

[15] Michael Stone and Gary Brucato, *The New Evil: Understanding Modern Violent Crime* (Guilford, CT: Prometheus Books, 2019), 258.

[16] Marc Riedel and Wayne Welsh, *Criminal Violence: Patterns, Causes, and Prevention*, 2nd ed. (New York, NY: Oxford University Press, 2008), 266.

[17] Harold V. Hall, "Criminal-Forensic Neuropsycholgy of Disorders of Executive Functions," in *Disorders of Executive Functions: Civil and Criminal Law Applications*, ed. Harold V. Hall and Robert J. Sbordone (Boca Raton, FL: St. Lucie Press, 1998), 65.

[18] See: Curt R. Bartol and Anne M. Bartol, *Criminal Behavior: A Psychological Approach*, 9th ed. (San Francisco, CA: Prentice Hall, 2011), 512-515; and Jennifer L. Tackett and Robert F. Krueger, "Dispositional Influences on Human Aggression," in *Human Aggression and Violence: Causes, Manifestations, and Consequences*, ed. Phillip R. Shaver and Mario Mikulincer, (Washington D.C: American Psychological Association, 2011): 89-104.

[19] Bianca Castro, "Brain Damage Results from Substance Abuse," NBCDFW.com, posted March 28, 2017, http://www.nbcdfw.com/news/health/Brain-Damage-Results-From-Substance-Abuse-417382733.html. The piece is based on an interview with Dr. Joshua M. Masino, Director of Neurological Services at Enterhealth, based in Dallas, Texas. Additional sources uphold the same assertions: a) American Addiction Centers, "Neurological Disorders Caused by Substance Abuse," Sunrise House, http://sunrisehouse.com/addiction-demographics/neurological-disorders/; b) National Institute on Alcohol Abuse and Alcoholism, "Alcohol's Damaging Effects on the Brain," *Alcohol Alert* no. 63 (October 2004), https://pubs.niaaa.nih.gov/publications/aa63/aa63.htm; c) SAMHSA, "Chronic Substance Use and Cognitive Effects on the Brain: An Introduction," *In Brief* 9, no. 1 (Summer 2016).

[20] Marc A. Schuckit, "Comorbidity between Substance Use Disorders and Psychiatric Conditions," *Addiction* 101, supplement 1 (September 2006): 84.

[21] Ibid.

[22] Rosemary E.F. Kingston, Christina Marel, and Katherine L. Mills. "A Systematic Review of the Prevalence of Comorbid Mental Health Disorders in People Presenting for Substance Use Treatment in Australia," *Drug and Alcohol Review* 36, no. 4 (July 20217): 527-539.

[23] Wilson M. Compton, Yonette F. Thomas, Fredrick S. Stinson, and Bridget F. Grant, "Prevalence, Correlates, Disability, and Comorbidity of DSM-IV Drug Abuse and Dependence in the United State: Results from the National Epidemiologic Survey on Alcohol and Related Conditions," *Archive of General Psychiatry* 64, no. 5 (May 2007): 570-571, table 3. Adjustments included "age, race or ethnicity, sex, education, income, marital status, urbanicity, geographic region, and other psychiatric disorders." Ibid, table 3. Diagnostic labels were from the American Psychiatric Association, *Diagnostic and Statistical Manual of Mental Disorders*, 4th ed. (*DSM-IV* – Washington DC, 1994).

[24] Ismene L. Petrakis, Gerardo Gonzales, Robert Rosenheck, and John H. Krystal, "Comorbidity of Alcoholism and Psychiatric Disorders: An Overview," *Alcohol Research and Health* 26, no. 2 (January 2002): 81-89. The paper does not mention if there were controls for demographics. Diagnostics were based on interviews. Two data sources were used: The Epidemiologic Catchment Area Study involving people 15-54 in 1990-91 and the NIMH Epidemiologic Catchment Area Program, with subjects 18 years of age and older interviewed 1980-1984. Ibid, under "Rates of Psychiatric Disorders in Patients with Alcohol Use Disorders."

[25] Az Hakeem and Brian Fitzgerald, "A Survey of Violent and Threatening Behaviours within an In-Patient Learning Disability Unit," *Psychiatric Bulletin* 26 (2002): 424-427, http://pb.rcpsych.org/content/26 /11/424.full.

[26] Deb Shoumitro and Katherine Roberts, "The Evidence Base for the Management of Imminent Violence in Learning Disability Settings," (occasional paper 57, Royal College of Psychiatrists, March 2005), 13.

[27] Ibid, 15.

[28] One involved fourth and fifth graders and the other third, fourth, and fifth. Ruth Pearl, Tanis Bryan, and Mavis Donahue, "Social Behaviors of Learning Disabled Children: A Review," T*opics in Learning and Learning Disabilities* 3, no. 2 (July 1983): 3-4. The reviewers summarized Tanis H. Bryan and James H. Bryan. "Social Interactions of Learning Disabled Children," *Learning Disabilities Quarterly* 1, no. 1 (February 1978): 33-38; and Tanis H. Bryan, Roslyn Wheeler, Judith Felcan, and Tomacene Henek, "'Come on Dummy': An Observational Study of Children's Communications," *Journal of Learning Disabilities* 9, no. 10 (December 1976): 661-669.

[29] Keith A. Hawkins and Krista K. Trobst, "Frontal Lobe Dysfunction and Aggression: Conceptual Issues and Research Findings," *Aggression and Violent Behavior* 5, no. 2 (March-April 2000): 155.

[30] Caroline Skirrow, Gráinne McLoughlin, Jonna Kunsti, and Phillip Asherson. "Behavioral, Neurocognitive, and Treatment Overlap between Attention-Deficit/Hyperactivity Disorder and Mood Instability," *Expert Review Neurotherapeutics* 9, no. 4 (2009): 492. Additional information on cognition and behavioral traits of young people with mild/moderate learning impairments may be found in Eileen B. Raymond, *Learners with Mild Disabilities: A Characteristic Approach*, 3rd ed. (Boston, MA: Allyn & Bacon, 2008). For more on ADD/ADHD and impulsivity, there is a classic text: Russell A. Barkley, *ADHD and the Nature of Self-Control* (New York, NY: The Guilford Press, 1997, afterword, 2005).

[31] Anette GM Johansson, Malin Källman, Lennart Högman, Marianne Kristiansson, Håkan Fischer, and Sven Bölte, "Psychotically Driven Aggression Is Associated with Greater Mentalizing Challenges in Psychotic Spectrum Disorders," *BMC Psychiatry* 20, article no. 470 (2020), https://bmcpsychiatry.biomedcentral.com/articles/10.1186/s12888-020-028 68-7.

[32] Hawkins and Trobst, "Frontal Lobe Dysfunction and Aggression," 149.

[33] See: a) Clare S. Allely, Helen Minnis, Lucy Thompson, Phillip Wilson, and Christopher Gillberg, "Neurodevelopmental and Psychosocial Risk Factors in Serial Killers and Mass Murderers," *Aggression and Violent Behavior* 19, no. 3 (May-June 2014): 290-297; b) Jana L. Bufkin and Vickie R. Luttrell, "Neuroimaging Studies of Aggressive and Violent Behavior: Current Findings and Implications for Criminology and Criminal Justice," *Trauma, Violence, and Abuse* 6, no. 2 (April 2005): 180, table 1; c) Frank A. Elliott, "Neurological Factors in Violent Behavior (The Dyscontrol Syndrome)," *Bulletin of the American Academy of Psychiatry and the Law* 4, no. 4 (December 1976): 304-307; d) Katherine A. Larson, "A Research Review and Alternative Hypothesis Explaining the Link Between Learning Disability and Delinquency," *Journal of Learning Disabilities* 21, no. 6 (June/July 1988): 359-361.

[34] Claudia Rinaldi, "Language Competence and Social Behavior of Students with Emotional or Behavioral Disorders," *Behavioral Disorders* 29, no. 1 (November 2003): 35.

[35] Ibid, 39.

[36] Kathleen M. McDonough, "Analysis of the Expressive Language Characteristics of Emotionally Handicapped Students in Social Interactions," *Behavioral Disorders,* 14, no. 2 (February 1989): 132-134.

[37] Ibid, 135.

[38] For confirmation: a) Diana L. Rogers-Adkinson, "Language Processing in Children with Emotional Disorders," *Behavioral Disorders* 29, no. 1 (November 2003): 43-57; b) Barkley, *ADHD and the Nature of Self-Control*, 260-362; c) David P. Farrington, "Life-Course and Developmental Theories in Criminology," in *The Sage Handbook of Criminological Theory*, ed. Eugene McLaughlin and Tim Newburn (Thousand Oaks, CA: Sage Publications Inc., 2010), 250-251, 253-256, 261-263; d) Jane M. Healy, *Endangered Minds: Why Children Don't Think and What We Can Do about It* (New York, NY: Simon & Schuster, 1990), 183-191; e) Robin Karr-Morse and Meredith S. Wiley, *Ghosts from the Nursery: Tracing the Roots of Violence* (New York, NY: The Atlantic Monthly Press, 1997), 99-114; f) Larson, "A Research Review and Alternative," 359-362; e) Raymond, *Learners with Mild Disabilities*, 147-148; g) Rinaldi, "Language Competence and Social Behavior," 39-141; h) Donna M. Schwartz-Watts, "Asperger's Disorder and Murder," *Journal of the American Academy of Psychiatry and the Law Online* 33, no. 3, posted September 1, 2005, 390-393, http://www.jaapl.org/content/33/3.toc; i) Skirrow, McLoughlin, Kunsti, and Asherson, "Behavioral, Neurocognitive, and Treatment Overlap," 491.

[39] A few samples: a) Pekka-Eric Auvinen, "Natural Selector's Manifesto," School Shooters.info, s.v. "Pekka-Eric Auvinen Online," https://schoolshooters.info/; b) Alvaro Castillo journal excerpts, in State of North Carolina v. Alvaro Rafael Castillo, COA 10-814 North Carolina Court of Appeals, Defendant-Appellant's Brief 15-B 2009, (submitted September, 19, 2010), 11-14; b) Eric Harris, scan from *Journal* written entries, May 20, 1998 and June 12, 1998, in Dave Cullen, *Columbine* (New York, NY: Hachette Book Group, 2009), appendix B; Dylan Klebold, scan from journal, *A Virtual Book of Existences*, March 1997 and October 14, 1997, in Cullen, *Columbine*, appendix B. Throughout this book, there are many other examples, notably Blaze, Kinkel, Gill, and Rodger.

[40] Hawkins and Trobst, "Frontal Lobe Dysfunction and Aggression," 151-152.

[41] Raymond, *Learners with Mild Disabilities*," 302.

[42] Dr. Richard J. Konkol's Testimony, in *Frontline*, "111 Years Without Parole," Public Broadcasting System (PBS), posted January 2000, under "Read Excerpts from Konkol's Testimony," https://www.pbs.org/wgbh/pages/frontline/shows/kinkel/. Dr. Konkol testified as an expert witness for the defense during Kinkel's sentencing hearing. Kinkel was sentenced on November 9, 1999. Elisa Swanson, "Comment: 'Killers Start Sad and Crazy': Mental Illness and the Betrayal of Kipland Kinkel," *Oregon Law Review* 79, no. 4 (Winter 2000), under "B. Craziness," https://scholarsbank.uoregon.edu/xmlui /bitstream/handle/1794/4583/79olr1081.pdf.

[43] Eric B. Elbogen and Sally C. Johnson, "The Intricate Link Between Violence and Mental Disorder: Results from the National Epidemiologic Survey on

Alcohol and Related Conditions," *Archive of General Psychiatry* 66, no. 2 (February 2009): 159.

[44] *Frontline*, "Who is Kip Kinkel?" PBS, posted January 2000, under "Chronology," https://www.pbs.org/wgbh/pages/frontline/shows/kinkel/.

[45] Jonathan Fast, *Ceremonial Violence: A Psychological Explanation of School Shooting* (Woodstock, NY: Overlook Press, 2008), 52; *Frontline,* "Who is Kip?" under "Chronology."

[46] Dr. Richard J. Konkol's Testimony, in *Frontline,* "111 Years Without Parole."

[47] Jan Davidson and Bob Davidson, with Laura Vanderkam, *Genius Denied: How to Stop Wasting Our Brightest Young Minds* (New York, NY: Simon and Schuster, 2004), 84.

[48] With a Ph.D. from the University of Iowa in neuroanatomy and a Medical Degree from Georgetown University, Dr. Konkol specializes in pediatric neurology. Dr. Richard J. Konkol's Testimony, in *Frontline,* "111 Years Without Parole," box.

[49] Dr. Richard J. Konkol's Testimony, in *Frontline,* "111 Years Without Parole."

[50] Dr. Orin Bolstad's Testimony, in Frontline, "111 Years Without Parole," under "Read Excerpts from Bolstad's Testimony"; Dr. William Sack's Evaluation of Kinkel, in *Frontline,* "111 Years Without Parole," under "Read Excerpts of Sack's Testimony." Dr. Bolstad is a clinical psychologist who treated young killers in Oregon's juvenile prisons. At the time of Kinkel's trial, he was also a consultant at the MacLaren Youth Correctional Facility, the state juvenile prison where Kinkel served the first part of his sentence. Dr. Orin Bolstad's Testimony, in *Frontline,* "111 Years Without Parole," box. Dr. William Sack is a child and adolescent psychiatry specialist in Portland, Oregon with decades of experience. Healthgrades National Index, "Learn about Dr. Sacks," Healthgrades Operating Company, Inc © 2023, https://www.healthgrades.com/physician/dr-william-sack-y42c6.

[51] Jeff Barnard, "A Familiar Tragedy," *South Coast Today*, posted May 22, 1998, updated Jan 11, 2011, https://www.southcoasttoday.com/article/19980522/news/305229999; David Foster, Julia Prodis, and Associated Press (AP), "Warning Signs Were Plentiful," *Sun*, posted May 23, 1998; *Guardian*, "How 'Schizoid' Kid From Good Home Turned to Murder at Oregon School," posted May 22, 1998, https://www.theguardian.com/world/1998/may/23/3; Margot Hornblower, "The Boy Who Loved Bombs," *Time*, posted June 24, 2001, http://content.time.com/time/magazine/article/0,9171,139242,00.html.

[52] Maxine Bernstein, "Kipland P. Kinkel: A Clear Path Toward Destruction," *Oregonian*, published in paper on August 30, 1998, posted May 16, 2008, updated January 11, 2019, https://www.oregonlive.com/pacific-northwest-news/2008/05/kipland_p_kinkel_a_clear_path.html; *Guardian*, "How 'Schizoid' Kid."

[53] *Guardian*, "How 'Schizoid' Kid"; Lisa Popyk, "Zero Guilt, Zero Remorse," *Washington Post*, originally published November 11, 1999, Murderpedia: The Encyclopedia of Murderers, last updated June 4, 2017, s.v. "Kipland P. Kinkel," https://murderpedia.org/.

[54] Bernstein, "Kipland P. Kinkel: A Clear Path."

[55] Demonstrated in: a) Henrik Belfrage, "A Ten-Year Follow-Up of Criminality in Stockholm Mental Patients: New Evidence for a Relation between Mental Disorder and Crime," *British Journal of Criminology* 38, no. 1 (Winter 1998): 145–155, abstract, https://doi.org/10.1093/oxfordjournals.bjc.a014217; b) Josanne D. M. Van Dongen, Nicole M. L. Buck, Marko Barendregt, Nico M. Van Beveren, Edwin De Beurs, and Hjalmar J. C. Van Marle, "Anti-Social Personality Characteristics and Psychotic Symptoms: Two Pathways Associated with Offending in Schizophrenia," *Criminal Behaviour and Mental Health* 25, no. 3 (July 2015): 185; c) Simone Ullrich, Robert Keers, and Jeremy W. Coid, "Delusions, Anger, and Serious Violence: New Findings From the MacArthur Violence Risk Assessment Study," *Schizophrenia Bulletin* 40, no. 5 (September 2014): 1174–1181; d) Dean J. Wilkinson and Laura S. Caulfield, "Delusional Ideation, Cognitive Processes and Crime Based Reasoning," *Europe's Journal of Psychology* 13, no. 3 (August 2017): 503–518.

[56] Shown in: a) Valentina Candini, Marta Ghisi, Gioia Bottesi, Clarissa Ferrari, Viola Bulgari, Laura Iozzino, Maria Elena Boero, Alessandra De Francesco, Paolo Maggi, Beatrice Segalini, Vanessa Zuccalli, Gian Marco Giobbio, Giuseppe Rossi, and Giovanni de Girolamo, "Personality, Schizophrenia, and Violence: A Longitudinal Study," *Journal of Personality Disorders* 32, no. 4 (August 2018): 465-481; b) J. Reid Meloy, *The Psychopathic Mind: Origins, Dynamics and Treatment* (Northvale, NJ: Jason Aronson Inc., 1988), 245-279; c) Katharina Nymo Engelstad, Bjørn Rishovd Rund, Bjørn Lau, Anja Vaskinn and Anne-Kari Torgalsbøen, "Increased Prevalence of Psychopathy and Childhood Trauma in Homicide Offenders with Schizophrenia Compared to Nonviolent Individuals with Schizophrenia," *Nordic Journal of Psychiatry* no. 3 (July 2015), posted August 23, 2019, 181–191, abstract, https://www.tandfonline.com/doi/abs/10.1080/08039488.2019.1656777?src=recsys&journalCode=ipsc20&; d) Josanne D. M. Van Dongen, Nicole M. L. Buck, Marko Barendregt, Nico M. Van Beveren, Edwin De Beurs, and Hjalmar J. C. Van Marle, "Anti-Social Personality Characteristics and Psychotic Symptoms: Two Pathways Associated with Offending in Schizophrenia," *Criminal Behaviour and Mental Health* 25, no. 3 (July 2014): 181-191; e) Karen A. Nolan, Jan Volavka, Pavel Mohr, and Pál Czobor, "Psychopathy and Violent Behavior among Patients with Schizophrenia or Schizoaffective Disorder," *Psychiatric Services* 50, no. 6 (June 1999): 787-792; f) Ottilie Sedgwick, Susan Young, David Baumeister,

Ben Greer, Mrigendra Das, and Veena Kumari, "Neuropsychology and Emotion Processing in Violent Individuals with Antisocial Personality Disorder or Schizophrenia: The Same or Different? A Systematic Review and Meta-Analysis," *Australian & New Zealand Journal of Psychiatry* 51, no. 12 (December 2017): 1178 –1197.

[57] See: a) S. L. Dunaif and P.H. Hoch, "Pseudopsychopathic Schizophrenia," in *Psychiatry and the Law*, ed. Paul H. Hoch and Joseph Zubin (New York, NY: Grune & Stratton, 1955), 108-121; b) Louis De Page and Jérôme Englebert, "Heboidophrenia and Pseudo-Psychopathic Schizophrenia: Current Knowledge and Critical Perspective," *Psychopathology* 51, no. 4 (September 2018): 227–233; c) Nolan, Volavka, Mohr, and Czobor, "Psychopathy and Violent," 791; d) Adrian Raine, "Antisocial Personality as a Neurodevelopmental Disorder," *Annual Review of Clinical Psychology* 14 (2018): 259–289.

[58] Hodgins Sheilagh, A. Cree, J. Alderton, and Terrence Mak, "From Conduct Disorder to Severe Mental Illness: Associations with Aggressive Behaviour, Crime and Victimization," *Psychological Medicine* 38, no. 7 (July 2008): 977, 979-980. Subjects were 18-65, 120 men and 85 women, on average 38.5 years of age, diagnosed with schizophrenia, schizoaffective disorder, bipolar disorder, major depression, and non-toxic psychosis. Aggression was defined as one or more incidents of assault. $p = 0.000$. Ibid, table 2.

[59] Van Dongen et al., "Anti-Social Personality Characteristics," 185.

[60] For research supporting a developmental course of psychopathy with schizophrenia, see: a) Paul Moran and Sheilagh Hodgins, "The Correlates of Comorbid Antisocial Personality Disorder in Schizophrenia," *Schizophrenia Bulletin*, 30 no. 4 (2004): 791-802; b) Raine, "Antisocial Personality as a Neurodevelopmental"; c) Adrian Raine, Kenneth Dodge, Rolf Loeber, Lisa Gatzke-Kopp, Don Lynam, Chandra Reynolds, Magda Stouthamer-Loeber, and Jianghong Liu, "The Reactive–Proactive Aggression Questionnaire: Differential Correlates of Reactive and Proactive Aggression in Adolescent Boys," *Aggressive Behavior* 32, no. 2 (February 2006): 159–171; d) Edelyn Verona and Christopher J. Patrick, "Psychobiological Aspects of Antisocial Personality Disorder, Psychopathy, and Violence," *Psychiatric Times* 32, no. 3 (March 25, 2015): 2-3, https://www.psychiatrictimes.com/view/psychobiological-aspects-antisocial-personality-disorder-psychopathy-and-violence.

[61] Verona and Patrick, "Psychobiological Aspects of Antisocial," 3. The author's base their insight on '[a] hierarchical biometric … of the origins of comorbidity among substance dependence, antisocial behavior, and a disinhibited personality style." See also, Robert F. Krueger, Brian M. Hicks, Christopher J. Patrick, Scott R. Carlson, William G. Iacono, and Matt McGue, "Etiologic Connections Among Substance Dependence, Antisocial

Behavior, and Personality: Modeling the Externalizing Spectrum," *Journal of Abnormal Psychology* 111, no. 3 (January 2002), abstract.

[62] Bernstein, "Kipland P. Kinkel: A Clear Path"; Fast, *Ceremonial Violence*, 51.

[63] Bernstein, "Kipland P. Kinkel: A Clear Path"; Foster, Prodis, and AP, "Warning Signs Were Plentiful."

[64] Maxine Bernstein and Janet Filips, "A Springfield Tribute: Kinkels Remembered with Joy," *Oregonian*: posted May 30, 1998, https://www.oregonlive.com/special/2008/05/a_springfield_tribute_kinkels.html; Hornblower, "The Boy Who Loved."

[65] Bernstein, "Kipland P. Kinkel: A Clear Path"; Foster, Prodis, and AP, "Warning Signs Were Plentiful."

[66] Kristen was born December 22, 1976, and Kip August 30, 1982. *Frontline,* "Who Is Kip Kinkel?" PBS, posted January 2000, under "Chronology," https://www.pbs.org/wgbh/pages/frontline/shows/kinkel/.

[67] "An Interview with Kristin Kinkel," in *Frontline,* "Who Is Kip Kinkel?"

[68] Bernstein, "Kipland P. Kinkel: A Clear Path"; Lisa Grace Lednicer and Maxine Bernstein, "Suspect's Sister Impresses Friends after Return Home," *Oregonian,* posted May 28, 1998, https://www.oregonlive.com/special/2008/05/suspects_sister_impresses_frie.html.

[69] Karen Brandon and V. Dion Haynes, "Accused Youth Had Good Home, Caring Folks," *Chicago Tribune*, posted May 24, 1998, https://www.chicagotribune.com/news/ct-xpm-1998-05-24-9805240181-story.html; comments by Peter J. Boyer, Kristen Kinkel, and Bryan Mabe, in Michael Kirk, dir. and writ., and Peter J. Boyer, writ, transcript for *The Killer at Thurston High* [90 min. version], in *Frontline,* "Who Is Kip Kinkel," under "Tapes & Transcripts."

[70] Hornblower, "The Boy Who Loved."

[71] Comments by Kristen Kinkel, in Kirk and Boyer, transcript for *The Killer at Thurston High.*

[72] Kip Kinkel, *Journal*, School Shooters .info: Resources on School Shootings, Perpetrators, and Prevention, updated March 5, 2024, s.v. "Kip Kinkel," https://schoolshooters.info/. Spelling conforms with entry.

[73] Comments by Peter J. Boyer, Dick Bushnell, and Marcia Bushnell, in Kirk and Boyer, transcript for *The Killer at Thurston High*; Fast, *Ceremonial Violence*, 52; Don Terry and Frank Bruni, "Shootings in a Schoolhouse: The Suspect; Lethal Fantasies of a 15-Year-Old Became a Reality," *New York Times*, posted May 24, 1998, https://www.nytimes.com/1998/05/24/us/shootings-schoolhouse-suspect-lethal-fantasies-15-year-old-became-reality.html?auth=login-email&login=email. One narrative states he was enrolled in karate classes as early as six or seven. Maxine Bernstein, "Kipland P. Kinkel Chronology," *The Oregonian*, posted August 30, 1998, s.v. "Age 6 or 7," https://www.oregonlive.com/special/2008/05/kinkels_boyhood_troubles_explo.html. That observation is contradicted by multiple sources including

Brandon and Haynes, "Accused Youth Had Good Home," in addition to those already cited.

[74] Fast, *Ceremonial Violence*, 52; Kristin Kinkel, in "An Interview with Kristen Kinkel"; Terry and Bruni, "Shootings in a Schoolhouse."

[75] Bernstein, "Kipland P. Kinkel Chronology," s.v. "Middle School"; Peter Langman, *School Shooters: Understanding High School, College, and Adult Perpetrators* (Boulder, CO: Rowman & Littlefield, 2015), 41. Bernstein reports Kinkel was called a name and Langman says he was pushed.

[76] Bernstein and Filips, "A Springfield Tribute: Kinkel's Remembered"; comments by Peter J. Boyer, Bryan Mabe, and Don Stone, in Kirk and Boyer, transcript for *The Killer at Thurston High*; Terry and Bruni, "Shootings in a Schoolhouse."

[77] Lauren Dodge, "School Shooting: Boy's Rampage Leaves Wake of Death, Fear," *Sun*, posted May 22, 1998, https://products.kitsapsun.com/archive/1998/05-22/0016_school_shooting__boy_s_rampage _le.html; Bryan Mabe, in Kirk and Boyer, transcript for *The Killer at Thurston High*.

[78] Kinkel, *Journal*. Spelling and punctuation as written.

[79] Fast, *Ceremonial Violence*, 52; *Frontline*, "Who Is Kip Kinkel?" under "Chronology."

[80] Fast, *Ceremonial Violence*, 52-53.

[81] Dr. Orin Bolstad's Testimony, in *Frontline*, "111 Years Without Parole."

[82] Ibid.

[83] Frontline, "Who is Kip Kinkel?" under "Chronology."

[84] Encyclopedia.com, s.v. "Kip Kinkel," under "The Trial," updated April 12, 2020, https://www.encyclopedia.com/law/encyclopedias-almanacs-transcripts-and-maps/kinkel-kip; Brandon with Haynes, "Accused Youth Had Good Home."

[85] *Frontline*, "Who is Kip Kinkel?" under "Chronology,"; Laura L. Finley, ed., *Encyclopedia of School Crime and Violence* (Santa Barbara, CA: ABC-CLIO, 2011), 177.

[86] Bernstein, "Kipland P. Kinkel Chronology"; Encyclopedia.com, s.v. "Kip Kinkel," under "Special Education"; Fast, *Ceremonial Violence*, 52; *Frontline*, "Who is Kip Kinkel?" under "Chronology."

[87] *Frontline*, "Who is Kip Kinkel?" under "Chronology."

[88] Dr. Hicks Treatment Notes on Kip Kinkel, in *Frontline*, "111 Years without Parole," under "Read His Treatment Notes on Kip."

[89] Georges Han, Bonnie Klimes-Dougan, Susie Jepsen, Kristin Ballard, Megan Nelson, Alaa Houri, Sanjiv Kumra, and Kathryn Cullen, "Selective Neurocognitive Impairments in Adolescents with Major Depressive Disorder," *Journal of Adolescence* 35 no. 1 (February 2012): 11.

[90] Thomas G. Conover, reviewer, "Depressive Disorders DSM-IV Criteria," Medical Home Portal, posted and updated April 2000, https://www.medicalhomeportal.org/.

[91] Dr. Hicks Treatment Notes on Kip Kinkel, in *Frontline*, "111 Years without Parole."

[92] Kip Kinkel, "Love Sucks," School Shooters. info: Resources on School Shootings, Perpetrators, and Prevention, last updated March 21, 2024, s.v. "Kip Kipland," https://schoolshooters.info/. Grammar as shown on site. See also, Peter Langman, "Shakespeare and School Shooters, Part 2 (Romeo and Juliet)," *Psychology Today*, posted February 5, 2010, https://www.psychologytoday.com/us/blog/keeping-kids-safe/201002/shakespeare-and-school-shooters-part-2-romeo-and-juliet.

[93] Kinkel, *Journal*.

[94] *Frontline*, "Who is Kip Kinkel?" under "Chronology."

[95] Dr. Hick's Treatment Notes on Kip Kinkel.

[96] Fast, *Ceremonial Violence*, 53; *Frontline*, "Who is Kip Kinkel?" under "Chronology," s.v. "June 27, 1997." Due to its magazine capacity, light trigger pull, reliability, and relative low-cost, the weapon has come to be favored throughout the United States. Erin McCarthy, "Why the Glock Became America's Handgun," *Popular Mechanics*, posted January 12, 2012; also, interview with Paul Barrett, in the same article, https://www.popularmechanics.com/military/weapons/a7445/why-the-glock-became-americas-handgun/.

[97] Fast, *Ceremonial Violence*, 53; *Frontline*, "Who is Kip Kinkel?" under "Chronology."

[98] Jeffrey L. Hick's Testimony, in *Frontline*, "111 Years without Parole," under "Read Excerpts from Hick's Testimony."

[99] Bernstein, "Kipland P. Kinkel Chronology,"; Fast, *Ceremonial Violence*, 53; *Frontline*, "Who is Kip Kinkel?" under "Chronology."

[100] *Frontline*, "Who is Kip?" under "Chronology."

[101] Bernstein, "Kipland P. Kinkel Chronology"; Fast, *Ceremonial Violence*, 53. There is some evidence, though inconclusive, that Kip Kinkel, not his father, had the .22 in his room on the night he killed his parents. Dr. Orin Bolstad's Testimony, in *Frontline*, "111 Years Without Parole."

[102] Comment by Kristin Kinkel, in Kirk and Boyer, transcript for *The Killer at Thurston High.*

[103] Fast, *Ceremonial Violence*, 53; Joseph Lieberman, *School Shootings: What Every Parent and Educator Needs to Know to Protect Our Children* (New York, NY: Kensington Publishing Corp., 2008), 55, 156.

[104] Dr. Hicks Treatment Notes on Kip Kinkel, in *Frontline*, "111 Years without Parole."

[105] *Frontline*, "Who is Kip Kinkel?" under "Chronology."

[106] Fast, *Ceremonial Violence*, 54.
[107] Fast, *Ceremonial Violence*, 55; *Frontline*, "Who is Kip Kinkel?" under "Chronology"; Lieberman, *School Shootings: What Every Parent and Educator Needs to Know*, 56
[108] Fast, *Ceremonial Violence*, 55.
[109] *Frontline*, "Who is Kip Kinkel?" under "Chronology"; David Postman and Arthur Santana, "Bombs in Home of Ore. Boy Whose School Attack Killed 2 – Two More Found Dead Are His Parents," *Seattle Times*, posted May 22, 1998, https://archive.seattletimes.com/archive/?date=19980522 &slug=2752170.
[110] *Frontline*, "Who is Kip Kinkel?" under "Chronology."
[111] Bernstein, "Kipland P. Kinkel: A Clear Path"; Postman and Santana, "Bombs in Home."
[112] Bernstein, "Kipland P. Kinkel: A Clear Path"; Fast, *Ceremonial Violence*, 55.
[113] Kinkel, *Journal*.
[114] Dr. Orin Bolstad's Testimony, in *Frontline*, "111 Years Without Parole."
[115] Dr. Orin Bolstad's Testimony, in *Frontline*, "111 Years Without Parole." Certain sources give "Corey Ewert" as the supplier of Kinkel's final gun purchase. Ibid; Fast, *Ceremonial Violence*, 56. Others say "Korey Ewert." Bernstein, "Kipland P. Kinkel Chronology," May 20; *Frontline*, "Who is Kip Kinkel?" under "Chronology" The content and timing of the statements prove they are the same person with different spellings of the first name.
[116] Bernstein, "Kipland P. Kinkel: A Clear Path"; Bernstein, "Kipland P. Kinkel Chronology"; commentary by Boyer, in Kirk and Boyer, transcript for *The Killer at Thurston High*; *Frontline*, "Who is Kip Kinkel?" under "Chronology."
[117] Bernstein, "Kipland P. Kinkel: A Clear Path."
[118] Bernstein, "Kipland P. Kinkel Chronology"; *Frontline*, "Who is Kip Kinkel?" under "Chronology"; commentary by Det. Al Warthen, Springfield Police Department, in Kirk and Boyer, transcript for *The Killer at Thurston High.*
[119] Commentary by Det. Warthen in Kirk and Boyer, transcript for *The Killer at Thurston High.*
[120] Bernstein, "Kipland P. Kinkel: A Clear Path."
[121] Bernstein, "Kipland P. Kinkel: A Clear Path." Twenty years later Don Stone recalled the exchange a little differently, though with substantially the same content. "'I can remember him looking up at me, his eyes were … I just couldn't see anything in his eyes,' says Stone. 'But nonetheless, he said, "Coach, what's going to happen?" And I said, "Well Kip, we don't have any tolerance for guns on campus. I'm not sure you're going to be with us anymore."'" In Brian Bull, with Alec Cowan and Deonna Anderson, "KLCC Special Documentary: The Thurston High School Shooting - 20 Years Later," National Public Radio (NPR) KLC.org: posted May 21, 2018, https://

www.klcc.org/post/klcc-special-documentary-thurston-high-school-shooting-20-years-later.

[122] Commentary by Det. Warthen.

[123] Bernstein, "Kipland P. Kinkel: A Clear Path."

[124] Ibid.

[125] Fast, *Ceremonial Violence*, 56.

[126] Ibid.

[127] Bernstein, "Kipland P. Kinkel Chronology"; *Frontline*, "Who is Kip Kinkel?" "Chronology."

[128] Although they may differ with respect to the origin of pressure, the various renditions of "strain theory" hold that criminal conflict is incentivized by misguided attempts to cope with frustrating social, political, or economic conditions that are seemingly unyielding. Maria João Lobo Antunes and Michelle Manasse, "Social Disorganization and Strain: Macro and Micro Implications for Youth Violence," *Journal of Research in Crime and Delinquency* 59, no. 1 (February 2022): 82-127; Marcin Jurczyk, "Relation between the Sense of Strain, Social Control, Differential Associations and Juvenile Delinquency Amongst Adolescents: An Empirical Test of Robert Agnew's General Strain Theory," Research Square, posted March 8, 2022, https://doi.org/10.21203/rs.3.rs-1252590/v1; Scot Wortley, with Randy Seepersad Andrea Mcalla, Rashmee Singh, Natasha Madon, Carolyn Greene, Nicole Myers, and Terrance Roswell, *The Review of the Roots of Youth Violence* (Ontario, Canada: Service Ontario Publications, 2008), 81-98. A penetrating article published over a decade ago applied the general premise associated with societal stress to a sequence of school massacres based on "cumulative strain." Jack Levin and Eric Madfis, "Mass Murder at School and Cumulative Strain: A Sequential Model," *American Behavioral Scientist* 52, no. 9 (May 2009): 1227-1245. (The phrase is first used on page 1229). With important distinctions regarding origin, sequence, and momentum, the proposed model has similarities to the one formulated in *How Rampage Killers Interpret Their Worlds*. Levin and Madfis suggest that "some loss perceived to be catastrophic in the mind of the killer … serves as a catalyst or precipitant." Levin and Madfis, "Mass Murder at School," 1235. They designate it as "acute strain." The contention advanced in this book's companion is that there is no single situation boosting the final succession of crimes. Rather, planning is sustained for a period that is often prolonged. The attack is nudged forward by a series of events with exaggerated importance for the rampageous individual. Eventually a combination of circumstances dictates the fulfillment of intent. The distinction is subtle, but nevertheless important for understanding the role of external influences.

[129] Springfield Police Department, Kip Kinkel's Confession as Told to Detective Al Warthen, recorded May 21, 1998, transcript 4-5, 15, School Shooters. info, s.v. "Kip Kinkel."

[130] Commentary by Mabe, in Kirk and Boyer, transcript for *The Killer at Thurston High.*

[131] *Frontline*, "Who is Kip?" under "Chronology"; Springfield Police Department, Kip Kinkel's Confession, 5.

[132] *Frontline*, "Who is Kip Kinkel?" under "Chronology."

[133] Ibid.

[134] Ibid.

[135] Fast, *Ceremonial Violence*, 57; narration by Boyer, in Kirk and Boyer, transcript for *The Killer at Thurston High*; Springfield Police Department, Kip Kinkel's Confession, 7-9, 15-16; *Frontline* "111 Years without Parole," under "The State's Case."

[136] Springfield Police Department, Kip Kinkel's Confession, 9. Ellipsis in original.

[137] Ibid, 4, 5, 8, 9, 15, 19.

[138] Lilianne Rivka Mujica-Parodi, Dolores Malaspina, and Harold A. Sackeim, "Logical Processing, Affect, and Delusional Thought in Schizophrenia," *Harvard Review of Psychiatry* 8, no. 2 (July-August 2000): 73-83, abstract. See also: a) Lilianne Rivka Mujica-Parodi, Tsafrir Greenberg, Robert M. Bilder, and Dolores Malaspina, "Emotional Impact on Logic Deficits May Underlie Psychotic Delusions in Schizophrenia," University of California Merced: *Proceedings of the Annual Meeting of the Cognitive Science Society* 23 no. 23 (2001), http://citeseerx.ist.psu.edu/viewdoc/download?doi=10.1.1.123.8056&rep=rep1&type=pdf; and Stephen A. Selesnick and Gareth S. Owen, "Quantum-Like Logics and Schizophrenia," *Journal of Applied Logic*, 10, no. 1 (March 2012): 115-126.

[139] Tom Adams and News Staff, "'I for One Am Very Tired of Having This Wound Picked Open,'" KATU 2, posted September 12, 2013, https://katu.com/news/local/i-for-one-am-very-tired-of-having-this-wound-picked-open-11-19-2015; Springfield Police, Kip Kinkel's Confession, 10. A documentary film states he carried the extra ammunition in a gym bag. Narration by Boyer, in Kirk and Boyer, transcript for *The Killer at Thurston High.* Other sources say it was a backpack. *Frontline*, "Who Is Kip Kinkel?" under "Chronology," s.v. "May 21, 1998 – Day of Shooting at Thurston High, 7:30 a.m., Kip Leaves House"; Irvin H. Perline and Jona Goldschimdt, *The Psychology and Law of Workplace Violence: A Handbook for Mental Health Professionals and Employers* (Springfield, Il: Charles C. Thomas, LTD, 2004), 323. Another reference says, "[h]e filled a black backpack *and* gray military bag. …" Lieberman, *The Shooting Game*, 10, emphasis added.

[140] *Frontline*, "Who is Kip Kinkel?" under "Chronology," s.v. "May 21, 1998, 7:30 a.m."; Springfield Police Department, Kip Kinkel after Being Taken into Custody by Springfield Police, photo with caption, in Brian Bull with Alec Cowan and Deonna Anderson, "KLCC Special Documentary: The Thurston High School Shooting – 20 Years Later," NPR, posted May 21, 2018, https://www.klcc.org/post/klcc-special-documentary-thurston-high-school-shooting-20-years-later; Springfield Police Department, Kip Kinkel's Confession, 10-11.

[141] Narration by Boyer, in Kirk and Boyer, transcript for *The Killer at Thurston High*; *Frontline*, "Who is Kip Kinkel?" under "Chronology"; Springfield Police Department, Kip Kinkel's Confession, 12-13. For the relevance of Nine Inch Nails, as well as the general fascination that sudden mass assailants have for edifying extreme violence, refer to the work that accompanies this book, *How Rampage Killers Interpret Their Worlds*, with particular attention to Chapter Four.

[142] *Frontline*, "Who is Kip Kinkel?" under "Chronology."

[143] Commentary by Bryan Mabe, in Michael J. Kirk, dir. and writ., and Peter J. Boyer, writ., broadcast of *Frontline,* "The Killer at Thurston High," PBS, originally aired January 18, 2000, rebroadcast May 2004, https://www.pbs.org/wgbh/pages/frontline/shows/kinkel/.

[144] Cullen, *Columbine*, 42. Harris and Klebold, as a team, will be discussed in the next chapter.

[145] Maxine Bernstein, "Silenced Grief Finds A Voice," *Oregonian*, posted May 16, 1999, under "Son on List of Wounded," https://www.oregonlive.com/special/2008/05/silenced_grief_finds_a_voice.html; Fast, *Ceremonial Violence*, 57.

[146] Cynthia M., original creator, maintained by A. J., memorial page for Benjamin Allen "Ben" Walker (4 Oct 1981–21 May 1998), Find a Grave Memorial no. 7649469, citing Springfield Memorial Gardens, Springfield, Lane County, Oregon, USA, https://www.findagrave.com.

[147] Maxine Bernstein, "Thurston 20 Years Later: 'We Know Exactly How They Feel,'" *Oregonian*, posted May 20, 2018, updated January 30, 2019, https://www.oregonlive.com/pacific-northwest-news/2018/05/thurston_20_years_later_we_kno.html.

[148] Adams and News Staff, "'I for One.'"

[149] The reported number of pupils on the scene at that point ranges from 200 to 400: 200 – Adams and News Staff, "'I for One'"; 270 – Lieberman, *The Shooting Game*, 12; 400 – Barnard, "A Familiar Tragedy."

[150] Narration by Boyer, in Kirk and Boyer, transcript for *The Killer at Thurston High*; Lieberman, *The Shooting Game*, 12-13.

[151] Barnard, "A Familiar Tragedy"; Cynthia M., writ., memorial page for Mikael Erik Nickolauson (26 Dec 1980–21 May 1998), Find a Grave Memorial no.

7649473, citing Sunset Hills Cemetery, Eugene, Lane County, Oregon, USA, https://www.findagrave.com/memorial/7649473/mikael-erik-nickolauson; *Register-Guard*, "Remembering the Victims of The May 1998 Thurston Shooting," posted May 19, 2018, updated May 20, 2018, under "Mikael Nickolauson, 17," https://www.registerguard.com/news/20180519/remembering - victims-of-may-1998-thurston-shooting.

[152] Barnard, "A Familiar Tragedy"; Lieberman, *The Shooting Game*, 15.

[153] Lieberman, *The Shooting Game*, 15.

[154] *Frontline*, "Who is Kip Kinkel?" under "Chronology," s.v. "May 21, 1998, 7:55 a.m."; Lieberman, *The Shooting Game*, 15-16.

[155] Narration by Boyer, in Kirk and Boyer, transcript for *The Killer at Thurston High*; Fast, *Ceremonial Violence*, 58; Lieberman, *The Shooting Game*, 16.

[156] Barnard, "A Familiar Tragedy." The exact wording changes in other accounts. This quotation was chosen because the story appeared the day after the shooting at school.

[157] Fast, *Ceremonial Violence*, 58; *Frontline*, "Who is Kip Kinkel?" under "Chronology."

[158] Hawkins and Trobst, "Frontal Lobe Dysfunction and Aggression,"152.

[159] Fast, *Ceremonial Violence*, 75-76; Johnathan Fast, "Unforgiven and Alone: Brenda Spencer and Secret Shame," in *School Shootings: International Research, Case Studies, and Concepts for Prevention*, ed. Nils Böckler, Peter Sitzer, Thorsten Seeger, and Wilhelm Heitmeyer (New York, NY: Springer, 2013), 251-252. "A positron emission tomography, or PET, scan is an imaging technique that uses positively charged particles (radioactive positrons) to detect subtle changes in the body's metabolism and chemical activities. ... PET scans can be used to evaluate neurological illnesses, especially epilepsy, and Alzheimer's disease and other dementias." Harvard Medical School, "Positron Emission Tomography (PET Scan)," Harvard Health Publishing, posted April 2014, https://www.health.harvard.edu/medical-devices-and-technology/positron-emission-tomography-pet-scan-.

[160] Robert J. Sbordone, "Epileptic-Related Executive Dysfunction and Violent Crime," in *Disorders of Executive Functions: Civil and Criminal Law Applications*, ed. Harold V. Hall and Robert J. Sbordone (Boca Raton, FL: St. Lucie Press, 1998), 129, citing his own work as follows: a) "Assessment and Treatment of Cognitive Communicative Impairments in the Closed Head Injury Patient: A Neurobehavioral-Systems Approach," *Journal of Head Trauma Rehabilitation* 3, no. 2 (June 1988): 55-62; b) "Psychotherapeutic Treatment of the Client with Traumatic Brain Injury: A Conceptual Model," in *Community Integration Following Traumatic Brain Injury*, ed. Jeffrey S. Kreutzer and Paul Wehman (Baltimore, MD: Brookes, 1990), 139-156; c) "Rehabilitative Neuropsychological Approach for Severe Traumatic-Brain

Injury Patients," *Professional Psychology Research* and Practice 15, no. 2 (April 1984): 165-175.

[161] Saku Luukkainen, Kaisa Riala, Matti Laukkanen, Helinä Hakko, and Pirkko Räsänen, "Association of Traumatic Brain Injury with Criminality in Adolescent Psychiatric Inpatients from Northern Finland," *Psychiatry Research* 200 no. 2–3 (December 2012): 767-772, abstract, https://www.sciencedirect.com/science/article/abs/pii/S016517811200203X ?via%3Dihub. Information on TBI came from the Finnish Hospital Discharge Register and on criminality from the Legal Register Center. Ibid, abstract. Conduct disorder determination was based on semi-structured Schedule for Affective Disorder and Schizophrenia for School-Age Children – Present and Lifetime, diagnosed according to *DSM-IV* criteria; Joan Kaufman, Boris Birmaher, David Brent, Paula Moreci, Douglas Williamson, Neal Ryan, "Schedule for Affective Disorders and Schizophrenia for School-Age Children - Present and Lifetime version (K-SADS-PL): Initial Reliability and Validity Data," *Journal of American Academy of Child & Adolescent Psychiatry* 36, no. 7 (July 1997): 980-988. Confidence intervals as follows: criminality, 95%; CD, 95%; concomitant, 95%. Luukkainen et al., "Association of Traumatic Brain Injury," abstract.

[162] Gina Christopher and Jacqueline Kiefel, "When A Child Has Epilepsy and Attention Problems: The Role of Neuropsychology," Children's Healthcare of Atlanta, *Neuro Update* 5, no. 3: 2-3. For further evidence, see: a) Ann Abramowitz and Petrina Hollingsworth, reviewed by Joseph I. Sirven and Patricia O. Shafer, "Epilepsy and ADHD," Epilepsy Foundation, posted July-August, 2018, https://www.epilepsy.com/learn/challenges-epilepsy/moods-and-behavior/mood-and-behavior-101/epilepsy-and-adhd; b) John M. Pellock, "Understanding Co-Morbidities Affecting Children with Epilepsy," *Neurology* 25, no 5, suppl. 2 (March 2004), abstract, https://n.neurology.org /content/62/5_suppl_2/S17; c) Amy E Williams, Julianne M Giust, William G Kronenberger, and David W Dunn, "Epilepsy and Attention-Deficit Hyperactivity Disorder: Links, Risks, and Challenges," *Neuropsychiatric Disease and Treatment* 12 (2016): 287–296, doi: 10.2147/NDT.S81549.

[163] Narration and interview with District Attorney Richard Sacks, in John Dower, dir. and writ., *I Don't Like Mondays,* (September Films, 2006), IMDb TV; Denise Noe, "Girl Who Shot Up Her School and Said 'I Don't Like Mondays,'" Crime Library, posted May 19, 2014, part 1, http://www.crime library.com/blog (pages discontinued).

[164] Fast, *Ceremonial Violence*, 73; Noe, "Girl Who Shot," part 1.

[165] Fast, *Ceremonial Violence*, 74; *New York Times*, "San Diego Girls Slays 2 with Rifle and Wounds Nine on School Grounds," 128, no. 44,113 (January 30, 1979): A10.

[166] John Durham, "Girl in Custody After Two Slain at School Here," *San Diego Union-Tribune*: from the archives, January 29, 1979, posted January 29, 2018, https://www.sandiegouniontribune.com/news/150-years/sd-me-150-years-january-29-htmlstory.html. The exact wording of this comment varies between reports. This version was selected because it was locally sourced and published on the actual day of event.

[167] "I Don't Like Mondays," *The Fine Art of Surfacing* (United Kingdom: Ensign, 1979).

[168] Noe, "Girl Who Shot," part 1. Or something to that effect; again, accounts vary. A deputy district attorney at a parole hearing described the ending of her second conversation with a newsman in this way: "And then she said something to him about wanting to shoot a pig, and hung up the phone." California Board of Prison Terms, Subsequent Parole Consideration Hearing in the Matter of Brenda Spencer, CDC Number W – 14944, California Institution for Women, Corona, August 13, 2009, 81, School Shooters. Info, s.v. "Brenda Spencer."

[169] Gene Cubbison, in Dower, *I Don't Like Mondays*.

[170] Fast, *Ceremonial Violence*, 68-69; Eric D. Hart, *Does Anybody Like Mondays? The Brenda Spencer Murder Case* (Hart Publishing, 2012), chap. 2, Kindle Cloud Reader; Noe, "Brenda Spencer, The Girl Who Shot," pt. 1.

[171] Comments by Dot Spencer, in Dower, *I Don't Like Mondays*.

[172] Fast, *Ceremonial Violence*, 68; Hart, *Does Anybody Like Mondays?* chap. 12.

[173] Fast, *Ceremonial* Violence, 69; Langman, *School Shooters: Understanding High School,* 10.

[174] Statement by representative for Spencer, Christopher Cowan, Law Student, in California Board of Prison Terms, Subsequent Parole Consideration Hearing in the Matter of Brenda Spencer, CDC Number W – 14944, California Institution for Women, Frontera, September 27, 2005, 64, School Shooters. info, s.v. "Brenda Spencer."

[175] Comments by Dot Spencer, in Dower, *I Don't Like Mondays*.

[176] Hart, *Does Anybody Like Mondays?* chap. 12.

[177] California Board, Subsequent Parole Hearing for Brenda Spencer, 2005, 14.

[178] Funk, *How Rampage Killers Interpret Their Worlds*, Chapter Seven; Peter Langman, "Brenda Spencer: Sorting Out the Contradictions," version 1.1 (May 17, 2016), School Shooters .info.

[179] Hart, *Does Anybody Like Mondays?* chap. 12.

[180] Dot Spencer, in Dower, *I Don't Like Mondays*.

[181] Hart, *Does Anybody Like Mondays?* chap. 12.

[182] Ibid.

[183] Ibid, chap. 13, referring to *Los Angeles Times* article, "Lonely Girl Conceals a Violent Fantasy," February 4, 1979.

[184] Commissioner's summations of juvenile hall report and psychological evaluations, California Board of Prison Terms, Subsequent Parole Consideration Hearing in the Matter of Brenda Spencer, CDC Number W – 14944, California Institution for Women, Frontera, January 21, 1993, 15-17, 20-21; interchange between Spencer and presiding commissioner, in California Board, Parole Hearing for Spencer, 2009, 32-33; Hart, *Does Anybody Like Mondays?* chap. 13; Noe, "Brenda Spencer, The Girl Who Shot," pt. 3; *Washington Post*: "Classmates Say Alleged Sniper Seemed Lonely, Friendless Girl," originally published January 31, 1979, https://www.washingtonpost.com/archive/politics/1979/01/31/classmates-say-alleged-sniper-seemed-lonely-friendless-girl/54e24de0-c539-46e3-9518-8e1f488d7c52/.

[185] Referenced in these sources: a) Julie A. Dopheid, "Clinical Reviews: Recognizing and Treating Depression in Children and Adolescents," *American Journal of Health-System Pharmacy* 63, no. 3 (February 2006): 235-236; b) Edith "Emma" Dundon, "Adolescent Depression: A Metasynthesis," *Journal of Pediatric Health Care* 20, no. 6 (November/December 2006): 384-392; c) Michael J. Kofler, Michael R. McCart, Kristyn Zajac, Kenneth J. Ruggiero, Benjamin E. Saunders, and Dean G. Kilpatrick, "Depression and Delinquency Covariation in an Accelerated Longitudinal Sample of Adolescents," author manuscript, PubMed Central (PMC), U.S. Department of Health and Human Services (HHS), posted July 3, 2015, https://www.ncbi.nlm.nih.gov/pmc/articles/PMC4490863/; d) Naomi R Marmorstein, "Longitudinal Associations Between Depressive Symptoms and Alcohol Problems: The Influence of Comorbid Delinquent Behavior," *Addictive Behaviors* 35, no. 6 (June 2010): 564-571; e) Anita Thapar, Stephan Collishaw, Daniel S. Pine, and Ajay K. Thapar, "Depression in Adolescence," author manuscript, PMC, HHS, posted November 3, 2012, figure 1, https://www.ncbi.nlm.nih.gov/pmc/articles/PMC3488279/; f) A. Hyatt Williams, "Depression, Deviation and Acting Out In Adolescence," *Journal of Adolescence* 1, no. 4 (December 1978): 309-317.

[186] Dot Spencer, in Dower, *I Don't Like Mondays*; Hart, *Does Anybody Like Mondays?* chap. 16.

[187] Hart, *Does Anybody Like Mondays?* chap. 16.

[188] Dot Spencer, in Dower, *I Don't Like Mondays*.

[189] Hart, *Does Anybody Like Mondays?* chap. 13.

[190] Observation by Michael McGlinn, in Dower, *I Don't Like Mondays*. McGlinn also implied that Spencer's mother spent very little time with her. As her lawyer he, of course, became acquainted with the parents following the shooting and so he only would have been aware of the familial interactions during the period immediately preceding the rampage and thereafter. His

knowledge of the relationships around the time of the couple's breakup would have been cursory at best.

[191] Hart, *Does Anybody Like Mondays?* prologue, chap. 32.

[192] John T. Cacioppo and William Patrick, *Loneliness: Human Nature and the Need for Social Connection* (New York, NY: W. W. Norton & Company, 2008), 14-15.

[193] Elizabeth Kate Hughes, Eleonora Gullone, and Shaun D. Watson, "Emotional Functioning in Children and Adolescents with Elevated Depressive Symptoms," *Journal of Psychopathology and Behavioral Assessment* 33, no. 3 (September 2011): 335, referencing Jessica L. Tracy and Richard W. Robins, "Putting the Self Into Self-Conscious Emotions: A Theoretical Model," *Psychological Inquiry: An International Journal for the Advancement of Psychological Theory* 15, no. 2 (2004): 103-125.

[194] Hughes, Gullone, and Watson, "Emotional Functioning in Children," 337-343.

[195] For more on this idea, peruse Darcia Narvaez and Jenny L. Vaydich, "Moral Development and Behaviour under the Spotlight of the Neurobiological Sciences," *Journal of Moral Education* 37, no. 3 (September 2008): 289-313.

[196] Jorge Moll, Ricardo de Oliveira-Souza, Paul J. Eslinger, Ivanei E. Bramati, Janaína Mourão-Miranda, Pedro Angelo Andreiuolo, and Luiz Pessoa, "Neural Correlates of Moral Sensitivity: A Functional Magnetic Resonance Imaging Investigation of Basic and Moral Emotions," *Journal of Neuroscience* 22, no. 7 (April 2020): 2730.

[197] Fast, *Ceremonial Violence*, 75; narration, in Listen Notes (ParcastNetwork), "'I Don't Like Mondays' Part 2 – Brenda Spencer," *Female Criminals*, first aired May 15, 2019, https://www.listennotes.com/podcasts/female-criminals/i-dont-like-mondays-pt-2-hEb8vGSrBLz/. Spencer was 16 years of age and a junior in high school when she assaulted the school yard, meaning she would have been injured during or prior to her freshman year. Comments by Presiding Commissioner Lee, in California Board, Subsequent Parole Hearing for Brenda Spencer, 2005, 5, 6; Langman, *School Shooters: Understanding High School*, 10. Spencer has blamed her father for the head injury, claiming he kicked her in the head while severely beating her. Statement by Spencer to presiding commissioner in California Board, Subsequent Parole Hearing for Brenda Spencer, 2005, 10; statement by counsel to board in California Board, Subsequent Parole Hearing for Brenda Spencer, 2009, 93. Her brother, sister, and mother all say otherwise. Hart, *Does Anybody Like Mondays?* chap. 20, 21, 22.

[198] Hart, *Does Anybody Like Mondays?* chap. 20, 21, 22; narration, in Listen Notes, "'I Don't Like Mondays' Part 2."

[199] Fast, *Ceremonial Violence*, 75; narration, in Listen Notes Network, "'I Don't Like Mondays' Part 2."

[200] Fast, Ceremonial Violence, 75; Hart, *Does Anybody Like Mondays?* chap. 17. Spencer has stated that she had "headaches and blackout spells" prior to the bike mishap and she had hit her head on a wall suffering a cut above one eye when she was five and one-half years of age. Review of records by presiding commissioner, in California Board, Subsequent Parole Hearing for Spencer, 2005, 6, 10. Regardless, of timing, her epileptic condition and probable damage to her frontal lobe have been well documented.

[201] Interchange between Spencer and presiding commissioner, in California Board, Subsequent Parole Hearing for Spencer, 2005, 6; interchange between Spencer and presiding commissioner, in California Board, Subsequent Parole Hearing for Spencer, 2009, 34-35. The minutes for the hearing in 2009 spell the drug as "Tegritol."

[202] Brenda Spencer, Letter to ed. Jennifer Furio, in *Letters from Prison: Voices of Women Murderers* (New York, NY: Algora Publishing, 2001), 134.

[203] Robert Fisher, "A Revised Definition of Epilepsy," Epilepsy Foundation, written April 20, 2014, https://www.epilepsy.com/article/2014/4/revised-definition-epilepsy.

[204] Observation by David Basset, in Dower, *I Don't Like Mondays*.

[205] Research showing lack of causal connection between epileptic seizures and violent aggressive acts: a) Laura Marsh and Gregory L. Krauss, "Aggression and Violence in Patients with Epilepsy," *Epilepsy & Behavior* 1, no. 3 (June 2000): 160-168; b) James D. Seward, "Epilepsy, Violence and Aggression: Legal Implications," *Journal of Police and Criminal Psychology* 3, no. 1 (March 1987): 35–43; c) David M. Treiman, "Epilepsy and Violence: Medical and Legal Issues," *Epilepsia* 27, suppl. 2 (1986): 77-104; d) A. James Fessler and David M. Treiman, "Epilepsy and Aggression Proceed with Caution," *Neurology* 73, no. 21 (November 2009): 1720-1721.

[206] Martin J. Brodie, Frank Besag, Alan B. Ettinger, Marco Mula, Gabriella Gobbi, Stefano Comai, Albert P. Aldenkamp, and Bernhard J. Steinhoff, "Epilepsy, Antiepileptic Drugs, and Aggression: An Evidence-Based Review," *Pharmacological Reviews* 68, no. 3 (July 2016): 563–602; and Treiman, "Epilepsy and Violence," 81-98.

[207] Consider: Kousuke Kanemoto, Jun Kawasaki, and Etsuko Mori, "Brief Communication: Violence and Epilepsy: A Close Relation between Violence and Postictal Psychosis," *Epilepsia* 40, no. 1 (January 1999): 107-109; and David M. Treiman, "Psychobiology of Ictal Aggression," *Advances in Neurology* 55 (February 1991): 341-356. More on Spencer's presence of mind during the mass assault in *How Rampage Killers Interpret Their Worlds*, Chapter Seven.

[208] See: American Psychiatric Association, *DSM-5*, 466-467; and L. Tebartz van Elst, G. Woermann, L. Lemieux, P. J. Thompson, and M. R. Trimble, "Affective Aggression in Patients with Temporal Lobe Epilepsy: A

Quantitative MRI Study Of The Amygdala," *Brain: A Journal of Neurology* 123, no. 2 (February 2000): 234-235.

209 Paul J. Eslinger, Claire V. Flaherty-Craig, and Arthur L. Benton, "Developmental Outcomes after Early Prefrontal Cortex Damage," *Brain and Cognition* 55, no. 1 (June 2004): 100. Onset of the lesions was congenital to seven years with the ages of the subjects at the time of study ranging from 7 to 33 years of age. Data were derived from published reports. Ibid, 84-85, 88-89, table 1.

210 Paul J. Eslinger, "Review: Neurological and Neuropsychological Bases of Empathy," *European Neurology* 39, no. 4 (May 1998): 193-199.

211 Deputy commissioner summation of records, in California Board, Subsequent Parole Hearing for Brenda Spencer, 2009, 61. Refer to the following internal sources for clarification on sociopathy and psychopathy visa-vis ASPD: the biographical analysis for Patrick Purdy in Chapter Three, the opening portion of the next chapter (5), and the Appendix. Also: Curt R. Bartol and Anne M. Bartol, *Criminal Behavior: A Psychological Approach*, 9th ed. (San Francisco, CA: Prentice Hall, 2011), 171-175; and David T. Lykken, "The Case for Parental Licensure," in *Psychopathy: Antisocial, Criminal, and Violent Behavior*, ed. Theodore Millon, Erik Simonsen, Morten Birket-Smith, and Roger D. Davis (New York, NY: Guilford Press, 1998), 122-133.

212 Closing statement by attorney for Spencer, in California Board, Subsequent Parole Hearing for Brenda Spencer, 1993, 32. Hyphens added.

213 Tom Leonard, "'I Don't Like Mondays': School Shooter's Brenda Spencer's Bid for Freedom," *The Advertiser*, posted April 18, 2019, https://www.adelaidenow.com.au/lifestyle/sa-weekend/i-dont-like-mondays-school-shooter-brenda-spencers-bid-for-freedom/news-story/edc28524f11afaa7bbee4583d163955c.

214 James P McGee and Caren R. DeBernardo "The Classroom Avenger: A Behavioral Profile of School Based Shootings," *The Forensic Examiner* 8, nos. 5 and 6 (May-June 1999): 16-18.

215 The site's banner read: "Join the web's largest community for gothic-industrial culture." VampireFreaks.com, http://vampirefreaks.com/. Gill's participation was suspended by site administrators. Beta People Pill, s.v. "Kimveer Gill," under "Vampirefreaks Online Profile," last updated December 27, 2019, https://peoplepill.com/. A site with the same name continues but it is now merely a costume shop and no longer an imaginary on-line coven of enthusiasts for the dark arts.

216 Ros Taylor and Agencies, "College Gunman Wanted to Die 'in a Hail of Gunfire.'" *Guardian*, posted September 14, 2006, http://www.theguardian.com/world/2006/sep/14/highereducation.internationaleducationnews.

217 Kimveer Gill, *fatality666*, VampireFreaks.com (scans of printed pages) and (electronic version), Peter Langman, transcriber, School Shooters .info, s.v.

"Kimveer Gill." Unless otherwise noted, all quotations from Gill retain the same spelling and punctuation as his posts.

[218] London, UK: EMI Records, Ltd., 1982

[219] Gill, *fatality666,* profile.

[220] Gill, *fatality666.*

[221] Ibid.

[222] Ibid.

[223] Ibid.

[224] Ibid.

[225] Gill, *fatality666*. Ellipsis after "happening" added to show sentences left out of quotation.

[226] Murderpedia, s.v. "Patrick Henry Sherrill"; Mara Bovsun, "Mailman Massacre: 14 Die After Patrick Sherrill 'Goes Postal' in 1986 Shootings," *New York Daily News*, posted August 15, 2010, http://www.nydailynews.com/news/crime/mailman-massacre-14-die-patrick-sherrill-postal-1986-shootings-article-1.204101; Storer Rowley, "Postal Worker Kills 14, Himself," *Chicago Tribune*, posted August 21, 1986, http://articles.chicagotribune.com/1986-08-21/news/8603020471_1_vince-furlong-postal-workers-letter-carrier. More on Sherrill in *How Rampage Killers Interpret Their World.*

[227] Gill, *fatality666.*

[228] Ibid, s.vv. "February 15, 2006," "May 3, 2006," "May 20, 2006," "July 13, 2006," "August 24, 2006."

[229] Gill, *fatality666*. Ellipses represent passages edited for brevity.

[230] It is the seventh cut on *The Funeral Album* (Century Media, released May 2005). As the name implies, it was the last recording by the ensemble. Other than artistic expression there is no evidence that the band encouraged violence.

[231] Oslo District Court, Indictment against Anders Behring Breivik, March 7, 2012, and Judgment of Anders Behring Breivik, August 24, 2012, both on Murderpedia, s.v. "Anders Behring Breivik." Due to confusion immediately following the killings and difficult conditions when searching for the dead, the initial casualty reports deaths ranged from 68 to 93. American Broadcasting Company (ABC) News, "Norway Terror Attacks Toll Upped to 87: Norwegian Man Arrested," ABC, posted July 22, 2011, https://abcnews.go.com/Blotter/oslo-norway-terror-attacks-toll-upped-87-norwegian/story?id=14135844; Views and News Staff, "Death Toll Declines after Confusion," News in English.no, posted July 26, 2011, https://www.newsinenglish.no/2011/07/26/death-toll-declines-after-early-confusion/.

[232] *Daily Mail* Reporter, "Norwegian Mass killer Anders Breivik Pleads to Be Let Out of Prison to Attend His Mother's Funeral," *Daily Mail*, posted March 23, 2013, updated March 25, 2013, http://www.dailymail.co.uk/news/article-

2298067/Anders-Breivik-Norwegian-mass-killer-pleads-let-prison-attend-mothers-funeral.html; Kelsey Campbell-Dollaghan, "Norway's Lovely Memorial to the Worst Mass Shooting in Modern History," Gizmodo, posted March 5, 2014, http://gizmodo.com/norways-lovely-memorial-to-the-worst-mass-shooting-in-1536842749.

[233] Stephanie Pappas, "What 'Insanity' Means for Norwegian Gunman," *Live Science*, posted April 18, 2012, http://www.livescience.com/19767-insanity-norway-shooting-trial.html.

[234] Oslo District Court (Oslo tingrett), Judgment of Anders Behring Breivik, August 24, 2012, under "6.2 The work and Conclusions of The Expert Witnesses."

[235] Ibid, under "6.3 On psychosis in General," "6.4 Paranoid Schizophrenia," "6.5 Paranoid Psychosis," "6.6 Other Health Personnel," "6.8 Summary."

[236] Anders Breivik, "Anders Breivik's Opening Statement, Day 2, April 17, 2012," trans. Andrew Hamilton, Counter-Currents Publishing, originally posted in *North American New Right*, May 11, 2012, http://www.counter-currents.com /2012/05/anders-breiviks-opening-statement/print/. Intended as a political polemic published by extremists, this translation, admittedly, may be biased. However, it generally aligns with the content in another source: Anders Behring Breivik Court Statement 2012-04-17 (Opening Statement), in Murderpedia, s.v. "Anders Behring Breivik." It corresponds with summaries in a news report and an historical account. Diana Magnay, "Admitted Norway killer Boasts of 'Spectacular Political Attack,' Cable News Network (CNN), posted April 17, 2012, https://www.cnn.com/2012/04/17/world/europe/ norway-breivik-trial/index. html; Douglas O. Linder, "Anders Breivik (Norway Massacre) Trial: An Account," Famous Trials, posted 2020, under "The Trial," https://famous-trials.com/Breivik/2570-anders-breivik-norway-massacre-trial-an-account. In addition, it aligns in tone, structure, and much of the phrasing with his manifesto, *2083 – A European Declaration of Independence*, some of which is presented in *How Rampage Killers Interpret Their Worlds*, Chapter Seven. Breivik's obsessional focus on racial heritage and nationalism in his first presentation for his trial is obvious. The version used was quoted because it seemed to be the most complete.

[237] British Broadcasting Corporation (BBC), "Timeline: How Norway's Terror Attacks Unfolded," posted April 17, 2012, updated December 29, 2019, https://www.bbc.com/news/world-europe-14260297; Beatrice de Graaf, Liesbeth van der Heide, Sabine Wanmaker, and Daan Weggemans, *The Anders Behring Breivik Trial: Performing Justice, Defending Democracy* (International Centre for Counterterrorism – The Hague: June 2013), 3, https://icct.nl/publication/the-anders-behring-breivik-trial-performing-justice-defending-democracy/; Cato Hemmingby and Tore Bjørgo, "Terrorist Target Selection: The Case of Anders Behring Breivik," *Perspectives on Terrorism*

12, no. 6 (December 2018): 169-170; ABC News, "Norway Terror Attacks Toll; Åsne Seierstad, trans. Sarah Death, *One of Us: The Story of Anders Breivik and the Massacre in Norway* (New York: Farrar, Straus, and Giroux, 2014), pt. 1, Kindle Cloud.

[238] Hemmingby and Bjørgo, "Terrorist Target Selection," 170.

[239] Overall content for this sentence: Sean Flynn, "Is He Coming? Is He? Oh God, I think He Is," *GQ*, posted July 30, 2012, https://www.gq.com/story/anders-behring-breivik-norway-massacre-story; Hemmingby and Bjørgo, "Terrorist Target Selection," 168; Jacob Aasland Ravndal, "A Post-Trial Profile of Anders Behring Breivik," *CTC Sentinel* (published by the Combating Terrorism Center at West Point) 5, no. 10 (October 2012): 17-18. Comments by Breivik during court proceedings: "political indoctrination," "cultural Marxists," from Ravndal, "A Post-Trial Profile," 18. All other succeeding excerpts or paraphrases or descriptions from Oslo District Court, no: 11-188627 MED-05 (the trial for the bombing and subsequent shooting), unless otherwise sourced, are from transcripts by TV2 Norway, Breivik Report, http://ecofeminist-v-breivik.weebly.com/oslo-dist-crt-trial.html.

[240] Anders Breivik witness testimony, in TV2 Norway, Breivik Report, Oslo District Court: no: 11-188627 MED-05, s.v. "20 April 2012, 11:56 a.m."

[241] Brian Palmer, "What Happens at a Norwegian Political Youth Camp?" *Slate*, posted July 25, 2011, https://slate.com/news-and-politics/2011/07/norway-killing-spree-questions-about-political-youth-camps-christian-martyrs-and-confirmed-death-tolls.html.

[242] 22nd of July Court Transcript, "Transcript 2012-08-24," Oslo District Court (24 August 2012), as translated, in Graaf, Heide, Wanmaker, and Weggemans, *The Anders Behring Breivik Trial*," 9.

[243] Helen Pidd, "Anders Breivik Prefers Execution over 'Pathetic' Jail Term," *Guardian*, posted April 18, 2012, https://www.theguardian.com/world/2012/apr/18/anders-breivik-execution-pathetic-jail-term.

[244] Max Fisher, "A Different Justice: Why Anders Breivik Only Got 21 Years for Killing 77 People," *Atlantic*, posted August 24, 2012, https://www.theatlantic.com/international/archive/2012/08/a-different-justice-why-anders-breivik-only-got-21-years-for-killing-77-people/261532/; Smith-Spark, "Norway Killer Anders Breivik Ruled Sane, Given 21-Year Prison Term."

[245] In Sinead O'Carroll, "21-Year-Sentence Does Not Mean Breivik Will Walk Free in 2033. Here's Why: There Is Actually No Limit to the Number of Times the Court Can Extend the Sentence," *Journal*, posted August 24, 2012, http://www.thejournal.ie/21-years-breivik-trial-sentence-norway-570722-Aug2012/. Also, see Agence France-Presse (AFP), "Why Norway's maximum sentence is just 21 years," *The Local*, posted August 24, 2012, https://www.thelocal.no/20120824/why-norways-maximum-sentence-is-just-21-years.

[246] O'Carroll, "21-Year-Sentence Does Not Mean Breivik Will Walk Free."

[247] Global Legal Research Directorate, *Norway: Norwegian Criminal Law and the July 22, 2011 Massacre*, (The Law Library of Congress, August 2011), 4-5, https://tile.loc.gov/storage-services/service/ll/llglrd/2018298786/2018298786.pdf.

[248] The Legal Definition (United Nations Prevention and Punishment of the Crime of Genocide), in *Genocide: A Reader*, ed. Jens Meierhenrich (Oxford University Press, 2014), 62-63.

[249] The Legal Definition Revised (Rome Statute of the International Criminal Court and Elements of Crimes), in *Genocide: A Reader*, 68.

[250] As interpreted by Professor William Schabas, an expert on international law and human rights, in Global Legal Research Directorate, *Norway: Norwegian Criminal Law and the July 22, 2011 Massacre*, (The Law Library of Congress, August 2011), 4-5, https://tile.loc.gov/storage-services/service/ll/llglrd/2018298786/2018298786.pdf.

[251] AP, "Anders Breivik Questioned about 'Knights Templar' Group," *Independent*, posted April 18, 2012, http://www.independent.co.uk/news/world/europe/anders-breivik-questioned-about-knights-templar-group-7657101.html; Editors of Encyclopedia Britannica, "Templar Religious Military Order," *Encyclopedia Britannica*, updated May 11, 2006; Kelly Knauer, ed., *Secret Societies: Decoding the Myths and Facts of History's Most Mysterious Organizations* (New York, NY: Time Inc. Books, 2016), 9-10.

[252] Brian Van Brunt and W. Scott Lewis, "Costuming, Misogyny, and Objectification as Risk Factors in Targeted Violence," *Violence and Gender* 1, no. 1 (December 2014): fig. 2, https://cdn.nabita.org/website-media/nabita.org/wordpress/wp-content/uploads/2016/08/gender-and-violence.pdf; Murderpedia, "Anders Behring Breivik," s.v. "Anders Behring Breivik"

[253] Psychiatrist Michael Setsaas, in Neil Syson, "Killer Breivik's Uniform a Sham," *Sun*, posted August 1, 2011, https://www.thesun.co.uk/archives/news/693773/killer-breiviks-uniform-a-sham/. Spelling and punctuation (except ellipsis) copied from *Sun*.

[254] Kaczynski's case is summarized on an FBI webpage that states early on: "The man that the world would eventually know as Theodore Kaczynski came to our attention in 1978 with the explosion of his first, primitive homemade bomb at a Chicago university. Over the next 17 years, he mailed or hand delivered a series of increasingly sophisticated bombs that killed three Americans and injured 24 more. Along the way, he sowed fear and panic, even threatening to blow up airliners in flight." FBI: History, "Unabomber," https://www.fbi.gov/history/famous-cases/unabomber. The page has a video with commentary by agents that shows his cabin. A disconcerting chronicle of his pivot toward solitude and murder is offered by an acquaintance who is also a former academician. See Alston Chase, "Harvard and the Making of

the Unabomber," *Atlantic*, posted June 2000, https://www.theatlantic.com/magazine/archive/2000/06/harvard-and-the-making-of-the-unabomber/378239/. The manifesto was published in a special report by the *Washington Post*, https://www.washingtonpost.com/wp-srv/national/longterm/unabomber/ manifesto.text.htm.

[255] BBC News, "'Breivik Manifesto' Details Chilling Attack Preparation," posted July 24, 2011, http://www.bbc.com/news/world-europe-14267007; Andrew Berwick [presumably intended as an anglicized version of Ander Breivik], *2083: A European Declaration of Independence* (London, UK: self-pub, 2011), https://www.rai.it/dl/docs/13115255886322083-A-European-Declaration -of-Independence.pdf; William Boston, "Killer's Manifesto: The Politics Behind the Norway Slaughter," *Time*, posted July 24, 2011; http://content.time.com/time/world/article/ 0,8599,2084901,00.html; Macy Halford, "Anders Breivik, Reader," *New Yorker*, posted July 24, 2011, https://www.newyorker.com/books/page-turner/anders-breivik-reader; Mark Juergensmeyer, "Why the Year 2083 Is the Title of Norwegian Terrorist Anders Breivik's Manifesto," *Huffington Post*, posted July 28, 2011, updated August 27, 2011, http://www.huffingtonpost.com/mark-juergensmeyer/ anders-breivik-manifesto_b_910229.html; Karl Ove Knausgaard, "Letter from Norway: The Inexplicable – Inside the Mind of a Mass Killer," *New Yorker*, posted May 25, 2015, http://www.newyorker.com/magazine/2015/ 05/25/the-inexplicable; Robert Mackey, "Online, Clues to a Suspected Attacker's Motives," *Lede*, posted July 23, 2011, https://archive .nytimes. com/thelede.blogs.nytimes.com/2011/07/23/scouring-the-web-for-clues-to-a-suspected-attackers-motives/.

[256] Stephen A. Diamond, "Psychosis – The Breivik Verdict: Forensic Commentary," *Psychology Today*, posted August 26, 2012, https://www.psychologytoday.com/us/blog/evil-deeds/201208/the-breivik-verdict-forensic-commentary.

[257] Ibid.

[258] See "The Insanity Defense and the Question of Competence," later in this chapter.

[259] AP, "Anders Breivik Questioned"; Graaf, Heide, Wanmaker, and Weggemans, *The Andres Behring Breivik Trial*, 9.

[260] BBC, "Anders Breivik Pleads Not Guilty at Norway Murder Trial," posted April 16, 2012, http://www.bbc.com/news/world-europe-17724535.

[261] Ian Johnson and Alastair Jamieson, "Anders Breivik to Norway Court: I Killed 77 People but Am Not Guilty," NBC News, posted April 16, 2012, http://worldnews.nbcnews.com/_news/2012/04/16/11220262-anders-breivik -to-norway-court-i-killed-77-people-but-am-not-guilty?lite; Tony Paterson, "A Clenched Fist and A Smirk as Court Declares Anders Breivik Sane," *Independent News*, posted August 24, 2012, http://www.independent.co.uk/

news/world/europe/a-clenched-fist-and-a-smirk-as-court-declares-anders-breivik-sane-8079554.html.

[262] James Waller, *Becoming Evil: How Ordinary People Commit Genocide and Mass Killing* (New York, NY: Oxford University Press, 2002), 184

[263] Ibid.

[264] Donald G. Dutton, Katherine R. White, and Dan Fogarty, "Paranoid Thinking in Mass Shooters," *Aggression and Violent Behavior* 18, no. 5 (September–October 2013): 551.

[265] John Junginger, Judith Parks-Levy, and Lynanne McGuire, "Delusions and Symptom-Consistent Violence," *Psychiatric Services* 49, no. 2 (February 1988): 218.

[266] Henry Richards, "Evil Intent: Violence and Disorders of the Will," in *Psychopathy: Antisocial, Criminal, and Violent Behavior*, 74.

[267] Video and audio of interview with Dr. Reid, court appointed psychiatrist in 2014, in Daily Mail TV, "Chilling James Homes Sanity Evaluation Video," posted February 7, 2019, https://www.dailymail.co.uk/video/dailymailtv/video-1858640/Video-Chilling-video-James-Holmes-sanity-evaluation. html.

[268] "During my examination of Mr. Homes, I obtained more information from him regarding the concept of human capital. … Mr. Holmes explained that it is more important for a killer to kill more than just one person because it increases the worth of the person doing the killing in a mathematical way. He stated that it included the following factors:

1. number of people killed
2. your own perception of what life is worth
3. your contribution to society (e.g., in a meaningful and positive way)"

James L. Metzner, James Eagan Holmes: Sanity Evaluation, Arapahoe Colorado Mental Health Institute at Pueblo, Colorado, Case no. 12CR1522, September 3, 2013, 10, School Shooters .info, s.v. "James Holmes." Punctuated as written.

[269] *The Week*, compiled from reports by James Dao, Dan Frosch, Jack Healy, and Serge F. Kovaleski in the *New York Times* and by Joel Achenbach, David A. Fabrenthold, Thomas Heath, and Carol D. Leonnig in the *Washington Post*, "The Last Word: Who Is James Holmes? The Gunman Who Allegedly Killed 12 People at a Colorado Movie Theatre Was Once Bound for Great Things," 12, no. 577 (August 3, 2012): 41.

[270] Evidenced by data and explanatory descriptions presented in: a) Renato Alarcón, Edward F. Foulks, and Mark Vakkur, *Personality Disorders and Culture: Clinical and Conceptual Interactions* (New York, NY: John Wiley & Sons, Inc., 1998), 87-89; b) Lynn F. Alden, Judith M. Laposa, and Charles T. Taylor, "Avoidant Personality Disorder," in *Practitioners Guide to Evidence-Based Psychotherapy*, ed. Jane E. Fisher and William T. O'Donohue (New York, NY: Springer Science and Business Media, 2006),

115-121; c) Regina T. Dolan-Sewell, Robert F. Krueger and M. Tracie Shea. "Co-Occurrence with Syndrome Disorders," in *Handbook of Personality Disorders: Theory, Research, and Treatment*, ed. W. John Livesley, (New York, NY: The Guilford Press, 2001), 84-104; d) Mark F. Lenzenweger, Michael C. Lane, Armand. W. Loranger, and Ronald Kessler, "DSM-IV Personality Disorders in the National Comorbidity Survey Replication," *Biological Psychiatry: A Journal of Neuroscience and Therapeutics* 62, no. 6 (September 15, 2007), 553-564, posted online January 9, 2007, https://www.ncbi.nlm.nih.gov/pmc/articles/PMC2044500/; e) Out of the Fog, "Personality Disorder Statistics," 2007-2015, http:// outofthefog. website/personality-disorder-statistics/; f) Thomas Widiger and James H. Rogers, "Prevalence and Comorbidity of Personality Disorders," *Psychiatric Annals* 19, no. 3 (March 1989): 132-136.

[271] D. L. Fogelson, R.A. Asarnow, C.A. Sugar, K.L. Subotnik, K.C. Jacobson, M.C. Neale, K.S. Kendler, H. Kuppinger, and Keith H. Nuechterlein, "Avoidant Personality Disorder Symptoms in First-Degree Relatives of Schizophrenia Patients Predict Performance of Neurocognitive Measurers: The UCLA Family Study," *Schizophrenia Research* 120, no. 1-3 (July 2010): 113.

[272] D. L. Folgeson, K.H. Nuechterlein, R. A. Asarnow, D. L. Payne, K. L. Subotnik, K. C. Jacobson, M. C. Neale, and K. S. Kendler, "Avoidant Personality Disorder is a Separable Schizophrenia Spectrum Personality Disorder when Controlling for the Presence of Paranoid Schizotypal Personality Disorders – The UCLA Family Study," *Schizophrenia Research* 91, no. 1-3 (March 2001), 192-199, posted online February 15, 2007, abstract and under "Discussion," doi: 10.1016/j.schres.2006.12.023.

[273] Charles A. Sanislow, Ellen Bartolini, and Emma C. Zoloth, "Avoidant Personality Disorder," in *Encyclopedia of Human Behavior*, 2nd ed., ed. V. S. Rmachandran, (San Diego, CA: Academic Press, 2012), 260. The mutuality is also discussed at length in Michelle L. Esterberg, Sandra M. Goulding, and Elaine F. Walker, "Cluster A Personality Disorders: Schizotypal, Schizoid, and Paranoid Personality Disorders in Childhood and Adolescence," *Journal of Psychopathology and Behavioral Assessment* 32, no. 4 (December 2010): 515-528, doi: 10.1007/s10862-010-9183-8.

[274] In this paragraph all references to writings are from James Holmes, *Computation Book: Course of Life*, Colorado Judicial Department: James Holmes 12CR1522, Peoples Exhibit #341, 9, 11-13, https://assets .document cloud.org/documents/2089833/james-holmes-notebook.pdf. Pagination notes here and elsewhere for this diary correspond to pdf, not numbers in original, which appear sporadic.

[275] Jordan Steffen, "A Guide to Mental Health Professionals Who Saw Theater Shooting Gunman," *Denver Post*: posted July 8, 2015, under "Unnamed

Counselor," https://www.denverpost.com/2015/07/10/a-guide-to-mental-health-professionals-who-saw-theater-shooting-gunman/.

[276] Ann O'Neill, "James Holmes' Life Story Didn't Sway Jury," CNN, posted August 11, 2015, under "How a Boy 'Lost His Joy,'" http://www.cnn.com/2015/08/02/us/13th-juror-james-holmes-aurora-shooting/.

[277] Carol D. Leonnig and Joel Achenbach, "James Holmes, Held in Colorado Shooting, Known as Shy but Pleasant," *Washington Post*, posted July 20, 201, https://www.washingtonpost.com/national/health-science/james-eagan-holmes-held-in-colorado-shooting/2012/07/20/gJQA213UyW_story.html.

[278] CNN Wire, "From Happy Boy to Mass Murderer: James Holmes' Life Story Weighed by Jury," Q13 Fox, posted August 3, 2015, under "A Traumatic Move," http://q13fox.com/2015/08/03/from-happy-boy-to-mass-murderer-james-holmes-life-story-weighed-by-jury/; O'Neill, "James Holmes' Life," under "How a 'Boy Lost.'"

[279] O'Neill, "James Holmes Life," under "A traumatic move."

[280] American Psychiatric Association, *DSM-5*, 765, 769.

[281] Steffen, "A Guide to Mental Health Professionals," under "Mel Lipsey."

[282] James L. Metzner, James Eagan Holmes: Sanity Evaluation, 41.

[283] James Holmes, *Computation Book: Course of Life*, 30.

[284] American Psychiatric Association, *DSM-5*, 765-766, 780.

[285] Recruit for the neuroscience program, in Erica Goode, Serge F. Kovaleski, Jack Healy, and Dan Frosch, "Before Gunfire, Hints of 'Bad News,'" *New York Times*, posted August 26, 2012, under "Cool and Detached," http://www.nytimes.com/2012/08/27/us/before-gunfire-in-colorado-theater-hints-of-bad-news-about-james-holmes.html.

[286] Goode, Kovaleski, Healy, and Frosch, "Before Gunfire.'"

[287] Dan Frosch, "James Holmes's Psychiatrist Testifies in Colorado Theatre Shooting Trial: Lynne Fenton Treated Him While He Was a Student at the University of Colorado, Denver," *Wall Street Journal*, updated June 16, 2015, http://www.wsj.com/articles/james-holmess-psychiatrist-testifies-in-colorado-theater-shooting-trial-1434484324.

[288] American Psychiatric Association, *DSM-5*, 765-766.

[289] *Denver Post*, "James Holmes Was Among Elite in Neuroscience before Aurora Theater Massacre," posted August 4, 2012, updated May 1, 2016, http://www.denverpost.com/2012/08/04/james-holmes-was-among-elite-in-neuroscience-before-aurora-theater-massacre/; Goode, Kovaleski, Healy, and Frosch, "Before Gunfire," under "Cool and Detached"; Jack Healy and Serge F. Kovaleski, "Before and After Massacre, Puzzles Line Suspect's Path," *New York Times*, posted July 21, 2012, http://www.nytimes.com/2012/07/22/us/pain-and-puzzles-in-wake-of-deadly-colorado-attack.html; *The Week*, "The Last Word: Who is James Holmes?" 40.

[290] *The Week*, "The Last Word: Who is James?" 40.

[291] CNN Wire, "From Happy Boy to Mass Murderer," under "A Traumatic Move"; O'Neill, "James Holmes' Life Story," under "How a 'Boy Lost'"; Dan Frosch, "James Holmes's Psychiatrist Testifies"; Jason Silverstein, "James Holmes' Ex-Girlfriend Testifies in Death Penalty Trial," *New York Daily News*, updated June 11, 2015, http://www.nydailynews.com/news/national/james-holmes-ex-girlfriend-testifies-shooting-trial-article-1.2254303; *The Week*, "The Last Word: Who is James?" 41.

[292] Jack Healy, "James Holmes's Ex-Girlfriend Recalls Awkwardness and Ghoulish Remarks," *New York Times*, posted June 11, 2015, https://www.nytimes.com/2015/06/12/us/at-james-homes-colorado-theater-shooting-trial-ex-girlfriend-recalls-unnerving-comments.html.

[293] Gargi Datta, in AP, "Colorado Shooter's Ex-Girlfriend Describes Him as 'Shy and Closed Off,'" CBS News, posted June 10, 2015, http://www.cbsnews.com/news/james-holmes-trial-colorado-shooter-ex-girlfriend-describes-him-as-shy/.

[294] American Psychiatric Association, *DSM-5*, 765-766; AP, "Colorado Shooter's Ex-Girlfriend Describes Him"; Datta, in Anica Padilla, "Theater Shooting Trial: James Holmes' Ex-Girlfriend Says, 'He Liked Me More Than I Liked Him,'" 7 News, posted June 10, 2015, updated, June 11, 2015, http://www.thedenverchannel.com/news/movie-theater-shooting/theater-shooting-trial-james-holmes-ex-girlfriend-gargi-datta-testifies-wednesday.

[295] Adult Friend Finder, http://adultfriendfinder.com/; *The Week*, "The Last Word: Who is James?" 41.

[296] Leonnig and Achenbach, "James Holmes, Held in Colorado Shooting,"; *The Week*, "The Last Word: Who is James?" 41.

[297] Holmes, *Computation Book: Course of Life*, 6.

[298] Ibid, cover.

[299] Ibid, 9.

[300] Ibid, 10.

[301] Ibid, 17, underlining in original.

[302] Ibid, 18-25.

[303] Ibid, 33, underlining in original.

[304] American Psychiatric Association, *DSM-5*, 766.

[305] Holmes, *Computation Book: Course of Life*, 10.

[306] a) Joseph J. Campos, Rosemary G. Campos, and Karen C. Barrett, "Emergent Themes in the Study of Emotional Development and Emotion Regulation," *Developmental Psychology* 25, no. 3 (May 1989): 397-40; b) Stephan Moratti, "Low Emotional Arousal in Depression as Explained by the Motivated Attention Approach," *Escritos de Psicología* 5, no. 2 (May-August 2012): 20-26, https://www.researchgate.net/publication/230816311_Low_emotional_arousal_in_depression_as_explained_by_the_motivated_attention_approach/link/00463532373d5084bc000000/download; c) Rolland S.

Parker, "Forensic Neuropsychology and Claims of Personal Injury," in *Disorders of Executive Functions: Civil and Criminal Law Applications* ed. Harold V. Hall and Robert J. Sbordone, (Boca Raton, FL, St. Lucie Press, 1998), 9-10; d) Jonathan Waldron and Angela Scarpa "Biosocial Perspective of Proactive Aggression: Applications to Perpetuators of Mass Shootings," in *The Wiley Handbook of the Psychology of Mass Shootings*, ed. Laura C. Wilson (Malden, MA: John Wiley & Sons, 2017), 79.

[307] Hugo Critchley, "Review: Electrodermal Responses: What Happens in the Brain," *Neuroscientist*, posted April 1, 2002, abstract, https://doi.org/10.1177/107385840200800209.

[308] Hans J. Eysenck, *The Biological Basis of Personality* (New Brunswick, NJ: Transaction Publishers, 2006), 245-249.

[309] Waldron and Scarpa, "Biosocial Perspective of Proactive Aggression," 79.

[310] Holmes, *Computation Book: Course of Life*, 31-32.

[311] Eric Berne, frequently lauded as the father of transactional analysis, popularized the perspective that people protect their self-image or advance personal agendas by plotting encounters according to psychological dramas of which they are barely aware. His landmark book on the subject is *Games People Play* (New York, NY: Ballantine Books, 1964). While Berne's theoretical basis can be criticized as a reworking of Freud's ideas on subconscious motivations, it would be difficult to deny that individuals engage in repetitive social contests to preserve a sense of well-being or engage in one-upmanship. In *Games* Berne calls out a charade he calls "Wooden Leg" where a person expects others to overlook his or her shortcomings because they supposedly cannot be helped due to some defect. *Games People Play*, 159-162. He delivers the following commentary: "The 'Plea of Insanity,' played as a legal game is acceptable to American culture and is different from the almost universally respected principle that an individual may be suffering from a psychosis so profound that no reasonable person would expect him to be responsible for his actions. In Japan drunkenness, and in Russia war-time military service are accepted as excuses for evading responsibility for all kinds of outrageous behavior…." Ibid, 159-160. The following articles scrutinize the moral formulations of a psychotic mind or the ways in which intellectual dishonesty may be associated with aggression: a) Anita L. Allen, Mental Disorders and the "System Of Judgmental Responsibility," *Boston University Law Review* 90 no. 2 (April 2010), 621-640; b) Gregory Bateson, Don D. Jackson, Jay Haley, and John Weakland, "Toward a Theory of Schizophrenia," *Behavioral Science* 1 no. 4 (1956), 251-254; c) Richard P. Bentall, Georgina Rowse, Nick Shryane, Peter Kinderman, Robert Howard, Nigel Blackwood, Rosie Moore, and Rhiannon Corcoran, "The Cognitive and Affective Structure of Paranoid Delusions: A Transdiagnostic Investigation of Patients with Schizophrenia Spectrum

Disorders and Depression," *Archives of General Psychiatry* 66 no. 3 (2009): 236-247; d) Quinn Hiroshi Gibson, "Self-deception in and out of Illness: Are Some Subjects Responsible for Their Delusions?" *Palgrave Communication* 3, no. 15 (October 2017), https://doi.org/10.1057/s41599-017-0017-0.

[312] Holmes, *Course of Life*, 30-32.

[313] Ibid, 32.

[314] For support of that assertion: a) Katherine S. Lau, "Exploring Narcissism, Psychopathy, and Machiavellianism in Youth: An Examination of Associations with Antisocial Behavior and Aggression" (master's thesis, University of New Orleans, 2010), 11-22, 63-65; b) Jon T. Mandracchia and Robert D. Morgan, "Understanding Criminals' Thinking: Further Examination of the Measure of Offender Thinking Styles–Revised," *Assessment* 18, no. 4 (December 2011), 448-449; c) Jon T. Mandracchia, Robert D. Morgan, Sheila Garos, and Travis Garland, "Inmate Thinking Patterns: An Empirical Investigation," *Criminal Justice and Behavior* 34, no. 8, (August 2007), 1029-1043; d) Glenn D. Walters, "Criminal Thinking," in *Personality, Personality Disorder, and Violence*, ed. Mary McMurran and Richard Howard (West-Sussex, UK: John Wiley & Sons, Ltd., 2009), 281-295.

[315] Stanton E. Samenow, *Inside the Criminal Mind* (New York, NY: Crown Publishers, 1984), 87.

[316] Clayton Sandell with Carol McKinley, "Psychiatrist Called James Holmes 'Danger to the Public' before Killings," ABC News, posted April 5, 2013, https://abcnews.go.com/blogs/headlines/2013/04/psychiatrist-called-james-holmes-danger-to-the-public-before-killings/.

[317] Video of legal analyst observations, in CBS News, "Co. Theater Shooting Trial: Holmes Psychiatrist Takes the Stand," embedded in AP, CBS News, "Strained Family Relationships Cut to Heart of Theater Gunman's Defense," posted July 6, 2015, https://www.cbsnews.com/news/strained-family-relationships-cut-to-heart-of-theater-gunman-james-homles-defense/; Sandell with McKinley, "Psychiatrist Called James Holmes 'Danger to the Public.'"

[318] As phrased in Claudia Koerner, "James Holmes Psychiatrist Breaks Silence in Court, Tells of His Desire to Kill," *BuzzFeed.News*, posted June 16, 2015, https://www.buzzfeednews.com/article/claudiakoerner/psychiatrist-james-holmes-thought-about-killing-3-or-4-times.

[319] "Koerner, "James Holmes Psychiatrist Breaks Silence."

[320] Healy and Kovaleski, "Before and After Massacre."

[321] Ibid.

[322] Gordon Rayner, Mark Hughes, and Nick Allen. "Batman Cinema Shooting: Killer Said He Was 'The Joker," *Telegraph*, posted July 20, 2012,

http://www.telegraph.co.uk/news/worldnews/northamerica/usa/9416606/Batman-cinema-shooting-killer-said-he-was-The-Joker.html.

[323] Nina Strochlic, "James Holmes: 6 Reported Facts about the Alleged Aurora Shooter," *Daily Beast*, posted July 23, 2012, under "He Began Preparations Two Months Ago," https://www.thedailybeast.com/james-holmes-6-reported-facts-about-the-alleged-aurora-shooter; *The Week*, "The Last Word: Who Is James?" 41.

[324] There were two slightly distinct descriptions: "bizarre, guttural, freakish at best," Strochlic, "James Holmes: 6 Reported Facts," under "He Began Preparations"; "It was a very bass, very deep-sounding guttural voice … bizarre or freakish," *The Week*, "The Last Word: Who Is James?" 41.

[325] *The Week*, "The Last Word: Who Is James?" 41.

[326] Strochlic, "James Holmes: 6 Reported Facts," under "He Began Preparations"; *The Week*, "The Last Word: Who Is James?" 41.

[327] Stephen Singular and Joyce Singular, *The Spiral Notebook: The Aurora Shooter and the Epidemic of Mass Violence Committed by American Youth* (Berkley, CA: Counterpoint, 2015), 109-111; Jana Winter, "Exclusive: Movie Massacre Suspect Sent Chilling Notebook to Psychiatrist before Attack," Fox News.com, posted July 25, 2012, https://www.foxnews.com/us/exclusive-movie-massacre-suspect-sent-chilling-notebook-to-psychiatrist-before-attack.

[328] Ann O'Neill, Ana Cabrera and Sara Weisfeldt, "A Look Inside the 'Broken' Mind of James Holmes," CNN, updated June 10, 2015, under "James Holmes Trial: His Parents, Changing Hair Color, "Medication," https://www.cnn.com/2015/06/05/us/james-holmes-theater-shooting-trial/index.html.

[329] Sadie Gunman, "The Colorado Theater Shooter Gave Some Horrifying Answers During His Psych Evaluation," *Business Insider*, posted June 2, 2015, https://www.businessinsider.com/the-colorado-theater-shooter-gave-some-horrifying-answers-during-his-psych-evaluation-2015-6.

[330] Sky News US Team, "Cinema Killer Called Hospital Before Rampage," *Sky News*, posted May 4, 2015, http://news.sky.com/story/cinema-killer-called-hospital-before-rampage-10360924; *Telegraph*, "Batman Shooting: James Holmes Tried to Call Psychiatrist Nine Minutes before Attack," posted December 20, 2016, http://www.telegraph.co.uk/news/worldnews/northamerica/usa/9510809/Batman-shooting-James-Holmes-tried-to-call-psychiatrist-nine-minutes-before-attack.html.

[331] Mark Strassmann, "James Holmes Recalls His State of Mind Before Colorado Shooting," CBS News, posted May 29, 2015, https://www.cbsnews.com/news/james-holmes-recalls-his-state-of-mind-before-colorado-shooting/.

[332] Keith Coffman and Reuters, "Colorado Theater Shooter Believed Suicidal Thoughts Would Go Away if He Killed Others," *Business Insider*, posted

May 29, 2015, https://www.businessinsider.com/r-colorado-gunman-believed-suicide-thoughts-would-go-away-if-he-killed-others-2015-5.

[333] Melanie Asmar, "James Holmes: Read Timeline of His Actions Before and After Aurora Theater Shooting," *Westword*, posted January 10, 2013, s.v. "July 20, 12:03 a.m.," https://www.westword.com/news/james-holmes-read-timeline-of-his-actions-before-and-after-aurora-theater-shooting-5880120; William H. Reid, *A Dark Night in Aurora: Inside James Holmes and the Colorado Mass Shooting* (New York, NY: Sky Horse Publishing, 2018), 114; *The Week*, "The Last Word: Who Is James," 40.

[334] Asmar, "James Holmes: Read Timeline"; Reid, *A Dark Night*, 114.

[335] Amanda Holpuch, "Colorado Movie Theater Shooting as It Unfolded – Timeline," *Guardian*, posted July 20, 2012, s.v. "12:30 MDT," https://www.theguardian.com/world/2012/jul/20/colorado-movie-theater-shooting-timeline; *The Week*, "The Last Word: Who Is James?" 40.

[336] Terrell Brown narration, in CBS News, "Aurora Shooting Victims Update," YouTube, posted July 22, 2012, https://www.youtube.com/watch?v=sWi_McggpcQ; CBS News, "Powerful Photos Released from Aurora Theater Shooting," posted September 11, 2015, https://www.cbsnews.com/pictures/powerful-photos-released-from-aurora-theater-shooting/15/; Jordan Steffen, "Long-Awaited Trial Begins for Aurora Movie Theater Shooting Defendant," *Denver Post*, posted April 26, 2015, updated April 24, 2016, https://www.denverpost.com/2015/04/26/long-awaited-trial-begins-for-aurora-movie-theater-shooting-defendant/; CNN Editorial Research, "Colorado Theater Shooting Fast Facts," CNN, updated July 9, 2021, https://www.cnn.com/2013/07/19/us/colorado-theater-shooting-fast-facts/index.html; History.com Editors, "Aurora Shooting Leaves 12 Dead, 70 Wounded," History, posted December 2, 2013, updated July 19, 2021, https://www.history.com/this-day-in-history/12-people-killed-70-wounded-in-colorado-movie-theater-shooting.

[337] Healey and Kovaleski, "Before and After Massacre"; Sara C Nelson, "James Holmes: 'I Am the Joker,' Aurora Shooting Suspect 'Claimed to be Batman Nemesis,'" *Huffington Post*, posted July 23, 2012, http://www.huffingtonpost.co.uk/2012/07/20/james-holmes-i-am-the-joker-aurora-shooting-suspect-claimed-to-be-batman-nemesis-pictures_n_1690780.html; Raf Sanchez, Nickallen and Mark Hughes, "Batman Cinema Shooting: James Holmes 'Told Police He Was The Joker,'" *Telegraph*, posted July 20, 2012, http://www.telegraph.co.uk/news/worldnews/northamerica/usa/9416529/Batman-cinema-shooting-James-Holmes-told-police-he-was-The-Joker.html. Nelson, of the *Huffington Post*, alleges that Holmes announced that he was the Joker when conducting the shooting but the other sources state he made the declaration to police after he was arrested.

[338] Reid, *A Dark Night*, 143-144.

[339] Yohana Desta, "The Joker Didn't Inspire the Aurora Shooter, but the Rumor Won't Go Away," *Vanity Fair*, posted October 2, 2019, https://www.vanityfair.com/hollywood/2019/10/joker-aurora-shooting-rumor.

[340] George Brauchler, in Desta, "The Joker Didn't Inspire the Aurora Shooter."

[341] Kelsey Ray, "Psychiatrist: James Holmes Knew Right From Wrong; Court Shows Evaluation Video," News Corps, posted May 28, 2015, https://www.colorado.edu/initiative/newscorps/2015/05/28/psychiatrist-james-holmes-knew-right-wrong-court-shows-evaluation-video; Reid, *A Dark Night*, 189, 191.

[342] Reid, *A Dark Night*, 199. He references the *DSM-5*.

[343] Rachel Bozek, "The Aurora Theater Shooter: Insights from a Psychiatrist Who Interviewed Mass Murderer James Holmes," *True Crime Blog: Stories & News*, A&E Network, posted July 20, 2018, https://www.aetv.com/real-crime/james-holmes-aurora-colorado-theater-mass-shootings-psychiatrist-reid; Sadie Gurman, AP, "Defense: 20 Doctors Agree James Holmes Has Schizophrenia," CBS Denver, posted April 27, 2015, http://denver.cbslocal.com/2015/04/27/prosecutor-2-exams-found-james-holmes-to-be-sane/; Ben Markus, "Aurora Theater Trial: Schizophrenia Expert Says Holmes Was Insane," Colorado Public Radio (CPR) News, posted July 7, 2015, https://www.cpr.org/2015/07/07/aurora-theater-trial-schizophrenia-expert-says-holmes-was-insane/.

[344] Indeed, it can be argued that fashioning a distinction between certain dysfunctional personalities and schizophrenic traits is a somewhat artificial exercise. Evidence for such a viewpoint can be found in: a) Rachel Aviv, "Which Way Madness Lies: Can Psychosis Be Prevented?" *Harper's Magazine* (December 2010): 35-46; b) Esterberg, Goulding, Walker, "Cluster A Personality Disorders"; c) Rosemary Flanagan, "Shyness, Egocentricity, and Psychopathology: Their Relationships among Nonhospitalized Individuals and Mental Health Patients," *Psychological Reports* 70, no. 3 May 1992: 995-1004; d) Fogelson, et al., "Avoidant Personality Disorder Symptoms"; Simone Hoermann, "Schizotypal Personality Disorder and Schizophrenia," MentalHealth.net, posted August 29, 2009, updated September 7 2016, https://www.mentalhelp.net/blogs/schizotypal-personality-disorder-and-schizophrenia/; e) Nancy McWilliams, "Some Thoughts about Schizoid Dynamics," *Psychotherapy in Australia* 16, no. 4 (August 2010): 52-62, http://search.informit.com.au/documentSummary;dn=307705868971935;res=IELHE1323-0921; f) Alman Fanous, Charles Gardner, Dermot Walsh, and Kenneth S. Kendler, "Relationships Between Positive and Negative Symptoms of Schizophrenia and Schizotypal Symptoms in Nonpsychotic Relatives," *Archives of General Psychiatry* 58, no. 7 (August 2001): 669-673. From a neurological perspective, 30 years ago the research director at the University of Oslo in Norway concluded, "There

is reason to believe that schizotypals characterized by distant relationship to others, suspiciousness, eccentricity, peculiar communication, and dysfunctional school and work performance are within the schizophrenic sphere…." Svenn Torgersen, "Relationship of Schizotypal Personality Disorder to Schizophrenia: Genetics," *Schizophrenia Bulletin* 11, no. 4 (1985): 554-563, abstract. Today, that close association is widely accepted. "People with schizotypal personality disorder share common phenomenological, genetic, biological, outcome, and treatment response characteristics with more severely ill patients with chronic schizophrenia." Larry J. Siever and Kenneth L. Davis, "The Pathophysiology of Schizophrenia Disorders: Perspectives from the Spectrum," *American Journal of Psychiatry* 161, no. 3 (March 2004): 398, https://ajp.psychiatryonline.org/doi/pdf/10.1176/appi.ajp.161.3.398. Conceptually, this view is suggested by other researchers, "[T]he "spectra" of mental disorder may be more subtle than previously thought. Perhaps personality disorders in general are *sensitive* indicators of proneness to Axis I disorders (including psychosis), but Cluster A [which includes both avoidant and schizotypal] personality disorders reflect a more *specific* proneness to psychosis." Regina T. Dolan-Sewell, Robert F. Krueger, and M. Tracie Shea, "Co-Occurrence with Syndrome Disorders," in *Handbook of Personality Disorders: Theory, Research, and Treatment*, ed. W. John Livesley, (New York, NY: The Guilford Press, 2001), 90.

[345] N. M. Rath and B. Dash. "A Study on Insanity Related Homicide," *Indian Journal of Psychiatry* 32, no. 1 (January-March 1990): 69.

[346] Ibid, 70.

[347] Robert Keers, Simone Ulrich, Bianca L. DeStavoia, and Jeremy W. Cold, "Association of Violence with Emergence of Persecutory Delusions in Untreated Schizophrenia," *American Journal of Psychiatry* 171, no. 3 (March 2014): 323-339, posted online March 1, 2014, under "Discussion," http://dx.doi.org/10.1176/appi.ajp.2013.13010134. The research included adult male and female offenders who had served sentences of two years or more for violent or sexual assaults. Psychosis was ascertained by the following symptoms: "hallucinations, thought insertion, strange experiences, and delusions of persecution. …" Ibid, under "Method."

[348] Laurie Goodstein and William Glaberson, "The Well-Marked Roads to Homicidal Rage," *New York Times*, posted April 10, 2000. http://www.nytimes.com/2000/04/10/us/the-well-marked-roads-to-homicidal-rage.html?pagewanted=all.

[349] Mara Bovsun, "Sylvia Seegrist Went Psycho and Killed Three Innocent People at the Springfield, Pa., Mall: Seegrist Was Known in Her Neighborhood as Ms. Rambo, for Her Frightening Comments," *New York Daily News*, updated December 2, 2012, http://www.nydailynews.com/news/justice-story/ms-

rambo -kill-spree-article-1.1211691 (page no longer accessible); Goodstein and Glaberson, "The Well-Marked Roads."

[350] Bovsun, "Sylvia Seegrist Went Psycho."

[351] Bovsun, "Sylvia Seegrist Went Psycho"; Laura Hass, "Springfield Mall's 1985 Shooter: Where is She Now? A Springfield Resident Killed 3 and Injured 7 in a Delaware County Mass Shooting, 27 Years Ago," P Media, Patch Local Stream, posted July 24, 2012, http://patch.com/pennsylvania/media/spring field-malls-1985-shooter-where-is-she-now.

[352] AP, "Reno Woman Who Killed Six with Auto Sentenced to Die," *New York Times*, originally published March 30, 1982, http://www.nytimes.com/1982/03/30/us/reno-woman-who-killed-six-with-auto-sentenced-to-die.html.

[353] Brian D. Burghart, "The Day Terror Came Downtown: Pricilla Ford's Deadly Drive," *Reno News and Review*, posted July 7, 2013, archived, https://www.newsreview.com/reno/day-terror-came-downtown/content?oid =20584.

[354] Burghart, "The Day Terror Came Downtown"; Priscilla Ford, Appellant v. State of Nevada, Respondent. Supreme Court of Nevada, 717 P.2d 27, no. 14057, Justia U.S. Law, decided April 8, 1986, under "Opinion" and "1n," http://law.justia.com/cases/nevada/supreme-court/1986/14057-1.html.

[355] *Dessert News*, "Victims Still Suffer from Car Rampage: Memories, Injuries, Linger from Reno Thanksgiving in '80," posted November 25, 2015, https://www.deseret.com/2005/11/28/19924540/victims-still-suffer-from-car-rampage/.

[356] Burghart, "The Day Terror Came"; *Dessert News*, "Victims Still Suffer."

[357] AP, "Reno Woman Who Killed."

[358] AP, "Reno Woman Who Killed"; Burghart, "The Day Terror Came."

[359] Times Staff and Wire Reports, "Priscilla Ford, 75; Was the Only Woman on Nevada's Death Row," *Los Angeles Times* archives, originally posted February 1, 2005, https://www.latimes.com/archives/la-xpm-2005-feb-01-me-passings1.3-story.html.

[360] Jacqui Dillon, Lucy Johnstone, and Eleanor Longden, "Trauma, Dissociation, Attachment, and Neuroscience: A New Paradigm for Understanding Severe Mental Distress," *Journal of Critical Psychology, Counseling, and Psychotherapy* 12, no. 3 (September 2012): 147-148.

[361] American Psychiatric Association, *DSM-5*, 291-307. While it remains the single most universally accepted tool of clinicians, some researchers and practitioners have criticized the empirical bases of the various incarnations of the DSM. See Richard Noll, "When Psychiatry Battled the Devil," *Psychiatric Times*, posted December 6, 2013, http://www.google.com/search?client=safari&rls=en&q=when+psychiatry+battled+the+devil&ie=UTF-8&oe=UTF-8; Paul Verhaeghe, trans. Sigi Jöttkandt, *On Being Normal and Other Disorders: A Manual for Clinical Psychodiagnostics*, (New York, NY: Other Press, 2004), 19-70. *Psychiatric Times* retracted the original essay

by Noll and removed it from their website, citing possible liability as one reason. The periodical then reposted it on March 16, 2014. Ivan Oransky, "Psychiatric Times Reinstates Retracted Essay on 'Satanic Ritual Abuse,'" Retraction Watch, posted March 26, 2014, http://retractionwatch.com/2014/03/25/psychiatric-times-reinstates-retracted-essay-on-satanic-ritual-abuse/; Ivan Oransky, "Psychiatric Times Retracts Essay on 'Satanic Ritual Abuse,'" Retraction Watch: posted February 13, 2014, http://retractionwatch.com/2014/02/13/psychiatric -times-retracts-essay-on-satanic-ritual-abuse/.

362 American Psychiatric Association, *DSM-5*, 303.

363 Derived from a model for dissociated states: "Fragmented Sense of Self: Three Dimensions of Identity Disturbance," presented and discussed in Marlene Steinberg and Maxine Schnall, *The Stranger in the Mirror: Dissociation – The Hidden Epidemic* (New York, NY: Harper Collins Publications, Inc, 2000), 33-36, 100-117.

364 William DeJong, Joel C. Epstein, and Thomas E. Hart, "Bad Things Happen in Good Communities: The Rampage Shooting in Edinboro, Pennsylvania, and Its Aftermath," in *Deadly Lessons: Understanding Lethal School Violence*, ed. Mark H. Moore, Carol V. Petrie, Anthony A. Braga, and Brenda L. McLaughlin (Washington, D.C: The National Academies Press, 2003), 72, box 3-1.

365 Ibid, 73.

366 Ibid, 77.

367 Katherine Ramsland, "Female Mass Murderers: Major Cases and Motives," Crime Library: Criminal Minds and Methods, n.d., 1, http://www.crimelibrary.com/notorious_murders/mass/female_mass_murderer/1.html. The article is from a site that was a subsidiary of TruTV that no longer maintains it. For more see the thread under "Crime Library is Gone?" reddit, posted nine years ago as of March 2024, https://www.reddit.com/r/serialkillers/ comments/35mhu6/crime_library_is_gone/.

368 Dennis Tatz, "Amy Bishop's Sanity at Issue," *Patriot Ledger*, posted and updated on February 22, 2010, https://duckduckgo.com/?q=Amy+Bishop%27s+Sanity+at+Issue+site%3Awww.patriotledger.com&t=chromentp&atb=v234-1&ia=web.

369 Ronald Schouten, "The Insanity Defense: An Intersection of Morality, Public Policy, and Science.," *Psychology Today*, originally posted in "Almost a Psychopath" on August 16, 2012, http://www.psychologytoday.com/blog/almost-psychopath/201208/the-insanity-defense.

370 Sweeney and Associates, "The Insanity Defense," Offices of Sweeney and Associates, L.L.C., posted November 29, 2013, http://masslaw.wordpress.com/2013/11/29/the-insanity-defense/.

371 Ibid.

[372] Vic Dillinger, "Real Amityville Horror of Mass Murderer Ronald DeFeo, Jr: Northing to See Here; Amityville's Horrific History," InfoBarrel Lifestyle, posted July 2, 2012, edited November 13, 2013, http://www.infobarrel.com/Real_Amityville_Horror_of_Mass_Murderer_Ronald_DeFeo_Jr (site no longer secure); Lynne Murray, "Long Island's Own 'House of Horror,'" Examiner.com, posted November 1, 2009, http://www.examiner.com/article/long-island-s-own-house-of-horror; statement by Michael Ahearn, Suffolk Crime Bureau Chief, in A&E, "Amityville Horror Defeo [sic] Murders Full Documentary [excerpts]," posted by Herbert Devereaux, November 15, 2017, https://www.youtube.com/watch?v=0We7gcpbWBQ.

[373] Bob Keeler and D.J. Hill, "DeFeo's New Story: In His First Newspaper Interview Since the 1974 Murders that Spawned 'The Amityville Horror,' Ronald DeFeo Now Claims that He Did Not Massacre His Family. The House on Ocean Avenue," *Newsday*, posted March 19, 1986, http://amityvilletruth.freeservers.com/newsday.htm; Douglas B. Lynott, "The Real Life Amityville Horror," Crime Library, chapter 4, http://www.crimelibrary.com/notorious_murders/family/Amityville/1.html (site discontinued); Ric Osuna, *The Night the DeFeos Died: Reinvestigating the Amityville Murders* (NV: Noble Kai Media, 2003), 34, 188. Osuna's account is careful to state that this initial statement in the confession occurred when he "*supposedly* broke down" [emphasis added] and further on that the events transpired "*according* to Detective Rafferty" [emphasis added].

[374] Supreme Court of the State of New York, County of Suffolk, The People of the State of New York against Ronald Joseoph De Feo [sic], Jr., instructions to the jury by Justice Stark, in Hans Holzer, *The Amityville Curse: Fact and Fiction* (New York, NY: Barnes & Noble, 2007), 72; summary of notice of defense filed by Jacob Siegfried on May 15, 1975, in Osuna, *The Night the DeFeos Died*, 203. Holzer is obviously advancing a point of view, as the dust jacket of his book proclaims that he is "a leading authority on the paranormal" and intrigued by the "Amityville curse." This reference was utilized only to access transcribed statements and, in line with the protocol referred to in the Forward, the transcriptions have been verified by comparison with one or more additional references.

[375] Gerrard Sullivan and Harvey Aronson, *High Hopes: The Amityville Murders* (New York: Coward, McCann, & Geoghegan, 1981), 299-310. Sullivan was the lead prosecutor on the case. Later reflections of the defense counsel, William Weber, who represented DeFeo during the trial, corroborates the slant of the defense strategy suggested in *High Hopes*. Statement by William Weber, in Virginia Quinn, dir., *The Amityville Horror: The Real Story*, (Blink Films, 2008, Smithsonian Channel, released May 3, 2009). Further support for the assessment: "Behind the Camera: Extended Interview with Judge

Thomas Clark (Ret.)," taped on Long Island, New York, September 2007, cut from *Shattered Hopes: The True Story of the Amityville Murders*, (KatcoMedia); trial transcript read by Judge Stark, YouTube, posted January 6, 2012, http://www.youtube.com/watch?v=oJnSwdAQ2zA; Keeler and Hill, "DeFeo's New Story."

[376] Michael Ahearn, in "A&E, "Amityville Horror."

[377] DeFeo, in John Edginton, dir., "First Person Killers: Ronald DeFeo, Jr.," (Teale-Edwards Productions, Inc., 2006), *A&E Special Presentation*.

[378] Amelia Franza, in Edginton, "First Person Killers: Ronald DeFeo, Jr."

[379] Judge Stark, in Edginton, "First Person Killers: Ronald DeFeo, Jr."

[380] Ric Osuna with Christopher Berry-Dee, "The Parole Question," The Amityville Murders, n.d., http://www.amityvillemurders.com/paroleq.html; Sullivan and Aronson, *High Hopes*, 346.

[381] "The Murders: A Night of Hell," The Amityville Murders, n.d., http://www.amityvillemurders.com/murders.html; Sullivan and Aronson, *High Hopes*, 346.

[382] Tina Moore and Lia Eustachewich, "Amityville Horror' Killer Ronald DeFeo Dead in Prison at 69," *New York Post*, posted March 15, 2021, https://nypost.com/2021/03/15/amityville-horror-killer-ronald-defeo-dead-in-prison-at-69/.

[383] The elaborate formation of the Amityville legends is detailed in Quinn, *The Amityville Horror*.

[384] Marc C. Bardwell and Bruce A. Arrigo, *Criminal Competency on Trial: The Case of Colin Ferguson*, (Durham, NC: Carolina Academic Press, 2002), 24-31, 33-37, 41-47.

[385] U.S. Supreme Court, Faretta v. California, 4.22 U.S. 806 (1975), quoted and interpreted in Bardwell and Arrigo, *Criminal Competency on Trial*, 43.

[386] Recollection of Detective Brian Parpan (now retired), in Charlie Minn, dir. and writ., Aaron Michael Thomas, writ., Marvin Yoda, writ., *The Long Island Railroad Massacre* (J & M Productions, December 7, 2013), DVD; Contributed Content, "The Shame of 'Black Rage' Defense," *Chicago Tribune News*, posted June 6, 1994, https://www.chicagotribune.com /1994/06/06/the-shame-of-black-rage-defense/.

[387] Eric Hickey, ed., "Colin Ferguson" *Encyclopedia of Murder and Violent Crime* (Sage Publications, Inc., 2003), s.v. "Ferguson, Colin," posted online September 15, 2007, http://dx.doi.org/10.4135/9781412950619.n163.

[388] Parpan, in Minn, Thomas, and Yoda, *The Long Island Railroad*.

[389] *Saturday Night Live*, "Colin Ferguson Sketches: Colin Ferguson's Trial," National Broadcasting Company, aired February 11, 1995, season 20.

[390] Tom Smith, "Colin Ferguson Trial: 1995," Law Library - American Law and Legal Information: Notable Trials and Court Cases - 1995 to Present, n.d., https://law.jrank.org/pages/3671/Colin-Ferguson-Trial-1995.html. Smith

cites the following sources: a) Geraldine Baum, "Long Island Rail Road Shooting a Charade," *Detroit News* (February 13, 1995), IA, 8A; b) John T. McQuiston, "L. I. R. R. Trial Has Adviser Disgusted," *New York Times* (January 31, 1995): B5; c) Evelyn Nieves, "An Anguished Audience in a Theater of the Absurd," *New York Times* (January 31, 1995): B5

391 Bardwell and Arrigo, *Criminal Competency on Trial*, 149; Smith, "Colin Ferguson Trial."

392 David Stout, "William Kunstler, 76, Dies; Lawyer for Social Outcasts," *New York Times* 144, no. 50, 175 (September 5, 1995): B6.

393 Discover the Networks, "Ron Kuby," DiscoverTheNetworks.org – A Guide to the Political Left, © 2023, https://www.discoverthenetworks.org/individuals /ron-kuby; Alan Feuer, "Man Granted New Trial in Child Sexual Abuse Case," *New York Times*, posted August 13, 2013, http://www.nytimes.com /2013/08/14/nyregion/judge-grants-new-trial-to-man-convicted-of-child-sexual-abuse.html?ref=topics; Ron Kuby, interview with Doug Muzzio, *City Talk*, City University of New York, taped January 29, 2008, YouTube, posted Jun 24, 2011, https://www.youtube.com/watch?v=vJelJc4PPf0

394 William H. Grier and Price M. Cobbs, *Black Rage* (Eugene, OR: Wipf and Stock Publishers, 1992); Mills, "The Shame of 'Black Rage' Defense."

395 Kuby, in Minn, Thomas, and Yoda, *The Long Island Railroad.*

396 McQuiston, "Jury Finds Ferguson Guilty of Slayings on the L.I.R.R."

397 Bardwell and Arrigo, *Criminal Competency on Trial*, 149; McQuiston, "Jury Finds Ferguson Guilty of Slayings on the L.I.R.R."

398 Kuby, in Minn, Thomas, and Yoda, *The Long Island Railroad.*

399 Bardwell and Arrigo, *Criminal Competency on Trial*, 256-257.

400 Kuby, in Ashley Morris, dir., *Killer Trials – Judgment Day: The Long Island Massacre* (WMR Productions and IMG Entertainment for Investigation Discovery, MMXI World Media), *darkdocumentaries*, posted on YouTube, January 5, 2013, https://www.youtube.com/watch?v =8MPoz5DioPE.

401 Peck, in Minn, Thomas, and Yoda, *The Long Island Railroad.*

402 Ferguson Pretrial Hearing Transcripts, December 9, 1994, in Bardwell and Arrigo, *Criminal Competency on Trial*, 248, 251.

403 Ferguson Pretrial Hearing Transcripts, December 9, 1994, in Bardwell and Arrigo, *Criminal Competency on Trial*, 269-270; Kuby, in Morris, *Killer Trials – Judgment Day.*

404 Peck, in Morris, *Killer Trials – Judgment Day.*

405 Bardwell and Arrigo, *Criminal Competency on Trial*, 302-303; Smith, "Colin Ferguson Trial."

406 Kuby, in Minn, Thomas, and Yoda, *The Long Island Railroad.*

407 Jere Hester, "Counsel for the Defense Colin Ferguson Goes to Trial, 1995," *New York Daily News*, posted December 11, 1998, http://www.nydailynews.

com/archives/news/counsel-defense-colin-ferguson-trial-1995-article-1.817395.

[408] Bardwell and Arrigo, *Criminal Competency on Trial*, 303-304; Hester, "Counsel for the Defense."

[409] Smith, "Colin Ferguson Trial."

[410] Ibid.

[411] AP, "20 Years Later: Long Island Rail Road Shooting Remembered as Day Killer Colin Ferguson Went Off the Rails," *New York Daily News*, posted December 8, 2013, http://www.nydailynews.com/new-york/lirr-bloodbath-remembered-20-years-article-1.1539603.

[412] Bardwell and Arrigo, *Criminal Competency on Trial*, 305. *Pro se* is "[l]atin for 'for oneself, on one's own behalf.' When a litigant proceeds without legal counsel, they are said to be proceeding 'pro se.'" Legal Information Institute Cornell University Law School, s.v. "Pro se," n.d., https://www.law.cornell.edu/wex/pro_se. Surprisingly, it was not until 1975 that the Supreme Court ruled in Faretta v. California, 422 U.S. 806 that the right to counsel guaranteed in the sixth amendment to the Constitution of the United State implied the option of self-representation.

[413] Appellate Division New York State, People v. Ferguson, 248 N.Y.S. 2d 725 (1998), in Bardwell and Arrigo, *Criminal Competency on Trial*, 305.

Chapter Five

[1] In one study of 909 mass murders (not all necessarily rampage killings as defined in this work) taking place between 1900 and 1999, 22 percent of the perpetrators were killed at the scene while 47 percent were deemed to have suicidal tendencies. Grant Duwe, *Mass Murder in the United States: A History* (Jefferson, NC: McFarland & Company, Inc., 2007), 11, 101, 104, tables 13, 14. Suicidal inclinations vis-à-vis rampaging are analyzed in *How Rampage Killers Interpret Their Worlds*.

[2] American Psychiatric Association, *Diagnostic and Statistical Manual of Mental Disorders*, 5th ed. (*DSM-5* – Arlington, VA, 2013), 669.

[3] Mara Bovsun, "Crazy professor Valery Fabrikant kills 4 in Concordia University rampage," *Daily News*, posted April 21, 2013, http://www.nydailynews.com/news/justice-story/justice-story-college-prof-kills-4-article-1.1320928.

[4] Correspondence from Frema Engel, in Morris Wolfe, "Dr. Fabrikant's Solution," *Morris Wolfe: Essays, New and Selected*, Feature Articles, Lingua Franca, Saturday Night, posted July 1994, https://morriswolfe.com /fabrikant/; Tom Fennell, "Guilty as Charged: Valery Fabrikant Gets Life for Four Murders," *Maclean's* 106, no. 34 (August 23, 1993): 14; Independent Committee of Inquiry into Academic and Scientific Integrity, *Integrity in Scholarship* (Montreal, Quebec: Concordia University, April 1994),

Murderpedia, last updated June 4, 2017, s.v. "Valery I. Fabrikant," 55-70, https:// murderpedia.org/.

[5] Dave Cullen, *Columbine* (New York, NY: Hachette Book Group, 2009), 168-170, 247.

[6] Rachel Hirst, Krissy Leber, Hannah Brady, and Cecilia Imbus, "History of Mental Institutions," WordPress, n.d., http://psychologyshistory.umwblogs.org/hannahs-page/important-influences/#; J. Reid Meloy, *The Psychopathic Mind: Origins, Dynamics, and Treatment* (Northvale, NJ: Jason Aronson, Inc., 1988), 7.

[7] Hervey Cleckley, *The Mask of Sanity*, rev. ed. (St. Louis, MS: C.V. Mosby Company, 1982), 134.

[8] American Psychiatric Association, *DSM-5*, 461-462, 469-475, 659-663, 764-765.

[9] See: a) R. J. R. Blair, "Neurocognitive Models of Aggression, The Antisocial Personality Disorders, and Psychopathy," *Journal of Neurology, Neurosurgery & Psychiatry* 71, no. 6 (December 2001): 727-731; b) Robert D. Hare, *Without Conscience: The Disturbing World of The Psychopaths Among Us* (New York, NY: Guilford Press, 1993), 34-40, 157-163; c) Martha Stout, *The Sociopath Next Door: The Ruthless Versus the Rest of Us* (New York, NY: Broadway Books, 2005), 6-17; d) Michael Welner, "Classifying Crimes by Severity: From Aggravators to Depravity," in *Crime Classification Manual: A Standard System for Investigating and Classifying Violent Crime*, 2nd ed., ed. John E. Douglas, Ann W. Burgess, Allen G. Burgess, and Robert K. Ressler (San Francisco, CA: John Wiley & Sons, Inc., 2006), 63, table 4.2.

[10] Shortly before initiating their rampage, Klebold introduced their final video by saying, "Hey mom. Gotta go. It's about a half an hour before our little judgment day." Eric Harris and Dylan Klebold, "Transcript of the Columbine 'Basement Tapes,'" s.v. "20 April 1999 – About 30 Minutes before the Attack," 8, transcriber Peter Langman, School Shooters. info: Resources on School Shootings, Perpetrators, and Prevention, last updated March 21, 2024, s.vv. "Eric Harris," "Dylan Klebold," https://schoolshooters.info/.

[11] Elliot Rodger, *Retribution*, YouTube video, *New York Times*, posted May 24, 2014, https://www.nytimes.com/video/us/100000002900707/youtube-video-retribution.html.

[12] Rodger, *My Twisted World: The Story of Elliot Rodger,* manifesto, contributed by Lauren Johnston, *New York Daily News*, pt. 6, under "20 Years old," http://www.documentcloud.org/documents/1173808-elliot-rodger-manifesto.html.

[13] Hare, *Without Conscience*, 34.

[14] Consult these two sources for anecdotes and descriptions about Klebold's emotional discomfort and struggle with feelings of isolation: Cullen,

Columbine, 173-175, 186-188, 198; and Peter Langman, "Rampage School Shooters: A Typology," *Aggression and Violent Behavior* 14, no. 1 (January-February 2009): 82.

15 Associated Press (AP), "Sex Abuse Is Claimed in School Slayings Case," *New York Times* 147, no. 51,120 (April 7, 1998): A18; Cybelle Fox, Wendy D. Roth, and Katherine Newman, "A Deadly Partnership: Lethal Violence in an Arkansas Middle School," in *Deadly Lessons: Understanding Lethal School Violence,* ed. by Mark H. Moore, Carol V. Petrie, Anthony A. Braga, and Brenda L. McLaughlin (Washington, D.C: The National Academies Press: 2003), 102-103; Newman, Katherine, Cybelle Fox, David Harding, Jal Mehta, and Wendy Roth, *Rampage: The Social Roots of School Shootings* (New York, NY: Basic Books, 2004), 33-34; Times London, "Jonesboro Killer 'Was Molested," *Independent*, posted April 8, 1998, https://www.independent.ie/world-news/jonesboro-killer-was-molested-26189453.html.

16 AP, "Sex Abuse Is Claimed"; Fox, Roth, and Newman, "A Deadly Partnership," 105; Newman et al., *Rampage: The Social Roots*, 38.

17 Newman et al., *Rampage: The Social Roots*, 38.

18 Peter Langman, *Why Kids Kill: Inside the Minds of School Shooters* (New *York,* NY: Palgrave MacMillan, 2009), 108.

19 Newman et al., *Rampage: The Social Roots*, 37.

20 Fox, Roth, and Newman, "A Deadly Partnership," 105; Newman et al., *Rampage: The Social Roots*, 109. Some sources report that he was trying out for the team and did not make it because of the mutilation. However, Johnson, was athletic and adept at sports. It is more likely he was already on the team and was removed. Fox, Roth, and Newman, "A Deadly Partnership," 104; Newman et al., *Rampage: The Social Roots*, 35.

21 Aviva Laye-Gindhu and Kimberly A. Schonert-Reich, "Nonsuicidal Self-Harm among Community Adolescents: Understanding the 'Whats' and 'Whys' of Self-Harm," *Journal of Youth and Adolescence* 34, no. 5 (October 2005): 451, 453-455; John Peterson, Stacey Freedenthal, Christopher Sheldon, and Randy Andersen, "Nonsuicidal Self injury in Adolescents," *Psychiatry*, posted on PubMed Central (PMC) November 2008, under "Characteristics of Adolescents with NSSI," "Functions of Nonsuicidal Self-Injurious Behavior," https://www.ncbi.nlm.nih.gov/pmc/articles/PMC2695720/.

22 Fox, Roth, and Newman, "A Deadly Partnership," 104; Newman et al., *Rampage: The Social Roots*, 36.

23 Newman et al., *Rampage: The Social Roots*, 36.

24 Fox, Roth, and Newman, "A Deadly Partnership," 106.

25 Newman et al., *Rampage: The Social Roots*, 45. All ellipses, except the last were in the quotation.

26 Refer to: a) Arnold Arluke, Jack Levin, Carter Luke, and Frank Ascione, "The Relationship of Animal Abuse to Violence and Other Forms of Anti-Social

Behavior," *Journal of Interpersonal Violence* 14, no. 9 (September 1999): 963-975; b) Frank R. Ascione, "Animal Abuse and Youth Violence," *Juvenile Justice Bulletin* (U.S. Department of Justice, Office of Juvenile Justice and Delinquency Prevention, September 2001); c) Alan R. Felthous and Stephen R. Kellert, "Violence Against Animals and People: Is Aggression Against Living Creatures Generalized?" *Bulletin* [now *Journal*] *of the American Academy of Psychiatry and the Law* 14, no. 1 (March 1986): 55-69; d) Bill C. Henry, "The Relationship between Animal Cruelty, Delinquency, and Attitudes toward the Treatment of Animals," *Society & Animals* 12, no.3 (January 2004): 105-207; d) Ernest S. L. Luk, Petra K. Staiger, Lisa Wong, and John Mathai. "Children Who Are Cruel to Animals: A Revisit," *Australian and New Zealand Journal of Psychiatry* 33, no. 1 (February 1999): 29–36; e) John M. Macdonald, "The Threat to Kill," *American Journal of Psychiatry* 120, no. 2 (August 1963): 125-130; f) L. J. Warren, P. E. Mullen, S. D. M. Thomas, J. R. P. Ogloff, and P. M. Burgess, "Threats to Kill: A Follow-Up Study," *Psychological Medicine* 38, no. 4 (April 2008): 599–605.

[27] American Psychiatric Association, *DSM-5*, 469-470.

[28] Paul J. Frick, "Extending the Construct of Psychopathy to Youth: Implications for Understanding, Diagnosing, and Treating Antisocial Children and Adolescents," *Canadian Journal of Psychiatry* 54, no 12 (December 2009): 803-809; and Simone Pisano, Pietro Muratori, Chiara Gorga, Valentina Levantini, Raffaella Iuliano, Gennaro Catone, Giangennaro Coppola, Annarita Milone, and Gabriele Masi, "Conduct Disorders and Psychopathy In Children and Adolescents: Aetiology, Clinical Presentation and Treatment Strategies of Callous-Unemotional Traits," *Italian Journal of Pediatrics* 43, no. 44 (217): 1-3, 5-8, https://ijponline.biomedcentral.com/track/pdf/10.1186/s13052-017-0404-6.pdf.

[29] Newman et al., *Rampage: The Social Roots*, 40.

[30] Nadya Labi, "The Hunter and the Choirboy," *Time*, posted June 24, 2001, http://content.time.com/time /magazine/article/0,9171,138881,00.html.

[31] Fox, Roth, and Newman, "A Deadly Partnership," 107; Newman et al., *Rampage: The Social Roots*, 40.

[32] Newman et al., *Rampage: The Social Roots*, 40.

[33] Ibid, 41, 111.

[34] Fox, Roth, Newman, "A Deadly Partnership," 111; Newman et al., *Rampage: The Social Roots*, 41.

[35] Newman et al., *Rampage: The Social Roots*, 41.

[36] Fox, Roth, and Newman, "A Deadly Partnership: Lethal Violence," 105.

[37] Close friend of Johnson, Chris Jackson, in Newman et al., *Rampage: The Social Roots*, 37.

[38] Circuit Court of Craighead County, Arkansas, Mitchel K. Wright et al. v. Andrew Golden et al., Deposition of Andrew Golden A/KA Drew Grant, no. CIV98-394(B), December 22, 2008, 83. Punctuated as transcribed. Much of Golden's testimony strains credulity but this portion aligns with statements from Chris Jackson in Newman et al., *Rampage: The Social Roots*, 37.

[39] Labi, "The Hunter and the Choirboy."

[40] Rick Bragg, Dirk Johnson, John Kifner and Sam Howe Verhovek, "From Wild Talk and Friendship to Five Deaths in a Schoolyard," *New York Times* 147, no. 51,111 (March 29, 1998): A1, 30.

[41] Max Brantley, "Judge Opens Depositions of Shooters in Westside Case In 1998," *Arkansas Times*, posted August 15, 2017, https://arktimes.com/arkansas-blog/2017/08/15/judge-opens-depositions-of-shooters-in-westside-case-in-1998; Fox, Roth, and Newman, "A Deadly Partnership," 110.

[42] Deposition of Golden, *Wright v. Golden*, 67-70, School Shooters. info, s.v. "Drew Golden"; Meghan Keneally, "The Only Two Living US Mass School Shooters Who Are Not Incarcerated," American Broadcasting Company (ABC) News, posted February 17, 2016, under "Gun Possession and Freedom," https://abcnews.go.com/US/living-us-mass-school-shooters-incarcerated/story?id=36986507.

[43] Deposition of Golden, *Wright v. Golden*, 56; Lockman Foundation (trans.), *New American Standard Bible*. At 33 Golden was killed in July of 2019 in a head-on collision with another car on Highway 167 near Cave City, Arkansas. Region 8 Newsdesk, "Arkansas State Police Confirms, Westside School Shooter Killed in Crash," KAIT 8 ABC News, posted July 28, 2019, updated July 29, 2019. https://www.kait8.com/2019/07/28/westside-school-shooter-killed-crash-independence-county-asp-confirms/. At the time of this writing there was no reported connection between the crash and the rampage. Sharon Lynn Pruitt, "School Shooter Who Killed 4 Students, 1 Teacher, Killed in Car Crash More Than 20 Years Later," Oxygen, posted July 29, 2019, https://www.oxygen.com/crime-time/drew-grant-998-arkansas-school-shooter-andrew-golden-killed-highway-crash; Region 8 Newsdesk, "Arkansas State Police Confirms."

[44] Fox, Roth, and Newman, "A Deadly Partnership," 110.

[45] A reporter, Tim Roche, first came up with that label and used it in a story published in *Time* on December 20, 1999. C. Shepard, ed., "The Basement Tapes," A Columbine Site, established April 21, 1999, updated regularly, under "Basement Tapes and Home Videos," http://www.acolumbinesite.com/. There were five films, taped in two locations: the basement family room next to Harris's bedroom and Klebold's house. Cullen, *Columbine*, 326; Crime Video Archives, "Randy and Judy Brown Discuss the Basement Tapes," YouTube, posted July 25, 2017, https://www.youtube.com/watch?v=v3os4M8yygw. They have never been released to the public in their

entirety, though various abbreviated transcriptions have been pieced together by multiple sources. Langman, introduction to "Transcript of the Columbine," 1; Lost Media Archive, "The Columbine Killers' 3 Unreleased 'Basement Tapes' (Recorded in 1999)," Fandom, updated March 2, 2015, http://lostmediaarchive.wikia.com/wiki/The_ColumbineKillers%273_Unreleased _%22Basement _Tapes%22; Shepard, "The Basement Tapes." "The footage was shot in the last weeks of their short lives [for Klebold and Harris], the final segment just a few hours before the rampage…." Alan Prendergast, "Hiding in Plain Sight," *Westword*, posted April 13, 2006, http://www.westword.com/news/hiding-in-plain-sight-5088906. The recordings were seized by Jefferson County investigators immediately after the devastation. The *Denver Post* demanded their release, but the Colorado Supreme Court left the decision to the discretion of the Jefferson County Sheriffs Office (JCSO) which subsequently declined on the basis "that other troubled youths would see the tapes as a 'call to arms' and a 'how-to instruction video' to attack their own schools." Prendergast, "Hiding in Plain Sight"; Shepard, "The Basement Tapes" (internal quotation according to Shepard). However, other previously unreleased documents – with pages numbering close to one thousand – were made public. Shepard, "The Basement Tapes," introduction. The JCSO destroyed the so-called *Basement Tapes* along with other evidentiary items in early 2011. Alan Prendergast, "Columbine Killers' Basement Tapes Destroyed," *Westword*, posted February 2, 2015, https://www.westword.com/news/columbine-killers-basement-tapes-destroyed-6283043. Ted Mink, who was Sherriff at the time, offered a self-serving explanation that pretty much ignored the public's right to information: "That was my call. My decision. I can't tell you how to measure prevention. I feel in my own heart it was preventative." Ibid. *The Basement Tapes* are separate and distinct from the video recorded by the boys that features their practice with firearms. Fox News, "Columbine Killers Documented Training on Tape," posted October 22, 2003, https://www.foxnews.com/story/columbine-killers-documented-training-on-tape; C. Shepard, transcriber, partial transcript, "Rampart Range Video," A Columbine Site, under "Columbine Video Archive," s.v. "March 6, 1999," http://www.acolumbinesite.com/ (video now "unavailable").

[46] Cullen, *Columbine*, 326.

[47] Harris and Klebold, "Transcript of the Columbine 'Basement Tapes,'' s.v. "15 March 1999," 1. Second ellipsis in transcript.

[48] Cullen, *Columbine*, 221, 275-278, 295, 280, 293, 305-306, 335-337; Jonathan Fast, *Ceremonial Violence: A Psychological Explanation of School Shootings* (Woodstock, NY: The Overlook Press, 2008), 208; Trent Seibert, "Harris, Klebold Tapes Chilling," Denver Post.com, *Colorado News*, posted December 13, 1999, http://extras.denverpost.com/news/shot1213a.htm.

[49] See "Timeline: Before," in Cullen, *Columbine*, 371-372.

[50] In Prendergast, "Hiding in Plain Sight."

[51] Ibid.

[52] Meloy, *The Psychopathic Mind*, 120.

[53] Sue Klebold, interview with Diane Sawyer, *ABC 20/20*, in Margaret Dawson, Tess Scott, Christina Ng, and Lauren Effron, "Columbine killer's Mother Sue Klebold on Relationship with Her Son, Warning Signs She Missed, What She Went Through after the Tragedy," ABC News, posted February 12, 2016, https://abcnews.go.com/US/columbine-killers-mother-sue-klebold-relationship-son-warning/story?id=36891650.

[54] Klebold, in "Transcript of the Columbine," s.v. "15 March 1999," 2.

[55] Klebold, *A Virtual Book*, s.v. "July 23rd, 1997," in *A Teenage Philosophy of Awareness and Existence: Analysis of the Columbine Shooters Worldview*, transcriber and ed. Mathijs Koenraadt, (Amsterdam, The Netherlands: Morningtime, 2015), 84.

[56] Harris, "reb the juvey," A Columbine Site, under "Eric's Harris," "Notebooks, Journals, and Drawings," "Eric Harris' [sic] Writing," Eric Harris' [sic] Websites." Punctuation and capitalization match source.

[57] Klebold, *A Virtual Book*, s.v. "September 5, 1997," in Koenraadt, *A Teenage Philosophy*, 87. Formatting matches transcription.

[58] Harris, *Journal*, s.v. "April 10, 1998," in *Koenraadt, A Teenage Philosophy*, 41.

[59] Klebold, *A Virtual Book*, in Koenraadt, *A Teenage Philosophy*, 77.

[60] Harris, *Journal*, s.v. "April 10, 1998," in Koenraadt, *A Teenage Philosophy*, 41. "V" is short for VoDKa, Dylan Klebold's self-adopted nickname, after his preferred alcoholic beverage with the mid-capitalization of his initials. Cullen, *Columbine*, 9; Koenraadt, *A Teenage Philosophy*, 41.

[61] Klebold, *A Virtual Book*, s.vv. "October 14, 1997," "November 3, 1997," "February 2, 1998," "June 10, 1998," in Koenraadt, *A Teenage Philosophy*, 89, 90, 91, 94, 95, 99.

[62] Klebold, *A Virtual Book*, s.v. "April 15, 1997," in Koenraadt, *A Teenage Philosophy*, 94.

[63] Stone, dir. and writ., Quentin Tarantino, David Veloz, and Richard Rutowski, writ., *Natural Born Killers* (Warner Bros, Regency Enterprises, Alcor Films, Ixtlan, New Regency Pictures, and J D Productions, 1994).

[64] Shepard, transcriber, A Columbine Site, s.v. "Eric Harris' Writings."

[65] Klebold, *A Virtual Book*, s.v. "January 20, 1999," in Koenraadt, *A Teenage Philosophy*, 100. Spelled as transcribed.

[66] Jack Katz, *Seductions of Crime: Moral and Sensual Attractions in Doing Evil* (United States of America: Basic Books, 1988), 297, 309. The cases involved Dale Pierre, Gary Gilmore, Dick Hickock with Perry Smith, and Gregory Powell with Jimmy Lee Smith, chronicled respectively in: Gary Kinder,

Victim: The Other Side of Murder (New York, NY: Laurel Books, 1982); Norman Mailer, *The Executioner's Song* (New York, NY: Warner Books, 1979); Truman Capote, *Cold Blood* (New York, NY: New American Library, 1965); Joseph Wambaugh, *The Onion Field* (New York, NY: Dell, 1973). All involved ruthless violence with little or no financial gain.

[67] J. Pete Blair, and Katherine W. Schweit, *A Study of Active Shooter Incidents in the United States between 2000 and 2013* (U.S. Department of Justice, Texas State University, Federal Bureau of Investigation, 2014), 6, 7. The study used the "agreed-upon definition of an active shooter by U.S. government agencies." That is "an individual actively engaged in killing or attempting to kill people in a confined and populated area." Ibid, 5. As the identifier implies, these events do not include killing with other weapons besides firearms, (that is, knives, vehicles, etc.). Ibid, 4fn.

[68] Blair and Schweit, *A Study of Active Shooter Incidents,* 7, 37.

[69] Ibid, 37.

[70] Bill Braun and Dylan Goforth, "Shooters Get Life without Parole," *Tulsa World*, posted December 17, 2013, https://www.tulsaworld.com/news/courts/shooters-get-life-without-parole/article_0d34eeb7-1991-5471-be80-8291bb13929a.html.

[71] Manny Fernandez and Channing Joseph, "Arrests in Shootings End a Terrifying Weekend in Tulsa," *New York Times*, posted April 8, 2012, https://www.nytimes.com/2012/04/09/us/tulsa-police-arrest-2-men-in-shootings.html.

[72] Ibid.

[73] AP, "Pair Plead Guilty in Tulsa Shooting Rampage," *USA Today*, posted December 16, 2013, https://www.usatoday.com/story/news/nation/2013/12/16/tulsa-shooting-guilty-plea/4045901/.

[74] *Daily Mail Reporter*, "Two Tulsa Shooting Suspects Confess to Good Friday Gun-Spree Which Left Three Dead and Two Seriously Injured," posted April 9, 2012, updated April 10, 2012, https://www.dailymail.co.uk/news/article-2127506/Tulsa-shootings-Two-shooting-suspects-confess-Good-Friday-gun-spree-left-dead-seriously-injured.html.

[75] a) Meagan J. Brem, Autumn Rae Florimbio, JoAnna Elmquist, Ryan C. Shorey, and Gregory L. Stuart, "Antisocial Traits, Distress Tolerance, and Alcohol Problems as Predictors of Intimate Partner Violence in Men Arrested for Domestic Violence," *Psychology of Violence* 8, no. 1 (January 2018): 132-139; b) Nicole M. L. Buck, Ellie P. E. M. Leenaars, Paul M. G. Emmelkamp, and Hjalmar J. C. van Marle, "Explaining the Relationship Between Insecure Attachment and Partner Abuse: The Role of Personality Characteristics," *Journal of Interpersonal Violence* 27, no. 16 (April 2012): 3149–3170; c) James E. Hastings and Kevin L. Hamberger, "Personality Characteristics of Spouse Abusers: A Controlled Comparison," *Violence and Victims* 3, no. 1 (January 1988): 31-48; d) Marcela, Madalena, Lucas de Francisco Carvalho,

and Denise Falcke, "Intimate Partner Violence: The Predictive Power of Experiences in the Family of Origin and of Personality Disorder Traits," *Trends in Psychology* 26, no.1 (January/March 2018): 93-109; e) Corinne Peek-Asa, C. Zwerling, Tracy Young, A. M. Stromquist, L. F. Burmeister, and J. A. Merchant, "A Population Based Study of Reporting Patterns and Characteristics of Men Who Abuse Their Female Partners," *Injury Prevention* 11, no. 3 (June 2005): 180-185; f) Danuta Rode, Magdalena Rode, and Maciej Januszek, "Psychosocial Characteristics of Men and Women as Perpetrators of Domestic Violence," *Polish Psychological Bulletin* 46, no. 1 (March 2015): 53-64; g) Richard M. Tolman and Larry W. Bennett, "A Review of Quantitative Research on Men Who Batter," *Journal of Interpersonal Violence* 5, no. 1 (March 1990): 87-118.

[76] Stephen Fisher, *From Violence to Coercive Control: Renaming Men's Abuse of Women*, publication no. 3 (White Ribbon Foundation, January 2011), 6, https://vawnet.org/material/violence-coercive-control-renaming-mens-abuse-women. In addition, see: a) Donald G. Dutton and Andrew J. Starzomski, "Personality Predictors of the Minnesota Power and Control Wheel," *Journal of Interpersonal Violence* 12, no. 1 (February 1997): 70–82; b) Anthony F. Greene, and Charlton J. Coles, "Psychopathology and Anger in Interpersonal Violence Offenders," *Journal of Clinical Psychology* 50, no. 6 (November 1994): 906-912; c) Pamela C. Regan and Ramani S. Durvasula, "A Brief Review of Intimate Partner Violence in the United States: Nature, Correlates, and Proposed Preventative Measures," *Interpersona: An International Journal on Personal Relations* 9, no. 2 (2015): 127-134; d) John G. Taylor, "Behind the Veil: Inside the Mind of Men 'That Abuse,'" *Psychology Today*, posted February 5, 2013, https://www.psychologytoday.com/us/blog/the-reality-corner/201302/behind-the-veil-inside-the-mind-men-abuse; e) Richard M. Tolman and Larry W. Bennett, "A Review of Quantitative Research on Men Who Batter," *Journal of Interpersonal Violence* 5, no. 1 (March 1990): 87-89, 94-95, 98-99; f) Roger Tweed and Donald G. Dutton, "A Comparison of Impulsive and Instrumental Subgroups of Batterers." *Violence and Victims* 13, no. 3 (February 1998): 217-30.

[77] Everytown for Gun Safety Support Fund, *Mass Shootings in the United States* (November 21, 2020), under "Domestic Violence Was a Part of Most Mass Shootings," https://maps.everytownresearch.org/massshootingsreports/mass-shootings-in-america-2009-2019/. A mass shooting was defined "as any incident in which four or more people are shot and killed, excluding the shooter." Ibid, "Definition of a Mass Shooting," box.

[78] "Deconstructing the 'Power and Control Motive': Developing and Assessing the Measurability of Internal Power" (doctoral diss., University of South Florida, 2012), 37, https://scholarcommons.usf.edu/etd/4248/.

[79] Ibid, 56-60; 95-96, tables 15 -17, 97, table 18, 98, appendices A-G.

[80] Ibid, 99-100.

[81] Eric W. Hickey, *Serial Killers and Their Victims*, 5th ed. (United States: Wadsworth Cengage Learning, 2010), 35, 226.

[82] Ibid, 232.

[83] MentalHelp.net, "The Most Significant, Defining Featured of Personality Disorders: Interpersonal Difficulties," © 2024, https://www.mentalhelp.net/personality-disorders/most-significant-defining-feature-interpersonal-difficulties/, referring to MentalHelp.net, "Defining Features of Personality Disorders: Problematic Emotional Response Patterns," © 2024; and Brindusa Vanta, "Defining Features of Personality Disorders: Impulse Control Problems," MentalHelp.net, © 2024.

[84] American Psychiatric Association, *DSM-5*, 776, 775.

[85] Mario Mikulincer and Phillip R. Shaver, "Attachment, Anger, and Aggression," in H*uman Aggression and Violence: Causes, Manifestations, and Consequences*, ed. Phillip R. Shaver and Mario Mikulincer, (Washington D.C: American Psychological Association, 2011), 245.

[86] Ibid, referencing Mario Mikulincer, "Adult Attachment Style and Individual Differences in Functional Versus Dysfunctional Experiences of Anger," *Journal of Personality and Social Psychology* 74, no. 2 (March 1998): 513-524.

[87] Joseph E. McEllistrem, "Affective and Predatory Violence: A Bimodal Classification System of Human Aggression and Violence," *Aggression and Violent Behavior* 10, no. 1 (November 2004): 3-4. The author is interpreting and synthesizing the following articles in the description: a) W.R. Hess and M. Brugger, "Das Subkortikale Zentrum der Affektiven Abwehrreaktion [The Subcortical Center for Affective Defense Reactions]," *Helvetica Physiologica et Pharmacolgica Acta* 1, no. 1 (1943): 33-52; b) Jules H. Masserman, "Is the Hypothalamus a Center of Emotion?" *Psychosomatic Medicine* 3, no. 1 (January 1941): 3-25; c) Marvin Wasman and John P. Flynn, "Directed Attack Elicited from Hypothalamus," *Archives of Neurology* 6, no. 3 (March 1962): 635-644

[88] Mark Zimmerman, "Overview of Personality Disorders," *Merck Manual Professional Version*, review/revision, reviewed/revised September 2023, https://www.merckmanuals.com/professional/psychiatric-disorders/personality-disorders/overview-of-personality-disorders.

[89] Sadie F. Dingfelder, "Treatment for the 'Untreatable,'" *Monitor on Psychology* 35, no. 3 (March 2004), 46, https://www.apa.org/monitor/mar04/treatment.

[90] Sander Thomaes and Brad J. Bushman, "Mirror, Mirror on the Wall, Who's the Most Aggressive of Them All? Narcissism, Self-Esteem, and Aggression," in *Human Aggression and Violence: Causes, Manifestations, and Consequences*, ed. Phillip R. Shaver and Mario Mikulincer (Washington D.C: American Psychological Association, 2014), 213.

[91] Donald G. Dutton, "Attachment and Violence: An Anger Born of Fear," in *Human Aggression and Violence: Causes, Manifestations, and Consequences*, ed. Phillip R. Shaver and Mario Mikulincer, (Washington D.C: American Psychological Association, 2011), 265.

[92] Seena Fazel and John Danesh, "Serious Mental Disorder in 23,000 prisoners: A Systematic Review of 62 Surveys," *Lancet* 359, no. 9306 (March 2002): 545.

[93] Stanton E Samenow, *The Myth of the Out of Character Crime* (Westport, CT: Praeger, 2007), 18-19.

[94] The so-called "Cluster B" (e.g., anti-social or histrionic) as opposed to "Cluster A" encompassing those who are considered "odd or "eccentric" (e.g., schizotypal) or "Cluster C" individuals who appear hampered by extreme anxiety (e.g., avoidant or dependent). American Psychiatric Association, *DSM-5*, 646.

[95] Ibid, 649, 652, 655, 659, 663, 667, 679, 672, 675, 678.

[96] Ibid, 646.

[97] Joyce Egginton, *Day of Fury: The Story of the Tragic Shootings that Forever Changed the Village of Winnetka* (New York, NY: William Morrow and Company, Inc., 1991), 135-136.

[98] Ashley B. Johnson, Julie P. Gentile, and Terry L. Correll, "Accurately Diagnosing and Treating Borderline Personality Disorder." *Psychiatry* 7, no. 4 (April 2010): 21-30, PMC, posted April 2010, under "Introduction," https://www.ncbi.nlm.nih.gov/pmc/articles/PMC2877618/. For more on the overlap between BPD and BD: David. M. Allen, "A Matter of Personality: Bipolar or Borderline? A Rampant Case of Diagnonsense," Psychology Today.com, posted December 11, 2011, https://www.psychologytoday.com/blog/matter-personality/201112/bipolar-or-borderline; and Antonia S. New, Joseph Triebwasser, and Dennis S. Charney, "Review: The Case for Shifting Borderline Personality Disorder to Axis I," *Biological Psychiatry*, Biological Psychiatry 64, no. 8 (October 2008): 653-659.

[99] Robert S. Biskin and Joel Paris, "Comorbidities in Borderline Personality Disorder," *Psychiatric Times* 30, no. 1 (January 9, 2013), under "Diagnosis," https://www.psychiatrictimes.com/view/comorbidities-borderline-personality-disorder. The authors cite: Thomas H. McGlashan, Carlos M. Grilo, Andrew E. Skodol, John G. Gunderson, M. Tracie Shea, Leslie C. Morey, Mary C. Zanarini, and Robert L. Stout, "The Collaborative Longitudinal Personality Disorders Study: Baseline Axis I/II and II/II Diagnostic Co-occurrence," *Acta Psychiatrica Scandinavica* 102 no. 4 (November 2000): 256-64; and Mary C. Zanarini, Frances R. Frankenburg, Elyse D. Dubo, Amy E. Sickel, Anjana Trikha, Alexandra Levin, and Victoria Reynolds, "Axis I Comorbidity of Borderline Personality Disorder," *American Journal of Psychiatry* 155, no. 12 (December 1998): 1733-1739.

[100] The follow-up diagnoses were conducted "using a joint-interview design, where one rater observed the other and both made independent ratings." Camilo J. Ruggero, Mark Zimmerman, Iwona Chelminski, and Diane Young, "Borderline Personality Disorder and the Misdiagnosis of Bipolar Disorder," author manuscript, PMC, National Institutes of Health Public (NIH) Access, under "Procedures and Measures," https://www.ncbi.nlm.nih.gov/pmc/articles/PMC2849890/. "[N]early 40% (20/52) of the patients diagnosed with *DSM-IV* borderline personality disorder reported having been misdiagnosed with bipolar disorder compared to slightly more that 10% (62/558) of the patients without personality disorder." Ibid, under "Results."

[101] It is safe to assume the determination was based on the *DSM III-R* because it was made between November 1987 and March 1988 and that version of the manual was the latest during that interval, copyrighted in 1987 (Washington D.C: American Psychiatric Association). Egginton, *Day of Fury*, 135-136; American Psychiatric Association, *DSM III-R*, copyright page. It is possible, however, the diagnostician, might have referred to the edition prior to the revision, which was published in 1980. American Psychiatric Association, Diagnostic and Statistical Manual, 3rd ed. (*DSM-III* – Washington D.C: American Psychiatric Association). The distinction is insignificant, though, since relevant adjectives for manic-depressive episodes in both overlap with the *DSM-5* traits identified for BPD. See: a) American Psychiatric Association, *DSM-III*, 208-209, 214; b) *DSM III-R*, 217, 222; c) *DSM-5*, 663.

[102] Egginton, *Day of Fury*, 274.

[103] Rick Kogan, "Documentary Re-Creates Dann's Day of Terror, but Can't Give Us the Why." *Chicago Tribune*, originally published May 3, 1989, http://articles.chicagotribune.com/1989-05-03/features/8904090304_1_ ocd-obsessive-compulsive-disorder-laurie-dann.

[104] American Psychiatric Association, *DSM-5*, 766-767.

[105] Joel Kaplan, George Papajohn, and Eric Zorn, *Murder of Innocence: The Tragic Life and Final Rampage of Laurie Dann, "The Schoolhouse Killer"* (New York, NY: Warner Books, Inc., 1990), 159-161.

[106] Kaplan, Papajohn, and Zorn, *Murder of Innocence*, 161. Her treatment is also described in George Papajohn and Joel Kaplan, with contributors Ray Gibson, William Recktenwald, John O'Brien, Steve Johnson, Barbara Mahany, and Steven Swanson, "The Many Faces of Laurie Dann," *Chicago Tribune*, published June 5, 1988, 1, 16.

[107] American Psychiatric Association, *DSM-5*, 766-767.

[108] Ibid, 679.

[109] "Obsessive-Compulsive Personality Disorder," *MedlinePlus*, updated by Fred K. Berger, reviewed by David C. Dugdale, Brenda Conaway, and the Animated Dissection of Anatomy for Medicine Editorial Team, November 6, 2022, https://medlineplus.gov/ency/article/000942.htm.

[110] Kaplan, Papajohn, and Zorn, *Murder of Innocence*, 43-47, 51.

[111] Papajohn et al., "The Many Faces." Also, relevant: Barbara Van Noppen, "Obsessive Compulsive Personality Disorder (OCPD)," International OCD Foundation, 2010, under "What is the difference between OCPD and OCD?" https://iocdf.org/wp-content/uploads/2014/10/OCPD-Fact-Sheet.pdf.

[111] Fred K Berger, reviewed by David C. Dugdale, Brenda Conaway, and the Animated Dissection of Anatomy for Medicine Editorial Team, "Obsessive-Compulsive Personality Disorder," *MedlinePlus*, updated on November 6, 2022, https://medlineplus.gov/ency/article/000942.htm.

[112] Simon Baron-Cohen, *The Science of Evil: On Empathy and the Origins of Cruelty*, (New York: NY: Basic Books, 2011), 43-64. According to Baron-Cohen there are two other personality types that may lack the capacity to empathize: psychopathic and narcissistic. Ibid, 44-45. The author, along with others, designed a scale known as the "Empathy Quotient," Ibid, 20-23, appendix 1.

[113] Randy A. Sansone and Lori A. Sansone, "The Interface: Borderline Personality and Externalized Aggression," *Innovations in Clinical Neuroscience* 2, no. 9 (March 2012): 25.

[114] Ibid, table 1.

[115] Kaplan, Papajohn, and Zorn, *Murder of Innocence*, 10.

[116] Ibid, 11.

[117] Ibid.

[118] American Psychiatric Association, *DSM-5*, 766.

[119] Papajohn et al, "The Many Faces."

[120] Ibid.

[121] Kaplan, Papajohn, and Zorn, *Murder of Innocence*, 18-19.

[122] Kaplan, Papajohn, and Zorn, *Murder of Innocence*, 20-26, 28; Papajohn et al., "The Many Faces."

[123] Papajohn et al., "The Many Faces."

[124] Kaplan, Papajohn, and Zorn, *Murder of Innocence*, 22.

[125] Ibid, 24-27

[126] Montgomery Bower with Bonnie Bell, Dennis Breo, Jody Brott, Judy Hevrdejs, Barbara Kleban Mills, Chris Tamarkin, and Justin Greenberg, "Mad Enough to Kill," *People Weekly* (June 6, 1988): 46.

[127] American Psychiatric Association, *DSM-5*, 767.

[128] Kaplan, Papajohn, and Zorn, *Murder of Innocence*, 35, 41-42.

[129] Ibid, 42.

[130] Ibid, 42-45.

[131] Ibid, 48.

[132] Ibid.

[133] Papajohn et al., "The Many Faces."

[134] Kaplan, Papajohn, and Zorn, *Murder of Innocence*, 73, 77, 82.

[135] Baron-Cohen, *The Science of Evil*, 56.

[136] See: a) American Psychiatric Association, *DSM-5*, 663-664; b) Kim Bartholomew, Marilyn J. Kwong, and Stephen D. Hart, "Attachment," in *Handbook of Personality Disorders: Theory, Research, and Treatment*, ed. W. John Livesley (New York: Guilford Press, 2001), 212-215; c) Dr. Ramani Durvasula interview with Kyle Kittleson, in MedCircle, "How to Spot the 9 Traits of Borderline Personality Disorder," YouTube, posted August 19, 2018, https://www.youtube.com/watch?v=to5qRLRSS7g&t=188s; d) Kenneth N. Levy, Benjamin N. Johnson, Tracy L. Clouthier, J. Wesley Scala, and Christina M. Temes, "An Attachment Theoretical Framework for Personality Disorders," *Canadian Psychology* 56, no. 2 (May 2015): 197-207; e) Vijaya Manicavasagar and Derrick Silove, *Separation Anxiety Disorder in Adults: Clinical Features, Diagnostic Dilemmas and Treatment Guidelines* (University of New South Wales, Sydney, Australia: Academic Press, 2020), 151-170.

[137] Bower et al., "Mad Enough to Kill," 46-47; Egginton, *Day of Fury*, 122-127.

[138] Papajohn et al., "The Many Faces of Laurie Dann."

[139] Bower et al., "Mad Enough to Kill," 46-47; Egginton, *Day of Fury*, 122-127; Papajohn et al., "The Many Faces of Laurie Dann."

[140] Egginton, *Day of Fury*, 132; Kaplan, Papajohn, and Zorn, *Murder of Innocence*, 82-83; Papajohn et al., "The Many Faces of Laurie Dann."

[141] Egginton, *Day of Fury*, 269, 270, 271, 273-274.

[142] Decompensation in medical or psychological terminology refers to a patient's reaction to interrupted stasis often due to stress. "Decompensation ... *Medicine* The inability of a bodily organ or system, especially the circulatory system to maintain physiological function in the presence of a disease. ... *Psychology* The inability to maintain defense mechanisms in response to stress, resulting in personality disturbance or psychological imbalance." *The American Heritage Medical Dictionary*, Harper Collins Publishers, 2022, s.v. "Decompensation," https://ahdictionary.com/word/search.html?q=decompensation.

[143] American Psychiatric Association, *DSM-5,* 664.

[144] W. John Livesley, "Conceptual and Taxonomic Issues," in *Handbook of Personality Disorders*, 6.

[145] Katrin Schroeder, Helen L. Fisher, and Ingo Schäfer, "Review: Psychotic Symptoms in Patients with Borderline Personality Disorder – Prevalence and Clinical Management," *Current Opinion in Psychiatry* 26, no. 1 (2013): 114, 117, http://journals.lww.com/copsychiatry/Abstract/2013/01000/Psychotic_symptoms_in _patients_with_borderline.21.aspx.

[146] Egginton, *Day of Fury,* 270, 275.

[147] Kaplan, Papajohn, and Zorn, "Murder of Innocence," 175.

[148] Bower et al., "Mad Enough to Kill," 47; Egginton, *Day of Fury,* 275.

[149] Substance Abuse and Mental Health Services Administration, U.S. Department of Health and Human Services, *Report to Congress on Borderline Personality Disorder*, (Publication no. SMA-11-4644, 2010), 16, https://integratedrecovery.org/wp-content/uploads/2021/07/BPDreportToCongress.pdf.

[150] Mary C. Zanarini, Frances R. Frankenburg, John Hennen, D. Bradford Reich, and Kenneth R. Silk, "Axis I Comorbidity in Patients with Borderline Personality Disorder: 6-Year Follow-Up and Prediction of Time to Remission," *American Journal of Psychiatry* 161, no. 11 (November 2011): 2109, 2112.

[151] Elements Behavioral Health, "Borderline Personality Disorder and Eating Disorders," 2014, http://www.borderline-personality-disorder.com/co-occuring-disorders/eating-disorders/.

[152] Egginton, *Day of Fury*, 276.

[153] Egginton, *Day of Fury*, 259; *Encyclopedia of School Crime and Violence, A-N*, ed. Laura L. Finley (Santa Barbara, CA: ABC-CLIO, 20110), s.v. "Dann, Laurie."

[154] *Encyclopedia of School Crime*, s.v. "Dann, Laurie"; Papajohn et al., "The Many Faces of Laurie Dann."

[155] Egginton, *Day of Fury*, 259-260; AP, "Police Still Unraveling Trail Left by Woman in Rampage," *New York Times*, published May 22, 1988, http://www.nytimes.com/1988/05/22/us/police-still-unraveling-trail-left-by-woman-in-rampage.html.

[156] Kaplan, Papajohn, and Zorn, *Murder of Innocence*, 1, 219-221.

[157] Bower et al., "Mad Enough to Kill," 48-49.

[158] Bower et al., "Mad Enough to Kill," 42; Murderpedia, s.v. "Laurie Dann," under "Laurie Wasserman Dann (c. 1958 - 20 May 1988)."

[159] Kaplan, Papajohn, and Zorn, *Murder of Innocence*, 231.

[160] Brower et al., "Mad Enough to Kill," 43-45; Kaplan, Papajohn, and Zorn, *Murder of Innocence,* 232-234.

[161] Bower et al., "Mad Enough to Kill," 44; Kaplan, Papajohn, and Zorn, *Murder of Innocence*, 234-235.

[162] Bower et al., "Mad Enough to Kill," 44.

[163] Bower et al., "Mad Enough to Kill," 44-45; Patricia Calhoun, "School Shooter Laurie Dann Only Killed One, But Her Crime Was Memorable for Other Reasons, Too," *Westword*, posted December 28, 2012, https://www.westword.com/news/school-shooter-laurie-dann-only-killed-one-but-her-crime-was-memorable-for-other-reasons-too-5865565; *Encyclopedia of School Crimes*, s.v. "Dann, Laurie."

[164] See American Psychiatric Association, *DSM-5*, 649. Categorical criteria rather than alternate descriptors were used when considering PPD because the alternative model does not, for reasons that are unexplained, mention it as a syndrome distinct from other PDs. Ibid, 761-781.

[165] He started work at the Hammermill Paper Company in 1948 and his SMASI was on October 23, 1967. Don Sarvey, *Day of Rage: Model Citizen Turns Cold Blooded Killer in a Pennsylvania Small Town* (Mechanicsburg, PA: Stackpole Books, 2011), 1, 2, 5, 92.

[166] Ibid, front jacket.

[167] Sarvey, *Day of Rage*, front jacket; *Time Magazine*, "Pennsylvania: The Revolt of Leo Held," originally published November 3, 1967, Murderpedia, s.v. "Leo Held," under "No More Bull."

[168] Katherine Ramsland, *Inside the Minds of Mass Murderers: Why They* Kill (Westport, CT: Praeger Publishers, 2005) 91; Sarvey, *Day of Rage,* 2, 91-92.

[169] Ronald D. Brown, *Dying on the Job: Murder and Mayhem in the American Workplace* (Lanham, MD: Rowan & Littlefield Publishers, Inc., 2013), 76.

[170] Sarvey, *Day of Rage*, 88.

[171] Ibid.

[172] *Time*, "Pennsylvania: The Revolt."

[173] Brown, *Dying on the Job*, 77.

[174] Sarvey, *Day of Rage*, 89.

[175] Ibid, 92-95.

[176] Sarvey, *Day of Rage*, 39; *Time Magazine*, "Pennsylvania: The Revolt."

[177] Sarvey, *Day of Rage*, 94. Rigidity, as a trait, transverses multiple PDs and certainly aligns with a paranoid perspective.

[178] *Time*, "Pennsylvania: The Revolt," under "One to Go." The magistrate dismissed the case.

[179] Sarvey, *Day of Rage,* 94.

[180] Ibid. Sarvey only notes that the report came from that newspaper but does not directly cite the author or article.

[181] American Psychiatric Association, *DSM-5*, 649.

[182] Ibid, 90.

[183] Ronald D. Brown, *Dying on the Job: Murder and Mayhem in the American Workplace* (Lanham, MD: Rowan & Littlefield Publishers, Inc., 2013), 76-77; Sarvey, *Day of Rage*, 91.

[184] *Time*, "Pennsylvania: The Revolt."

[185] Ramsland, *Inside the Minds*, 91; Sarvey, *Day of Rage*, 18, 38-39; *Time*, "Pennsylvania: The Revolt," under "No More Bull."

[186] Sarvey, *Day of Rage*, 38-39; *Time*, "Pennsylvania: The Revolt," under "No More Bull."

[187] *Time*, "Pennsylvania: The Revolt," under "No More Bull."

[188] Sarvey, *Day of Rage*, 52-54.

[189] *Time*, "Pennsylvania: The Revolt." Sarvey reports that a police sergeant told him he was going to get Held's daughter to talk. To which Held replied, "I don't want my daughter. … I'm tired of taking all this bull." Sarvey, *Day of Rage*, 54. Either way the accusatory tone suggests paranoia.

[190] Sarvey, *Day of Rage*, 55-56, 73.

[191] *Time*, "Pennsylvania: The Revolt."

[192] American Psychiatric Association, *DSM-5*, 646, 669-670.

[193] AP, "Timeline of Events Leading Up to and Including Killings of 6 in Chaotic Santa Barbara Rampage," Fox News, posted February 19, 2015, updated May 3, 2016, s.v. "May 23," https://www.foxnews.com/us/timeline-of-events-leading-up-to-and-including-killings-of-6-in-chaotic-santa-barbara-rampage.

[194] AP, "Timeline of Events," s.v. "May 23 at 7:38 p.m."; Jonelle Lawrence, "Isla Vista Shooting Rampage: Crime Scene Locations, Timeline," Eye Witness News ABC 7, posted May 25, 214, https://abc7.com/isla-vista-shooting-rampage-timeline-locations-mass-shootings-santa-barbara/77039/; Office of the District Attorney County of Santa Barbara, *Public Report on Officer-Involved Shooting of Elliot Rodger by Santa Barbara County Deputy Sheriffs on May 23, 2014*, released September 4, 2015, 1, http://media.independent.com/news/documents/2015/09/09/PublicReportonOfficerInvolvedShootingofElliotRodgerbySheriffDeputiesonMay23_2014.PDF; Phillip Rucker. "Elliot Rodger's Killing Spree: What Happened," *Washington Post*, posted May 24, 2014, https://www.washingtonpost.com/politics/elliot-rodgers-killing-spree-what-happened/2014/05/24/207778ec-e3b2-11e3-810f-764fe508b82d_story.html; Nicky Woolf, "Chilling Report Details How Elliot Rodger Executed Murderous Rampage," Guardian, posted February 20, 2015, https://www.theguardian.com/us-news/2015/feb/20/mass-shooter-elliot-rodger-isla-vista-killings-report. Some sources (including AP and Lawrence) indicate that Rodger, after knocking at the sorority, walked across the street, and shot at a group of women, killing two and wounding one, then resumed driving. The official version states only that the episode involved "a series of drive-by shootings." Office of the district Attorney, *Public Report on Officer-Involved Shooting*, 1.

[195] Huffy Yan, Pamela Brown, and Alan Duke. "New Details Emerge abut California Killer and His Victims." Cable News Network (CNN), updated May 27, 2014, http://www.cnn.com/2014/05/26/justice/california-killing-spree/; Arjun Varma, "Elliot Rodger Emailed Manifesto Titled 'My Twisted World' Before Going on Killing Spree, *International Business Times*, posted May 26, 2014, updated June 25, 2014. The first story states that there were two dozen recipients. The second gives the number cited.

[196] Kashmir Hill, "The Disturbing Internet Footprint of Santa Barbara Shooter Elliot Rodger," *Forbes*, posted May 24, 2014, https://www.forbes.com/sites/kashmirhill/2014/05/24/the-disturbing-internet-footprint-of-santa-barbara-shooter-elliot-rodger/?sh=4ad91bf77c31; Richard Winton, Rosanna Xia, Rong-Gong Lin II, "Isla Vista Shooting: Read Elliot Rodger's Graphic, Elaborate Attack Plan," *Los Angeles Times*, posted May 25, 2014,

https://www.latimes.com/local/lanow/la-me-ln-isla-vista-document-20140524-story.html.

[197] Elliot Rodger, *My Twisted* World; Winton, Xia, and Rong-Gong "Isla Vista Shooting."

[198] Rodger, *My Twisted World*, intro. Ellipsis in original.

[199] Ibid, pt. 1, under "A Blissful Beginning: Age 0-5."

[200] Ibid.

[201] American Psychiatric Association, *DSM-5*, 669.

[202] Rodger, *My Twisted World*, pt. 2, under "Growing up in America: Age 5-9."

[203] Ibid, pt. 6, under "22 Years Old."

[204] American Psychiatric Association, *DSM-5*, 670.

[205] Rodger, *My Twisted World*, pt. 2, under "6 Years Old.'

[206] Ibid, pt. 2, under "6 Years Old"; pt.4, under "Stuck in the Void: Age 13-17," "14 Years Old," "16 Years Old"; pt. 5, under "18 Years Old"; pt. 6, under "19 Years Old," "21 Years Old," "22 Years Old."

[207] Susan Harter, "Causes and Consequences of Low Self-Esteem in Children and Adolescents," in *Self-Esteem: The Puzzle of Low Self-Regard*, ed. Roy F. Baumeister (New York, NY: Plenum Press, 1993), 97.

[208] Rodger, *My Twisted World*, pt. 3, under "10 Years Old."

[209] Ibid, pt. 3, under "11 Years Old."

[210] Ibid, pt. 4, under "Stuck in the Void: Age 13-17."

[211] Ibid.

[212] Sam Vaknin, *The Soul of a Narcissist: The State of the Art*, last updated March 11, 2024, under "Chapter 4: The Tortured Self, The Inner World of the Narcissist," https://www.healthyplace.com/personality-disorders/malignant-self-love/soul-of-a-narcissist-intro. In a short autobiographical piece accompanied by a range of blogs, interviews, and videos on his website Vaknin candidly discloses how covetousness stoked by utter egocentrism led to his imprisonment: "Malignant Self Love - Narcissism Revisited Homepage," last updated May 13, 2019, https://www.healthyplace.com/ personality-disorders/malignant-self-love/narcissism-narcissistic-personality-disorder-npd. The contents were reviewed by Harry Croft, MD, Medical Director of HealthyPlace.com, which supports Vaknin's webpages and claims to be "the largest consumer mental health site on the net." Natasha Tracy, "About Healthy Place.com," updated February 23, 2022, https://www.healthyplace.com/about-healthyplace/about-us/about-healthyplace.

[213] Rodger, *My Twisted World*, pt. 4, under "Stuck in the Void: Age 13-17."

[214] Ibid, pt. 4, under "14 Years Old," "15 Years Old."

[215] Ibid, pt. 4, under "15 Years Old."

[216] Ibid.

[217] Ibid.

[218] Ibid.

[219] Ibid, pt. 5, under "22 Years Old."
[220] Ibid, pt. 5, under "18 Years Old."
[221] Ibid, pt. 4, under "17 Years Old."
[222] Ibid.
[223] Ibid.
[224] Ibid.
[225] American Psychiatric Association, *DSM-5*, 669.
[226] Rodger, *My Twisted World*, pt. 5, under "19 Years Old."
[227] Ibid.
[228] Ibid, pt. 6, under "Age 19-22."
[229] Ibid, under "Age 19-22," "20 Years Old."
[230] Caroline Logan, "Narcissism," in *Personality, Personality Disorder and Violence*, ed. Mary McMurran and Richard C. Howard (Malden, MA: John Wiley & Sons, 2009), 91.
[231] "Research suggests core features of the disorder are associated with poor prognosis in therapy, including slow progress to behavioral change, premature patient-initiated termination, and negative therapeutic alliance." Elizabeth L. Kacel, Nicole Ennis, and Deidre B. Pereira, "Narcissistic Personality Disorder in Clinical Health Psychology Practice: Case Studies of Comorbid Psychological Distress and Life-Limiting Illness," *Behavioral Medicine* 43, no. 3 (2017): 156-164, abstract, https://doi.org/10.1080/08964289.2017.1301875. See also: Eve Caligor, Kenneth N. Levy, Frank E. Yeomans, "Narcissistic Personality Disorder: Diagnostic and Clinical Challenges," *American Journal of Psychiatry* 172, no. 5 (May 2015), https://ajp.psychiatryonline.org/doi/pdf/10.1176/appi.ajp.2014.14060723; and Otto F Kernberg, "The Almost Untreatable Narcissistic Patient," *Journal of the American Psychoanalytic Association* 55, no. 2 (February 2007): 503-39.
[232] Yan, Brown, and Duke, "New Details Emerge about California Killer."
[233] Rodger, *My Twisted World*, pt. 6, under "22 Years Old."
[234] Jen Heger, "UCSB Shooter Eliot Rodger Refused Psychiatric Medicines, His Parents Now in Hiding," RadarOnline.com, posted May 25, 2014, https://radaronline.com/exclusives/2014/05/ucsb-mass-shooter-refused-psychiatric-medicines-parents-in-hiding/.
[235] Rodger, *My Twisted World*, pt. 6, under "22 Years Old."
[236] Ibid, pt. 6, under "21 Years Old."
[237] Ibid.
[238] Ibid.
[239] Ibid.
[240] Ibid.
[241] Ibid.
[242] Ibid, pt. 6, under "22 Years Old."

[243] Ibid, pt. 6, under "21 Years Old."
[244] Ibid. Grammar matches posted document.
[245] Ibid.
[246] Ibid.
[247] Ibid.
[248] Vaknin, *Malignant Self Love*, 128.
[249] Rodger, *My Twisted World*, pt. 6, under "21 Years Old."
[250] Ibid, pt. 6, under "22 Years Old."
[251] Rodger, *My Twisted World*, pt. 6, under "22 Years Old." Rodger produced and published 22 videos throughout his life. They range in length from 27 seconds ("Throwback: July 4th, 2011 Party," posted April 5, 2011) to 9 minutes, 29 seconds ("Awesome View of L.A. from Landing Plane," March 28, 2014). Besides his last, twelve were uploaded in May 2014. Hanne Wolsgård, "Imagined Injustice: Elliot Rodger, Masculinity, and Fantasies of Perceived Victimhood," (master's thesis, University of Southern Denmark, 2015), 8, appendix b. The last, "Retribution," was posted the day of his rampage. Elliot Rodger, "Retribution," video and audio in *New York Times*, "YouTube Video: Retribution," posted May 24, 2014, https://www.nytimes.com/video/us/100000002900707/youtube-video-retribution.html.
[252] Rodger, *My Twisted World*, pt. 6, under "22 Years Old."
[253] Ibid. Ellipsis in circulated document.
[254] According to Simon Astaire, a family friend, in Joe Mozingo, "Frantic Parents of Shooting Suspect Raced to Isla Vista," *Los Angeles Times*, posted May 25, 2014, https://www.latimes.com/local/lanow/la-me-ln-frantic-parents-isla-vista-shootings-20140525-story.html; Kate Mather, Richard Winton, and Adolfo Flores, "Deputies Didn't View Elliot Rodger's Videos in Welfare Check," *Los Angeles Times*, posted May 29, 2014, https://www.latimes.com/local/la-me-rodger-welfare-20140530-story.html; interview with County Sheriff Bill Brown, on *Face the Nation*, embedded in Rebecca Kaplan, "Sheriff: Elliot Rodger Long Concealed Mental Health Issues," *Face the Nation*, last updated May 25, 2014, https://www.cbsnews.com/news/elliot-rodger-long-concealed-mental-health-issues-sheriff-says/.
[255] Mather, Winton, and Flores, "Deputies Didn't View Elliot Rodger's Videos."
[256] According to a statement by the Sheriff, reported in Mather, Winton, and Flores, "Deputies Didn't View Elliot Rodger's Videos."
[257] Kaplan, "Sheriff: Elliot Rodger Long Concealed Mental Health Issues."
[258] Rodger, *My Twisted World*, pt. 6, under "22 Years Old." Spelling and grammar as posted.
[259] Timothy Levine, "Truth-Default Theory (TDT): A Theory of Human Deception and Deception Detection," *Journal of Language and Social Psychology* 33, no. 4 (May 2014): 378-392.

[260] Interview with County Sheriff Bill Brown on *Face the Nation*, embedded in Kaplan, "Sheriff: Elliot Rodger Long Concealed Mental Health Issues."

[261] Joe Navarro with Toni Sciarra Poynter, *Dangerous Personalities: An FBI Profiler Shows You How to Identify and Protect Yourself from Harmful People* (United States of America: Rodale, 2017), 25.

[262] Vaknin, *Malignant Self Love*, 371.

[263] Rodger, "Retribution," in *New York Times*, "Elliot Rodger's 'Retribution' Video"; Peter Langman, transcriber, "Transcript of Elliot Rodger's 'Retribution' Video," School Shooters. info, s.v. "Elliot Rodger."

Chapter Six

[1] Jessica M. Craig, Stephanie M. Cardwell, and Alex R. Piquero, "The Effects of Criminal Propensity and Strain on Later Offending," *Crime & Delinquency* 63, no. 13 (August 2016): 1655-1681.

[2] Jonathan Fast, *Ceremonial Violence: A Psychological Explanation of School Shootings* (Woodstock, NY: Overlook Press, 2008), 28.

[3] Annemarie C.J. Köhne and Adela-Maria Isvoranu, "A Network Perspective on the Comorbidity of Personality Disorders and Mental Disorders: An Illustration of Depression and Borderline Personality Disorder," *Frontiers in Psychology*, posted July 6, 2021, under "Discussion," https://www.frontiersin.org/articles/10.3389/fpsyg.2021.680805/full. Besides data in the study and references throughout the article, two specific sources supporting these conclusions are mentioned: Mark J. Hilsenroth, Michael Katz, and Annalisa Tanzilli, "Psychotherapy Research and the Psychodynamic Diagnostic Manual (PDM–2)," *Psychoanalytic Psychology* 35, no. 3 (July 2018): 320-327; and Vittorio Lingiardi and Nancy McWilliams, "The Psychodynamic Diagnostic Manual – 2nd edition (PDM-2)," *World Psychiatry* 14, no. 2 (June 2015): 237-239.

[4] See Table 1.1, under the heading "Pathological Personality."

[5] Hervey Cleckley, *The Mask of Sanity* (St. Louis, Mo: C. V. Mosby Co., 1982), 137-145. Also: a) W. John Livesley, "Conceptual and Taxonomic Issues" in *Handbook of Personality Disorders: Theory, Research, and Treatment*, ed. W. John Livesley (New York, NY: Guilford Press, 2001), 3-38; b) Theodore Millon, Sarah E. Meagher, and Seth D. Grossman, "Theoretical Perspectives," in *Handbook of Personality Disorders*, 39-59; c) Peter Mulders, Alberto Llera, Indira Tendolkar, Philip van Eijndhoven, and Christian Beckmann, "Personality Profiles Are Associated with Functional Brain Networks Related to Cognition and Emotion," *Scientific Reports* 8, article no. 13874 (2018), posted September 17, 2018, https://www.nature.com/articles/s41598-018-32248-x; d) Regina T. Dolan-Sewell, Robert F. Krueger, and M. Tracie Shea, "Co-Occurrence with Syndrome Disorders," in *Handbook of Personality Disorders*, 84-104.

[6] Alv A. Dahl, "Psychopathy and Psychiatric Comorbidity," in *Psychopathy: Antisocial, Criminal, and Violent Behavior*, 293, referring to Eli Robins, Kathye A. Gentry, Rodrigo A. Munoz, and Sue Marten, "A Contrast of the Three More Common Illnesses with the Ten Less Common in a Study and 18-Month Follow-up of 314 Psychiatric Emergency Room Patients," *Archive of General Psychiatry* 34, no. 3 (1977): 285-291.

[7] M. C. J. Swanson, R. C. Bland, and S. C. Newman, "Antisocial Personality Disorders," *Acta Psychiatrica Scandinavica* 89, no. s376 (January 1994): 63-70, abstract, https://doi.org/10.1111/j.1600-0447.1994.tb05792.x.

[8] T. J. Maanasa, C. Sivabackiya, B. Srinivasan, Shajahan Ismail, Sabari Sridhar, and S. Kailash, "A Cross Sectional Study on Prevalence and Pattern of Personality Disorders in Psychiatric Inpatients of a Tertiary Care Hospital," *International Archives of Integrated Medicine* 3, no. 5 (May 2016): 94-97, table 3, http://iaimjournal.com/wp-content/uploads/2016/05/iaim_2016_0305_16.pdf.

[9] Estimates for the number of patrons and staff members inside the eatery at the time of Huberty's rampage range from 45 to 50. History.com Editors, "Twenty-One People Are Shot to Death at McDonald's," History, posted November 13, 2009, updated July 20, 2020, https://www.history.com/this-day-in-history/twenty-one-people-are-shot-to-death-at-mcdonalds; Bill O'Brien, *Killing for Pleasure: Unique Profiles of Nine Mass Murderers from One of the World's Leading Police officers* (London, UK: John Blake, Ltd., 2009), 42.

[10] Arthur S. Brisbane, "To Father of Mass Murderer, Son's Violence Is Inexplicable," *Washington Post*, published July 21, 1984, https://www.washingtonpost.com/archive/politics/1984/07/21/to-father-of-mass-murderer-sons-violence-is-inexplicable/377d77bd-97ff-4f22-b2a3-15c747f70ea3/?utm_term=.0ec0278d1f59; John Holusha, "Mass Killer is Recalled as a Gun Loving Youth," *New York Times* 133, no. 46,112 (July 21, 1984): A8; Murderpedia: The Encyclopedia of Murderers, last updated June 4, 2017, "James Huberty," s.v. "James Oliver Huberty," https://murderpedia. org/; O'Brien, *Killing for Pleasure*, 33.

[11] Huberty's father gave that explanation, adding, "She wanted to be a missionary in Jamaica. She did go with the Indians out West." Brisbane, "To Father of Mass Murderer." A different account states that she left to work as a Southern Baptist street preacher. Murderpedia, "James Oliver Huberty," s.v. "James Oliver Huberty." While still another says simply that she became a "street missionary." Robert Keller, *The World's Deadliest Rampage Killer*s (self-pub., 2016), 9.

[12] Holusha, "Mass Killer Is Recalled."

[13] Steven Carley, *Serial Killers, Mass Murderers, & Disorders* (Brockton, MA: SGC Production, 2013), 20; *Philadelphia Daily News*, "Killers Rage Was Long Simmering."

[14] Holusha, "Mass Killer Is Recalled."

[15] Brisbane, "To Father of Mass Murderer."

[16] Esther Calvete, Izaskun Orue, and Benjamin L. Hankin, "Early Maladaptive Schemas and Social Anxiety in Adolescents: The Mediating Role of Anxious Automatic Thoughts," *Journal of Anxiety Disorders* 27, no. 3 (April 2013), 278; and Kim Killu, R. Marc, and A. Crundwell, "Students with Anxiety in the Classroom: Educational Accommodations and Interventions," *Beyond Behavior* 25, no. 2 (August 2016), 30.

[17] Judith L. Rapoport and Deborah R. Ismond, *DSM-IV Training Guide for Diagnosis of Childhood Disorders* (New York, NY: Routledge, 1996), 227.

[18] Killu and Marc, "Students with Anxiety," 30. Also, see: Esther Calvete, Izaskun Orue, and Benjamin L. Hankin, "O-43 – Early Maladaptive Schemas and Social Anxiety in Adolescents: The Mediating Role of Anxious Automatic Thoughts," *Journal of Anxiety Disorders* 27, no. 3 (April 2013): 278-279; and Eliot A. Layden, John T. Cacioppo, Stephanie Cacioppo, Stefano F. Cappa, Alessandra Dodich, Andrea Falini, and Nicola Canessa, "Perceived Social Isolation Is Associated with Altered Functional Connectivity in Neural Networks Associated with Tonic Alertness and Executive Control," *NeuroImage* 145 (January 2017): 58-73.

[19] Carl F. Weems, Wendy K. Silverman, Ronald M. Rapee, and Armando A. Pina, "The Role of Control in Childhood Anxiety Disorders," *Cognitive Therapy and Research* 27, no. 5 (October 2003), abstract.

[20] Alte Miller, in John Holusha, "Mass Killer is Recalled."

[21] Murderpedia, "Killer Talked of 'Shooting Somebody,'" originally published July 20, 1984, s.v. "James Oliver Huberty."

[22] Carley, *Serial Killers, Mass*, 20, 21; Keller, *The World's Deadliest*, 9, 10; *Washington Post*, "I Never Really Believed that He Would Do Anything Like This," July 21, 1984, https://www.washingtonpost.com/archive/politics /1984/07/21/i-never-really-believed-that-he-would-do-anything-like-this/6e 96d1aa-65b1-456a-a999-86c0121e3449/?utm_term=.c89553d8a540 (page discontinued); Murderpedia, "James Oliver Huberty," s.v. "James Oliver Huberty."

[23] Murderpedia, "James Huberty," s.v. "James Oliver Huberty"; *Washington Post*, "I Never Really Believed."

[24] Brisbane, "To Father of Mass Murderer"; Bill Cardoso, "Mass Murderer: 'Always Very Sad and Very Lonely,'" United Press International (UPI) Archives, originally published July 22, 1984, https://www.upi.com/ Archives /1984/07/22/Mass-murderer-always-very-sad-and-very-lonely/4891459316

800/#:~:text=SAN%20DIEGO%20%2D%2D%20One%20day,proclaimed%20himself%20a%20war%20criminal.; Keller, *The World's Deadliest*, 10.

[25] *Philadelphia Daily News*, "Killers Rage Was Long Simmering," originally published July 19, 1984, Murderpedia, s.v., "James Oliver Huberty."

[26] Carley, *Serial Killers, Mass Murderers*, 21; Keller, *The World's Deadliest*, 10; "James Oliver Huberty," Murderpedia, s.v. "James Oliver Huberty."

[27] Mark Z. Barabak, "James Huberty, The Loner Who Killed 21 People at…," UPI Archives, originally published July 20, 1984, https://www.upi.com/Archives/1984/07/20/James-Huberty-the-loner-who-killed-21-people-at/6288459144000/.

[28] Creative Commons "James Oliver Huberty," Real Life Villains Wiki, s.v. "James Oliver Huberty," last updated June 16, 2021, under "Biography," https://reallifevillains.miraheze.org/wiki/JamesOliver_Huberty (site terminated); Murderpedia, "James Oliver Huberty," s.v. "James Oliver Huberty."

[29] Carley, *Serial Killers, Mass Murderers*, 21; Keller, *The World's Deadliest*, 11; Creative Commons "James Oliver Huberty," under "Biography."

[30] Judith Cummings, "Neighbors Term Mass Slayer A Quiet but Hotheaded Loner," *New York Times* archives, originally published July 20, 1984, https://www.nytimes.com/1984/07/20/us/neighbors-term-mass-slayer-a-quiet-but-hotheaded-loner.html; Time-Life Editors, *True Crime: Mass Murderers* (Alexandria, VA: Time Life Books, 1992), 122.

[31] Cummings, "Neighbors Term Mass Slayer."

[32] Time-Life Editors, *True Crime: Mass Murderers*, 119.

[33] *Philadelphia Daily News*, "Killer Fit Soldier of Fortune Profile," originally published July 20, 1984, Muderpedia, s.v. "James Oliver Huberty"; Creative Commons "James Oliver Huberty," under "Biography."

[34] Murderpedia, "Killer Talked of 'Shooting Somebody,'" s.v. "James Oliver Huberty." The observation is substantiated in James Alan Fox and Jack Levin, *Extreme Killing: Understanding Serial and Mass Murder*, (Thousand Oaks, CA: Sage Publications, 2005), 248.

[35] Mark Z. Barabak, "James Huberty, the loner who killed 21 people at …," UPI Archives, originally posted July 20, 1984, https://www.upi.com/Archives/1984/07/20/James-Huberty-the-loner-who-killed-21-people-at/6288459144000/.

[36] Brisbane, "To Father of Mass Murderer."

[37] *Washington Post*, "I Never Really Believed."

[38] According to Etna Huberty, in Murderpedia, "James Huberty"; Keller, *The World's Deadliest*, 11;

[39] Keller, *The World's Deadliest*, 11; Time-Life Editors, *True Crime: Mass Murderers*, 119.

[40] According to a story in the *Akron Beacon Journal*, as reported in Murderpedia, s.v. "James Oliver Huberty."

[41] James Aslanes, in Murderpedia, "Killer Talked of 'Shooting Somebody,'" s.v. "James Oliver Huberty."

[42] Carley, *Serial Killers, Mass Murderers*, 21; Murderpedia, "Killer Talked of 'Shooting Somebody.'" The second reference states it was a car accident, while the first says it involved a motorcycle.

[43] Fandom, "James Huberty," Criminal Minds Wiki, n.d., under "Background," https://criminalminds .fandom.com/wiki/James_Huberty; Etna Huberty, in Murderpedia, "James Huberty."

[44] Carley, *Serial Killers, Mass Murderers*, 21; Time-Life Editors, *True Crime: Mass Murderers*, 118.

[45] R.M. Beard, "The Pre-Conceptual Sub-Stage," in *An Outline of Piaget's Developmental Psychology* 1st ed., (London, England: Routledge, 2006), abstract, https://www.routledge.com/An-Outline-of-Piagets-Developmental-Psychology/Beard/p/book/9780415402293; Oxford Reference, in *A Dictionary of Psychology*, 2023, s.v. "Transductive Reasoning," https://www.oxfordreference.com/view/10.1093/oi/authority.20110803105323835.

[46] Steve Burns, "What Is Transductive Reasoning?" New Trader U, © 2024 New Trader U, https://www.newtraderu.com/2020/05/20/what-is-transductive-reasoning/. To pursue the relationship to cognitive maturation, see John H. Flavell, *The Developmental Psychology of Jean Piaget*, (New York, NY: D. Van Nostrand Co., Litton Educational Publishing, Inc., 1963), 160. Unfortunately, this type of short-circuited reasoning is not always limited to children.

[47] See: a) Gene G. Ano and Erin B. Vasconcelles, "Religious Coping and Psychological Adjustment to Stress: A Meta-Analysis," *Journal of Clinical Psychology* 61, no. 4 (April 2005): 461-480; b) Giora Keinan, "Effects of Stress and Tolerance of Ambiguity on Magical Thinking," *Journal of Personality and Social Psychology* 67, no. 1 (July 1994): 48-55; c) Richard Wiseman and Caroline Watt, "Belief in Psychic Ability and the Misattribution Hypothesis: A Qualitative Review," *British Journal of Psychology* 97, no. 3 (August 2006): 323-338.

[48] Cardoso, "Mass Murderer: 'Always Very Sad,'"; Carley, *Serial Killers, Mass Murderers*, 21; Fandom, "James Huberty," under "Background"; Murderpedia, "James Huberty," s.v. "James Oliver Huberty"; Time-Life Editors, *True Crime: Mass Murderers*, 121.

[49] "A Haunting Memory: Survivors of McDonald's Massacre Cope," originally published July 17, 1994, Murderpedia, s.v. "James Oliver Huberty,"; substantiated by Keller, *The World's Deadliest Killers*, 12. Partially because of Huberty's crimes, the state legislature passed a law requiring more rigorous screening for security personnel. IMDb, "James Oliver Huberty

Biography," IMDb.com, Inc., updated 1990-2021, under "Trivia (6)," https://www.imdb.com/name/nm1272041/bio.

[50] Keller, *The World's Deadliest*, 12; Murderpedia, "James Huberty," s.v. "James Oliver Huberty"; Time-Life Editors, *True Crime: Mass Murderers*, 121, 122, 123.

[51] Daisy Yuhas, "Psychology Reveals the Comforts of the Apocalypse," *Scientific American*: posted December 18, 2012, https://blogs.scientificamerican.com/observations/psychology-reveals-the-comforts-of-the-apocalypse/.

[52] Cardoso, "Mass Murderer: 'Always Very Sad.'"

[53] Cardoso, "Mass Murderer: 'Always Very Sad.'"; Murderpedia, "James Huberty," s.v. "James Oliver Huberty."

[54] Fox and Levin, *Extreme Killing: Understanding*, 248; Holusha, "Mass Killer is Recalled"; *New York Times*, "Coast Man Kills 20 in Rampage at a Restaurant," 133, no. 46,110 (July 19, 1984): A1; narration, in *Real Crime*, "Minute by Minute: Hunting Humans - San Ysidro McDonald's Massacre," YouTube, posted November 24, 2016, https://www.youtube.com/watch?v=AXCvEslZRVY.

[55] Carley, *Serial Killers, Mass Murderers*, 21; Fandom, "James Huberty," under "The Massacre"; narration, in *Real Crime*, "Minute by Minute"; Time-Life Editors, *Mass Murders*, 123.

[56] Katherine Ramsland, *Inside the Minds of Mass Murderers: Why They* Kill (Westport, CT: Praeger Publishers, 2005), 41.

[57] Keller, *The World's Deadliest*, 12-13; Murderpedia, s.v. "James Oliver Huberty."

[58] Keller, *The World's Deadliest*, 13"; Time-Life Editors, *Mass Murderers*, 123.

[59] Keller, *The World's Deadliest*, 13.

[60] Carley, *Serial Killers, Mass Murderers*, 22; Fandom, "James Huberty," under "The Massacre"; Fox and Levin, *Extreme Killing: Understanding*," 248; Keller, *The World's Deadliest*, 13-14; Murderpedia, "One Man's Massacre," s.v. "James Oliver Huberty."

[61] Narration, in *Seriously Strange*, Rob Gavagan, host, Rob Dyke, writ., "Massacre at McDonald's - James Huberty: Anatomy of Murder #5," YouTube, posted May 22, 2016, https://www.youtube.com/watch?v=LGpym2LagOk&t=55s; Editors of Time-Life, *Mass Murderers*, 124.

[62] David Freed, "'Going Hunting Humans,' Slayer Told Wife," *Los Angeles Times*, July 20, 1984, 1, as quoted in Ramsland, *Inside the Minds*, 42, 5en. An almost identical quotation appears in another story, "going hunting…hunting for humans." George Pallas, "The McDonald's Massacre," *20/20*, posted July 27, 2020, https://georgepallas.com/blog/2020/07/mcdonalds-massacre/. The exact phrasing of the farewell may have been slightly different. Here are some samples: a) "I'm going to hunt humans," as recalled by Etna Huberty, in Debbie Baker, "Daughter of McDonald's Killer

Has Advice for San Bernardino Shooters' Baby," *San Diego Tribune*: posted August 23, 2016, https://www.sandiegouniontribune.com/opinion/the-conversation/sdut-daughter-mcdonalds-killer-james-huberty-interview-2015 dec15-story.html; b) "Going hunting humans," Keller, *The World's Deadliest*, 13 and Murderpedia, "James Huberty," s.v. "James Oliver Huberty"; c) "Hunting humans"; narration, in *Seriously Strange*, Gavagan and Dyke, "Massacre at McDonald's"; d) "I'm going hunting," James Alan Fox and Jack Levin, *Overkill: Mass Murder and Serial Killing Exposed* (New York, NY: Plenum Press, 1994), 230; e) "I'm going hunting humans," Violence Policy Center, *Where'd They Get Their Guns? An Analysis of the Firearms Used in High-Profile Shootings, 1963 to 2001*, April 2001 75, http://www.vpc.org/graphics/where.pdf. It hardly matters, the foreboding nonchalance prevails in all versions.

[63] Baker, "Daughter of McDonald's Killer"; Editors of Time-Life, *Mass Murderers*, 124.

[64] IMDb, "James Oliver Huberty Biography," under "Trivia (6)"; *New York Times,* "The Gun Collector," 133 no. 46,113 (July 22, 1984): E 20; *Real Crime*, "Minute by Minute." An Uzi is a hand-held sub-machine gun designed by Israeli Captain Uziel Gal for an international competition to design a new automatic weapon during the 1940s. Three variants have been developed in the years since. Orvelin Valle, "11 Facts about the Legendary Uzi Submachine Gun," We Are the Mighty, posted November 24, 2015, https://www.wearethemighty.com/mighty-tactical/11-facts-about-the-legendary-uzi-submachine-gun/.

[65] *Real Crime*, "Minute by Minute."

[66] Murderpedia, "One Man's Massacre," s.v. "James Oliver Huberty"; narration, in *Seriously Strange*, Gavagan and Dyke, "Massacre at McDonald's."

[67] Murderpedia, "One Man's Massacre," s.v. "James Oliver Huberty"; *New York Times,* "Coast Man Kills 20"; Jerry Sanders interview with Itica Milanes, in ABC 10 News, "Remembering the McDonald's Massacre," YouTube, posted July 16, 2014, https://www.youtube.com/watch?v=99JnMxyvL-E&t=116s.

[68] Narration, in *Seriously Strange*, Gavagan and Dyke, "Massacre at McDonald's"; *Seriously Strange*, narration, in Gavagan and Dyke, "Massacre at McDonald's."

[69] Comments by Charlie Minn, filmmaker, in KPBS News, "77 Minutes – 1984 McDonald's Mass Murder," YouTube, posted September 20, 2016, https://www.youtube.com/watch?v=thgXWb97B4c.

[70] Time-Life Editors, *Mass Murderers*, 127. The *New York Times* stated there was an unconfirmed report that Huberty exclaimed, "he had killed many in Vietnam and he wanted to kill more." "Coast Man Kills 20."

[71] Mike McPadden, "'Society Had Their Chance': James Huberty and the 1984 'Hunting Humans' McDonald's Massacre," Investigation Discovery Crime

Feed, posted July 18, 2017, http://crimefeed .com/2017/07/im-going-to-hunt-humans-james-huberty-and-the-1984-mcdonalds-massacre/ (video no longer accessible).

[72] Karla Felix, in ABC 10 News San Diego and Itica Milanes, "Shot in the Head: 32 Years Later, McDonald's Massacre Survivor Shares Her Story," https://www.10news.com/news/shot-in-the-head-32-years-later-mcdonalds-massacre-survivor-shares-her-story; commentary by Steve Fiorina, reporter in ABC 10 News, "'77 Minutes' Explores McDonald's Massacre," YouTube, posted July 18, 2016, https://www.youtube.com/watch?v=WDWBzpZTrRU; comments by Minn, in KPBS News. "77 Minutes – 1984 McDonald's Mass Murder"; *Philadelphia Daily News*, "Critical after Massacre, Healthy Baby Goes Home," originally published August 8, 1984, Murderpedia, s.v. "James Oliver Huberty"; narration, in *Seriously Strange*, Gavagan and Dyke, "Massacre at McDonald's."

[73] Replay of undated news cast hosted by Marty Levin, in *Morbid Minds*, "The 1984 McDonald's Massacre: James Huberty," YouTube, posted January 16, 2018, https://www.youtube.com/watch?v= 25QkdMy889o&t=46s.

[74] Report by Milanes, in ABC 10 News, "Remembering the McDonald's Massacre"; Sign on San Diego, "Time of Terror," Murderpedia, s.v. "James Oliver Huberty"; Dana Littlefield, "New Documentary Explores 1984 McDonald's Massacre in San Ysidro," *San Diego Union-Tribune*, posted September 21, 2016, http://www.sandiegouniontribune.com/sd-me-mcdonalds -documentary-20160920-story.html. Because they do not to count the murdered fetus, many reports state that, besides, Huberty only 20 died that day.

[75] Ramsland, *Inside the Minds*, 41; narration, in *Seriously Strange*, Gavagan and Dyke, "Massacre at McDonald's."

[76] *New York Times*, "Coast Man Kills"; *New York Times,* "Mass Slayings and Toll: McDonald's Case Biggest," 136, no. 47,120 (April 25, 1987): A9. Tragically, that number was surpassed in the Mandalay Bay massacre in Las Vegas.

[77] Mei Fong, "Newtown and Guangshan county: A tale of two massacres," *Salon*, posted December 17, 2012, https://www.salon.com/2012/12/17/the_chinese _lanza_had_a_knife_all_22_schoolkids_survived/. An online magazine (that specializes in the interpretation of Chinese media) complained, "Incredibly, days after the occurrence … reporters still do not know the names of the children attacked." Ibid, quoting *Tea Leaf Nation*. A few months before that, a nurse was seriously lacerated by a frustrated patient. A doctor, a security guard and a guide were also injured. The attack occurred after the Ministry of Health and the Ministry of Public Security issued a stern statement warning of criminal penalties for such actions. After the incident, a professor at Capital Medical University countered that the government should be providing support for patients who are struggling with the emotional

repercussions of serious illness. Sina, "Man Detained in Brutal Stabbing," *China Daily*, posted September 5, 2012, http://english.sina.com/china/p/2012/0904/503362.html (site no longer accessible). Chinese authorities have consistently explained that mass attacks were instigated by people who have mental illness or a history suggesting that possibility. David Brenan, "Mentally Ill Man Goes on Knife Rampage, Attacks and Stabs Early Morning Commuters and Students," *Newsweek*, posted February 21, 2019, https://www.newsweek.com/mass-stabbing-knives-china-jian-commuters-students-wounded-1338629. However, some have suggested that the gulf between the wealthy and those in poverty is responsible and others have indicated that the increase in psychological problems may be linked to accelerating economic pressure and the decrease in social support systems. Agence France-Presse, "15 Killed in New Year Knife Rampage and Arson Attack In China," *Jakarta Post*, posted February 8, 2019, https://www.thejakartapost.com/news/2019/02/08/15-killed-in-new-year-knife-rampage-and-arson-attack-in-china.html; Brennan, "Mentally Ill Man Goes On Knife Rampage." When an ex-convict rammed his Land Rover into crowds at a public square in Hengyang then assaulted people with a dagger and shovel, leaving 15 dead, police said simply, "he wanted revenge against society." Kelsey Cheng, "Rampage Driver Is Sentenced to Death in China after Ramming His Car into Crowds on a Busy Square, Killing 15," *Daily Mail Online*, posted and updated December 2018, https://www.dailymail.co.uk/news/article-6492151/Driver-sentenced-death-China-ramming-car-crowds-busy-square-killing-15.html. Within months the 54-year-old man was sentenced to death and executed. Tom Livingstone, China Executes Man Just Months after Rampage Killed 15 People," 9News, posted January 29, 2019, https://www.9news.com.au/world/china-news-yang-zanyun-executed-just-months-after-rampage-kills-15-people/52f3530b-216b-4261-8136-75d4ac96d623.

[78] Consider: a) David Bamman, Brendan O'Connor, and Noah A. Smith, "Censorship and Deletion Practices in Chinese Social Media," *First Monday: Peer Reviewed Journal on the Internet* 17, no. 3 (March 5, 2012), doi: 10.5210/fm.v17i3.3943; b) Beina Xu and Eleanor Albert, "Media Censorship in China," Council on Foreign Relations, updated February 17, 2017, https://www.cfr.org/backgrounder/media-censorship-china; c) Dan Blumenthal and Linda Zhang, "China's Censorship, Propaganda & Disinformation," American Enterprise Institute, posted July 10, 2020, https://www.aei.org/articles/chinas-censorship-propaganda-disinformation/.

[79] Because of that government's multiple attempts to render the probability of psychological degeneration into simplistic bromides, the appendix disregards every case from the People's Republic, save one, which is included because adequate background information was available.

Appendix

[1] Lara Cooper, "Hearings Continue on Possible Release of David Attias, Driver Who Killed 4 in Isla Vista," *Noozhawk*, posted June 1, 2012, https://www.noozhawk.com/article/060112_court_hearings_driver_who_killed_4.

[2] Investigation Commission, *Jokela School Shooting on 7 November 2007* (Finland: Ministry of Justice, 2009), 50, School Shooters. info, s.v. "Pekka-Eric Auvinen."

[3] Investigation Commission, *Jokela School Shooting*, 50; Tuulikki Petäjäniemi, Chairperson of Investigation Commission, in interview for TV Nelonen News, February 26, 2009, embedded in Bit Chute, "What Kind of Person Was Pekka-Eric Auvinen – An Interview with Tuulikki Petäjäniemi," posted October 24, 2021, https://www.bitchute.com/video/cyDVhEQB9RSg/.

[4] Tuomas Hulkkonen, peer, in Associated Press (AP), "Police: Finland Teen Shooter Left a Suicide Note," National Broadcasting Company (NBC) News, posted November 8, 2007, https://www.nbcnews.com/id/wbna21686096; Investigation Commission, *Jokela School Shooting*, 50-51.

[5] A&E Encyclopedia Dramatica, s.v. "Pekka-Eric Auvinen/Archive," edited June 7, 2018, https://encyclopediadramatica.online/Pekka-Eric_Auvinen/archive; Harry de Quetteville, "Biography of a Teen Killer," originally published by Telegraph.co.uk, posted August 11, 2007, Murderpedia, s.v. "Pekka-Eric Auvinen."

[6] Auvinen, *Channel of Truth and Justice*, originally posted on YouTube, joined October 2007, School Shooters. info, s.v. "Pekka-Eric Auvinen."

[7] Sakari Suoninen, "Finland School Shooter Admired Hitler, Nietzsche," Reuters, posted November 8, 2007, https://www.reuters.com/article/idUSL083199 81/.

[8] Patrick Radden Keefe, "A Loaded Gun: A Mass Shooter's Tragic Past," *The New Yorker Reader True Crime*, Special Edition (December 2015): 91, 97-98.

[9] He would deliberately display the butt. The habit eventually resulted in the offer of a severance package. Michael D. Kelleher, *Profiling the Lethal Employee: Case Studies of Violence in the Workplace* (Westport, Connecticut: Praeger, 1997), 75-76.

[10] Murderpedia, "Luther Casteel," s.v. "Luther V. Casteel.

[11] An interviewer asked him to describe his feelings when he took up his gun and decided to kill. Casteel replied: "Fear. Loneliness... Yeah. Depressed. It's hard to explain." Alex Hannaford, "We Asked 12 Mass Killers: 'What Would Have Stopped You?'" *GQ*, posted September 11, 2018, https://www.gq-magazine.co.uk/article/mass-shootings-in-america-interviews. Presented as written. An article from the *Kane County Chronicle*, reprinted in *SSRI Stories*, states a doctor diagnosed Casteel with "bipolar disorder, also known

as manic-depressive disease." The original is not accessible. Victoria A.F. Camron, "Suspect Takes Stand in Pub Shooting Trial," originally published November 27, 2001, posted with editor's note: "Man Prescribed Zoloft Drinks, Goes on Shooting Spree in Bar Killing 2, Injuring 16. Sentenced to Death," now on Scribd, as "Man Kills Two: Injures 16," under "Index To SSRI Stories."

[12] AP, "Suspect in Shooting of 18 Is Ex-Convict," *New York Times*, posted April 16, 2001, https://www.nytimes.com/2001/04/16/national/suspect-in-shooting-of-18-is-exconvict.html; oral transcript of letter by Casteel, in Stories from the Penitentiary, "Speaking to Inmate Luther Casteel," YouTube, posted February 26, 2001, https://www.youtube.com/watch?v=-awLeLfObz0. Regarding the low arousal threshold, criminal history, and promiscuity, see: American Psychiatric Association, DSM-5, 659-661; Robert D. Hare, *Without Conscience: The Disturbing World of The Psychopaths Among Us* (New York, New York: Guilford Press, 1993), 52-56, 67-68; Thomas A. Widiger and Donald R. Lynam, "Psychopathy and the Five-Factor Model of Personality," in *Psychopathy: Antisocial, Criminal, and Violent Behavior*, ed. Theodore Millon, Erik Simonsen, Morten Birket-Smith, and Roger D, Davis (New York, NY: Guilford Press, 1988), 176, 178-179.

[13] Murderpedia, "Luther Casteel."

[14] Beth Karas, "Man Obsessed with Columbine Convicted of Murder," Cable News Network (CNN), posted August 21, 2009, http://www.cnn.com /2009/CRIME/08/21/north.carolina.castillo.trial/index.html#; North Carolina Court of Appeals, State of North Carolina v. Alvaro Rafael Castillo, Defendant-Appellant's Brief, no. COA 10-814, submitted September 19, 2010, 5, School Shooters. info, s.v. "Alvaro Castillo."

[15] Alvaro Castillo, "Self-Made Video 5-31-06 pt. 2," posted on *MrAlvarocastillo*, You Tube, August 16, 2009, https://www.youtube.com/watch?v=x7Sp9H2 qIm0; Court of Appeals, *North Carolina v. Castillo*, 6-7; Karas, "Man Obsessed with Columbine."

[16] Virginia Tech Review Panel, *Mass Shootings at Virginia Tech – April 16, 2007* (Commonwealth of Virginia: presented to Governor, August 2007), 31-32, https://scholar.lib.vt.edu/prevail/docs/VTReviewPanelReport.pdf.

[17] Evan Thomas, "Tragedy at Virginia Tech," *Newsweek*, posted April 29, 2007, https://www.newsweek.com/tragedy-virginia-tech-98053; Virginia Tech Review Panel, *Mass Shootings at Virginia Tech*, 33, 37.

[18] Cho Seung-hui, "Fiction and Poetry," School Shooters. info, s.v. "Seung-hui Cho"; Michael Fitzgerald, "Autism and School Shootings — Overlap of Autism (Asperger's Syndrome) and General Psychopathy," posted April 2, 2015, from the edited volume *Autism Spectrum Disorder – Recent Advances*, under "5. Virginia Tech Shootings," https://www.intechopen.com/chapters/

47518; Virginia Tech Review Panel, *Mass Shootings at Virginia Tech*, 31-35.

[19] CBS News, "Police: Cho Stalked 2 Women In 2005," posted April 18, 2007, https://www.cbsnews.com/news/police-cho-stalked-2-women-in-2005/; Cho Seung-hui, "Fiction and Poetry"; Dave Cullen, "Psychopath? Depressive? Schizophrenic? Was Cho Seung-Hui Really Like the Columbine Killers?" *Slate*, posted April 20, 2007, https://slate.com/technology/2007/04/was-cho-a-psychopath-a-depressive-or-a-psychotic.html; National Public Radio (NPR), *Morning Edition*, "Cho Was Accused of Stalking in 2005," transcript and audio report, April 18, 2007, https:// www.npr.org/templates/story /story.php?storyId=9645423; Johnathan Watts, "Gunman's brooding disturbed his family," *Guardian*, posted April 19, 2007, https://www. theguardian.com/world/2007/apr/19/usgunviolence.usa4.

[20] Alexis Shaw and Michael S. James, in American Broadcasting Company (ABC) News, "LAX Suspect Paul Ciancia Told Officials He Acted Alone in Airport Shooting," posted November 2, 2017, http://abcnews.go.com/US/lax-suspect -paul-ciancia-told-officials-acted-airport/story?id =20770658.

[21] Josh Hicks, "Police: Alleged LAX Gunman Ciancia Texted Brother with Suicidal Thoughts," *Washington Post*, posted November 2, 2013, https:// www.washingtonpost.com/local/crime/police-alleged-lax-gunman-ciancia-texted-brother-with-suicidal-thoughts/2013/11/01/58a81120-435a-11e3-8b74-d89d714ca4dd_story.html.

[22] Ibid.

[23] Matt Hamilton, "LAX Shooter's Plea Agreement Reveals He Did Not Consider Himself a Terrorist, But A 'Patriot,'" *Los Angeles Times*, posted September 1, 2016, https://www.latimes.com/local/lanow/la-me-ln-lax-shooter-guilty-plea-20160901-snap-story.html.

[24] Joyce H. Gallegos, *The Untold Truth about 2019 El Paso Shooting: All You Need to Know about Patrick Crusius's Trials* (self-published, 2023), 6; Latifa Yedroudj, "Who Is Patrick Crusius? Loner, 21, Suspected of 'Anti-Mexican' El Paso Mass Shooting," *Mirror*, posted August 4, 2019, https://www. mirror.co.uk/news/us-news/patrick-crusius-everything-know-el-18825659.

[25] Attorneys for Crusius, in Jake Bleiberg, "Lawyer: El Paso Shooting Suspect Has 'Mental Disabilities,'" AP, posted July 13, 2020, https://apnews. com/article/167c0dc9a34a7094569b4cb7b08e470a; [Patrick Crusius?], "The Inconvenient Truth about Me," posted [August 3-6?], https:// egbertowillies.com/wp-content/uploads/2019/08/Patrick-Crusius-The-Inconvenient-Truth-Evil-Manifesto.pdf; Gallegos, *The Untold Truth*, 5, 7.

[26] Maria Perez and Brett Murphy, "A Timeline of Nikolas Cruz's Activities Leading Up to the Mass School Shooting in Parkland, Florida," *Naples Daily News*, posted and updated February 27, 2018, under "November 1, 2017," "November 24, 2017," "February 14, 2018," https://www.naplesnews.

com/story/news/crime/2018/02/27/timeline-nikolas-cruzs-activities-leading-up-mass-school-shooting-broward-county/377021002/; Brittany Wallman, Paula McMahon, Megan O'Matz, and Susannah Bryan, "A Lost and Lonely Killer," *Sun Sentinel*, posted February 24, 2018, https://www.sun-sentinel.com/local/broward/parkland/florida-school-shooting/fl-florida-school-shooting-nikolas-cruz-life-20180220-story.html.

[27] Collaborative Educational Network, Inc., *Independent Review of "Nc's"* [Nikolas Cruz's] *Educational Record* (Broward County Public Schools, June 16, 2018), 19-43, School Shooters. info, s.v. "Nikolas Cruz"; Perez and Murphy, "A Timeline of Nikolas Cruz's Activities," under "February 27, 2018," "November 27, 2012," "January 1, 2013," "September 28, 2016," "January 19, 2017," "September 24, 2017"; Beatrice Thomas, Protective Investigator and Bernadette Harding, Supervisor, Confidential Investigative Summary Adult In-Home Investigation, Florida Department of Children and Families, Intake Number 2016-271667-01, September 28, 2016-November 12, 2016, School Shooters. info, s.v. "Nikolas Cruz"; Tribune News Service, "Parkland School Shooter Nikolas Cruz Writes Disturbing Love Letters from Jail to 'Miley': I Want to Name My Sons after Guns," *South China Morning Post*, posted April 9, 2019, https://www.scmp.com/news/world/united-states-canada/article/3005353/parkland-school-shooter-nikolas-cruz-writes.
Although he manifested developmental delays, it is doubtful, as his defense attorneys argued, that Cruz had fetal alcohol syndrome (FAS). He lacked the physical features associated with FAS as well as the attendant fine-motor abnormalities. Eric Levenson, Denise Royal and Sara Weisfeldt, "Nikolas Cruz's Defense Says His Brain Was 'Poisoned' by Birth Mother's Addictions In Death Penalty Trial," CNN, posted August 23, 2022, https://www.cnn.com/2022/08/22/us/nikolas-cruz-trial-defense/index.html; Terry Spencer, "Expert: School Shooter Faked Fetal Alcohol Symptoms," AP, posted October 4, 2022, https://apnews.com/article/health-education-florida-fort-lauderdale-parkland-school-shooting-88ca67eca27858858ba376f09bfdbb44.

[28] Broward County Sheriff's Office, Contact Summary with Nikolas Cruz, under "Event 14, November 20, 2014," "Event 15, February 5, 2016," "Event 21, November 30, 2017," School Shooters. info, s.v. "Nikolas Cruz"; Carol Marbin Miller and Kyra Gurney, "Therapy files reveal dark dreams of Parkland school shooter," *Miami Herald*, posted March 9, 2018, updated March 10, 2018, https://www.miamiherald.com/news/local/crime/article204450699.html; Carol Marbin Miller and Nicholas Nehamas, "Nikolas Cruz's Birth Mom Had a Violent, Criminal Past. Could It Help Keep Him Off Death Row?" *Miami Herald*, posted September 05, 2018, updated January 28, 2019, https://www.miamiherald.com/news/local/community/broward/article216909390.html.

[29] Miller and Gurney, "Shooter Revealed Gory Fantasies."

[30] AP, "The Latest: Police Have Found No Motive for Shooting Rampage," 9&10 News, posted and updated February 25, 2016, Wayback Machine, https://web.archive.org/web/20160226084253/http://www.9and10news.com/story/31316664/the-latest-police-have-found-no-motive-for-shooting-rampage.

[31] Johnathan Carlson, reporter, in Live 7 Investigators, "Who Is Jason Dalton?" WXYZ TV Detroit, Channel 7, posted on YouTube, February 21, 2016, https://www.youtube.com/watch?v=oSaVM19ritE; Cody Combs, "Neighbors Say Shooting Suspect, Dalton, Became Paranoid," News Channel 3, posted February 21, 2016, https://wwmt.com/news/local/neighbors-say-shooting-suspect -dalton-became-paranoid; Cody Combs, "New Details about Dalton's Past Emerge," News Channel 3, posted February 22, 2016, https://wwmt.com/news/local/new-details-about-daltons-past-emerge; Scripps, "15 Guns Removed from Home of Jason Dalton," WXYZ Detroit, posted and updated February 24, 2016, https://www.wxyz.com/news/15-guns-removed-from-home-of-accused-kalamazoo-gunman-jason-dalton; Kyle Sparks and Jeremy Marr, "The Latest: Six killed in String of Shootings, Suspect Was Uber driver," News Channel 3, posted February 21, 2016, Wayback Machine, https://web.archive.org/web/20160222092301/http://wwmt.com/news/local/suspect-in-custody-following-string-of-shootings-7-dead.

[32] Robert Allen, "Botched Uber Request Preceded Kalamazoo Killing Spree," *Detroit Free Press*, posted March 19, 2016, updated March 20, 2016, https://www.freep.com/story/news/local/michigan/2016/03/19/uber-call-botched-kalamazoo-shootings/81915560/; Combs, "New Details about Dalton's Past Emerge"; Mark Cottingham in Jason Colthorp, "Kalamazoo Rampage," Local 4 WDIV News, posted on YouTube as "New Details about Who Jason Dalton Is," April 6, 2018, https://www.youtube.com/ watch?v =95T0M4hrLVM; Janet Fay-Dumaine, Consulting Forensic Examiner, letter to Judge Tiffany A. Ankley, Re: Competence to Stand Trial, to Kalamazoo, Michigan: 8th Judicial Court, April 13, 2016, 3, 4, https://media.mlive.com/kzgazette_impact/other/Dalton%20competency%20exam.pdf; analysis by Dr. Todd Grande, in "Jason Dalton Case Analysis: Uber Driver Turned Murderer," YouTube, posted April 24, 2021, https://www.youtube.com/watch?v=QoUykMWq-p8; Chris Heath, "The Uber Killer: The Real Story of One Night of Terror," *GQ*, posted August 22, 2016, https://www.gq.com/story/the-uber-killer; Jennifer Mascia, "Kalamazoo Shooting Spree: What We Know about the Killer's Guns," *The Trace*, posted February 23, 2016, https://www.thetrace.org/2016/02/kalamazoo-shooting-jason-dalton-guns/; Ryan Felton, "Kalamazoo Shooter Saw 'Devil' on Uber App and Blames Visions for Killing Spree," *Guardian*, posted March 14, 2016, https://www.theguardian.com/us-news/2016/mar/14/kalamazoo-shooter-jason-dalton-uber-iphone-takes-over-body.

[33] Psychopathy is suggested by Delgado Morales's verbal fluency (as indicated by his employment as a tutor), his social pretention, and the evident non-sexual sadism of his final acts. Relevant to that assumption: a) Hare, *Without Conscience*, 33-38; b) Mary McMurran and Richard C. Howard, "Personality, Personality Disorder and Violence: Implications for Future Research and Practice," in *Personality, Personality Disorder and Violence*, ed. Mary McMurran and Richard C. Howard (West Sussex, UK: John Wiley & Sons, Ltd., 2009), 302-303; c) Millon and Davis, "Ten Subtypes of Psychopathy," 163; d) Michael H. Stone, *The Anatomy of Evil* (Amherst, NY: Prometheus Books, 2009), 123-124; e) Leah Thomas and Vincent Egan, "Subclinical Sadism: Examining Temperamental Predispositions and Emotional Processing," *Personality and Individual Differences* 196 (October 2022), https://doi.org/10.1016/j.paid.2022.111756; f) Brent E. Turvey, "Psychopathy and Sadism: Interpreting Psychopathic and Sadistic Behavior in the Crime Scene," in *Criminal Profiling: An Introduction to Behavioral Evidence Analysis*, 4th. ed., ed. Brent E. Turvey (San Diego, CA: Academic Press, 2012), 447-479. "[T]he deceptions of psychopaths are generalized and pervasive, part of the natural stratagem that ranges from cool indifference to the malevolent intent to deceive and control." Paul Babiak and Robert D. Hare, *Snakes in Suits: When Psychopaths Go to Work* (New York, NY: Regan, 2007), 130.

[34] Narration and observation of bookstore owner, in Sirius Rust, writ. and ed., "Case 23: The Aramoana Massacre (Part I)," *True Crime New Zealand: A NZ Podcast*, posted November 4, 2020, chaps. 1, 2, https://truecrimenz.com/2020/11/04/case-23-the-aramoana-massacre-part-i/.

[35] Narration, in Rust, "Case 23: The Aramoana Massacre (Part I)."

[36] Andrew Frost and John Pratt, "Causes of the Aramoana Massacre, 1990," https://aramoanmassacre.weebly.com/causes-of-the-aramoana-massacre.html; narration and observation by community member, in Rust, "Case 23: The Aramoana Massacre (Part I)," chap. 1.

[37] Frost and Pratt, "Causes of the Aramoana Massacre"; Murderpedia, "Killer A Loner Fascinated by Weapons," s.v. "David Malcolm Gray"; narration and observation of bookstore owner, in Rust "Case 23: The Aramoana Massacre (Part I)," chaps. 1, 2.

[38] W. Douglas Cullen, *The Public Inquiry into the Shootings at Dunblane* (Scotland: Parliament, October 1996), ¶ 4.15, 4.42, 5.48, app. 3, School Shooters .info, s.v. "Thomas Hamilton"; Murderpedia, "Police Activity," s.v. "Thomas Watt Hamilton."

[39] Nick Cohen, "The life and Death of Thomas Watt Hamilton," *Independent*, posted March 17, 1996, https://www.independent.co.uk/news/uk/home-news/the-life-and-death-of-thomas-watt-hamilton-1672323.html; Joanne Kavanagh, "Face of Pure Evil: Who Was Dunblane Shooter Thomas

Hamilton and Why Did He Do It?" *Sun*, posted and updated March 13, 2021, under "Who Was Thomas Hamilton?" https://www.thesun.co.uk/news/14282766/thomas-hamilton-dunblane-shooter-killer/.

[40] CBS, AP, "What we know about Oregon Shooter Chris Harper Mercer," CBS News, posted October 1, 2015, https://www.cbsnews.com/news/umpqua-community-college-shooting-chris-harper-mercer/; First Post, "Oregon Shooter Christopher Harper-Mercer Was Army Boot Camp Drop Out and Awkward Loner," posted and updated October 3, 2015, https://www.firstpost.com/world/oregon-shooter-christopher-sean-harper-mercer-was-army-boot-camp-drop-out-and-awkward-loner-2453726.html.

[41] Chris Harper-Mercer, *Manifesto* [as labeled on site], under "My Story," School Shooters .info, s.v. "Chris Harper-Mercer."

[42] Erin Calabrese, Miguel Almaguer and Phil Helsel, "Mother of Oregon College Shooter Wrote about Guns, Autism," NBC News, posted October 6, 2015, https://www.nbcnews.com/storyline/oregon-college-shooting/mother-oregon-college-shooter-wrote-about-guns-autism-n439766.

[43] Harper-Mercer, "Manifesto," under "My Story."

[44] Kaitlin Durbin and Jakob Rodgers, "Family Stymied by 'Imminent Threat Law' in Trying to Avert Halloween Shooting Rampage," *Colorado Springs Gazette*, posted October 30, 2016, https://gazette.com/crime/family-stymied-by-imminent-threat-law-in-trying-to-avert/article_b496913d-8eaf-5b50-ba3e-fc226da01a0c.html.

[45] At least 4 moves prior to high school. Jonathan Fast, *Ceremonial Violence: A Psychological Explanation of School Shootings* (New York: The Overlook Press, 2008), 178.

[46] AP, "Mall Gunman Admitted He Was Satanic, Attempted Suicide," Fox News, posted December 27, updated January 13, 2015, https://www.foxnews.com/story/mall-gunman-admitted-he-was-satanic-attempted-suicide; Jeff Zeleny and Maria Newman, "Details of Omaha Shooting Emerge," *New York Times*, posted December 6, 2007, https://www.nytimes.com/2007/12/06/us/06cnd-shoot.html.

[47] AP, "Mall Gunman Admitted He Was Satanic"; Lynn Safranek, "Understanding Tragedy: Teen Robbie Hawkins Had No Remorse, Empathy after Threatening Stepmom's Life," *World Herald*, posted August 17, 2008, updated October 16, 2019, https://omaha.com/news/local/understanding-tragedy-teen-robbie-hawkins-had-no-remorse-empathy-after-threatening-stepmoms-life/article_5f9366dc-c4da-11e7-b5bc-eb3f5c40ffb2.html.

[48] Safranek, "Understanding Tragedy: Teen Robbie Hawkins Had No Remorse."

[49] Ibid.

[50] Ibid.

[51] Hawkins, in AP, "Transcript of Robert Hawkins' Suicide Note," *Herald Net*, posted December 7, 2007, https://www.heraldnet.com/news/transcript-of-robert-hawkins-suicide-note/.

[52] Tim Madigan, John Gonzalez, and Karen Potter, "Killer 'Was Like a Raging Volcano Ready to Explode,'" New York Times News Service, posted October 27, 1991, updated Jan 28, 2015, https://greensboro.com/killer-was-like-a-raging-volcano-ready-to-explode/article_cb9eace9-328a-5a7c-9bdd-a6f5b1edc59a.html.

[53] Ronald M. Holmes and Stephen T. Holmes, *Mass Murder in the United States* (Upper Saddle River, New Jersey: Prentice Hall, 2001), 101.

[54] Editors of Time-Life Books, *True Crime: Mass Murderers* (Alexandria, VA: Time-Life Books, 1992), 80; Madigan, Gonzalez, and Potter, "Killer 'Was Like a Raging Volcano'"; Don Terry, "Portrait of a Texas Killer: Impatient and Troubled," *New York Times* 141, no. 48,757 (October 18, 1991): A14.

[55] Based on evidence of flat affect and unusual posture when walking. She emphasized in her writing that she was self-conscious about the way others viewed her.

[56] Maria L. La Ganga, "James Holmes Speaks: 'I Just Considered Them Numbers Really, Not People,'" *Los Angeles Times*, posted June 3, 2015, https://www.latimes.com/nation/la-na-james-holmes-quotes-20150603-story.html; Jason Oviatt, in AP, "Cops Testify How Colorado Gunman Acted after Arrest," CBS News, posted April 30, 2015, https://www.cbsnews.com/news/colorado-theater-gunman-james-holmes-interested-massacre-aftermath/.

[57] James Alan Fox, Ann W. Burgess, Jack Levin, Marleen Wong, and Allen G. Burgess, "Capitol Hill Mass Murder Case," *Brief Treatment and Crisis Intervention* 7, no. 2 (May 2007), 141, https://web.northeastern.edu/jfox/Documents/CapHillRepBTCI.pdf.

[58] Narration and visual of suicide note, in Infamous Crime Locations, "Capitol Hill Massacre Leaves 6 Dead (Rave Party Shooting)," YouTube, posted July 9. 2021, https://www.youtube.com/watch?v=mqw3ELRGIxI.

[59] James Alan Fox, Ann W. Burgess, Jack Levin, and Marleen Wong, *Panel Report on the March 25, 2006 Capitol Hill Shooting* (Seattle, WA: Submitted to Seattle Police Department, July 17, 2002), 17-18, 22-23, Murderpedia, s.v. "Kyle Aaron Huff."

[60] Huff, suicide note excerpt, in Thomas Francis, "Parting Shot," *The Stranger*, posted June 1, 2006, https://www.thestranger.com/seattle/parting-shot/Content?oid=37331.

[61] Some of the people who knew Huff prior to his rampage portray him as polite, approachable, and somewhat passive at times. CBS and AP, "No Warnings on Seattle Shooter," CBS News, posted March 27, https://www.cbsnews.com/news/no-warnings-on-seattle-shooter/; Phuong Le, Angela Galloway, and Mike Lewis, "Killer Was a 'Gentle Giant,' 'Quick to Anger,'" *Seattle pi*,

posted March 27, 2006, https://www.seattlepi.com/local/article/Killer-was-a-gentle-giant-quick-to-anger-1199600.php. The ability to project agreeability, even gentleness, while withholding hostility is part of the characterological masquerade of a psychopath. In addition, it is apparent that Huff's genteel presentations were usually performed in the presence of his twin brother. In the absence of an internalized moral code, it is likely Huff relied on his sibling as a psychological cue to restrain aggressive impulsivity. Family members can exert checks with immature or maladaptive personalities and a twin is particularly influential. For context, see: a) Greg J. Duncan, Johanne Boisjoly, and Kathleen Mullan Harris, "Sibling, Peer, Neighbor, And Schoolmate Correlations as Indicators of The Importance of Context for Adolescent Development," *Demography* 38 no. 3 (August 2001): 437–447; b) David Álvarez-García, Paloma González-Castro, José Carlos Núñez, Celestino Rodríguez, and Rebeca Cerezo, "Impact of Family and Friends on Antisocial Adolescent Behavior: The Mediating Role of Impulsivity and Empathy," *Frontiers in Psychology*, posted September 10, 2019, https://www.frontiersin.org/journals/psychology/articles/10.3389/fpsyg.2019.02071/full; c) Kenneth N. Levy, Benjamin N. Johnson, Tracy L. Clouthier, J. Wesley Scala, and Christina M. Temes, "An Attachment Theoretical Framework for Personality Disorders," *Canadian Psychology* 56, no. 2 (2015): 197-207, https://www.apa.org/pubs/journals/features/cap-0000025.pdf; d) Susan M. McHale, Kimberly A. Updegraff, and Shawn D. Whiteman, "Sibling Relationships and Influences in Childhood and Adolescence," author manuscript, Health and Human Services public access, PubMed Central, posted September 21, 2012, https://www.ncbi.nlm.nih.gov/pmc/articles/PMC3956653/. When the murders took place the connection between the brothers had become more distant than ever before. Kane, Kyle's brother, had graduated from community college and was enjoying relations with women. Kyle, meanwhile, had been employed in a series of menial jobs and was unable to form attachments (romantic or otherwise) since their relocation from Montana to Seattle. Fox, Burgess, Levin, and Wong, *Panel Report*, 20. The eventual killer would have been experiencing "psychopathic" degeneration, wherein the balance between affectation and aggressive preferences is tilting. Boris Sidis, *The Causation and Treatment of Psychopathic Diseases* (Boston, MA: Richard G. Badger, 1916), chap. x, Kindle. The behaviors itemized in this row make a compelling case for Huff's anti-social conduct and commensurate deception. Further substantiation for the possibility that Huff was psychopathic may be found in the following: a) Hervey Cleckley, *The Mask of Sanity*, Rev. ed. (St. Louis, Missouri: C.V. Mosby Company, 1982), 204-205, 211-212, 24-242; b) Alexandra Junewicz and Stephen Bates Billick, "Preempting the Development of Antisocial Behavior and Psychopathic Traits," *Journal of the American Academy of*

Psychiatry and the Law Online, posted January 2021, JAAPL.200060-20, doi: https://doi.org/10.29158/JAAPL.200060-20; c) Linda Mealey, "The Sociobiology of Sociopathy: An Integrated Evolutionary Model," abstract, Cambridge University Press, posted February 4, 2010, https://www.cambridge.org/core/journals/behavioral-and-brain-sciences/article/abs/sociobiology-of-*f*horesey-an-integrated-evolutionary-model/A5F1DDC8F0D32E036B725FE7BFA761AF#access-block; d) J. Reid. Meloy, *The Psychopathic Mind: Origins, Dynamics, and Treatment* (Northvale, NJ: Jason Aronson, Inc., 1988), 132-141; e) Theodore Millon and Roger D. Davis, "Ten Subtypes of Psychopathy," in *Psychopathy: Antisocial, Criminal, and Violent Behavior*, 166-167.

[62] Fox, Burgess, Levin, and Wong, *Panel Report*, 5; Fox, Burgess, Levin, Wong, and Burgess, "Capitol Hill Mass Murder Case," 137, 141, 142, 143, 144; Le, Galloway, and Lewis, "Killer Was a 'Gentle Giant,'"; *Seattle Post Intelligencer*, "'We're Hiding,' Girl Whispered in 911 Call," originally posted March 30, 2006, Murderpedia, s.v. "Kyle Aaron Huff."

[63] Francis, "Parting Shot."

[64] CBS and AP, "Seattle Gunman: 'Plenty for Everyone,'" CBS News, posted March 27, 2006, https://www.cbsnews.com/news/seattle-gunman-plenty-for-everyone/.

[65] Murderpedia, "Worker's Rampage Spills from Hotel," s.v. "Silvio Izquierdo-Leyva"; *St. Petersburg Times,* "He killed … for No Reason," originally published April 18, 2002, Murderpedia, s.v. "Silvio Izquierdo-Leyva."; Kathryn Wexler, Jo Becker, Sarah Schweitzer, and Steve Huettel, contributor, "Trouble Lay Hidden in Shooting Suspect's Past," *St. Petersburg Times Online*, posted January 1, 2000, http://www .sptimes.com/News/010100/TampaBay/Trouble_lay_hidden_in.shtml (no longer accessible).

[66] *St. Petersburg Times,* "He killed … for No Reason"; Wexler, Becker, Schweitzer, and Huettel, "Trouble Lay Hidden."

[67] Ellen Cranley, Rosie Perper, and Kelly McLaughlin, "3 Dead, Including Gunman, after Mass Shooting at Madden Video Game Tournament in Jacksonville, Florida," *Business Insider*, posted August 27, 2018, https://www.businessinsider.com/jacksonville-landing-mass-shooting-florida-madden-tournament-2018-8.

[68] Jose Pagliery, Curt Devine, and Drew Griffin, "Jacksonville Shooter Had History of Mental Illness and Police Visits to Family Home," CNN Investigates, updated August 28, 2018, https://www.cnn.com/2018/08/28/us/jacksonville-madden-shooter-katz-mental-health-invs/index.html.

[69] Pagliery, Devine, and Griffin, "Jacksonville Shooter Had History of Mental Illness"; Ellyn Santiago and Tom Cleary, "David Katz: 5 Fast Facts You Need to Know," Heavy, posted August 27, 2018, https://heavy.com/news/2018/08/david-katz-bread-ravenschamp/; Chris Riotta, "Florida Shooting

Suspect Had History of Mental Illness, Court Records Show," *Independent*, posted August 27, 2018, https://www.independent.co.uk/news/world/americas/florida-shooting-david-katz-baltimore-twitch-shooter-mental-illness-gun-laws-a8510311.html.

[70] Murderpedia, s.v. "Stephen Phillip Kazmierczak"; Northern Illinois University Department of Public Safety, *Report of the February 14, 2008 Shootings at Northern Illinois University* (State of Illinois, n.d.), 26-27, https://schoolshooters.info/sites/default/files/Northern%20Illinois%20University%20Official%20Report.pdf.

[71] Northern Illinois University Department of Public Safety, *Report of the February 14, 2008 Shootings*, 27-33; David Vann, "Portrait of the School Shooter as a Young Man," *Esquire*, originally published in August 2008 issue, posted February 12, 2009, https://www.esquire.com/news-politics/a4863/steven-kazmierczak-0808/.

[72] Tim Stelloh, Caitlin Fichtel and Tracy Connor, "Who Is Devin Kelley, the Texas Church Shooter?" NBC News, posted November 5, 2017, updated November 6, 2017, https://www.nbcnews.com/storyline/texas-church-shooting/who-devin-kelley-alleged-texas-church-shooter-n817806.

[73] Camila Domonoske, "Before His Military Trial, Texas Shooter Escaped Mental Health Facility," NPR, posted November 7, 2017, https://www.npr.org/sections/thetwo-way/2017/11/07/562607996/before-his-military-trial-texas-shooter-escaped-mental-health-facility; Tom Dart, "Texas Gunman Fled Mental Health Clinic and Smuggled Weapons on to Military Base," *Guardian*, posted November 7, 2017, https://www.theguardian.com/us-news/2017/nov/07/texas-gunman-shooting-sutherland-springs-devin-kelley; Kirk Mitchell and *Denver Post*, "Gunman Who Killed 26 People in Texas Cited for Cruelty to Animals in Colorado," *Daily Camera*, posted November 6, 2017, https://www .dailycamera.com/2017/11/06/gunman-who-killed-26-people-in-texas-cited-for-cruelty-to-animals-in-colorado/.

[74] Alan Blinder, Dave Phillips, and Richard A. Oppel, Jr., "In 2012 Assault, Texas Gunman Broke Skull of Infant Stepson," *New York Times*, posted November 6, 2017, https://www.nytimes.com/2017/11/06/us/devin-patrick-kelley-texas.html; Domonoske, "Before His Military Trial, Texas Shooter Escaped"; Mitchell and *Denver Post*, "Gunman Who Killed 26 People in Texas Cited."

[75] AP, "Church Killer Left Note Predicting War," *Lakeland Ledger*, June 24, 1980, 8A; AP, "5 Killed, 10 Shot in Church Service," *Ocala Star-Banner*, June 23, 1980, 1, 14A; *Time*, "Nation: This Is War!" originally published July 7, 1980, 1, http://content.time.com/time/magazine/article/0,9171,952699,00.html.

[76] Jan Reid, "Blood of the Lamb," *Texas Monthly* (March 1983): 193; *Time*, "Nation: This Is War!" 1-2; United Press International (UPI), "Man Charged

in Church Killings Called an Egotistical Eccentric," *Sarasota Herald Tribune*, June 24, 1980, 8A.

77 Murderpedia, s.v. "Julian Knight"; Christopher Knaus, "Nurse Says She Watched Military Abandon Hoddle Street Killer before Massacre," *Canberra Times*, posted January 17, 2015, https://www.canberratimes.com.au/story/6073188/nurse-says-she-watched-military-abandon-hoddle-street-killer-before-massacre/; narration, statements by Dr. David Sime, Forensic Psychiatrist, Tim Watson-Monroe, Forensic Psychologist, in David Morgan, dir., Jonathan Holmes, writ. and narrator, "Hoddle Street 1988," *Documentary Australia* (Melbourne, Australis: Australian Broadcasting Corporation, 1988), YouTube, posted July 9, 2015, https://www.youtube.com/watch?v=48IXtyHoQSM&t=11s; Andrew Rule, "Dark Trail of Brutality That Led to Hoddle St," *Herald Sun*, posted January 24, 2015, https://www.heraldsun.com.au/news/opinion/andrew-rule/dark-trail-of-brutality-that-led-to-hoddle-st/news-story/74c08cd6d38424eb7be11637033fc648.

78 James Alan Fox and Jack Levin, *Overkill: Mass Murder and Serial Killing Exposed* (New York, NY: Plenum Press, 1994), 234; police interrogation and narration, in Holmes and Morgan, "Hoddle Street 1988"; narration, in *True Crime Worldwide*, "The Nightmare of Hoddle Street …," YouTube, posted May 9, 2022, https://www.youtube.com/watch?v=cLID3fpoS5o.

79 Marshall Cavendish and Colin Wilson, consultant, "Julian Knight: Highway Madness," *Murder in Mind: The Killers, Their Crimes, Their Psychology*, no. 46: 21; Graham Kent, "Hoddle Street Massacre," State Library of Victoria, © 2024, https://ergo.slv.vic.gov.au/explore-history/rebels-outlaws/city-criminals/hoddle-street-massacre; Murderpedia, "Julian's Life," s.v. "Julian Knight."

80 Observations by Dr. Kenneth Byrne, Forensic Psychologist, police interrogation, narration, in Holmes and Morgan, "Hoddle Street 1988"; Sime, in Murderpedia, "Julian's Life."

81 Testimony by Forensic psychiatrist Allen Bartholomew, reported in Terri Daley, "The ADF and Julian Knight: A Lesson On Defence's [sic] Culture Reform," *The Conversation*, posted February 28, 2014, https://theconversation.com/the-adf-and-julian-knight-a-lesson-on-defences-culture-reform-23480; narration, statements by Dr. Kenneth Byrne, Forensic Psychologist, in Holmes and Morgan, "Hoddle Street 1988"; John Silvester, "Inside the mind of Hoddle Street killer Julian Knight," *The Age*, posted August 4, 2017, https://www.theage.com.au/national/victoria/inside-the-mind-of-hoddle-street-killer-julian-knight-20170803-gxodxc.html.

82 Reed Coleman (aka Matthew Nolan), compiler, "Adam Lanza: Timeline," reprinted from the Sandy Hook Lighthouse blog (since modified, now dormant) in School Shooters .info, with permission, s.v. "Adam Lanza,"; Peter Lanza, "Adam Lanza's First Psychotic Episode," *Psychology Today*, posted July 26, 2015, https://www.psychologytoday.com/us/blog/keeping-

kids-safe/201507/adam-lanzas-first-psychotic-episode; Peter Langman, "The Enigma of Adam Lanza's Mind and Motivations for Murder," version 1.2 (December 30, 2018), School Shooters .info, s.v. "Adam Lanza"; Matthew Lysiak, *Newton: An American Tragedy* (New York, NY: Gallery Books, 2013), 207-227; Office of the Child Advocate, *Shooting at Sandy Hook Elementary School* (State of Connecticut: November 21, 2014), 16-18, 36, 38-41, 71; Jamie Turndorf, "Was Adam Lanza an Undiagnosed Schizophrenic?" *Psychology Today*, posted December 20, 2012, https://www.psychologytoday.com/us/blog/we-can-work-it-out/201212/was-adam-lanza-undiagnosed-schizophrenic. To gain more perspective on autism spectrum disorder relative to forensic science, consider: Daniel C. Murrie, Janet I. Warren, Marianne Kristiansson, and Park E. Dietz, "Asperger's Syndrome in Forensic Settings," *International Journal of Forensic Mental Health* 1, no.1 (2002): 59-70, https://img1.wsimg.com/blobby/go/6a7d9703-1c11-490e-a8ca-6fef2394564a/downloads/Aspergers_Syndrome _in_Forensic_Settings.pdf?ver=1637262107554;
and Marianne Kristiansson and Karolina Sörman, "Autism Spectrum Disorders: Legal and Forensic Psychiatric Aspects and Reflections," *Clinical Neuropsychiatry* 5, no. 1 (2008): 55-61.

83 Lanza, "Granny's Clubhouse of Happy Children," Lanza and Coauthor [?], "Adventures of Granny," School Shooters.info, s.v. "Adam Lanza," under "The Adventures of Granny 8"; Office of the Child Advocate, *Shooting at Sandy Hook*, 29; Michael A. Downs, Investigating Officer and Daniel E. Jewiss, Primary Officer, Supplement Investigation Report no.1200704559-00180670, in Office of the State's Attorney Judicial District of Danbury, *Appendix to Report on the Shootings at Sandy Hook Elementary School and 36 Yogananda St., Newtown, Connecticut on December 14, 2012* (November 25, 2013), A220-221, School Shooters.info, s.v. "Adam Lanza." The appendix was released on the same date as the *Report on the Shootings at Sandy Hook Elementary School* (by the same office), but as a separate document. It contains evidentiary materials. The standard method has been used in citation.

84 Lee Mellor, *Rampage: Canadian Mass Murder and Spree Killing* (Toronto, Ontario, Canada: Dundurn, 2013), 255.

85 Ibid.

86 Lebrun, note to mother and father, in Mellor, *Rampage: Canadian Mass Murder*, 257-258.

87 CBS/AP, "What We Know about Gilroy Garlic Festival Shooter Santino William Legan," CBS News, posted July 29, 2019, https://www.cbsnews.com/news/santino-william-legan-what-we-know-about-the-gilroy-garlic-festival-shooter/;

[88] Alia E. Dastagir, "Mass Shootings and Misogyny: The Violent Ideology We Can't Ignore," *USA Today*, posted and updated August 6, 2019, https://www.usatoday.com/story/news/nation/2019/08/06/shooting-ohio-dayton-el-paso-texas-shooter-gilroy-california/1924532001/; NBC Bay Area Staff, "Festival Gunman Identified; Had Referred to Neo-Nazi Manifesto before Shooting," NBC Bay Area, posted July 29, 2019, updated July 30, 2019, https://www.nbcbayarea.com/news/local/gunman-identified-in-gilroy-garlic-festival-mass-shooting/152470/; Susan Scutti, "Festival Shooter Santino Legan Wore Tactical Gear, Sunglasses and a Ballcap. He 'Seemed Confident in His Use of the Gun,'" CNN, updated July 30, 2019, https://www.cnn.com/2019/07/29/us/food-garlic-festival-shooting/index.html.

[89] Peter Langman, "Adult School Shooters," version 1.1 (February 1, 2016), 2, School Shooters. info, s.v. "Marc Lépine."

[90] In his suicide note Lépine wrote: "Depuis 7 ans que la vie ne m'apporte plus de joie et étant totalement blasé, j'ai décidé de mettre des bâtons dans les roues à ces viragos"; translated as: "For seven years life has brought me no joy and being totally blasé, I have decided to put an end to those viragos." Lépine, "Suicide Note," ed. Peter Langman, School Shooters. info, s.v. "Marc Lépine."

[91] Langman, "Adult School Shooters," 3-4.

[92] Gregory Gibson, *Gone Boy: A Father's Search for Truth in His Son's Murder* (Berkeley, CA: North Atlantic Books, 2011), Kindle Cloud Reader, chap. 22.

[93] Jonathan Fast, *Ceremonial Violence*, 105; Gibson, *Gone Boy*, chap. 21.

[94] Aimee Houser, with Thomas L. Hafemeister, content consultant, *Tragedy in Tucson: The Arizona Shooting Rampage* (Minneapolis, MN: ABDO Publishing Company, 2012), 8, including caption below photo, 10-12, 28-29, 33; Michael Martinez and Kyung Lah, "Loughner Pleads Guilty to 19 Counts in Tucson, Arizona, Mass Shooting," CNN, updated August 8, 2012, https://www.cnn.com/2012/08/07/us/arizona-loughner-plea/index.html.

[95] Classitup10 [pseud. for Loughner], "Introduction: Jared Loughner," YouTube, posted December 15, 2010, https://www.youtube.com /watch?v=nHoaZaLbqB4; John Cloud, "The Troubled Life of Jared Loughner," *Time*, posted January 15, 2011, https://content.time.com/time/magazine/article/0,9171,2042358-2,00.html; A. J. Daulerio, "Lucid Dreams Deferred: Jared Loughner's Extraordinary Email Madness," *Gawker*, posted November 9, 2012, http://gawker.com/5959006/lucid-dreams-deferred-jared-loughners-extraordinary-email-madness (no longer accessible); Alan R. Felthous, "Analysis and Commentary: The Involuntary Medication of Jared Loughner and Pretrial Jail Detainees in Nonmedical Correctional Facilities," *Journal of the American Academy of Psychiatry and the Law* 40, no. 1 (January 2012): 99; Dr. Christina Pietz, forensic psychologist, in Martinez and Lah, "Loughner Pleads Guilty"; summation of reporting, in Mark Memmott,

"Loughner: 'Social Outcast' with 'Indecipherable Beliefs,'" The Two Way, NPR, posted January 10, 2011, https://www.npr.org/sections/thetwo-way/2011/01/10/132810483/loughner-social-outcast-with-indecipherable-beliefs; ReallyRick [pseud. for Loughner], "'Genocide School' Rant Video," YouTube posted January 15, 2011, https://www.youtube.com/watch?v=bLYeSwMVg_0; Rong-Gong Lin II, Maeve Reston, and Rick Rojas. "School Releases YouTube Post from Loughner," *Los Angeles Times*, posted January 15, 2011, https://www.latimes.com/archives/la-xpm-2011-jan-15-la-na-arizona-shooting-20110115-story.html; A. G. Sulzberger and Jennifer Medina, "Shooting Suspect Had Been Known to Use Potent, and Legal, Hallucinogen," *New York Times*, posted January 17, 2011.

96 ABC News, "8 Children Dead in Japanese School Stabbing," posted January 6, 2006, https://abcnews.go.com/International/story?id=80964&page=1; "Death for Japanese school killer," originally posted August 28, 2003, Murderpedia, s.v. "Mamoru Takuma"; *Japan Times Weekly*, "Killer of Eight Children Hanged," originally posted September 18, 2004, Murderpedia, s.v. "Mamoru Takuma"; Valerie Reitman, "Accused Killer's Dad Lays Blame," *Los Angeles Times*, posted June 12, 2001, https://www.latimes.com/archives/la-xpm-2001-jun-12-mn-9408-story.html.

97 CNN, "Japan Mourns School Victims," CNN.com, posted June 10, 2001, under "Suspect Mentally Ill," WayBack Machine https://web.archive.org/web/20071117121020/http://archives.cnn.com/2001/WORLD/asiapcf/east/06/09/japan.stabbing.02/index.html; narration in *Dire Trip*, "The Disturbing Case of Mamoru Takuma and Ikeda Elementary School," YouTube, posted September 10, 2020, https://www.youtube.com/watch?v=dyM2rKddRrA&t=33s; *Japan Weekly Monitor*, "No Words Of Apology From Defendant in School Stabbing Spree," posted June 13, 2002, Free Library by Farlex, https://www.thefreelibrary.com/No+words+of+ apology+from+defendant+in+school +stabbing +spree.-a087377067; *Japan Weekly Monitor*, "Osaka Massacre Suspect Takuma Not Schizophrenic: Psychiatrist," posted March 28, 2002, Free Library by Farlex, https://www.thefreelibrary.com/Osaka+massacre+suspect+Takuma+not+schizophrenic%3A+psychiatrist.-a084532275; Mr. K. [pseud.], "Mamoru Takuma, The Man Who Committed Mass Murder in Elementary School," Medium, posted April 16, [2021?], https://medium .com/short-time/mamoru-takuma-the-man-who-committed-mass-murder-in-elementary-school-4fe2cf9db098; Murderpedia "Osaka School Killer Says He Targeted Elite Kids," compiled from *Mainichi* and wire stories, published June 11, 2002, s.v. "Mamoru Takuma."

98 Narration, in *Dire Trip*, "The Disturbing Case of Mamoru Takuma"; Mr. K., "Mamoru Takuma, The Man Who Committed Mass Murder." As the time for the administration of his death sentence drew near Mamoru wrote in a letter

to his attorney: "'I apologize from the bottom of my heart to the deceased children, their relatives and the state." *Japan Weekly Monitor*, "Alleged School Killer Apologized, Attempted Suicide: Lawyer," posted August 3, 2001, Free Library by Farlex, https://www.thefreelibrary.com/Alleged+school+killer+apologized%2c+attempted+suicide%3a+lawyer.-a077497323.

[99] Murderpedia, "The life and death of Clifton McCree," s.v. "Clifton McCree."

[100] According to supervisors, in William Booth, "Fired Worker Shoots 5 Dead, Kills Himself," *Washington Post*, posted February 10, 1996, https://www.washingtonpost.com/archive/politics/1996/02/10/fired-worker-shoots-5-dead-kills-himself/fe3750b6-0748-4f95-a3b6-bb8948705e80/; *Miami Herald*, "Additional Test to Pinpoint when Killer Used Marijuana," originally published February 13, 1996, Murderpedia, s.v. "Clifton McCree"; Murderpedia, "The life and death of Clifton McCree," s.v. "Clifton McCree."

[101] Murderpedia, "The life and death of Clifton McCree," s.v. "Clifton McCree."

[102] "The district attorney said a piece of paper found in the house he shared with his mother also included the names of nine lawyers in the area. He said Michael McLendon apparently wanted to hire a lawyer in a dispute with members of his family over getting a family Bible returned to him, but the details weren't clear." Jessica Gresko and Desiree Hunter, "Ala. Gunman Left List of Those Who Wronged Him," originally posted March 11, 2009, Murderpedia, s.v. "Michael Kenneth McLendon." Among the ten people McLendon killed, five were relatives and he also burned down the house he shared with his mother. Ibid. "'He cleaned his family out,' Coffee County coroner Robert Preachers said." Emily Friedman, "Alabama Shooter Michael McLendon Was 'Quiet,'" ABC News, posted March 11, 2009, https://abcnews.go.com/US/story?id=7056936&page=1. The pursuit of an attorney to sue relatives over an item imbued with sentimental and religious significance, along with demolition by fire of the home where he resided with his mother, announces intense family discord.

[103] Liam Casey, "Alek Minassian Incapable of Rational Choice at Time Of Toronto Van Attack, Defense Argues," Canadian Broadcasting Corporation (CBC), posted and updated December 17, 2020, https://www.cbc.ca/news/canada/toronto/closing-arguments-alek-minassian-1.5845340; Liam Casey, "Alek Minassian's 'Way of Thinking' Similar To Psychosis, Murder Trial Hears," CBC, posted and updated November 12, 2020, https://www.cbc.ca/news/canada/toronto/alek-minassian-van-attack-trial-november-12-1.5799525; Amy Dempsey, "Inside the Life of Alek Minassian, The Toronto Van Rampage Suspect No One Thought Capable of Murder," *Hamilton Spectator*, posted May 14, 2018, updated March 1, 2020, https://www.thespec.com/news/ontario/2018/05/14/inside-the-life-of-alek-minassian-the-toronto-van-rampage-suspect-no-one-thought-capable-of-murder

.html. As previously emphasized, the precursors are foundational, not causal. For Minassian, ASD was only one of three dispositional conditions. The prosecutor said in his closing argument: "This is about a person who committed mass murder who happened to have ASD, not that the ASD made him commit murders." AP, "Prosecutor: Autism Didn't Make Toronto Van Attacker Kill 10," WTOP News, posted December 18, 2020, https://wtop.com/canada/2020/12/prosecutor-autism-didnt-make-toronto-van-attacker-kill-10/.

104 In the Minassian case, isolation of pathological personal characteristics is vitally important for distinguishing the restrained expressivity symptomatic of ASD from the absence of remorse. The two attributes are hardly sympatico. The appearance of detachment among individuals with autism (notwithstanding the indulgent cruelty of Lanza and Minassian) does not equate to indifference. "An unfortunate myth about the disorder [Asperger's – a syndrome usually considered to be part of the autistic continuum, marked by greater verbal fluency than is apparent in most cases of autism] is that diagnosed individuals have no emotions whatsoever, which is simply not the case. They can have a harder time identifying and fully expressing their emotions. Yet, most are able to do so to a certain degree. Being autistic doesn't mean you are at a greater risk of evil deeds. If this character [Alek Minassian] didn't have Asperger's, his moral compass would still be corrupt and would still be void of empathy for the victim, but more able to fake empathy for his own self-preservation." Voice over, in "The Case of Alek Minassian," JCS - Criminal Psychology, Internet Archive, publication date October 10, 2019, posting date March 25, 2020, https://archive.org/details /thecaseofalekminassian. For substantiation, see: Rebecca McKenzie and Rudi Dallos, "Autism and Attachment Difficulties: Overlap of Symptoms, Implications and Innovative Solutions," *Clinical Child Psychology and Psychiatry* 22, no. 4: 632-648; and Geoffrey Bird and Essi Viding, "The Self to Other Model of Empathy: Providing a New Framework for Understanding Empathy Impairments in Psychopathy, Autism, And Alexithymia," *Neuroscience & Biobehavioral Reviews* 47 (November 2014): 520-532. Also, refer to the commentary with accompanying note of Lanza's parental support and home environment in Chapter Three of this book.

105 Incel: involuntary celibate. Consult Table 1.1, left column and *HRKITW,* Appendix A. The amorality is an essential component of his personality and, again, is not, definitionally, associated with ASD. A person on the spectrum – at least one as functional as Minassian – is capable of distinguishing social standards and norms, regardless of his or her aptitude in empathizing with others. The discernment of moral expectations is an intellectual act and, therefore, an investiture of personality. A highly regarded scholar and well-published author in cognitive science, Jonathan Baron, remarks, almost

offhandedly in a paper on personal habits and intellectual capacity: "[P]ropensities are potentially under voluntary control." Later he affirms, "[P]eople may create their own general traits by constructing rules for themselves and teaching themselves to follow these rules, just as parents do for children." "Personality and Intelligence," in *Handbook of Human Intelligence*, ed. Robert J. Sternberg (New York, NY: Cambridge University Press, 1982), 316, 342. For background on Baron, consult Jonathan Baron, https://www.sas.upenn.edu/~baron/. If nothing else, Minassian, who demonstrated verbal astuteness during his police interrogation, would have recognized that killing was illegal. Alek Minassian in "Alek Minassian — Full Police Interrogation of Incel Van Attack Driver," posted by The Mob Reporter, YouTube, September 27, 2019, https://www.youtube.com/watch?v=VyHgtSy41VM. Refer to Table 3.1 and discussion on lingual capacity in 4 under "Restricted, or Distorted, Cognition." Also, see: a) Liam Casey and Canadian Press, "Alek Minassian Knew Van Attack Was Morally Wrong, Psychiatrist Testifies," CP24, posted and updated December 11, 2020, https://www.cp24.com/news/alek-minassian-knew-van-attack-was-morally-wrong-psychiatrist-testifies-1.522 6771; b) Cathy M. Grant, Jill Boucher, Kevin J. Riggs, and Andrew Grayson, "Moral Understanding in Children with Autism," *Autism* 9, no. 3 (August 2005): 317–331;); c) Michelle Hartley-McAndrew and Donald Crawford, "A Commentary on Autism and Moral Development: What Can We Learn from the Sandy Hook School Shooting?" *North American Journal of Medicine and Science* 6, no 3 (2013): 163-166; d) Sarah Kurchak, "The Danger in Alek Minassian's Autism Defense," *Fashion*, November 25, 2020, https:// fashionmagazine.com/flare/the-danger-in-alek-minassians-autism-defence/.

[106] Jesse McKinley and Marc Santora, "Upstate Man Who Fatally Shot 4 Dies in Standoff; Motive Remains Unclear," *New York Times*, posted March 14, 2013, https://www.nytimes.com/2013/03/15/nyregion/man-sought-in-upstate-new-york-shootings-is-killed.html.

[107] Jon Campbell and Doug Stanglin, "Cops Kill Suspect in Deadly N.Y. Shooting Rampage," *USA Today*, posted and updated March 14, 2013, https://www.usatoday.com/story/news/2013/03/14/upstate-new-york-herkimer-mohawk-suspect-surrounded/1986913/; Michael Hill and John Kekis, AP, "Kurt Myers, Suspected Gunman in New York Shooting Rampage, Killed by Police," *Huffington Post*, posed March 14, 2013, updated May 14, 2013, https://www.huffpost.com/entry/kurt-myers-killed_n_287498 1; McKinley and Santora, "Upstate Man Who Fatally Shot 4 Dies"; *Observer-Dispatch*, "Newly Discovered Love Notes Reveal Kurt Myers' Personal Life," posted March 13, 2014, https://www.uticaod.com/article/20140313/News/140319690.

[108] CBS News Staff, "Law School Shooter Arraigned," CBS News, posted January 16, 2002, http://www.cbsnews.com/news/law-school-shooter-arraigned/.

[109] AP, "Families of Victims Injured in Law School Shooting Sue School," *Elizabeth Star*, published January 13, 2004, https://news.google.com/newspapers?nid=1204&dat=20040113&id=v7QOAAAAIBAJ&sjid=w4IDAAAAIBAJ&pg=5564,916591&hl=en; Peter Langman, *School Shooters: Understanding High School, College, and Adult Perpetrators* (New York, NY: Rowman & Littlefield, 2015), 96, citing Chris Kahn, "Appalachian School of Law Killer Still Haunted by Paranoia, Delusions," AP, June 11, 2004.

[110] Paul Farrell, "Dimitrios Pagourtzis: 5 Fast Facts You Need to Know," Heavy, posted May 21, 2018, under "4. Pagourtzis Is Reported to Have also Been Armed with Pipe Bombs," https://heavy.com/news/2018/05/dimitrios-pagourtzis/.

[111] British Broadcasting Corporation (BBC), "Dimitrios Pagourtzis: What we Know about Texas Shooting Suspect," BBC News, posted May 18, 2018, https://www.bbc.com/news/world-us-canada-44173960; Samantha Raphelson and Brakkton Booker, "What We Know About the Alleged Texas High School Shooter," NPR, posted May 19, 2018, https://www.npr.org/sections/thetwo-way/2018/05/19/612468377/what-we-know-about-dimitrios-pagourtzis-the-alleged-texas-high-school-shooter.

[112] A friend said he sometimes appeared "sad" and a "little bit sluggish." Michael Biesecker, Jeff Horwitz, and Juan A. Lozano, "Here's What We Know about Dimitrios Pagourtzis, The Student Charged in the Santa Fe High School Shooting," Boston.com, posted May 18, 2018, https://www.boston.com/news/national-news/2018/05/18/dimitrios-pagourtzis.

[113] Recorded thoughts of suicide in his journal, reported in Jennifer Emily, "What We Know about Accused Santa Fe High Gunman Dimitrios Pagourtzis," *Dallas Morning News*, posted May 18, 2018, https://www.dallasnews.com/news/crime/2018/05/18/what-we-know-about-accused-santa-fe-high-gunman-dimitrios-pagourtzis/.

[114] Evan Perez, Jason Morris, and Ralph Ellis, "What we know about Dimitrios Pagourtzis, the alleged Santa Fe High School shooter," CNN, updated May 21, 2018, https://www.cnn.com/2018/05/18/us/dimitrios-pagourtzis-santa-fe-suspect; Julie Turkewitz and Jess Bidgood, "Who Is Dimitrios Pagourtzis, The Texas Shooting Suspect?" *New York Times*, posted May 18, 2018, https://www.nytimes.com/2018/05/18/us/dimitrios-pagourtzis-gunman-texas-shooting.html.

[115] Pemberton was joined in his rampage by Ryan Williams for whom there is in inadequate information to isolate dispositional predilections.

[116] BBC, "Devon Police Apologise for 'Failings' over Murderer," BBC News, posted March 4, 2020, https://www.bbc.com/news/uk-england-devon-

51735016; BBC, "Murderer Donald Pemberton Found with 'Knife' in Prison Cell," BBC News, posted August 23, 2017, https://www.bbc.com/news/uk-england-leeds-41026912; Simon Carr, "'Axe Murder' Suspect Gives Finger at Court," *Sun*, posted January 5, 2015, https://www.thesun.co.uk/archives /news/4948/axe-murder-suspect-gives-finger-at-court (no longer accessible); Simon Hall, "Tanis Bhandari Murder: 'Random and Unprovoked,'" BBC News, posted December 10, 2015, https://www.bbc. com/news/uk-england-devon-35054221; photos in "Family of Man Stabbed to Death in Plymouth Receive Apology from Police Five Years Later," ITV Presents, West Country News, posted March 4, 2020, https://www.itv.com/news/westcountry/2020-03-04/family-of-man-stabbed-to-death-in-plymouth-receive-apology-from-police-five-years-later.

[117] Hall, "Tanis Bhandari Murder."

[118] BBC, "Murderer Donald Pemberton Found with 'Knife.'"

[119] Fast, *Ceremonial Violence*, 28.

[120] Ibid.

[121] Jerry Buckley, "The Tragedy in Room 108," *U.S. News and World Report*, posted October 31, 1993, https://www.usnews.com/news/articles/1993/10/ 31/the-tragedy-in-room-108; Peter Langman, "School Shooters: Nine Brief Sketches," version 1.1 (February 12, 2016), 1-2, School Shooters.info, s.v. "Gary Scott Pennington."

[122] Fast, *Ceremonial Violence*, 111-115; Peter Langman, "Rampage School Shooters: A Typology," version 1.2 (February 12, 2016), 3, School Shooters .info; Langman, *School Shooters*, 66.

[123] Fast, *Ceremonial Violence*, 115-117.

[124] State psychologist, in Fast, *Ceremonial Violence*, 112.

[125] Fast, *Ceremonial Violence*, 115, 119; Langman, *School Shooters*, 66.

[126] Sarah Netter, "Suspected Orlando Office Shooter Jason Rodriguez Captured at Mom's House," ABC News, posted November 6, 2009, under "Shooting Victims Described as 'Trauma Red' Patients," https://abcnews.go.com/US/ shooting-downtown-orlando-office-building/story?id =9016169.

[127] Jason Rodriguez v. State of Florida, Fifth District, Case No. 5D14-41, Opinion filed August 14, 2015, Justia U.S. Law, 2, https://law.justia.com/cases /florida/fifth-district-court-of-appeal/2015/5d14-41.html.

[128] Laura Burnip and David Boroff, "Church Massacre: Who Is Dylann Roof and What Did He Do?" *Sun*, posted and updated December 11, 2020, under "Who Is Dylann Roof," https://www.the-sun.com/news/1955593/dylann-roof-crimes-white-supremacist-south-carolina/; Frances Robles and Nikita Stewart, "Dylann Roof's Past Reveals Trouble at Home and School," *New York Times*, posted July 16, 2015, https://www.nytimes.com /2015/07/17/us/ charleston-shooting-dylann-roof-troubled-past.html.

[129] United States Court of Appeals for The Fourth Circuit, no. 17-3, United States of America v. Dylann Storm Roof, argued May 25, 2021, decided August 25, 2021, III.A.1, https://www.ca4.uscourts.gov/opinions/173.P.pdf.

[130] Ibid.

[131] Alakananda Bandyopadhyay, "Dylann Roof's Chilling Letters, Videos from Jail Show Charleston Shooter's Lack of Remorse: 'Not Shed A Tear,'" Media, Entertainment, and Arts Worldwide, posted May 25, 2021, https://meaww.com/dylann-roof-letters-videos-jail-charleston-church-shooter-no-remorse-im-not-sorry-mentall-illness; Eric Levenson and Tina Burnside, "Dylann Roof Believed He'd Be Freed from Prison after a Race War, Attorneys Say in Appeal," CNN, updated "January 29, 2020," https://www.cnn.com/2020/01/29/us/dylann-roof-appeal/index.html.

[132] Roof, in Bandyopadhyay, "Dylann Roof's Chilling Letters," under "'I Am Not Sorry.'"

[133] Crime Investigation, "The Hungerford Massacre Crime Files," last updated 2022, under "Beginnings of a Mass Murderer," https://www.crimeandinvestigation.co.uk/crime-files/michael-ryan-and-the-hungerford-massacre; Jeremy Josephs, *Hungerford: One Man's Massacre*, (London, England: Smyth Gryphon, Ltd., 1993), 23.

[134] Claire Carter, "Inside the Indulgent but Lonely Childhood of The Hungerford Massacre Gunman before His Mass Bloodbath," *Mirror*, posted September 16, 2017, updated September 22, 2017, https://www.mirror.co.uk/news/uk-news/inside-indulgent-lonely-childhood-hungerford-11162474; Crime Investigation, "The Hungerford Massacre," under "Beginnings of a Mass Murderer"; Josephs, *Hungerford: One Man's Massacre*, 24; Sylvia Pascoe, neighbor, Pan Pantziarka, writer, unidentified family acquaintance, in *Real Crime*, "This Man Massacred 16 People," posted on YouTube as "Why Did a Former Antiques Dealer His Own Mother and 15 People [sic]? Killing Spree," February 20, 2020, https://www.youtube.com/watch?v=uskzmhod XQI; Thorson, "Britain's Worst Mass Murderer."

[135] Carter, "Inside the Indulgent but Lonely Childhood"; Dr Gregory Moffat, childhood aggression specialist, in Crime Investigation, "The Hungerford Massacre," under "But Why?"

[136] The possibility that Ryan was struggling with a severe thought disorder was, for purposes of this categorization, dismissed as speculative. Although the history of avoidance would suggest the eventual development of schizophrenia in a fashion that might resemble the progression of James Holmes (*WRKE*, Chapter Four), Ryan did not manifest the jumbled reasoning that was exhibited by his psychotic counterparts such as Ford, Holmes, Loughner, Seegrist, or San Marco (among others). The imaginary encounters that Ryan spun into yarns to impress associates were fanciful, but still coherent and were, themselves, indicative of APD. "They desire affection and

acceptance and may fantasize about idealized relationships with others." American Psychiatric Association, *DSM-5*, 674. The attempted rape that preceded his rampage was in line with the spineless sadism that was associated with his suppressed aggression and social cowardice (summarized in the rightmost column and accompanying notes). Dr. John Hamilton, medical director for a high security psychiatric facility (Broadmoor Hospital) at the time (1987), believed that Ryan was suffering from acute schizophrenia and was undoubtedly psychotic. Josephs, *Hungerford: One Man's Massacre*, 167-168. Today, though, after more than three decades with data on dozens of SMASIs, it is certain that highly personalized motives are functional to autogenic killings and are not, as this book and others demonstrate, necessarily symptomatic of insanity. A foremost consulting forensic psychiatrist for Mersey Regional Health Authority, Dr. Jim Higgins, noting that Ryan's mother was a victim opined, "Matricide is the schizophrenic crime – that is an aphorism in forensic psychiatry." Josephs, *Hungerford: One Man's Massacre*, pref., ix, 168. There is a high rate of violence toward family members by individuals with neuropsychological disturbances, but a mathematical correlation between matricide (or patricide for that matter) has yet to be demonstrated. Besides, the crime itself does not equate to a diagnosis any more than the cognitive malfunction would necessitate the crime. "Most matricides suffered from psychotic disorders, especially schizophrenia. Nevertheless, not all the perpetrators had psychotic symptoms at the time of the crime. … [M]ental illness is not the only variable related to matricide and, taken alone, is not enough to explain the crime. Several factors in the history of the mother and son need to be probed. … The peculiar dynamics of the mother-son relationship and the unique personalities and life experiences of both subjects are the real key to cases of matricide." Roberto Catanesi, Gabriele Rocca, Chiara Candelli, and Felice Carabellese, "Matricide by Mentally Disordered Sons: Gaining a Criminological Understanding Beyond Mental Illness – A Descriptive Study," International *Journal of Offender Therapy and Comparative Criminology* 59, no. 14 (2015): 1550-63, abstract, https://pubmed.ncbi.nlm.nih.gov/25100768/. For more on this topic: a) Robert E. Hanlon, Joseph J. Coda, Derin Cobia, and Leah H. Rubin, "Psychotic Domestic Murder: Neuropsychological Differences between Homicidal and Nonhomicidal Schizophrenic Men," *Journal of Family Violence* 27 (2012: 105-113; b) A. Ogunwale and O. Abayomi, "Matricide and Schizophrenia in the 21st Century: A Review and Illustrative Cases," *African Journal of Psychiatry* 15, no. 1 (2012): 55-57, https://www.longdom.org/open-access/matricide-and-schizophrenia-in-the-st-century-a-review-and -illustrative-cases-jop-15-421.pdf; c) Robert A. Schug, "Schizophrenia and Matricide: An Integrative Review," *Journal of Contemporary Criminal Justice* 27, no. 2 (May 2011): 204-229.

[137] To check markers on avoidant personality disorder (APD), see American Psychiatric Association, *DSM-5*, 672-675. For evidence of Ryan's pathological characteristics: a) Carter, "Inside the Indulgent but Lonely Childhood"; b) Crime Investigation, "The Hungerford Massacre," under "Beginnings of a Mass Murderer"; c) Professor Craig Jackson, criminal psychologist, unidentified family acquaintance, in Real Crime, *This Man Massacred*; d) Peter Bullock, pub owner, Gary Devin, acquaintance, Edred Gwilliam, business associate, Vic Lardner, physical education teacher, Brian Meikle, peer, John Mitchell, workmate, Constance Ryan, aunt, in Josephs, *Hungerford: One Man's Massacre*, 16, 22-23, 26; e) Thorson, "Britain's Worst Mass Murderer a Polite Loner." Also, review note regarding stalking under Cho Seung-hui.

[138] To access information on spineless sadism relative to APD refer to: Suzanne Degges-White, "Is It Sadistic Personality or Just Everyday Sadism?" *Psychology Today,* posted July 7, 2023," https://www.psychologytoday.com/us/blog/lifetime-connections/202307/sadistic-personality-disorder-or-just-an-everyday-sadist; Suzanne Degges-White, reviewed by Rajy Abulhosn, "Sadistic Personality Disorder: Signs, Traits, & Treatment," Choosing Therapy, posted June 15, 2023, https://www.choosingtherapy.com/sadistic-personality-disorder/; Theodore Millon, Seth Grossman, Carrie Millon, Sarah Meagher, and Rowena Ramnath, *Personality Disorders in Modern Life*, 2nd ed. (Hoboken, NJ: Wiley & Sons, Inc., 2004), table 15.2; Michael Stone, "Sadistic Personality in Murders," in *Psychopathy: Antisocial, Criminal, and Violent Behavior*, 349-355.

[139] Investigation Commission of the Kauhajoki School Shooting, *Kauhajoki School Shooting on 23 September 2008 – Report of the Investigation Commission* (Vantaa, Finland: Ministry of Justice, 2010), 54, trans. School Shooters .info, s.v. "Matti Saari."

[140] Ibid, 54-55.

[141] Ibid, 55, 58-59.

[142] Satoshi Uematsu, Letter to Lower House Speaker Tadamori Oshima, embedded in Sarah Dean and Matt Hunter for *MailOnline*, Alexander Ward and Glen Keogh for *Daily Mail*, "Killer Who Butchered 19 in Their Sleep at Japanese Disabled Care Home Smiles in Back of a Police Van … As It Is Revealed He Wanted to Slaughter 470 and His Body Is Covered in Demonic Tattoos," *Daily Mail*, posted July 25, 2016, updated July 27, 2016, under "The Disturbing Warning Letter Sent by Killer Satoshi Uematsu before Japan Stabbing," https://www.dailymail.co.uk/news/article-3707721/Stabbing-horror-Japan-leaves-19-dead-45-injured-knifeman-attacks-centre-disabled-people.html#ixzz4FWo7VWNe.

[143] Ibid.

[144] Dean, Hunter, Ward, Keogh, "Killer Who Butchered 19"; David McNeill, "Man Who Killed 19 In Japan Knife Attack Had Threatened Disabled," *Irish Times*, posted July 26, 2016, https://www.irishtimes.com/news/world/asia-pacific/man-who-killed-19-in-japan-knife-attack-had-threatened-disabled-1.2734732.

[145] As quoted in *Kyodo News*, "Care Home Mass Murderer Will Not Appeal Death Penalty Ruling," posted March 18, 2020, https://english.kyodonews.net/news/2020/03/84352d0758f5-care-home-mass-murderer-will-not-appeal-death-penalty-ruling.html.

[146] Ibid.

[147] According to court testimony of Ruth Seegrist, mother, in Kathleen Clute, "Seegrist Was Sexually Abused, Her Mother Says," United Press International Archives, originally posted June 21, 1986, https://www.upi.com/Archives/1986/06/21/Seegrist-was-sexually-abused-her-mother-says/3460519710400/.

[148] Peel Regional Police Force, Follow-up Investigation Report, June 6, 1975, Incident Date: May 28, 1975, 3, School Shooters .info, s.v. "Michael Slobodian."

[149] His sister stated he wore platform shoes to make himself appear taller. starviego [pseudonym], "5-28-75 Centennial Secondary School in Brampton, Canada," Echoes of Columbine, posted August 4, 2007, under "Psychological Background," https://www.tapatalk.com/groups/signofthetimes/5-28-75-centennial-secondary-school-in-brampton-ca-t729.html#.U6xWAV5UgpE.

[150] Both of Slobodian's parents were out of work. His father had suffered his second heart attack, and his grandfather had passed away earlier in the month. He cried while relaying his troubles to his English teacher, who was one of his victims. Jankie Devi Ramnaraine, "Michael Slobodian: The Forgotten School Shooter – An Examination of the On-Scene Offense Characteristics of the First Canadian School Shooting, Brampton, Ontario, 1975," (master's major paper, University of Ontario Institute of Technology, 2014), 26, https://ir.library.dc-uoit.ca/bitstream/10155/495/1/Ramnaraine_Jankie.pdf, using the following sources: a) J. Beaufoy, "'Fed Up with Life,' Youth Wrote He Planned to Eliminate Some People," *Globe and Mail*, May 29, 1975; b) Globe and Mail Staff, "School Superintendent Shocked: Michael Slobodian: Average in Almost Every Way," *Globe and Mail*, May 30, 1975; c) J. Sallot, "The life and Death of Mike Slobodian," *Globe and Mail*, June 21, 1975. His suicide message also showed signs of a depressed state of mind. See HRKTW, Fig. 5.2.

[151] He alleged that the notes were from his parents. Mary S. Martin, "The 1990 Kirpan Case: Cultural Conflict and the Development of Equity Policy in the Peel District School Board," (doctoral thesis, University of Toronto, 2011),

42, https://tspace.library.utoronto.ca/bitstream/1807/29806/9/Martin_Mary_S-201106_EDD_thesis.pdf.pdf.pdf. One note even included a fake medical certificate. Ramnaraine, "Michael Slobodian: The Forgotten School Shooter," 27-28, referencing K. Faught, "It did happen here," *Toronto Star*, posted May 1, 1999. In an essay on *Death of a Salesman*, he wrote that Willy Loman "died the death of a deluded fool and not that of a tragic hero." Ramnaraine, "Michael Slobodian: The Forgotten School Shooter," sourced to J. Shallot, "The life and Death of Mike Slobodian," *Globe and Mail*, June *21,* 1975. His physics teacher described a science project in this way: "It was the dissection of 13 frogs and it involved stimulation of the hearts to keep them alive after they had been killed." *Lewiston Daily Sun*, "Lad in Ontario Shooting Spree Called Above Average Student," May 30, 1975, 11. The instructor did not let him participate because the experiment involved a living animal. Ibid. In addition, Langman presents a compelling case for probable psychopathy. See his study: "Michael Slobodian: A Case History," version 1.1 (February 12, 2016) 2-3, School Shooters. info, s.v. "Michael Slobodian." The premise that Slobodian could be both depressed and psychopathic may seem incongruous on the surface. However, psychopaths do experience depression, even though the state may stem from their emotional distance from others and, therefore, is based on their own relational vacuity, not empathic concerns. A compelling case can be made for comorbidity of depressed feelings and anti-social tendencies. See: a) Mark Holder, "Are Psychopaths Happy? Psychopaths Get What They Want and Don't Feel Guilty. So Are They Happy?" *Psychology Today*, posted January 7, 2017, https://www.psychologytoday.com/us/blog/the-happiness-doctor/201701/are-psychopaths-happy; b) Christian Keysers, "Inside the Mind of a Psychopath – Empathic, But Not Always: Brain Imaging Shows Psychopaths Can Empathize but Do Not Empathize Spontaneously," *Psychology Today*, posted July 24, 2013, https://www.psychologytoday.com/us/blog/the-empathic-brain/201307/inside-the-mind-psychopath-empathic-not-always; c) Willem H. J. Martens, "The Hidden Suffering of the Psychopath." *Psychiatric Times* 31, no. 10 (October 7, 2014), http://www.psychiatrictimes.com/psychotic-affective-disorders/hidden-suffering-psychopath; d) Zlatko Šram, "The Comorbidity of Psychopathy and Depression: Across Different Ethnic and Sex Groups," *The International Journal of Indian Psychology* 4, no. 3 (April-June 2017): 98-109.

[152] Mara Bovsun, "Beauty Salon Massacre," *New York Daily News*, posted March 25, 2008, under "Retreated into Books," http://www.nydailynews.com/news/crime/beauty-salon-massacre-article-1.273663; Christa Mackey, "The Rose-Mar Killings," BellaOnline: The Voice of Women, n.d., http://www.bellaonline.com/articles/art22876.asp; Time.com, "Nation: Slaughter in the College of Beauty," originally posted November 18, 1966, Murderpedia, s.v.

"Robert Benjamin Smith"; Editors of Time-Life Books, *True Crime: Mass Murderers*, 60.

[153] George Sodini, *Blog*, May 5, 2009, in ABC News, "George Sodini's Blog: Full Text by Alleged Gym Shooter," posted August 5, 2009, http://abcnews.go.com/US/story?id=8258001&page=1.

[154] Ibid.

[155] Edmund L. Andrews, "Shooting Rampage at German School," *New York Times* 150, no. 51,736 (April 27, 2002): A1, A9; AP, "Gunman Hid Expulsion from Parents," Murderpedia, s.v. "Robert Steinhäuser"; David Hancock, "German Police Learn More of Gunman," CBS News, posted May 3, 2002, https://www.cbsnews.com/news/german-police-learn-more-of-gunman/; Toby Helm, "Double Life of Massacre Gunman," *Telegraph*, posted April 29, 2002, https://www.telegraph.co.uk/news/worldnews/europe/germany/1392594/Double-life-of-massacre-gunman.html; John Hooper, "Killer's Secret behind Revenge Attack," *Guardian*, posted April 29, 2002, https://www.theguardian.com/world/2002/apr/29/schools.education; *St. Louis Post-Dispatch*, "German Teen Apparently Planned School Attack," originally posted May 1, 2002, Murderpedia, s.v. "Robert Steinhäuser."

[156] Joe Bauman, "Ex-relative Calls Talovic [sic] Vicious, Troubled," *Deseret News*, posted March 23, 2007, https://www.deseret.com/2007/3/23/20009001/ex-relative-calls-talovic-vicious-troubled; Zeljko Debelnogic, "Utah Gunman Was Srebrenica Siege Survivor – Cousin," Reuters, posted August 9, 2007, https://www.reuters.com/article/us-shooting-utah-srebrenica/utah-gunman-was-srebrenica-siege-survivor-cousin-idUSL1461950520070214/; Chantelle Janelle, "Acquaintances Shed Light on Life of Utah Gunman," WIS News 10, posted February 15, 2007, updated June 30, 2007, https://www.wistv.com/story/6090074/acquaintances-shed-light-on-life-of-utah-gunman/; Ben Winslow, Nedim Hasic, and *Slobodna Bosna*, "A child of Violence: Talovic Survived Genocide," *Deseret News*, posted February 21, 2007, https://www.deseret.com/2007/2/21/20002309/a-child-of-violence-talovic-survived-genocide/.

[157] Bauman, "Ex-relative Calls Talovic [sic]"; excerpt from an FBI report on Sulejman Talović, in Nate Carlisle, "FBI found Talovic [sic] Had a History with Trolley Square," *Salt Lake Tribune*, posted June 25, 2009, https://archive.sltrib.com/story.php?ref=/ci_12382259; Stephen Hunt, "Utah Shooter Had a Record," *Star Tribune*, posted February 17, 2007, archived, https://trib.com/news/state-and-regional/utah-shooter-had-a-record/article_6cdef6dd-4399-5c6f-8e87-d665b211c46f.html.

[158] Brenton Harrison Tarrant, *The Great Replacement: Towards a New Society, We March Ever Forward* (self-published), posted [March 15, 2019?], under prompt "1. Who are you?" https://gatesofvienna.net/wp-content/uploads/2019/03/tarrant-manifesto.pdf. Posting date is based on court record: The

Queen v. Brenton Harrison Tarrant, CRI-2019-009-2468 [2020] NZHC 2192, "Sentencing Remarks of Mander J," August 27, 2020, [1], [4], https://www.courtsofnz.govt.nz/assets/cases/R-v-Tarrant-sentencing-remarks-20200827.pdf. However, a news story said he uploaded it at 7.20 pm on March 14, 2019. Sam Sherwood, "How Australian Terrorist Spent His Final Months before Christchurch Mosque Attack," 9News, posted December 8, 2020, under "The Reconnaissance," https://www.9news.com.au/world/brenton-tarrant-how-christchurch-terrorist-spent-final-months-before-attack/ca366435-03c8-4981-b382-051abec79f56.

159 According to New Zealand Prime Minister Jacinda Ardern, in Adrianna Zappavigna, "How the Christchurch Shooter Obtained Powerful Military-Style Weapons," News.com.au, posted March 17, 2019, https://www.news.com.au/world/pacific/how-the-christchurch-shooter-obtained-powerful-militarystyle-weapons/news-story/eaeec3112cefe61cf995397e1565304a.

160 Sherwood, "How Australian Terrorist Spent His Final Months."

161 Tarrant, *The Great Replacement: Towards a New Society*, under "Numbers Aren't Everything."

162 Tarrant, *The Great Replacement: Towards a New Society*, under "Democracy is the Only Solution, Why Are You Committing to Force?"

163 Jessica McBride, "Brenton Tarrant: 5 Fast Facts You Need to Know," Heavy, posted March 16, 2019, under "1. Brenton Tarrant, A Former Fitness Trainer," https://heavy.com/news/2019/03/brenton-tarrant/.

164 Tarrant, *The Great Replacement: Towards a New Society*, under "This is White Genocide."

165 McBride, "Brenton Tarrant: 5 Fast Facts You Need to Know"; *Queen v. Brenton Harrison Tarrant*, "Sentencing Remarks of Mander J," [7]-[17], [21].

166 Tarrant, *The Great Replacement: Towards a New Society*, after prompts, "Do You Feel Any Remorse for The Attack?" "Did You Commit the Attack to Receive Media Coverage and to Propagate Your Own Writings/Beliefs/Ideals?" "You Are a Bigot, Racist, Xenophobe, Islamophobe, Nazi, Fascist!" and heading, "Accept Death, Embrace Infamy." Spelling, capitalization, grammar, and punctuation, copies post.

167 Guest [pseud.], "Subject: Dion Terres (Kenosha McDonald's, 1993," Columbine High School Massacre Discussion Forum, posted April 9, 2021, under "Other Mass Shootings," https://columbinemassacre.forumotion.com/forum; News clip and commentary in, *JamesEdward 123*, "Kenosha Shooting," YouTube, posted September 21, 2017, https://www.youtube.com/watch?v=GTebqFiMIss&list=PLUoyRq2UlrY7-o0pMNcLOokxBiWB68rUl&index=5.

168 Terres, in *JamesEdward 123*, "Dion Terres Last Moments," YouTube, posted September 21, 2017, https://www.youtube.com/watch?v=jNL-F__Qe3g;

commentary and Terres, in *ThatOddGuyFromDallas*, "Dion Terres on Documentary," YouTube, posted February 26, 2021, https://www.youtube.com/channel/UCE0M-ihMchwrsCwBw4EesaQ (channel no longer carries content).

[169] Narration with visuals, in Mere Blather [pseud.], "Japan's Knife Laws," YouTube, posted July 19, 2012, https://www.youtube.com/watch?v=1YSSaXk29a4; *Japan Times,* "Eight Dead in School Stabbing Spree," posted June 9, 2001, https://www.japantimes.co.jp/news/2001/06/09/national/eight-dead-in-school-stabbing-spree/; Norimitsu Onishi, "Man Kills 7 on Tokyo Street in Rampage," *New York Times*, posted June 9, 2008, https://www.nytimes.com/2008/06/09/world/asia/09japan.html; Park Dietz & Associates, "News Analysis: Mass Murder in Japan," http://www.parkdietzassociates.com/mass-murder-in-japan-pda-news-analysis/ (page no longer accessible).

[170] Agence France-Presse (AFP), "Japan Massacre Suspect Said He Was Ugly, Lonely," originally posted June 10, 2008, Murderpedia, s.v. "Tomohiro Kato."

[171] AFP, "Japan Massacre Suspect"; BBC, "Tomohiro Kato Sentenced to Death Over Tokyo Stabbings," BBC News, posted March 24, 2011, https://www.bbc.com/news/world-asia-pacific-12844673; *Kyodo News*, *JIJI Press,* Japan Times Staff, "Akihabara Marks 10 Years Since Deadly Stabbing Rampage," *Japan Times*, posted June 8, 2018, https://www.japantimes.co.jp/news/2018/06/08/national/akihabara-marks-10-years-since-deadly-stabbing-rampage/; *Kyodo News*, "Motive for Akihabara Massacre Hinted At," posted July 28, 2012, https://www.japantimes.co.jp/news/2010/07/28/national/motive-for-akihabara-massacre-hinted-at/; Tomohiro Osaki, "Death Sentence Upheld for Akihabara Rampage Killer," *Japan Times*, posted February 2, 2015, https://www.japantimes.co.jp/news/2015/02/02/national/crime-legal/death-sentence-confirmed-akihabara-rampage-killer/; *Mainichi Japan*, "Akihabara Stabbing Spree Shocks Japan," originally posted June 9, 2008, Murderpedia, s.v. "Tomohiro Kato"; *Mainichi Japan*, "Missing Work Clothes at Factory May Have Sparked Akihabara Stabbing Rampage," originally posted June 9, 2008, Murderpedia, s.v. "Tomohiro Kato"; Eric Talmadge, "Japan Stabbing Suspect Cries During Interrogation," AP, originally posted June 10, 2008, Murderpedia, s.v. "Tomohiro Kato"; Timesonline.co.uk, "Tokyo knifeman Tomohiro Kato recorded murder blog before rampage," originally posted June 10, 2008, Murderpedia, s.v. "Tomohiro Kato."

[172] *Mainichi Japan*, "Missing Work Clothes at Factory."

[173] Patrick Sauer, "The Story of the First Mass Shooting in U.S. History," *Smithsonian*, posted October 14, 2015, https://www.smithsonianmag.com/history/story-first-mass-murder-us-history-180956927/.

[174] Unruh was open about his homosexuality, but believed people, including a group of teens in his neighborhood, gossiped about it. His SMASI was enacted in New Jersey in 1949. Sauer, "The Story of the First Mass Shooting." His sexuality at that time in that state would have been more than socially unacceptable. In most quarters, it would have been considered "sodomy" and was actually illegal as well as punishable with time in prison. George Painter, "The Sensibilities of Our Forefathers: The History of Sodomy Laws in the United States – New Jersey," edited August 10, 2004, https://www.glapn.org/sodomylaws/sensibilities/new_jersey.htm.

[175] Roberto A. Ferdman, "The Unusual Story of America's First Mass Shooting," *Washington Post*, posted December 3, 2015, https://www.washingtonpost.com/news/wonk/wp/2015/12/03/the-unusual-motive-that-provoked-americas-first-mass-shooting/; writing by unidentified psychiatrist, in Sauer, "The Story of the First Mass Shooting"; Katherine Ramsland, *Inside the Minds of Mass Murderers: Why They Kill* (Westport, CT: Praeger Publishers, 2005), 10-11.

[176] Editors of Time-Life Books, *True Crime, Mass Murderers*, 58-59; Sauer, "The Story of the First Mass Shooting." Charged with thirteen counts of "willful and malicious slayings' and three counts of "atrocious assault and battery," Unruh underwent psychiatric evaluation at the New Jersey Hospital for the Insane (now Trenton Psychiatric Hospital). Four Board Certified Psychiatrist signed off on the report. He was diagnosed with "dementia praecox, mixed type, with pronounced catatonic and paranoid coloring" or, in today's terms, paranoid schizophrenia. Ramsland, *Inside the Minds of Mass Murderers*, 12. However, he never exhibited any of the features associated with that mental disease – e.g., hallucinatory episodes, prolonged delusions, disorganized language, catatonia, lack of affect. See American Psychiatric Association, *DSM-5*, 99-100. Dr. Richard Noll, a psychology professor at DeSales University, author of *The Encyclopedia of Schizophrenia and the Psychotic Disorders* (New York, NY: Facts of Life, Inc. 1992, 2000, 2007), and a psychiatry historian has observed: "It sounds more like schizoid personality disorder or paranoid personality disorder, in modern *DSM-IV* [the edition in use when Noll's assessment was made] parlance. When someone was violent back then, they always invoked the diagnosis of paranoid schizophrenia. If someone was distraught (from emotional trauma, for example), that might be called pseudo-neurotic schizophrenia. … [T]he diagnostic criteria for paranoid schizophrenia have tightened up considerably since the 1940s when this incident took place, and back then the term paranoid schizophrenia was liberally dispensed in a forensic context as almost a euphemism for raving madman." Noll, in, Katherine Ramsland, "Rampage in Camden," Crime Library, n.d., 8, https://www.crimelibrary.org /notorious_murders/mass/howard_unruh/index.html. The site was independently founded in 1988, later

acquired by truTv, then discontinued in 2014. Noll's analysis is paraphrased in Ramsland, *Inside the Minds of Mass Murderers*, 13-14.

[177] The latter two were police issued weapons taken from Weise's grandfather after he killed him.

[178] Kelleher, *Profiling the Lethal Employee*, 56; David Lester, *Mass Murder: The Scourge of the 21st Century* (Hauppauge, NY: Nova Science Publishers, Inc., 2004), 48.

[179] Steven Carley, *Serial Killers, Mass Murderers, & Disorders* (Brockton, MA: SGC Production, 2013), 56; Kelleher, *Profiling the Lethal Employee*, 56; Lester, *Mass Murder*, 49.

[180] Carley, *Serial Killers, Mass Murderers,* 56; Lester, *Mass Murder*, 49

[181] Statements by C. A. Whitman, Father: "I did on many occasions beat my wife, but I loved her"; and "With all three of my sons it was 'yes, sir' and 'no, sir.' They minded me. The way I looked at it, I am not ashamed of any spankings." In Gary M. Lavergne, *A Sniper in the Tower: The Charles Whitman Murders* (New York: Bantam Books, paperback edition, 1998) 3.

[182] Commentary by Dr. Kobolinsky and narration, in Boris Ivanov, dir., "Deranged Killers: Charles Whitman 2009," *Discovery Channel*, posted on *darkdocumentaries*, YouTube, Jan 3, 2013, https://www.youtube.com/watch?v=Jy1B5mfzCBA; Editors of Time-Life Books, *True Crime: Mass Murderers*, 48-49, 54, 55. The extent to which the tumor may have contributed to Whitman's actions is unknowable. The pathologist and neuropathologist who performed his autopsy were ambivalent about its neurological effects or even the amount of pain it may have produced. Editors of Time-Life Books, *True Crime: Mass Murderers*, 54. It is listed because it must have factored into the killer's overall mental state, not because it was conclusively recognized as a primary cause of the rampage.

[183] Among the notes Whitman left behind are these ponderings: "I wonder if I will ever taste the sweet honey of success. ... Will I ever accomplish anything I set forth to do?" Narration, in Ivanov, "Deranged Killers: Charles Whitman." His wife was concerned about his depression and sometimes was reluctant to leave him alone. Editors of Time-Life Books, *True Crime: Mass Murderers*, 50.

[184] Editors of Time-Life Books, *True Crime: Mass Murderers*, 46, 48, 49-50; narration and commentary by Dr. Ramsland, in Ivanov, "Deranged Killers: Charles Whitman."

[185] Fast, *Ceremonial Violence*, 139.

[186] Ibid, 139-140.

[187] Luke T. Woodham v. State of Mississippi, Supreme Court of Mississippi, no. 1998-KA-01689-SCT, decided November 29, 2001, ¶3, FindLaw, https://caselaw.findlaw.com/ms-supreme-court/1439843.html.

[188] Woodham court testimony, quoted in, CNN.com, "Teen Guilty in Mississippi School-Shooting Rampage," posted June 12, 1998, Murderpedia, s.v. "Luke Woodham."

[189] United States District Court, S.D. Mississippi, Jackson Division, Luke Woodham v. Michael Wilson and Jim Hood, no. 3:04cv48-HTW-JCS, November 3, 2006, *8 Issue Eleven, School Shooters .info, s.v. "Luke Woodham."

[190] James L. Cooper, Detective, Seattle Police Department, Certification of Probable Cause, June 10, 2014, 2, School Shooters .info, s.v. "Aaron Ybarra."

[191] Mike Baker and Caitlin Cruz, "SPU Shooting Suspect Raised in Home of Tumult," *Seattle News*, posted July 19, 2014, updated July 20, 2014, under "The Brother," "The Father," https://www.seattletimes.com/seattle-news/spu-shooting-suspect-raised-in-home-of-tumult/; Mountlake Terrace Police Department, Mental Health Contact Report – Involuntary, case no. 13-2287, August 15, 2013, School Shooters .info, s.v. "Aaron Ybarra."

[192] Sara Jean Green, "Aaron Ybarra Found Guilty of First-Degree Murder in Seattle Pacific University Shooting," *Seattle Times*, posted and updated November 16, 2016, https://www.seattletimes.com/seattle-news/crime/ybarra-found-guilty-of-seattle-pacific-university-shootings/; Peter Langman, "Aaron Ybarra: An Analysis," version 1.1 (July 14, 2015), School Shooters .info, s.v. "Aaron Ybarra"; Mountlake Terrace Police Department, Mental Health Contact Report – Involuntary, case no. 12-2887, October 8, 2012, School Shooters .info, s.v. "Aaron Ybarra"; Mountlake Terrace PD, MH Contact Report – Involuntary, case no. 10-2892, October 10, 2010, School Shooters .info, s.v. "Aaron Ybarra." "Prosecutors acknowledged during the trial that Ybarra is mentally ill, but insisted he was driven by hatred and anger, and understood that what he was doing was wrong." Green, "Aaron Ybarra Found Guilty."

[193] According to court filings and statements by mother. AP, "Santa Monica Gunman Underwent Mental Evaluation," *USA Today*, posted June 11, 2013, updated June 12, 2013, https://www.usatoday.com/story/news/nation/2013/06/11/santa-monica-gunman-mentally-evaluated/2413563/.

[194] "A neighbor near the Zawahri home … told the AP: 'It was not an easy breakup. It was a bitter divorce.'" Emma G. Gallegos, "What We Know So Far about Santa Monica Rampage Suspect John Zawahri," *LAist*, posted June 9, 2013, https://laist.com/news/john-zawahri-was-fascinated-with-gu.

[195] Tami Abdollah, "Santa Monica Gunman Was Mentally Evaluated," *Ottumwa Courier*, posted June 12, 2013, updated June 27, 2013, https://www.ottumwacourier.com/archives/santa-monica-gunman-was-mentally-evaluated/article_fdcdef2e-576e-5ccc-b997-6fde6836fa96.html; Pamela Engel, "The Santa Monica Shooter Had A Troubled Past," *Insider*, posted June 11, 213, bullets, https://www.businessinsider.com/john-zawahri-had-a-troubled-past-2013-6;

Gallegos, "What We Know So Far"; Marc Haefele, "The Gun on the Pavement: Marc Haefele on the Santa Monica shootings and John Zawahri's gun," 89.3 KPCC, posted June 14, 2013, https://www.scpr.org/blogs/offramp/2013/06/14/13994/the-gun-on-the-pavement-marc-haefele-on-the-santa/.

Index

Note on organization and functions: Locators pertain to information, not necessarily source material, except to the extent that a note may contain additional content. Topical listings are for locations about that subject. Exemplative anecdotal examinations (in keeping with the theory validation offered in the introduction) are contained in the accounts of cases, which are indexed, but are also summarized in the Appendix. The directives, "*see* under," or "*see also*," or simply "*see*" are for locating a word or phrase in this index. Whereas, the instruction, "*refer to*," advises pursuit of the connotation of a term embedded in another locution by perusing the page(s) cited.

L

M

N

www.ingramcontent.com/pod-product-compliance
Lightning Source LLC
LaVergne TN
LVHW010718210926
848485LV00008B/1435/J
* 9 7 8 1 6 8 0 5 3 5 4 4 0 *